Investor Protection and Corporate Governance

Investor Protection and Corporate Governance

Firm-Level Evidence across Latin America

Foreword by

Andrei Shleifer

Edited by

Alberto Chong and
Florencio López-de-Silanes

A COPUBLICATION OF STANFORD ECONOMICS AND FINANCE,
AN IMPRINT OF STANFORD UNIVERSITY PRESS, THE WORLD BANK, AND
THE INTER-AMERICAN DEVELOPMENT BANK.

1300 New York Avenue, NW
Washington DC 20577
Telephone: 202-623-1000
Internet: www.iadb.org
E-mail: res@iadb.org

1 2 3 4 10 09 08 07

A copublication of Stanford Economics and Finance, an imprint of Stanford University Press, the World Bank, and the Inter-American Development Bank.

Stanford University Press
1450 Page Mill Road
Palo Alto CA 94304

The World Bank
1818 H Street NW
Washington DC 20433

The Inter-American
Development Bank
1300 New York Avenue, NW
Washington, DC 20577

ISBN-10: 0-8213-6913-X (World Rights except North America)
ISBN-13: 978-0-8213-6913-5 (World Rights except North America)
eISBN-10: 0-8213-6914-8 (World Rights except North America)
DOI: 10.1596 / 978-0-8213-6913-5 (World Rights except North America)
ISBN-13 (Hardcover): 978-0-8047-0001-6 (North America)
ISBN-13 (Softcover): 978-0-8047-0007-8 (North America)
ISBN 0-8047-0001-X ISBN 0-8047-0007-9
Library of Congress Cataloging-in-Publication Data

Investor protection and corporate governance : firm-level evidence across Latin America / edited by Alberto Chong and Florencio Lopez-de-Silanes.
p. cm.—(Latin American development forum)
Includes bibliographical references and index.
ISBN-13: 978-0-8213-6913-5
ISBN-10: 0-8213-6913-X
ISBN-10: 0-8213-6914-8 (electronic)
ISBN-13: 978-0-8047-0001-6 (Stanford Hardcover)
1. Corporate governance. 2. Investments. I. Chong, Alberto. II. Lopez-de-Silanes, Florencio.
HD2741.I63 2007
338.6098—dc22

2007003700

Latin American Development Forum Series

This series was created in 2003 to promote debate, disseminate information and analysis, and convey the excitement and complexity of the most topical issues in economic and social development in Latin America and the Caribbean. It is sponsored by the Inter-American Development Bank, the United Nations Economic Commission for Latin America and the Caribbean, and the World Bank. The manuscripts chosen for publication represent the highest quality in each institution's research and activity output and have been selected for their relevance to the academic community, policy makers, researchers, and interested readers.

Advisory Committee Members

About the Contributors

Ricardo Bebczuk teaches regularly at the universities of La Plata, Di Tella, CEMA, and San Andres in Argentina. He is also chief economist at the Center for Financial Stability, Buenos Aires.

André L. Carvalhal-da-Silva is assistant professor of finance at the Coppead Graduate Business School, Federal University of Rio de Janeiro.

Alberto Chong is a principal research economist in the Research Department of the Inter-American Development Bank.

Juan José Cruces is an assistant professor in the Department of Economics at the Universidad de San Andrés, Buenos Aires; he was also chairman of the Master's Program in Finance at the same university until August 2005.

Urbi Garay is assistant professor of finance, coordinator of the Finance Department, and member of the Academic Council at the Instituto de Estudios Superiores de Administración, Caracas.

Maximiliano González is assistant professor at the Finance Center of the Instituto de Estudios Superiores de Administración, Caracas.

Luis Hernando Gutiérrez is an associate professor in the Faculty of Economics, Universidad del Rosario, Bogotá.

Enrique Kawamura is assistant professor of economics at the Universidad de San Andrés, Buenos Aires.

Ricardo P. C. Leal has been associate professor of finance at the Coppead Graduate Business School, Federal University of Rio de Janeiro, since 1998. He is also the chair of the Center for Insurance Studies and Research.

Fernando Lefort is an associate professor in the Business School of the Pontificia Universidad Catolica in Santiago de Chile. He is also the director of the Center of Corporate Governance and director of the Journal of the Department of Business and Economics at the same university.

Florencio López-de-Silanes is professor of finance and governance and chairman of the Master's Program in Business Administration and International Master's Committees at the University of Amsterdam Business School; he is also a faculty research fellow at the National Bureau of Economic Research, Cambridge, MA.

Carlos Pombo is an associate professor at the Department of Economics and director of Graduate Studies in Economics, Universidad del Rosario, Bogotá.

Eduardo Walker is a professor in the School of Business Administration, Pontificia Universidad Catolica, Santiago de Chile.

Contents

Figures

Foreword

Over the last 10 years, both financial research and public policy have increasingly focused on the problem of corporate governance. This focus has been pervasive, from Eastern to Western Europe, from East to South Asia, from North to South America.

The renewed interest is based on a fresh approach to the problem of corporate governance. This approach holds that the crucial failure of corporate governance is the expropriation of outside investors, be they shareholders or creditors, by those who are in control of firms. The problem of expropriation, also known as tunneling, often takes on enormous proportions. Billions of dollars of wealth are siphoned away from outside investors to controlling shareholders and their private company allies. The expropriation prevents investors from devoting funds in the corporate sector, thus leading to low valuations of corporate assets, stunted capital markets, and slowed economic growth.

Low valuations and underdeveloped financial markets are only two of the symptoms of investor expropriation. Other symptoms include concentrated corporate ownership, large spreads between cash flow ownership and the voting rights of dominant shareholders, pyramids, and low dividend payments. When financial markets exhibit these symptoms, the likely underlying problem is investor expropriation.

One of the most important mechanisms through which societies deal with investor expropriation and the various financial problems it entails is the law, including corporate, securities, and bankruptcy law. Legal rules, if they are enforced by courts, have the power to stop or, at least, slow investor expropriation, with substantial benefits for outside investors and markets. Some of the rules explicitly address the problem of self-dealing by corporate insiders; others require the disclosure of financial information. Good laws are probably the single most important element of good corporate governance.

The new approach to corporate governance is wonderfully illustrated in the studies collected in this volume. Latin America has been among the key parts of the world where the legal protection of outside investors is weakest, where the problems of investor expropriation are most severe, and where, therefore, financial markets are significantly underdeveloped.

The essays collected in this volume put together a compelling picture showing that many of the symptoms of investor expropriation and poor corporate governance are present in Latin America. In Latin America, in companies where these symptoms are more serious, the failures of corporate governance are more extreme. In an unfortunate way, Latin America fits well into the common, worldwide pattern in which poor corporate governance goes hand in hand with financial underdevelopment. The evidence is loud and clear in every chapter of this book.

But there are also benefits to collecting this detailed proof. The evidence suggests recipes for improvement as well. In many instances, Latin American countries have lagged behind their counterparts in other regions of the world in their pursuit of financial reform and, in particular, in enhancing the legal protection of outside investors. Both at the country level and at the company level, the corporate governance practices pursued by Latin American firms are not conducive to financial development. The message of this book is as unambiguous as is its analysis: a critical goal in the agenda of financial reform in Latin America must be improvement in corporate governance through legal reform.

Andrei Shleifer
Professor of Economics
Harvard University

Acknowledgments

This book was written with the support of the Latin American Research Network at the Inter-American Development Bank (IDB). Created in 1991, this network aims to leverage the capabilities of the IDB's Research Department, improve the quality of research performed in the region, and contribute to the policy agenda in Latin America and the Caribbean. Through a competitive bidding process, the network provides grant funding to leading Latin American research centers to conduct studies on the economic and social issues of greatest concern to the region today. The network currently comprises nearly 300 research institutes in the region and has proven to be an effective vehicle for financing quality research to enrich the policy debate in Latin America and the Caribbean.

Many individuals provided comments and suggestions: Cesar Calderón, Guillermo Calvo, Bruno Chong, Marco Chong, Virgilio Galdo, Gianmarco Leon, Magdalena López-Morton, Eduardo Lora, Ugo Panizza, Enrico Perotti, Anna Serrichio, Andrei Shleifer, Guillermo Zamarripa, and Luisa Zanforlin. The editors also want to thank the Bank and colleagues who participated in formal and informal discussions and workshops on background papers, and who provided comments during the revisions. Valuable input was provided in the production of this book by Norelis Betancourt, Rita Funaro, Raquel Gómez, John Dunn Smith, Maria Helena Melasseca, and Mariela Semidey. Book editing, design, and print production were coordinated by Shana Wagger, Dana Vorisek, and Denise Bergeron in the World Bank's Office of the Publisher.

The views and opinions expressed in this book are those of the authors and do not necessarily reflect the official position of the IDB, its Board of Directors, or the Advisory Committee.

Acronyms and Abbreviations

ADR	American depositary receipt
BVC	Caracas Stock Exchange (Bolsa de Valores de Caracas)
CEO	Chief executive officer
CGI	Corporate governance index
CLSA	Credit Lyonnais Securities Asia
CNV	National Securities Commission (Comisión Nacional de Valores) (República Bolivariana deVenezuela)
CVM	Brazilian Securities Commission (Comissão de Valores Mobiliários)
GDP	Gross domestic product
GNP	Gross national product
IBGC	Brazilian Institute of Corporate Governance
IPO	Initial public offering
ITP	Informed trading probability
Nafinsa	Nacional Financiera, S.A. (Mexico)
NAFTA	North American Free Trade Agreement
NM	Novo Mercado (dummy) (Brazil)
OLS	Ordinary least squares
P/B	Ratio of price to book
P/CF	Ratio of price to cash flow
P/S	Ratio of price to sales
ROA	Return on assets
ROE	Return on equity
SSOC	Superintendence of Commercial Companies (Superintendencia de Sociedades) (Colombia)
SVAL	Superintendence of Securities (Superintendencia de Valores) (Colombia)
SVS	Securities and Insurance Commission (Superintendencia de Valores y Seguros) (Chile)
TDI	Transparency and disclosure index

Overview: Corporate Governance in Latin America

*Alberto Chong and Florencio López-de-Silanes**

As a result of a series of corporate shocks over the last 10 years, starting with the East Asian and Russian financial crises and followed by corporate governance scandals in Europe and the United States, countries in these regions have started to introduce corporate governance reform. But the pace of reform has not been uniform across nations. For the most part, Latin America has not engaged in institutional reform in financial markets, leaving firms in the region in a difficult position in terms of raising capital in an increasingly competitive global market.

Latin America has been surprisingly spared from a generalized wave of corporate scandals. One possible explanation is that the region's level of investor protection is adequate or has consistently improved based on the lessons drawn from governance crises elsewhere. The evidence reviewed in this chapter does not support this view, though. The status of shareholder protection in Latin America has somewhat improved in the last decade, but the region's low place in shareholder protection still holds. An alternative explanation for the absence of public governance scandals in the region is that the low level of protection and transparency has prevented the creation of an environment where problems may be detected or are worthwhile pursuing. The poor penetration of financial markets and the unsubstantial levels of participation by individuals and institutional investors in these markets seem to suggest this is a possibility. Latin American

* The authors would like to thank the Inter-American Development Bank for the financial support provided for this project. They also want to thank Gianmarco Leon for his invaluable research assistance during this project. If you have any comments, please send them to Professor Florencio López-de-Silanes (f.lopez@uva.nl or florens@nber.org) or Alberto Chong (albertoch@iadb.org).

capital markets are still among the least developed, and this imposes heavy burdens on firms as they try to restructure and face increasingly integrated capital and product markets. The evidence presented in this book suggests that even the largest capital markets in the area are being confronted by the challenge of extinction.

The purpose of this chapter is threefold. First, we review the recent history of Latin American capital markets and the reasons behind their poor development. We extend the empirical evidence on the institutions required to support large capital markets, presenting the situation of Latin America in contrast to the rest of the world. There is a large body of literature that has now established a causal empirical link between legal institutions and financial markets.[1] This chapter extends some of the previous work to include a larger sample of Latin American countries of all sizes and areas within the region.[2] The results in this chapter and in several other chapters in the book reveal a systematic pattern of capital market underdevelopment in the region and a slow movement toward legal reform. Legal reform in the region has faced opposition because of the stubbornness of the status quo. It has been implemented in some countries, but, for the average nation in the region, there is still a long way to go to reach the effective legal protection offered by developed countries and the closest competing developing economies.

In a weak regulatory environment, firms need to adapt to overcome an institutional framework that leaves them at a disadvantage in terms of their ability to raise finance. Companies need to work more assiduously to attract capital by providing a better bundle of protective measures for their investors. For this reason, within-country corporate governance characteristics may make a difference in lowering the cost of capital for firms in the region. Improving firm-level corporate governance practices is a clear need.

The second goal of this chapter is therefore to provide a review and analysis of firm-level studies that have gathered the largest data sets on this topic in Latin America. Until now, firm-level data on governance have been almost nonexistent. The literature reviewed in this chapter fills the gap. We review main findings to show that appropriate firm-level corporate governance characteristics are linked to lower costs for capital, better performance, and better dividend payments across countries. The data gathered include data on corporate governance characteristics, ownership structures, dividend policies, and performance measures. The effort at data collection has also involved a coordinated endeavor to establish a homogeneous corporate governance questionnaire, which has been sent to firms in most of the countries examined in the book. The results show that, on top of the countrywide legal protection of investors, higher firm-level protection and better corporate governance practices have a positive effect in valuation and performance. The evidence matches previous research on the subject in other regions of the world.[3] The first set of results in the book reveals the very high levels of ownership and voting rights concentrations and monolithic governance structures in the largest samples of Latin American companies up to now. Several of the chapter authors have also carried out comprehensive, homogeneous firm-level corporate governance assessments periodically. The book presents the first analyses of such data on the region. The series of new data in the book emphasizes the importance of the specific characteristics of the investor protection regimes in several Latin American countries. By and large, the results across chapters show that those firms with better governance measures in several dimensions are granted higher valuations and thus lower costs for capital.

The third goal of this chapter is to analyze the current threats to Latin American stock markets. If legal reform is slow to come in Latin America, functional reform may be a viable alternative for some firms and may bring improved governance. A second alternative open to firms is to look for capital elsewhere. Cross-listing in U.S. capital markets is an alternative available at least to some Latin American firms. Issuing American depositary receipts (ADRs) may be a large threat to the development of capital markets in the region, as suggested by Moel and Tufano (2002) and Karolyi (2004, 2005).[4] The evidence on the substantial growth of firms issuing equity in international markets in the last 10 years and on the stagnant local markets in the region support this view. Finally, a third alternative is to sell out or join forces with foreign companies that do have access to lower-cost capital. Again, the large wave of foreign acquisitions in some countries in the region shows that such a movement is real. This situation presents problems for the development of local Latin American markets and for the growth of the region. Firm migration and the acquisition of Latin American corporations by cash-rich international firms that are able to raise capital at better terms pose serious threats to the growth of local markets in the region if reform continues to progress so slowly. Although firm-level efforts to improve internal governance and to access foreign sources of capital may alleviate the situation, they do not constitute a sustainable long-run strategy for private sector development. In the end, firms and regulators need to actively engage in the transformation of governance structures and shareholder protection if they are to meet the improved benchmarks of developed nations brought about because of the Asian, European, and U.S. scandals in recent years.

This chapter is organized as follows. In the next two sections, we place the region in the context of the rest of the world and analyze country-level factors of investor protection. These sections also look at the last decade of corporate governance reform across Latin America, emphasizing the experience of some of the countries covered in the book that are representative of what has happened in the region as a whole. The slow pace of reform explains part of the poor development of stock markets across Latin America, which is reviewed in the subsequent section. The section thereafter presents a summary of the evidence on firm-level corporate governance gathered in the various chapters in this book. The studies in this volume represent the largest data set collected on Latin American firms so far. They portray the state of Latin American firms in terms of their ownership structures, internal organization, corporate governance mechanisms, shareholder rights, valuations, performance, and dividend payout policies. The evidence shows a potential positive role for firm-level efforts to escape a poor institutional environment. The penultimate section focuses on the large external threats to the development of capital markets in the region. The increasing financial and product market integration of the last two decades has pushed firms to look for foreign alternatives to raise capital. This observed migration may have serious permanent effects on the growth of local markets. The last section concludes with policy recommendations at the country and firm levels.

Investor Protection and Its Evolution

Capital markets in Latin America are lagging behind those in the rest of the world. Figures 1, 2, and 3 show that a simple look at basic statistics on stock market development puts the region far behind not only developed countries, which may be expected, but also developing and emerging markets. With the notable exception of Chile, as several chapters of this book explain, there has been little dynamism in the rest of the markets of the region in the last couple of decades. For the case of the larger economies in the region, such as Argentina, Brazil, and Mexico, market growth has not matched the growth of the economy.

Although still far behind most of the world, the region seems to have shown upward movement in terms of market capitalization as a proportion of gross domestic product (GDP) over the last 15 years (see figure 1). But a more careful look at the numbers in figure 2 shows that the bulk of the increase in recent times is not occurring because more firms are entering the market, but rather because some large companies are capturing the market and are cross-listed in foreign exchanges (more on this elsewhere below). In sharp contrast to other emerging market regions of the world such as Asia and Eastern Europe, the number of listed firms has plummeted in Latin America. Since 1970, Africa and Latin America are the only regions of the world exhibiting a decline in the number of firms per million inhabitants. The incredibly low levels of trading activity portrayed in figure 3 are also a reflection of the poor state of capital markets in the region. Today, Latin American stock exchanges are among the smallest and least active markets in the world relative to the size of the economies.

Figures 1–3 reflect some concern that capital markets in the region are not a real source of finance and have not developed at the appropriate pace to sustain business growth. There are several hypotheses that may explain the history depicted in figures 1–3. One of the first candidates is

Figure 1 Market Captitalization Relative to GDP, 1990, 1994, 2005

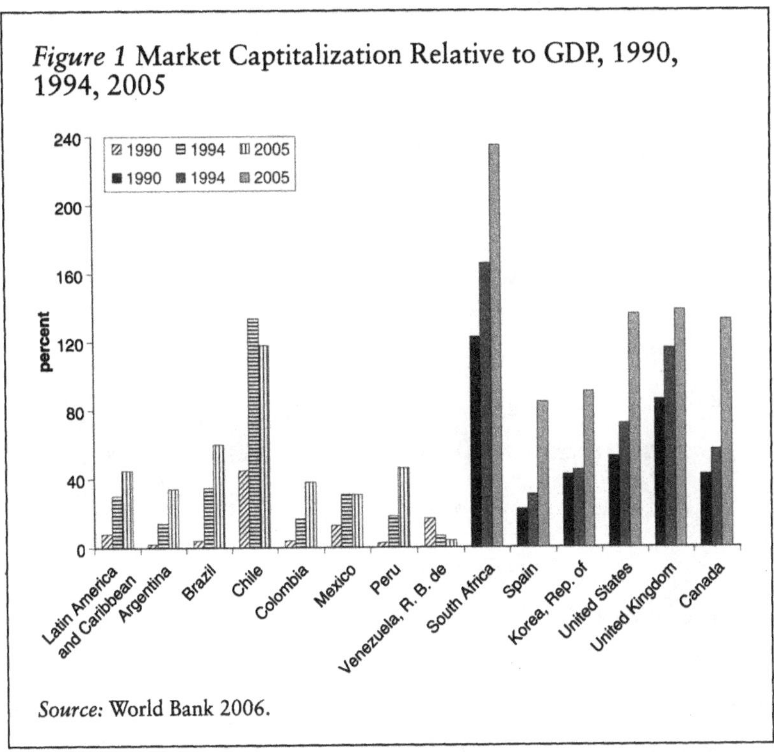

Source: World Bank 2006.

the poor record of past economic and political stability. It is well known that there is an important relationship among macroeconomic stability, political stability, and a country's financial market development.[5] The 1970s and 1980s continued a history of macroeconomic instability, large government deficits, and economic imbalances that could hardly foster sufficient domestic savings to finance firms. Currency devaluations across the region also triggered extensive capital flight and uncertainty in company investment programs. But these arguments should also mean that, when economic and political stability are reached, one would expect better conditions mapping into bigger markets. This is not the case of the average country in Latin America, however. The relatively more stable macroeconomic environment and transition to democracy in many countries have not materialized into a consolidation of capital markets as a serious source of financing. Many other countries and regions around the world have undergone experiences similar to those in the average Latin American country. Yet, the capital markets in these nations have performed much more effectively, as figures 1–3 illustrate.

The persistently low penetration of Latin American capital markets calls for more analysis that digs into structural explanations. In the rest of the section, we look at the fundamentals of investor protection in a global

Figure 2 Listed Companies, 1990, 1994, and 2005

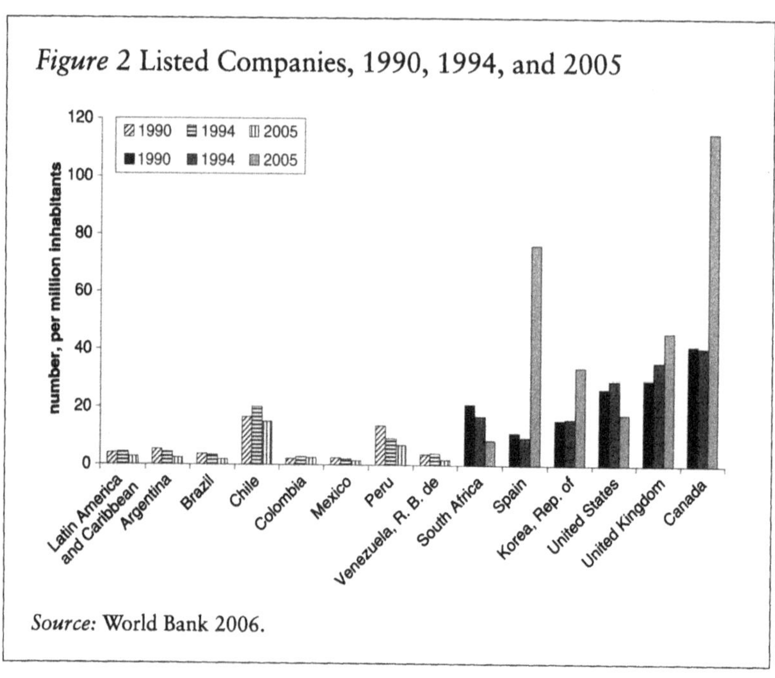

Source: World Bank 2006.

Figure 3 Trading Value Relative to GDP, 1994 and 2004

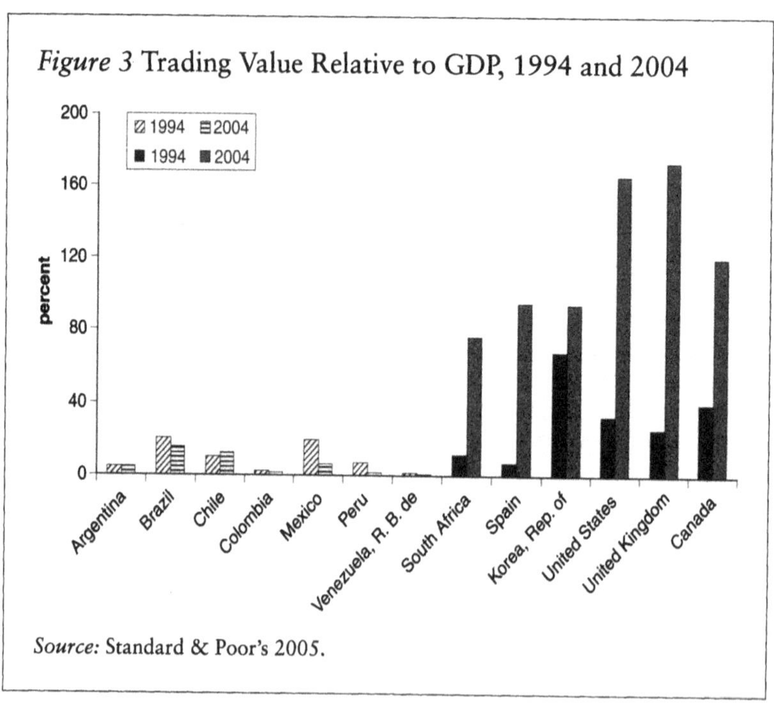

Source: Standard & Poor's 2005.

context to try to understand part of Latin America's lackluster capital market performance. One explanation is provided by an examination of the quality of financial market institutions and a comparison with similar institutions in the rest of the world. Such a comparative approach, rooted in agency theory, holds that better investor protection should translate into lower costs for capital and more access to finance.[6]

To understand the tenets and evolution of the legal approach to finance, we need to depart from the basic premise that the separation between ownership and control may have a large effect on the size of capital markets as we depart from the Modigliani-Miller assumptions.[7] In a simple Modigliani-Miller framework, the size of capital markets is determined only by the cash flows that accrue to investors. Therefore, roughly speaking, the size of capital markets should be proportional to gross national product (GNP). To explain the large discrepancies in the size of financial markets across countries with similar GNPs, one needs to recognize that securities are more than the cash flows they represent, because they entitle investors to exercise certain rights. Shares entitle investors not only to receive dividend payments, but also to exercise control over management through the voting process. To take an extreme view, outside equity would have no value if shareholders did not have control rights to force managers to pay out dividends. In the same vein, creditors would be unwilling to lend money at any interest rate if their control rights did not allow them to punish debtors who default on financial obligations.

Both financiers and management would benefit from the elimination of the agency conflict if they were able to write a complete contract that specified what the manager should do with the funds and how he or she would give them back to investors in all states of the world and under all conditions. Of course, such a complete contract cannot be implemented in practice, making it necessary for management to have some level of discretion.[8] Although it is a cost-effective way of dealing with the separation of ownership and control, management discretion may, unfortunately, be used to expropriate financiers through outright expropriation, transfer pricing, or asset stripping.

The agency model might, in principle, explain why some countries have much larger capital markets than others since it is apparent that countries differ enormously in the extent to which they afford legal protection to investors. Not only do shareholders in Peru, for example, have a different bundle of rights from those in the United States, but also their recourse to redress is likely to be significantly weaker. The agency model predicts larger capital markets in countries where agency costs are reined in by laws and by institutions built to support legal enforcement.

Shareholder Rights in the 1990s

La Porta et al. (1998) systematically assess the rights of investors, as well as the quality of rights enforcement in 49 countries. La Porta et al.

(1997, 1998) and La Porta, López-de-Silanes, and Shleifer (1999) relate legal institutions around the world to the size and breadth of external capital markets, as well as to corporate ownership concentration. There are numerous differences among company laws in different countries. But, for the purpose of understanding the status of minority investors who are facing the decision to invest in a firm, one might focus on basic rules that scholars believe to be essential to corporate governance. Annex 1 provides a detailed description of all the variables used in this chapter; table 1 presents the evidence on shareholder rights for the cross-section of 49 countries included in the original La Porta et al. (1998) paper and for the expanded set of 59 countries included in López-de-Silanes (2003), which updates and expands the Latin American countries included in the original La Porta et al. work. Naturally, laws in different countries are typically not written from scratch, but rather transplanted—voluntarily or coincidentally—from a few legal families or traditions. In general, *commercial* laws come from two broad traditions: common law and civil law. Table 1 includes all available Latin American countries in each case, as well as the means for the other legal families in the world, namely, common law and the rest of the civil law families.[9]

Shareholders in a firm have residual rights over the cash flows of the firm. The right to vote is the main source of power of the shareholders. This right to vote in the general meeting to elect directors and make major corporate decisions guarantees shareholders that management will channel the firm's cash flows to shareholders through the payment of dividends rather than divert the funds to give themselves higher compensation, undertake poor acquisitions, or adopt other measures not in the interest of the shareholders. Therefore, voting rights and the rights that support voting mechanisms are the defining features of equity. Institutional investors and those associations that sell analyses of corporate practices around the world to such investors pay close attention to these measures. They do so because the measures constitute some of the main tools available for monitoring firms and ensuring that returns flow properly toward investors.

Shareholder protection in common law countries is significantly better than it is in French civil law countries. The data in both panels of table 1 show that, while the incidence of cumulative voting for directors and preemptive rights are not statistically different across English and French legal origins, the remaining four measures showed marked differences in the 1990s. If we focus on the data for 1999, for example, common law countries more frequently allow shareholders to exercise their vote by mail than do French-origin countries (40 percent versus 3 percent). No common law country blocks shares before shareholders meetings, while 59 percent of French civil law countries do this. On average, 9 percent of the share capital is sufficient to call an extraordinary shareholders meeting in common law countries, whereas 15 percent of share capital is required in French civil law nations. Finally, 95 percent of common law countries

Table 1 Shareholder Protections in the 1990s

Country	*Proxy by mail allowed*	*Shares not blocked*	*Cumulative vote, proportional representation*	*% capital to call an extraordinary shareholders meeting*	*Preemptive rights*	*Oppressed minority*	*Antidirector rights*
a. Shareholder rights in 1995							
Common law average	0.39	1.00	0.28	0.09	0.44	0.94	4.00
Argentina	0.00	0.00	1.00	0.05	1.00	1.00	4.00
Brazil	0.00	1.00	0.00	0.05	0.00	1.00	3.00
Chile	0.00	1.00	1.00	0.10	1.00	1.00	5.00
Colombia	0.00	1.00	1.00	0.25	1.00	0.00	3.00
Ecuador	0.00	1.00	0.00	0.25	1.00	0.00	2.00
Mexico	0.00	0.00	0.00	0.33	1.00	0.00	1.00
Peru	0.00	1.00	1.00	0.20	1.00	0.00	3.00
Uruguay	0.00	0.00	0.00	0.20	1.00	1.00	2.00
Venezuela, R. B. de	0.00	1.00	0.00	0.20	0.00	0.00	1.00
Latin American average	0.00	0.67	0.44	0.18	0.78	0.44	2.67
Rest of French-origin average	0.08	0.50	0.17	0.12	0.50	0.17	2.08
French-origin average	0.05	0.57	0.29	0.15	0.62	0.29	2.33
German-origin average	0.00	0.17	0.33	0.05	0.33	0.50	2.33
Scandinavian-origin average	0.25	1.00	0.00	0.10	0.75	0.00	3.00
Civil law average	0.18	0.71	0.27	0.11	0.53	0.53	2.65
World average	0.18	0.71	0.27	0.11	0.53	0.53	2.65

(continued)

Table 1 Shareholder Protections in the 1990s *(continued)*

Country	*Proxy by mail allowed*	*Shares not blocked*	*Cumulative vote, proportional representation*	*% capital to call an extraordinary shareholders meeting*	*Preemptive rights*	*Oppressed minority*	*Antidirector rights*
b. Shareholder rights in 1999							
Common law average	0.40	1.00	0.30	0.09	0.40	0.95	4.00
Argentina	0.00	0.00	1.00	0.05	1.00	1.00	4.00
Bolivia	0.00	0.00	0.00	0.20	1.00	0.00	1.00
Brazil	0.00	1.00	0.00	0.05	0.00	1.00	3.00
Chile	0.00	1.00	1.00	0.10	1.00	1.00	5.00
Colombia	0.00	1.00	1.00	0.25	1.00	0.00	3.00
Costa Rica	0.00	0.00	1.00	0.25	0.00	0.00	1.00
Dominican Republic	0.00	1.00	0.00	0.25	0.00	1.00	3.00
Ecuador	0.00	0.00	0.00	0.25	1.00	0.00	1.00
El Salvador	0.00	0.00	0.00	0.05	0.00	0.00	1.00
Guatemala	0.00	0.00	1.00	0.25	0.00	0.00	1.00
Honduras	0.00	0.00	0.00	0.25	1.00	0.00	1.00
Mexico	0.00	0.00	0.00	0.33	1.00	0.00	1.00
Panama	0.00	0.00	1.00	0.05	0.00	0.00	2.00
Paraguay	0.00	0.00	0.00	0.05	0.00	1.00	2.00
Peru	0.00	1.00	1.00	0.20	1.00	0.00	3.00
Uruguay	0.00	0.00	0.00	0.20	1.00	1.00	2.00
Venezuela, R. B. de	0.00	1.00	0.00	0.20	0.00	0.00	1.00

(continued)

Table 1 Shareholder Protections in the 1990s *(continued)*

Country	*Proxy by mail allowed*	*Shares not blocked*	*Cumulative vote, proportional representation*	*% capital to call an extraordinary shareholders meeting*	*Preemptive rights*	*Oppressed minority*	*Antidirector rights*
Latin American average	0.00	0.35	0.41	0.18	0.53	0.35	2.06
Rest of French-origin average	0.09	0.45	0.18	0.13	0.45	0.18	2.00
French-origin average	0.03	0.41	0.31	0.15	0.52	0.28	2.07
German-origin average	0.00	0.17	0.33	0.05	0.33	0.50	2.33
Scandinavian-origin average	0.25	1.00	0.00	0.10	0.75	0.00	3.00
Civil law average	0.05	0.43	0.28	0.13	0.51	0.29	2.21
World average	0.17	0.63	0.29	0.12	0.47	0.51	2.80

Sources: Panel a: La Porta et al. 1998; Panel b: López-de-Silanes 2003.

Note: This table classifies countries by legal origin. Definitions for each of the variables may be found in annex 1. Panel a includes data for 42 countries. Panel b has data on 59 countries. 1.00 = investor protection is covered in the law.

have an oppressed minority mechanism in place, while only 28 percent of French-origin countries have such a mechanism in place. The differences between English- and French-origin countries are captured in the antidirector index, which has an average of 4.00 for common law countries, but only 2.07 for French civil law nations (a t-statistic of 6.09).

Latin America scores somewhat higher than the average of all French-origin countries in many shareholder rights. Latin America has a higher incidence of one share–one vote (59 percent versus 41 percent) and a higher incidence of proportional representation (41 percent versus 31 percent). Latin America is also a bit less likely to block shares (35 percent versus 41 percent), is not statistically different in terms of granting preemptive rights (53 percent versus 52 percent), and has only a slightly higher incidence of oppressed minority remedies (35 percent versus 28 percent). On the other hand, Latin America never allows proxy by mail (versus 3 percent for all French-origin systems) and requires a higher fraction of the share capital to call for an extraordinary shareholders meeting (18 percent versus 15 percent). With the exception of the one share–one vote rule, these differences are not statistically significant when taken in isolation. Although not statistically significant, the differences add up to marginally better shareholder rights in Latin America than in all French civil origin countries when rights are aggregated in the antidirector index (2.06 versus 2.07). However, Latin America's antidirector rights index is statistically significant at a lower level relative to the index for common law countries.

German civil law countries share the lack of protection of shareholder rights with the French-origin countries. Although German-origin countries have a significantly higher incidence of oppressed minority mechanisms, they block shares more often than French countries do. The average antidirector scores for the German and French families are very similar (2.33 versus 2.07). Finally, Scandinavian-origin countries, although clearly inferior to common law countries in shareholder protection, are the best within the civil law tradition. The average Scandinavian antidirector rights score is 3. In short, compared to the rest of the world, common law countries have the package of laws most protective of shareholders.

Legal rules are only one element of investor protection; the enforcement of these rules may be equally or even more important. If good laws are not enforced, they cannot be effective. Likewise, investors may enjoy high levels of protection despite bad laws if an efficient judiciary system is able to redress expropriations by management. In this way, strong legal enforcement may serve as a substitute for weak rules. Table 2 presents several proxies for the quality of the enforcement of laws in different countries. These measures are collected by private credit-risk agencies for the use of foreign investors interested in doing business in the respective countries (Business International Corporation, Political Risk Services). We use five measures: efficiency of the judicial system, rule of law, corruption, risk of expropriation, and risk of contract repudiation. The first two of these proxies pertain to law enforcement, while the last three capture the government's general attitude toward business. In addition to these measures, we also use the data collected in Djankov et al. (2003) to provide an objective, rather than subjective measure of the efficiency of a legal system. This measure creates an index of restrictions or complexities in the resolution of disputes through courts. Finally, we also have another objective measure of enforcement deriving from collected data on the quality of the accounting standards of publicly traded firms in different countries. Accounting is central to corporate governance; it may be difficult to assess management performance without reliable accounting standards. More broadly, cash flows may be very difficult to verify in countries with poor accounting standards; consequently, the menu of financial contracts available to investors may be substantially narrower in such countries. The index of accounting standards in table 2 is provided by the Center for International Financial Analysis and Research based on an examination of the company reports of firms in each country. It is available for 41 of the 59 countries in our sample.

We may begin the discussion of these data by focusing on the Latin American average. Compared with the English-origin average, Latin America has very weak legal institutions and accounting standards. A corrupt or inefficient legal system, coupled with poor disclosure standards, might render legal rules ineffective.

While the Latin American average of most enforcement variables is below the French-origin average, it turns out that the French civil law family shares Latin America's weak legal-enforcement mechanisms. The French family has the weakest quality of legal enforcement and accounting standards. Scandinavian countries have the strongest enforcement mechanisms, and German civil law and common law countries are close behind. Common law countries, although behind Scandinavian nations, are still ahead of the French civil law countries. Note that rule of law is the only measure where differences in means between common law and French legal origin are not statistically significant. An inspection of table 2 suggests that, for the enforcement measures, the level of per capita income may have a more important confounding effect than it does relative to the laws themselves. Regression analysis shows that, in most measures of enforcement, richer countries have a higher quality of enforcement (La Porta et al. 1998). Nonetheless, even when one controls for per capita income, the legal family is relevant to the quality of enforcement and accounting standards. The Latin American subgroup of French civil law is consistently associated with lower enforcement across the board, even controlling for per capita income.

These results do not support the conclusion that the quality of law enforcement substitutes or compensates for the quality of laws. An investor in Latin America and, more generally, in a French civil law country is

Table 2 Enforcement of Laws in the 1990s

Country	*Efficiency of judicial system*	*Rule of law*	*Corruption*	*Accounting standards*	*Court formalism to collect bounced check*
Common Law Average	8.10	6.10	6.46	69.62	2.76
Argentina	6.00	5.36	6.01	45.00	5.40
Bolivia	—	1.32	1.68	—	5.75
Brazil	5.75	6.31	6.31	54.00	3.06
Chile	7.25	7.02	5.30	52.00	4.57
Colombia	7.25	2.08	5.00	50.00	4.11
Costa Rica		6.67	8.33	—	5.48
Dominican Republic	6.75	3.14	3.00	—	4.08
Ecuador	6.25	6.67	5.18	—	4.92
El Salvador	—	2.38	3.69	—	4.60
Guatemala	—	1.43	2.00	—	5.68
Honduras	—	2.07	2.00	—	4.90
Mexico	6.00	5.36	4.76	60.00	4.71
Panama	6.75	2.11	2.11	—	5.84
Paraguay	—	4.11	2.14	—	5.91
Peru	6.75	2.50	4.70	38.00	5.60
Uruguay	6.50	5.00	5.00	31.00	4.05
Venezuela, R. B. de	6.50	6.37	4.70	40.00	6.01

(continued)

Table 2 Enforcement of Laws in the 1990s *(continued)*

Country	*Efficiency of judicial system*	*Rule of law*	*Corruption*	*Accounting standards*	*Court formalism to collect bounced check*
Latin American average	6.52	4.11	4.23	46.25	4.98
Rest of French-origin average	6.62	6.38	5.95	55.10	3.78
French origin-average	6.57	5.05	4.94	51.17	4.29
Socialist-origin average	8.90	8.11	7.57	62.67	3.93
German-origin average	10.00	10.00	10.00	74.00	3.15
Scandinavian-origin average	7.36	6.03	5.86	56.89	3.15
Civil law average	7.65	6.05	6.07	60.93	3.38
World average	8.10	6.10	6.46	69.62	3.53

Sources: La Porta et al. 1997, 1998; Djankov et al. 2003; López-de-Silanes 2003.

Note: This table classifies countries by legal origin. Definitions for each of the variables may be found in annex 1. Data are available on 49 countries for all variables except the "Court formalism to collect bounced checks," which is available for 109 countries.

poorly protected by both the laws and the system that enforces the laws. The converse is true for an investor in a common law country, on average. Poor enforcement and accounting standards aggravate rather than cure the difficulties faced by investors in French civil law countries. The weak scores obtained by Latin America in shareholder and creditor rights may actually understate the severity of the corporate governance problem in the region.

The Evolution of Shareholder Protection to 2005

The past decade has been plagued by scandals involving conflicts of interest and a political agenda that has prominently displayed corporate governance across countries. The initial indicators presented in the first panel of table 1 were, in fact, the first available measurements of shareholder protection across countries. However, almost a decade has passed since the initial calculation of these indicators. The wave of corporate governance scandals during the East Asian crisis, followed by Russia's crisis and the poor corporate governance practices of firms in Europe and the United States, propelled investor protection to the headlines of newspapers and the top of the policy agenda in many countries. Therefore, to get a complete picture of what has happened, it is important to analyze the recent evolution of investor protection in Latin America.

In the rest of this section, we will review the most recent data evidence from various sources that paint a fuller picture of the state of shareholder protection in Latin America and other regions of the world. We will also analyze several of the reform measures that have been undertaken in the core Latin American countries that are analyzed in this book and that are trying to reach the ever more rapidly upward moving target in corporate governance best practice.

Table 3 summarizes the main efforts carried out in the six countries analyzed in this book in terms of corporate law reform since 1950 and in terms of securities law reform since 1975. The table reveals a bipolar pattern. It seems that securities law, partly as a result of the consolidation of stock markets over the last 30 years across the region, has been the source of changes. In certain cases, such as Mexico, countries have even reissued laws, sometimes after a series of gradual, partial changes. Basically, all countries in the sample have been active on this front.

On the other hand, table 3 also shows that no corporate law reform has taken place in half the countries in the sample for several decades. No country has issued any new corporate law in almost 30 years. Only Brazil, Chile, and Colombia have partially reformed corporate regulations. The table suggests that legal reform has been slow and that countries have opted for the possibly easier route of changing securities law, which may require less political conflict with parliament. The danger of this strategy, assuming it might succeed in passing substantial reform, is that the

Table 3 Legal Reforms in Latin America

Reform	*Argentina*	*Brazil*	*Chile*	*Colombia*	*Mexico*	*Venezuela, R. B. de*
New code of commerce, corporation law	n.a.	n.a.	1981	1987	n.a.	1955
Partial reform of the code of commerce, corporation law	n.a.	1999	1989, 1994, 2000[a]	1995, 1997	n.a.	n.a.
New security market law	n.a.	n.a.	1981	n.a.	2005	1975
Partial reform of the security market law	2004	1997, 2001	1989, 1994, 2000,[a] 2001	n.a.	2001	1988
Committee on corporate governance, code of best practices	n.a.	n.a.	n.a.[b]	n.a.	January 2000	n.a.

Source: Compiled by the authors.

Note: n.a. = not applicable.

a. This amendment was known as the corporate governance law (Law 19,705).

b. Although Chile has a code of best practices, the date of introduction is unclear.

dichotomous paths are likely to hurt small and medium firms in the region because they may not be able to gain adequate access to markets.

To analyze the content of the changes brought about by the reform measures that have been implemented, one must look at the actual shareholder rights embedded in the new rules. The first natural candidate for analysis is shareholder rights because these have recently been recalculated in Djankov et al. (2006) for a wide range of countries in many regions for 2005. The sample is now 72 countries (rather than 49), representing more than 99 percent of the world's market capitalization. The numbers are shown in table 4. The revised index relies on the same basic dimension of corporate law as the earlier index, but defines the variables with more precision and eliminates enabling clauses from actual shareholder protective measures. It also focuses on the impact of law on publicly traded firms when different regulations apply to publicly traded versus nonpublicly traded firms.

Table 4 shows that the level of investor protection in the average country in the world has increased from 3 to 3.4 points on the antidirector scale. This seems to be consistent with the view that corporate governance scandals may have triggered reform that has impacted this rough measure of protection to investors. But the differences in the level of shareholder protection between common and civil law countries remain virtually intact. For the case of Latin American countries, the revised index shows an aggregate score of 2.54, virtually identical to the score in 1995. Although the number of countries is different in both panels of table 1 and in table 4, the numbers across the region are virtually identical if we average the common countries in the tables. These numbers corroborate what table 3 has previewed: there has been no major revamping of corporate law in the region, and, where partial reform has taken place, it has not significantly changed the environment of investor protection.[10]

A comparison across countries within table 4 also shows that the relative situation of the region has not materially changed. As in table 1, common law countries and the German and Scandinavian civil law families show higher indicators of shareholder protection than do the countries in Latin America. Perhaps the most surprising fact comes from the comparison between Latin American countries and the rest of the countries that belong to the French civil law family. While the average French civil law nation outside Latin America has improved its score from 2.00 to 2.91, the countries in Latin America have simply stagnated on this front.

It is possible that the political realities in most Latin American nations have made it difficult for governments to pass swift reform in the area of corporate law. For this reason and based on the partial picture drawn from table 3 of reform dates, we need to look at securities law to complement the picture. Securities law may complement corporate law and tort law and provide additional incentives to keep market issuers from taking advantage of investors, thus reducing the cost of contracting and of dispute resolution and encouraging the search for external financing.

Table 4 Shareholder Protections in 2005

Country	*Vote by mail*	*Shares not deposited*	*Cumulative voting*	*Oppressed minority*	*Preemptive rights*	*Capital to call meeting*	*Antidirector index*
Common law average	0.76	1.00	0.10	0.90	0.52	0.09	4.19
Argentina	0	0	0	0	1	0.05	2.00
Bolivia	0	0	0	1	1	0.20	2.00
Brazil	1	0	1	1	1	0.05	5.00
Chile	0	1	1	0	1	0.10	4.00
Colombia	0	1	1	0	1	0.20	3.00
Ecuador	0	1	0	0	1	0.25	2.00
El Salvador	0	0	0	0	1	0.05	2.00
Mexico	0	1	0	0	1	0.10	3.00
Panama	0	0	0	0	1	0.05	2.00
Peru	0	1	1	0.5	1	0.05	3.50
Uruguay	0	0	0	0	1	0.20	1.00
Venezuela, R. B. de	0	1	0	0	0	0.20	1.00
Latin American average	0.08	0.50	0.33	0.21	0.92	0.13	2.54
Rest of French-origin average	0.30	0.50	0.35	0.33	0.90	0.10	3.13
French-origin average	0.22	0.50	0.34	0.28	0.91	0.11	2.91

(continued)

Table 4 Shareholder Protections in 2005 *(continued)*

Country	*Vote by mail*	*Shares not deposited*	*Cumulative voting*	*Oppressed minority*	*Preemptive rights*	*Capital to call meeting*	*Antidirector index*
German-origin average	0.29	0.43	0.29	0.32	0.71	0.06	3.04
Scandinavian-origin average	0.00	1.00	0.20	0.60	1.00	0.09	3.80
Civil law average	0.22	0.53	0.31	0.32	0.86	0.09	3.03
World average	0.38	0.67	0.25	0.49	0.76	0.09	3.37

Source: Djankov et al. 2006.

Note: This table classifies countries by legal origin. Definitions for each of the variables may be found in annex 1. Data are available for 72 countries.

Securities law may benefit the enforcement of good conduct through the provision and regulation of market mechanisms and the resulting litigation on private contracts.

As table 3 shows, securities regulations is an area in which there has been recent activity in investor protection reform. Several reforms have improved transparency and shareholder rights among publicly traded firms in the region. Chile was the first country to revamp its securities law (in the early 1980s), followed by most of the other countries only in the 1990s. The details of the reforms in this area are outlined in each of the chapters in this book.

Securities law aims at regulating the behavior of market participants and providing incentives for issuers not to abuse their information advantages over simple investors. As La Porta, López-de-Silanes, and Shleifer (2006) detail, these objectives may be achieved by empowering the supervisor of the market or by improving disclosures and reinforcing liability standards that facilitate private enforcement against those who take advantage of investors.

To establish specific investor protective measures through securities law, it is useful to concentrate on the promoter problem. The promoter problem has been the focus of many of the analyses of securities regulations because it is a problem that may be full of agency conflicts between prospective investors in an initial public offering (IPO) and the promoters or issuers who offer shares for sale. La Porta, López-de-Silanes, and Shleifer (2006) have collected data on the regulation of IPOs covering three groups of measures in the context of the new issuance of securities in the market. Table 5 shows these measures for all countries in their sample of 49 nations and for the average country in the various legal families described above.[11] The first two columns of the table show an index on the compulsory disclosure of potential conflicts of interests in the IPO and an index of the liability standards in cases against issuers, directors, distributors, and accountants involved in the offering. The last column reports an index of the characteristics and the investigative and sanction powers of the regulator or public enforcer. The exact definitions of the variables are found in annex 1. All indicators are standardized to fall between zero and one, whereby higher numbers mean higher standards. The cutoff date for the regulations measured here is 2003; so, some of the reforms in the past couple of years are not reflected among the indicators.

In the area of the disclosure of potential conflicts of interest, Latin America as a whole ranks last, even behind the rest of the French civil law nations. The average country in the region has few regulations requiring disclosures of the terms of material contracts outside the ordinary course of business, disclosures of transactions in which related parties have an interest, and disclosures involving shareholders themselves. Argentina, Chile, and Mexico manage to get close to the mean of the world in disclosures, but the rest of the countries lag behind. The first column of table 5

Table 5 Securities Laws in 2001

Country	*Disclosure requirements*	*Liability standard*	*Public enforcement*
Common law average	0.78	0.58	0.62
Argentina	0.50	0.22	0.58
Brazil	0.25	0.33	0.58
Chile	0.58	0.33	0.60
Colombia	0.42	0.11	0.58
Ecuador	0.00	0.11	0.55
Mexico	0.58	0.11	0.35
Peru	0.33	0.66	0.78
Uruguay	0.00	0.11	0.57
Venezuela, R. B. de	0.17	0.22	0.55
Latin American average	0.31	0.24	0.57
Rest of French-origin average	0.55	0.49	0.51
French-origin average	0.45	0.39	0.53
German-origin average	0.60	0.42	0.25
Scandinavian-origin average	0.56	0.47	0.38
Civil law average	0.49	0.40	0.46
World average	0.60	0.47	0.52

Source: La Porta et al. 2006.

Note: This table classifies countries by legal origin. Definitions for each of the variables may be found in annex 1. Data are available for 49 countries.

shows that the disclosure strength is superior in other nations of the civil legal family, as well as in most countries of common law origin.

Unfortunately, the picture in terms of liability standards for participants in IPOs is no better. With the rare exception of Peru, the rest of the Latin American nations shown in table 5 exhibit some of the highest levels of burden of proof in the world. The liability standards for issuers, directors, and underwriters are low, and investors find it virtually impossible to recover losses from any of these parties due to the extremely difficult requirement to show wrongful intent or gross negligence. This contrasts sharply with the situation in other developed countries, such as the United States, where investors need to prove only that a prospectus contains misleading information. Similarly, the burden of proof is much less significant in other developing nations, such as the Republic of Korea and Malaysia, where investors are only required to show that they have relied on a prospectus or that their losses have been caused by the misleading information.

The bleak picture portrayed in the indicators of the first two columns in table 5 may make the reader wonder if the wave of recent reforms in securities law in Latin American countries has really amounted to a substantial initiative that has improved the environment. Answering this question involves looking at the other two areas where most reform in the region seems to have been concentrated: the power of market regulators and laws pertaining to self-dealing (transactions with potential conflicts of interest) or related party transactions.

Latin America does fare better in the area of public enforcement than in the areas of disclosure and private enforcement via liability standards. The third column of table 5 shows that the average capital market regulator in Latin America has as many rule-making powers and as much authority to impose sanctions as the average regulator in other nations. There are, in fact, no statistically significant differences between Latin America and the rest of the groups included in column 3 of table 5 (the t-statistics are not shown).

In terms of the regulation of self-dealing, some of the main changes during the recent wave of reform in securities law have been motivated by the scandals in developed countries and the acute emphasis that policy makers around the world have placed on improving corporate governance. Although securities law and corporate law seem to have different targets and purposes, the reality is that these two sets of regulations interact in many ways. Some areas of corporate law apply to privately and publicly held firms. For this reason and with the aim of painting the most comprehensive view of investor protection in Latin America, one must adopt an approach that allows a focus on the regulation of self-dealing because this is the main problem area in corporate governance, and it will allow us to gain an understanding of all regulations and their interactions. The corporate governance scandals that have occurred in East Asia, Italy, Russia, and the United States have all involved some kind of self-dealing transaction such as excessive executive compensation or loans, transfer pricing, targeted repurchases, corporate opportunities, and the purchase and sale of assets under other than arm's-length terms.

The regulation of self-dealing involves corporate law and securities law, as well as other regulatory areas, even including civil procedure (that is, rules of evidence and so on). As in the case of an offer of securities to investors through the market, self-dealing transactions may be monitored through public and private enforcement mechanisms. Public enforcement on this issue has been on the rise, as evidenced by the recent U.S. Sarbanes-Oxley Act, which provides for higher fines and for prison terms for those found guilty. We have also seen an increase in measures that facilitate private enforcement, as several countries have established better corporate disclosure standards and approval procedures, and a few have also tried to facilitate private litigation aimed at countering unfair transactions.

Table 6 presents the results of the analysis of the regulation of self-dealing. The data are based on the recent work by Djankov et al. (2006). The table attempts to summarize the measures available to try to stop or to obtain redress from a classic transaction with potential conflicts of interest

Table 6 Anti–Self-Dealing Regulations in 2005

Country	*Ex ante private control of self-dealing*	*Ex post private control of self-dealing*	*Anti–self-dealing index*	*Public enforcement index*
Common law average	0.34	0.45	0.40	0.33
Argentina	0.33	0.35	0.34	0.00
Brazil	0.22	0.33	0.27	0.50
Chile	0.50	0.75	0.63	1.00
Colombia	0.83	0.31	0.57	0.00
El Salvador	0.83	0.03	0.43	0.00
Mexico	0.19	0.15	0.17	0.50
Panama	0.17	0.15	0.16	0.00
Peru	0.25	0.65	0.45	0.25
Uruguay	0.08	0.28	0.18	0.50
Venezuela, R. B. de	0.08	0.10	0.09	0.00
Latin American average	0.35	0.31	0.33	0.28
Rest of French-origin average	0.36	0.55	0.45	0.50
French-origin average	0.35	0.48	0.42	0.43
German-origin average	0.44	0.69	0.57	0.52
Scandinavian-origin average	0.24	0.60	0.42	0.35
World average	0.36	0.52	0.44	0.41

Source: Djankov et al. 2006.

Note: This table classifies countries by legal origin. Definitions for each of the variables may be found in annex 1. Data are available for 72 countries.

characterized by the existence of a single controlling shareholder on both sides of the deal, in this case, the purchase of an asset by a corporation. As in table 5, measures are covered that facilitate private enforcement before or after the transaction takes place and that provide powers to a regulator. The table shows the available numbers for Latin American countries included in the 72-nation study and the mean scores for legal families around the world.

The first column shows data on ex ante measures against self-dealing. These measures address the approval requirements that need to be fulfilled and the mandatory disclosures that need to be made before a transaction occurs. The disclosures may be made by the acquiring company or the conflicted party. The index also takes into consideration the existence of an independent review of the transaction before it actually occurs. The column reveals that the average Latin American country lacks the bells and whistles that are found in a transparent system for the control of this type of transaction. Latin American countries and other French civil law countries are behind the average common law nation, which makes greater disclosure and the implementation of arm's-length approval a priority in attacking this potential problem.

The second column of table 6 tries to summarize the situation that shareholders would face if they were to attempt to seek redress once the self-dealing transaction has taken place. Shareholders may use disclosures that are required after the transaction, such as in the annual report, and all other legal means to find evidence, prove wrongdoing, and seek compensation. The scores for Latin America show that, on average, shareholders would face more difficulties in obtaining standing to sue, gaining access to evidence, and seeking redress relative to investors in the average common law country and even in other civil law families. Although some Latin American nations have recently instituted changes in this area, investors still do not have sufficient power to act if they fear expropriation through this kind of conflicted transaction.

Overall, the lack of ex ante bells and whistles, the lower-than-average ex post disclosure requirements, and the difficulties in seeking redress in Latin America are responsible for the low total score in the regulation of self-dealing. Some Latin American countries score among the lowest 10 countries in the world. Contrast this with the average nation in the common law family, which includes high- and low-income countries. In the median common law country, related party transactions are reviewed by independent financial experts and approved by disinterested shareholders. The disclosures are extensive both before and after a transaction is approved. Moreover, establishing liability, although costly, is relatively easier than in the average Latin American nation because of lower ownership requirements, a less cumbersome burden of proof, and substantial access to evidence. The situation in the United Kingdom and the United States, the countries with the largest immigration of firms in the form of depositary receipts, is also much better.

The last column of table 6 shows an aggregate index of public enforcement mechanisms that groups the penalties imposed by the public regulator on those who are found liable in the area of self-dealing. Half of the countries in Latin America impose fines on directors who are found liable, but not on the controlling shareholders. The average country in the region also imposes prison terms of more than 10 years for such crimes. The penalties are among the highest in the world, but there is virtually no record of the actual application of these penalties to a case such as the self-dealing transaction in the study. The risk is that, as in many other countries, existing penalties are hardly a deterrent because it is virtually impossible to prove wrongdoing. Additionally, the region may be facing serious problems in enforcement by regulators. Despite the recent progress in securities regulations in some countries in the region, the data in table 6 suggest that there is a lot of room for improvement in shareholder protection.

A skeptic may argue that Latin American countries are simply different from common law countries and that a high level of shareholder protection against self-dealing and abuse by promoters of securities is simply unattainable in the region. The answer to such claims is Chile, which belongs to the French civil law family, like the rest of Latin America, and shares many of the same geographical, political, and economic characteristics with other countries in the region. The various scores for shareholder protection across tables 1 through 6 reveal the strength of corporate governance in Chile relative to the region. Of course, this is only one observation, but it goes to the heart of the critique that substantial reform within the region is infeasible.

Access to External Finance

The ultimate question is whether countries with poor investor protection actually suffer because of this. If laws and their enforcement matter, then countries that offer entrepreneurs better terms of external finance would have both higher-valued and broader capital markets. We also predict that countries that offer entrepreneurs better terms would have more widely held corporations. Consequently, this section compares external finance and ownership concentration across countries as a function of the origin of their laws, the quality of legal investor protection, and the quality of law enforcement.

There are at least two reasons why legal institutions may have no effect on the pattern of external financing among firms. First, laws may not be necessary to support external financing if, for example, companies deliver on their promises not because they are forced to do so, but because they want to build a good reputation to facilitate their access to capital markets.[12] Reputations unravel if there is ever a time when the gains from cheating exceed the value of keeping external financing open because investors, through backward induction, would never extend financing to such a firm to begin with.

Second, poor laws and poor enforcement may have no real consequences anyway if firms may easily opt out of laws in their legal jurisdictions. Easterbrook and Fischel (1991) are skeptical that legal rules are binding in most instances because entrepreneurs may offer better investor rights, when it is advantageous to, through corporate charters that effectively serve as contracts between entrepreneurs and investors. In practice, however, opting out of rights may be costly both for firms that need to write nonstandard contracts and for investors who need to study them. In addition, courts may be unwilling or unable to enforce nonstandard contracts, further limiting the scope for opting out.

Alternatively, if legal institutions matter, ownership concentration in countries with poor investor protection should be higher than it is in countries with strong investor protection. This is so for at least two reasons. First, agency problems may call for large shareholders to monitor managers and thus prevent or minimize expropriation. Second, minority shareholders may be unwilling to pay high prices for securities in countries with weak legal protection. At the same time, entrepreneurs are going to be more reluctant to offer shares at discounted prices, thus resulting in higher ownership concentration, as well as smaller and narrower markets for external equity.[13]

Ultimately, the question of whether legal institutions matter is fundamentally empirical. If opting out were cheap and simple, the patterns of ownership and external financing among firms would not be affected by differences in legal institutions across countries.[14] Accordingly, we now examine two types of evidence regarding the influence of legal institutions on external finance: ownership concentration and the size and breadth of capital markets.

The Size and Breadth of Capital Markets

There are several, now standard measures of external equity financing and stock market development.[15] Table 7 summarizes the results from application of the three widely used measures of equity financing. The first measure is the ratio of equity financing to GNP between 2000 and 2005. The procedure we follow may overestimate the level of external financing in countries with poor protection, because ownership concentration is likely to be higher in these markets. A conceptually better measure involves looking at the corrected measure of true equity financing that considers ownership concentration levels.[16] The remaining two measures of external equity financing capture market breadth. The first is the number of domestic firms listed in the stock exchange of a country relative to the country's population. The second is the value of IPOs as a proportion of the size of the economy between 2000 and 2005. We look at both the stock and flow of new companies obtaining equity financing because the development of financial markets has accelerated greatly over the last 10 years, and, hence, the IPO data provide a more recent picture of external equity financing.

Several interesting patterns emerge from an examination of our proxies for external equity financing in table 7. First, access to external equity financing is most limited in French civil law countries. Specifically, the ratio of total capital and external capital to GDP and the ratio of domestic firms to population are both roughly two-thirds of the world mean. The ratio of domestic quoted companies to population and the IPO-GDP ratio are also roughly two-thirds of the world mean. Equity markets are particularly

Table 7 Market Outcomes

Country	*Stock market capitalization to GDP*	*Listed firms per million population*	*IPOs to GDP*	*Block premium*	*Ownership concentration*
Common Law Average	85.54	32.56	3.71	0.04	0.44
Argentina	58.08	3.10	0.56	0.12	0.53
Bolivia	15.59	3.17	—	—	—
Brazil	38.35	2.48	0.05	0.49	0.57
Chile	89.70	16.72	0.51	0.15	0.45
Colombia	14.27	2.89	0.01	0.15	0.63
Ecuador	5.77	2.38	0.00	—	0.54
El Salvador	17.26	5.62	—	—	—
Mexico	21.87	1.73	0.22	0.47	0.64
Panama	25.21	9.68	—	—	—
Peru	22.85	8.17	0.04	0.17	0.56
Uruguay	1.21	4.37	0.00	—	0.78
Venezuela, R. B. de	5.51	2.81	0.68	0.28	0.51
Latin American average	26.31	5.26	0.23	0.26	0.58
Rest of French-origin average	51.35	28.18	2.86	0.08	0.54
French-origin average	41.96	19.59	1.73	0.16	0.55
German-origin average	48.95	24.22	4.81	0.15	0.34
Scandinavian-origin average	90.37	69.40	3.38	0.02	0.37
Civil law average	48.62	25.74	2.54	0.14	0.49
World average	59.39	27.73	2.97	0.11	0.47

Sources: Djankov et al. 2006; Dyck and Zingales 2004.

Note: This table classifies countries by legal origin. Definitions for each of the variables may be found in annex 1. Data are available for 72 countries.

narrow in Latin America. In fact, Latin American countries are well below the rest of the French civil law countries, and this explains a large portion of the low ratios of this legal family. For Latin American countries, the ratio of the number of firms to population is roughly one-fourth of the world mean, whereas the ratio of the number of IPOs to population is almost 10 times smaller than the world mean. The first column shows that the size of the stock market in the average Latin American country is less than half the world mean. If we compare the Latin American numbers to the numbers of the average common law country, the results are even more striking. The median country in the region has capital markets that are one-third of those of the median common law nation.

Table 7 shows results without controlling for other country characteristics. As argued above, it is possible that macroeconomic, geographical, or political conditions have had an impact on the size and breadth of capital markets. To take these factors into consideration, tables 8 through 13 present regressions of external financing measures on investor protection, controlling for country-specific characteristics. Tables 8 and 10 use data for the mid-1990s from the sample that includes 19 Latin American countries. Tables 9, 11, 12, and 13 use more recent data on capital markets and include the samples in La Porta, López-de-Silanes, and Shleifer (2006) and Djankov et al. (2006). The latter tables have the advantage of using more recent data and sometimes a larger sample of countries, but they do not include as many countries from Latin America as the first two regression tables. Another reason for presenting these two sets of regressions is to illustrate that results are robust to alternative samples, time periods, and indicators of shareholder protection.

In all specifications, we regress our measures of capital markets on macroeconomic variables and law enforcement. All regressions include economy-wide controls. We control for different sets of measures to show robustness. The first of these controls is the growth rate of GDP on the theory that growth affects valuation, which, in turn, may affect ownership patterns because entrepreneurs are more willing to issue at attractive prices. We also control for the logarithm of total GNP on the theory that the creation of capital markets may be subject to increasing returns to scale. If this theory is true, we should observe that larger economies have larger firms and might therefore show lower ownership concentrations. In some tables, we present the log of GNP per capita as an alternative economy-wide control. All regressions also control for different indicators of law enforcement across the tables. Tables 8 and 10 use the average index of the rule of law for the past 20 years as a measure of the quality of enforcement. These results are representative of other specifications with alternative subjective measures of enforcement used in the literature. In tables 9, 11, 12, and 13, we use an objective measure of court efficiency found in Djankov et al. (2003). This variable measures the average duration

Table 8 Regressions of External Financing in the Mid-1990s and Legal Origin

Independent variables	Dependent variables: Ratio: external capitalization to GDP	Ratio: domestic firms to population	Ratio: IPOs to population
GNP per capita growth	3.6913 (4.7899)	4.5809 (2.8052)	0.4554 (0.4242)
Log GDP	9.0294 (4.1605)**	-0.9642 (1.8683)	0.1074 (0.1820)
Rule of law	5.2318 (2.0867)**	3.6805 (1.3250)***	0.3558 (0.1026)***
French origin, Latin America	-29.7382 (10.2542)***	-19.2761 (6.9754)***	-1.0812 (0.4395)**
Rest of French origin	-36.6155 (14.8308)**	-22.6474 (9.3752)**	-1.2178 (0.7977)
German origin	-28.5638 (18.7438)	-27.3288 (11.2920)**	-2.6202 (1.0341)**
Scandinavian origin	-1.1080 (36.6125)	-13.4163 (10.8309)	-0.2844 (1.4286)
Constant	-82.7251 (40.0524)**	13.3160 (19.9450)	-1.9039 (1.5455)
Observations	56	58	58
Adjusted R^2	0.49	0.42	0.43

Sources: Data from La Porta et al. 1997, 1998; López-de-Silanes 2003.

Note: The table shows ordinary least squares regressions of a cross-section of 58 countries around the world. Robust standard errors are shown in parentheses.

* significant at 10 percent

** significant at 5 percent

*** significant at 1 percent

of the civil procedures required to resolve the same simple claim for collection on a bounced check through the courts in each country.

We organize the discussion of the results across tables around five main areas. First, all indicators of economic conditions (that is, the growth of GDP, the size of the economy, and GDP per capita) have the signs predicted by the theory, but only GDP per capita consistently predicts larger capital markets with statistical significance. Second, enforcement measures, namely, the rule of law and the log of the number of days to collect on a bounced check through the courts, have a large and significant impact on all measures of development of capital markets. A move from the world mean to an almost perfect enforcement score or the lowest delay in the collection of a claim is associated with an increase of, respectively, close to

Table 9 Regressions of External Financing in Recent Years and Legal Origin

	Dependent variables		
Independent variables	*Ratio: stock market capitalization to GDP*	*Listed firms per million population*	*Ratio: IPOs to GDP*
Log (GDP per capita)	25.6852	10.0117	1.3024
	(5.35)***	(3.32)***	(4.76)***
Log (days to collect a check)	-11.3424	5.0761	0.6597
	(1.39)	(1.03)	(1.04)
Latin American–French legal origin	-51.6098	-30.2312	-3.7450
	(3.62)***	(4.50)***	(4.44)***
Rest of French legal origin	-39.1657	-6.7395	-1.3616
	(2.48)**	(0.47)	(1.42)
German legal origin	-48.6178	-23.0424	-1.0043
	(2.35)**	(2.44)**	(0.56)
Scandinavian legal origin	-50.7614	14.7840	-2.7117
	(1.45)	(0.44)	(1.86)*
Constant	-65.7859	-73.7803	-10.5211
	(1.32)	(2.40)**	(2.38)**
Observations	71	71	49
R-squared	0.46	0.22	0.46

Source: Djankov et al. 2003, 2006.

Note: The table shows ordinary least squares regressions of a cross-section of 72 countries around the world. Robust t-statistics are shown in parentheses.

* significant at 10 percent

** significant at 5 percent

*** significant at 1 percent

15 and 21 percentage points in the ratio of external market capitalization to GNP, an additional 11 to 12 firms per million population, and an additional 1.2 IPO to GDP ratio. All results are statistically significant.

The fourth set of results is derived from an examination of tables 8 and 9, which use the legal origin family of each country as a proxy for investor protection. The previous tables suggest that there are systematic differences across legal families. These regressions show that the differences still persist once we control for other country characteristics. Relative to common law countries, all civil law families tend to have smaller capital markets, but statistical significance is not reached in a few specifications for the German and Scandinavian civil law groups. The differences between common law and Scandinavian countries are, in fact, rarely statistically

Table 10 Regressions of External Financing in the Mid-1990s and Investor Protection Indicators

	Dependent variables		
Independent variables	*Ratio: external capitalization to GDP*	*Ratio: domestic firms to population*	*Ratio: IPOs to population*
GDP growth	2.0931 (4.0054)	4.1525 (2.7734)	0.3948 (0.4171)
Log GDP	4.9795 (3.5746)	-3.1838 (1.6264)*	-0.0989 (0.2081)
Rule of law	6.9628 (2.3713)***	4.0502 (1.0967)***	0.3797 (0.0965)***
Antidirector rights, 1995	11.9880 (3.8124)***	5.7608 (2.3183)**	0.4347 (0.1555)***
Constant	-95.4152 (32.5668)***	7.7958 (15.0785)	-1.6353 (0.1555)***
Observations	56	58	58
Adjusted R2	0.49	0.35	0.39

Sources: Data from La Porta et al. 1997, 1998; López-de-Silanes 2003.

Note: The table shows ordinary least squares regressions of a cross-section of 58 countries around the world. Robust standard errors are shown in parentheses.

* significant at 10 percent

** significant at 5 percent

*** significant at 1 percent

significant.[17] German and Scandinavian legal origin countries are also associated with smaller, narrower stock markets than are the English legal origin countries, but the effects are not as pronounced as they are with French legal origin.

For the purposes of making more specific statements about Latin America, we have split the French civil law countries into those that are located in Latin America and those that are not. The analysis of the results in tables 8 and 9 shows that, compared to common law countries, both groups of French civil law countries show smaller ratios of external equity to GNP and of total market capitalization to GDP. But the Latin American countries suffer the most from shallow markets, which translate into few listed firms and small IPO activity. Relative to the average common law country in the mid-1990s, Latin American countries exhibited a ratio of external equity to GDP that was lower by 30 percentage points, 19 fewer publicly traded firms per million people, and a ratio of IPOs per million people that was 1.2 lower (see table 8). As table 9 shows, Latin American–French civil law countries still have significantly smaller capital markets today than the average common law nation, with a ratio of total market capitalization to

Table 11 Regressions of External Financing in Recent Years and Investor Protection Indicators

Independent variables	*Dependent variable: ratio of stock market capitalization to GDP*						
Log (GDP per capita)	18.0808 (3.49)***	22.3815 (5.21)***	17.3902 (3.52)***	16.6213 (3.40)***	20.9151 (5.08)***	19.5489 (3.60)***	23.4120 (5.08)***
Log (days to collect a check)	−24.8784 (2.33)**	−13.2081 (1.48)	−16.1920 (1.39)	−22.5142 (1.70)*	−11.3748 (1.66)	−32.7852 (2.70)***	−17.4775 (1.77)*
Antidirectors rights index, 1995	14.3777 (2.58)**						
Antidirectors rights index, 2005		10.0716 (1.82)*					
Disclosure requirements			104.7693 (4.02)***				
Liability standards				72.6623 (3.87)***			
Anti–self-dealing index					83.3342 (2.51)**		
Public enforcement of securities laws						91.8696 (2.07)**	
Public enforcement of anti–self-dealing							−14.9931 (1.02)
Constant	2.4870 (0.04)	−94.3833 (1.50)	−55.9920 (0.68)	12.1254 (0.15)	−94.3996 (2.01)**	26.0813 (0.32)	−40.6648 (0.67)
Observations	49	71	49	49	71	49	71
R-squared	0.40	0.39	0.43	0.39	0.45	0.41	0.37

Sources: La Porta et al. 1998; La Porta, López-de-Silanes, and Shleifer 2006; Djankov et al. 2003, 2006.
Note: The table shows ordinary least squares regressions of a cross-section of 72 countries around the world.
Robust t-statistics are shown in parentheses.
* significant at 10 percent.
** significant at 5 percent.
*** significant at 1 percent.

Table 12 External Finance, Legal Origins, and Investor Protection Indicators

Independent variables	*Dependent variable: ratio of stock market capitalization to GDP*						
Log (GDP per capita)	19.8325	25.6157	19.3805	19.5868	23.9160	19.3932	26.1311
	(3.76)***	(5.35)***	(3.60)***	(3.47)***	(5.18)***	(3.96)***	(5.25)***
Log (days to collect a check)	−19.9349	−10.7815	−16.7589	−19.1477	−9.3195	−24.9885	−10.9255
	(1.64)	(1.33)	(1.29)	(1.38)	(1.32)	(2.02)**	(1.41)
Latin American–French legal origin	−33.4336	−49.0001	−9.7915	−31.6230	−36.1878	−40.2782	−51.7290
	(2.44)**	(3.60)***	(0.45)	(1.94)*	(2.85)***	(2.84)***	(3.54)***
Rest of French legal origin	−11.1381	−37.2631	−13.1866	−28.6891	−24.9001	−21.2748	−37.6057
	(0.65)	(2.57)**	(0.72)	(1.62)	(1.99)*	(1.31)	(2.47)**
German legal origin	−16.4804	−46.7572	−18.9645	−26.9448	−35.9018	0.2672	−47.0176
	(0.43)	(2.36)**	(0.48)	(0.67)	(2.37)**	(0.01)	(2.36)**
Scandinavian legal origin	−26.6563	−49.9317	−17.4479	−31.8183	−34.5417	−14.9158	−49.2607
	(0.60)	(1.44)	(0.40)	(0.73)	(1.03)	(0.36)	(1.45)
Antidirectors rights index 1995	11.5329						
	(2.23)**						
Antidirectors rights index 2005		1.7951					
		(0.40)					
Disclosure requirements			89.2059				
			(2.50)**				
Liability standards							
				(2.21)**			

(continued)

Table 12 External Finance, Legal Origins, and Investor Protection Indicators *(continued)*

Independent variables	*Dependent variable: ratio of stock market capitalization to GDP*						
Anti–self-dealing index					45.5373 (1.43)		
Public enforcement of securities laws						93.6562 (1.97)*	
Public enforcement of anti–self-dealing							−10.8972 (0.84)
Constant	−16.9507 (0.24)	−75.5425 (1.33)	−52.4460 (0.62)	−3.5120 (0.04)	−91.5774 (2.04)**	−0.1578 (0.00)	−67.9709 (1.43)
Observations	49	71	49	49	71	49	71
R-squared	0.43	0.46	0.44	0.43	0.48	0.46	0.47

Sources: La Porta et al. 1998; La Porta, López-de-Silanes, and Shleifer 2006; Djankov et al. 2003, 2006.

Note: The tables shows ordinary least squares regressions of a cross-section of 72 countries around the world.

Robust t-statistics are shown in parentheses.

* significant at 10 percent

** significant at 5 percent

*** significant at 1 percent

Table 13 Principal Components

Independent variables	*Dependent variable: ratio of stock market capitalization to GDP*			
Log (GDP per capita)	18.3803	22.1593	16.9974	21.5449
	(3.40)***	(3.94)***	(3.41)***	(3.64)***
Log (days to collect a check)	-14.1145	-20.8832	-13.4440	-29.0926
	(1.13)	(1.78)*	(1.26)	(2.50)**
Latin American–French legal origin	-12.3913	-42.6415		
	(0.69)	(2.74)***		
Rest of French legal origin	-8.1814	-28.6989		
	(0.47)	(1.83)*		
German legal origin	-11.7500	-11.9889		
	(0.30)	(0.35)		
Scandinavian legal origin	-14.7112	-18.3806		
	(0.34)	(0.49)		
Principal component, private enforcement	13.2660		15.7700	
	(2.77)***		(3.59)***	
Principal component, public enforcement		-17.7094		-18.2791
		(1.75)*		(1.75)*
Constant	-5.9628	6.9148	-4.2254	37.0918
	(0.08)	(0.09)	(0.06)	(0.46)
Observations	49	49	49	49
R-squared	0.44	0.45	0.44	0.40

Sources: La Porta et al. 1998; La Porta, López-de-Silanes, and Shleifer 2006; Djankov et al. 2003, 2006.

Note: The table shows ordinary least squares regressions of a cross-section of 49 countries around the world with all investor protection indicators. Robust t-statistics are shown in parentheses.

* significant at 10 percent
** significant at 5 percent
*** significant at 1 percent

GDP that is 50 percentage points lower, 30 fewer publicly traded firms per million people, and a ratio of IPO to GDP that is 3.7 percentage points lower. Simply put, the situation has not improved in the last 10 years.

The fifth set of results refers to the impact of the various measures of shareholder protection presented in tables 1 through 6. The results on all measures of shareholder protection are found in tables 10 and 11. The numbers are easy to summarize. All shareholder protection measures have a large impact on equity financing in both statistical and economical terms whether in the mid-1990s or in the more recent data for the period since 2000. To illustrate the magnitude of this impact, one might usefully consider that an increase by two standard deviations, equivalent to a jump from the level of protection found in a country such as República Bolivariana de Venezuela to the mean of common law countries, would be reflected in an increase by 33 percentage points in the ratio of external market capitalization to GDP, an additional 16 publicly traded firms per million population, and 1.2 additional IPOs per million population in the mid-1990s (see table 10). A similar jump by two standard deviations in the more recent data on antidirector rights recalculated for 2005 would be reflected in an increase by 23 percentage points in the ratio of total market capitalization to GDP (see table 11). The measures of IPO and anti–self-dealing regulation also have a large impact on the size of capital markets: an increase by two standard deviations in disclosure requirements and liability standards for the initiation of an IPO would translate into an increase in the ratio of the stock market to GDP of 49 and 37 percentage points, respectively. A similar jump in the anti–self-dealing index is reflected in an increase by 39 percentage points, or 65 percent of the mean stock market to GDP ratio (see table 11). Finally, public enforcement variables have a smaller or insignificant impact on the development of capital markets and a large impact on equity financing and are statistically significant almost everywhere.

Table 12 takes another look at the contribution of law and enforcement to the development of capital markets by controlling for legal origins and also the various indicators of shareholder protection. It represents an attempt to disassociate the link that the literature has documented between various legal origins and other negative characteristics. In table 12, we control for legal origin and then interpret the results in terms of the various indicators of shareholder protection as additional components that arise from the specific measures of the laws of investor protection captured by each index. The results in the table echo those of the previous table: French civil law countries, whether Latin American or not, have less well developed markets. But those countries that have higher levels of shareholder protection within these areas are able partly to escape their origin. In all regressions, the individual measures of shareholder protection are positive and significant.

One may argue that the different indicators of investor protection are closely related, and their impact is therefore not likely to be independent. For this reason, in table 13, we use all of our variables in the measurement of shareholder protection to construct two aggregate indexes that aim to capture the effectiveness of private measures and public measures of corporate governance. We use principal components analysis to construct these two indexes. The results suggest that the measures of the private enforcement of investor protection enhance external financing, while the measures of public enforcement seem to deter it. An increase by two standard deviations in our private enforcement index leads to an increase of about 43 to 51 percentage points in the ratio of stock market capitalization to GDP. This evidence supports the idea that, if reform is to take place in the region, the measures that facilitate disclosure and give investors the power to act have a more direct effect on the development of local capital markets.

Overall, the results of these five tables show that enforcement and shareholder rights have a large impact on the availability of external equity financing across countries. The regressions also confirm earlier results in the literature showing that the legal institutions of French and German civil law countries reduce the size and breadth of stock markets. Finally, the econometric estimates corroborate the hypothesis that part of the large underdevelopment in Latin American capital markets is due to the poor level of shareholder protection embedded in various laws and to the weak enforcement in the region.

Ownership Concentration

The image of the public corporation as a firm owned by dispersed shareholders, while control is concentrated in the hands of management, has been shown to be the exception rather than the rule in most countries around the world.[18] For the case of Latin America, the available empirical evidence is scant because of the difficulties in obtaining complete, reliable data on the structure of ownership beyond the largest companies. Some of the studies in this book fill this gap in the literature by providing a picture of the large ownership concentration in the region.

Information on ownership concentration represents a simple, alternative way to understand whether capital markets are broad and whether firms are able to place their stocks in the hands of investors. It is one of the most difficult types of statistics to obtain because ownership tends to be kept secret or disguised in many places. Latin America is, in fact, one of the regions in the world where this problem is exacerbated. One of the main contributions of the chapters in this book is to provide detailed information on levels of ownership concentration and deviations in cash flow and control rights among the largest samples of firms under study in Latin America today. The authors have used this information to examine in depth the ownership structures of firms and reveal, beneath the various layers of ownership, the "ultimate" owners of publicly traded firms. The methodology followed by the authors is similar to that applied in La Porta, López-de-Silanes, and Shleifer (1999). In many cases, the owners of firms are institutions or other corporations; thus, to discover the people who ultimately control the companies, we need to look for the owners of these firms and institutions. This is not an easy process; it requires a lot of information that has been unavailable until now.

Figure 4 summarizes the measures of ownership concentration found in this book. The columns on the left in each pair show the calculated concentration of the cash flow rights of the controlling groups in six countries for which data are available. The figure shows that, on average, the controlling group is sitting on 55 to 60 percent of the cash flow rights over the companies. This can hardly be said to help in the diversification of risk by the controlling group. But, more importantly, the figure also shows that minorities are barely present in the average corporation in Latin America. The chapters provide clear illustrations and examples of these facts.

Figure 4 Concentration of the Cash Flow Rights of Controlling Groups

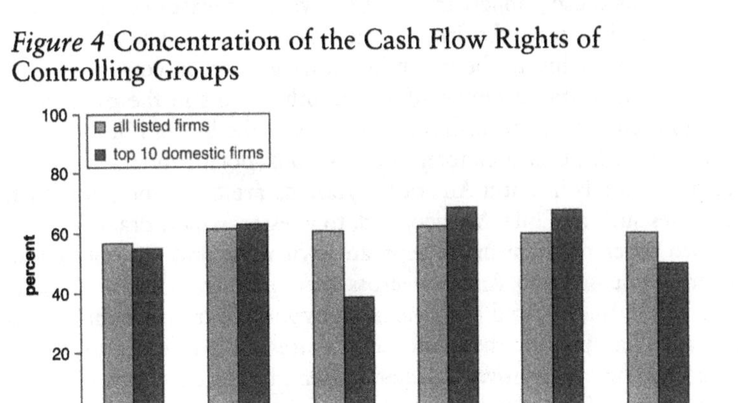

Source: Data from La Porta et al. 1998.

Note: "All listed firms" refers to all firms included in the samples under analysis in this book. For Brazil, Chile, and Colombia, data refer to the cash flow rights of the three major shareholders. For Argentina, they refer to the main ultimate shareholder. For República Bolivariana de Venezuela, they refer to the share owned by the major stockholder. The columns for the top 10 domestic firms refer to the cash flow rights of the three largest shareholders.

As confirmation for these findings, which cover all firms in the regional sample, we show the bars on the right in each pair in figure 4. These bars are based on the calculations in La Porta et al. (1998), who assembled data on the 10 largest publicly traded, nonfinancial private domestic firms in each country and measured ownership concentration as the median percentage share owned by the three largest shareholders in each of the 10 firms. The results echo the detailed comprehensive analysis of this book: ownership is highly concentrated even in the largest firms in the sample. The only country in which large firms appear to be an exception is Chile. In the case of Chile, the ownership concentration is almost half of that of the mean firm listed in the Santiago market. As other figures in the paper show, part of the difference between Chile and the rest of Latin America lies in the higher levels of protection offered to investors in Chile. This is documented in the tables in this introduction.

The separation of ownership and control in Latin American corporations is accomplished through the use of the two classic mechanisms: nonvoting shares and pyramids. In many countries, the law authorizes firms to issue stock that has no or only limited voting powers. Where this is the case, there is a distortion in the one share–one vote rule so that more powers are effectively given to those who have fuller voting rights. Pyramids are another such distortion of the one share–one vote principle. A pyramid is defined as those publicly traded firms where at least one other publicly traded firm is between the firm and the ultimate owner. The use of multiple layers of ownership in the pyramid allows insiders in control at the top also to control the resources of all the other firms in the pyramid even though their actual ownership in the firms at the bottom of the pyramid may be small. Several chapters in this book document the widespread use of pyramids in Latin America. Pyramids are a common approach in countries such as Chile, Mexico, and, to a lesser extent, Brazil.

Two other mechanisms to separate ownership and control appear to be prevalent in Latin America: cross-shareholding, whereby firms own each other's shares, and multiple or nonvoting share mechanisms. As in the case of a pyramid, the existence of shares with different voting rights facilitates the control over decision making by insiders with preferential voting rights. The nonvoting share mechanism is most common in Brazil, but it may also be found in other countries in the region and is widely used by firms that cross-list. All countries in the region, with the possible exception of Colombia, show significant frequency in the use of mechanisms to separate ownership and control.

Figure 5 shows that the value of the control block premiums for Latin American corporations is high. The data on block premiums in Dyck and Zingales (2004) indicate that Brazil, Mexico, and República Bolivariana de Venezuela have the highest block premiums in Latin America.

Figure 5 Block Premium Relative to Firm Equity

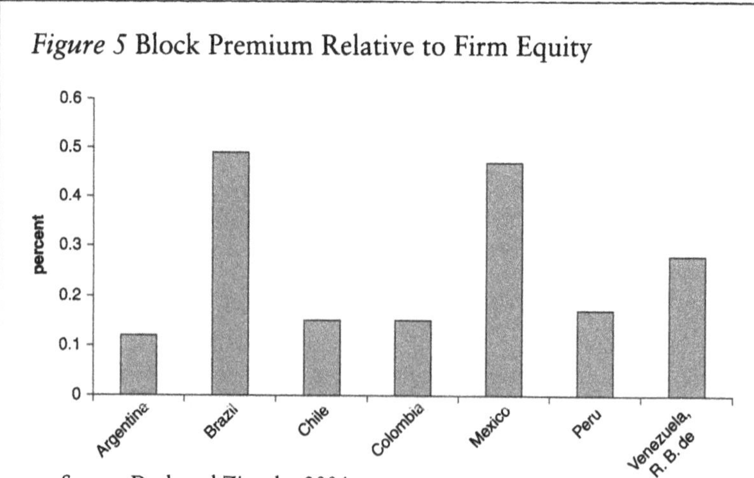

Source: Dyck and Zingales 2004.

Note: The block premium is computed as follows: the difference between the price per share paid for the control block and the exchange price two days after the announcement of the control transaction is divided by the exchange price two days after the announcement. The result is multiplied by the proportion of cash flow rights represented in the controlling block.

Some of these countries, in fact, show some of the highest numbers in the world. The value of the block premiums for firms in Argentina, Chile, and Colombia is lower. Several of these countries actually have better investor protection according to the measures outlined in the previous sections. Although there is variation, the data show that the concentration of ownership in Latin America may be linked to the great potential for the extraction of private benefits by exercising control.

Insider Trading

Another line of research that contributes to our understanding of the effects of poor shareholder protection across countries in Latin America is presented in the chapter by Cruces and Kawamura (chapter 1). The authors use intraday trading data on more than 1,400 tickers in Latin American companies to compute an insider or informed trading probability (ITP).[19] Previous work on the subject argues that the ITP might be a good proxy for the intensity of privately informed trading and thus be related to the quality of corporate governance among firms. Controlling groups may be able to trade using insider information, and such trading may be detrimental to outside investors. The data of Cruces and Kawamura show that the ITP is correlated with some of the countrywide investor protection variables used in the literature and presented in previous sections. The chapter also documents substantial increases in the ITP immediately before public corporate announcements, such as the release of financial statements or corporate governance announcements. These findings suggest that privately informed agents are trying to exploit their privileged information when it is most valuable.

Armed with this evidence, the chapter estimates the relationship between the ITP and corporate valuation. The authors find that, after controlling for company characteristics, the ITP is priced corresponding to the market: companies with higher ITPs fetch a lower Tobin's q.[20] A fall of one standard deviation in the ITP is associated with an increase by one or two percentage points in valuation measures. The authors conclude that the ITP proxies for the unobservable quality of corporate governance because the heterogeneity of firm behavior seems to be recognized by the market and priced accordingly. Another unintended consequence of poor corporate governance is the increased probability that those in control of a firm and having access to information will be able to abuse their information and benefit from trading on securities before the information becomes public and impacts the stock price. In such cases, small shareholders are hurt because they are not able to do the same.

The evidence in this chapter, the first evidence on Latin America and other emerging markets, suggests that there is substantial heterogeneity in firm behavior and, thus, corporate governance within a given institutional environment. Part of this heterogeneity seems to be recognized by the market and priced accordingly. The results concerning the ITP lead us to the next section in this chapter, on firm-level corporate governance characteristics beyond the countrywide measures.

Firm-Level Corporate Governance

To understand the options available to firms in Latin America, one might usefully follow Coffee (1999), who draws a distinction between legal and functional convergence. Legal convergence refers to the changes in rules and enforcement mechanisms that tend toward some desirable standard. According to the analysis of the evolution of legal investor protection in Latin America elsewhere above, to achieve a legal convergence to effective investor protection, most countries in the region will require more drastic legal, regulatory, and judicial reform. An alternative path to reaching higher standards is functional convergence, which refers to more decentralized, market-based, and firm-level changes. Functional convergence does not require legal reform per se, but still brings more firms and assets under the umbrella of effective legal protection for investors.

Functional convergence may be achieved through many mechanisms. First, firms may unilaterally try to improve their corporate governance practices and reform their statutes to adjust to the practices and rules followed by other companies inside or outside the country. The firm-level improvement of corporate governance practices that depart from current legislation and regulation in the country seems the simplest form of functional convergence available to firms. Firms may opt out of legal rules in their corporate charters, which serve as the ultimate contract between the firm and its investors.[21] Although opting out of the standard rules sounds simple, it may prove costly in practice if investors or courts have difficulty understanding these special contracts. Enforcement becomes critical if there are departures from the norm.

A second and probably less risky option for individual firms trying to provide higher investor protection is adherence to a common set of voluntary principles that have been designed by experts and authorities. Such approaches have now become more widely available because the wave of corporate governance scandals has translated into the adoption of voluntary codes of best governance practice throughout the world. These codes have sometimes been created to facilitate the transition of firms into higher standards without forcing legal reform. Adhering to a code of best practice or some of its principles has the advantage that other firms may also be adhering, the authorities have blessed the code, and the code has probably already passed the screening tests of lawyers in the country. This means that enforcement may be less of a problem than the unilateral adoption of different norms.

The third and final type of functional convergence involves foreign influences that may be exercised because a firm has listed abroad or has been acquired by a foreign firm that relies on a set of practices that are different from the local ones. In both of these cases, the probability of enforcement in support of the improved practices is greater because the courts and regulatory agencies of the other nations familiar with these norms possess certain powers to intervene in the case of disputes.

The use of one or more of these mechanisms of functional convergence means that firm-level corporate governance practices may differ within a country. If that is the case, we would find that, in countries with weak protection, some firms will not remain idle and will try to improve the local legal standard of corporate governance to gain greater access to capital. Functional convergence thus creates the need to analyze firm-level corporate governance practices within countries.

Firm-level Samples and Corporate Governance Indicators

Until recently, there were only a handful of studies that used firm-level data to measure the impact of corporate governance. La Porta et al. (2000a, 2000b) and Daines (2001) have established that country and state laws have an impact on firm valuation dividend payout ratios. A new generation of studies looks beyond country-level measures and collects data on firm-level characteristics and corporate governance practices to analyze the impacts.[22] The chapters in this book follow this approach by analyzing whether variations in firm-level governance practices are also associated with firm valuation, performance, and dividend payments.

The chapters represent pioneer studies on Latin America, a region with a virtual vacuum of firm-level information relative to other regions of the world. The studies here have involved the collection of the most comprehensive and detailed firm-level data that yet exist on Argentina, Brazil, Chile, Colombia, Mexico, and República Bolivariana de Venezuela. Because of the data limitations, detailed and comprehensive country studies of firm-level governance practices are still rare, particularly on developing countries. This sort of analysis needs to encompass detailed firm-level data, including information on financial statements, performance, board composition and functioning, disclosure levels, minority shareholder rights, enforcement procedures, and fees and compensations. The difficulty arises because some firms may not have the right incentives or may want to avoid disclosing this kind of information, especially in environments with weak financial markets or where there is little knowledge of the positive effects of good governance practices on corporate valuation and performance.

To address the issue of the measurement of corporate governance, the chapters look at the literature on firm-level analysis. Based on this information, the authors have developed a unique questionnaire, trying to keep the questions consistent across jurisdictions in the region to facilitate cross-country comparisons. In itself, this has represented an unprecedented step in the region. The additional effort at coordination among the research teams is a reflection on the quality of the data that have been generated.

Table 14 summarizes the types of efforts at convergence revealed through the questionnaire by firms across the Latin American countries covered in this book based on information supplied for 2003–04. The questionnaire was developed by the editors, in collaboration with the authors of the chapters. It has been based on the various indicators identified in other studies[23] and supplemented with additional questions to examine the poor level of investor protection in the region. This has meant that some basic questions about the legal protection of investors that may not have been necessary in other, more protective regions needed to be adapted and added to the questionnaire. Similarly, because of country differences in regulation and the level of protection, some questions are tailored to address the laws of particular countries.

The questionnaire was typically sent to officers and board members in each corporation. In most countries, the information was supplemented or corroborated through reliance on as many sources of publicly available information as possible. Table 14 shows that the questions covered nine basic areas of corporate governance: (1) the general characteristics of firm governance; (2) principles of corporate governance; (3) board structure and the characteristics of board meetings; (4) the characteristics and functions of board committees; (5) external auditors and other independent experts; (6) financial disclosures; (7) conflicts of interest, including related party transactions, as well as ownership structure, deviations from one share–one vote rules, compensation, and nomination; (8) shareholder rights and the workings of shareholder meetings; and (9) the experience with sanctions and recent, known governance problems in the firm. In general, the questions in each of these categories were tailored to all the countries. The number of questions across countries ranged from 20, in the case of Chile (which has the highest level of mandated disclosures and other shareholder protections in the region) to 70 in the case of República Bolivariana de Venezuela.

Despite the clear difficulties in gathering together such information, extensive groundwork and creative ways of using available information have allowed the researchers to collect firm-level longitudinal data on at least half the listed firms in each country, which represents around 70 percent of the total market capitalization in these countries (see figures 6 and 7). In terms of financial and operational measures, the authors of all the chapters have used several sources to create panel data sets that cover quantitative variables and that, in some cases, span more than a decade.

The studies in this book are largely homogeneous in their analysis on issues related to the effects of corporate governance in terms of various performance and valuation measures, but each study also departs from the others and investigates additional questions that are relevant to specific markets. The authors provide a descriptive analysis of ownership structures and of the separation of ownership and control in Brazil, Chile, and Colombia. In the case of República Bolivariana de Venezuela, the authors try to assess the relationships among performance, the earnings of chief executive officers, and the role of boards in monitoring chief executive officers.

Table 14 Questions in Each Category on the Corporate Governance Questionnaire

No.	*Question category*	*Argentina*	*Brazil*	*Chile*	*Colombia*	*Costa Rica*	*Mexico*	*Venezuela, R. B. de*
1	Company structure and governance characteristics	0	2	1	1	3	0	5
2	General governance principles	1	0	1	4	4	0	4
3	Board structure and board meetings	2	4	4	6	10	14	11
4	Board committees: structure and functions	4	2	3	0	6	20	4
5	External auditors and other independent experts	1	1	1	1	1	6	4
6	Financial disclosure	13	2	2	6	8	1	8
7	Conflicts of interest (related party transactions, ownership structure, compensation, and nomination)	11	7	4	8	13	5	13
8	Shareholder rights and meetings	0	3	3	5	15	8	16
9	Sanctions and recent governance problems	0	3	1	0	5	0	5
	Corporate governance index	32	24	20	31	65	54	70

Source: Chapters in this volume.

Figure 6 Listed and Sampled Firms

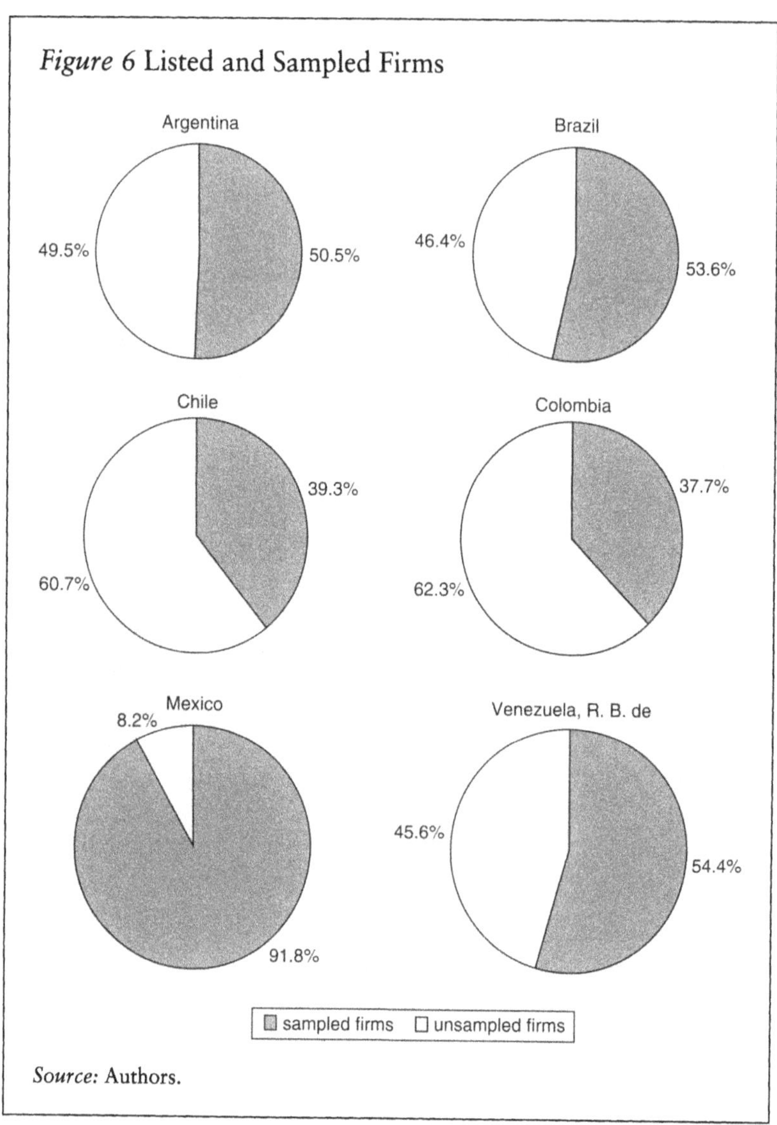

Source: Authors.

Firm-level Corporate Governance Practices and their Impact

In this section, we briefly describe the most salient differences in corporate governance among firms within each of the countries examined in the book and the impact of the related measures on valuation, performance, and dividend payout ratios. Using the data samples described in the previous section, we highlight interesting facts regarding the corporate governance of firms within each country and its relationship with firm performance.

Figure 7 Market Capitalization of Listed Firms and Total Market Capitalization

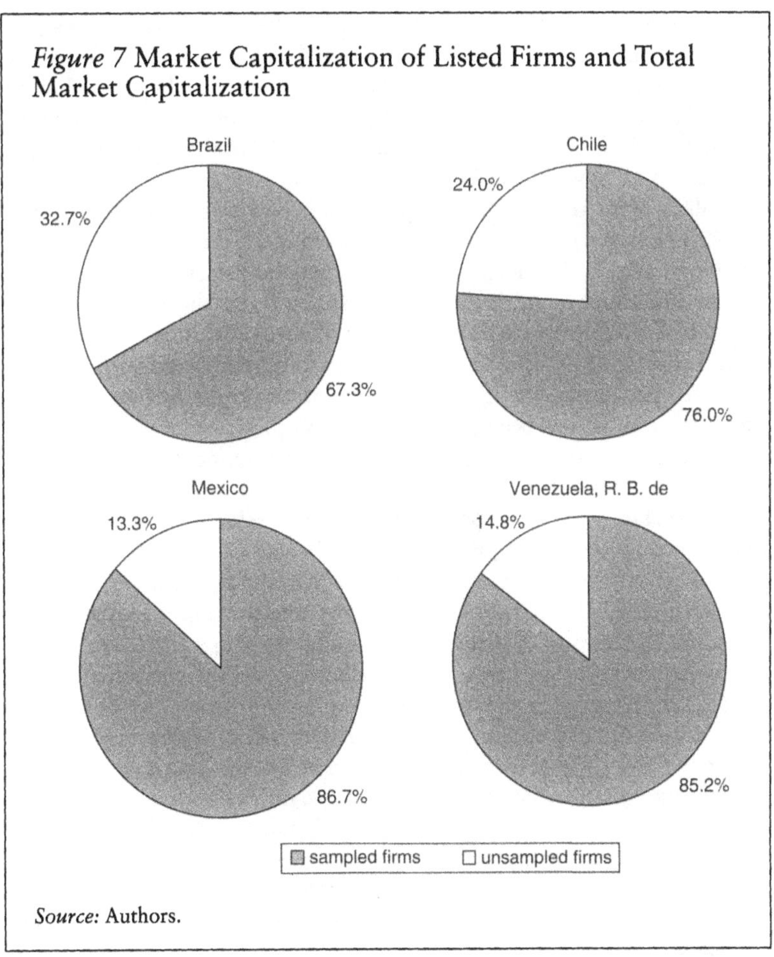

Source: Authors.

There are two patterns that are common across the six countries that have reported a firm-level corporate governance index for this book (Argentina, Brazil, Chile, Colombia, Mexico, and República Bolivariana de Venezuela): (1) the average firm in most countries exhibits a low overall score, and (2) there is wide variation in the practices across firms within each country.

Firms in all three southern cone countries (Argentina, Brazil, and Chile) show higher scores in the disclosure of the index. Argentine firms seem to perform poorly when we look at the average index computed; they score only 39.1 of a possible 100 points. As in most countries, there is wide variation in the index across firms, ranging from 18.8 to 84.4 points. On subindexes, the highest average score is the one on disclosure (49.4), and the lowest is the one on board characteristics (28.4).

Meanwhile, in Brazil, the average index in the sample was 10 of a possible 24 points, and the range was between 4 and 19. Brazilian firms also score relatively better on disclosure. On the other hand, they score low on the shareholder rights subindex. Despite improvements in recent years, compliance with good practices by boards and avoidance of conflicts of interest remain low in Brazil.

Chilean firms also show better performance in disclosure and information (5.14). The score on boards and officers is relatively high, too (4.54). The worst area in the index is the one on general principles (2.63).

The other three countries in the region show larger differences. Firms in Colombia and República Bolivariana de Venezuela exhibit relatively low overall scores, while firms in Mexico seem to have improved over time.

More specifically, the implementation of corporate governance practices in Colombia has been poor: half the sample scores fewer than 47 of 100 points. The independence of boards and discipline do not seem to be fostered by the average Colombian firm.

Venezuelan public companies also exhibit relatively low corporate governance scores overall, with an average score of 3.79 out of 7. As in the case of Argentina, Brazil, and Chile, the best performance is on the disclosure and information section of the questionnaire. In the section on general principles, the results are similar to those for Chile: a large number of Venezuelan firms do not adhere to the international code of conduct. In terms of the questions pertaining to officers and boards, the most salient finding is that, in almost half the companies surveyed, the chief executive officers were also the chairmen of the board and belonged to the same family or control group. Finally, only slightly more than half the companies acknowledged having independent board members, and only a handful had corporate governance committees.

The creation of the corporate governance code for publicly traded firms has been a significant source of improvement in firm-level practices in Mexico. By 2003, the average listed company met 78.4 percent of all the recommendations in the code. A year later, more than 90 firms in the sample (150 firms) met more than 80 percent of the code's recommendations. Although compliance is increasing, there is still a lot of variation: firms comply with between 30 and 98 percent of the recommendations. Among the specific areas, compliance ranged from 53 percent regarding the recommendation on the evaluation committee and on compensation to 90.3 percent on the recommendations related to the duties of directors.

Each chapter includes a set of econometric results that relate corporate governance indicators to various outcome measures. But the most distinctive feature of this book is that all the authors have sought to reach a common ground to be able to analyze the impact of firm-level corporate governance practices in terms of measures of valuation, performance, and dividend payout ratios. We should clarify that, because of the various data limitations in each country, all the outcome measures are not available for all the chapters, and the econometric procedures that the authors have been able to use have also differed in some cases. All the authors have performed their analyses following the ordinary least squares methodology. However, because it is possible that certain types of firms are more likely to adopt better corporate governance practices, most chapters discuss alternative econometric procedures to address the endogeneity issue.[24]

Several characteristics relating to the intrinsic nature of firms, their assets, or their cash flows may be a source of endogeneity in this kind of study. The size or the age of a firm likewise might affect corporate practices. The operations of a small firm may be more easily understood and monitored, while larger firms or firms in multiple industries would have potentially larger agency problems and might thus seek to adopt better corporate governance. Similarly, firms with lower tangible assets may be more difficult for investors to monitor and would thus require better governance practices.[25] Additionally, firms with large, free cash flows might cause investors to become more concerned about potential expropriation and might thus adopt better corporate governance measures to keep investors happy.[26] Probably one of the larger sources of concern are unobserved future growth opportunities that might lead controlling shareholders and managers to improve corporate governance to increase their chance of tapping capital markets or reduce the cost of capital. In such cases, valuation measures are likely also to be determined with a view to anticipated future growth.

As elsewhere in the literature, the chapters in this book try to disentangle the corporate governance effect on performance and valuation measures by controlling for several company characteristics likely to be associated with higher growth prospects and greater needs for monitoring because of the nature of firm assets, cash flows, and firm size. All regressions control for key company characteristics that the theory predicts should have an impact on valuation or performance measures. The regressions in each chapter typically include measures of size, indebtedness, profitability, and growth. The analysis also tries to take into account potential endogeneity problems emerging from the nature of firm assets or cash flows, especially in light of the differences across industries; industry-level fixed effects are considered whenever possible. Most authors also rely on methods involving some instrumental variables to provide robustness to the results from ordinary least squares.

Although the samples and econometric methodology of each of the studies vary, some numbers may be compared across countries. To provide a rough overview of the analysis of the effects of corporate governance, we summarize some comparable results in figures 8 and 9. These two figures look at the impact of the corporate governance index developed in each country on Tobin's q and dividend payouts, respectively.

There are several potential outcome variables at the firm level that fall in the categories of valuation, performance, and payout ratios. Among valuation measures, the most commonly used in the literature is Tobin's q,[27] but several chapters also analyze the price-to-book ratio for robustness purposes. An argument might be made that valuation measures are the prime variable for capturing the effect of firm-level corporate governance. According to the model in La Porta, López-de-Silanes, and Shleifer (2002), improved valuations deriving from better corporate governance are the result of the higher confidence of investors that controlling shareholders will have fewer means to expropriate the cash flows of the firm. Better firm-level governance makes investors more willing to provide capital to firms at lower cost, and this is reflected in higher valuation multiples.

Controlling for endogeneity issues as carefully as possible for each data set, figure 9 shows that there is a positive impact on the valuation of firms across the region. The graph illustrates the percentage change in firm valuation that would arise from an increase by two standard deviations in the corporate governance index of each country. The largest impact is in the case of Mexico, which shows large returns. Mexico is followed by Argentina and República Bolivariana de Venezuela, where a jump of two standard deviations in the index would increase Tobin's q by 30 percent. The results in the chapters that

Figure 8 Effect of Corporate Governance on Tobin's q

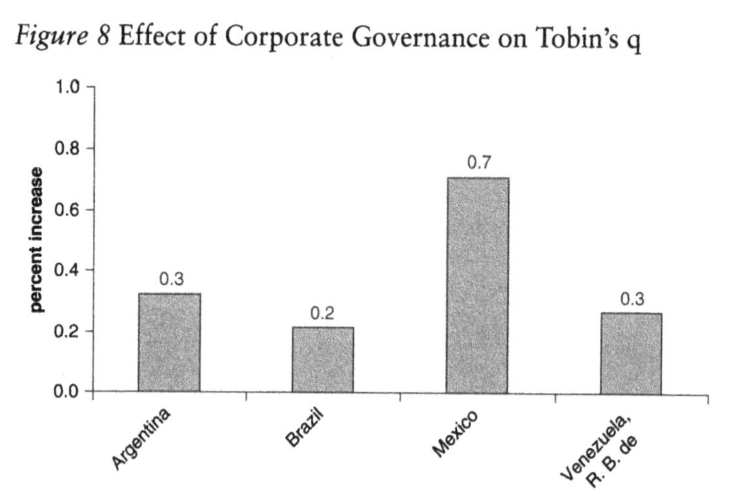

Source: Calculations of the authors based on the results of regression analyses discussed in the chapters.

Note: The figure shows the percentage increase in each country's Tobin's q caused by an increase in the corporate governance index of two standard deviations. The numbers for each country are not the result of the same calculation or methodology. Argentina uses the transparency and disclosure index instead of the corporate governance index, and the data cover the period 2000–03. The data on Brazil are for 2002, on Mexico for 2002–03, and on República Bolivariana de Venezuela for 2004. The results for this last country come from an ordinary least squares model. The coefficients for Brazil are estimated using a three stage least squares model to deal with endogeneity problems. Argentina and Mexico use a two stage least squares model to deal with endogeneity.

Figure 9 Effect of Corporate Governance on Dividend Payout

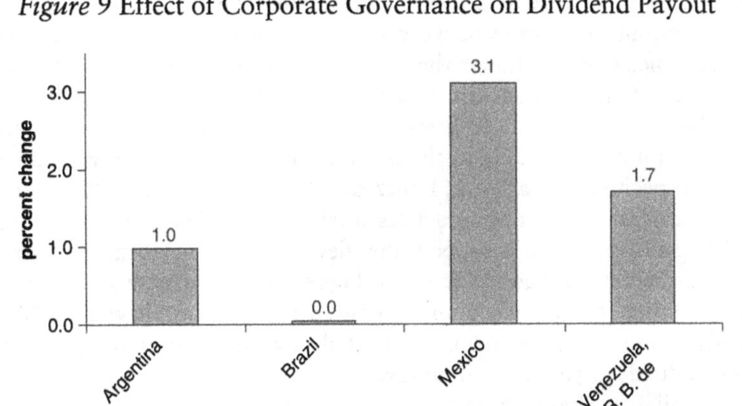

Source: Calculations of the authors based on the results of regression analyses discussed in the chapters.

Note: The results are from regression analyses that are not strictly the same for each country. Argentina uses a pooled Tobit regression for the years 2000–03. To deal with potential endogeneity, Brazil uses a three stage least squares model for 2002, and Mexico uses a two stage least squares procedure for data from 2002–03. República Bolivariana de Venezuela, using data for 2004, estimates ordinary least squares models.

use price-to-book ratios are also very similar (Brazil, Mexico, and República Bolivariana de Venezuela). The findings regarding the impact of corporate governance practices on valuation are large and significant. They support earlier results for samples of firms in emerging markets examined in Klapper and Love (2002) and, for Korea, in Black, Jang, and Kim (2006a, 2006b).

Although valuation ratios are likely to be the best measure for capturing the impact of better firm-level governance, performance measures might also be affected. One might argue that more well-governed firms are also better run, probably because better mechanisms are used to face changing conditions or new opportunities. If this is the case, then these firms would show higher returns. Following this logic, several chapters also analyze the impact of corporate governance on performance ratios that include the return on assets and the return on equity. It is worthwhile noting that the rationale behind a positive association between performance and governance relies on a notion of market inefficiency whereby investors tend to underestimate the full impact of higher agency costs in poorly governed firms. Some recent papers have tested this hypothesis in other countries and have found that governance exerts a positive effect on operating performance.[28] The authors have sufficient data on Argentina, Mexico, and República Bolivariana de Venezuela to analyze the association between the corporate governance index and the return on assets and the return on equity. The results are positive, but smaller than those for valuation measures. In the case of Colombia, the authors use data for 2004 and find a significant association between the return on assets and the corporate governance index, although the economic effect of the findings is small.

Figure 9 summarizes the results across the chapters that perform an analysis of the impact of firm-level corporate governance on dividend payout ratios. According to the outcome agency model of dividend payments specified by La Porta, López-de-Silanes, and Shleifer (2002), firms with stronger governance practices should have higher dividend payouts. The results in figure 9 support the view that stronger firm-level governance practices are associated with higher dividend payouts. To provide a magnitude for the effect, an increase by two standard deviations in the corporate governance index is reflected in a doubling or tripling of the mean dividend payout ratio in three of the four countries for which data are available. These effects are twice as large as those for regressions that do not account for endogeneity. The only country where the impact of dividends is small, but still positive, is Brazil.

Overall, these figures are revealing and embody the basic message of the book: individual firm-level corporate governance measures do have an effect on firm valuation and on the amounts of dividends that are delivered to shareholders. In line with evidence on other countries, these results support the view that firms providing a better package of governance measures are more well appreciated by markets and distribute more profits to shareholders.

Firm Migration and Disappearing Stock Markets

The challenges facing Latin American stock markets are huge because of the proximity of Wall Street. The existence of cross-listing programs in the United States and other countries with large stock markets provides firms with an alternative mechanism to escape the low levels of general legal protection in their local markets. The most common form of cross-listing is a depositary receipt program. These programs exist in the main stock exchanges in the United States and other places such as Hong Kong (China), London, Luxembourg, and Singapore. Depositary receipts are negotiable certificates that are denominated in the currency of the market where they are traded and that represent the ownership of shares in a foreign company. These certificates may be traded over the counter or in organized exchanges, and they may be either capital raising or not.[29]

Cross-listing abroad has been perceived by some as a mechanism to foster improvements in firm-level corporate governance practices because of the links to U.S. markets, which have higher corporate governance and disclosure standards than the average Latin American country. Coffee (1999) and others (for example, Karolyi 2004, 2005) argue that cross-listings represent an important movement toward functional convergence to U.S.-style corporate governance. The recent gains in Hong Kong (China) and London as favorite cross-listing locations mean that, except for Luxembourg, the largest cross-listing centers are located in common law countries, which rank systematically higher in measures of legal protection for investors.

The quality of the laws and of law enforcement seems to be an important factor among firms wanting to cross-list. Sarkissian and Schill (2004) provide empirical evidence that foreign firms list in markets with better investor protection where they are provided with higher liquidity and a larger shareholder base. Firms may also wish to migrate to avoid certain exchange controls, transaction costs, trading taxes, or clearance and settlement risks in local markets. Differences in tax regimes may also be a motive for listing abroad. To lure them to their capital markets, tax havens and markets in Hong Kong (China), Luxembourg, and Singapore offer tax concessions for foreign firms.

Thus, cross-listing may bring several advantages for firms. First, entering an international capital market may send a signal to investors about the firm's quality and commitment to increased disclosure and protection, leading to higher equity valuations. Second, because financial markets are not fully integrated, entering foreign markets may simply lower the cost of capital as the premium on once hard-to-get stocks is reduced. Third, diversifying and increasing the investor base through a foreign listing may also improve a company's capacity to access capital and exploit growth opportunities. A fourth advantage may arise from the additional publicity that is attached to the cross-listing and that tends to enhance the visibility of a firm's products. A larger investor base and increased investor recognition lower information costs and may therefore affect the cost of capital.[30] Higher liquidity is a fifth reason for listing abroad; this may allow a firm to avoid funding reductions during periods of negative domestic shocks and local market contraction. Finally, although less common, cross-listed shares are easier to use as currency for foreign acquisitions.

However, cross-listing is not simple and may also be costly. First, there is the classic home bias of investors, who have a demonstrated preference for familiar assets.[31] Reducing this bias is simpler for firms in countries with significant cultural, language, institutional, geographical, or trade ties. Sarkissian and Schill (2004) show that all these factors facilitate crossborder listings. Second, for controlling groups, the flip side of increased investor protection is more transparency, less flexibility in exerting power over shareholders, and a greater probability of losing dominance in the firm.[32] The recent wave of improvements in corporate governance standards and the potential penalties imposed for violations also increase the threat to controlling shareholders if they enter foreign markets. Higher disclosure standards likewise mean higher financial costs for reconciling and adopting international accounting standards. Recent evidence shows that accounting costs in the United States have nearly doubled since passage of the Sarbanes-Oxley Act.

The empirical evidence suggests that, despite the potentially high costs, firms that cross-list are perceived by markets as benefiting overall. Foerster and Karolyi (1999) were among the first to illustrate these benefits in a series of studies on a large cross-section of countries. The data indicate that a firm listing shares in the United States experiences a positive change in its share price at home and improves its subsequent access to external capital markets. There is also evidence that listing in U.S. markets is perceived as a commitment by the firm to higher shareholder protection. Lins, Strickland, and Zenner (2005) show that there is a decline in the sensitivity of investment to cash flow when an American depositary receipt (ADR) is issued by a company from a country with a weak legal system and a less well-developed capital market. Reese and Weisbach (2001) find that companies in French and Scandinavian civil law countries are more likely to list ADRs on an organized exchange in the United States. This means that ADRs seem to be used as a partial substitute for weak legal institutions because they represent a commitment by firms to greater disclosure. The increased protection mainly comes through the stricter disclosure requirements,[33] but it may also be the result of the threat of action by the foreign regulatory authorities, who may undertake damaging investigations and legal suits that might end in delisting and other financial penalties.

Probably as a result of a combination of improved investor protection and the other market-access arguments outlined above, firms from all parts of the world have been cross-listing in the United States and, more recently, in other large exchanges. The movement toward Wall Street by firms in other jurisdictions has been significant over the last 50 years (see figure 10). After an early period of little growth in cross-listings, foreign listings on the New York Stock Exchange began surging around 1986. The 1990s were the years with the largest growth in this market as firms moved away from issuing the traditional over-the-counter or level 1 depositary receipts and started to engage more in exchange-listed (levels 2 and 3), Rule 144A, and global depositary receipts. From 1990 to 1996, the number of depositary receipt programs doubled to almost 1,500. Figure 10 shows this explosion: the number of ADR programs listed on the New York Stock Exchange reached an all-time high of more than 450 in 2001–02.

Figure 11 takes a closer look at the change in the composition of depositary receipt programs in recent years. The figure shows continuous growth at first and a small setback in 2003–04. By mid-2006, the market had recovered and reached a new record of 1,943 depositary receipt programs in 75 countries available to investors. The figure illustrates that foreign issuers have continued to increase their participation in the depositary receipt market, but the bulk of the increase has not come from U.S.-listed programs. Instead, the increase is explained by level 1 ADRs in the United States and, above all, global depositary receipts going to Hong Kong (China), London, and Luxembourg.

Figure 10 Non-U.S. Firms Cross-Listing on the New York Stock Exchange

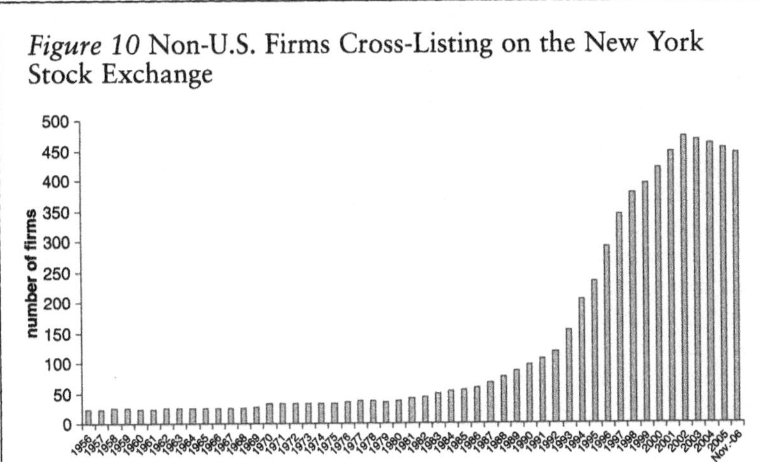

Source: White 2002 for data up to 2001. For data after 2001, compiled by the authors from data of the New York Stock Exchange, http://www.nyse.com/marketinfo/datalib/ 1022221393065.html.

Figure 11 Sponsored Depositary Receipt Programs

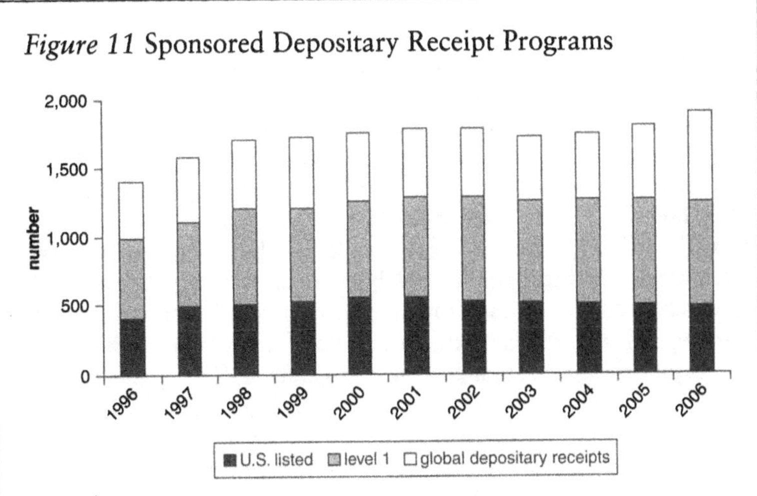

Source: Compiled by the authors based on data from NYSE 2005, 2006.

Note: U.S.-listed stocks include level 2 and level 3 ADRs. Level 1 refers to over-the-counter ADRs. Global depositary receipts are depositary receipt programs that are established under private placement and non-U.S. offering rules and that are often listed on international stock exchanges. The data for 2006 correspond to the data available until July 2006.

Since 2001, the number of U.S.-listed depositary receipt programs has shrunk by more than 10 percent, reaching a nine-year low of 473 in June 2006. There are new listings every year, but more issuers have left U.S. exchanges. The reasons for this phenomenon include mergers, acquisitions, and financial difficulties. The U.S. market downturn of 2002 may have been another important reason behind the reduction in listed ADRs. But the change in the composition of cross-listings observed in the past few years may also have other, more structurally related causes. The expansion of foreign stock markets and the reduced attractiveness of the U.S. economy as a whole translate into a reduced advantage for U.S. markets in attracting capital. Additionally, levels of investor protection, supervision, regulatory burden, and liability risk have risen in the United States, notably with the passage of the Sarbanes-Oxley Act in 2003 and a stream of litigation that followed the collapse of Enron. Indeed, there are fears that some features of the new rules are too expensive, particularly for small firms. These concerns have already led regulators to analyze rule changes to lighten the burden. In November 2006, a special independent committee on capital market regulation issued its first report, which proposed that more cost-effective regulation and a reform of the U.S. litigation and enforcement system may be needed to regain competitiveness relative to other big markets. This does not mean less regulation or lower levels of protection. In fact, some of the recommendations call for stronger shareholder rights to bolster the market for corporate control. But it does suggest reconsidering the costs and the benefits of existing rules that have generated a substantial increase in litigation, which may also harm investors.

Although there seems to be a push for reform in U.S. capital markets, the recent numbers should provide some comfort. The past two years have seen higher levels of activity, similar to the levels of the late 1990s. Figure 12 shows that the annual capital-raising value of primary and follow-on depositary receipt offerings have surpassed the previous record set in 2000. The figure illustrates two important points. First, it is clear that, today, a few markets outside the United States are attracting foreign cross-listings. Unfortunately, none of these markets are in Latin America. Second, although the number of new U.S. listings is not rising rapidly, U.S. markets are still raising large amounts for return issuers. The capital raised through depositary receipts on U.S. exchanges in 2005 was the second-largest annual amount in the last decade, behind only the effort in 2000. Additionally, although competition from other exchanges has impacted U.S. exchanges, more than 90 percent of the cross-listers still choose to market their shares to investors in the United States under Rule 144A.

Latin American firms have additional incentives to enter U.S. markets because of the product market, the investor base, or simply geographical reasons that render trading more synchronous with their own local markets. For all these reasons, companies in the region are flocking to U.S.

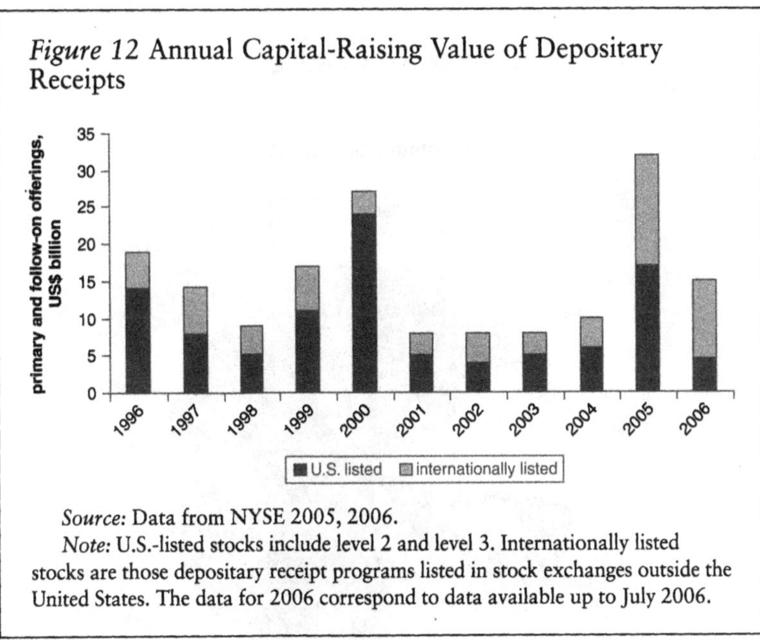

Figure 12 Annual Capital-Raising Value of Depositary Receipts

Source: Data from NYSE 2005, 2006.

Note: U.S.-listed stocks include level 2 and level 3. Internationally listed stocks are those depositary receipt programs listed in stock exchanges outside the United States. The data for 2006 correspond to data available up to July 2006.

listings or are going over the counter. The United States is still the most relevant choice for firms in Latin America that want to migrate.[34] Over the last 15 years, there has been a large, steady movement of cross-listings by Latin American firms. Figure 13 shows the composition of the ADR listings in 1990 and in 2003. The increasing participation of Latin America in this market is impressive. In 1990, the only Latin American country that showed a significant participation was Mexico, which ranked 19th, with less than 1 percent of all ADR listings. The situation had completely changed a decade later. By 2003, Mexico and Brazil were the sixth and seventh largest contributors to ADR listings, respectively. That year, these two countries had more than 9 percent of all cross-listings.

Hong Kong (China), India, and Taiwan (China) have recently moved to the top of the list in depositary receipt listings. Meanwhile, the share of Latin America in the overall market has not really changed. Nonetheless, Latin American depositary receipt programs represent close to 13 percent of all available programs in the world. In 2005–06, Latin American companies accounted for five of the largest 15 depositary receipt programs in the world and five of the top 20 most actively traded U.S.-listed ADRs.[35]

Figure 14 illustrates this trend. It indicates the large number of new firms in Brazil, Mexico, and, to a lesser extent, Argentina and Chile, that are entering the cross-listings market. The figure shows that firms in the region are still using U.S. markets as an important mechanism to access

Figure 13 Composition of ADR Listings in the United States

a. Composition in 1990

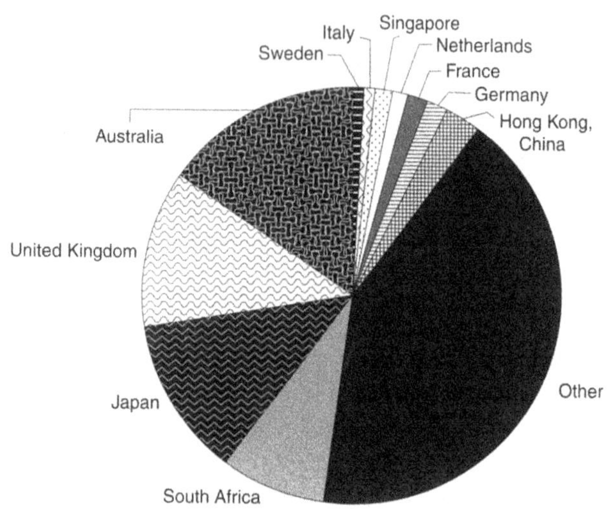

b. Composition in 2003

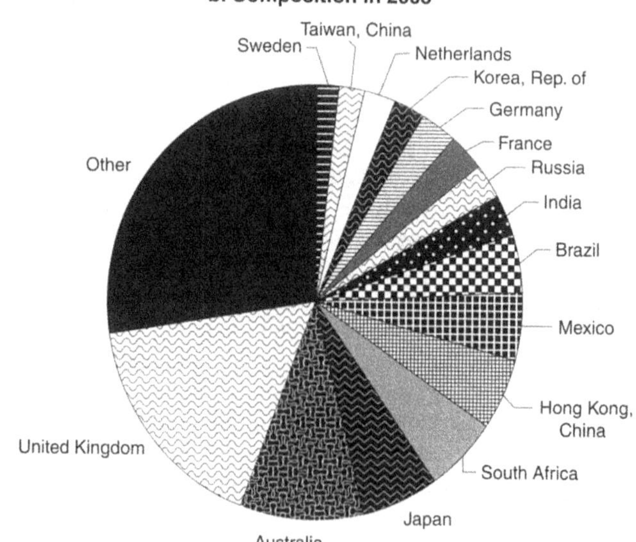

Source: Data from Karolyi 2005.

Figure 14 New Latin American Firms with ADRs

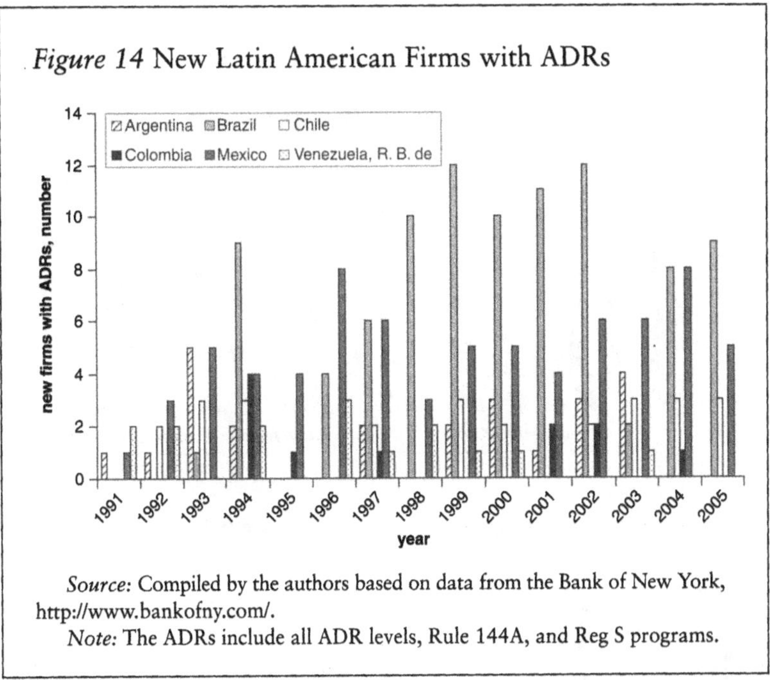

Source: Compiled by the authors based on data from the Bank of New York, http://www.bankofny.com/.

Note: The ADRs include all ADR levels, Rule 144A, and Reg S programs.

investors and raise capital. In 2005, two of the top 20 capital-raising depositary receipts were Latin American, and that number doubled in 2006.[36] For the majority of the past 15 years, capital raising via ADRs has been larger or similar to the capital raising by Latin American firms in their respective local markets.[37]

Firms in Latin America favor U.S. markets for the simple reason that these markets provide them with access to the capital they need at a lower cost. There is empirical support for the idea that firms in countries with poor shareholder protection may want to migrate or cross-list in places with stronger investor protection because these markets are larger, more inclusive, and more valuable and give them higher valuations.[38] The bonding theory of international cross-listings proposed by Coffee (1999) and Stulz (1999) seems to be borne out in the data: the lower cost of capital experienced by U.S. cross-listers derives mainly through the benefits accrued by bonding to the laws and regulations that govern firms in more protective markets.[39] Figure 15 illustrates the evidence on this issue for a large sample of foreign firms cross-listing in the United States from all over the world. The first chart shows that there is a positive valuation premium, or lower cost of capital, for firms with cross-listed securities. The average Tobin's q of firms that cross-listed in the United States between 1997 and 2004 was 14.6 percent for all countries and 13.3 percent for Latin American firms. These numbers are even higher for those firms that cross-listed

Figure 15 The Valuation Premiums of U.S. Cross-Listings

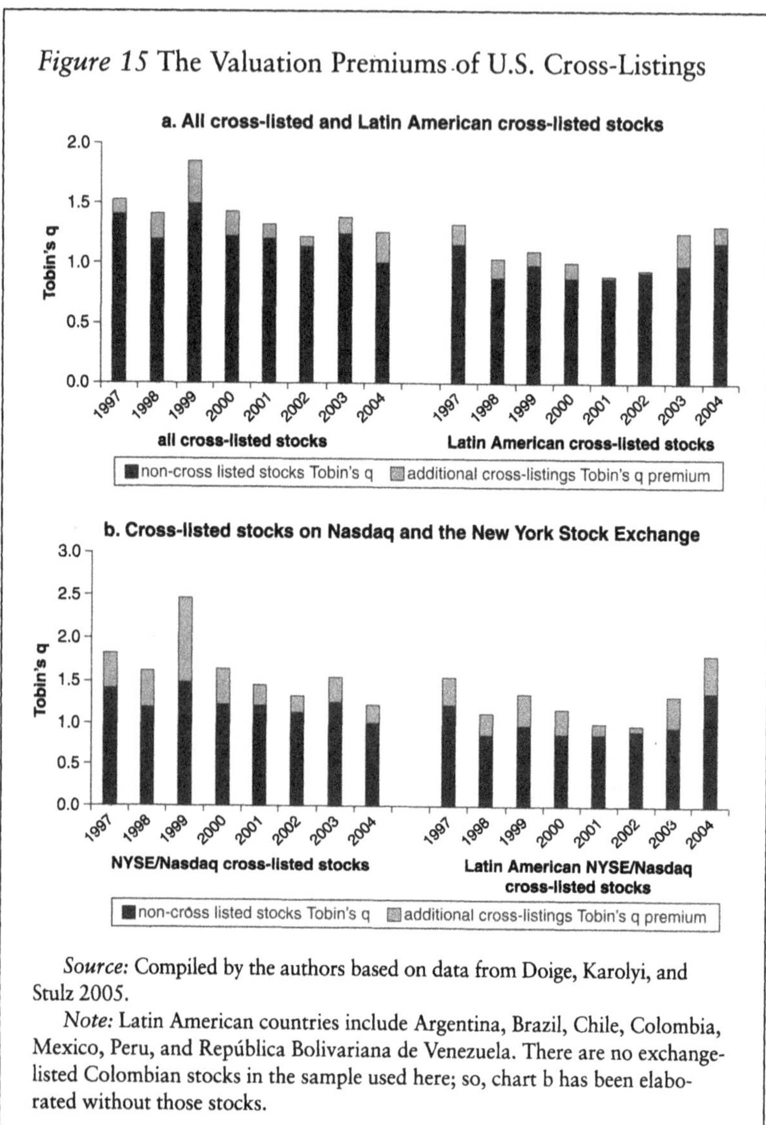

Source: Compiled by the authors based on data from Doige, Karolyi, and Stulz 2005.

Note: Latin American countries include Argentina, Brazil, Chile, Colombia, Mexico, Peru, and República Bolivariana de Venezuela. There are no exchange-listed Colombian stocks in the sample used here; so, chart b has been elaborated without those stocks.

on U.S. exchanges (ADR levels 2 and 3), reaching 31.7 and 29.6 percent for all foreign and Latin American companies, respectively.

The current debate about the decline of U.S. markets is partly fueled by the observation that the valuation premium on cross-listing has severely decreased since 2001.[40] The data in figure 15 show that, if we compare the average premiums of the period before and after 2000, the average pre-2000 premium falls by about 45 percent for all firms cross-listed and by about 58 percent for those firms cross-listing on a U.S. exchange. The source of the reduction in the premium is still an open question. It might include the reduced benefits of higher regulatory costs in the United States or the improvement in corporate governance in stock markets outside the United States. What is important for Latin American markets is that, for whatever reason, the premium for Latin American firms has not been reduced at the same rate. In fact, the post-2000 valuation premium reduction for cross-listers in the region has been reduced by between 20 and 23 percent. These findings go hand in hand with the findings outlined elsewhere above that the corporate governance environment in Latin America is still lagging. The lower rate of premium reduction may reflect the relatively limited improvement in corporate governance in Latin American countries.

Figures 16, 17, and 18 show additional statistics that portray the large migration to northern markets.[41] The data in these figures also indicate that Latin American markets are highly connected and synchronized with U.S. markets through cross-listings. Measured as a percentage of issuers, or of market capitalization, or of value traded, ADR firms are growing at an increasing pace. Mexico has the largest percentage of locally listed firms that have ADRs in the United States. Figure 16 shows that, for the average Latin American country, close to 50 percent of the most important stocks have a U.S. cross-listing. The number reached 80 percent of all the large issuers in Mexico and República Bolivariana de Venezuela included in the Standard & Poor's–International Finance Corporation Global index in 2000. The number of Brazilian and Chilean firms also rose substantially. This evidence supports the view that, in countries with weak investor

Figure 16 ADR Holders as a Share of Listed Firms

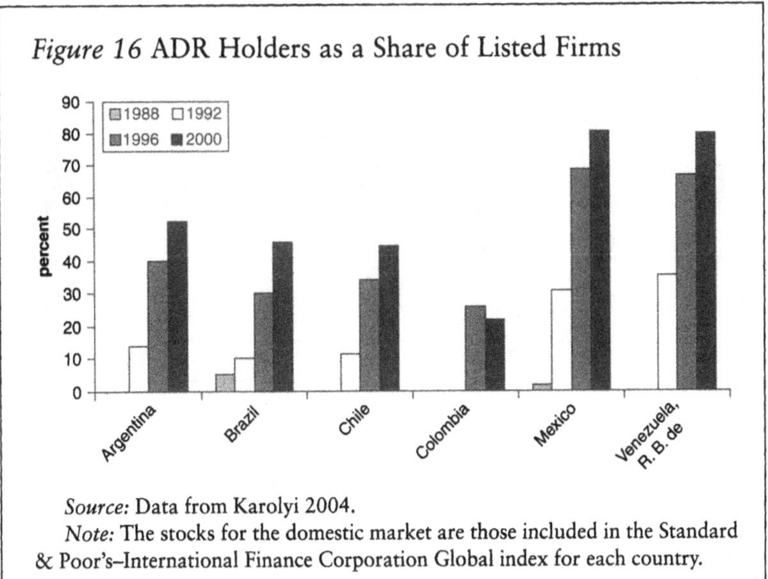

Source: Data from Karolyi 2004.

Note: The stocks for the domestic market are those included in the Standard & Poor's–International Finance Corporation Global index for each country.

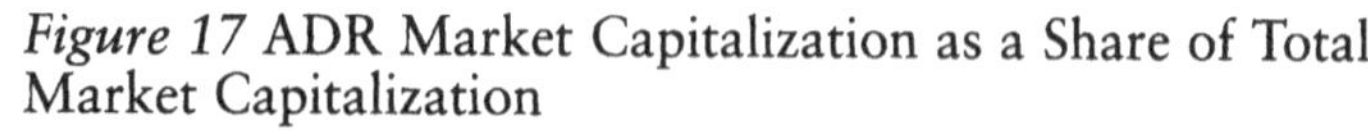

Figure 17 ADR Market Capitalization as a Share of Total Market Capitalization

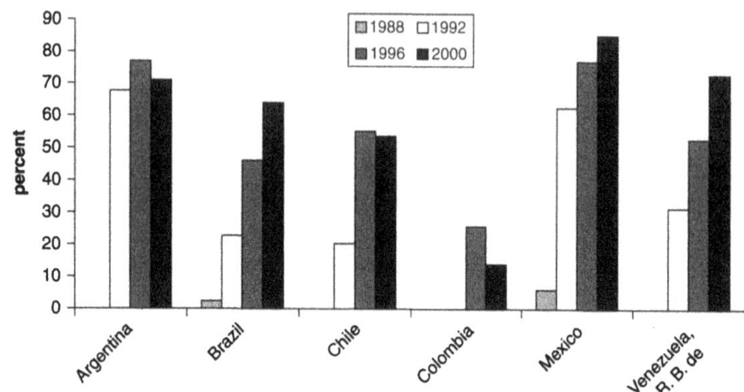

Source: Data from Karolyi 2004.

Note: The stocks for the domestic market are those included in the Standard & Poor's–International Finance Corporation Global index for each country.

Figure 18 ADR Value Traded as a Share of Total Value Traded

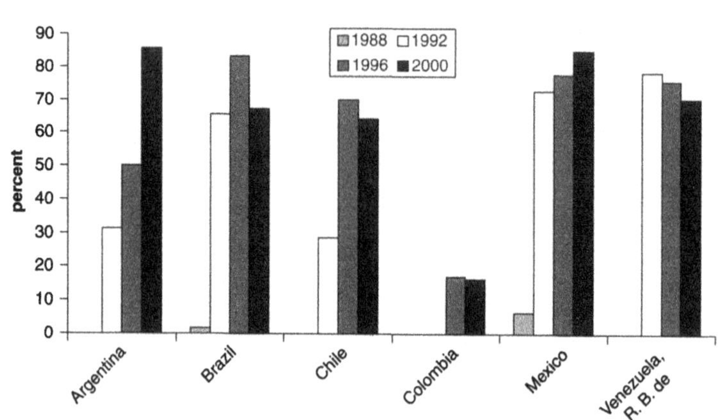

Source: Data from Karolyi 2004.

Note: The stocks for the domestic market are those included in the Standard & Poor's–International Finance Corporation Global index for each country.

protection, firms seek ways to gain access to external capital markets. The numbers in figure 17 and 18 are even more startling. With the exception of Colombia, the capitalization of firms with ADRs was above 60 percent of the total capitalization of firms in the Standard & Poor's–International Finance Corporation Global index, and the proportion of value traded of firms with ADRs was, on average, 70 percent of the value traded among the firms included in the same index. The share reached more than 80 percent for Argentina and Mexico in 2000.

Listing abroad seems to be a good alternative for Latin American firms. The evidence shows that, in addition to the lower cost of capital, firms that cross-list experience a reduction in capital constraints and are able to tap more easily into domestic and foreign debt markets. Overall, there seems to be a large positive impact on financial costs and a reduction in local market volatility. One might wonder, then, if the positive impact on cross-listers has any positive externality in terms of local issuers.

Theoretically, the impact of cross-listings on local market development may be positive or negative. It seems that, if investors learn more about several firms in a market, they might use some of that information to assess firms that have remained listed only locally; this would have a positive spillover effect. The migration of companies to the ADR market would represent a first step in the integration of the local market with the more liquid and well-developed U.S. market. As more firms cross-list, local financial intermediaries would face more competition, which would force them to improve. Cross-listers would start a positive spiral leading to financial innovation by intermediaries and market development overall.[42] The pressure from ADRs may also be expected to have a positive impact on investor protection because authorities and regulators would face the challenge of competition and be pushed to improve disclosure standards and shareholder rights.

The predictions of this theory do not seem to square with the concern of policy makers in many countries who perceive the growth of depositary programs as a threat. An alternative theory on the effects of cross-listing predicts, in fact, an effect that is exactly the opposite of the effect described above. Firm migration abroad may hurt the liquidity of the firms that remain in the local market.[43] As firms cross-list, there might be a diversion of local activity to the foreign market that would lead to a fragmentation of local markets and a reduction in local liquidity. Instead of being a source of the local development of local markets and intermediaries, depositary programs would be the catalysts of investment and trading diversion. The result would be an inhibition in growth as the local market becomes less relevant.[44]

Unfortunately for Latin America, the bulk of evidence points to negative, rather than positive, externalities on local markets from large firm migrations through depositary programs. Using different samples with different country coverage and time spans, most of the authors represented in this volume find that cross-listing leads to lower local liquidity and the reduced ability of nonmigrant firms to access capital. ADR growth has a negative impact on new local listings and overall market growth.[45] The impact varies across regions; African and Latin American markets are the most negatively affected by depositary receipt programs. Moel and Tufano (2002) find that the impact is quite severe for the listing of new firms in local markets. Their estimates suggest that a local IPO is lost every time a new firm cross-lists. Karolyi (2005) confirms these results: ADR activity, measured in terms of the number of programs and their market or trade value, has a negative impact on domestic markets, though this impact is confined to the non-ADR issuers. His results also show that it is the exchange-listed ADRs, rather than the Rule 144A ADRs, that are the drivers.

There is additional evidence showing that the process of international market integration through cross-listings is more complex and that there are unexpected, negative side effects. Melvin and Valero-Tonone (2003) analyze the impact of a cross-listing firm on home-market rival firms. Theoretically, this impact would be positive if there is a positive spillover effect in the cost of capital for all firms in the same sector because one of them has started a depositary program. The empirical results of Melvin and Valero-Tonone show the opposite, however: there are negative cumulative abnormal returns for local rival firms at the announcement of the new program and on the listing dates. Investors perceive that firms without depositary receipts are less transparent and represent poorer growth opportunities. This negative effect is at least twice as large for firms in emerging markets, such as in Latin America.

The past five years have seen other stock markets competing more vigorously against the hegemonic position of Wall Street. Asian and European markets are taking ground and have started to list more and more global issuers. Latin American markets contrast sharply with these newcomers: virtually no foreign firm lists in Latin American markets. Although ADRs are facilitating the integration of local markets in world capital markets,[46] this greater synchronicity among markets has arisen through the link provided by Latin American companies that are going the other way around by cross-listing elsewhere. The data show that the degree of regional integration is also close to zero. With the exception of a few Argentine companies that list in Brazil, there is no regional stock market integration to speak of. No Latin American market has become an attractive alternative pole to compete with U.S. markets or to begin generating regional integration. The isolation of Latin American stock markets should be a matter of policy concern. The greater competition among markets may lead to consolidation through alliances, mergers, or market shutdowns in emerging markets.

In summary, the search for capital by Latin American firms that are trying to gain access on Wall Street through cross-listings has been successful. Latin American cross-listers are among the largest and most traded securities on this market. Foreign markets are thus serving as a valve for some firms by facilitating their access to external finance. But such opting in cannot fully replace legal reform in the region because the vast majority of Latin American firms are not sufficiently large to access U.S. markets, particularly given the new regulations. If local markets dry up, many firms will be deprived of a vital source of capital for facing foreign competition. For most countries in Latin America, the threat posed by Wall Street should alert policy makers to the urgent need to improve local investor protection standards. The effort would require changes in regulations and improved judicial mechanisms to enforce rights.

Conclusions and Policy Implications

The basic argument running through the chapters in this volume is that, even under distorted conditions, with insufficient legal shareholder protection and poor enforcement, as in most Latin American countries today, capital market access may be improved if firms depart from the norm and begin adopting better corporate governance practices. Improvements in firm-level governance foster reductions in the margin for conflict between large and minority shareholders as companies become more transparent. Companies that take this path are welcomed by the markets, which attach to them higher relative valuations and thus lower the cost of capital.

This overview chapter sets the framework for understanding the trends in and the limitations of firm-level corporate governance reform in the region. As the cross-country evidence shows, investor rights are not inherent to securities, but are determined by laws. Investors in different legal jurisdictions have different bundles of rights. Countries in Latin America suffer from a generally lower level of protection, partly inherited from their legal traditions. The weaknesses of the region's capital markets are exacerbated by the relatively low enforcement levels in most of the countries under analysis. The inadequacies of the legal institutions in Latin America generate high levels of ownership concentration, poor access to external equity financing, and narrow equity markets.

A first level of policy recommendations suggested in this volume is directed at improving corporate governance by putting it at the top of the policy agenda in Latin America. The evidence surveyed in this book calls out for wholesale legal reform. Cross-country studies show that minority shareholders would benefit from the existence of disclosure mechanisms that improve transparency and from mechanisms to address expropriation.[47] This chapter shows that there is plenty of room to strengthen voting rights and to enhance disclosure requirements in the region.

One of the key challenges in Latin America is the effective enforcement of legal standards. Improving the judicial means of enforcement should be viewed as a policy step that reinforces legal reform. A well-functioning, politically independent judiciary reduces the danger that regulators may be captured. However, to the extent that improving the efficiency of the judicial system and asserting the rule of law are slow processes, it is important to incorporate tools to address these constraints in the policy design. Sometimes, standards and rules are too difficult or too impractical to enforce. In such cases, it may be appropriate to adopt simpler bright-line rules. An example would be the adoption of an oppressed minority mechanism, perhaps similar to that in Chile, that minimizes the involvement of the courts even if its more mechanical nature results in outcomes that are less than fair. Similarly, mandating enhanced disclosure requirements may not be sufficient in countries with weak legal institutions. In such instances, it may be desirable, for example, to require that institutional investors only be allowed to invest in companies that meet minimum corporate governance standards as determined by independent best-practice commissions. Similarly, as López-de-Silanes (2002) shows, legal reform must also be politically feasible.

In the absence of a good legal environment, the evidence surveyed in this chapter suggests that access to financing by firms in the region requires that companies undertake significant efforts to protect financiers. Expropriation by entrepreneurs may be considered a serious threat because of the lack of good enforcement mechanisms.

The studies in this book portray what may be regarded as the demand side as local firms seek capital. The firm-based analyses suggest that domestic and foreign capital is available to sustain larger stock markets that are more active in valuation and to make viable the investment projects of firms that decide to reform and seek public capital. In this respect, there is an implicit assumption that supply forces may work their way in to the markets if providers of capital are permitted entry. Although the economies in the region are not characterized by an abundance of idle capital, the experience of several emerging markets that have opened up in recent decades suggests that capital will flow if the barriers are lowered.

There are reasons to believe that the situation is more promising in most Latin American countries today than it was 25 years ago. Throughout the 1980s and 1990s, most countries in the region underwent a series of market reforms and macroeconomic stabilization measures that opened up their economies to competition. A series of legal reforms encouraged investment in what had been considered strategic investment areas and allowed foreigners to take part in the large privatization programs of the late 1980s.[48] In some instances where access to the privatization of state-owned enterprises was restricted to domestic capital, the financial crises of the 1990s in Argentina, Brazil, and Mexico led to a relaxation of the rules and permitted foreigners to enter these sectors. A notable example is the case of the Mexican banking sector, where foreign capital was not allowed in during the initial round of privatization; 10 years later, virtually no major bank remained under domestic control.[49]

There are two exceptions to this generalized process, however. First, key mineral sectors and oil have not yet become fully liberalized to outside capital. Second, in the last few years, countries such as Bolivia and República Bolivariana de Venezuela have turned their backs on liberalization policies. In both cases, the isolation that industries and countries are facing will come at the cost of additional lags in the access to the resources needed to achieve a healthy level of competitiveness. It remains to be seen if such policies are viable in an interconnected world.

The growing interconnectedness of markets is creating additional problems in the development of capital markets in the region. Reform in the region is engaged in an uphill battle because of the increasing connectivity of capital markets across countries. Chile represents a good example for others in the region because of its reforms and transparency, as well as the adequacy of its legal environment and enforcement. Yet, it seems that all these attributes have not spared Chile from a recent shrinkage in the number of listings. This pattern of fewer listings and more delistings is also evident in Colombia, Mexico, and República Bolivariana de Venezuela.

Skeptics of the benefits of reform have pointed to the recent trend toward delisting as a failure of efforts at improved investor protection and governance. The chapters on Argentina and Mexico voice this concern. Of course, the alternative hypothesis is that reforms have not gone far enough to prevent the massive exodus of firms to other markets. The access to U.S. capital markets through ADRs has provided an additional source of funds for some firms in the region. Such alternatives provide some explanation for the shrinkage in Latin American capital markets and are a stimulus for firms in the region to adopt better governance practices unilaterally. What matters to firms is access to finance, irrespective of the origin of the finance.

But integration with international financial markets does not eliminate the need for vibrant local financial markets. International markets are not appropriate for all firms. The constant threat of Wall Street poses real challenges for policy makers in the region. Although the gap between the level of protection of the average Latin American country and that in the large capital markets of the United Kingdom and the United States is large, stagnation and lack of change and reform in the region would do nothing except foster an even larger exodus over the medium and long run, putting countries in the region at the mercy of foreign investment. The experience of the recent governance reforms in U.S. markets has even prompted European economies to support reform to reduce the reliance of their firms on U.S. markets. In the end, reforms in other markets trickle down through firms that want to access those markets and hurt firms that have not yet taken the leap. If governments in Latin America do not want to create a two-tier structure in regulation, which would hurt medium-size firms the most, the imperative to catch up with the reforms abroad is paramount.

It took a series of financial crises in Brazil, Russia, Thailand, and the United States to heighten the concern for corporate governance reform. Since these crises, the perceived threat of a global financial meltdown has waned. The danger for Latin America is that local because improve corporate governance in the region will lose momentum because of the more stable financial markets. If this turns out to be the case, it is hard to foresee how local markets will be able to survive the next series of shocks.

Annex 1 Variable Definitions

The table below describes the variables collected for the 49 countries included in our study. The first column gives the name of the variable. The second column describes the variable and gives the range of possible values. The third column provides the sources from which the variable has been collected.

Variable	*Description*	*Sources*
Legal origin	Identifies the legal origin of the company law or commercial code of each country. Equals 1 if the origin is English common law, 2 if the origin is the French commercial code, and 3 if the origin is the German commercial code.	La Porta et al. (1998), collected from "Foreign Law Encyclopedia of Commercial Laws of the World"
Proxy by mail allowed	Equals 1 if the company law or commercial code allows shareholders to mail their proxy vote to the firm; 0 otherwise.	La Porta et al. (1998)
Vote by mail	Equals 1 if the law explicitly mandates or sets as a default rule that: (1) proxy solicitations paid by the company include a proxy form allowing shareholders to vote on the items on the agenda, (2) a proxy form to vote on the items on the agenda accompanies the notice of the meeting, or (3) shareholders vote by mail on the items on the agenda (that is, postal ballot); 0 otherwise.	Djankov et al. (2006)
Shares not blocked	Equals 1 if the company law or commercial code does not allow firms to require that shareholders deposit their shares prior to a general shareholders meeting, thus preventing them from selling those shares for a number of days; 0 otherwise.	La Porta et al. (1998)
Shares not deposited	Equals 1 if the law does not require nor explicitly permit companies to require shareholders to deposit with the company or another firm	Djankov et al. (2006)

(continued)

Annex 1 Variable Definitions *(continued)*

Variable	*Description*	*Sources*
	any of their shares prior to a general shareholders meeting.	
Cumulative voting or proportional representation	Equals 1 if the company law or commercial code allows shareholders to cast all their votes for one candidate standing for election to the board of directors (cumulative voting) or if the company law or commercial code allows a mechanism of proportional representation on the board by which minority interests may name a proportional number of directors to the board; 0 otherwise.	La Porta et al. (1998); Djankov et al. (2006)
Capital to call a meeting	The minimum percentage of ownership of share capital that entitles a shareholder to call for an extraordinary shareholders meeting. It ranges from 1 to 33 percent.	La Porta et al. (1998); Djankov et al. (2006)
Preemptive rights	Equals 1 if the company law or commercial code grants shareholders the first opportunity to buy new issues of stock, and this right may only be waved by a shareholders vote; 0 otherwise.	La Porta et al. (1998); Djankov et al. (2006)
Oppressed minorities	Equals 1 if the company law or commercial code grants minority shareholders either a judicial venue to challenge the decisions of management or of the assembly or the right to step out of the company by requiring the company to purchase their shares when they object to certain fundamental changes, such as mergers, assets, dispositions, and changes in the articles of incorporation. The variable equals 0 otherwise. Minority shareholders are defined as those shareholders who own 10 percent of share capital or less.	La Porta et al. (1998); Djankov et al. (2006)

(continued)

Annex 1 Variable Definitions *(continued)*

Variable	*Description*	*Sources*
Antidirector rights index	An index aggregating the shareholder rights that we labeled antidirector rights. The index is formed by adding 1 when: (1) the country allows shareholders to mail their proxy vote to the firm, (2) shareholders are not required to deposit their shares prior to the general shareholders meeting, (3) cumulative voting or proportional representation of minorities on the board of directors is allowed, (4) an oppressed minorities mechanism is in place, (5) the minimum percentage of share capital that entitles a shareholder to call for an extraordinary shareholders meeting is less than or equal to 10 percent (the sample median), or (6) shareholders have preemptive rights that may only be waved by a shareholder vote. The index ranges from 0 to 6.	La Porta et al. (1998); Djankov et al. (2006)
Disclosure requirements index	The index of disclosure equals the arithmetic mean of: (1) prospect, (2) compensation, (3) shareholders, (4) inside ownership, (5) contracts irregular, (6) and transactions.	La Porta, López-de-Silanes, and Shleifer (2006)
Liability standards index	The index of liability standards equals the arithmetic mean of (1) the liability standard for the issuer and its directors, (2) the liability standard for distributors, and (3) the liability standard for accountants.	La Porta, López-de-Silanes, and Shleifer (2006)
Public enforcement index	The index of public enforcement equals the arithmetic mean of (1) the supervisor characteristics index, (2) the rulemaking power index, (3) the investigative powers index, (4) the orders index, and (5) the criminal index.	La Porta, López-de-Silanes, and Shleifer (2006)

(continued)

Annex 1 Variable Definitions *(continued)*

Variable	*Description*	*Sources*
Ex ante private control of self-dealing	Index of ex ante control of self-dealing transactions. Average of approval by disinterested shareholders and ex ante disclosure.	Djankov et al. (2006)
Ex post private control of self-dealing	Index of ex post control over self-dealing transactions. Average of disclosure in periodic filings and ease of proving wrongdoing. Ranges from 0 to 1.	Djankov et al. (2006)
Anti–self-dealing index	Average of ex ante and ex post private control of self-dealing.	Djankov et al. (2006)
Public enforcement of self-dealing	Index of public enforcement. Ranges from 0 to 1. One-quarter point when each of the following sanctions is available: (1) fines for the approving body, (2) jail sentences for the approving body, (3) fines for Mr. James, and (4) jail sentence for Mr. James.	Djankov et al. (2006)
Efficiency of judicial system	Assessment of the efficiency and integrity of the legal environment as it affects business, particularly foreign firms. It is produced by the country-risk rating agency, Business International Corporation. It may be taken to represent investor assessments of conditions in the country in question. Average between 1980 and 1983. Scale from 0 to 10, with lower scores indicating lower efficiency levels.	La Porta et al. (1998)
Rule of law	Assessment of the law-and-order tradition in the country produced by the country-risk rating agency International Country Risk. Average of the months of April and October of the monthly index between 1982 and 1995. Scale from 0 to 10, with lower scores indicating less tradition for law and order. (We have changed the scale from its original range of 0 to 6.)	La Porta et al. (1998)

(continued)

Annex 1 Variable Definitions *(continued)*

Variable	*Description*	*Sources*
Corruption	International Country Risk's assessment of the corruption in government. Lower scores indicate high government officials are likely to demand special payments, and illegal payments are generally expected throughout lower levels of government in the form of bribes connected with import and export licenses, exchange controls, tax assessment, policy protection, or loans. Average of the months of April and October of the monthly index between 1982 and 1995. Scale from 0 to 10, with lower scores indicating higher levels of corruption. (We have changed the scale from its original range of 0 to 6.)	La Porta et al. (1998)
Accounting standards	Index created by examining and rating the 1990 annual reports of companies on their inclusion or omission of 90 items. These items fall into seven categories (general information, income statements, balance sheets, funds flow statement, accounting standards, stock data, and special items). A minimum of three companies in each country have been studied. The companies represent a cross-section of various industry groups whereby industrial companies represent 70 percent, while financial companies represent the remaining 30 percent.	La Porta et al. (1998)
Court formalism to collect a bounced check	The index measures substantive and procedural statutory intervention in judicial cases at lower-level civil trial courts and is formed by adding up the following indicators: (1) professionals versus laymen, (2) written versus oral elements, (3) legal justification, (4) statutory regulation of evidence,	Djankov et al. (2003)

(continued)

Annex 1 Variable Definitions *(continued)*

Variable	*Description*	*Sources*
	(5) control of superior review, (6) engagement formalities, and (7) independent procedural actions. The index ranges from 0 to 7, where 7 means a higher level of control or intervention in the judicial process.	
Stock market capitalization to GDP	Ratio of the market capitalization (also known as market value, which is the share price, multiplied by the number of shares outstanding) of listed domestic companies (the domestically incorporated companies listed on the country's stock exchanges at the end of the year), divided by the GDP (in millions).	La Porta et al. (1998) for table II.6; World Bank (2005) for figure III.1
Listed firms per million population	Ratio of the listed domestic companies are the domestically incorporated companies listed on the country's stock exchange at the end of the year relative to the country's population (in millions). (This indicator does not include investment companies, mutual funds, or other collective investment vehicles.)	La Porta et al. (1998) for table II.6; World Bank (2005) for figure III.2
IPOs to GDP	Average of the ratio of the equity issued by newly listed firms in a given country (in thousands) to the country's GDP (in millions) over the period 1996–2000.	La Porta, López-de-Silanes, and Shleifer (2006)
Block premium	The block premium is computed taking the difference between the price per share paid for the control block and the exchange price two days after the announcement of the control transaction, divided by the exchange price, and multiplying by the ratio of the proportion of cash flow rights represented in the controlling block. We use the country's sample media.	La Porta, López-de-Silanes, and Shleifer (2006); taken from Dyck and Zingales (2004)

(continued)

Annex 1 Variable Definitions *(continued)*

Variable	*Description*	*Sources*
Ownership concentration	Average percentage of common shares not owned by the top three shareholders in the 10 largest nonfinancial, privately owned domestic firms in a given country. A firm is considered privately owned if the state is not a known shareholder in it.	La Porta, López-de-Silanes, and Shleifer (1999); Hartland-Peel (1996) for Kenya; Bloomberg and various annual reports for Ecuador, Jordan, and Uruguay
Trading volume to GDP	Total trading volume, divided by the GDP (expressed in 2001 US$) of a certain country in a given year.	World Bank (2005)
Price-to-book value of equity	Quotient between the market value of equity and the book value of equity.	Standard & Poor's (2005)
External capitalization relative to GNP	The ratio of the stock market capitalization held by minorities to GNP for 1999. The stock market capitalization held by minorities is computed as the product of the aggregate stock market capitalization and the average percentage of common shares not owned by the top three shareholders in the ten largest nonfinancial, privately owned domestic firms in a given country. A firm is considered privately owned if the state is not a known shareholder in it.	Moody's International, CIFAR, EXTEL, WorldScope, 20-Fs, PriceWaterhouse, and various country sources
Domestic firms relative to population	Ratio of the number of domestic firms listed in a given country to the country's population (in millions) in 1999.	Emerging Market Factbook; World Bank (1999)
IPOs relative to population	Ratio of the number of IPOs of equity in a given country to the country's population (in millions) in 1999.	López-de-Silanes (2003)
GDP growth	Average annual percent growth of per capita GDP for the period 1960–98.	World Bank (2001)
Log GNP	Logarithm of the GNP in 1999.	World Bank (2001)

Source: Compiled by the authors.

Annex 2 Variable Definitions

	Argentina	*Brazil*	*Chile*	*Colombia*	*Costa Rica*	*Mexico*	*Venezuela, R. B. de*
Tobin's q	The market value of equity, plus the book value of liabilities to the book value of assets.	Ratio of the market value to the book value of assets. The market value of assets is computed as the market value of equity, plus the book value of assets, minus the book value of equity at year-end values. The numerator "market value of equity" was computed directly by Economática as the most liquidity stock type (voting or nonvoting) market price, times the total number of shares (voting and nonvoting).	The market book of assets, divided by the book value of assets at the end of each calendar year. We estimate the market value of assets as the book value of debt, plus the book value of preferred stock, plus the market value of common stock.	Ratio between the market value of assets and the book value of assets.	Yes.	Defined as the market value of equity (actual shares outstanding, times the closing price of the period), plus total liabilities, divided by total assets.	The ratio of the market value to the book value of assets. The market value is the market value of equity, plus the book value of assets, minus the book value of equity. They are all computed as of the end of 2004.

(continued)

Annex 2 Variable Definitions *(continued)*

	Argentina	*Brazil*	*Chile*	*Colombia*	*Costa Rica*	*Mexico*	*Venezuela, R. B. de*
Return on assets	Earnings before interest and taxes relative to total assets.	Ratio of operating income to total assets (return on assets) at year-end.	Return on assets. Net income, divided by the book value of total assets.	Return on assets.		Ratio between net income and total assets. Expressed in percentage points.	The ratio of earnings before interest and taxes to the end of year total assets for each firm i and for each year t.
Return on equity	Earnings before interest and taxes relative to total equity.			Return on equity.		Ratio between net income and the book value of equity (total assets, minus total liabilities). Expressed in percentage points.	For each firm i and for each year t, the ratio of earnings before interest and taxes to the end-of-year total equity.
Dividend payout	Dividends relative to cash flow: cash dividends relative to the sum of total earnings and depreciation.	Cash and stock dividends relative to the net income ratio with year-end values.			Dividends-to-earnings ratio.	Ratio between the dividends paid and net income. Expressed in percentage points.	Cash and stock dividends, divided by net income. Data correspond to 2003. They are all computed at year-end values and are obtained from BVC (2003).

(continued)

Annex 2 Variable Definitions *(continued)*

	Argentina	*Brazil*	*Chile*	*Colombia*	*Costa Rica*	*Mexico*	*Venezuela, R. B. de*
Market-to-book ratio		The market value of stock, divided by the book value of stock.		The market value of common stock and the book value of common stock.		Ratio between the market value of equity and the book value of equity.	The market value, divided by the book value at the end of 2004. The market value and book value have been obtained from Economática and Datastream.
Corporate governance index	Transparency and disclosure index: 32 binary items grouped in 3 subindexes. Scaled between 0 and 100.	24 binary items on 4 dimensions. Scaled value between 0 and 24.	67 questions grouped in 4 sections and scaled from 0 to 20.	31 questions grouped in 6 different aspects and scaled from 0 to 100.	57 binary questions scaled from 0 to 100.	Mean of the corporate governance index for 2003 and 2004. The variable is between 0 and 1, and it represents the accomplishment of the corporate governance principles stated in the questionnaire that all listed companies must present to the Mexican Stock Exchange every year.	

Source: Compiled by the authors from the chapters in this volume.

Notes

1. See Claessens, Klingebiel, and Schmukler (2006); Kumar, Rajan, and Zingales (2001); La Porta, López-de-Silanes, and Shleifer (1999, 2002, 2006); La Porta et al. (1997, 1998, 2000a, 2000b); Wurgler (2000).

2. Countries have been included in the analysis generally only if they possess a stock exchange. This restriction gives the following list of Latin American countries: Argentina, Bolivia, Brazil, Chile, Colombia, Costa Rica, Dominican Republic, Ecuador, El Salvador, Guatemala, Honduras, Jamaica, Mexico, Panama, Paraguay, Peru, Trinidad and Tobago, Uruguay, and República Bolivariana de Venezuela.

3. See Klapper and Love (2002); Gompers, Ishii, and Metrick (2003); Black, Jang, and Kim (2006a, 2006b).

4. ADRs are negotiable certificates that are denominated in dollars. They stand in for the ownership of shares in foreign companies and may be traded on U.S. exchanges. For more on depositary receipts, see the section on Firm Migration and Disappearing Stock Markets.

5. La Porta et al. (1997, 1998) capture some of these effects in cross-country analyses by looking at institutional quality over the past 20 years and the impact of GDP per capita, which is a good summary measure of political and economic success.

6. See La Porta et al. (1997, 1998).

7. See Modigliani and Miller (1958).

8. See Grossman and Hart (1986).

9. Most English-speaking countries belong to the common law tradition based on the British Company Act. The common law family includes former British colonies and other nations such as Israel and Thailand that have modeled their initial corporate laws on the laws of England. There are 20 common law countries in the sample. The rest of the world belongs to the civil law tradition, derived from Roman law, which has three main families: the French family based on the Napoleonic Code of 1804, the German family based on Bismarck's Code of 1896, and the Scandinavian family, which legal scholars describe as less derivative of Roman law and distinct from the other two civil families. The French legal family includes France, Portugal, Spain, and their colonies. There are 29 French legal origin countries in our sample, including 19 in Latin America. The German tradition has had less influence, and we have only six countries in this family: Austria, Germany, Japan, the Republic of Korea, Switzerland, and Taiwan (China). Finally, the Scandinavian family includes the four Nordic countries of Denmark, Finland, Norway, and Sweden. For a fuller explanation, see La Porta et al. (1998).

10. We should be careful about strictly comparing the specific variables in tables 1 and 4 since the definition of some of the variables in these two tables has been refined for the numbers in 2005.

11. The La Porta, López-de-Silanes, and Shleifer (2006) sample is the 49 countries with the largest stock market capitalization in 1993 (the La Porta et al. 1998 original sample).

12. See Diamond (1989, 1991); Gómes (1996).

13. Ownership concentration per se may be efficient because the existence of large shareholders monitoring management reduces the agency problem between management and shareholders (Jensen and Meckling 1976; Shleifer and Vishny 1986). But large concentration comes at a cost because it creates another agency problem: the expropriation of minority shareholders by large ones. An additional cost of heavily concentrated ownership is that the core investors are not diversified.

14. La Porta et al. (2000a) find that, for a cross-section of countries around the world, various measures of dividend payout ratios are lower in countries with poor

investor protection than in countries with high investor protection. This evidence suggests that companies in countries with poor laws and poor enforcement of those laws do not build reputations by paying high dividends to their shareholders.

15. See La Porta, López-de-Silanes, and Shleifer (2006); Djankov et al. (2006).

16. To compute a rough proxy of truly external equity financing, we first need a measure of ownership concentration. We multiply the total market value of common stock of all publicly traded firms by the average fraction of the equity not held by the largest three investors (that is, the complement of the ownership variable already described). We scale the total market value of common stock by the fraction of equity held by minority shareholders to avoid overestimating the availability of external financing. For example, if 90 percent of a firm's equity is held by insiders, then the market capitalization of the whole firm gives a 10-fold overestimate of how much has actually been raised externally. Therefore, an alternative measure is the ratio of external (outside the control group) equity financing to GNP in each country. The results presented in the text hold for this corrected ratio as well.

17. Note that there are only four countries in the Scandinavian family.

18. See La Porta, López-de-Silanes, and Shleifer (1999).

19. The chapter is a cross-country study of nations in the region. The study uses data on stocks and ADRs from Argentina, Brazil, Chile, Colombia, Mexico, Peru, and República Bolivariana de Venezuela. Interday data (time, price, and volume) from more than 1,400 tickers in about 1,000 corporations were obtained from Bloomberg for 42 weekdays in late 2003. The database was completed using market data on best offers, changes at each point in time, highest bids, total volumes, ask prices, and so on.

20. Tobin's q is a classic measure of valuation that results from dividing the market value of debt and equity by the book value.

21. See Easterbrook and Fischel (1991).

22. See Gompers, Ishii, and Metrick (2003); Klapper and Love (2002); Black, Jang, and Kim (2006a); Doidge, Karolyi, and Stulz (2007).

23. See, for example, the Credit Lyonnais Securities Asia index used by Klapper and Love (2002).

24. Endogeneity is certainly a concern in the chapters, as well as in other papers on firm-level practices. See, for example, Gompers, Ishii, and Metrick (2003); Klapper and Love (2002); Black, Jang, and Kim (2006a, 2006b).

25. See Klapper and Love (2002).

26. Jensen and Meckling (1976).

27. See Demsetz and Lehn (1985); Morck, Shleifer, and Vishny (1989); La Porta et al. (2001b); Gompers, Ishii, and Metrick (2003).

28. See Gompers, Ishii, and Metrick (2003); Klapper and Love (2002).

29. Depositary receipts are typically divided into two groups: (1) global depositary receipts, which are programs established outside the United States; these depository receipts are often listed on other international exchanges; and (2) ADRs, which are depositary receipt programs in the United States. Among ADRs, there are four basic types according to the level of disclosure and the capital-raising ability. Rule 144A ADRs, which have become more important since 2003, give access to the U.S. market, but without the full registration and compliance costs. These ADRs are designed for firms that seek private U.S. placements for qualified institutional buyers. They do not require reconciliation with the U.S. Generally Accepted Accounting Principles or full U.S. Securities and Exchange Commission disclosure. Level 1 ADRs trade over the counter, involve minimal disclosure to the Securities and Exchange Commission, and do not require reconciliation with the Generally Accepted Accounting Principles. Level 2 ADRs are used by firms that want to list on a U.S. exchange, but do not raise new capital. Level 3 ADRs are used by firms that want to list on an exchange and do want to raise new capital. Levels

2 and 3 require large amounts of disclosure—similar, but not identical to U.S. firms—and reconciliation with the Generally Accepted Accounting Principles.

30. See Merton (1987).
31. See Poterba and Warshawsky (1999).
32. See Coffee (1999); La Porta, López-de-Silanes, and Zamarripa (2003).
33. See Coffee (1999).
34. Basically, all Chilean and Mexican companies and the vast majority of Brazilian and Venezuelan firms choose to cross-list in the United States. The second market for Latin American cross-listings is Luxembourg, which attracts a handful of Argentine and Brazilian firms and a large proportion of the few Colombian cross-listers.
35. Calculations based on data of the Bank of New York, http://www.bankofny.com/.
36. Calculations based on data of the Bank of New York, http://www.bankofny.com/.
37. See Moel and Tufano (2002).
38. See La Porta et al. (1997, 1998); La Porta, López-de-Silanes, and Shleifer (2002); Doidge (2004); Doidge, Karolyi, and Stulz (2005).
39. See Doidge (2004); Doidge, Karolyi, and Stulz (2005).
40. See Zingales (2007).
41. These three figures reflect the most updated data with consistent definitions across time. The data have been obtained by calculating the proportion of firms in the Standard & Poor's–International Finance Corporation Global index (which includes the largest and most visible firms in each country) that have ADRs in the United States.
42. See Moel and Tufano (2002).
43. See Levine and Schmukler (2005).
44. See Karolyi (2005).
45. Moel and Tufano (2002) and Hargis and Ramanlal (1998) focus on Latin American markets. Claessens, Klingebiel, and Schmukler (2006) and Karolyi (2005) look at larger samples of countries and firms.
46. See Karolyi (2005).
47. See La Porta, López-de-Silanes, and Shleifer (2006); Djankov et al. (2006).
48. See López-de-Silanes (1997).
49. See López-de-Silanes and Zamarripa (1995); La Porta, López-de-Silanes, and Zamarripa (2003).

References

Black, B. S., H. Jang, and W. Kim. 2006a. "Does Corporate Governance Predict Firms' Market Values?: Evidence from Korea." *Journal of Law, Economics, and Organization* 22 (2): 366–413.

———. 2006b. "Predicting Firms' Corporate Governance Choices: Evidence from Korea." *Journal of Corporate Finance* 12 (3): 660–91.

BVC (Bolsa de Valores de Caracas). 2003. *Anuario 2003*. Caracas: Bolsa de Valores de Caracas.

Claessens, S., and J. P. H. Fan. 2002. "Corporate Governance in Asia: A Survey." *International Review of Finance* 3 (2): 71–103.

Claessens, S., D. Klingebiel, and S. L. Schmukler. 2006. "Stock Market Development and Internationalization: Do Economic Fundamentals Spur Both Similarly?" *Journal of Empirical Finance* 13 (6): 316–50.

Coffee, J. C., Jr. 1999. "The Future as History: The Prospects for Global Convergence in Corporate Governance and Its Implications." *Northwestern University Law Review* 93 (3): 631–707.

Daines, R. 2001. "Does Delaware Law Improve Firm Value?" *Journal of Financial Economics* 62 (3): 525–58.

Demsetz, H., and K. Lehn. 1985. "The Structure of Corporate Ownership: Causes and Consequences." *Journal of Political Economy* 93 (6): 1155–77.

Diamond, D. W. 1989. "Reputation Acquisition in Debt Markets." *Journal of Political Economy* 97 (4): 828–62.

———. 1991. "Debt Maturity Structure and Liquidity Risk." *Quarterly Journal of Economics* 106 (3): 709–37.

Djankov, S., R. La Porta, F. López-de-Silanes, and A. Shleifer. 2003. "Courts." *Quarterly Journal of Economics* 118 (2): 453–517.

———. 2006. "The Law and Economics of Self-Dealing." Unpublished working paper, November 13, World Bank, Washington, DC.

Doidge, C. 2004. "U.S. Cross-Listings and the Private Benefits of Control: Evidence from Dual Class Firms." *Journal of Financial Economics* 72 (3): 519–53.

Doidge, C., G. A. Karolyi, and R. M. Stulz. 2005. "The Valuation Premium for Non-U.S. Stocks Listed in U.S. Markets." Unpublished working paper, Rotman School of Management, University of Toronto, Toronto.

———. 2007. "Why Do Countries Matter So Much for Corporate Governance?" *Journal of Financial Economics*. Forthcoming.

Dyck, A., and L. Zingales. 2004. "Private Benefits of Control: An International Comparison." *Journal of Finance* 59 (2): 537–600.

Easterbrook, F., and D. Fischel. 1991. *The Economic Structure of Corporate Law*. Cambridge, MA: Harvard University Press.

Foerster, S. R., and G. A. Karolyi, 1999. "The Effects of Market Segmentation and Investor Recognition on Asset Prices: Evidence from Foreign Stocks Listing in the United States." *Journal of Finance* 54 (3): 981–1013.

Gómes, A. 1996. "The Dynamics of Stock Prices, Manager Ownership, and Private Benefits of Control." Unpublished working paper, Harvard University, Cambridge, MA.

Gompers, P. A., J. L. Ishii, and A. Metrick. 2003 "Corporate Governance and Equity Prices." *Quarterly Journal of Economics* 118 (1): 107–55.

Grossman, S. J., and O. D. Hart. 1986. "The Costs and Benefits of Ownership: A Theory of Vertical and Lateral Integration." *Journal of Political Economy* 94 (4): 691–719.

Hargis, K., and P. Ramanlal. 1998. "When Does Internationalization Enhance the Development of Domestic Stock Markets?" *Journal of Financial Intermediation* 7 (3): 263–92.

Hartland-Peel, C. 1996. *African Equities: A Guide to Markets and Companies*. London: Euromoney Publications.

Jensen, M. C., and W. H. Meckling. 1976. "Theory of the Firm: Managerial Behavior, Agency Costs, and Ownership Structure." *Journal of Financial Economics* 3 (4): 305–60.

Karolyi, G. A. 2004. "The Role of ADRs in the Development of Emerging Equity Markets." *Review of Economics and Statistics* 86 (3): 670–90.

———. 2005. "The World of Cross-Listings and Cross-Listings of the World: Challenging Conventional Wisdom." Unpublished working paper, Fisher College of Business, Ohio State University, Columbus, OH.

Klapper, L. F., and I. Love. 2002. "Corporate Governance, Investor Protection, and Performance in Emerging Markets." Policy Research Working Paper 2818, World Bank, Washington, DC.

Kumar, K. B., R. G. Rajan, and L. Zingales. 2001. "What Determines Firm Size?" CRSP Working Paper 496, Center for Research in Security Prices, University of Chicago, Chicago.

La Porta, R., F. López-de-Silanes, and A. Shleifer. 1999. "Corporate Ownership around the World." *Journal of Finance* 54 (2): 471–517.

———. 2002. "Government Ownership of Banks." *Journal of Finance* 57 (1): 265–301.

———. 2006. "What Works in Securities Laws?" *Journal of Finance* 61 (1): 1–32.

La Porta, R., F. López-de-Silanes, A. Shleifer, and R. W. Vishny. 1997. "Legal Determinants of External Finance." *Journal of Finance* 52 (3): 1131–50.

———. 1998. "Law and Finance." *Journal of Political Economy* 106 (6): 1113–55.

———. 2000a. "Agency Problems and Dividend Policies around the World." *Journal of Finance* 55 (1): 1–33.

———. 2000b. "Investor Protection and Corporate Governance." *Journal of Financial Economics* 58 (1–2): 3–27.

La Porta, R., F. López-de-Silanes, and G. Zamarripa. 2003. "Related Lending." *Quarterly Journal of Economics* 118 (1): 231–68.

Levine, R., and S. Schmukler. 2005. "Internationalization and Stock Market Liquidity." NBER Working Paper 11894, National Bureau of Economic Research, Cambridge, MA.

Lins, K. V., D. Strickland, and M. Zenner. 2005. "Do Non-U.S. Firms Issue Equity on U.S. Stock Exchanges to Relax Capital Constraints?" *Journal of Financial and Quantitative Analysis* 40 (1): 109–33.

López-de-Silanes, F. 1997. "Determinants of Privatization Prices." *Quarterly Journal of Economics* 112 (4): 966–1028.

———. 2002. "The Politics of Legal Reform." *Economia* 2 (2): 91–152.

———. 2003. "Latin America: Status of Investor Protection." Unpublished working paper, Inter-American Development Bank, Washington, DC.

López-de-Silanes, F., and G. Zamarripa. 1995. "Deregulation and Privatization of Commercial Banking." *Review of Economic Analysis* 10 (2): 113–64.

Martinez, L., and A. Werner. 2002. "Capital Markets in Mexico: Recent Developments and Future Challenges." Paper prepared for the Banco de México seminar, "Estabilidad Macroeconómica, Mercado Financieros, y Desarrollo Económico," November 12–13.

Melvin, M., and M. Valero-Tonone. 2003. "The Effects of International Cross-Listing on Rival Firms." Unpublished working paper, University of Arizona, Tempe, AZ.

Merton, R. C. 1987. "Presidential Address: A Simple Model of Capital Market Equilibrium with Incomplete Information." *Journal of Finance* 42 (3): 483–510.

Modigliani, F., and M. Miller. 1958. "The Cost of Capital, Corporation Finance, and the Theory of Investment." *American Economic Review* 48 (3): 261–97.

Moel, A., and P. Tufano. 2002. "When Are Real Options Exercised?: An Empirical Study of Mine Closings." *Review of Financial Studies* 15 (1): 35–64.

Morck, R., A. Shleifer, and R. W. Vishny. 1989. "Characteristics of Hostile and Friendly Takeover Targets." NBER Working Papers 2295, National Bureau of Economic Research, Cambridge, MA.

NYSE (New York Stock Exchange). 2005. *The Depositary Receipts Market.* New York: NYSE.

———. 2006. *The Depositary Receipts Market.* New York: NYSE.

Poterba, James, and Mark Warshawsky. 1999. "The Costs of Annuitizing Retirement Payouts from Individual Accounts." NBER Working Paper 6918, National Bureau of Economic Research, Cambridge, MA.

Reese, W. A., Jr., and M. S. Weisbach. 2001. "Protection of Minority Shareholder Interests, Cross-Listings in the United States, and Subsequent Equity Offerings." *Journal of Financial Economics* 66 (1): 65–104.

Sarkissian, S., and M. J. Schill. 2004. "The Overseas Listing Decision: New Evidence of Proximity Preference." *Review of Financial Studies* 17 (3): 769–809.

Shleifer, Andrei, and Robert W. Vishny. 1986. "Large Shareholders and Corporate Control." *Journal of Political Economy* 94 (3): 461–88.

Siegel, J. 2005. "Can Foreign Firms Bond Themselves Effectively by Renting U.S. Securities Laws?" *Journal of Financial Economics* 75 (2): 319–59.

Standard & Poor's. 2005. *Global Stock Markets Factbook.* New York: McGraw-Hill.

Stulz, R. M. 1999. "Globalization, Corporate Finance, and the Cost of Capital." *Journal of Applied Corporate Finance* 12 (3): 8–25.

White, L. J. 2002. "The New Economy and Banks and Financial Institutions." In *New Economy Handbook*, ed. D. C. Jones, 419–37. London: Academic Press.

World Bank. 1999. *World Development Report 1999/2000: Entering the 21st Century*. Washington, DC: World Bank; New York: Oxford University Press.

———. 2001. *World Development Report 2002: Building Institutions for Markets*. Washington, DC: World Bank; New York: Oxford University Press.

———. 2005. *World Development Indicators 2005*. World Bank, Washington, DC.

———. 2006. *World Development Indicators*. Washington, DC: World Bank. http://www.worldbank.org/.

Wurgler, J. 2000. "Financial Markets and the Allocation of Capital." *Journal of Financial Economics* 58 (1–2): 187–214.

Zingales, L. 2007. "Is the U.S. Capital Market Losing Its Competitive Edge?" *Journal of Economic Perspectives*. Forthcoming.

1

Insider Trading and Corporate Governance in Latin America

*Juan J. Cruces and Enrique Kawamura**

Introduction

If illegal insider (informed) trading goes unpunished, as it does in most countries in Latin America, controlling groups may periodically confiscate the wealth of minority shareholders in a politically low-cost way by trading on their privileged access to information.[1] The expected probability that the wealth of outside investors will be confiscated through poor governance and informed trading is a crucial determinant of the portfolio allocation of such investors and the ensuing cost of capital for corporations.

Two questions remain, however: How prevalent is insider trading in Latin America? And to what extent is it connected to corporate governance? All the questionnaires that form the basis of the known corporate governance ratings include sections related to fair and timely disclosure of information to the market.[2] But, aside from the individual analyst's judgment of the corporation's common practice, there is presently no independent, objective, quantitative, and theory-based assessment of the extent to which informed trading effectively takes place. This chapter provides such estimates for the universe of liquid stocks of Latin America. It then uses them as both an explained and an explanatory variable in regression analysis.

Is informed trading a deterministic function of the corporate and countrywide institutional controls in the literature, or does it provide substantial

* The authors wish to thank Alberto Chong, Kevin Cowan, and Florencio López-de-Silanes for valuable comments, Hernán Finkelstein, Esteban Giraldo, and Tomás Romero for excellent research assistance, and John D. Smith for editorial help. All remaining errors are their own.

additional information? What corporate observables are more likely to be correlated with higher informed trading intensity? In the time-series dimension, does informed trading peak some time before material corporate announcements are disclosed to the market, or is it flat and close to zero throughout the sample? Moreover, might estimated informed trading intensity help explain corporate valuations above and beyond countrywide institutional variables in the literature? Would such intensity also provide a better measure, in this sense, than analyst-based rankings intended to measure governance quality? As shown by Klapper and Love (2002) and La Porta et al. (2002), the market sets prices according to the quality of corporate governance. However, do markets charge a premium for informed trading above and beyond the punishment for bad governance?

This chapter addresses these questions using high-quality, ultrahigh-frequency data from Bloomberg comprising more than 80 million records of individual transactions and best offer quotes from October 2, 2003 to September 29, 2004.

In addition, the framework of Easley, Kiefer, and O'Hara (1996, 1997a, 1997b) and of those authors with Paperman (Easley et al. 1996) is used to estimate the informed trading probability (ITP) for each individual stock at various points throughout the sample. As far as the authors of this chapter know, this is the only method that allows direct estimation of how likely it is that each observed transaction arises from a privately informed party. This method contrasts with others in the literature (for example, Keown and Pinkerton 1981, John and Lang 1991, Meulbroek 1992, Cornell and Sirri 1992, and Estrada and Peña 2002) that only provide an indirect methodology to infer informed trading and is better suited for countries where insider trading prosecutions are rare. It is noteworthy that the method adopted here estimates the intensity of *privately informed* trading, a category that includes, but is not limited to, *illegal insider* trading. Legal private information trading includes acting on the basis of analysts' reports, proprietary industry, or macro forecasts.

In related work, Grishchenko, Litov, and Mei (2002) use a test based on the theoretical model of Llorente et al. (2002) to estimate informed trading in 19 emerging markets from almost seven years of daily closing price and volume data. According to the model, the higher the correlation among lagged volume times, lagged return, and current return, the higher the intensity of privately informed trading. Grishchenko, Litov, and Mei find that the coefficient is statistically significant for 14 percent of the firms in their sample.[3] There does not seem to be a formal way to evaluate whether the Easley et al. (1996) or the Llorente et al. (2002) method is better. The method proposed here seems more powerful. For example, the Grishchenko, Litov, and Mei method would not detect informed trading if markets were weakly efficient at daily intervals. In this case, however, the focus is on transaction-by-transaction data that might still detect informed trading. In the model adopted here, it is the composition of the buy and sell orders and no-trade intervals within the day and not the return data that indicates whether some agents are more informed than others.

The key findings are as follows. There is substantial heterogeneity in the ITP across stocks, and this dispersion occurs mainly within groups (such as countries, volume quintiles, industrial sectors, security types, and American depository receipt [ADR] classifications), but not between them. Despite this, several patterns emerge. First, the ITP is much higher when stocks are less liquid. Second, Brazil and Mexico show lower mean ITPs, while Colombia and República Bolivariana de Venezuela show mean ITPs higher than the average. Importantly, the stocks of firms with ADR programs have lower mean ITPs than those without, and countries with better information-related legal variables on investor protection tend to show lower ITPs.

The chapter next analyzes whether the ITP peaks that occur immediately before material corporate announcements are disclosed to the market and finds that this is true in general, though the magnitude and the lead time of anticipation seem higher for acquisition and divestiture announcements than for earnings and cash-dividend announcements. There is evidence of information leakage in Argentina, Chile, and Mexico, but not in Brazil. Investors might also care to know that some industrial sectors are subject to significant spikes in the ITP immediately before public announcements.

Last, the chapter finds that the market recognizes, in part, the heterogeneity of the ITP across firms and over time: a fall of one standard deviation in the ITP raises Tobin's q by around 1 or 2 percentage points.

The rest of the chapter is organized as follows. The next section discusses the hypotheses tested in the chapter, and the following section describes the informed trading estimation method. The subsequent section describes the data sources and sample construction, and the penultimate section discusses the empirical results. The last section concludes, analyzes the policy implications of the findings, and highlights directions for future research. Annex 1.1 reports the liquidity characteristics of the sample, describes the corporate announcements data and the investor protection variables used in the chapter, and presents the results of a robustness check for the event study.

Testable Hypotheses

The theme of this chapter is that, given the unobservability of illegal insider trading, the detrimental effect of this sort of trading on the returns of minority shareholders, and the history of the impunity of this fraud in Latin America, controlling groups may actually choose the extent to which they will exploit their informational advantage in securities trading.[4] This may result in heterogeneity in informed trading behavior across stocks subject to the same institutional or technological environment (such as nationality, industry, and so on). Moreover, controlling groups might signal to the market that they will abstain from exploiting their informational advantage, and the market might react to this signal by assigning higher valuations.

The discretionary powers of controlling groups might hurt minority shareholders, but they might also have a benefit for minority shareholders. For instance, a more powerful controlling group may internalize the benefits of monitoring that are beneficial to all shareholders, or they might react more effectively to unexpected changes in the economic environment. However, insider trading is an explicit use of the discretion option that is harmful to outside investors. The presence of nationwide regulations reflects the truth that controlling groups have options to do harm. Insider trading proxies indicate to what extent controlling groups actually exercise these options at the expense of outsiders.

Three sets of tests of these hypotheses are proposed. The first set attempts to assess the degree of heterogeneity of firm behavior regarding insider trading activity within a given institutional environment and the cross-sectional covariates of the ITP. Also, if corporations use the listing of ADRs as a signal to convey to the market a fairer treatment of inside information, then those corporations that do not list abroad will have a higher ITP. Also tested is whether the ITP is related to the investor protection or legal environment variables used in the literature to proxy for corporate governance quality. The hypothesis is that this new measure of governance quality contains more information than previously used measures.

The second set of tests focuses on the time pattern of the ITP around material corporate announcements. If insiders are indeed exploiting their informational advantage, the ITP should peak immediately before these announcements. Additionally analyzed is whether the quantitative importance of this effect depends upon the observable characteristics of firms.

The first two sets of tests document that there is substantial heterogeneity in privately informed trading within countries, within investor protection environments, and over time. The third and final set of tests assesses the extent to which the market recognizes this heterogeneity. If so, when companies manage to reduce their ITP levels, the market should respond with higher valuations. This hypothesis is tested by expressing the market value regression in La Porta et al. (2002) in panel form and adding each firm's quarterly ITP to it instead of the cash flow rights.

An important recent literature pioneered by La Porta et al. (1998), among others, has estimated how the quality of the nationwide investor protection environment affects the cost and availability of outside financing for corporate investment. This chapter attempts to extend this literature by following the lead of Klapper and Love (2002) and Grishchenko, Litov, and Mei (2002) in analyzing whether there is significant heterogeneity of controlling group behavior within a given institutional environment and the extent to which such behavior is recognized by the market.

Klapper and Love (2002) find that the quality of individual corporate governance is priced above and beyond countrywide controls. Their estimates, however, rely on the governance quality ratings of Credit Lyonnais Securities Asia (CLSA), found in Gill (2001), an analyst-based and therefore potentially subjective or endogenous measure. Moreover, because these ratings are fixed over time, they are unable to be used to compute the market valuation response to a given corporation's change in governance quality. By the same token, they are unable to be used to determine whether information-based trading finds a peak before public announcements, as this chapter attempts to do.

Grishchenko, Litov, and Mei (2002) also precede this chapter. Unlike the procedure used here, their method would not detect informed trading if markets are weakly efficient at daily intervals.[5] Moreover, they do not compute the extent to which market valuations respond to different ratings of the quality of corporate governance, as Klapper and Love (2002) and this chapter do.

To the best of the authors' knowledge, this chapter is the first study to provide objective, quantitative, and theory-based assessments of the probability of informed trading using ultrahigh-frequency data and to use these data to address questions about corporate governance.

Estimation of Informed Trading Probability

Methodological Review

The ITP is estimated by using the discrete time theoretical framework developed by Easley and O'Hara (1987, 1992) and implemented in several applications for U.S. markets by Easley, O'Hara, and their coauthors.[6] This appears to be the only theoretical model that generates a structural equation allowing direct estimations of the probability of privately informed trading. This section briefly surveys the model's basic elements.

The intuition underlying the model is that sudden increases in the gap between buy and sell orders (that is, order imbalance) may be associated with the more active participation by informed parties that results from the arrival of private information. In the model, once informed parties observe a signal, they always trade as long as they may extract a rent. If trading is not caused by private information, one would expect a more stable and balanced flow of buy and sell orders.

More formally, the model considers that a signal perfectly correlated with the value of the asset may be realized before the beginning of the trading day. The true value of the asset will be publicly known only at the end of the day. Both the signal and the value of the firm may take only two realizations, either high or low. However, there may be days with no signal realization at all. The trading day is divided into many discrete time periods. The asset is traded in a market with competitive market makers. Agents execute all buy and sell orders from investors at prices quoted by the market makers. There are two types of investors: privately informed traders (or *insiders*) know the realization of the signal; liquidity or *noise* traders may buy or sell for reasons other than information. Investors and market makers are assumed to be risk neutral.[7] There may also be no trade in some periods.

Transactions take place sequentially over the many time periods in one day, as illustrated in figure 1.1. In every period, nature chooses only one trader to place an order. If nature chooses an informed trader (which happens with probability μ), this agent buys (if the signal indicated a high value) or sells (if the signal indicated a low value) one unit of the asset.[8] Nature chooses a noise trader with the remaining probability $(1 - \mu)$. This agent may

Figure 1.1 The Probability Structure of Trade

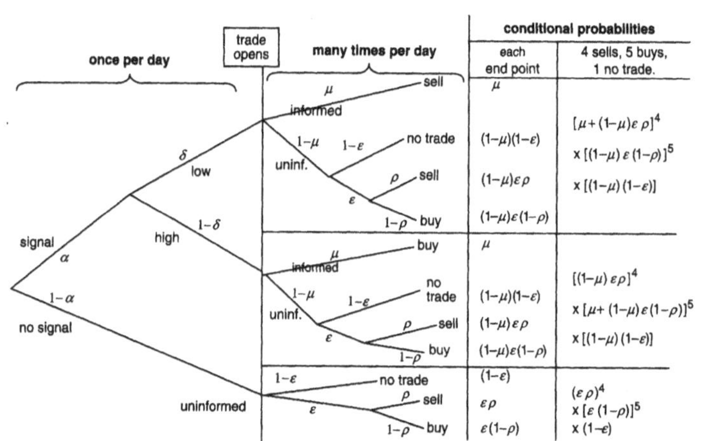

Source: Authors.

Note: This figure shows the tree diagram of the trading process. α is the probability of new information (a signal) occurring. Conditional on the appearance of new information, δ denotes the probability of a bad signal. Given any signal, μ is the probability that nature chooses an informed trader to trade. If nature chooses an uninformed trader, the latter trades with probability ε. Given that an uninformed trader trades, he or she sells with probability ρ and buys with probability $(1 - \rho)$. Nodes to the left of the vertical Trade Opens line occur only at the beginning of the trading day, while nodes to the right occur in every possible trading period within the day. As an example, the rightmost column computes the probability, for a given trading day, of observing 4 sells, 5 buys, and 1 no-trade period, conditional on the existence and type of signal at each trade-opening node. The likelihood for that day is equation (1.1) with the value of observed trades in this day in place of *S*, *B*, and *N*.

either trade with probability ε or not trade. If the agent trades, he or she sells one unit with probability ρ and buys with the remaining probability $1 - \rho$.

In equilibrium, given perfect competition, market makers set bid and ask quotes equal to the expected value of the asset conditional on either a sell or a buy, respectively. Glosten and Milgrom (1985) have shown that these are, indeed, the optimal quote policies by these market makers. Thus, each market maker extracts information from the order flow. Glosten and Milgrom (1985) and Easley and O'Hara (1992) have shown that, if all probabilities are bounded by (0,1), the market price converges in probability to the true value of the firm by the end of the trading day.

While μ is the ITP conditional on the existence of private information, the object of interest in this chapter is the probability that a given observed trade is generated by an informed investor, that is, the probability that, conditional on a trade, that trade arises from an informed investor. This equals the probability of observing an informed trade divided by the total probability of observing a trade, whether informed or uninformed, as follows:

$$ITP = \frac{\alpha\mu}{\alpha\mu + (1-\alpha\mu)\varepsilon}. \tag{1.1}$$

This probability depends on α (the probability that an information event takes place), on μ (the joint probability of a trade and that the trade comes from an informed investor, given that an information occurs), and on ε (the probability that an uninformed investor decides to trade when nature chooses him or her). For any given α and μ, the greater the propensity of the uninformed investor to trade ε, the lower the probability that a given trade originates from an informed investor.[9]

In the model, the number of trades is ex ante random. For illustration, the last column of figure 1.1 shows the probability of observing five buys, four sells, and one no-trade period in one day given three different scenarios: there is bad (private) information, there is good (private) information, or there is no new (private) information. The unconditional probability of observing five buys, four sells and one no-trade period during that day is simply the weighted average of these three probabilities, whereby the weights are the probabilities of observing bad information ($\alpha\delta$), good information ($\alpha(1-\delta)$), and no information ($1-\alpha$). Generalizing this, one may write the probability of observing a given amount of B buys, S sells, and N no trades as,

$$\begin{aligned} L[\theta \mid B, S, N] = P[B,S,N \mid \theta] = \alpha\delta P[B,S,N \mid \text{low signal}] \\ +\alpha(1-\delta)P[B,S,N \mid \text{high signal}] \\ +(1-\alpha)P[B,S,N \mid \text{no signal}] \end{aligned} \tag{1.2}$$

where:

$$\theta = (\alpha, \delta, \mu, \varepsilon, \rho),$$

$$P[B,S,N \mid \text{low signal}] = [\mu + (1-\mu)\varepsilon\rho]^S \, [(1-\mu)(1-\varepsilon)]^N \times [(1-\mu)\varepsilon(1-\rho)]^B,$$

$$P[B,S,N \mid \text{high signal}] = [(1-\mu)\varepsilon\rho]^S \, [(1-\mu)(1-\varepsilon)]^N \times [\mu + (1-\mu)(1-\rho)]^B, \text{ and}$$

$$P[B,S,N \mid \text{no signal}] = [\varepsilon\rho]^S \, [(1-\varepsilon)]^N [\varepsilon(1-\rho)]^B.$$

Equation (1.2) shows the likelihood of observing a trade pattern during a given day. To estimate the model's parameters, the literature assumes that these are fixed during a period of time and that the number of daily buys, sells, and no trades observed during that period is a random sample from this distribution.[10] With these assumptions, the problem reduces to maximizing the log likelihood, as follows:

$$l = \sum_{t=1}^{T} \ln L(\theta | B_t, S_t, N_t). \tag{1.3}$$

The solution to this maximization problem provides the parameter estimates used to compute the ITP in (1.1).

Does Informed Trading Probability Really Measure what we want to Measure?

As described above, the ITP estimation procedure relies exclusively on the observed pattern of buys, sells, and no trades. This pattern, however, may result from factors other than private information, such as market humor and pure heterogeneous beliefs. This section argues that the ITP is a good measure of the intensity of privately informed trading; a survey of findings in the literature indirectly validates this approach. Alternative measures of asymmetric information in stock markets include the bid-ask spread, the adverse selection component of the spread, and the price impact of trades and volume.

A large portion of the literature relies on the bid-ask spread to proxy for the degree of asymmetric information, including the framework used here.[11] The idea is that the higher the degree of asymmetric information,

Colombia and República Bolivariana de Venezuela make up the remaining 1 percent (see table 1A in the annex). For the region as a whole, there is about as much trading in the ADR market as there is at home.[17] Table 1B in the annex looks at the industrial sector breakdown of the tickers by country, while tables 1C through 1F analyze the distribution of liquidity in the sample. Table 1G analyzes the distribution of traded volume by quintile.

While every transaction involves a purchase by one party and a sale by another party, transactions are classified in this chapter as a buy or a sell according to the action actually triggering the transaction. Accordingly, this chapter follows Lee and Ready (1991) by classifying each transaction as a transaction initiated by a seller or as a transaction initiated by a buyer. This method classifies a trade observed at the ask (bid) price as a buy (sell) and a trade above (below) the midpoint of the bid-ask spread as a trade initiated by a buyer (seller).[18] For each day in the sample, the number of buys, sells, and no-trade periods is computed (B_t, S_t, and N_t in equation 1.3). Following Easley, Kiefer, and O'Hara (1997a), this chapter defines the number of no-trade periods between two subsequent trades as the maximum integer number of five-minute-long intervals between them.

With these data in hand, one estimates the parameters of the model by maximum likelihood using the Newton-Raphson algorithm on a fine grid.[19] Easley, Kiefer, and O'Hara (1996, 1997a, 1997b) and Easley et al. (1996) proceed in this way to estimate the parameters using data from periods that range from six to twelve weeks. Equation 1.3 is estimated for each calendar quarter in the sample for these 288 tickers. With those estimates, equation 1.1 is used to compute the ITPs, which provide the basis for all of the empirical tests except for the event study.[20]

Country Data

This chapter follows the literature in using several measures of the quality of the nationwide investor protection environment. Besides the original La Porta et al. (1998) variables, this chapter uses the March 2004 reading of the law and order index and the corruption index of the *International Country Risk Guide*,[21] to which is added the investment profile, also in the guide. In addition to these variables, this chapter uses the legality index of Berkowitz, Pistor, and Richard (2003), which is a linear combination of judicial efficiency, law and order, corruption, risk of expropriation, and risk of contract repudiation from La Porta et al. (1998) and the *International Country Risk Guide*. Also consulted is a second reading of this index using the updated arguments in PRS Group (2004). According to Bhattacharya and Daouk (2002), from whom the insider trading enforcement dummy is borrowed, the seven countries in the sample have regulations banning illegal insider trading. This variable equals 1 if at least one person had been prosecuted under these laws as of March 1999, and it is zero otherwise. Mexico stands out as a paradigmatic case of nonenforcement: although it banned illegal insider trading in 1975, no one had been prosecuted for the crime by the end of the 1990s.

Corporate Announcements Data

The comprehensive list of corporate announcements used for the event study is from Bloomberg. Four types of announcements are considered: acquisitions, divestitures, cash dividends, and earnings announcements, which make up the majority of public statements by firms. The annex describes the announcement data in detail.

It is possible that the patterns of informed trading before periodic announcements are different relative to those before nonperiodic or aperiodic announcements. On the one hand, the market knows that a corporation will announce earnings about six weeks after the end of the quarter. While, in an ideal world, the magnitude of the earnings figure is secret, the approximate timing of the release is common knowledge. The situation differs for aperiodic announcements. In an ideal world, not only is the content of these announcements secret, but also the frequency of their public release. It is thus conjectured that the ratio of illegally over legally privately informed trades is higher before aperiodic announcements than before periodic announcements. Earnings and cash dividends announcements are therefore classified as periodic, while acquisition and divestiture announcements are classified as aperiodic, and potentially different event effects are calculated for each type.

For each announcement in the sample, three ITPs are estimated during adjacent periods, each 20 trading days long: a control period from $\tau = -40$ to $\tau = -21$, a preannouncement period from $\tau = -20$ until $\tau = -1$, and a postannouncement period from $\tau = 1$ to $\tau = 20$.[22] Given the requirement that there must be 40 trading days before the first announcement and 20 trading days after the last, announcements in the event study sample run from November 24, 2003, until September 10, 2004.

The total number of announcements during this period for all the exchanges in the sample was 1,310. Eight stocks in the sample of 288 tickers did not release any announcements during the announcement sample. From Colombia, Peru, and República Bolivariana de Venezuela, 14 stocks made 58 announcements in total; these are excluded to avoid making inferences on country effects based on too small a sample. This leaves 266 tickers, which made a total of 1,252 announcements. Furthermore, the algorithm did not converge in the estimation of equation 1.3 for two other stocks that had made a total of five announcements. Therefore, the event study is based on 1,247 announcements from 264 stocks.

Figures 1A and 1B in the annex plot the frequency over time by type of announcement and by country. About 90 percent of the announcements pertain to earnings and cash dividends, and the remaining share corresponds to acquisitions and divestitures. The average ticker made about 4.7 announcements during the sample period.

Firm-specific Variables

The variables of country, industrial sector, common or preferred stock classification, and stock ADR status are from Bloomberg. Some researchers (for example, Leal and Carvalhal-da-Silva 2005) argue that Brazilian preferred stocks (for instance, PN, PA, or PB shares) are, in fact, nonvoting common stocks with no material dividend payments. They and others (such as Gledson de Carvalho 2000) find that control in Brazilian corporations is so concentrated that controlling groups may easily divert net income from outside shareholders. While this chapter uses the Bloomberg classification, the terms preferred and nonvoting shares are used interchangeably, because the only such stocks in the sample of 288 tickers are from Brazil. It should be noted, though, that ADR and common or preferred status are independent groupings. ADR tickers were classified as common or preferred stocks according to each ADR's underlying security. The ADR classification consists of four exhaustive and mutually exclusive categories: (1) the ticker corresponds to an ADR; (2) the ticker corresponds to an ADR underlying security; (3) the ticker corresponds to a company that has an ADR program, although the ticker itself is neither the ADR nor the underlying; and (4) the ticker is from a company that does not have an ADR program.[23]

Individual corporate governance ratings, here referred to as CLSA ratings, are taken from Gill (2001). The average rating for each firm and for several of the subindexes—management transparency, management discipline, and management independence—are used. Because this chapter's market value regression expands on the one employed in La Porta et al. (2002), the relevant procedure is followed in measuring Tobin's q and average sales growth for the four quarters in the sample, for which balance sheet data from Economática are used. A proxy measure of q is defined as the ratio of the market value of assets to the book value of assets.[24] Figures 1A and 1B in the annex show that most firms release their quarterly accounting data before the eighth week in the next quarter, so it is assumed that the quarterly balance sheet data have been fully incorporated into market prices two months after the closing of the quarter. Therefore, the first quarterly measure of Tobin's q corresponds to accounting data for the third quarter of 2003, matched with the market value of equity as of December 1, 2003. In the market value regressions, these measures of q are aligned with ITPs estimated from trades taking place during the fourth quarter of 2003. Similarly, the fourth reading of Tobin's q uses accounting data from the second quarter of 2004, matched with the market value of equity as of September 1, 2004, and with ITPs estimated from transaction data from the third quarter of 2004.[25] As pointed out by La Porta et al. (2002, 1998), this measure of equity value is assessed from the point of view of outside shareholders, investors who do not necessarily have access to the firm's control or inside information. To reduce the weight of outliers, Tobin's q is censored at the 5th and 95th percentiles by setting extreme values to the 5th and 95th percentiles, respectively.

To proxy for the value of growth opportunities, the annual U.S. dollar sales growth rate is computed for each quarter and firm in the sample for the three years ending 11 months before the reading of the market value of equity. So, the first observation of the sales growth rate is an average of annual sales growth from January 1999 to December 2002; this is matched with Tobin's q as of December 1, 2003. The geometric annual average growth rate from up to three years is used.[26] Again, sales growth is capped at the 5th and 95th percentiles to avoid problems with outliers.

The 288 tickers used in the rest of this study correspond to 207 unique firms, and the market value regression is run at the firm (not at the ticker) level. After dropping firms with missing data, 175 firms remain, and these form the basis for the estimation.

Like La Porta et al. (2002), this chapter runs the market value regression expressing sales growth and q in deviation from the industry medians. Following their procedure, all firms in Economática are used, excluding the 205 firms in the present sample, and q and average sales growth are computed for the 1,135 remaining firms for which data are available.[27] These firms are in 19 different industries according to the Economática classification, and all sectors have at least five remaining firms. The median q and average sales growth are determined for each of the 19 sectors, and the industry-adjusted variables of these are computed for the firms in the sample.

Results

Distribution of Informed Trading Probability

Table 1.1 presents summary statistics on the distribution of the ITP by ticker-quarter. The top panel in table 1.1 reports the breakdown by the country where the corporate headquarters are located. For example, the mean of the ITP over time across Brazilian stocks was 16 percent.[28] The Brazilian stock with the smallest average ITP gauged 2.9 percent, while that with the largest ITP gauged 76.2. This means that there was a 76.2 percent chance that any randomly selected trade in that stock-quarter was initiated by a privately informed agent.

The ranking of countries, from lowest to highest median ITP, is the following: Brazil, Mexico, Peru, Argentina, Chile, República Bolivariana de Venezuela, and Colombia. One should be cautious, however, about inferring that the degree of the ITP across the universe of Colombian and Venezuelan firms is large, given that only three stocks from each of these countries appears in the sample. The most important insight from the top panel is that there is a substantial heterogeneity in the ITP across stocks, and that the variability occurs mainly within countries and not across them.

To place these results within the context of the earlier literature, the mean and standard deviation of the ITP across 150 stocks of U.S. corporations estimated by Easley, Kiefer, and O'Hara (1996) and Easley et al. (1996) are 17.7 and 8.8, respectively (the minimum and maximum are 0.0 and 68.4). Although the U.S. distribution tends to be shifted to the left relative to that of the Latin American countries, the gap is much smaller than expected.

Table 1.1 Distribution of ITP by Group of Stock

	N	*Mean*	*Std. dev.*	*Min.*	*5th pctl.*	*Median*	*95th pctl.*	*Max.*
a. Country								
Argentina	165	20.5	10.5	3.3	10.5	18.3	42.4	68.4
Brazil	540	16.0	7.8	2.9	7.1	14.6	27.7	76.2
Chile	174	22.3	7.9	6.6	11.9	20.6	37.9	53.0
Colombia	12	28.7	8.4	16.5	16.5	30.6	45.9	45.9
Mexico	186	17.0	6.0	5.8	7.9	17.0	27.5	35.4
Peru	33	19.3	7.1	6.7	7.1	18.2	31.2	37.2
Venezuela, R.B. de	12	23.8	9.3	13.1	13.1	23.2	45.1	45.1
Total	1,122							
b. Industrial sector								
Basic materials	203	16.6	6.8	4.7	7.7	16.2	27.7	46.9
Communications	239	16.1	8.7	2.9	6.7	14.6	30.1	76.2
Consumer, cyclical	98	20.5	6.1	6.2	10.9	19.9	29.0	41.5
Consumer, noncyclial	123	19.3	9.2	3.3	8.7	17.5	35.1	60.1
Diversified	48	20.0	7.9	3.5	9.9	19.0	31.6	52.7
Energy	40	16.6	5.8	4.8	7.8	15.9	26.4	28.8
Financial	129	19.9	11.0	3.9	8.5	17.2	38.2	68.4
Industrial	102	19.1	8.6	7.0	8.0	18.1	35.6	55.3
Utilities	140	18.4	8.0	4.4	8.8	16.7	34.4	48.4
Total	1,122							

(continued)

Table 1.1 Distribution of ITP by Group of Stock *(continued)*

	N	*Mean*	*Std. dev.*	*Min.*	*5th pctl.*	*Median*	*95th pctl.*	*Max.*
c. Security type								
Prefered	405	15.3	7.8	2.9	7.0	14.0	26.4	76.2
Common	717	19.7	8.4	3.3	9.1	18.5	35.4	68.4
Total	1,122							
d. ADR status								
ADR	306	16.8	10.2	3.3	7.2	14.9	33.0	76.2
ADR underlying	255	16.1	7.6	5.8	7.1	14.7	30.4	52.7
Co. has ADR, but this is not the underlying	137	18.5	6.0	6.2	9.7	18.2	30.5	38.6
Co. just trades at home (no ADR program)	424	20.1	7.8	2.9	10.3	19.1	36.9	55.3
Total	1,122							

Source: Authors.

Note: This table shows summary statistics of the distribution of ITP within each category. All tables are based on 100 times ITP, which is computed for each of 288 tickers during each quarter from October 2, 2003, until September 30, 2004. So we have 1,122 ticker-quarters—the algorithm based on the discrete time model did not converge for a few ticker-quarters. Note that in the top panel, ADRs are pooled with the other stocks from their home country. ADRs were classified as common or preferred stock based on the relevant category for their underlying securities. In the ADR classification (bottom panel) a ticker can either be an ADR, an ADR underlying security, the stock of a company that has an ADR program, although this is not the underlying stock, or the stock of a company that only trades at home. The figures show that ITPs are fairly diverse within countries, industrial sectors, and security types.

This prior expectation is based on the relative degree of investor protection and enforcement of insider trading bans and on the evidence in Bhattacharya et al. (2000) that Mexican corporate announcement news has already been fully incorporated into prices by the time it is officially disclosed to the market. However, Easley, Kiefer, and O'Hara (1996) and table 1.2 show that the distribution of the ITP depends critically on the liquidity of each security; so, ignoring this dependence may significantly bias comparisons. Moreover, the substantial discrepancy in sample periods (the U.S. estimates are from the early 1990s) may underlie differences in the worldwide systematic component of α in equation 1.1. In general, an appropriate comparison of the ITP across markets that are so different should be based on a matched sample of firms, as Easley, Kiefer, and O'Hara do. This type of careful comparison is left for future research.

The second panel in table 1.1 groups stocks by industrial sector. While communications has the lowest median ITP (14.6 percent), and cyclical consumer products has the highest median ITP (19.9 percent), there seems to be even lower variability in median ITPs across industrial sectors than there is across countries. The third panel in table 1.1 reports that preferred stocks have a much lower ITP than common stocks. Given that all preferred stocks in the sample are from Brazil and that these make up three-fourths of the stocks from that country, this finding is related to the lower ITP of Brazilian stocks and is addressed in detail in the discussion on table 1.4.

Assuming that the U.S. Securities and Exchange Commission scrutinizes ADR transactions as well as it does U.S. domestic stocks, one may expect a higher punishment for trading with private information in the United States relative to Latin American exchanges. Also, if one assumes that firms listing ADRs are thereby signaling their commitment to better corporate governance practices, one might also expect lower ITPs for ADRs. The fourth panel in table 1.1 shows that this is the case on average. ADRs and ADR underlying stocks have ITPs that are lower than the ITPs of stocks that trade only in their home countries. In line with the results from other partitionings of the ITP set, it is found that, although ADRs have lower ITPs, these are also more widely dispersed than are the ITPs for the other categories.

Table 1.2 presents the distribution of the ITP by volume quintiles, defined for each quarter. Two measures of volume are used: quintiles defined relative to the amount of trading in each of the eight exchanges (intraexchange quintiles) and quintiles defined relative to the amount of trading in all exchanges combined (interexchange quintiles). Whatever the measure, the findings confirm the finding of Easley, Kiefer, and O'Hara (1996) that, in the United States, less liquid stocks are prone to substantially higher ITPs: the figure for the lowest volume quintile (23 points in the index) is about twice as large as that for the highest volume quintile (12 points). While the econometric exercises below show that volume is one of the most robust determinants of differences in the ITP, table 1.2 shows that even this partitioning of the sample leaves much within-group variance: the top 5 percent of stocks in the most liquid quintile have higher ITPs than the median stock from the lowest volume quintile.

Finally, table 1.3 shows the variation in the ITP across quarters; it also shows that the time pattern differs across categories (for example, some are higher at the beginning, while others are higher near the end of the sample).

The main message so far is that there is a substantial heterogeneity of the ITP within categories commonly controlled for in the literature. This underscores the importance of computing company-specific proxies of governance quality, as is done in this chapter.

Table 1.2 Distribution of the ITP by Volume Quintile

Quintiles Defined within Each Exchange-Quarter

Intraexchange	N	*Mean*	*Std. dev.*	*Min.*	*5th pctl.*	*Median*	*95th pctl.*	*Max.*
1st quintile (highest vol.)	230	13.7	6.9	4.4	6.7	11.4	27.7	45.9
2nd quintile	226	14.6	5.6	3.3	7.7	13.6	25.2	37.0
3rd quintile	232	19.3	8.3	7.2	10.4	17.8	31.6	68.4
4th quintile	227	20.5	7.0	9.2	12.5	19.3	33.0	60.1
5th quintile (lowest vol.)	207	22.9	10.3	2.9	9.5	20.6	44.6	76.2
Total	1,122							

Quintiles Defined across All Exchanges in Each Quarter

Interexchange	N	*Mean*	*Std. dev.*	*Min.*	*5th pctl.*	*Median*	*95th pctl.*	*Max.*
1st quintile (highest vol.)	222	11.7	4.8	4.4	6.6	10.6	21.7	30.8
2nd quintile	230	15.6	8.0	3.3	7.9	14.1	26.4	68.4
3rd quintile	227	19.6	6.8	7.4	11.3	18.7	30.7	60.1
4th quintile	230	21.2	6.5	9.2	12.8	20.6	34.5	52.7
5th quintile (lowest vol.)	213	22.6	10.4	2.9	9.5	20.1	45.0	76.2
Total	1,122							

Source: Authors.

Note: This table shows statistics of the distribution of ticker-quarter ITPs by volume quintiles. Quintiles are defined for each calendar quarter based on the volume traded in each security during that time. In the top panel, quintiles are exchange specific, so that volume classification thresholds differ across the eight exchanges (that is, the seven countries in the sample, plus the ADR market). In the bottom panel, a uniform volume classification is used across all exchanges. Daily volumes in local currency are converted in U.S. dollars at each day's closing exchange rate from Economática. So a security that is relatively liquid in a low volume exchange may be in the top quintile in the top panel, but in a lower quintile in the bottom panel. The number of tickers is not constant across quintile bins because it was impossible to estimate ITPs during some ticker-quarters. Regardless of the classification used, these figures confirm the finding of Easley et al. (1996b) that ITPs are substantially higher for lower volume stocks (for example, it is about twice as high in the lowest volume quintile relative to the highest volume quintile).

Cross-sectional Determinants of Informed Trading

Categorical decomposition of informed trading. An attempt is first made to identify categorical covariates of the ITP using the pooled ordinary least squares regression, as follows:

$$\begin{aligned} ITP_{it} &= \alpha + \boldsymbol{\beta}^{V\prime}\mathbf{I}(\text{Vol. Quintile}_{it}) + \boldsymbol{\beta}^{C\prime}\,\mathbf{I}(\text{Country}_i) + \boldsymbol{\beta}^{S\prime}\,\mathbf{I}(\text{Sector}_i) + \\ &+ \boldsymbol{\beta}^{P\prime}\,\mathbf{I}(\text{Common/Preferred}_i) + \boldsymbol{\beta}^{A\prime}\,\mathbf{I}(\text{ADR status}_i) + \boldsymbol{\beta}^{t\prime}\,\mathbf{I}(t) + \varepsilon_{it}; \\ & i = 1,.., 288; \quad t = 1, 2, 3, 4 \end{aligned} \tag{1.4}$$

where every *I( )* is a matrix of dummy variables for each classification. Because several sets of dummy variables are included, the standard procedure

Table 1.3 Quarterly Distribution of the ITP

	2003–IV	*2004–I*	*2004–II*	*2004–III*
Country				
Argentina	18.7	18.5	22.0	22.6
Brazil	14.9	15.7	15.9	17.5
Chile	20.9	22.7	23.3	22.2
Colombia	27.3	27.5	32.6	27.5
Mexico	17.0	15.2	16.8	19.2
Peru	22.5	17.5	18.3	19.0
Venezuela, R.B. de	22.9	18.9	30.5	22.9
Average across countries	20.6	19.4	22.8	21.6
Industrial sector				
Basic materials	16.6	16.2	17.0	16.6
Communications	15.6	15.1	15.5	18.2
Consumer, cyclical	19.0	18.9	22.3	21.7
Consumer, noncyclial	17.0	18.0	20.8	21.5
Diversified	18.8	17.8	21.6	22.0
Energy	14.5	16.9	16.4	18.6
Financial	19.9	19.8	18.8	21.0
Industrial	17.9	19.8	19.9	18.7
Utilities	16.9	16.9	19.2	20.7
Average across industries	17.4	17.7	19.1	19.9

(continued)

Table 1.3 Quarterly Distribution of the ITP *(continued)*

	2003–IV	*2004–I*	*2004–II*	*2004–III*
Security type				
Prefered	14.7	15.1	15.3	16.2
Common	18.6	18.6	20.3	21.3
Average across security types	16.7	16.9	17.8	18.8
ADR status	*2003–IV*	*2004–I*	*2004–II*	*2004–III*
ADR	16.4	16.2	16.4	18.4
ADR underlying	15.2	14.6	17.4	17.5
Co. has ADR, but this is not the underlying	17.7	17.5	18.3	20.9
Co. just trades at home (no ADR program)	18.8	19.7	20.8	20.9
Average across ADR status	17.0	17.0	18.2	19.4

Source: Authors.

Note: This table shows, for each quarter, the mean of ITP across stocks in each category. Note that in the top panel, ADRs are pooled with the other stocks from their home country. See notes to table 1A for details on security type and ADR classifications. The figures show that ITP display some variation over time (e.g., they were 17 percent higher on average during the second than during the first quarter of 2004 looking at country grouped data). The bottom line of each panel reports the equally weighted average of the figures in the other lines of that panel. Those averages differ from panel to panel because they imply a different weighting of the original ticker-quarter ITPs. For example, in the top panel and for each quarter, the average of the three Colombian ticker ITPs (note from table 1A that there are 12 Colombian ticker-quarters, which amounts to three tickers per quarter) get the same weight as that of the 135 Brazilian tickers in obtaining the average ITP across countries. Because Colombia has a high mean ITP, this hikes the cross-country average relative to the average across sectors in which these Colombian firms (which are all from the financial sector, see table A2) are pooled with the ITPs of about 26 other tickers to obtain the financial sector average.

of reporting the results for each group as a difference relative to a control group is departed from to facilitate the interpretation of the results. In other words, dummies are used that span the full set of possibilities of a given partition of the sample so that the coefficient on each dummy reflects the extent to which behavior for that category deviates from the global average.[29] The *t*-ratios assess whether the difference is statistically significant.[30] The coefficient on the global intercept is the mean of the ITP for the average stock. Given the evidence in tables 1.2

and 1.3, time and volume fixed effects and volume effects are included in all regressions. Table 1.4 reports the results.

The first important result is that volume is inversely related to the ITP. While the ITP for the average stock is 21.6 percent (model 1 in table 1.4), the estimate is 17.2 percent for the most liquid stocks, and it rises to about 26.8 percent for the least liquid stocks from the average country. The result is robust to different specifications and is consistent with those in the received literature.[31]

Model 1 also shows that Brazilian, Mexican, and Peruvian companies have statistically significantly lower ITPs than the average stock. The (few) firms from Colombia and República Bolivariana de Venezuela in the sample, in contrast, have systematically higher average ITPs, while the ITPs of Argentine and Chilean companies are not significantly different from the overall mean.

Model 2 analyzes economic sector effects and shows that the ITPs of financial and cyclical consumer products firms are higher than average, while communications firms have lower ITPs.[32] Model 3 shows that common stocks have higher ITPs than do preferred stocks. The Brazilian coefficient in model 1 may be low because informed trading is not as prevalent there or because 75 percent of Brazilian tickers in the sample are preferred stocks, which are themselves characterized by low ITPs, as model 3 shows. Model 5 checks for this possibility by including all controls simultaneously.[33]

It may seem puzzling that the estimate for Brazil is 5 percentage points lower than that for Chile, while Chile scores better in several corporate governance quality measures.[34] Various authors argue that there is an extraordinary concentration of voting power in Brazilian companies represented in common shares that are usually not traded in public stock markets, while, in the case of 90 percent of the stocks that are traded, there are nonvoting or preferred shares that do not pay material dividends.[35] If this is true, the value of such preferred shares may be disentangled from corporate outcomes. Insiders may therefore not participate in public markets and may potentially choose to profit from their informational advantage in private transactions.[36] This situation notably contrasts with that in Chile, where firms rarely issue nonvoting shares.[37] Moreover, about 15 percent of the issued stocks are actively traded in the local market, whereas about 8 percent of such stocks are kept in custody for depositary receipts traded in foreign markets. These numbers suggest that, for Chilean companies, a much higher proportion of voting power is traded in public stock markets relative to Brazilian firms. It may thus be possible that insiders in Chilean firms trade in public stock markets more actively than is the case in Brazil.

This chapter's country ranking differs from that of Grishchenko, Litov, and Mei (2002). They find that Argentina and Brazil show a much higher prevalence of informed trading than does Chile. This contrast may result

Table 1.4 Categorical Decomposition of ITPs

Model	*1*	*2*	*3*	*4*	*5*
Intercept	21.6*** (0.6)	18.5*** (0.3)	17.8*** (0.2)	18.1*** (0.2)	21.1*** (0.6)
1st quintile (highest vol.)	–4.4*** (0.4)	–4.5*** (0.4)	–4.5*** (0.4)	–4.4*** (0.4)	–4.1*** (0.4)
2nd quintile	–3.5*** (0.4)	–3.6*** (0.4)	–3.3*** (0.4)	–3.6*** (0.4)	–3.3*** (0.3)
3rd quintile	0.6 (0.5)	0.8 (0.5)	1.1** (0.5)	0.9* (0.5)	0.5 (0.5)
4th quintile	2.1*** (0.4)	2.1*** (0.4)	2.0*** (0.4)	2.1*** (0.4)	2.0*** (0.4)
5th quintile (lowest vol.)	5.2*** (0.7)	5.3*** (0.7)	4.7*** (0.7)	4.9*** (0.7)	4.9*** (0.7)
Argentina	–0.9 (0.96)				–1.2 (0.96)
Brazil	–5.3*** (0.7)				–4.6*** (0.7)
Chile	0.4 (0.8)				0.4 (0.7)
Colombia	8.0*** (2.5)				7.7*** (2.3)
Mexico	–4.6*** (0.7)				–4.7*** (0.6)
Peru	–2.1* (1.2)				–2.4** (1.1)
Venezuela, R.B. de	4.6** (2.3)				4.7** (2.2)
Basic materials		–0.2 (0.6)			
Communications		–2.1*** (0.5)			
Consumer, noncyclical		0.3 (0.7)			
Diversified		0.4 (0.9)			
Energy		–0.6 (0.9)			

(continued)

Table 1.4 Categorical Decomposition of ITPs *(continued)*

Model	*1*	*2*	*3*	*4*	*5*
Financial		2.3*** (0.8)			
Industrial		–0.5 (0.7)			
Utilities		–0.6 (0.6)			
Common stock			1.8*** (0.2)		0.6** (0.3)
Preferred stock			–1.8*** (0.2)		–0.6** (0.3)
ADR				–1.2*** (0.4)	–1.5*** (0.4)
ADR underlying				0.1 (0.4)	–0.2 (0.3)
Co. has ADR, but this is not the underlying				–0.2 (0.4)	0.5 (0.4)
Co. only trades at home (no ADR program)				1.3*** (0.4)	1.2*** (0.4)
R-squared	0.27	0.20	0.22	0.19	0.29
No. of ticker-quarters	1,123	1,123	1,123	1,123	1,123

Source: Authors.

Note: This table shows the output of pooled ordinary least squares regressions controlling for time fixed effects. The dependent variable is the ITP for each ticker, times 100. Dummies are used for each possible category within a classification. So, the coefficient on a dummy shows how different the average stock is in that category from the overall average stock (Suits 1984). See note to Table1.1 for details on the security type and ADR classifications. Volume quintiles are defined by exchange-quarter (intraexchange classification). The industry effects are dropped in model 5 because they are jointly insignificant. The time fixed effects are jointly significant in all specifications and are not reported. White (1980) heteroskedasticity-consistent standard errors are in parentheses (see equation 1.4).

* significant at 10 percent
** significant at 5 percent
*** significant at 1 percent

from the difference in the sample periods and from the alternative methods used to infer informed trading. Note, however, that, although these authors document a positive relationship between return autocorrelation and volume, which may be interpreted as evidence of informed trading, they do not perform the test indicated in Llorente et al. (2002) to show that the correlation coefficient effectively depends on informed trading measures. The approach used here is more direct because the ITP is the probability that each trade originates with an informed trader.

Another important result from table 1.4 is that the gap between ADRs and stocks that only trade at home is significant (2.7 percentage points) relative to an overall ITP average of about 21.1. This is consistent both with the hypothesis of better enforcement of insider trading rules in the United States and with the signaling hypothesis discussed above, and it also confirms the results in Von Furstenberg and Tabora (2004). These authors use price data for Telmex and Televisa stocks that are traded both at the Bolsa Mexicana de Valores and, as ADRs, in New York. They find that price discovery generally takes place in Mexico, which conforms to a higher presence of informed traders in the home market. Model 5 shows that ADRs have an average ITP that is 1.3 points lower than that of the underlying securities.

Informed trading and corporate governance measures used in the literature. The relationship between privately informed trading and the governance quality variables used in the literature is analyzed next. The hypothesis proposed is that this chapter's measure contains more information than do earlier metrics. Table 1.5 reports the results of estimations of the panel regression, as follows:

$$\begin{aligned} ITP_{ijt} &= \alpha + \beta^{G}\ \textit{Governance Quality}_{ij} \\ &\quad + \boldsymbol{\beta}^{t\prime}\ \mathbf{I}(t) + \boldsymbol{\beta}'\,\mathbf{I}(\text{Vol. Quintile}_{it}) + \varepsilon_{ijt} \\ i &= 1,\ldots,288;\quad j = \text{Arg., Bra., Chi., Col., Per., Mex., Ven.};\quad t = 1,\ldots,4 \end{aligned} \tag{1.5}$$

with one *Governance Quality*$_{ij}$ variable at a time, including volume quintile and time dummies, and using random effects at the stock exchange level. In most cases, *Governance Quality*$_{ij}$ uses only the country subscript (j) because it is a nationwide measure. Consequently, there are only seven effective observations of the quality variable in the regressions; the results should thus be interpreted with care.[38] The individual corporation subscript (i) is included because four lines in table 1.5 use the individual corporation ratings of CLSA.[39] The first four columns of the table report the coefficients and standard errors using intraexchange and interexchange volume quintiles, respectively.[40] The last two columns report the effect on the ITP of either a one standard deviation increase in *Governance Quality*$_{ij}$ or a change in the variable from zero to one when it is binary. For most explanatory variables, a higher value implies better investor protection or a better corporate governance environment (for example, a higher value in the risk of expropriation index means less risk). The exceptions are percentage of share capital to call an extraordinary shareholders' meeting (a higher value means that it is more difficult for minorities to accomplish this), the median shares of the three largest shareholders (a higher value implies more concentrated ownership), and mandatory dividend (the fraction of net income that a corporation is forced to pay out as dividends, which may be ambiguous for governance quality). To facilitate interpretation, regression results ranked from the lowest to the highest coefficients are reported.

Several variables yield the expected results. Higher values in the risk of expropriation, accounting standards, CLSA management transparency,[41] corruption in 1998, or the introduction of one share–one vote or mandatory dividends clauses imply a lower ITP. A one standard deviation increase or a change in each of these variables from zero to one leads to a fall of between 0.6 and 2.3 percentage points in the ITP. When controlling for interexchange quintiles, insider trading enforcement is also relevant, with a substantial fall of 2.4 percentage points in the ITP in those markets. Some of these variables are directly related to informational issues; so, these results seem reasonable.

Table 1.5 ITP and Investor Protection Environment

Governance quality/investor protection variables	*Definition of volume quintiles*				*Effect on ITP of increase in explanatory variable*	
	Intraexchange		*Interexchange*			
Ownership concentration (median shares of the 3 largest shareholders in 10 largest privately owned nonfinancial firms)	–21.1	(3.7)***	–17.0	(3.7)***	–2.26	–1.82
Mandatory dividend	–5.0	(1.6)***	–4.1	(1.6)***	–1.20	–0.99
Risk of expropriation	–2.0	(0.6)***	–0.7	(0.6)	–1.58	–0.59
Corruption in 1998[a]	–1.7	(0.6)***	–2.2	(0.5)***	–1.14	–1.45

(continued)

Table 1.5 ITP and Investor Protection Environment *(continued)*

Governance quality/ investor protection variables	*Definition of volume quintiles*				*Effect on ITP of increase in explanatory variable*	
	Intraexchange		*Interexchange*			
One share–one vote (binary)	−1.7	(0.8)**	−1.4	(0.7)*	−1.69	−1.36
Shares not blocked before meeting (binary)	−0.8	(0.8)	−0.8	(0.8)	−0.82	−0.75
Insider trading enforcement[b] Bhattacharya et al. (2000), Binary	−0.8	(1.1)	−2.4	(1.1)**	−0.81	−2.36
Risk of contract repudiation	−0.6	(0.6)	0.7	(0.6)	−0.58	0.68
Legality in 1998[c] (Berkowitz et al. 2002)	−0.5	(0.4)	−0.1	(0.3)	−0.77	−0.15
Rule of Law in 1998[d] (Law and Order from ICRG)	−0.4	(0.4)	−0.1	(0.4)	−0.80	−0.16
Accounting standards	−0.3	(0.1)***	−0.1	(0.1)	−2.29	−0.70
Oppressed minorities mechanism (binary)	−0.1	(0.9)	−1.1	(0.9)	−0.09	−1.15
CLSA management transparency	−0.1	(0.03)*	0.0	(0.03)	−0.77	−0.60
CLSA management discipline	0.0	(0.02)	0.0	(0.02)	−0.29	−0.19
Investment profiled	0.0	(0.2)	0.5	(0.2)***	0.03	1.22
CLSA management independence	0.1	(0.02)***	0.1	(0.02)***	1.08	0.90

(continued)

Table 1.5 ITP and Investor Protection Environment *(continued)*

Governance quality/ investor protection variables	*Definition of volume quintiles*				*Effect on ITP of increase in explanatory variable*	
	Intraexchange		*Interexchange*			
CLSA average rating	0.1	(0.1)	0.1	(0.1)*	0.56	0.73
Rule of law in 2004[d]	0.6	(0.2)***	0.7	(0.2)***	1.46	1.83
Legality in 2004[c]	0.8	(0.2)***	1.0	(0.2)***	1.36	1.76
Percentage of share capital to call an extraordinary shareholders' meeting	0.9	(3.5)	6.7	(3.4)*	0.10	0.71
Shareholder rights	1.2	(0.3)***	0.7	(0.3)***	1.79	1.02
Preemptive rights to new issues (binary)	3.6	(0.7)***	3.3	(0.7)***	3.61	3.27

Source: Authors.

Note: This table shows the output of panel regressions using exchange-ticker random effects and controlling for time and volume fixed effects. The first two columns use intraexchange volume quintiles, while the second two columns use interexchange quintiles. Each line corresponds to a regression that uses only that investor protection variable. All variables except the CLSA individual corporation (i) ratings are fixed within a country (j). See annex table A5 for a definition of the explanatory variables and their sample moments. For most explanatory variables, a higher value implies better investor protection or corporate governance environment (for example, a higher risk of expropriation index means less risk). The exceptions are the following: percentage of share capital to call an extraordinary shareholders' meeting (a higher value means that it is more difficult for minorities to accomplish this), the median shares of the three largest shareholders (a higher value implies more ownership concentration), and mandatory dividend (the fraction of net income that a corporation is forced to pay out as dividends, which may be ambiguous for governance quality). The last two columns report the effect on 100 times ITP of either a one standard deviation rise in the explanatory variable or, if it is binary, the effect of it changing from 0 to 1. The time fixed effects are jointly significant in all specifications and are not reported. Volume effects are likewise not reported. Standard errors are in parentheses beside each coefficient (see equation 1.5).

a. PRS Group (2004).

b. Bhattacharya et al. (2000).

c. Berkowitz et al. (2002).

d. Law and Order PRS Group (2004).

* significant at 10 percent

** significant at 5 percent

*** significant at 1 percent

However, there are other variables that yield the opposite result: Shareholder rights, a better representation of minorities (for instance, the existence of cumulative voting or proportional representation rules), judicial efficiency, preemptive rights to new issues, ownership concentration, as well as the 2004 scores of rule of law, corruption, and legality. These variables seem to be unrelated to private information.

The finding that higher ownership concentration leads to lower ITP is the Brazil versus Chile result in a new disguise. Brazil is at the top of the concentration scale, while Chile is at the bottom; in fact, the latter is about two standard deviations below the sample mean.

The sign change of the coefficients on rule of law and on corruption between the 1998 and 2004 observations merits an explanation. Brazil was about half a standard deviation above the cross-country mean in 1998, and it went down to about half a standard deviation below the mean in 2004 on both of these variables. This fact—given that Brazil has the lowest mean ITP in the sample—helps explain the sign reversal in these variables in equation 1.5. As noted above, this is essentially a regression with seven observations in the $Governance\ Quality_j$ dimension; so, this big reversal in the score of Brazil may cause the unexpected sign change.

The findings of Grishchenko, Litov, and Mei (2002) and of this chapter agree on some important points, but they disagree on others. On the one hand, the enforcement of insider trading bans, better accounting standards, less risk of expropriation, and the existence of one share–one vote legislation imply less prevalence of asymmetric information trading in both the paper and this chapter. There are also some counterintuitive results that coincide: existence of cumulative voting or proportional representation rules imply higher informed trading intensity in both the paper and the chapter.

On the other hand, while the effect of the percentage of shares needed to call an extraordinary meeting has a counterintuitive effect in Grishchenko, Litov, and Mei (2002), this chapter finds no effect on the ITP. Moreover, countries with more concentrated ownership structures exhibit asymmetric information trading according to those authors, while, in the present exercise, those countries have lower ITPs. Of course, this comparison is limited by the fact that, with a sample of 19 countries, those authors have more degrees of freedom than are available here to identify the effect of countrywide variables.

Although the regressions involving CLSA ratings are exempt from the degrees of freedom problem that pervades those regressions relying on nationwide controls, the use of variables based on CLSA ratings gives mixed results. Management independence and average rating from CLSA have the wrong sign in at least one of the specifications, though, as mentioned above, management transparency did have the right sign in one of the specifications.

In summary, while some of the often-used measures of the quality of corporate governance quality are associated with ITPs, there seems generally to be an important degree of heterogeneity in the ITPs that is not captured by the variables used in the literature.

Event Study: The ITP Around Corporate Announcements

In the time series dimension, inside information is most valuable immediately prior to the information's public release. Next, an event study is run in an attempt to analyze if, indeed, the ITP rises during the 20 trading days before a public announcement relative to a control period and a postannouncement period. Then, an assessment is made whether this time pattern differs across categories (for example, volume quintiles, countries, industries, common and preferred stocks, and ADR status). As usual in these types of experiments, this is a test of the joint hypothesis that the ITP is a good measure of insider trading and that insiders take advantage of their privileged access to information. After computing the ITP for the three periods around each announcement, the following equation is estimated:

$$\begin{aligned} ITP_{ikt} = {} & \alpha_0 + \alpha'\mathbf{Z}_i + \left(\beta_0 + \beta'\mathbf{Z}_i\right)\ I_{it}^{PERIODIC-PRE} + \left(\gamma_0 + \gamma'\mathbf{Z}_i\right)\ I_{it}^{PERIODIC-POST} \\ & + \left(\delta_0 + \beta'\mathbf{Z}_i\right)\ I_{it}^{APERIODIC-PRE} + \left(\phi_0 + \phi'\mathbf{Z}_i\right)\ I_{it}^{APERIODIC-POST} + \upsilon_{ikt} \end{aligned} \tag{1.6}$$

where $i = 1,\ldots, 264$; $k = 1,\ldots, K_i$; $t = 1,\ldots, T_i$; K_i is the number of announcements for firm i during the sample; and t indicates calendar time measured in days.[42] I_{it} represents an indicator function that equals 1 when day t, during which the ITP of the kth announcement of stock i is estimated, corresponds to I's superscript.[43]

In some cases, two announcements of a given firm are not sufficiently spaced; then, the data for a given day are used to estimate two different ITPs. For example, if there are fewer than 40 trading days between two consecutive announcements, some days will fall in the postannouncement period relative to the first statement and in the preannouncement period relative to the second. Therefore, the underlying ITP-generating process will be affected by these confounding effects. To handle this problem, each of the three ITPs pertaining to each announcement is multiplied by a 20-by-1 unit vector, whereby each entry pertains to the calendar day from which the number of buys, sells, and no-trade periods is taken to estimate that ITP. This is the reason the dependent variable in equation 1.6 has 60 different values for the t subscript for the kth announcement of firm i. On the right-hand side of the regression, the potentially different data-generating processes are addressed by turning on *both* indicator functions because day t falls in the range that activates I^{POST} relative to the first announcement and I^{PRE} relative to the second announcement. Moreover, there will be two observations for that day t. In one of them, the dependent variable will be the ITP of the postannouncement period relative to the first statement, while, in the other, the dependent variable will be the ITP of the preannouncement period relative to the second announcement. This procedure appears to address the potentially confounding information in the data-generating process without resorting to dropping announcements. Whenever announcements by a firm are spaced more than 40 days apart, only one indicator function will be turned on for each day.[44]

Table 1.6 reports the results of estimations for equation 1.6. Note that a specific dummy is not used for the control period. Thus α_0 reflects the mean value of the ITP during the control period, and all other coefficients in the table report the incremental value of the ITP during either a pre- or a postannouncement period or for stocks in a specific category or both. The vector Z_i contains dummies for every possible category within a classification: intraexchange volume quintile, country of domicile, industrial sector, security type, and ADR status. So, in each column, the coefficient on each line shows the difference between the behavior of stocks in that category and the behavior of the overall average stock during the corresponding event period.[45]

The coefficients on the top row show the behavior of the average stock so that the ITP has a benchmark value of 19.8 percent during the control period. During the preperiodic announcement period, this rises by 0.8 points (the increase being statistically significant). The ITP is 0.2 points higher during the postperiodic announcement period relative to the control period, but this difference is not statistically significant. So, the point estimates indicate that the ITP rises from 19.8 to 20.6 percent and falls back to 20 percent around periodic announcements precisely as if informed parties were speculating with private information prior to the public release of the information. The evidence is not as compelling for aperiodic announcements, though the ITP falls by a statistically significant amount after the announcement. This indicates that there is more informed trading during the 40 days prior to an announcement relative to after the announcement. If the true window width were greater than 20 days, this might imply that there is also speculative trading prior to these aperiodic announcements.

Table 1.6 reports the incremental coefficients of a category or announcement type relative to the control period. To facilitate interpretation, figures 1.2–1.6 report *total* ITP during each period for each category. Each figure consists of four charts. Those on the left correspond to periodic announcements, and those on the right correspond to aperiodic ones. Charts at the top in each figure are based on an unreported regression wherein the only dummies included in Z_i are the volume quintiles and at most the set of dummies for one other classification at a time (for example, figure 1.2 focuses on volume alone; 1.3 focuses on volume and countries; 1.4 on volume and industries, and so on). Charts at the bottom of each figure report the results of the addition of the coefficients in table 1.6; so, they measure the *partial* effects of a given category when Z_i includes

Table 1.6 ITP around Corporate Announcements

Explanatory variable	*Control period*	*Periodic announcement*		*Aperiodic announcement*	
		Pre	*Post*	*Pre*	*Post*
Intercept effect in each window (α_0, β_0, γ_0, δ_0, ϕ_0)	19.8*** (0.1)	0.8*** (0.1)	0.2 (0.1)	–0.2 (0.3)	–2.5*** (0.3)
1st quintile (highest vol.)	–5.6*** (0.1)	0.0 (0.1)	–0.4*** (0.1)	–1.2*** (0.2)	1.6*** (0.2)
2nd quintile	–3.2*** (0.1)	–0.2* (0.1)	–0.5*** (0.1)	–2.4*** (0.3)	–1.4*** (0.3)
3rd quintile	0.5*** (0.1)	–0.5*** (0.1)	0.7*** (0.1)	–0.2 (0.3)	–1.1*** (0.3)
4th quintile	2.5*** (0.1)	0.4*** (0.1)	0.6*** (0.1)	1.6*** (0.3)	–0.4 (0.3)
5th quintile (lowest vol.)	5.8*** (0.1)	0.3** (0.2)	–0.4*** (0.2)	2.2*** (0.3)	1.2*** (0.3)
Argentina	1.5*** (0.2)	-0.3 (0.2)	-1.7*** (0.2)	-0.5 (0.5)	0.2 (0.5)
Brazil	-2.6*** (0.1)	-0.8*** (0.2)	1.2*** (0.2)	-1.3*** (0.3)	2.8*** (0.3)
Chile	2.0*** (0.1)	2.2*** (0.2)	1.8*** (0.2)	2.2*** (0.3)	-3.2*** (0.3)
Mexico	-0.9*** (0.1)	-1.2*** (0.2)	-1.3*** (0.2)	-0.4 (0.3)	0.3 (0.3)
Basic materials	1.4*** (0.2)	-1.3*** (0.2)	-2.2*** (0.2)	0.2 (0.3)	0.4 (0.4)
Communications	-0.7*** (0.1)	-0.3** (0.2)	-0.8*** (0.2)	-0.6** (0.3)	1.3*** (0.3)
Consumer, cyclical	0.5** (0.2)	-1.4*** (0.2)	-1.5*** (0.2)	-2.1*** (0.5)	2.8*** (0.5)
Consumer, noncyclical	-1.4*** (0.2)	2.3*** (0.2)	1.3*** (0.2)	5.1*** (0.4)	-1.0** (0.4)
Diversified	0.6** (0.3)	1.6*** (0.3)	0.6* (0.3)	-2.9*** (0.5)	-1.6*** (0.6)
Energy	-0.2 (0.3)	-0.3 (0.4)	1.1*** (0.4)	1.3** (0.5)	-0.1 (0.5)
Financial	0.8*** (0.2)	-0.5** (0.2)	0.2 (0.2)	-0.1 (0.4)	-1.0** (0.4)
Industrial	-0.5** (0.2)	1.9*** (0.2)	1.9*** (0.2)	-2.9*** (1.1)	-3.4*** (1.3)

(continued)

Table 1.6 ITP around Corporate Announcements *(continued)*

Explanatory variable	*Control period*	*Periodic announcement* Pre		*Aperiodic announcement* Pre	
		Pre	*Post*	*Pre*	*Post*
Utilities	-0.4**	-2.1***	-0.5***	2.1***	2.6***
	(0.2)	(0.2)	(0.2)	(0.4)	(0.4)
Common stock	0.3***	-0.9***	0.4***	-0.2	1.1***
	(0.1)	(0.1)	(0.1)	(0.2)	(0.2)
Preferred stock	-0.3***	0.9***	-0.4***	0.2	-1.1***
	(0.1)	(0.1)	(0.1)	(0.2)	(0.2)
ADR	-1.5***	-0.8***	-0.4***	2.0***	0.8***
	(0.1)	(0.1)	(0.1)	(0.2)	(0.2)
ADR underlying	0.0	-0.8***	-0.1	0.2	-1.8***
	0.1	0.1	0.1	0.2	0.2
Co. has ADR, not underlying	0.3**	1.5***	0.5***	-1.9***	-2.5***
	0.2	0.2	0.2	0.4	0.4
Home only	1.2***	0.0	-0.1	-0.3	3.5***
	0.1	0.1	0.1	0.3	0.3

Source: Author.

Note: This table shows the results of an event study analyzing the behavior of ITP around corporate announcements controlling for volume, country, industrial sector, security type, and ADR status of each stock. The dependent variable is ITP (in percentage points) estimated during a control, a preannouncement and a postannouncement period relative to each announcement date. Each estimation period is 20 trading days long. I_{it} is an indicator function that equals 1 on those days t (the data for which are used to compute the ITP of the k th announcement of stock i) that fall in the range of I 's superscript. Periodic announcements comprise earnings and cash dividends news, while aperiodic ones consist of acquisitions and divestiture reports. The top row reports the intercept coefficients: α_0 is the average ITP during the control period, β_0 shows the difference between ITP during the preperiodic announcement period, and ITP during the control period, and γ_0 shows the gap between ITP during postperiodic announcement days and control days, and soon. The vector Z_i contains dummies for every possible category within a class So, in each column of the table, the coefficient on each line shows the difference between the behavior of the average stock in that category and that of the overall average stock during the corresponding event period (Suits 1984). The model is estimated by ordinary least squares, so, the mean ITP during the sample of a top-volume Argentinean common stock from the noncyclical consumer sector that trades only at home was 15.8 percent during the control period, rising to 17.7 percent before a periodic announcement, and falling back to 15.5 percent after the announcement. This table uses the universe of announcements made between November 26, 2003 and September 8, 2004, as recorded in Bloomberg, a total of 1,247 announcements from 264 stocks. Colombia and Peru are excluded to avoid small-sample bias. Standard errors are in parenthesis (See equation 1.6).

* significant at 10 percent

** significant at 5 percent

*** significant at 1 percent

Figure 1.2 ITP around Corporate Announcements, by Volume Quintile

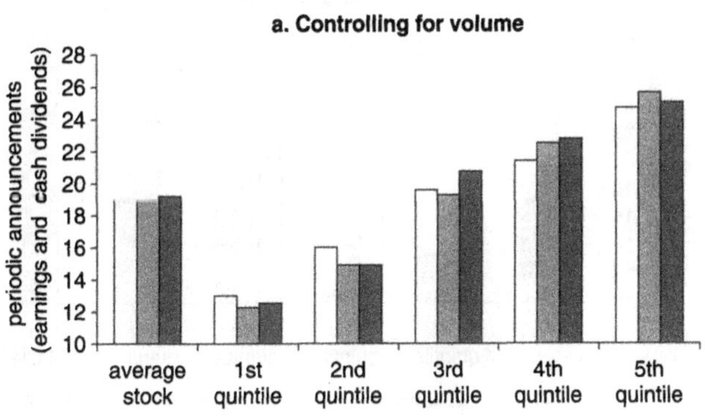

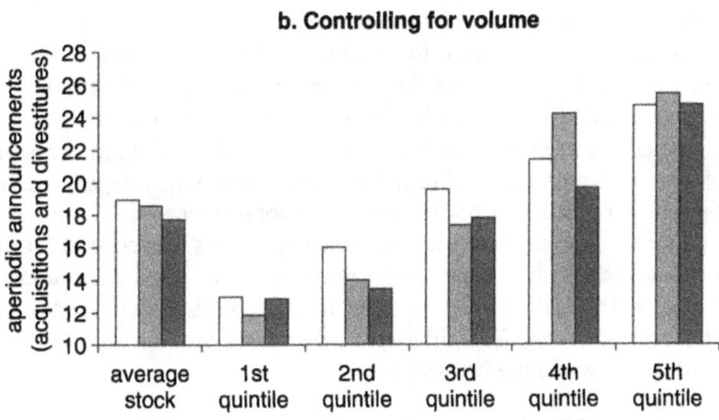

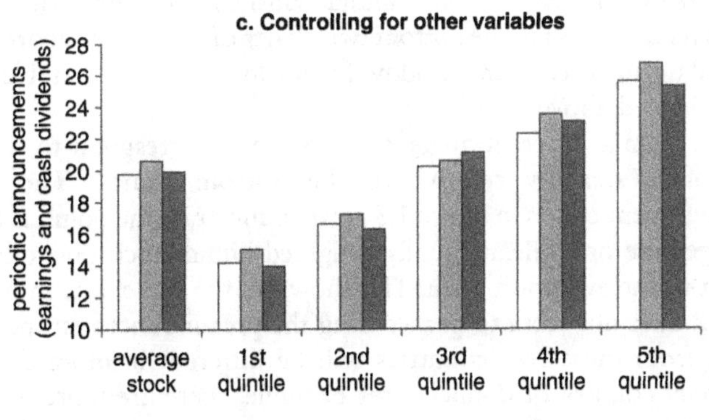

Figure 1.2 (continued)

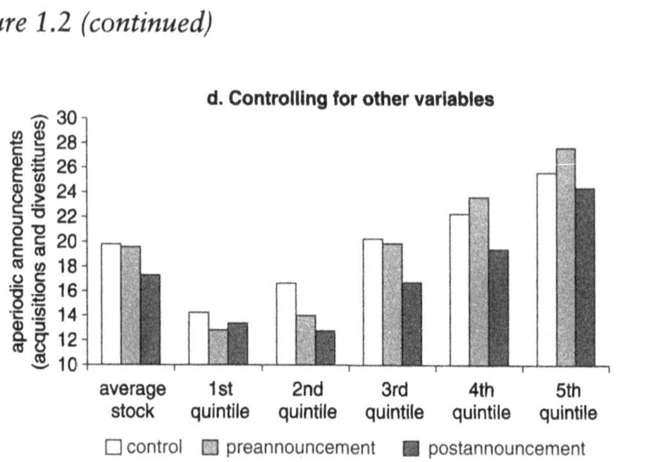

Source: Authors.

Note: Figures 1.2.A through 2.E show the mean total informed trading probability estimated in the event study (for the control, preannouncement, and postannouncement periods) for stocks in different categories. Each figure contains four graphs. Graphs on the left correspond to periodic announcements (earnings and cash dividends), while those on the right pertain to aperiodic announcements (acquisitions and divestitures). Graphs at the top correspond to OLS regressions that control only for volume beside the category analyzed in the graph. Graphs at the bottom report the total estimated ITP for stocks in the indicated category but resulting from regressions that control for other categories not explicitly depicted in the graph (i.e., they result from adding the coefficients in Table 3). The ITP in the bottom graphs is thus purged of factors other than the one being explicitly shown that could also have affected the ITP of the stocks shown in the top graph.

dummies for all classifications simultaneously. For example, the first three bars (average stock) in the bottom two charts of figure 1.2 report the average ITP during each event window for the average stock in table 1.6 that was discussed above.

Seen from a different angle, the top charts correspond to a different investment strategy relative to the bottom charts. The periodic announcement charts in figure 1.3 serve to illustrate the point. If one buys an Argentine or Chilean equally weighted liquid stock portfolio, one is subject to the evolution of the ITP shown in the top chart. In particular, the ITP does not seem to peak during the preannouncement period. But stocks from these two countries will be different in more dimensions than only country of domicile; for example, there are more noncyclical consumer product companies and fewer energy companies in the Chilean sample than in its Argentine counterpart (see table 1B in the annex for a

Figure 1.3 ITP around Corporate Announcements, by Country

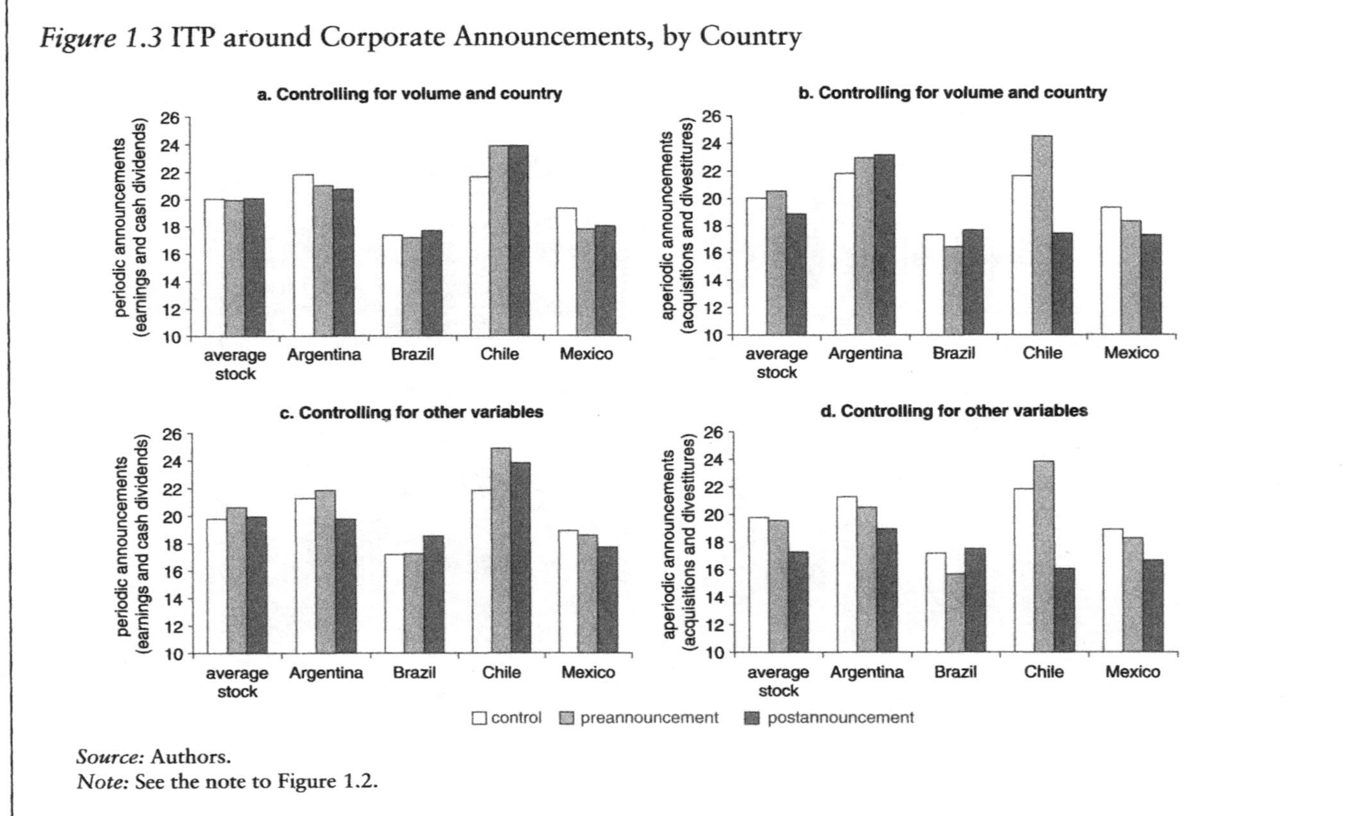

Source: Authors.

Note: See the note to Figure 1.2.

Figure 1.4 ITP around Corporate Announcements, by Industrial Sector

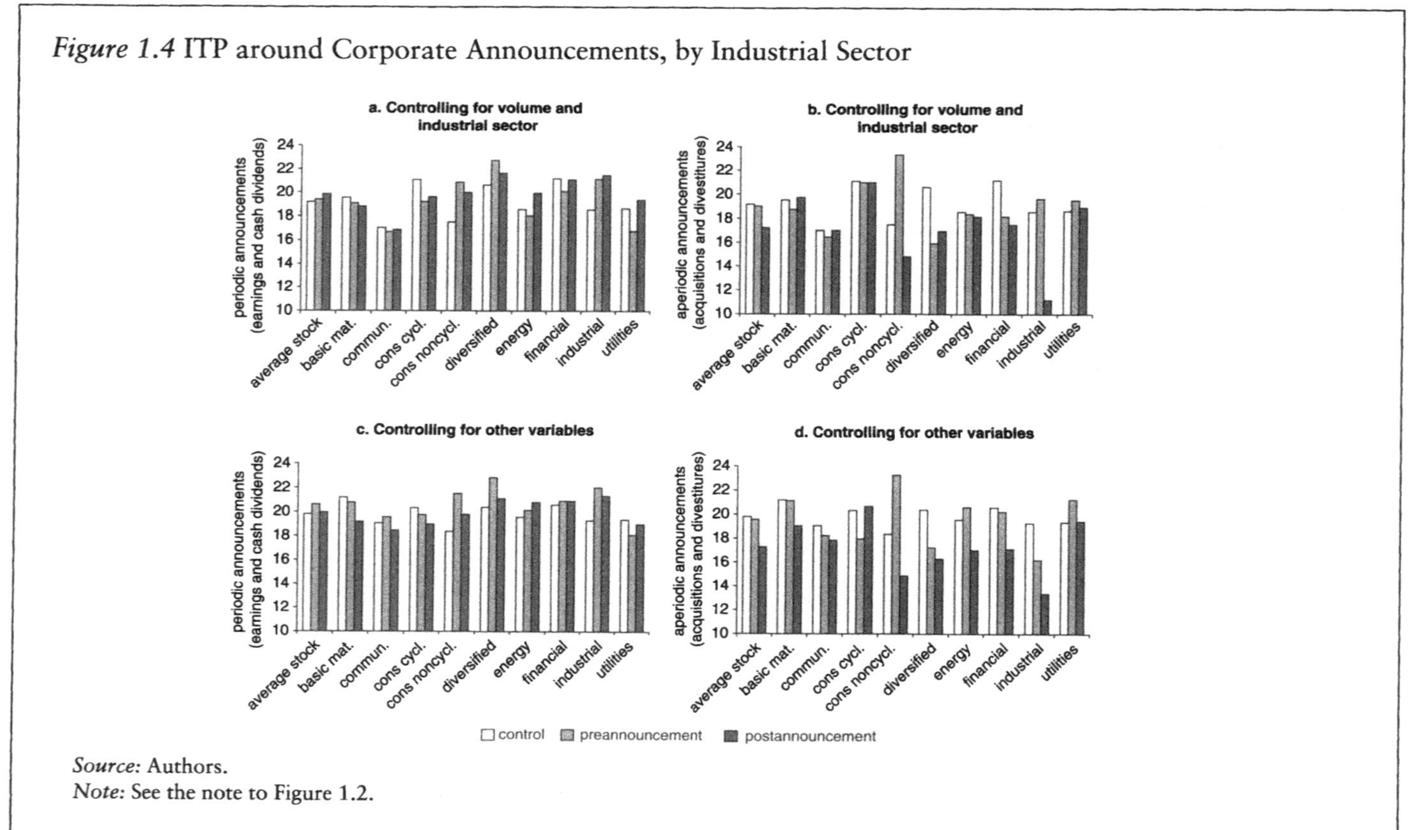

Source: Authors.
Note: See the note to Figure 1.2.

Figure 1.5 ITP around Corporate Announcements, by Security Type

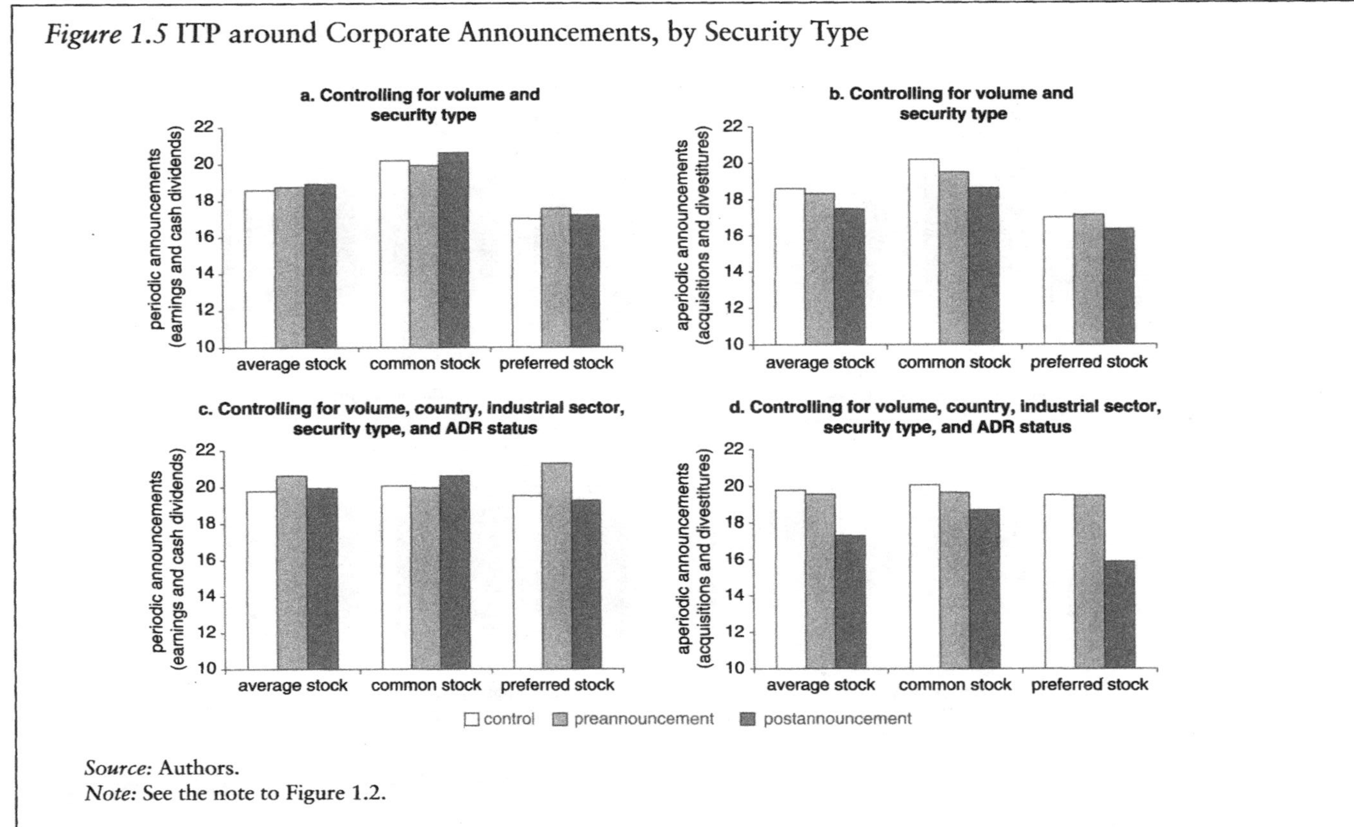

Source: Authors.
Note: See the note to Figure 1.2.

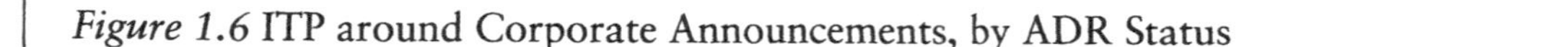

Figure 1.6 ITP around Corporate Announcements, by ADR Status

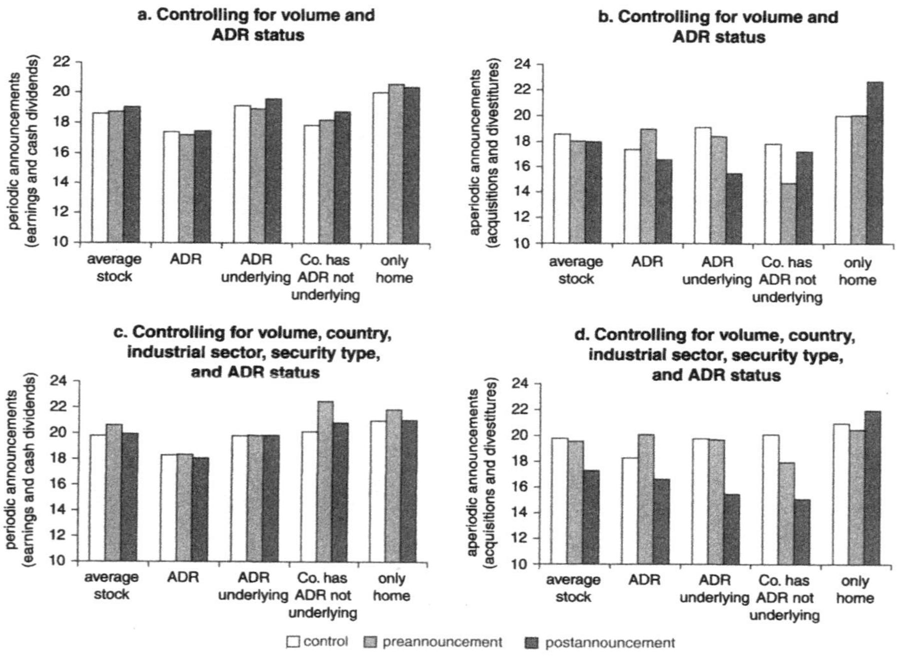

Source: Authors.
Note: See the note to Figure 1.2.

breakdown). The relative importance of stocks that trade only at home is also different. The bottom charts show the pure country *partial* effect (that is, purged of the influence of these other variables). This reflects the results of a strategy that is long in the country in question, but short in the various components of the portfolio that differ from the average stock in the sample of the four countries considered. In focusing on the pure country effect, the bottom charts show that there is substantial private information speculation in the preannouncement period in both Argentina and Chile, something that is hidden by other factors in the top charts.

For expository simplicity the discussion focuses on the bottom charts in figures 1.2–1.6. Interested readers may check the results with the coefficients in table 1.6, which is the basis of these figures.

The bottom charts in figure 1.2 confirm that periodic announcements are subject to private information trading in all quintiles but the third. For aperiodic announcements, only stocks in the two lowest quintiles are subject to speculative trading.

The bottom row in figure 1.3 shows that Chilean stocks are subject to information-based trading before both types of announcements, while Argentine stocks suffer the same problem before periodic announcements. Mexican stocks (and Argentine stocks prior to aperiodic announcements) have the peculiar pattern that the ITP peaks during the control period and falls thereafter. If the true window length were longer than 20 days, this might also indicate speculative trading there. There is no evidence of information-based trading in Brazil. The Chilean versus Brazilian patterns are fully consistent with the findings of table 1.4 discussed elsewhere above.

Speculative trading prior to public announcements also seems to differ across industrial sectors (see figure 1.4). Communications, noncyclical consumer products, diversified, and the industrial sector proper have the hump-shaped pattern peaking in the preperiodic announcement period.[46] Noncyclical consumer products, energy, and utilities replicate the pattern for aperiodic announcements.

The bottom row in figure 1.5 shows that there seems to be more speculative trading in preferred stocks than there is in common stocks, a feature that is not fully consistent with this chapter's explanation of the preferred effect in the discussion of table 1.4. There is not a coherent explanation for this figure.

The bottom charts in figure 1.6 are also telling. The information-based trading of periodic announcements seems to focus on stocks that trade only at home and on stocks that are not ADR underlying securities, although their issuers have ADR programs. The picture is different for mergers and acquisitions, in which the ITP seems substantially higher before announcements than after announcements, and this is particularly so for the stocks of companies with ADR programs. Unfortunately, the evidence in Von Furstenberg and Tabora (2004) does not make it possible to determine whether the price discovery taking place locally (which is confirmed to be the case generally and for periodic announcements) switches to New York immediately before aperiodic announcements are released, as documented here.

Two reasons may underlie the lack of speculative trading related to aperiodic announcements for stocks that trade only at home. It may be that firms without ADR programs release low-quality information regarding these announcements, and so analyst-based privately informed traders may become more active after such a release. It may also be that, because a mere 25 of the 163 aperiodic announcements were released by companies that trade only at home, the sample is too small for drawing any useful inferences.

As a robustness check, the same exercise is performed using a window length of only 10 trading days. Figures 1C and 1D in the annex show the counterpart results of those in table 1.6 and figures 1.2 through 1.6. The figures tend to confirm the finding of the benchmark experiment that the ITP before announcements is higher than the ITP after announcements. This is reflected in the first three bars of each figure, which show the situation of the average stock. However, in many cases in this experiment, the total ITP during the control period is higher than the ITP during the preannouncement period. On the assumption that the ITP correctly measures true informed trading, this is interpreted as evidence that the specified window length is shorter than the true window length. This is because the observed informed trading during the control period should be, at most, as high as the observed informed trading during the preannouncement period. If there is privately informed trading, then the observed informed trading during the preannouncement period should be lower, and, if there is no privately informed trading, it should be as high. The results indicate that, in many cases, the ITP is highest during the control period. The case of ADRs during aperiodic announcements illustrates the point (shown in the charts on the bottom right in figures 1.6 and 1D [annex]): with the window width of 20 trading days, the ITP has the expected hump in the middle, while it is always decreasing with the window width of 10 days. The latter result is attributed to window misspecification. More evidence that a window width of 10 trading days is too short is the fact that both Vega (2004) and Aktas et al. (2004) use event windows that are at least 40 trading days. Given that only 250 trading days of data and one announcement every 53 trading days are available on average, it has been decided, in this instance, not to use a window width greater than 20 days.

In summary, the event study set out to analyze whether the time pattern of the ITP around material corporate announcements is consistent with the hypothesis that privately informed parties exploit this information when it is most valuable. The ITP was decomposed during three periods, and notable differences were found across volume ranges, countries, industrial sectors, security type, and the ADR status of the securities in question. The overall evidence is consistent with the hypothesis proposed.

The Market Value of Informed Trading

Thus far, this chapter has documented the substantial heterogeneity in the ITP both within and among categories that have been examined through regression analysis. To complete the findings, an assessment is now carried out on whether the market does indeed recognize both this heterogeneity and the fact that informed trading is harmful to outside investors, as reflected in the prices of the securities traded by outside investors. La Porta et al. (2002) focus on nationwide controls and on corporation-specific cash-flow rights measured at one point in time. Klapper and Love (2002) use corporation-specific measures of governance that are analyst based (and so potentially subjective and endogenous) and are also fixed over time. The present contribution is to postulate that the ITP measured during each quarter in the sample is an indicator of the quality of corporate governance at the firm-quarter level. A panel regression is thus estimated, as follows:

$$
\begin{aligned}
q_{ijt} &= \alpha + \beta^I \, ITP_{ijt} + \beta^G \, Governance\ Quality_{ij} \\
&\quad + \beta^S \, Sales\ Growth_{ijt} + \boldsymbol{\beta}^{t\prime}\mathbf{I}(t) + \varepsilon_{it} \\
i &= 1,\ldots,175;\ \ j = \text{Arg., Bra., Chi., Col., Per., Mex., Ven.}\ \ t = 1,\ldots,4
\end{aligned} \tag{1.7}
$$

where Tobin's q_{ijt} proxies for the value of the firm i in country j during quarter t, and *Sales Growth*$_{ijt}$ attempts to capture the value of the firm's growth opportunities. Several regressions are run using all the governance quality or investor protection variables examined in table 1.5 both alone and interacted with the ITP with time fixed effects. Few of these variables turned out to be significant; so, the tables focus on those cases in which they were significant. Following La Porta et al. (2002), table 1.7 presents the results using raw data, while, for robustness, table 1.8 uses q and *Sales Growth* in deviation from industrial sector medians. The bottom line of each table reports the percentage rise in Tobin's q that accompanies a fall of one standard deviation in the ITP.

The key result is that the ITP has a negative contemporaneous effect on market value in all specifications: a fall of one standard deviation in the ITP is accompanied by a rise in Tobin's q of between 0.99 and 2.11 percentage points depending on the model. The effect is significant economically and statistically at the 10 percent level in most specifications, and it is slightly stronger with industry-adjusted data.[47]

The first two columns in each table report the benchmark specifications, in which the ITP is used alongside *Sales Growth* and a constant.[48] The first column uses firm fixed effects, while the second column uses country random effects. In three of the four cases, the ITP is significant at the 10 percent level.

Table 1.7 The Market Value of Informed Trading, Raw Data

	Base model		*Type of investor protection variable in each specification (firm random effects)*		
Explanatory variable	*Firm fixed effects*	*Country random effects*	*Legality*	*Rule of law*	*CLSA average*
Informed trading probability	-0.15* (0.09)	-0.33* (0.21)	-0.17* (0.09)	-0.17* (0.09)	-0.03 (0.18)
Governance quality			0.03 (0.02)	0.02* (0.0 1)	0.03*** (0.01)
Average sales growth	0.01 (0.08)	0.63*** (0.13)	0.07 (0.07)	0.07 (0.07)	0.16 (0.15)
Intercept	1.31*** (0.02)	1.36*** (0.06)	1.03*** (0.21)	1.22*** (0.07)	-0.48 (0.44)
Rise in q for a one standard deviation fall in ITP	0.99%	2.11%	1.06%	1.06%	0.21%

Source: Authors.

Note: This table shows panel regression output for a sample of 175 firms from seven countries (except the CLSA column, which uses 60 firms from five countries) measured once per quarter between October 2, 2003, and September 30, 2004. The dependent variable q for each quarter. The explanatory variables are the ITP for the most liquid ticker of each company during each quarter, investor protection proxies as defined in La Porta et al. (1998) and Berkowitz, Pistor, and Richard (2002), but updated using data from PRS (2004), and the average corporate governance quality rating from Gill (2001). Sales growth is three-year geometric annual growth in U.S. dollars lagged three quarters relative to the measure of Tobin's q. The bottom line reports the percentage rise in Tobin's q for a one standard deviation fall in the ITP. Standard errors are in parentheses (see equation 1.7).

* p-value <10 percent

** p-value < 5 percent

*** p-value <1 percent

The regressions in the last three columns use governance quality variables that are fixed over time. Therefore, fixed effects are not feasible, and random effects are used. For rule of law and legality (both assessed during 2004), the ITP coefficients are in the vicinity of the benchmark specifications and are statistically significant in three of the four cases. The ITP is therefore priced above and beyond the measures of nationwide investor protection in this seven-country sample.

Table 1.8 The Market Value of Informed Trading, Industry-Adjusted Data

	Base model		*Type of investor protection variable in each specification (firm random effects)*		
Explanatory variable	*Firm fixed effects*	*Country random effects*	*Legality*	*Rule of law*	*CLSA average*
Informed trading probability	-0.20*	-0.12	-0.20*	-0.20*	-0.10
	(0.11)	(0.22)	(0.1)	(0.1)	(0.22)
Investor protection			0.03*	0.03*	0.03***
			(0.02)	(0.02)	(0.01)
Average sales growth	-0.03	0.56***	0.04	0.04	0.08
	(0.09)	(0.13)	(0.09)	(0.09)	(0.17)
Intercept	0.29***	0.23**	-0.03	0.19***	-1.36***
	(0.02)	(0.1)	(0.22)	(0.07)	(0.49)
Rise in q for a one standard deviation fall in ITP	1.28%	0.78%	1.28%	1.28%	0.62%

Source: Authors.

Note: This table shows panel regression output for a sample of 175 firms from seven countries (except the CLSA column, which uses 60 firms from five countries) measured once per quarter between October 2, 2003, and September 30, 2004. The dependent variable is industry adjusted Tobin's q for each quarter. The explanatory variables are the ITP for the most liquid ticker of each company during each quarter, investor protection proxies as defined in La Porta et al. (1998) and Berkowitz, Pistor, and Richard (2002), but updated using data from the PRS (2004), and the average corporate governance quality rating from Gill (2001). Sales growth is three-year geometric annual growth in U.S. dollars lagged three quarters relative to the measure of Tobin's q. The bottom line reports the percentage rise in Tobin's q (not industry adjusted q) for a one standard deviation fall in ITP. Standard errors are in parentheses below each coefficient (see equation 1.8).

* p-valve <10 percent

** p-value <5 percent

*** p-value <1 percent

The last column of each table reports the results of a regression using the CLSA average rating for each corporation. These data, however, are available for only 60 firms of the 175 used in the previous regression. Although the point estimate of the coefficient on the ITP remains negative, it is no longer statistically significant. A similar result obtained using other CLSA measures of governance quality. This may result, in part, from the correlation between the average rating and the ITP documented in table 1.5, a fact that has interesting policy implications (discussed in the next section).

Klapper and Love (2002) also regress Tobin's q on CLSA governance ratings and find a coefficient between 0.02 and 0.025, quite similar to this chapter's point estimates of 0.03 and 0.027, respectively.

Conclusions, Policy Implications, and Directions for Future Research

For all practical purposes, illegal insider trading goes unpunished in Latin America. The theme of this chapter is that, given the invisibility of illegal insider trading from the viewpoint of outside investors, its detrimental effect on the returns of minority shareholders, and the history of impunity of this fraud in Latin America, controlling groups actually choose the extent to which they will exploit their informational advantage in securities trading. Corporate governance and insider trading are therefore intimately related.

While the discretionary powers of controlling groups might hurt minority shareholders, they might also benefit these shareholders. For instance, a more powerful controlling group may internalize the benefits of monitoring that are beneficial to all shareholders. However, insider trading is an explicit use of the discretion option that is harmful to outside investors. Nationwide regulations that permit this discretion give controlling groups the option to harm. Insider trading proxies indicate the extent to which controlling groups actually exercise this option at the expense of outsiders.

This chapter uses a well-established method to estimate the probability of informed trading (ITP) for each of 288 Latin American stocks. The behavior of the ITP is analyzed in the cross-section and around corporate announcements. The chapter also assesses whether the market sets a price on this risk. One caveat to all of the findings is that the ITP provides estimates of *privately* informed trading, which is more general and not necessarily restricted to illegal insider trading.

The results show that there is substantial heterogeneity in the ITP across stocks and that this dispersion occurs mainly within groups (such as countries, volume quintiles, industrial sectors, security types, and ADR classifications) rather than between them. This valuable new information may be used in assessing individual corporate behavior, which is not easily captured by groupings usually controlled for in the literature.

Despite this, it is possible to estimate the effects of some control variables. Thus, it is found that the ITP varies greatly across volume categories; the least liquid stocks have about twice the median rate (20 percent) of the most liquid stocks (11 percent). Brazil and Mexico have lower mean ITPs, while Colombia and República Bolivariana de Venezuela have higher mean ITPs than the average stock. The stocks of firms with ADR programs have lower ITPs than those without, similar to preferred stocks, which show amounts lower than those for common stocks. Also, countries with better information-related legal variables on investor protection tend to have lower ITPs.

The chapter then analyzes whether the ITP rises immediately before material corporate announcements are disclosed to the market, and this hypothesis is generally confirmed, although the magnitude and the lead of the anticipation seems higher for acquisition and divestiture (aperiodic) announcements than for earnings and cash-dividend (periodic) announcements. While ADRs have low information leakage relative to periodic announcements, they seem to have substantial leakage relative to aperiodic announcements. Tangible information leakage is found in Argentina, Chile, and Mexico, but no evidence of information leakage is found in Brazil. Some industrial sectors are subject to significant spikes in the ITP immediately before public announcements, a fact that might interest investors.

Last, the chapter checks whether the market value of firms responds to changes in the ITP, and it is found that a fall of one standard deviation in this variable raises corporate value by about 1 to 2 percentage points. This pricing seems low compared with the expected loss to an outsider from trading with a privately informed agent. The gap is attributed to the fact that the market may not be sufficiently aware of the distribution of informational asymmetries among different stocks.

It is concluded that the ITP does indeed proxy for unobservable corporate governance quality and that there is substantial heterogeneity of firm behavior within a given institutional environment. Part of this heterogeneity seems to be recognized by the market and priced accordingly.

In a nutshell: different stocks within a country display substantially different rates of private information trading, and the market recognizes this to some extent by trading less and reducing the market value of those firms with higher ITPs. These findings have important policy implications. While the literature to date emphasizes the benefits of *macro* (legal) reforms, this chapter shows that the *micro* components of the corporate governance measure are far from trivial. The traditional adverse selection literature (for example, Leland and Pyle 1977) shows that, with asymmetric information, the absence of signaling technologies induces uninformed investors to charge higher financing rates to all firms, precluding funding for some otherwise profitable projects. Moreover, a signal variable may be sufficient for investors to discriminate correctly across firms and projects, restoring the Pareto-efficiency of market equilibrium. This chapter proposes the creation of a corporate integrity score to fill the role of such a signal variable. By publicly disclosing the score of different companies, spontaneous market separation mechanisms would be relied upon to improve the corporate investment funding role of public securities markets.[49]

Although the ITP would be an ingredient of this score, other asymmetric-information measures such as the bid-ask spread, its adverse selection component, or the price impact of trades should also be contemplated. Moreover, like this chapter, one might conduct an event study of the ITP around corporate announcements, but using two or three years of data, and compute the mean increase of the ITP during the preannouncement period for each individual corporation. Furthermore, it would be interesting to counterpart these trade- and offer-based data with the price impact of data on announcements. While Bhattacharya et al. (2000) show that Mexican stock prices are, on average, unresponsive to corporate announcements, it may be conjectured that the distribution of these responses is heterogeneous within countries, as is the distribution of the ITP.

Because controlling groups may evolve over time in the management of inside information, due partly to the pressure caused by the integrity score, the latter might be updated once or twice a year to reflect this change in behavior.

These measures have the advantage of being objective, quantitative, theory-based proxies for corporate behavior. They are also less expensive to compute than the alternative, analyst-based measures, which are potentially subjective and endogenous.

This score might provide palpable benefits by encouraging investor interest in those companies that are making a genuine effort to improve the quality of and access to information. Moreover, it would induce companies that have problems with inside information management to be more proactive in this area. For example, in choosing a target for a merger or an acquisition, a company may care to know how likely it is that the partner will begin trading (illegally) in the public market to tilt the negotiation in his or her favor before the deal is completed. Also, multilateral financial organizations would be able to screen companies on this score when accepting them as contractors for investment projects that they help fund. But, before this happens, more research is clearly needed to assess the specific construction and robustness of this proposed individual corporation integrity score.

Annex 1.1 Additional Figures and Tables

Table 1A Traded Volume in Latin American Stocks

a. Average daily volume of transactions in sample

	Average daily volume from IVQ03–IIIQ04					
Countries	*Home market*	*ADRs in the United States*	*Total*	*Country's share of total trade in Latin American stock*	*Ratio of ADR volume to home market volume*	*Sample coverage ratio*
Argentina	14,473	14,885	29,358	3.6%	1.03	0.98
Brazil	217,521	239,229	456,750	55.6%	1.10	0.82
Chile	33,666	16,879	50,545	6.2%	0.50	0.85
Colombia	888	723	1,611	0.2%	0.81	0.30
Mexico	143,509	116,197	259,706	31.6%	0.81	0.80
Peru	1,048	18,271	19,319	2.4%	17.44	0.89
Venezuela, R.B. de	742	3,702	4,444	0.5%	4.99	0.77
Total	411,846	409,886	821,732	100.0%	1.00	0.82

(*continued*)

Table 1A Traded Volume in Latin American Stocks (*continued*)

b. Average daily volume of transactions in all stocks

	Average daily volume from IVQ03–IIIQ04					
Countries	*Home Market*	*ADRs in the United States*	*Total*	*Country's share of total trade in Latin American stock*	*Ratio of ADR volume to home market volume*	*Sample coverage ratio*
Chile	40,321	18,848	59,169	5.9%	0.47	0
Colombia	4,670	723	5,392	0.5%	0.15	0
Mexico	148,091	176,059	324,149	32.3%	1.19	4,547
Peru	3,373	18,271	21,645	2.2%	5.42	218
Venezuela, R.B. de	2,045	3,734	5,779	0.6%	1.83	0
Total	529,980	474,994	1,004,974	100.0%	0.90	7,597

Source: Complied by the authors based on data from World Federation of Exchanges 2004 and from Economática, http://www.economática.com/index_fla.htm.

Note: This table shows, for each country, the average daily dollar amount of transactions in domestic stocks that took place in its home market and in the United States in the ADR market. This is as reported by Economática for the period between October 2, 2003, and September 30, 2004. Figures are expressed in thousands of dollars. The bottom panel shows that the average daily trading volume in Latin American securities is about US$ billion dollars. This compares with US$1.8 billion in Hong Kong (China), US$2.6 billion in the TSX Group (Toronto Stock Exchange and TSX Venture Exchange), US$4.8 billion in Spain, US$6.1 in Germany, US$9.7 billion in Euronext (the merger of the Amsterdam, Paris, Brussels, Lisbon, and London International Financial Futures exchanges, though only spot stock trading is considered here), US$13.1 billion in Japan, US$20.5 billion in the United Kingdom, and US$83.2 billion in the United States (New York Stock Exchange, American Stock Exchange, and Nasdaq combined during 2004 according to the World Federation of Exchanges Annual Report [2004].

Table 1B Number of Tickers by Country and Sector

	Argentina	*Brazil*	*Chile*	*Colombia*	*Mexico*	*Peru*	*Venezuela, R. B. de*	*Total*
Basic materials	6	34	4	0	3	6	0	53
Communications	4	40	3	0	12	1	2	62
Consumer, cyclical	3	5	7	0	10	0	0	25
Consumer, noncyclical	4	9	8	0	9	1	0	31
Diversified	1	4	3	0	4	0	0	12
Energy	5	5	0	0	0	0	0	10
Financial	9	9	7	3	4	1	0	33
Industrial	4	10	5	0	8	0	0	27
Utilities	6	21	7	0	0	0	1	35
Total	42	137	44	3	50	9	3	288

(continued)

Table 1B Number of Tickers by Country and Sector *(continued)*

Source: Compiled by the authors based on data from Bloomberg.

Note: The rows reports the total number of tickers for each country-sector among the 288 tickers. Bloomberg provides an industry-subsector classification. The following contains all included subsectors:

Basic materials: Agricultural chemicals, Chemicals–diversified, Chemicals–plastics, Chemicals–specialty, Coatings/Paint, Diversified Minerals, Gold mining, Metal–aluminum, Metal–copper, Metal–diversified, Nonferrous metals, Paper and related products, Petrochemicals, Silver mining, Steel–producers, Steel–specialty.

Communications: Broadcast Serv/Program, Cable TV, Cellular telecom, Publishing–books, Radio, Telecom services, Telephone–integrated.

Consumer, cyclical: Airlines, Apparel Manufacturers, Appliances, Audio/Video Products, Auto–Cars/Light Trucks, Auto/Trk Prts and Equip–orig, Auto/Trk Prts and Equip–repl, Bldg–residential/Commer, Distribution/Wholesale, Footwear and Related Apparel, Hotels and Motels, Housewares, Import/Export, Music, Retail–Appliances, Retail–Consumer Electron, Retail–Discount, Retail–Drug Store, Retail–Hypermarkets, Retail–Major Dept. Store, Retail–Misc/Diversified, Retail–Petroleum Prod, Retail–Restaurants, Textile–Apparel, Textile–Products, Toys.

Consumer, noncyclical: Agricultural biotech, Agricultural operations, Beverages-Non-alcoholic, Beverages-Wine/Spirits, Brewery, Fisheries, Food–Baking, Food–Canned, Food–Confectionery, Food–Flour and Grain, Food–Meat Products, Food–Misc/Diversified, Food–Retail, Food–Wholesale/Distrib, Medical–Hospitals, Medical–Whsle Drug Dist, Poultry, Printing–Commercial, Public Thoroughfares, Soap and Cleaning Prepar, Sugar, Tobacco, Veterinary Diagnostics, Whsing and Harbor Trans Serv.

Diversified: Diversified Operations, Specified purpose acquis.

Energy: Oil Comp–Integrated, Oil Refining and Marketing, Oil–Field Services, Pipelines.

Financial: Commer Banks Non–US, Diversified Finan Serv, Finance–Invest Bnkr/Brkr, Finance—Other Services, Investment Companies, Money Center Banks, Real Estate Mgmnt/Servic, Real Estate Oper/Develop, Regional Banks–Non United States.

Industrial: Aerospace/Defense, Airport Develop/Maint, Bldg Prod–Cement/Aggreg, Bldg Prod–Wood, Bldg and Construct Prod–Misc, Building and Construct–Misc, Building–Heavy Construct, Ceramic Products, Containers–Metal/Glass, Containers–Paper/Plastic, Diversified Manufact Op, Electronic Compo–Misc, Engines–Internal Combust, Explosives, Firearms and Ammunition, Mach Tools and Rel Products, Machinery–Constr and Mining, Machinery–Electric Util, Machinery–Farm, Machinery–General Indust, Machinery–Therml Process, Metal Processors and Fabrica, Miscellaneous Manufactur, Steel Pipe and Tube, Transport–Marine.

Utilities: Electric–Distribution, Electric–Generation, Electric–Integrated, Electric–Transmission, Gas–Distribution, Water.

Table 1C Number of Sample Stocks by Liquidity Range, Home Market

a. Number of stocks in each presence range[a]

Country	*Range of percentage of trading days during which the stock traded*									*Total*
	0–30	*30–40*	*40–50*	*50–60*	*60–70*	*70–80*	*80–90*	*90–99.9*	*100*	
Argentina				1				14	15	30
Brazil		1					1	15	88	105
Chile								13	18	31
Colombia								1	1	2
Mexico			1	1		1		5	27	35
Peru	1		1					2	1	5
Venezuela, R.B. de									2	2
Total	1	1	2	2	0	1	1	50	152	210

b. Number of stocks in each volume range

Country	*Range of average daily trading volume (in thousands of US$)*								
	0–25	*25–50*	*50–100*	*100–250*	*250–500*	*500–1M*	*1M–3M*	*3M+*	
Argentina	2	9	3	4	5	2	4	1	30
Brazil	3	5	8	15	12	15	23	24	105
Chile				4	5	10	10	2	31
Colombia					2				2
Mexico				2	2	5	13	13	35

(continued)

Table 1C Number of Sample Stocks by Liquidity Range, Home Market (*continued*)

b. Number of stocks in each volume range

	Range of average daily trading volume (in thousands of US$)								
Country	*0–25*	*25–50*	*50–100*	*100–250*	*250–500*	*500–1M*	*1M–3M*	*3M+*	*Total*
Peru			1	2	1			1	5
Venezuela, R.B. de			1			1			2
Total	5	14	13	27	27	33	50	41	210

c. Number of stocks in each range of number of trades[b]

	Range of average daily number of trades[b]							
Country	*0–10*	*10–25*	*25–50*	*50–75*	*75–150*	*150–300*	*300+*	*Total*
Argentina		11	4	2	8	2	3	30
Brazil	1	17	17	10	11	24	25	105
Chile		10	10	7	4			31
Colombia			1	1				2
Mexico			9	8	6	7	4	34
Peru	2		2		1			5
Venezuela, R.B. de			1	1				2
Total	3	38	44	29	30	33	32	209

Source: Compiled by the authors based on data from Economática, http://www.economatica.com/index_fla.htm.
Note: The sample period is October 2, 2003, to September 30, 2004.
a. Presence is the fraction of trading days during which a stock actually traded.
b. The number of trades of Wal-Mart de Mexico C is not available in Economática.

Table 1D Number of Sample Stocks by Liquidity Range, ADR Market

a. Number of stocks in each presence range[a]

Country	Range of percentage of trading days during which the stock traded									Total
	0–30	30–40	40–50	50–60	60–70	70–80	80–90	90–99.9	100	
Argentina								3	9	12
Brazil								6	26	32
Chile							2	5	6	13
Colombia								1		1
Mexico								4	11	15
Peru			1					1	2	4
Venezuela, R.B. de									1	1
Total	0	0	1	0	0	0	2	20	55	78

b. Number of stocks in each volume range

Country	Range of average daily trading volume (in thousand of dollars)								Total
	0–25	25–50	50–100	100–250	250–500	500–1M	1M–3M	3M+	
Argentina			1		3	2	5	1	12
Brazil			1	2	3	4	3	19	32
Chile				2	4	2	3	2	13
Colombia						1			1

(continued)

Table 1D Number of Sample Stocks by Liquidity Range, ADR Market (*Continued*)

b. Number of stocks in each volume range

	Range of average daily trading volume (in thousand of dollars)								
Country	*0–25*	*25–50*	*50–100*	*100–250*	*250–500*	*500–1M*	*1M–3M*	*3M+*	*Total*
Mexico			2	1	5		1	6	15
Peru			1		1			2	4
Venezuela, R.B. de								1	1
Total	0	0	5	5	16	9	12	31	78

c. Number of stocks in each range of number of trades[b]

	Range of average daily number of trades							
Country	*0–10*	*10–25*	*25–50*	*50–75*	*75–150*	*150–300*	*300+*	*Total*
Argentina		1	2	2	3	3	1	12
Brazil		1	4	2	4	8	13	32
Chile		3	4	1	3	2		13
Colombia				1				1
Mexico		1	7		1	2	4	15
Peru			2				2	4
Venezuela, R.B. de						1		1
Total	0	6	19	6	11	16	20	78

Source: Compiled by the authors based on data from Bloomberg and from Economática, http://www.economatica.com/index_fla.htm.

Note: The sample period is October 2, 2003, to September 30, 2004.

a. Presence is the fraction of trading days during which a stock actually traded.

b. Number of trades data for ADR is from Bloomberg.

Table 1E Statistics of the Liquidity of Sample Stocks, Home Market

Country	N	*Mean*	*Standard deviation*	*Minimum*	*Q1*	*Median*	*Q3*	*Maximum*
a. Presence								
Argentina	30	97.4	8.4	53.8	98.4	99.8	100.0	100.0
Brazil	105	99.1	6.1	38.8	100.0	100.0	100.0	100.0
Chile	31	99.0	1.8	93.7	99.2	100.0	100.0	100.0
Colombia	2	99.6	0.6	99.2	99.2	99.6	100.0	100.0
Mexico	35	96.2	13.0	40.3	100.0	100.0	100.0	100.0
Peru	5	69.8	43.0	6.0	44.2	99.2	99.6	100.0
Venezuela, R.B. de	2	100.0	0.0	100.0	100.0	100.0	100.0	100.0
Total	210	97.7	10.6	6.0	99.6	100.0	100.0	100.0
b. Average daily trading volume (in US$ thousands)								
Argentina	30	485.4	808.0	20.6	38.6	136.7	481.1	3,314.6
Brazil	105	2,074.6	2,988.7	6.1	185.9	695.6	2,744.0	14,403.7
Chile	31	1,089.4	1,001.5	142.8	423.8	826.4	1,364.9	4,155.1
Colombia	2	446.1	30.6	424.5	424.5	446.1	467.8	467.8
Mexico	35	4,299.6	5,583.6	105.7	907.8	1,994.7	5,167.6	22,866.0
Peru	5	937.1	1,621.4	64.9	191.7	194.8	404.8	3,829.3
Venezuela, R.B. de	2	370.8	387.0	97.1	97.1	370.8	644.5	644.5
Total	210	2,014.2	3,349.4	6.1	191.7	688.8	2,146.1	22,866.0

(continued)

Table 1E Statistics of the Liquidity of Sample Stocks, Home Market (*continued*)

Country	*N*	*Mean*	*Standard deviation*	*Minimum*	*Q1*	*Median*	*Q3*	*Maximum*
c. Average daily number of trades[b]								
Argentina	30	100.5	119.3	14.1	21.8	48.6	118.7	470.7
Brazil	105	197.2	207.0	8.7	34.4	137.9	294.3	928.5
Chile	31	44.2	25.3	16.1	24.6	37.5	61.2	112.0
Colombia	2	52.5	3.7	49.9	49.9	52.5	55.1	55.1
Mexico	34	135.6	114.2	26.7	47.6	71.8	218.6	442.0
Peru	5	35.2	32.9	2.3	6.0	37.3	48.1	82.3
Venezuela, R.B. de	2	40.1	16.1	28.7	28.7	40.1	51.5	51.5
Total	209	143.9	171.0	2.3	31.9	63.0	204.4	928.5

Source: Compiled by the author based on data from Economática, http://www.economatica.com/index_fla.htm.

Note: The sample period is October 2, 2003, to September 30, 2004.

a. Presence is the fraction of trading days during which a stock actually traded.

b. The number of trades of Wal-Mart de Mexico C is not available in Economática.

Table 1F Statistics of the Liquidity of Sample Stocks, ADR Market

Country	N	Mean	Standard deviation	Minimum	Q1	Median	Q3	Maximum
a. Presence[a]								
Argentina	12	99.7	0.8	97.2	99.8	100.0	100.0	100.0
Brazil	32	99.4	1.8	91.2	100.0	100.0	100.0	100.0
Chile	13	96.3	5.3	85.3	92.8	99.6	100.0	100.0
Colombia	1	99.6		99.6	99.6	99.6	99.6	99.6
Mexico	15	99.5	1.2	95.6	99.6	100.0	100.0	100.0
Peru	4	84.8	29.4	40.6	69.5	99.2	100.0	100.0
Venezuela, R.B. de	1	100.0		100.0	100.0	100.0	100.0	100.0
Total	78	98.2	7.1	40.6	99.6	100.0	100.0	100.0
b. Average daily trading volume (in US$ thousands)								
Argentina	12	1,241.2	1,196.5	60.6	381.9	916.1	1,604.9	4,145.5
Brazil	32	7,477.5	9,746.7	72.5	886.2	3,390.0	10,840.9	38,855.9
Chile	13	1,307.6	1,560.6	189.4	326.3	600.2	1,517.1	5,199.5
Colombia	1	725.5		725.5	725.5	725.5	725.5	725.5
Mexico	15	7,747.1	13,533.9	65.7	257.4	436.1	13,021.8	48,185.9
Peru	4	4,582.4	5,296.0	89.5	200.7	3,681.3	8,964.0	10,877.4
Venezuela, R.B. de	1	3,702.5		3,702.5	3,702.5	3,702.5	3,702.5	3,702.5
Total	78	5,258.2	9,052.7	60.6	326.3	1,237.0	5,199.5	48,185.9

(continued)

Table 1F Statistics of the Liquidity of Sample Stocks, ADR Market (*continued*)

Country	*N*	*Mean*	*Standard deviation*	*Minimum*	*Q1*	*Median*	*Q3*	*Maximum*
c. Average daily number of trades[b]								
Argentina	12.0	130.3	100.7	21.7	48.7	87.4	224.7	297.9
Brazil	32.0	300.7	251.7	20.7	106.4	227.8	458.0	1069.1
Chile	13.0	87.2	87.4	21.6	27.9	42.3	102.1	296.4
Colombia	1.0	62.3		62.3	62.3	62.3	62.3	62.3
Mexico	15.0	236.0	305.4	20.4	32.5	49.0	348.8	948.4
Peru	4.0	317.1	327.9	35.0	35.7	290.2	598.4	652.8
Venezuela, R.B. de	1.0	262.2		262.2	262.2	262.2	262.2	262.2
Total	78.0	223.7	239.0	20.4	42.3	123.4	297.9	1069.1

Source: Compiled by the authors based on data from Bloomberg and from Economática, http://www.economatica.com/index_fla.htm.

Note: Sample period: October 2, 2003, to September 30, 2004.

Data are from Economática and Bloomberg.

a. Presence is the fraction of trading days during which a stock actually traded.

b. Number of trades data for ADR is from Bloomberg.

Table 1G Dollar Volume of Trading by Exchange and Quintile

a. Dollar volume of transactions (in millions)

Exchange	*1st quintile (highest volume)*	*2nd quintile*	*3rd quintile*	*4th quintile*	*5th quintile (lowest volume)*	*quintiles 1 to 5*	*Total in sample / total in exchange*
Argentina	2,728.6	594.7	187.2	61.0	32.1	3,604	96%
Brazil	37,807.5	10,949.2	3,977.2	1,349.6	296.6	54,380	69%
Colombia	123.6	0.0	93.2	0.0	0.0	217	19%
Chile	4,940.3	1,660.	1,013.3	609.6	213.8	8,442	83%
Mexico	24,087.6	6,876.4	3,216.1	1,647.1	480.6	36,308	97%
Peru	123.0	57.6	47.2	31.7	1.4	261	31%
United States (ADR market)	78,187.3	17,337.2	5,111.3	1,738.8	506.7	102,881	86%
Venezuela, R.B. de	156.6	0.0	23.6	0.0	0.0	180	36%

b. Fraction of sample volume accounted for by each quintile, %

Exchange	*1st quintile (highest volume)*	*2nd quintile*	*3rd quintile*	*4th quintile*	*5th quintile (lowest volume)*
Argentina	75.7	16.5	5.2	1.7	0.9
Brazil	69.5	20.1	7.3	2.5	0.5
Colombia	57.0	0.0	43.0	0.0	0.0
Chile	58.5	19.7	12.0	7.2	2.6
Mexico	66.3	18.9	8.9	4.5	1.3
Peru	47.1	22.1	18.1	12.1	0.5
United States (ADR market)	76.0	16.9	5.0	1.7	0.5
Venezuela, R.B. de	86.9	0.0	13.1	0.0	0.0

(continued)

Table 1G Dollar Volume of Trading by Exchange and Quintile (*continued*)

c. Cumulative fraction of sample volume accounted for up to each quintile

Exchange	*1st quintile (highest volume)*	*2nd quintile*	*3rd quintile*	*4th quintile*	*5th quintile (lowest volume)*
Argentina	76	92	97	99	100
Brazil	70	90	97	99	100
Colombia	57	57	100	100	100
Chile	59	78	90	97	100
Mexico	66	85	94	99	100
Peru	47	69	87	99	100
United States (ADR market)	76	93	98	100	100
Venezuela, R.B. de	87	87	100	100	100

Source: Authors.

Note: Panel A shows the dollar volume (in millions) of transactions that took place from October 2, 2003, to September 30, 2004 in the 288 tickers of the sample across the eight exchanges considered. The columns correspond to the different quintiles within each exchange. The last column shows that the sample covers more than 80 percent of total exchange trading volume for Argentina, Chile, Mexico, and the ADR market for Latin American stocks. Panel B shows the fraction of the total sample trading volume accounted for by each quintile. Panel C shows the accumulated trading volume accounted for up to each quintile. There is a high concentration of trading in the 40 percent of stocks that trade the most. They account for more than 70 percent of trading in all but one exchange.

Figure 1A Temporal Distribution of Announcements

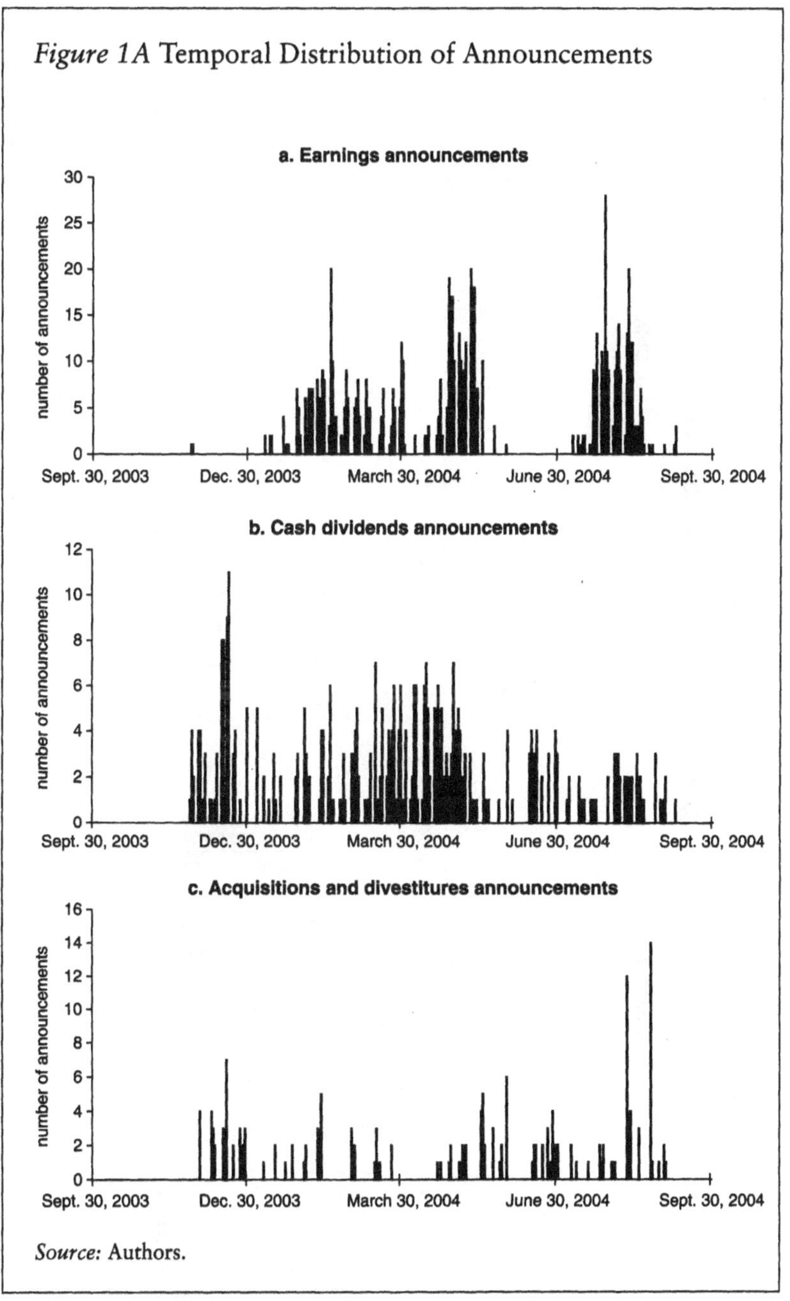

Source: Authors.

Figure 1B Temporal Distribution of Earnings Announcements by Country and Date

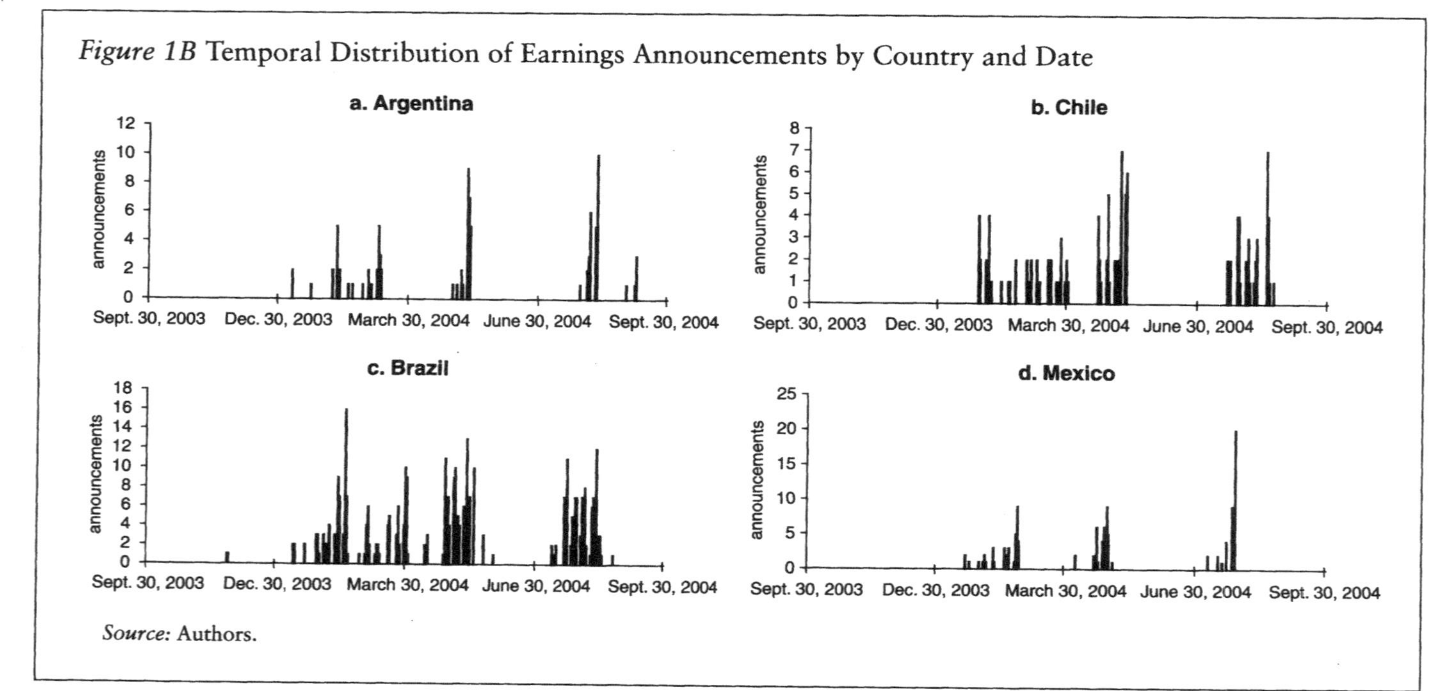

Source: Authors.

Figure 1C ITP around Corporate Announcements by Security Type, 10 Trading Days

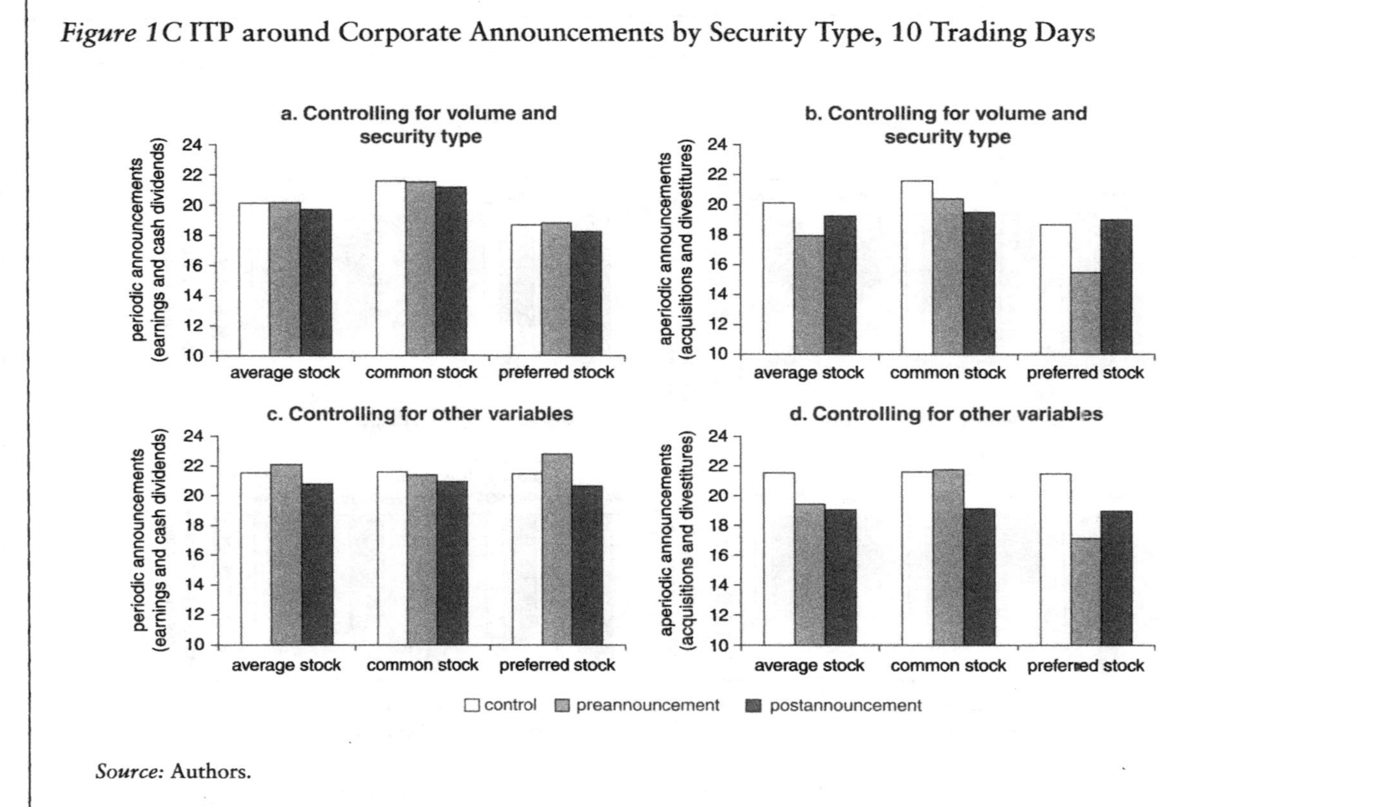

Source: Authors.

Figure 1D ITP around Corporate Announcements by ADR Status, 10 Trading Days

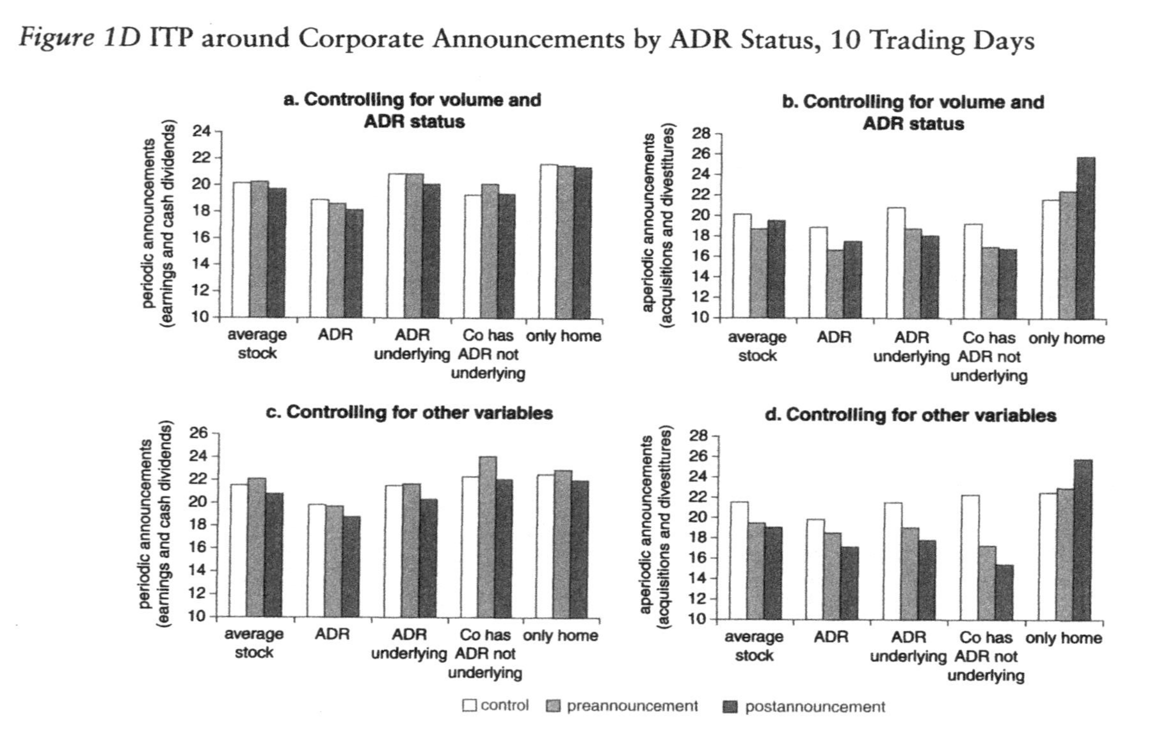

Source: Authors.

Notes

1. See Maug (2002); Bhattacharya et al. (2000); Bhattacharya and Daouk (2002); Beny (1999).

2. Examples include questions 14, 15, 17, and 18 in Gill (2001), questions 1 and 3 in the information disclosure section in Grandmont, Fry, and Iragui (2001), and the section on financial transparency and information disclosure in Standard & Poor's (2002).

3. Although this positive correlation is interpreted as evidence of private information trading, the authors do not perform the test shown in Llorente et al. (2002) to show that the correlation coefficient effectively depends on informed trading measures.

4. Bhattacharya and Daouk (2002) report that, while the seven countries in the present sample have regulations banning insider trading, Colombia, Mexico, and República Bolivariana de Venezuela have never had any prosecutions on this basis. A cursory look at the Web sites of the national securities commissions of the countries in the present sample confirms the infrequency of insider trading accusations in Latin America.

5. While Grishchenko, Litov, and Mei (2002) examine a wider cross-section of countries, the stocks from Latin America that they use are fewer in number than those used in this chapter.

6. See Easley, Kiefer, and O'Hara (1996, 1997a, 1997b); Easley et al. (1996, 2002).

7. Most Latin American exchanges are organized as auction markets, not as dealer markets; so, the price-setting mechanisms are not exactly the same as in the model (or in the New York Stock Exchange). For a comparison between both types of markets see, for example, Heidle and Huang (2002).

8. A more general model (for example, Easley and O'Hara 1987) considers two different trade sizes. However, the empirical evidence on the relevance of trade size in U.S. stock markets is somewhat ambiguous. Therefore, the simplest version of the model is estimated, ignoring size information.

9. The empirical exercises are based on the 288 most liquid Latin American stocks in a universe of more than 1,000 listed stocks. Even within this relatively liquid sample, there is substantial heterogeneity of trading activity: 100 stocks traded more than 300 times a day on average during the sample period, while 94 stocks traded fewer than 75 times a day (see tables 1C and 1D in the annex). Therefore, it is crucial to take into account differences in trading frequency in any assessment of the prevalence of informed trading among Latin American stocks.

10. Easley et al. (2002) is the only paper that explicitly estimates time-varying ITPs.

11. See Glosten and Milgrom (1985), Kyle (1985), and Easley and O'Hara (1987) for a theoretical analysis of this relationship.

12. To the best of the authors' knowledge, Aktas et al. (2004) provide the strongest criticism of the Easley and O'Hara (1987, 1992) measure of informed trading. These authors compute the ITP for a sample of 87 French companies listed on the Paris Bourse around merger and acquisition announcements that took place between 1995 and 2000. They find that the ITP drops in periods previous to the public announcement date relative to a control and postannouncement window. (In this chapter, the control window comprises the period of between 270 and 181 days previous to each announcement; the remote preannouncement period includes the period of between 180 and 66 days before the announcement; the near preannouncement period runs from 65 to 6 days previous to the announcement; and the postannouncement period runs from 3 to 63 days after the announcement.)

13. Note that analysts may, in principle, study a wide cross-section of firms, but insiders will only know about their own. In the empirical analysis, sector, country, or stock-specific controls are used to remove some of the informed analyst effects that are constant across stocks or over time.

14. Stock and ticker are hereafter used interchangeably because both refer to a unique security-exchange combination. Note that an ADR and its underlying stock have different tickers, similar to the situation of the preferred and common stock of a single corporation.

15. The bid and ask prices are used to facilitate the identification of transactions as initiated by buyers or sellers. The bid and ask volumes are useful in identifying possible measurement errors in transaction volumes. Offer data for Colombia and for ADRs are not available.

16. Transaction records that are flagged with condition codes are unusual in some sense (for example, if they pertain to the official closing price of a market, which is not a real trade, or they pertain to a trade that is subject to nonstandard delivery terms).

17. The exceptions are Peru and República Bolivariana de Venezuela, for which there is about 5.5 and 1.8 times as much trading in the United States as there is at home, respectively. The bottom panel in table 1A in the annex covers all listed stocks, not only those in the sample.

18. When offer data are unavailable, Lee and Ready propose to use the tick test. This test declares a given trade to be buyer initiated (seller initiated) when its price is higher (lower) than that of the last preceding trade with a price that was different from the given trade's price. Because this criterion proves to be precise relative to the case with offer data, only transaction data for Colombia and the United States are used. When offer data are available, but the trade price is exactly at the midpoint of the spread, Lee and Ready suggest the use of the tick test.

19. The estimation procedure comprises a possibly nonconcave optimization problem because the expression inside the logs is of the form $f(\psi)^X$, where X is greater than one (X is the number of buys, sells, or no-trade periods). These functions are strictly convex for $X>1$. Even if one applies the natural log to these functions, the convexity may remain. As standard in this literature, possible multiple local maxima are addressed by using each grid point as the initial value of the algorithm and then choosing the highest among the local maxima attained from each starting point.

20. It has not been possible to estimate the model for some ticker-quarters. This may be due to sudden drops in the liquidity of a security (including outright delisting) or to convergence failure of the algorithm. Therefore, the number of ticker-quarters (N) in the first column of table 1.1 is not necessarily a multiple of four.

21. See PRS Group (2004).

22. Here τ indicates time measured in trading days. Note that transactions taking place on the day of the announcement are discarded because it is not known whether the announcement was made before or after the opening of trading. The annex reports the results of a robustness check using event windows that are 10 trading days long.

23. International depository receipts and global depository receipts trading in the United States are coded as ADRs. A few stocks labeled "unit" in Bloomberg (instead of common or preferred) are coded as common stocks. Tenaris and Quilmes of Argentina, which are legally headquartered in Luxembourg, are coded as Argentine corporations. Also, Credicorp Ltd. and Southern Peru Copper Co. are two Peruvian-coded firms that Bloomberg shows as headquartered in Bermuda and the United States, respectively.

24. The market value of assets results from summing the book value of liabilities and the market value of equity. From an accounting identity, the book value of

liabilities equals the book value of assets, minus the book value of equity. This is used as a proxy for the market value of liabilities, which is not easily observable. Data on deferred taxes are unavailable for the firms in the present sample, so the La Porta et al. (2002, 1158) definition of q cannot be perfectly replicated. The present measure approximates that in Klapper and Love (2002).

25. Economática only reports the sum of total shares outstanding: the result of adding all classes of common shares with different voting rights and preferred shares. Given the inability to discriminate within the different classes of common and preferred shares and across both categories of stocks, to compute the market value of equity, one must multiply the total number of shares by the price of the issue that was most heavily traded during the full sample period. Note that, for the majority of companies with liquid common and preferred shares included in the 288-ticker sample (all of them from Brazil), the traded volume of preferred shares exceeded that of common shares by a factor of between 10 and 40. The 288 tickers correspond to 207 corporations. Two were dropped for lack of data: Embratel (Brazil) and La Polar (Chile).

26. This computation and alignment procedure for sales growth and q mimics that in La Porta et al. (2002).

27. In practice, though both active and cancelled firms in Economática are used, for a total of 1,135, the cancelled firms lack data. The count of the active-firm subset was 815.

28. The ITP figures in the tables in the text are reported in percentages.

29. See Suits (1984). When using a control group, one imposes the constraint that the coefficient on that group's dummy is zero. The constraint imposed here is that the sum of the coefficients of all group dummies is zero. The problem is mathematically identical, but the results are more easily interpreted in this way, especially when more than one set of dummy variables is used. The test that all the coefficients on the dummies are jointly equal to zero is a test of equality of the group means.

30. Given the strong indication from tables 1.1 and 1.2 that the volatility of the ITP differs substantially across groups of stocks, White (1980) heteroskedasticity-consistent standard errors are used.

31. See, for example, Easley, Kiefer, and O'Hara (1996).

32. One possible justification for these results is that it is more difficult for outsiders properly to assess the value of financial firms (the expertise of which is precisely the handling of critical information about borrowers) as opposed to the heavily regulated communications firms.

33. The industrial sector effects are jointly insignificant in the combined regression and, so, are dropped in model 5.

34. Examples include investor protection in La Porta et al. (1998) and legality in Berkowitz, Pistor, and Richard (2003).

35. This is discussed in Leal and Carvalhal-da-Silva (2005) and Gledson de Carvalho (2000), among others.

36. One caveat to this explanation is that the Brazil effect in model 5 is much stronger than the preferred effect. One possibility for this result is that the common Brazilian shares, representing a negligible fraction of voting power, are also not the means of choice among insiders in trading on information.

37. See Lefort and Walker (2005).

38. All pertinent variables in La Porta et al. (1998), the legality index in Berkowitz, Pistor, and Richard (2003), the insider trading enforcement dummy in Bhattacharya et al. (2002), and the investment profile measure in PRS Group (2004) are used. When country attributes are measured periodically, the original values in La Porta et al. (1998) and the 2004 readings using the more current *International Country Risk Guide* data are included. See the section on Data Sources and Sample Construction for more details.

39. These are management transparency, management discipline, management independence, and the average rating.

40. The two specifications amount to different ways of controlling for volume effects. If markets are segmented (perfectly integrated), the appropriate control is intraexchange (interexchange) quintiles. For example, an illiquid Brazilian stock would be in the low-liquidity quintile in the intraexchange (that is, segmented) classification, but in a higher quintile in the interexchange (that is, integrated) partitioning. It is reassuring that the signs of the estimated coefficients are the same across both specifications.

41. These two variables are statistically significant only in the case of intraexchange volume quintiles.

42. Naturally, only the calendar days in the 60 trading days around each announcement are used.

43. Periodic announcements comprise earnings and cash dividends news, while aperiodic announcements consist of acquisitions and divestiture reports. See the data sources section for details.

44. Naturally, the width of 20 trading days in the event window is arbitrary. Vega (2004) estimates the ITP using data corresponding to the 40 days prior to each earnings announcement made during 15 years. Aktas et al. (2004) compute the ITP in four different windows, each lasting 60 days, around announcements made during five years. Because data for only one year are available, a smaller window width is used here.

45 For example, the mean ITP during the sample period of a top-volume Argentine common stock from the noncyclical consumer sector that trades only at home was 15.8 percent during the control period, rising to 17.7 percent before a periodic announcement, and falling back to 15.5 percent after the announcement. Again, the average of the effects within a classification is zero, because this is the identification constraint that is imposed on the model. See Suits (1984).

46. Table 1B in the annex lists the subsectors in each sector.

47. To the extent that the ITP is correlated with some other, albeit more general measure of corporation-specific governance quality, these coefficients are biased measures of the effects of the ITP on value. Given the inexistence to date of such an ideal measure, the contribution in this chapter is precisely to compute a proxy for the measure and to assess its market value. This problem is common to the other papers that have attempted to construct corporation-specific governance quality measures (for example, La Porta et al. 2002 and Klapper and Love 2002).

48. The choice of random versus fixed effects in these two cases was determined by a Hausman test. Naturally, using firm effects reduces the importance of *Sales Growth* in all specifications.

49. Bhattacharya et al. (2000) propose creating a nationwide market integrity score. Aitken and Siow (2004) show one implementation of that idea. Again, this chapter's results show that there is wide variation of informed trading *within* countries, hence the benefit of the individual corporation ratings proposed here.

References

Aitken, M., and A. Siow. 2004. "Ranking World Equity Markets on the Basis of Market Efficiency and Integrity." Unpublished working paper, University of New South Wales, Sydney.

Aktas, N., E. de Bodt, F. Declerck, and H. Van Oppens. 2004. "The PIN Anomaly around M&A Announcements." Unpublished working paper, Université Catholique de Louvain, Louvain, Belgium.

Aslan, H. 2004. "The Effect of Regulation Fair Disclosure on the Information Environment." Unpublished working paper, Cornell University, Ithaca, NY.

Beny, L. 1999. "A Comparative Empirical Investigation of Agency and Market Theories of Insider Trading." Harvard Law School Discussion Paper 264, Harvard Law School, Cambridge, MA.

Berkowitz, D., K. Pistor, and J. Richard. 2003. "Economic Development, Legality, and the Transplant Effect." *European Economic Review* 47 (1): 165–95.

Bhattacharya, U., and H. Daouk. 2002. "The World Price of Insider Trading." *Journal of Finance* 57 (1): 75–108.

Bhattacharya, U., H. Daouk, B. Jorgenson, and C.-H. Kehr. 2000. "When an Event Is Not an Event: The Curious Case of an Emerging Market." *Journal of Financial Economics* 55 (1): 69–101.

Brown, S., M. Finn, and S. Hillegeist. 2001. "Disclosure Quality and the Probability of Informed Trade." Unpublished working paper, Kellogg School of Management, Northwestern University, Evanston, IL.

Gledson de Carvalho, A. 2000. "Ascensão e Declínio do Mercados de Capitais no Brasil: A Experiência dos Anos 90." *Economía Aplicada* 4 (3): 595–632.

Cornell, B., and E. Sirri. 1992. "The Reaction of Investors and Stock Prices to Insider Trading." *Journal of Finance* 47 (3): 1031–59.

Dennis, P., and J. Weston. 2001. "Who's Informed?: An Analysis of Stock Ownership and Informed Trading." Unpublished working paper, University of Virginia, Charlottesville, VA, and Rice University, Houston.

Easley, D., R. F. Engle, M. O'Hara, and L. Wu. 2002. "Time-Varying Arrival Rates of Informed and Uninformed Trades." Paper presented at the American Finance Association Meetings, Atlanta, January.

Easley, D., N. M. Kiefer, and M. O'Hara. 1996. "Cream-Skimming or Profit-Sharing?: The Curious Role of Purchased Order Flow." *Journal of Finance* 51 (3): 811–33.

———. 1997a. "One Day in the Life of a Very Common Stock." *Review of Financial Studies* 10 (3): 805–35.

———. 1997b. "The Information Content of the Trading Process." *Journal of Empirical Finance* 4: 159–86.

Easley, D., N. M. Kiefer, M. O'Hara, and J. B. Paperman. 1996. "Liquidity, Information, and Infrequently Traded Stocks." *Journal of Finance* 51 (4): 1405–36.

Easley, D., and M. O'Hara. 1987. "Price, Trade Size, and Information in Securities Markets." *Journal of Financial Economics* 19 (1): 69–90.

———. 1992. "Time and the Process of Security Price Adjustment." *Journal of Finance* 47 (2): 577–605.

Estrada, J., and I. Peña. 2002. "Empirical Evidence on the Impact of European Insider Trading Regulations." *Studies in Economics and Finance* 20 (1): 12–34.

Gill, A. 2001. "Corporate Governance in Emerging Markets, Saints and Sinners: Who's Got Religion?" Emerging Markets Research Paper, April, Credit Lyonnais Securities Asia, Hong Kong, China.

Glosten, L. R., and P. R. Milgrom. 1985. "Bid, Ask, and Transaction Prices in a Specialist Market with Heterogeneously Informed Traders." *Journal of Financial Economics* 14 (1): 71–100.

Grandmont, R., V. Fry, and C. Iragui. 2001. "Who Has the Best Corporate Governance in Latin America?" Latin America Strategy Report. New York, Deutsche Bank.

Grishchenko, O., L. Litov, and J. Mei. 2002. "Private Information Trading and Corporate Governance in Emerging Markets." Unpublished working paper, New York University, New York.

Hasbrouck, J. 1991. "Measuring the Information Content of Stock Trades." *Journal of Finance* 46 (1): 179–207.

Heidle, H., and R. Huang. 2002. "Information-Based Trading in Dealer and Auction Markets: An Analysis of Exchange Listings." *Journal of Financial and Quantitative Analysis* 37 (3): 391–425.

John, K., and L. H. P. Lang. 1991. "Insider Trading around Dividend Announcements: Theory and Evidence." *Journal of Finance* 46 (4): 1361–89.

Keown, A., and Pinkerton, J. 1981. "Merger Announcements and Insider Trading Activity: An Empirical Investigation." *Journal of Finance* 36 (4): 855–69.

Klapper, L. F., and I. Love. 2002. "Corporate Governance, Investor Protection, and Performance in Emerging Markets." Policy Research Working Paper 2818, World Bank, Washington, DC.

Kyle, A. 1985. "Continuous Auctions and Insider Trading." *Econometrica* 53 (6): 1315–36.

La Porta, R., F. López-de-Silanes, A. Shleifer, and R. W. Vishny. 1998. "Law and Finance." *Journal of Political Economy* 106 (6): 1113–55.

———. 2002. "Investor Protection and Corporate Valuation." *Journal of Finance* 57 (3): 1147–70.

Leal, R. P. C., and A. L. Carvalhal-da-Silva. 2005. "Corporate Governance and Value in Brazil (and Chile)." Research Network Working Paper R-514, Research Department, Inter-American Development Bank, Washington, DC.

Lee, C., and M. Ready. 1991. "Inferring Trade Direction from Intraday Data." *Journal of Finance* 46 (2): 733–46.

Lefort, F., and E. Walker. 2005. "The Effect of Corporate Governance Practices on Company Market Valuation and Payout Policy in Chile." Research Network Working Paper R-515, Research Department, Inter-American Development Bank, Washington, DC.

Leland, H. E., and D. H. Pyle. 1977. "Informational Asymmetries, Financial Structure, and Financial Intermediation." *Journal of Finance* 32 (2): 371–87.

Llorente, G., R. Michaely, G. Saar, and J. Wang. 2002. "Dynamic Volume-Return Relation of Individual Stocks." *Review of Financial Studies* 15 (4): 1005–47.

Maug, E. 2002. "Insider Trading Legislation and Corporate Governance." *European Economic Review* 46 (9): 1569–97.

Meulbroek, L. 1992. "An Empirical Analysis of Illegal Insider Trading." *Journal of Finance* 47 (5): 1661–99.

Odders-White, E., and M. Ready. 2004. "Credit Ratings and Stock Liquidity." Unpublished working paper, University of Wisconsin, Madison, WI.

PRS Group. 2004. *International Country Risk Guide* 25 (3). East Syracuse, NY: Political Risk Services.

Standard & Poor's. 2002. "Standard & Poor's Corporate Governance Scores: Criteria, Methodology, and Definitions." Governance Services, Standard & Poor's, McGraw-Hill, New York, http://www2.standardandpoors.com/spf/pdf/products/CGSCriteria.pdf.

Straser, V. 2002. "Regulation, Fair Disclosure, and Information Asymmetry." Unpublished working paper, University of Notre Dame, South Bend, IN.

Suits, D. 1984. "Dummy Variables: Mechanics vs. Interpretation." *Review of Economics and* Statistics 66 (1): 177–80.

Vega, C. 2004. "Stock Price Reaction to Public and Private Information." Unpublished working paper, University of Rochester, Rochester, NY.

Von Furstenberg, G., and C. Tabora. 2004. "Bolsa or NYSE: Price Discovery for Mexican Shares." *Journal of International Financial Markets, Institutions & Money* 14 (4): 295–312.

Wang, F. A. 1998. "Strategic Trading, Asymmetric Information, and Heterogeneous Prior Beliefs." *Journal of Financial Markets* 1 (3–4): 321–52.

Wang, J. 1994. "A Model of Competitive Stock Trading Volume." *Journal of Political Economy* 102 (1): 127–68.

White, H. 1980. "A Heteroskedasticity-Consistent Covariance Matrix Estimator and a Direct Test for Heteroskedasticity." *Econometrica* 48 (1): 817–38.

World Federation of Exchanges. 2004. *Annual Report.* Paris: World Federation of Exchanges. http://www.world-exchanges.org/WFE/home.asp?menu=375&document=3495.

2

Corporate Governance, Ownership, and Dividend Policies in Argentina

Ricardo Bebczuk[*]

Introduction

Since the 1970s, a growing literature has emerged linking corporate policy and performance with governance and ownership structures. While profusely studied within academic circles, the resulting models did not gain widespread popularity until recently. Corporate scandals around the world have contributed to more awareness among managers, investors, and regulators, and an effort is under way in many countries to produce quantitative measures on ownership and governance and to estimate the impact of these on the value and decision-making processes of firms.

This chapter builds on this line of research by providing empirical evidence on the role of governance and ownership on corporate performance and dividend policies in Argentina in 1996–2003, with particular emphasis on the last years over that period (2000–03). Guided by this goal, we have assembled a unique set of corporate governance and ownership indicators on the available sample of 65 listed nonfinancial firms. The

* We are very grateful for comments from Alberto Chong, Florencio López-de-Silanes, Enrique Kawamura, and seminar participants at the IDB Research Network meetings, the Center for Financial Stability in Buenos Aires, and the universities of La Plata and San Andres, Argentina. The superb research assistantship of Horacio Pozzo and Máximo Sangiácomo is gratefully acknowledged. The usual disclaimer applies.

Argentine stock market is poorly developed, and so are the standards and practices of corporate governance; it is therefore of interest to determine whether the agency and information problems usually studied and found in more active markets also have a bearing on the functioning of much thinner markets, such as the one in Argentina. Equally relevant is the focus of this chapter on the severe financial crisis in 2001–02. In the midst of such a crisis, financial distress and uncertainty are exacerbated, rendering conflicts of interests and opportunistic behavior much more likely. Hence, a financial crisis is particularly appealing as a case study for the assessment of the disciplining role of corporate governance on company insiders.

The chapter is structured as follows. In the next section, we present our working hypotheses. In the subsequent section, we describe the corporate governance and ownership structure in Argentina as of 2003–04, relying on a set of measures specifically designed for this study. In the following section, we investigate the empirical link between these measures and corporate performance. The section thereafter is devoted to the link to dividend policies. Some concluding remarks close out the chapter.

Literature Review and Working Hypotheses

Corporate Governance, Ownership, and Performance

A great deal of attention has been paid to understanding how corporate governance and ownership structures affect firm performance. Corporate governance may influence a firm's performance whenever a conflict of interest arises between management and shareholders or between controlling and minority shareholders. In a management-shareholder conflict, the agency problem manifests itself in management's low effort and unproductive investments, usually known as perquisites. In the controlling-minority shareholder conflict, controlling shareholders use their power to benefit themselves at the expense of minority shareholders in what is called expropriation or the private benefits of control. The root of both conflicts is the fact that the manager in the first case and the controlling shareholders in the second case receive only a portion of the firm's net revenue, while they fully appropriate diverted resources. Thus, it is conceivable that, in light of this incentive structure, insiders will maximize their (pecuniary and nonpecuniary) utility even when the firm as a whole will not.

Of course, the ability to fulfill these goals is conditioned by the power insiders have in the company's decision-making process. Managers will enjoy more power because they are part of the board or act in connivance with the board and the controlling shareholders. In turn, the power of controlling shareholders lies in how effectively they are able to manipulate board decisions through voting majorities and other means; distortionary policies will then increase as the ratio of voting to cash flow rights becomes greater.[1] Outsiders have two main instruments to counterbalance this power: the enforcement of adequate corporate governance standards and the quality of the regulatory and legal environment, which should discourage detrimental actions by insiders and, if these occur, allow the affected stakeholders to challenge them through corporate and judicial channels.

While a wedge between control and cash flow rights is likely to harm minority shareholders and corporate valuation, Jensen and Meckling (1976) and Morck, Shleifer, and Vishny (1988) make the point that concentrated ownership may actually have an ambiguous effect: on the one hand, there may be a beneficial effect on performance and valuation (the so-called incentive effect) in that higher cash flow rights in the hands of a few shareholders tend to reduce the free riding problem that is associated with dispersed ownership during the process of monitoring and punishing opportunistic managers; on the other hand, the negative effect (the entrenchment effect) may come into play whenever there is a high concentration of control rights or a separation between control and cash flow rights.

There has been a surge in the international evidence in the last few years. Claessens et al. (1999), Klapper and Love (2002), and La Porta et al. (2002) represent prominent efforts in proving the nexus between corporate governance and performance using cross-country data, while other studies look at individual countries, such as the United States (Gompers, Ishii, and Metrick 2003), the Republic of Korea (Black, Jang, and Kim 2006), and Germany (Drobetz, Schillhofer, and Zimmermann 2003). By aiming to analyze the relationship between corporate governance and ownership structure, along with performance (as measured by the return on assets [ROA] and Tobin's q), in Argentina in 2000–03, the present chapter forms part of the latter country-level line of research.

Corporate Governance, Ownership, and Dividend Policies

The reasons firms pay dividends or not have been under heated debate ever since the seminal paper by Lintner (1956) five decades ago. This and many subsequent pieces of research have convincingly established that firms aim to avoid drastic changes in dividends over time. However, early dividend theories did not warrant such preference for smoothing cash distributions. As a matter of fact, Miller and Modigliani (1961) advanced the idea that, when financial markets are frictionless, investors are indifferent to whether they receive dividends or capital gains to the extent that they are able to substitute one for the other in reaching their desired level of cash dividends by selling or buying stock. The differences in tax rates usually observed between dividends and capital gains arose as the first argument against this proposition of dividend irrelevance. It was at this stage that Black (1976) coined the label "dividend puzzle" to illustrate the astonishing contrast between a body of theoretical work claiming either the irrelevance or the disadvantage of paying dividends and the indisputable fact that firms pay relatively high and stable dividends.

Since the early 1980s, a host of papers has offered alternative and appealing approaches to disentangle this enigma, most of them rooted in information asymmetries between firm insiders and outsiders and the bounded rationality of the latter. One such recent hypothesis holds that firms pay dividends to send a credible signal about their quality to the market to mitigate the undervaluation that arises in an adverse selection context. By paying high, stable dividends, high-quality companies might distinguish themselves from low-quality competitors for funds[3] that may be unable to mimic the first group; unlike poor-performance companies, profitable firms may replace diminished retained earnings through more expensive external funds. Another strand of literature focuses on the agency problems between managers and shareholders by making the point that higher dividends partially prevent managers from risking moral hazard at the expense of shareholders by reducing the free cash flow at the disposal of those running the firm.[4] Finally, other scholars have put forward behavioral explanations that support the investor preference for cash dividends, such as the psychological (but not necessarily rational from a purely financial standpoint) loss deriving from the reduction in principal from selling stock or the regret at liquidating stock immediately before the price rises.

The main insight of the asymmetric information theories is that insiders may be reluctant to pay dividends to outsiders. The underlying argument is as follows. For a given amount of cash flow generated by a firm, the controlling shareholders and managers must choose between fully appropriating the funds for themselves—the aforementioned private benefits of control—or distributing them equally among the universe of shareholders according to cash flow rights. Consequently, the testable predictions of this body of theoretical work are that dividend disbursements will be higher, (1) the better the corporate governance standards (that is, the better the protection to minority shareholders), (2) the higher the concentration of cash flow rights, (3) the lower the control rights, and (4) the lower the separation between control and cash flow rights.

At this point, it is imperative to establish the explanatory power of this theoretical framework for financially developed as opposed to emerging markets. The model implicit in the theories described above is one whereby the following three situations apply. (1) Ownership is highly dispersed, and the dividend recipients are not the company's decision makers. In this context, dividend policy is mostly driven by market value considerations in which dividends are a device to mitigate potential conflicts of interest between insiders and outsiders. The ultimate goal of the dividend policy is to maximize the stock price to reduce the cost of equity in future stock issues. (2) Capital markets are efficient, in that stock prices fully capture any value-related corporate change. (3) Firms do not appear to face important financial constraints in the present because they enjoy some freedom to determine how much to distribute from their net earnings, filling any gap through other sources of funding, such as external equity or debt.

Nevertheless, one must realize that some of these assumptions behind the theories (particularly the signaling approach) may not be entirely realistic for an emerging market, such as Argentina, that exhibits (1) a high ownership concentration (the leading minority shareholders are not a primary concern of the company's officers); (2) a negligible primary or issuance stock market (defusing the main incentive mechanism for improving governance, namely, the ability to issue more valuable stock in the future); (3) a questionable degree of market efficiency (though the evidence is mixed),[5] meaning that dividend announcements potentially may not be clearly reflected in stock prices; and (4) current financial constraints at the firm level,[6] as a result of which meeting the cash dividend demand from outside shareholders may mean that good investment opportunities must be passed up in response to the funding shortage. In other words, retained earnings may have no close (not even more onerous) substitutes at all.

For these reasons, when we search for the determinants of dividend payments, we will bear in mind that, besides governance and ownership considerations, dividend, financing, and investment policies are likely to be intertwined, regardless of whether the companies are governed by an owner-manager or display dispersed ownership with a separation between management and property.

Corporate Governance and the Ownership Structure in Argentina

This section describes the current status of corporate governance and ownership structure in Argentina to motivate the subsequent analytical work. Though we are initially reporting information on 103 listed companies as of November 2003, the usable sample for econometric purposes has been substantially reduced for the following reasons. (1) We have excluded listed financial institutions—because of the specificity of their line of business and their heavy regulation—and firms in general without complete information. This leaves 65 firms. (2) We have been able to gather complete ownership information for only 54 of these 65 companies.

As a preliminary remark, it must be said that Argentina's stock market is quite undeveloped, as shown in table 2.1. It is apparent from the table that Argentina ranks lower than the regions considered in terms of key variables such as domestic equity issues, value traded, market capitalization, number of listed companies, and fraction of delistings.

Table 2.1 Capital Market Indicators on Argentina and Selected Regions, 1997–2001 averages in percentage of gross domestic product, unless otherwise stated

	Argentina	*Developed countries*	*Latin America (excluding Argentina)*	*Other developing countries*
Domestic equity issues	0.23	3.60	1.10	2.35
Foreign equity issues	0.32	1.30	0.23	0.49
Number of listed companies (2000)	129	1093	409	410
Change in number of listed companies (in %, 1990–2000)	–30.2	37.0	–3.2	117.5
Value traded	4.7	61.4	10.5	40.6
Market capitalization	30.8	90.7	43.6	48.0

Source: Calculations of the author based on data from the International Federation of Stock Exchanges.

Historically, listed firms in Argentina have displayed poor standards of corporate governance. Nevertheless, a host of changes has taken place since the 1990s that have affected corporate governance standards in an a priori positive fashion: renewed access to foreign capital flows, moderate growth in domestic capital markets, the privatization of public utilities, the emergence of the institutional investment industry (led by private pension funds), the growing importance of foreign capital in the financial and nonfinancial sector, and the foreign listing of some domestic companies. These features induced the government to issue the so-called Transparency Decree (Decreto de Transparencia, No. 677/2001), whereby a number of governance guidelines, inspired by international best practices and standards, were established for listed companies. However, only modest progress has actually been achieved so far despite the well-intentioned goals of the reform. It is worth noting that the virtual inactivity of the primary stock markets both before and after the 2001–02 crisis has created no incentives for firms to upgrade their governance practices.

To deploy a quantitative and mostly objective measure of corporate governance, we are constructing, for the first time, a corporate governance index for listed companies in Argentina. The work closely relates to other work in this line of research.[7] The index has been designed to encompass two complementary measures: (1) a transparency and disclosure index (TDI) based on public information on each company and reflecting their norms of transparency and disclosure, which are a crucial element of corporate governance; this information has been gathered from a number of public information sources (balance sheets, annual reports, filings with domestic and foreign regulatory agencies, security issuance prospectuses, company Internet Web sites, and the like); (2) a complete corporate governance index based on a questionnaire sent out to each company to be answered either electronically or personally. The TDI was designed and completed between August and November 2003, while progress on the corporate governance index has been hindered due to the extremely low rate of response on the part of surveyed firms and thus will not be used in what follows.[8]

We are confident that the TDI is a comprehensive measure of corporate governance that will be highly correlated with the whole corporate governance index, as has occurred in other cases,[9] and we use it as our measure of corporate governance hereafter. Furthermore, the TDI has three distinctive advantages in that: (1) it is clearly objective and documented; (2) in a country such as Argentina where the disclosure requirements are easy and mostly limited to accounting information, it reflects voluntary rather than mandatory information, and it may thus display a desirable variability across firms; and (3) it is not affected by the frequently low response rate characteristic of company surveys, which, in the small universe of listed nonfinancial firms in Argentina, would represent an insurmountable obstacle to econometric analysis as a result of the small final sample. Conversely, it has the limitation of not providing information on any features of corporate governance that a company may have decided not to disclose.

Next, we discuss the most salient features and results from the TDI based on our usable sample of 65 listed firms. The TDI is used to try to assess the transparency of corporate information and the degree of protection of outside investors against expropriation, thus providing a measure of the balance of power between insiders and outsiders. The items in the TDI cover a broad range of governance topics, including the functioning of executive bodies, communication with outside stakeholders, and the flow of the information required for proper monitoring of the firm by minority shareholders. The TDI comprises 32 binary items; for each item, the company is given a value of 1 if there is partially or totally public information and a value of zero otherwise. We divide the index into three subindexes: board, disclosure, and shareholders. The board subindex measures the structure, procedures, and compensation of board and top management members. The disclosure subindex measures the degree to which the company informs relevant corporate facts to outside stakeholders. Finally, the shareholders subindex measures the quality of information regarding the compensation to minority shareholders. The TDI's structure and the percentage of positive entries for each item are presented in table 2.2.

Table 2.2 Structure of the Transparency and Disclosure Index

Item	Firms with public information on each item (%)
Board structure and procedures	
Independency criteria for directors	73.8
Years in office of present directors	18.5
Code of conduct for directors	6.2
Manager and director fees	52.3
Form of manager and director fee payment (cash, stock, stock options)	12.3
Rationale of manager and director fees	30.8
Information on whether manager and director fees are performance based	26.2
Shareholdings of managers and directors	15.4
Number and percentage of independent directors	86.2
Details on the nomination process of new directors	12.3
Report on issues by dissident directors	0.0
Composition of the different board committees	33.8
Details on activities of the different board committees	1.5
Disclosure	
Biography of main company officers	13.8
Biography of directors	20.0
Calendar of future events	3.1
English-translated corporate Web site	29.2
Financial indicators for the last five years	98.5
Strategic plan and projections for the following years	47.7
Publication of board meeting resolutions	89.2
Publication of shareholders meeting resolutions	93.8
Details on the appointment process of new directors	10.8
Details on attendance of minority and controlling shareholders in shareholders meetings	10.8
Reports on issues raised by dissident shareholders	30.8
Year of hiring of the external auditor	96.9
Report of the external auditor	96.9
Shareholders	
Details of corporate ownership (principal shareholders)	56.9
Type and amount of outstanding shares	98.5
Document on internal corporate governance standards	3.1

(continued)

Table 2.2 Structure of the Transparency and Disclosure Index (*continued*)

Item	*Firms with public information on each item (%)*
Dividend policy in the past five years	20.0
Projected dividend policy for the following years	27.7
Rationale of the past and/or future dividend policy	35.4

Source: Calculations of the author based on public sources.
Note: See the text for an explanation of the index.

Following the methodology outlined in the seminal paper by La Porta et al. (1998), we have also investigated the ownership structure of listed Argentine firms. The task has proved to be quite challenging as a result of data limitations. Companies are not legally required to disclose their ownership structures.[10] Accordingly, we have been obliged to rely on an array of dispersed resources, such as annual reports, issuance prospectuses, filings with local and foreign regulators, company and other Web sites, and newspapers and business magazines. The fieldwork was undertaken between September 2003 and May 2004.

La Porta et al. (1998), Claessens, Djankov, and Nenova (2000), and subsequent, related research look for the ultimate owners of each firm to establish the degree of ownership concentration and the difference between cash flow and voting rights; this difference is explained through the use of pyramiding, deviations from the one share–one vote rule, and cross holdings. If one goes through the various chains of ownership, four main types of ultimate owner emerge: families, the government, and widely held financial and nonfinancial corporations.

In the case of Argentina, because state enterprises have been privatized and because there are no widely held domestic companies, we identify two types of ultimate ownership, namely, national families and foreign firms. For each firm, starting from the direct shareholders, we trace back the shareholders of these shareholders until we find an Argentine family, an Argentine individual, or a foreign firm. In the last case, we have not identified the ultimate owners because this information was no longer especially relevant for our work.

We have defined the following variables: (1) cash flow rights of the main ultimate shareholder; (2) control rights of the main ultimate shareholder over the company; (3) the ratio of voting to cash flow rights of the main ultimate shareholder; (4) no one share–one vote rule; (5) pyramiding; (6) cross holdings; (7) domestically owned company; and (8) widely held company. For the precise definitions of these variables, as well as of the other variables used in this chapter, the reader is referred to table 2.3.

Table 2.3 Variable Definitions

Variable	*Definition*
Corporate governance variables	
TDI	See table 2.2
TDI board subindex	See table 2.2
TDI disclosure subindex	See table 2.2
TDI shareholders subindex	See table 2.2
Audit committee dummy	Takes the value 1 if the company created an audit committee as of May 2004; 0 otherwise
Trading intensity	Number of days the stock was traded in 2001–03 as a proportion of total trading days in that period; the variable ranges from 0 to 1
Corporate ownership variables	
Control rights of the main ultimate shareholder	The weakest link, in terms of voting rights, of the main ultimate shareholder along his or her control chain, based on a 20 percent cutoff (see hereafter the definition of widely held)
Cash flow rights of the main ultimate shareholder	The product of all voting rights of the main ultimate shareholder along the control chain
No one share–one vote rule dummy	Takes the value of 1 if there are shares of the main ultimate shareholder with higher voting power than others (at any link of the control chain); 0 otherwise
Pyramid dummy	Takes the value of 1 if the main ultimate shareholder exerts control through other companies along the control chain; 0 otherwise
Cross-holding dummy	Takes the value of 1 if the company owns shares in its main ultimate shareholder or in firms that belong to his or her control chain; 0 otherwise
Domestically owned dummy	Takes the value of 1 if the main ultimate shareholder is an Argentine individual or family and 0 if the shareholder is a company located abroad; the ultimate ownership of the foreign companies is not analyzed here
Widely held	Takes the value of 1 if no ultimate shareholder has at least 20 percent of control rights; 0 otherwise
Other dependent and control variables	
Return on assets (ROA)	Ratio of earnings before interest and taxes to total assets
Return on equity (ROE)	Ratio of earnings before interest and taxes to total equity

(continued)

Table 2.3 Variable Definitions *(continued)*

Variable	*Definition*
Return on sales	Ratio of earnings before interest and taxes to sales
Tobin's q	The market value of equity, plus the book value of liabilities, divided by the book value of assets
Dividends to cash flow	Ratio of cash dividends to total earnings and depreciation
Dividends to earnings	Ratio of cash dividends to total earnings
Dividends to sales	Ratio of cash dividends to sales
Ln(Age)	Logarithm of the company's age as of 2003
Ln(Assets)	Logarithm of the company's total assets
Size dummy	Takes the value of 1 if the company is in the highest 20 percent in terms of average total assets in 2000–01; 0 otherwise
Debt to assets	Ratio of total debt to assets
Sales growth	Percentage sales growth
American depositary receipt dummy	Takes the value of 1 if the company issued American depositary receipts before or during the period under analysis; 0 otherwise
Industry dummy	Takes the value of 1 if the company belongs to the industrial sector and 0 otherwise; the activity classification is taken from the Buenos Aires Stock Exchange
Utilities dummy	Takes the value of 1 if the company supplies utilities and 0 otherwise; the activity classification is taken from the Buenos Aires Stock Exchange
Primary products dummy	Takes the value of 1 if the company produces agricultural products, livestock, minerals, or other commodities and 0 otherwise; the activity classification is taken from the Buenos Aires Stock Exchange
Services dummy	Takes the value of 1 if the company provides services not included in the other three categories and 0 otherwise; the activity classification is taken from the Buenos Aires Stock Exchange

Source: Author.

Summary statistics on the TDI and the ownership variables appear in table 2.4. Out of a possible 100, the average TDI is only 39.1, with a low of 18.8 and a high of 84.4, revealing a low average quality of corporate governance. The three subindexes are equally low, on average. *Disclosure*

Table 2.4 Corporate Governance and Ownership: Descriptive Statistics

Variable	*Observations*	*Mean*	*Standard deviation*	*Minimum*	*Maximum*
Corporate governance variables					
TDI	65	39.13	14.53	18.75	84.38
TDI board	65	28.40	17.41	0.00	76.92
TDI disclosure	65	49.35	3.79	23.08	92.31
TDI shareholder	65	40.26	22.03	0.00	100.00
Audit committee dummy	65	0.72			
Trading intensity	64	0.46	0.35	0.00	1.00
Corporate ownership variables					
Control rights main ultimate shareholder	54	63.14	23.24	20.75	99.14
Cash flow rights main ultimate shareholder	54	56.90	26.58	4.31	99.14
Control-to-cash flow rights	54	1.30	0.74	1.00	5.43
Control-to-cash flow rights >1.02	22	1.74	1.03	1.03	5.43
No one share–one vote dummy	54	0.11			
Pyramid dummy	54	0.37			
Cross-holding dummy	54	0.00			
Widely held dummy	54	0.00			
Domestically owned dummy	54	0.46			

Source: Compiled by the author based on public sources.
Note: See table 2.3 for definitions of the variables.

shows the highest level (49.4 out of 100), and *board* the lowest (28.4 out of 100). Ownership appears to be quite concentrated, with the largest ultimate shareholder owning, on average, 63.1 percent of votes and 56.9 percent of cash flows. Ownership structures are relatively simple, and deviations of control and cash flow rights of 2 percentage points or more occur in only 22 of the 65 companies under study. In these 22 firms, the ratio of control to cash flow rights is 1.74 (1.30 for the 54 firms). It is known that this wedge may be attained through deviations from the one share–one vote rule, pyramiding, and cross holdings. In the Argentine case, pyramiding has been found in 20 companies, and dual-class shares in 6 companies; no cross holdings were detected in the sample. Argentine families and individuals are the largest ultimate owners in 25 firms (46 percent of the sample), and foreign firms are the largest ultimate owners in the remaining 29 firms (54 percent). No widely held companies exist in Argentina.

Table 2.5 shows the frequency of some of the measures discussed here. The TDI distribution is heavily skewed to the left, with a thick tail, because 60 percent of the sample is below a ranking of 37.5. The opposite applies to the distributions of control and cash flow rights, where only the first decile is below 30 percent. Likewise, the ratio of control to cash flow rights is above unity in only the last three deciles.

The pairwise correlation between governance and ownership indicators may be seen in table 2.6. The TDI is strongly correlated with each of the subindexes and has a weak, negative association with the control and cash flow rights variables (which, owing to the lack of separation between them, do have a high correlation to each other). The TDI and the ratio of control to cash flow rights show a positive and significant, but rather low correlation.

Table 2.5 Corporate Governance and Ownership: Deciles

Decile	*TDI*	*Control rights*	*Cash flow rights*	*Control-to-cash flow rights*
10	25.0	25.7	20.3	1.0
20	28.1	42.6	26.0	1.0
30	31.3	51.6	42.6	1.0
40	34.4	57.6	49.0	1.0
50	34.4	62.9	60.7	1.0
60	37.5	70.2	66.1	1.0
70	41.3	78.4	75.0	1.2
80	49.4	87.9	82.1	1.3
90	65.6	93.0	92.3	1.8
99	84.4	99.1	99.1	5.4

Source: Compiled by the author based on public sources.

Table 2.6 Corporate Governance and Ownership: Correlation Matrix

	TDI	*TDI-B*	*TDI-D*	*TDI-S*	*Control rights*	*Cash flow rights*	*Control-to-cash flow*
TDI	1						
TDI board	*0.9062*	1					
TDI disclosure	*0.8617*	0.6441	1				
TDI shareholder	*0.7979*	*0.6023*	*0.5722*	*1*			
Control rights	*-0.2129*	*-0.1918*	-0.1282	-0.2544	*1*		
Cash flow rights	-0.2008	-0.1303	*-0.1855*	*-0.2387*	*0.9173*	1	
Control-to-cash flow	*0.2649*	*0.2355*	*0.2003*	0.2624	*-0.3304*	*-0.5602*	1

Source: Author.
Note: Correlations statistically significant at 5 percent or less are shown in italics.

Determinants of Corporate Performance

We now turn to the determinants of corporate performance. The period of analysis is 2000–03.[11] Because the severe, full-blown financial crisis unraveled at the beginning of 2002 and may have affected the behavior and performance of firms, the sample has been broken down to run separate cross-section regressions for the whole period and for the 2000–01 and 2002–03 subperiods.

We follow previous studies by taking the ROA and Tobin's q as indicators of performance. The ROA is an accounting measure of profitability and efficiency, while Tobin's q captures market expectations about future earnings. Even though one would expect some correlation between them, this may not always be the case; in fact, the simple correlation in our sample is positive, but not significant. Furthermore, the implications are radically different in each case: while the ROA–corporate governance link reflects a tangible, balance-sheet effect, the q–corporate governance nexus has more to do with market perceptions about the value of corporate governance. In light of the absence of a primary capital market in Argentina, firms are largely unable to capitalize their governance quality, but may be encouraged to upgrade it as long as a direct effect on accounting profitability exists. In line with the arguments offered in the section on the literature review and working hypotheses, the key explanatory variables are the TDI (with a positive expected sign), cash flow rights (positive), the control rights of the largest shareholder (negative), and the ratio of control to cash flow rights (negative).

We include a set of controls in the regressions. We expect firm age to have a negative effect on performance as long as older firms are poorly managed under archaic rules dictated by members of the founding families. Firm size may have a negative effect if size is correlated with the exhaustion of growth opportunities, but may, in contrast, have a positive impact whenever size is correlated with greater diversification, greater economies of scale and scope, more professionalized management, and less severe financial constraints. The leverage ratio (debt to assets) may, on the one hand, improve performance by limiting managerial misbehavior and by serving as a signal of high quality, but, on the other hand, high leverage may lead to asset substitution and underinvestment.[12] Sales growth is a proxy for the product demand faced by the firm and its productivity. We also posit that issuers of American depositary receipts (ADRs) may exhibit comparatively better performance because they are driven by the need to compete with foreign firms for funds. Additionally, firms are classified into four broad sectors (industry, utilities, other services, and primary products) that vary in productive technology and international tradability. We use as regressors lagged values from the two years prior to the sample period of the debt ratio and the sales growth rate.

Tables 2.7 and 2.8 present summary statistics for the additional controls and their simple correlations with the ROA, q, and the governance and ownership variables. Visual inspection suggests that only the correlation

Table 2.7 Performance and Control Variables: Descriptive Statistics

Variable	*Observations*	*Mean*	*Standard deviation*	*Minimum*	*Maximum*
ROA	65	0.0073	0.0265	–0.0658	0.0650
q	56	0.8882	0.3096	0.3742	2.076
Age	59	51.2	28.4	11.0	119.0
Assets	65	1726542	4350881	1446	29000000
Debt to assets	65	0.209	0.158	0.000	0.544
Sales growth	65	0.355	2.101	–0.399	16.440
ADR dummy	59	0.237			
Industry dummy	65	0.338			
Utilities dummy	65	0.277			
Primary product dummy	65	0.215			

Source: Author.

Note: See table 2.3 for definitions of the variables.

Table 2.8 Performance and Explanatory Variables: Correlation Matrix

		1	*2*	*3*	*4*	*5*	*6*	*7*	*8*	*9*	*10*	*11*	*12*	*13*	*14*
ROA	1	1.00													
q	2	0.14	1.00												
TDI	3	*0.31*	–0.14	1.00											
Cash flow rights	4	–0.07	–0.01	–0.20	1.00										
Control rights	5	–0.11	–0.05	–0.21	*0.92*	1.00									
Control-to-cash flow	6	–0.09	–0.07	0.26	*–0.56*	*–0.33*	1.00								
Ln(age)	7	–0.07	0.02	–0.08	0.15	0.00	–0.04	1.00							
Ln(assets)	8	0.29	–0.19	*0.62*	–0.11	–0.05	0.19	*–0.42*	1.00						
Debt / assets	9	0.01	–0.18	–0.05	0.10	0.12	–0.01	–0.07	0.14	1.00					
Sales growth	10	–0.10	–0.03	0.00	–0.19	–0.25	–0.05	0.18	–0.14	–0.18	1.00				
ADR dummy	11	0.14	–0.12	*0.59*	*–0.34*	–0.17	*0.47*	–0.26	0.50	–0.11	–0.09	1.00			
Industry	12	0.22	–0.03	–0.10	–0.10	–0.18	–0.14	0.20	–0.22	–0.06	–0.11	–0.23	1.00		
Utilities	13	–0.06	–0.13	0.21	–0.06	0.06	0.05	*–0.75*	*0.43*	0.09	–0.08	*0.44*	*–0.44*	1.00	
Primary prod.	14	–0.16	0.17	–0.16	0.22	0.13	–0.19	0.34	–0.19	–0.05	0.21	–0.18	*–0.37*	*–0.32*	1.00

Source: Author.
Note: Correlations statistically significant at 5 percent or less are shown in italics.

between the ROA and the TDI (0.31) is significant. Also worth mentioning is the high correlation of 0.62 between ln(Assets) and the TDI. Because this gives rise to multicollinearity, preventing us from correctly estimating the independent contribution of each of them, we have replaced ln(Assets) in the reported regressions with a dummy variable that takes the value 1 if the company is in the highest 20 percent in terms of average total assets in 2000–01 and 0 otherwise.

Baseline Results

Tables 2.9 and 2.10 show the regression of the ROA and q, respectively, against the TDI without adding additional controls, while tables 2.11 and 2.12 show the regressions with such controls (except the ownership variables, which are included later on). The overall assessment is that the TDI has a positive and highly significant effect on both the ROA and q; in addition, the estimated coefficients remain reasonably stable across specifications and time periods. The quantitative effect is also remarkable. Looking at the estimates for the entire 2000–03 period with controls, one sees that, for a firm with the average TDI (39.13), an increase of 10 points in the firm's TDI to 49.13 would translate into a jump of 2.62 percentage point in the firm's ROA, that is, an increase of 1.9 percentage points

Table 2.9 The ROA and the TDI without Additional Controls

	Dependent variable: ROA		
Explanatory variables	*Reg 1*	*Reg 2*	*Reg 3*
TDI	0.0005344	0.0005029	0.0005647
	(3.11)***	(3.82)***	(2.18)**
Constant	–0.0147703	–0.0146024	–0.0148466
	(–1.91)*	(–2.32)**	(–1.36)
Adjusted R^2	0.1283	0.125	0.0816
No. of observations	65	65	65
F Statistic (p-value)	9.7(0.000)	14.63(0.000)	4.77(0.032)
Period	2000-I/2003-IV	2000-I/2001-IV	2002-I/2003-IV

Source: Author.

Note: The table shows ordinary least squares results for the whole period (2000–03) and two subperiods (2000–01 and 2002–03). The ROA is an average from quarterly data for each period. The TDI (on a 0–100 scale) is the same for all periods and is based on public corporate information for 2003. T-statistics based on robust standard errors are shown in parentheses.

* significant at 10 percent

** significant at 5 percent

*** significant at 1 percent

Table 2.10 Q and the TDI without Additional Controls

	Dependent variable: q		
Explanatory variables	*Reg 1*	*Reg 2*	*Reg 3*
TDI	0.0061043	0.0076789	0.0037968
	(3.28)***	(4.12)***	(1.78)*
Constant	0.5999676	0.4675686	0.733983
	(6.53)***	(5.36)***	(7.33)***
Adjusted R^2	0.0818	0.2098	
No. of observations	53	53	
F statistic (p-value)	10.75(0.002)	16.95(0.000)	3.18(0.08)
Period	2000-I/2003-IV	2000-I/2001-IV	2002-I/2003-IV

Source: Author.

Note: The table shows ordinary least squares results for the whole period (2000–03) and two subperiods (2000–01 and 2002–03). Q is an average from quarterly data for each period. Outlier observations with q > 2.5 have been dropped. The TDI (on a 0–100 scale) is the same for all periods and is based on public corporate information for 2003. T-statistics based on robust standard errors are shown in parentheses.

* significant at 10 percent

** significant at 5 percent

*** significant at 1 percent

Table 2.11 The ROA and the TDI with Controls

	Dependent variable: ROA		
Explanatory variables	*Reg 1*	*Reg 2*	*Reg 3*
TDI	0.0005449	0.0004813	0.0006292
	(2.61)**	(3.13)***	(1.79)*
Ln(Age)	–0.0154112	–0.0209034	–0.0072887
	(–2.11)**	(–2.63)**	(–1.03)
Size dummy	0.0069701	0.0099801	0.0038725
	(0.54)	(0.327)	(–0.23)
Debt to Assets	–0.0008561	–0.0041904	0.0042438
	(–0.06)	(–0.27)	(0.22)
Sales growth	4.20E–06	–2.11E–06	–0.0004995
	(0.12)	(–0.05)	(–0.74)
ADR dummy	–0.0025899	–0.0032994	–0.0009633
	(–0.41)	(–0.58)	(–0.1)

(continued)

Table 2.11 The ROA and the TDI with Controls *(continued)*

	Dependent variable: ROA		
Explanatory variables	*Reg 1*	*Reg 2*	*Reg 3*
Industry dummy	0.0015554	−0.0053865	0.008823
	(0.25)	(−1.04)	(0.94)
Utilities dummy	−0.0171923	−0.0198887	−0.0135516
	(−1.21)	(−1.25)	(−0.95)
Primary production dummy	−0.0049964	−0.0054604	−0.0069393
	(−0.63)	(−0.73)	(−0.66)
Constant	0.048235	0.0736632	0.0110886
	(1.65)	(2.37)	(0.35)
Adjusted R^2	0.1513	0.309	0.0551
No. of observations	62	62	59
F statistic (p-value)	2.51(0.000)	4.35(0.000)	3.72(0.000)
Period	2000-I/2003-IV	2000-I/2001-IV	2002-I/2003-IV

Source: Author.

Note: The table shows ordinary least squares results for the whole period (2000–03) and two subperiods (2000–01 and 2002–03). The ROA is an average from quarterly data for each period. The TDI (on a 0–100 scale) is the same for all periods and is based on public corporate information for 2003. The size dummy is a dummy variable with a value of 1 for firms in the upper 20 percent of firms according to total assets; 0 otherwise. Sales growth is the average quarterly sales growth in the two years previous to the sample period. Industry, utilities, and primary product dummies show the productive sector to which each firm belongs. The definition of the remaining variables may be found in table 2.3. T-statistics based on robust standard errors are shown in parentheses.

* significant at 10 percent
** significant at 5 percent
*** significant at 1 percent

on the 2000–03 average ROA (0.73 percent). Assuming a worst-to-best improvement in the TDI (18.75 to 84.38), one sees that the ROA increase would amount to 3.58 percentage points. If one repeats the exercise for q (for which the 2000–03 average is 0.89), the magnitudes are much more modest, but still noticeable. A 10 point improvement in the TDI would induce q to go up by 0.059, with a worst-to-best improvement of 0.38. For both the ROA and q, the TDI estimates are statistically more significant in the 2000–01 subperiod than in the 2002–03 subperiod, although the coefficient does not change much. In principle, the lost explanatory power might be blamed on the noise brought about by the financial crisis in the latter subperiod.

Table 2.12 Q and the TDI with Controls

	Dependent variable: q		
Explanatory variables	*Reg 1*	*Reg 2*	*Reg 3*
TDI	0.0058871	0.0054073	0.0050566
	(2.27)**	(2.73)***	(2.1)**
Ln(Age)	0.0329557	–0.0650277	–0.0077511
	(0.33)	(–1.71)*	(–0.1)
Size dummy	0.2214558	0.256726	0.2455017
	(2.11)**	(3.28)***	(2.62)**
Debt to assets	0.4502588	0.6344327	0.6112416
	(1.72)*	(3.01)***	(1.98)*
Sales growth	0.0007618	0.0001615	–0.0291134
	(0.74)	(0.32)	(–4.36)***
ADR dummy	–0.0387129	0.0035822	–0.0179075
	(–0.42)	(0.05)	(–0.21)
Industry dummy	0.1298286	–0.0183625	0.2894743
	(1.59)	(–0.25)	(2.78)***
Utilities dummy	0.0997021	–0.0471228	0.0802948
	(0.56)	(–0.53)	(0.65)
Primary production dummy	0.1634207	–0.0760166	0.3223821
	(1.13)	(–0.9)	(3.25)***
Constant	0.2775962	0.6843045	0.3910209
	(0.62)	(3.69)***	(1.21)
Adjusted R^2	0.0448	0.3784	0.247
No. of observations	54	53	50
F statistic (p-value)	5.24(0.000)	25.83(0.000)	14.94(0.000)
Period	2000-I/2003-IV	2000-I/2001-IV	2002-I/2003-IV

Source: Author.

Note: The table shows ordinary least squares results for the whole period (2000–03) and two subperiods (2000–01 and 2002–03). Q is an average from quarterly data for each period. Outlier observations with q > 2.5 have been dropped. The TDI (on a 0–100 scale) is the same for all periods and is based on public corporate information for 2003. The size dummy is a dummy variable with a value of 1 for firms in the upper 20 percent of firms according to total assets; 0 otherwise. Sales growth is the average quarterly sales growth in the two years previous to the sample period. Industry, utilities, and primary product dummies show the productive sector to which each firm belongs. The definition of the remaining variables may be found in table 2.3. T-statistics based on robust standard errors are shown in parentheses.

* significant at 10 percent

** significant at 5 percent

*** significant at 1 percent

No control variable reaches acceptable levels of significance in the ROA equations. In the q equations, in contrast, the size dummy enters positively at 5 percent, and the leverage ratio at 10 percent. For 2002–03, the industry and primary product dummies also become significant, which may be explained by the boost in profitability linked to the steep peso devaluation. Meanwhile, sales growth enters with a negative sign, which is difficult to explain.

Robustness Checks

In what follows, we carry out a battery of robustness checks to test the validity of the previous empirical findings. We start by running individual regressions, keeping the same control set as before, of each of the subindexes and other, alternative governance measures. As is apparent from table 2.13, *board* and *disclosure*, but not *shareholders*, have a positive and significant loading in the ROA equation for the whole 2000–03 period.

Table 2.13 The ROA and Alternative TDI Measures

	Dependent variable: ROA		
Explanatory variables	*2000-I/2003-IV*	*2000-I/2001-IV*	*2002-I/2003-IV*
TDI board	0.0003798	0.0003804	0.0004233
	(2.27)**	(3.13)***	(1.55)
TDI disclosure	0.0005578	0.0003138	0.0007863
	(2.38)**	(1.95)*	(2.14)**
TDI shareholders	0.0001353	0.0002087	0.0000662
	(1.22)	(2.11)**	(0.43)
TDI principal component	0.005078	0.0045892	0.0057355
	(2.5)**	(3.03)***	(1.7)*
TDI median	0.0116517	0.0137146	0.0152886
	(1.84)*	(2.51)**	(1.74)*

Source: Author.

Note: Each line of the table displays, for the three sample periods, the estimated coefficient (and robust t-statistic) on alternative TDI measures, namely, the three subindexes defined in the text (board, disclosure, shareholders), each measured, like the TDI, on a 0–100 scale, as well as the principal component of these three subindexes, and the median overall TDI. For each of the 15 ordinary least squares regressions, the controls are the same as in the baseline regressions with controls. Outlier observations with a q larger than 2.5 have been dropped. T-statistics based on robust standard errors are shown in parentheses.

* significant at 10 percent
** significant at 5 percent
*** significant at 1 percent

The coefficient on *disclosure* is the highest (0.00056) and is similar to that of the overall TDI; the coefficients on *board* and *shareholders* are 0.00038 and 0.00014, respectively. Again, the results seem to be much stronger in 2000–01 than in 2002–03, and, in fact, all coefficients are significant in the former two-year period, but not in the latter. Because it is to be expected that most governance provisions are interrelated and have some degree of commonality, we also use the first principal component of the three subindexes to minimize such overlapping. In this case, as when we take the median TDI, the estimates remain significant. The q regressions in table 2.14 reveal that board is the highest and most significant subindex and that the median TDI is the only one lacking significance across all time periods.

We may ask ourselves whether the TDI is the only proper measure of corporate governance. Although it is an objective and documented index, one caveat is that our TDI does not directly reflect actual governance practices, but rather how much about these practices the company chooses to disclose. To circumvent this possible criticism, we formulate two alternative measures. In the first place, we sent a detailed survey to all listed firms, which unfortunately was completed by only nine companies—an issue addressed in the paper elsewhere below. Later, we attempted to fill this informational void by running a short three-question phone survey,

Table 2.14 Q and Different TDI Measures

	Dependent variable: q		
Explanatory variables	*2000-I/2001-IV*	*2000-I/2003-IV*	*2002-I/2003-IV*
TDI board	0.0040451	0.0056068	0.004756
	(2.41)**	(2.22)**	(1.89)*
TDI disclosure	0.0030108	0.0042696	0.004586
	(1.82)*	(1.84)*	(2.44)**
TDI shareholders	0.0034545	0.0016843	0.0005941
	(2.19)**	(0.84)	(0.35)
TDI principal component	0.0536123	0.0536887	0.0449033
	(2.69)***	(2.16)**	(1.91)*
TDI median	0.1124944	0.1500073	0.1172497
	(1.3)	(1.33)	(1.42)

Source: Author.

Note: See the note to table 2.13. T-statistics based on robust standard errors are shown in parentheses.

* significant at 10 percent

** significant at 5 percent

*** significant at 1 percent

with similarly poor results.[13] Subsequently, we went over the charters of all the companies in the sample in search of distinctive features regarding corporate governance that are not legally binding (and that, hence, may display the desirable cross-section variability), such as the self-imposition of the one share–one vote rule and of minimum (1) dividends, (2) percentage of independent directors, or (3) percentage of votes to call an extraordinary shareholders meeting (in the latter case, below the legal requirement of 5 percent). Once again, this effort turned out to be fruitless because virtually all companies have standardized charters that merely adhere to the required legal framework.[14]

Ultimately, we constructed a compact corporate governance index that included three binary (0–1) variables, namely, whether the firm: (1) has a positive weight in the stock portfolio of an Argentine pension fund (the case of 40 percent of companies), (2) agreed to complete our governance survey (15 percent of companies), and (3) has a percentage of independent directors above the mean of our sample. Even though this index is restricted to only a few variables, it has a valuable informational content regarding governance. Item (1) is a useful proxy for the market perception of corporate governance by professional fund managers. Item (2) provides a notion of the willingness to disclose corporate information (and, due to some degree of self-selection, would most likely be correlated with good governance). Item (3) offers the most relevant information about governance practices that is not included in our TDI.[15]

Table 2.15 presents the results. It is apparent from the table that this new index is highly significant in the ROA regressions for 2000–03 and 2000–01 and in the q regression for 2002–03. Because the three components may be correlated and the new index may be, in turn, correlated with the TDI, we have additionally computed the principal component with and without the TDI. From the same table, we witness a greater significance in both the ROA and q regressions, especially when the TDI is included. This implies that the new index seems to complement rather than substitute for the TDI as a measure of corporate governance.

In another robustness check, we sent out a questionnaire to pension funds operating in Argentina to inquire about their perception of corporate governance practices in the companies they usually trade. We included only four general questions, each with a range of five answers from Very Good to Very Bad.[16] Eight of the 10 pension funds returned completed questionnaires. Even with a much smaller sample (26 companies), the baseline regressions continue to yield highly significant estimates on this index when the dependent variable is the ROA, but not when it is q, as shown in table 2.16.

Once the quality of our corporate governance measure had been tested, we went on to substitute the ROA and q for the return on equity and the return on sales as the dependent variable in unreported regressions where the TDI estimate is still significant, but only in 2000–01. In tables 2.17

Table 2.15 The ROA, Q, and Alternative Corporate Governance Measure, 1

	Period		
Explanatory variables	*2000-I/2001-IV*	*2000-I/2003-IV*	*2002-I/2003-IV*
Dependent variable: ROA			
Alternative corporate governance measure	0.0053662 (2.45)**	0.0055044 (2.17)**	0.0053446 (1.26)
Principal component	0.0043242 (2.73)***	0.0054439 (3.2)***	0.0067902 (2.28)**
Principal component with TDI	0.0060176 (3.28)***	0.0064885 (3.08)***	0.0068267 (1.89)*
Dependent variable: q			
Alternative corporate governance measure	0.0533555 (1.54)	0.0268823 (0.61)	0.0696259 (2.31)**
Principal component	0.0364547 (1.39)	0.0252562 (0.81)	0.0456212 (2.05)**
Principal component with TDI	0.062501 (2.73)***	0.0514405 (1.73)*	0.0689372 (2.71)***

Source: Author.

Note: Each line of the table displays, for the three sample periods, the estimated coefficient on an alternative corporate governance measure comprising whether the percentage of independent directors is above the mean for the sample, whether the firm stock is included in the pension funds portfolio, and whether the firm has participated in our corporate governance survey. Thus, the index range is 0–3. For each of the ordinary least squares regressions, the controls are the same as in the baseline regressions with controls. Outlier observations with a q larger than 2.5 have been dropped. T-statistics based on robust standard errors are shown in parentheses.

* significant at 10 percent

** significant at 5 percent

*** significant at 1 percent

and 2.18, we introduce several interaction terms. The square TDI seeks to capture a possible nonlinear effect of the TDI. Although the coefficient is negative, suggesting a positive, but decreasing effect, it is only significant at 10 percent for 2000–01. The TDI size interaction is intended to measure whether, in bigger firms, where management complexity may, a priori, create more acute agency problems, the role of good governance is reinforced. By the same token, good governance may be more valuable in older firms where founding shareholders or their relatives may exert

Table 2.16 The ROA, Q, and Alternative Corporate Governance Measure, 2

	Period		
Explanatory variables	*2000-I/2001-IV*	*2000-I/2003-IV*	*2002-I/2003-IV*
Dependent variable: ROA			
Corporate governance score by pension funds	0.0008149 (4.62)***	0.0013008 (3.21)***	0.0012313 (1.85)*
Dependent variable: q			
Corporate governance score by pension funds	0.0058265 (1.57)	0.004319 (1.57)	0.0020239 (0.37)

Source: Author.

Note: Each line of the table displays, for the three sample periods, the estimated coefficient statistic on an alternative corporate governance measure comprising the score given by pension funds to a subsample of firms they usually trade. The sample consists of 26 companies. For each of the ordinary least squares regressions, the controls are the same as in the baseline regressions with controls. Outlier observations with a q larger than 2.5 have been dropped. T-statistics based on robust standard errors are shown in parentheses.

* significant at 10 percent

** significant at 5 percent

*** significant at 1 percent

excessive and value-reducing power. Growing firms (as proxied by the growth of sales) may need adequate governance standards to enhance their access to financing and to avoid overinvestment. Finally, highly leveraged firms may, on the one hand, require proper governance as a disciplining device to mitigate the incentives for overinvestment and excessive risk taking; on the other hand, governance standards may have a less prominent effect to the extent that the default risk associated with fixed financial obligations may in itself be sufficient to mitigate conflicts of interest between large and minority shareholders. With the exception of a striking negative TDI sales growth interaction in the q regressions, none of these additional terms are significant for the whole period. The individual TDI significance is unchanged, except when interacted with age.

Endogeneity Checks

A recurring concern in econometric studies on corporate governance and performance is the potential presence of endogeneity. Specifically, if there exists a causal positive link from performance to governance, the estimated

Table 2.17 The ROA, the TDI, and Interaction Regressors

	Dependent variable: ROA		
Explanatory variables	*2000-I/2003-IV*	*2000-I/2001-IV*	*2002-I/2003-IV*
TDI	0.0019735	0.0018288	0.0022953
	(1.83)*	(2.39)**	(1.38)
TDI^2	–0.0000156	–0.0000147	–0.000018
	(–1.35)	(–1.76)*	(–1.07)
TDI	0.0005612	0.000504	0.0006386
	(2.59)**	(3.09)***	(1.68)*
TDI*size dummy	–0.0001358	–0.000189	–0.0000769
	(–0.17)	(–0.33)	(–0.07)
TDI	0.0003824	0.0000265	0.0007522
	(1.07)	(0.1)	(1.52)
TDI*age	2.69E–06	7.52E–06	–2.12E–06
	(0.62)	(1.94)*	(–0.4)
TDI	0.0005546	0.0004673	0.0006774
	(2.52)**	(2.93)***	(1.85)*
TDI*sales growth	–5.89E–06	8.54E–06	–0.0013834
	(–0.46)	(0.9)	(–0.82)
TDI	0.000442	0.0004291	0.0001384
	(1.39)	(1.79)*	(0.27)
TDI*debt to assets	6.47E–04	3.28E–04	0.0026687
	(0.40)	(0.32)	(0.97)

Source: Author.

Note: The table shows ordinary least squares results for the whole period (2000–03) and two subperiods (2000–01 and 2002–03). The ROA is an average from quarterly data for each period. The TDI (on a 0–100 scale) is the same for all periods and is based on public corporate information for 2003. For each of the ordinary least squares regressions, the controls are the same as in the baseline regressions. T-statistics based on robust standard errors are shown in parentheses.

* significant at 10 percent

** significant at 5 percent

*** significant at 1 percent

coefficient on governance would be upward biased, thus rendering the previous results anything but reliable. Among other reasons, good performance may encourage the adoption of a better governance framework because: (1) implementing governance reforms is costly; so, only profitable companies are capable of affording the associated expenses; and (2) there may be a multiple equilibrium problem at work, whereby there is a group of low-performance, bad governance companies, the insiders of which reap substantial private benefits of control and are struggling to perpetuate the status quo, and a second high-performance, good governance group of companies that

Table 2.18 Q, TDI, and Interaction Regressors

	Dependent variable: q		
Explanatory variables	*2000-I/2003-IV*	*2000-I/2001-IV*	*2002-I/2003-IV*
TDI	0.0162038	0.0080394	0.0158863
	(1.2)	(0.85)	(1.54)
TDI^2	–0.0001113	–0.0000283	–0.0001148
	(–0.89)	(–0.32)	(–1.23)
TDI	0.00637	0.0059362	0.0055036
	(2.21)**	(2.67)**	(1.96)*
TDI*size dummy	–0.0038428	–0.0041979	–0.0033814
	(–0.88)	(–1.12)	(–0.94)
TDI	0.0055717	0.0052771	0.0119218
	(0.95)	(1.94)*	(3.32)***
TDI*age	5.27E–06	2.21E–06	–0.0001216
	(0.05)	(0.06)	(–3.19)***
TDI	0.0065752	0.0054413	0.0050741
	(2.39)**	(2.55)**	(2.08)**
TDI*sales growth	–0.0004031	–0.0000196	0.0107459
	(–3.06)***	(–0.15)	(0.52)
TDI	0.0061942	0.0041172	0.0029627
	(1.42)	(1.24)	(0.82)
TDI*debt to assets	–0.0018984	0.0079738	0.0110808
	(–0.1)	(0.58)	(0.74)

Source: Author.

Note: The table shows ordinary least squares results for the whole period (2000–03) and two subperiods (2000–01 and 2002–03). Q is an average from quarterly data for each period. (Observations with q larger than 2 have been dropped.) The TDI (on a 0–100 scale) is the same for all periods and is based on public corporate information for 2003. For each of the ordinary least squares regressions, the controls are the same as in the baseline regressions. T-statistics based on robust standard errors are shown in parentheses.

* significant at 10 percent

** significant at 5 percent

*** significant at 1 percent

is aware of and enjoys the benefits of good governance rules and, hence, has incentives to continue along this path.

The use of an instrumental variable and the running of a simultaneous equation model are two popular devices for dealing with endogeneity. An instrumental variable is one that is correlated with the endogenous explanatory variable, but not with the dependent variable; meeting such binding conditions in financial economic studies is frequently difficult. However, we propose three possible options. The first is a dummy with a value of 1 if the company had established an audit committee as of May 2004 and 0 otherwise. Unlike other governance provisions, the creation of the audit committee has been imposed by law (through Decree 677/2001 cited in the Introduction), but the requirement, due to be fulfilled by May 2004, was only compulsory for big firms. Small firms (according to a classification dictated by Resolution 408/1993 of the Ministry of the Economy that establishes maximum levels of assets, sales, and employees by sector) were exempt from this requirement. In principle, because the audit committee is clearly part of a good governance framework and its creation was legally required (and, thus, by definition, exogenous with respect to firm performance), it stands out as a useful instrumental variable. Nevertheless, its use casts some doubt because we realize that its correlation with the TDI, though statistically significant, is rather low (0.32). Moreover, 60 percent of the firms with below average TDI have an audit committee, and 20 percent of the above average TDI companies do not, reinforcing the impression that this may not be as valuable an instrument as we had hoped. This observation suggests that firms choose their own governance regimes for reasons other than this particular legal duty. Anyway, as may be seen in table 2.19, we rerun the baseline regressions with this instrument in lieu of the TDI, without finding any significant coefficient.

Table 2.19 The ROA, Q, and Instrumental TDI, 1

	Period		
Explanatory variables	*2000-I/2001-IV*	*2000-I/2003-IV*	*2002-I/2003-IV*
Dependent variable: ROA			
Audit committee dummy	0.0074097 (1.1)	0.0073925 (1.27)	0.0068299 (0.73)
Dependent variable: q			
Audit committee dummy	0.0914799 (0.94)	0.0212256 (0.27)	0.0721781 (0.79)

Source: Author.

Note: The table shows ordinary least squares results, with the TDI instrumented according to whether the company had set up an audit committee by May 2004 for the whole period (2000–03) and two subperiods (2000–01 and 2002–03). The ROA is an average from quarterly data for each period. Q is an average from quarterly data for each period. (Observations with q larger than 2.5 have been dropped.) For each of the ordinary least squares regressions, the controls are the same as in the baseline regressions. T-statistics based on robust standard errors are shown in parentheses.

* significant at 10 percent
** significant at 5 percent
*** significant at 1 percent

The second alternative instrument has arisen from the fieldwork carried out to construct our index of corporate governance. As mentioned elsewhere above, we conducted a survey of corporate governance among all listed firms. After several reminders, we received no answers. At that point, we personally contacted top managers in 24 companies we knew before this study had been put in motion and asked them to complete the survey. As a result of this new, personal request, we managed to have the questionnaire completed, but only by nine companies. Predictably, the companies that agreed to respond in this instance had an average TDI (49.3) higher than that of the whole sample (39.1), indicating that participation in the survey is an indicator of good governance.[17] More importantly, the selection of these companies was totally unrelated to their performance. Consequently, we are able to claim that participation in the survey is a legitimate (dummy) instrumental variable. The regression output in table 2.20 for the ROA regressions, but not for q, yields a highly significant estimate for the whole 2000–03 period and also for 2002–03.

Next, we postulate yet another instrument, a trading intensity variable, defined as the number of days the stock was traded in 2001–03 as a proportion of the total trading days in that period. This variable ranges from

Table 2.20 The ROA, Q, and Instrumental TDI, 2

	Period		
Explanatory variables	*2000-I/2001-IV*	*2000-I/2003-IV*	*2002-I/2003-IV*
Dependent variable: ROA			
Survey participation dummy	0.0073902 (1.5)	0.0152633 (2.8)***	0.0230707 (2.81)***
Dependent variable: q			
Survey participation dummy	–0.0007394 (–0.01)	0.0167805 (0.2)	0.0441421 (0.68)

Source: Author.

Note: The table shows ordinary least squares results for the whole period (2000–03) and two subperiods (2000–01 and 2002–03), with the TDI instrumented according to whether the company has participated in our corporate governance survey. The ROA is an average from quarterly data for each period. Q is an average from quarterly data for each period. (Observations with q larger than 2.5 have been dropped.) For each of the ordinary least squares regressions, the controls are the same as in the baseline regressions. T-statistics based on robust standard errors are shown in parentheses.

* significant at 10 percent

** significant at 5 percent

*** significant at 1 percent

0 to 1.[18] Because we should expect that companies with good corporate governance are more attractive to and, thus, more actively traded by outside investors, the positive nexus between trading and governance is evident. In fact, the correlation with the TDI is 0.5. Nevertheless, trading may not be exogenous with respect to accounting performance, though the correlation in that case would not be positive, that is, it should not necessarily lead to the usual upward bias behind the endogeneity criticism. For instance, Chordia, Huh, and Subrahmanyam (2003) investigate the determinants of stock trading in the United States and argue that the ROA should actually reduce trading intensity because high ROA shares are preferred by investors following buy-and-hold strategies.[19] Their empirical finding, after controlling for a large number of variables, is that the ROA has no statistical effect on different measures of trading. Returning to our estimations, the baseline regressions presented in table 2.21 suggest that this instrumental variable enters significantly in all ROA regressions.

The independence of trading intensity and q is perhaps more questionable because investors may display loss aversion, leading them to

Table 2.21 The ROA, Q, and Instrumental TDI, 3

	Period		
Explanatory variables	*2000-I/2001-IV*	*2000-I/2003-IV*	*2002-I/2003-IV*
Dependent variable: ROA			
Trading intensity	0.0226526 (2.41)**	0.0166014 (2.21)**	0.0275019 (2.21)**
Dependent variable: q			
Trading intensity	0.1475558 (1.23)	0.162527 (1.71)*	0.0539047 (0.32)

Source: Author.

Note: The table shows ordinary least squares results, with the TDI instrumented according to trading intensity for the whole period (2000–03) and two subperiods (2000–01 and 2002–03). The ROA is an average from quarterly data for each period. Q is an average from quarterly data for each period. (Observations with q larger than 2.5 have been dropped.) For each of the ordinary least squares regressions, the controls are the same as in the baseline regressions. T-statistics based on robust standard errors are shown in parentheses.

* significant at 10 percent
** significant at 5 percent
*** significant at 1 percent

hold on to past losers and to trade past winners more actively. In line with this behavioral approach, Odean (1999) and Chordia, Huh, and Subrahmanyam (2003) document that high-return stocks are traded more. The expected positive correlation between q and trading intensity renders the latter an inappropriate instrument for corporate governance. In any event, we also run the same baseline q regressions in table 2.21, although no significant estimates have been obtained, except marginally for 2000–03.

As a final exercise, we confront potential endogeneity by running a two-stage least squares simultaneous equations model, that is, treating trading intensity as an endogenous variable. To save space, in table 2.22 we report only the estimates on trading intensity, where we observe significant coefficients in all cases with the exception of q in 2002–03. We have also gone back to our original regressions and apply this same technique for the TDI

Table 2.22 The ROA, Q, the TDI, and Trading Intensity: Simultaneous Equations

	Period		
Explanatory variables	*2000-I/2001-IV*	*2000-I/2003-IV*	*2002-I/2003-IV*
Dependent variable: ROA			
Trading intensity	0.0329259	0.0336572	0.0362385
	(2.67)***	(3.00)***	(2.21)**
TDI	0.0012004	0.0012271	0.001514
	(2.47)**	(2.81)***	(2.01)**
Dependent variable: q			
Trading intensity	0.4245126	0.2596319	0.1694634
	(2.47)**	(2.06)**	(0.97)
TDI	0.0154811	0.0098527	0.0077623
	(2.14)**	(2.05)**	(1.00)

Source: Author.

Note: The table shows two-stage, simultaneous equations for the whole period (2000–03) and two subperiods (2000–01 and 2002–03) for both (1) trading intensity and (2) the TDI. The ROA is an average from quarterly data for each period. Q is an average from quarterly data for each period. (Observations with q larger than 2.5 have been dropped.) For each of the ordinary least squares regressions, the controls are the same as in the baseline regressions. T-statistics based on robust standard errors are shown in parentheses.

* significant at 10 percent

** significant at 5 percent

*** significant at 1 percent

in the same table. Again, the estimations support the claim that endogeneity does not drive our econometric results.

Ownership and Performance

Resuming the discussion in the section on Literature Review and Working Hypotheses, we now report the results involving the ownership variables displayed in tables 2.23 and 2.24, where we show the estimated coefficients on the TDI and these indicators for the largest ultimate shareholder: control rights, cash flow rights, the ratio of control to cash flow rights, and nationality.[20] Most coefficients for both the ROA and q equations and for different sample periods turn out to be nonsignificant because the results do not change before the changes in the set of additional regressors. The exception is the ratio of control to cash flow rights, which has the expected negative, significant sign during the crisis period of 2002–03 for both performance measures. A plausible explanation for this finding is that conflicts of interest among shareholders are accentuated at times of financial distress and economic slump. Furthermore, macroeconomic instability (inflation, devaluation, abrupt relative price changes, and the like) allows controlling shareholders to expropriate minority shareholders and other stakeholders more easily because the ability to monitor the company and its managers is seriously undermined in a scenario where balance sheets and conventional analytical tools become less informative. In this sense, we also introduce a default dummy with a value of 1 if the company defaulted on its debt as a result of the 2002–03 crisis (which was the case of 9 of the 65 companies) and 0 otherwise. The incentive for self-dealing and other forms of expropriation is heightened under these circumstances; so, we would predict a negative sign on default. However, the estimation leads us to reject any noticeable effect.

Interaction terms of ownership variables with the TDI have been included in tables 2.25 and 2.26 to test whether the power of the TDI as a disciplining tool has anything to do with the power of controlling shareholders. Two contrasting hypotheses are sensible: (1) good governance is more valuable in firms with more powerful insiders because it helps to restrict the abusive actions that these insiders would otherwise commit; and (2) good governance is less valuable in firms with more powerful insiders because governance rules, no matter how good they are, are circumvented or plainly disregarded by controlling shareholders. Regression outcomes lend some support to hypothesis (2) in that the separation of control and cash flow rights attenuates, but does not neutralize whatsoever, the impact of the TDI on the ROA and q.[21] For instance, in the third column of table 2.25 (ROA in 2002–03), the overall TDI loading goes down to 0.00048 (for a control-to-cash flow ratio of 1.74, the average for the 22 firms for which the ratio exceeds 1.02) from 0.00058 (for no separation).

Table 2.23 The ROA, the TDI, and Ownership Variables

	Dependent variable: ROA		
Explanatory variables	*2000-I/2003-IV*	*2000-I/2001-IV*	*2002-I/2003-IV*
TDI	0.000409	0.0003322	0.0004598
	(1.88)*	(2.74)***	(1.24)
Domestically owned	0.0115982	0.0099056	0.0106716
	(2.16)**	(2.59)**	(1.24)
TDI	0.0004456	0.0003641	0.0004839
	(1.96)*	(2.65)**	(1.33)
Control rights	0.0000253	0.0000229	-0.0000503
	(0.22)	(0.26)	(-0.27)
TDI	0.0004412	0.0003569	0.0004899
	(1.98)*	(2.63)**	(1.38)
Cash flow rights	0.0000288	0.0000144	-0.0000177
	(0.26)	(0.17)	(-0.10)
TDI	0.0004365	0.0003528	0.0005157
	(1.97)*	(2.55)**	(1.41)
Control-to-cash flow rights	-0.0039524	0.0003507	-0.0073614
	(-1.89)*	(0.24)	(-2.27)**
TDI			0.000621
			(1.69)*
Default			-0.0040768
			(-0.32)

Source: Author.

Note: Each line of the table displays, for the three sample periods, the estimated coefficient (and t-statistic) of the TDI and the alternative ownership measures: (1) domestically owned: dummy variable with a value of 1 if the main ultimate shareholder is an Argentine family and 0 if the main ultimate shareholder is a foreign company; (2) control rights of the main ultimate shareholder over the company; (3) cash flow rights of the main ultimate shareholder over the company; and (4) the ratio of control to cash flow rights of the main ultimate shareholder. Default is a dummy variable with a value of 1 if the company declared default in 2002 and 0 otherwise. For each of the ordinary least squares regressions, the controls are the same as in the baseline regressions. T-statistics based on robust standard errors are shown in parentheses.

* significant at 10 percent

** significant at 5 percent

*** significant at 1 percent

Table 2.24 Q, the TDI, and Ownership Variables

	Dependent variable: q		
Explanatory variables	*2000-I/2003-IV*	*2000-I/2001-IV*	*2002-I/2003-IV*
TDI	0.0069655	0.006129	0.0053619
	(2.84)***	(3.80)***	(2.54)**
Domestically owned	-0.1360339	-0.0098623	0.0533931
	(-1.09)	(-0.17)	(-0.03)
TDI	0.0072879	0.0054797	0.005555
	(2.47)**	(2.9)***	(2.45)**
Control rights	0.0016564	-0.0010065	-0.0002549
	(0.71)	(-0.93)	(-0.15)
TDI	0.0068515	0.0057205	0.0056454
	(2.71)***	(3.27)***	(2.49)**
Cash flow rights	0.0014618	-0.0009766	-0.0001199
	(0.75)	(-1.01)	(-0.08)
TDI	0.0064649	0.0060841	0.0057941
	(3.01)***	(3.64)***	(2.61)**
Control-to-cash flow rights	-0.0659882	-0.0039019	-0.0761783
	(-1.27)	(-0.12)	(-2.35)**
TDI			0.0049681
			(1.97)*
Default			-0.0483392
			(-0.34)

Source: Author.

Note: Each line of the table displays, for the three sample periods, the estimated coefficient (and t-statistic) of the TDI and the alternative ownership measures: (1) domestically owned: dummy variable with a value of 1 if the main ultimate shareholder is an Argentine family and 0 if the main ultimate shareholder is a foreign company; (2) voting rights of the main ultimate shareholder over the company; (3) cash flow rights of the main ultimate shareholder over the company; and (4) the ratio of control to cash flow rights of the main ultimate shareholder. Default is a dummy variable with a value of 1 if the company declared default in 2002 and 0 otherwise. For each of the ordinary least squares regressions, the controls are the same as in the baseline regressions. Outlier observations with $q > 2.5$ have been dropped. T-statistics based on robust standard errors are shown in parentheses.

* significant at 10 percent

** significant at 5 percent

*** significant at 1 percent

Table 2.25 The ROA, the TDI, and Ownership: Interaction Regressors

	Dependent variable: ROA		
Explanatory variables	*2000-I/2003-IV*	*2000-I/2001-IV*	*2002-I/2003-IV*
TDI	0.0005468	0.0003577	0.0007089
	(2.28)**	(2.34)**	(1.80)*
TDI* control-to-cash flow	-0.000078 (-1.98)*	-0.0000318 (-0.12)	-0.0001345 (-2.30)**
TDI	0.0003855	0.0003033	0.0005016
	(1.58)	(1.93)*	(1.2)
TDI* control rights	0.0000	0.0000	0.0000
	(0.53)	(0.8)	(0.01)
TDI	0.0003764	0.0003089	0.0004644
	(1.52)	(1.98)*	(1.09)
TDI* cash flow rights	0.0000	0.0000	0.0000
	(0.64)	(0.71)	(0.25)
TDI	0.0003309	0.0002463	0.0004327
	(1.42)	(1.94)*	(1.08)
TDI* domestically owned	0.0001984 (1.62)	0.0002064 (2.33)**	0.0001157 (0.58)

Source: Author.

Note: The table shows ordinary least squares results for the whole period (2000–03) and two subperiods (2000–01 and 2002–03). The ROA is an average from quarterly data for each period. The TDI (on a 0–100 scale) is the same for all periods and is based on public corporate information for 2003. The alternative ownership measures are (1) domestically owned: dummy variable with a value of 1 if the main ultimate shareholder is an Argentine family and 0 if the main ultimate shareholder is a foreign company; (2) control rights of the main ultimate shareholder over the company; (3) cash flow rights of the main ultimate shareholder over the company; and (4) the ratio of control to cash flow rights of the main ultimate shareholder. For each of the ordinary least squares regressions, the controls are the same as in the baseline regressions. T-statistics based on robust standard errors are shown in parentheses.

* significant at 10 percent

** significant at 5 percent

*** significant at 1 percent

Determinants of Dividend Policies

Summary Statistics and Additional Regressors

We start by describing several summary measures of dividend activity, namely, the ratios of cash dividends to cash flow, earnings, and sales. We

Table 2.26 Q, the TDI, and Ownership: Interaction Regressors

	Dependent variable: q		
Explanatory variables	*2000-I/2003-IV*	*2000-I/2001-IV*	*2002-I/2003-IV*
TDI	0.0081147	0.0062605	0.0077512
	(3.06)***	(2.92)***	(3.12)***
TDI* control-to-cash flow	-0.0011564	-0.0001199	-0.0013212
	(-1.73)*	(-0.23)	(-3.00)***
TDI	0.0051433	0.0066116	0.0057072
	(2.19)**	(4.28)***	(1.90)*
TDI* control rights	0.000031	-0.000014	0.0000
	(0.73)	(-0.71)	(-0.03)
TDI	0.0052544	0.0066949	0.0056783
	(2.32)**	(4.36)***	(1.90)*
TDI* cash flow rights	0.000026	-0.000015	0.0000
	(0.72)	(-0.85)	(-0.00)
TDI	0.0081607	0.0058686	0.0048657
	(2.61)**	(3.43)***	(2.37)**
TDI*domestically owned	-0.0030955	0.0003422	0.0012361
	(-1.01)	(0.25)	(0.54)

Source: Author.

Note: The table shows ordinary least squares results for the whole period (2000–03) and two subperiods (2000–01 and 2002–03). Q is an average from quarterly data for each period. (Observations with q larger than 2.5 have been dropped.) The TDI (on a 0–100 scale) is the same for all periods and is based on public corporate information for 2003. The alternative ownership measures are (1) domestically owned: dummy variable with a value of 1 if the main ultimate shareholder is an Argentine family and 0 if the main ultimate shareholder is a foreign company; (2) control rights of the main ultimate shareholder over the company; (3) cash flow rights of the main ultimate shareholder over the company; and (4) the ratio of control to cash flow rights of the main ultimate shareholder. Default is a dummy variable with a value of 1 if the company declared default in 2002 and 0 otherwise. For each of the ordinary least squares regressions, the controls are the same as in the baseline regressions. T-statistics based on robust standard errors are shown in parentheses.

* significant at 10 percent

** significant at 5 percent

*** significant at 1 percent

will use only the first measure as our dependent variable in the subsequent econometric work because it most accurately reflects the decision to compensate shareholders from available firm revenues.[22] From a visual inspection of table 2.27, it may be observed that dividend ratios were more or less stable in 1996–2000, increased in 2001, and then shrank in 2002–03. The change in 2001 is allegedly attributable to the financial crisis initiated in 2001 that induced firms to pay high dividends as a means of allowing shareholders to cover themselves from the expected devaluation and the fragility of the banking system by buying external assets. In turn, during 2002–03, in the context of a marked contraction in sales and the balance sheet problems deriving from the currency crisis, companies seem to have partially adjusted through dividend cuts. For purposes of comparison, Faccio, Lang, and Young (2001) show that, for 14 Asian and European countries in 1992–96, the dividend to earnings, cash flow, and sales ratios were 34, 23.4, and 3.6 percent, respectively. For Argentina in 1996–2003, these values were 31.9, 12.9, and 3.4, respectively.

Our empirical strategy will assist in identifying fundamental factors that explain dividends for the whole period 1996–2003, and then, subsequently, we will concentrate on the 2000–03 subsample, including, at that stage, additional governance and ownership variables.[23] Following the corporate model in any standard textbook, we hypothesize that the core explanatory variables should encompass (1) the ROA: the higher the net revenues, the more dividends should be disbursed; (2) Tobin's q: the better the future growth opportunities, the less convenient it is to pay dividends whenever the firm has financial constraints on access to external sources of funds; (3) debt to assets: highly leveraged companies may prefer to pay less out in dividends (increasing equity financing) to contain default risk;[24] and

Table 2.27 Dividend Measures by Year, 1996–2003

	Dividends to cash flow		*Dividends to earnings*		*Dividends to sales*	
	Mean	*Std. dev.*	*Mean*	*Std. dev.*	*Mean*	*Std. dev.*
1996	0.153	0.222	0.245	0.330	0.046	0.089
1997	0.189	0.385	0.354	0.720	0.048	0.083
1998	0.152	0.207	0.283	0.388	0.047	0.083
1999	0.126	0.206	0.702	3.351	0.037	0.069
2000	0.153	0.210	0.387	0.730	0.036	0.055
2001	0.189	0.576	0.466	1.361	0.031	0.081
2002	0.021	0.065	0.038	0.119	0.010	0.040
2003	0.050	0.152	0.074	0.221	0.014	0.044
Average	0.13	0.25	0.32	0.90	0.03	0.07

Source: Author.

Note: The table shows, through yearly figures for 1996–2003, the mean and standard deviations for three alternative dividend measures. See the definitions in table 2.3.

(4) logarithm of assets: larger firms tend to be more diversified and thus less risky, to have more fluid access to credit, and to have fewer investment opportunities, thus rendering them more willing to pay dividends.

In addition, we test the effect of the following empirical counterparts of variables put forward in modern dividend theories. (5) The lagged dividend-to-cash flow ratio: from the empirical findings of Lintner (1956) and more recent signaling models, we should presume that firms attempt to maintain stable dividends, creating a persistent pattern over time. We include the host of governance and ownership variables, the predicted impact of which is discussed in the subsection on corporate governance, ownership, and dividend policies elsewhere above, namely: (6) the quality of corporate governance standards, (7) the cash flow rights of the largest shareholder, (8) the control rights of the largest shareholder, (9) the separation between control and cash flow rights, and (10) the nationality of the largest shareholder. It is sometimes presumed that foreign-owned firms are likely to face less stringent financial constraints and be able to overcome situations of financial distress more easily. This, coupled with an alleged desire of recovering investments in as short a period as possible in macroeconomic and politically unstable countries, may induce these firms to pay dividends that are higher than those paid by domestically owned companies. We also include (11) a dummy variable for issuers of ADRs because firms cross-listing in the U.S. may be induced to mimic the dividend policies of firms they compete with for funds in foreign markets.[25] Finally, we include (12) a default dummy, with a value of 1 if the company defaulted on its debt as a result of the 2002–03 crisis and 0 otherwise. The default should have a negative effect on dividends because, if controlling shareholders retain their power after a default or if covenants and legal mechanisms are in place to protect unpaid stakeholders, dividends are likely to be reduced. In the first case, controlling shareholders may feel even more encouraged to expropriate minority shareholders and creditors, while in the second case, dividends will be reduced to meet debt obligations. Along with these controls, we add year and sector dummies.

Summary statistics on these explanatory variables are shown in table 2.28. It must be highlighted that, while the ROA has decreased appreciably since 2002, Tobin's q has gone up, which should be associated with the bullish stock market in 2002–03. Equally shocking was the increase in the leverage ratio in 2002 at a time when bank credit was being cut back. In this case, the explanation is most likely related to the revaluation in pesos of dollar-denominated debt after the currency crisis. Tables 2.29 and 2.30 split the whole sample into dividend payers and nonpayers to test whether the means are different. In line with some of the theoretical predictions, table 2.29 shows that dividend-paying companies are larger, more profitable, and less leveraged, while table 2.30 shows that they have better corporate governance. The mean difference tests for the other variables are inconclusive.

Table 2.28 Balance Sheet Variables by Year, 1996–2003

	Ln(Assets)		*ROA*		*Tobin's q*		*Debt to assets*	
	Mean	*Std. dev.*	*Mean*	*Std. dev.*	*Mean*	*Std. dev.*	*Mean*	*Std. dev.*
1996	12.843	1.846	4.146	7.773	0.829	0.328	0.179	0.120
1997	12.968	1.716	4.636	7.027	0.911	0.307	0.181	0.126
1998	13.169	1.794	5.608	6.276	0.876	0.331	0.215	0.154
1999	13.285	1.767	5.102	6.149	0.840	0.293	0.229	0.159
2000	13.450	1.771	4.738	5.910	0.850	0.278	0.256	0.173
2001	13.529	1.590	4.467	6.302	0.766	0.219	0.214	0.163
2002	13.254	1.474	2.353	6.618	0.777	0.215	0.300	0.254
2003	13.082	1.698	2.846	7.982	0.914	0.249	0.246	0.220
Average	13.197	1.707	4.237	6.754	0.845	0.278	0.227	0.171

Source: Author.

Note: The table shows, through yearly figures for 1996–2003, the mean and standard deviations of the balance sheet regressors. See the definitions in table 2.3.

Table 2.29 Mean Difference Tests for Balance Sheet Variables

Test	*Mean dividend payers*	*Mean dividend nonpayers*
Ln(Assets)	13.46298***	12.18412
ROA	8.083471***	1.415236
q	2.852988	1.950592
Debt to assets	0.1465031	0.2207027***

Source: Author.

Note: The sample covers a maximum of 613 observations over 1996–2003. See the definitions in table 2.3.

*** statistically different from the mean of the other group at 1 percent

Econometric Results

Table 2.31 presents the baseline econometric results for 1996–2003. Because the dependent variable (cash dividends to cash flow) is censored at zero, a pooled Tobit procedure has been followed in the estimation. Size, leverage, q, and the ROA yield the expected signs at conventional confidence levels both when they enter individually (except q) or jointly. Time dummies are significantly negative for 2002 and 2003, and utilities appear to pay more dividends than other sectors. As usual, endogeneity

Table 2.30 Mean Difference Tests for Corporate Governance and Ownership

Test	*Mean dividend payers*	*Mean dividend nonpayers*
TDI	44.08***	37.43
TDI board	35.2***	26.07
TDI disclosurew	52.91***	48.19
TDI shareholders	44.19**	38.77
Control rights	61.95	63.63
Control-to-cash flow rights	1.258	1.32
Domestically owned	0.548	0.425
ADR	0.277	0.197

Source: Author.
Note: See the definitions in table 2.3.
** statistically different from the mean of the other group at 5 percent
*** statistically different from the mean of the other group at 1 percent

may cloud the reliability of most of the econometric work. In principle, this may not be a critical issue here because, at least a priori, dividend payments are decided by the firm immediately after each fiscal year has ended and when balance sheet variables are known. From this timeline structure, it is unlikely that year *t* dividends might cause changes in realized variables, such as earnings, sales, and the like. However, the leverage ratio and Tobin's q may be suspected of endogeneity under certain conditions. Leverage may be an endogenous variable if firms set a stable dividend target in advance to meet and adjust their debt ratio accordingly. This drawback may be ruled out by noting that, if this were the case, a positive bias should be expected between debt and dividends, while most regressions yield a negative and significant sign on debt. Therefore, this negative effect of debt is unlikely to be driven by the supposed endogeneity of debt.[26] As for Tobin's q, endogeneity may be present as long as investors have a preference for high dividends and correctly anticipate the payout to be announced after each fiscal year. Again, this positive bias is unlikely to be behind the negative sign encountered in the regressions. As can be seen in table 2.32, neither debt nor q loses explanatory power after being instrumented. Following most capital structure theories, debt is instrumented with tangibility, assets, and the ROA, as well as sector dummies, while q is instrumented with assets, the standard deviation of the ROA, and sector dummies.[27]

Table 2.31 Cash Dividends to Cash Flow: Balance Sheet Determinants

Explanatory variables	*Dependent variable: cash dividends to cash flow*				
	Reg 1	*Reg 2*	*Reg 3*	*Reg 4*	*Reg 5*
Ln(Assets)	0.139721				0.1208576
	(4.12)***				(3.68)***
ROA		0.0496856			0.0459259
		(4.98)***			(4.84)***
q			0.1179684		−0.3582527
			(1.03)		(−3.14)***
Debt to assets				−1.027093	−0.7139238
				(−3.86)***	(−2.95)***
Dummy 1997	0.0165076 (0.14)	0.0258632 (0.22)	0.0228356 (0.18)	0.0461027 (0.38)	0.0591087 (0.51)
Dummy 1998	−0.0238291 (−0.24)	−0.0174689 (−0.18)	0.0073206 (0.07)	0.0500902 (0.49)	0.0086075 (0.09)
Dummy 1999	−0.1866945 (−1.66)*	−0.1490408 (−1.46)	−0.1486515 (−1.33)	−0.0844999 (−0.76)	−0.1105616 (−1.07)
Dummy 2000	−0.0747963 (−0.64)	0.0010548 (0.01)	−0.0445119 (−0.39)	0.0090711 (0.08)	0.0163188 (0.15)
Dummy 2001	−0.1883885 (−1.27)	−0.0994918 (−0.67)	−0.1483344 (−0.95)	−0.1316112 (−0.86)	−0.1395932 (−0.97)
Dummy 2002	−0.6337873 (−3.42)***	−0.4875134 (−2.82)***	−0.6054717 (−3.29)***	−0.5184182 (−2.90)***	−0.4765879 (−2.65)***
Dummy 2003	−0.4314337 (−2.52)**	−0.3647389 (−2.37)**	−0.4119857 (−2.34)**	−0.3473336 (−2.07)**	−0.3450367 (−2.39)**
Industry dummy	0.123036 (1.12)	0.0277682 (0.28)	0.1085714 (0.99)	0.1182131 (1.1)	0.0579242 (0.6)
Utilities dummy	0.117748 (1.14)	0.1151168 (1.37)	0.3863711 (3.95)***	0.4217783 (4.37)***	−0.0554682 (−0.53)
Primary product dummy	−0.0179269 (−0.14)	0.015568 (0.13)	−0.0326666 (−0.25)	−0.0904107 (−0.74)	−0.0350659 (−0.31)
Constant	−2.003719 (−3.97)***	−0.405674 (−2.63)***	−0.3341172 (−1.83)*	−0.0586404 (−0.5)	−1.510991 (−3.40)

(continued)

Table 2.31 Cash Dividends to Cash Flow: Balance Sheet Determinants *(continued)*

Explanatory variables	*Dependent variable: cash dividends to cash flow*				
	Reg 1	*Reg 2*	*Reg 3*	*Reg 4*	*Reg 5*
Years	1996–2003	1996–2003	1996–2003	1996–2003	1996–2003
Observations	355	355	355	355	355
Companies	65	65	65	65	65
Method	Pooled Tobit	Pooled Tobit	Pooled Tobit	Pooled Tobit	Pooled Tobit
Wald test (p-value)	61.14 (0.000)	83.16 (0.000)	47.04 (0.000)	64.18 (0.000)	83.77 (0.000)
Observation left censored at 0	221	221	221	221	221

Source: Author.

Note: The table shows pooled Tobit results for yearly data 1996–2003 and a maximum of 65 listed nonfinancial firms. The yearly cash dividends are those announced once the company's fiscal year has ended, and the accounting variables (including the cash flow used to scale dividends) are calculated from that fiscal year's statements. Variable definitions may be found in table 2.3. Observations with percentage ROA smaller than –20 and greater than 20 have been dropped. T-statistics based on robust standard errors are shown in parentheses.

* significant at 10 percent

** significant at 5 percent

*** significant at 1 percent

Table 2.32 Cash Dividends to Cash Flow and Instrumented Q and Debt

Explanatory variables	*Dependent variable: cash dividends to cash flow*
Ln(Assets)	0.1208576 (3.68)***
ROA	0.0459259 (4.84)***
q	–0.3582527 (–3.14)***
Debt to assets	–0.7139238 (–2.95)***
Dummy 1997	0.0591087 (0.51)

(continued)

Table 2.32 Cash Dividends to Cash Flow and Instrumented Q and Debt *(continued)*

Explanatory variables	*Dependent variable: cash dividends to cash flow*
Dummy 1998	0.0086075 (0.09)
Dummy 1999	–0.1105616 (–1.07)
Dummy 2000	0.0163188 (0.15)
Dummy 2001	–0.1395932 (–0.97)
Dummy 2002	–0.4765879 (–2.65)***
Dummy 2003	–0.3450367 (–2.39)**
Industry dummy	0.0579242 (0.6)
Utilities dummy	–0.0554682 (–0.53)
Primary product dummy	–0.0350659 (–0.31)
Constant	–1.510991 (–3.40)
Years	1996–2003
Observations	299
Companies	65
Method	Pooled Tobit
Wald test (p-value)	50.05 (0.000)
Observation left censored at zero	196

Source: Author.

Note: The table shows pooled Tobit results for yearly data 1996–2003 and a maximum of 65 listed nonfinancial firms. Q is instrumented with ln(Assets), the standard deviation of the ROA in the previous three years, and sector dummies. Debt to assets is instrumented with ln(Assets), tangibility (fixed to total assets), the ROA, and sector dummies. The yearly cash dividends are those announced once the company's fiscal year has ended, and the accounting variables (including the cash flow used to scale dividends) are calculated from that fiscal year's statements. Variable definitions may be found in table 2.3. Observations with percentage ROA smaller than –20 and greater than 20 have been dropped. T-statistics based on robust standard errors are shown in parentheses.

* significant at 10 percent

** significant at 5 percent

*** significant at 1 percent

In table 2.33, we test whether firms prefer to keep stable dividends over time and find favorable evidence after including, alternatively, the lagged dividend-to-cash flow ratio and a dividend payment dummy that takes the value of 1 if the company paid any cash dividends in the previous year and 0 otherwise.

Before introducing our indicators of corporate governance and ownership, we check, in table 2.34, on the validity of our previous model for the shortened sample 2000-2003, which confirms the robustness of the initial specification.

Thereafter, we observe that the TDI enters with the predicted positive sign in the regressions reported in table 2.35. Nevertheless, it is somewhat difficult to claim an independent effect from the TDI because of the recurring problem of multicollinearity, which renders the TDI nonsignificant whenever the whole control set is used in the estimation. This problem is aggravated when the controls are size and the ROA, a result that should come as no surprise after the discussion in the section on Determinants of Corporate Performance. Focusing on the first column, where the only controls are the time and sector dummies, the estimate suggests a sizable effect: a 10-point increase of the TDI brings about an increase of 0.128 in the dividend-to-cash flow ratio, implying a twofold increase from the 1996–2003 average (0.129). This a priori large impact makes it advisable to treat these results with caution.

Table 2.33 Cash Dividends to Cash Flow: Balance Sheet Determinants and Lagged Dividends, 1996–2003

	Dependent variable: cash dividends to cash flow	
Explanatory variables	*Reg 1*	*Reg 2*
Lagged dividend-to-cash flow	0.3677375 (2.13)**	
Dividend payment dummy		0.4540746 (3.68)***
Ln (Assets)	0.1260323 (3.80)***	0.0813215 (2.85)***
ROA	0.0433225 (4.43)***	0.0391772 (4.63)***
q	–0.3310239 (–2.83)***	–0.3716614 (–3.24)***
Debt to assets	–0.5719821 (–2.41)***	–0.5242257 (–2.27)***
Dummy 1997	0.0428147 (0.37)	0.0511503 (0.43)
Dummy 1998	–0.038081 (–0.4)	–0.0141108 (–0.15)

(continued)

Table 2.33 Cash Dividends to Cash Flow: Balance Sheet Determinants and Lagged Dividends, 1996–2003 *(continued)*

	Dependent variable: cash dividends to cash flow	
Explanatory variables	*Reg 1*	*Reg 2*
Dummy 1999	–0.1349394 (–1.35)	–0.1540803 (–1.4)
Dummy 2000	0.0018235 (0.02)	0.0353736 (0.31)
Dummy 2001	–0.1631112 (–1.17)	–0.1736879 (–1.27)
Dummy 2002	–0.5978967 (–3.32)***	–0.4204837 (–2.72)***
Dummy 2003	–0.3163607 (–2.05)**	–0.1840429 (–1.28)
Industry dummy	0.0582177 (0.62)	0.1088636 (1.09)
Utilities dummy	–0.1349289 (–1.21)	–0.0604578 (–0.58)
Primary product dummy	–0.0804458 (–0.76)	–0.0361314 (–0.35)
Constant	–1.632618 (–3.60)***	–1.242202 (–3.14)***
Years	1996–2003	1996–2003
Observations	352	355
Companies	65	65
Method	Pooled Tobit	Pooled Tobit
Wald test (p-value)	90.05 (0.000)	100.65 (0.000)
Observation left censored at zero	220	221

Source: Author.

Note: The table shows pooled Tobit results for yearly data 1996–2003 and a maximum of 65 listed nonfinancial firms. The yearly cash dividends are those announced once the company's fiscal year has ended, and the accounting variables (including the cash flow used to scale dividends) are calculated from that fiscal year's statements. Variable definitions may be found in table 2.3. Observations with percentage ROA smaller than –20 and greater than 20 have been dropped. The lagged dividend-to-cash flow is the level of the variable in the previous fiscal year. (Negative values have been dropped.) The dividend payment dummy takes the value of 1 if the company paid any cash dividends in the previous year and 0 otherwise. T-statistics based on robust standard errors are shown in parentheses.

* significant at 10 percent

** significant at 5 percent

*** significant at 1 percent

Table 2.34 Cash Dividents to Cash Flow: Balance Sheet Determinants and Lagged Dividends, 2000–2003

	Dependent variable: cash dividends to cash flow	
Explanatory variables	*Reg 1*	*Reg 2*
Lagged dividend-to-cash flow	0.5937983 (2.35)**	
Dividend payment dummy		0.8558688 (2.88)***
Ln(Assets)	0.1930751 (2.51)**	0.1314615 (1.88)*
ROA	0.0816424 (3.17)***	0.064233 (3.29)***
q	–1.170026 (–2.64)***	–1.4488 (–2.87)***
Debt to assets	–1.131707 (–2.05)**	–0.8182062 (–1.69)*
Dummy 2001	–0.3673346 (–2.19)**	–0.4967385 (–2.92)***
Dummy 2002	–0.894018 (–2.77)***	–0.6531616 (–2.80)***
Dummy 2003	–0.4970166 (–2.06)**	–0.2253047 (–1.21)
Industry dummy	0.5154685 (1.88)*	0.4895822 (1.91)*
Utilities dummy	–0.2480822 (–0.96)	–0.1592987 (–0.66)
Primary product dummy	0.1348618 (0.53)	0.135574 (0.66)
Constant	–2.226291 (–2.33)**	–1.497589 (–1.73)*
Years	2000–2003	2000–2003
Observations	171	171
Companies	62	62
Method	Pooled Tobit	Pooled Tobit
Wald test (p-value)	25.34 (0.008)	30.44 (0.001)
Observation left censored at zero	125	125

Source: Author.

Note: See the note to table 2.33. The yearly data are from 2000 to 2003. T-statistics based on robust standard errors are shown in parentheses.

* significant at 10 percent

** significant at 5 percent

*** significant at 1 percent

Table 2.35 Cash Dividends to Cash Flow: TDI and Balance Sheet Determinants

	Dependent variable: cash dividends to cash flow						
Explanatory variables	*Reg 1*	*Reg 2*	*Reg 3*	*Reg 4*	*Reg 5*	*Reg 6*	*Reg 7*
TDI	0.0127588	0.0039001	0.0063895	0.0149198	0.0089636	0.0129927	0.0041633
	(2.28)**	(0.61)	(1.28)	(2.51)**	(1.7)*	(2.33)**	(0.78)
Ln(Assets)		0.1627004					
		(1.88)*					
ROA			0.0690156				
			(3.26)***				
q				−0.392965			
				(−1.22)			
Debt to assets					−1.73621		
					(−2.81)***		
Lagged dividend-to-cash flow						0.7371441	
						(2.05)**	
Dividend payment dummy							1.026434
							(3.19)***
Dummy 2001	−0.2116032	−0.2043868	−0.183809	−0.250894	−0.249116	−0.2507685	−0.3370484
	(−1.16)	(−1.1)	(−1.08)	(−1.39)	(−1.42)	(−1.43)	(−2.1)**
Dummy 2002	−0.7647883	−0.7536246	−0.6860092	−0.7772802	−0.7136279	−0.9052962	−0.698561
	(−2.95)***	(−2.92)***	(−2.56)**	(−2.97)***	(−2.80)***	(−2.90)***	
Dummy 2003	−0.4772231	−0.4793895	−0.5116594	−0.4400478	−0.5004413	−0.4372625	−0.183317
	(−2.05)**	(−2.09)**	(−2.24)**	(−1.94)*	(−2.18)**	(−1.77)*	(−0.81)

(continued)

Table 2.35 Cash Dividends to Cash Flow: TDI and Balance Sheet Determinants *(continued)*

	Dependent variable: cash dividends to cash flow						
Explanatory variables	*Reg 1*	*Reg 2*	*Reg 3*	*Reg 4*	*Reg 5*	*Reg 6*	*Reg 7*
Industry dummy	0.541146 (1.74)*	0.5440326 (1.77)*	0.3917792 (1.49)	0.5797464 (1.81)*	0.6272566 (1.97)**	0.5081307 (1.64)	0.4650673 (1.56)
Utilities dummy	0.3550852 (1.48)	0.0895996 (0.34)	0.0774173 (0.38)	0.4046428 (1.64)	0.5186541 (2.19)**	0.2047834 (0.85)	0.0988843 (0.42)
Primary product dummy	0.3529082 (1.13)	0.361681 (1.16)	0.4170981 (1.47)	0.3281751 (1.06)	0.2849596 (0.98)	0.2543225 (0.8)	0.207235 (0.73)
Constant	−1.14422 (−2.32)**	−2.869526 (−2.39)**	−1.072923 (−2.45)**	−0.9308687 (−1.89)*	−0.665306 (−1.53)	−1.196013 (−2.41)**	−1.132951 (−2.42)**
Years	2000–2003	2000–2003	2000–2003	2000–2003	2000–2003	2000–2003	2000-2003
Observations	171	171	171	171	171	171	171
Companies	65	65	65	65	65	65	65
Method	Pooled Tobit	Pooled Tobit	Pooled Tobit	Pooled Tobit	Pooled Tobit	Pooled Tobit	Pooled Tobit
Wald test (p-value)	15.2 (0.034)	15.96 (0.043)	25.69 (0.0012)	15.75 (0.046)	21.68 (0.0055)	19.02 (0.0148)	28.38 (0.004)
Observation left censored at zero	125	125	125	125	125	125	125

Source: Author.

Note: See the note to table 2.33. The TDI (on a 0–100 scale) is the same for all periods and is based on public corporate information for 2003. T-statistics based on robust standard errors are shown in parentheses.

* significant at 10 percent
** significant at 5 percent
*** significant at 1 percent

Table 2.36 Cash Dividends to Cash Flow and TDI, 2000–03

	Dependent variable: cash dividends to cash flow	
Explanatory variables	*2000–03*	*2002–03*
TDI	0.0127588 (2.28)**	0.0129488 (1.83)*
TDI board	0.0105979 (2.22)**	0.0136402 (1.96)**
TDI disclosure	0.0112709 (2.03)**	0.006726 (1.16)
TDI shareholder	0.0046088 (1.40)	0.0032187 (0.78)
TDI principal component	0.120073 (2.23)**	0.1154215 (1.77)*
TDI median	0.4375427 (1.73)*	0.4679927 (1.73)*

Source: Author.

Note: Each line of the table displays, for the two sample periods (2000–03 and 2002–03), the estimated coefficient (and robust t-statistic) on alternative TDI measures, namely, the three subindexes defined in the text (board, disclosure, shareholders), each measured, like the TDI, on a 0–100 scale, as well as the principal component of these three subindexes, and the median overall TDI. For each (pooled Tobit) regression, the controls are time and sector dummies. T-statistics based on robust standard errors are shown in parentheses.

* significant at 10 percent

** significant at 5 percent

*** significant at 1 percent

Table 2.37 Cash Dividends to Cash Flow and Ownership Variables, 2000–03

	Dependent variable: cash dividends to cash flow	
Explanatory variables	*2000–03*	*2002–03*
Domestically owned	0.3128624 (1.27)	0.0056998 (0.03)
Control rights	0.0043601 (0.96)	–0.0021286 (–0.56)
Cash flow rights	0.0029718 (0.81)	–0.0010807 (–0.34)

(continued)

Table 2.37 Cash Dividends to Cash Flow and Ownership Variables, 2000–03 *(continued)*

	Dependent variable: cash dividends to cash flow	
Explanatory variables	*2000–03*	*2002–03*
Control-to-cash flow rights	0.0107172 (0.11)	0.0087633 (0.1)
ADR	0.0570934 (0.32)	0.1517129 (0.76)
Default		0.0453669 (0.14)

Source: Author.

Note: Each line of the table displays, for the two sample periods (2000–03 and 2002–03), the estimated coefficient (and robust t-statistic) on alternative ownership measures: (1) domestically owned: dummy variable with a value of 1 if the main ultimate shareholder is an Argentine family and 0 if the main ultimate shareholder is a foreign company; (2) control rights of the main ultimate shareholder over the company; and (3) the ratio of control to cash flow rights of the main ultimate shareholder. ADR is a dummy variable with a value of 1 if the company issued an ADR and 0 otherwise. Default is a dummy variable with a value of 1 if the company declared default in 2002 and 0 otherwise. For each (pooled Tobit) regression, the controls are time and sector dummies. T-statistics based on robust standard errors are shown in parentheses.

* significant at 10 percent

** significant at 5 percent

*** significant at 1 percent

From table 2.36, another striking result emerges: all TDI subindexes are significant with only time and sector controls; the exception is shareholders, which should be the subindex most related to dividend policies.

Finally, in table 2.37, none of the ownership variables or the nationality and default dummies appears to be significantly correlated to dividends.

Conclusions

The goal of this chapter is twofold. First, we have put together, for the first time, quantitative measures on the quality of the corporate governance and the ownership structure in 65 listed nonfinancial companies in Argentina with information for 2003–04. A wide array of official and private sources has been used for this purpose. In summary, companies in Argentina seem to be poorly governed relative to international practices.

In turn, ownership appears to be quite concentrated at the level of the largest ultimate shareholder. Separation of control and cash flow rights prevails in fewer than half the companies. Pyramiding is the main mechanism for creating the wedge.

Second, we test the predictions of recent theories by linking these measures with corporate performance and dividend policy in 2000–03. Concerning performance, the results point to a sizable and robust effect of our governance measure on both the ROA and Tobin's q. Moreover, the separation of control and cash flow rights for the largest shareholder—an indicator of the incentives for expropriating minority shareholders—hinders performance directly and also attenuates the beneficial impact from good governance rules. For dividends, only our governance measure appears to exert a positive and marked effect on the cash dividend–cash flow ratio. However, the estimates prove fragile to the inclusion of some additional controls correlated to governance.

Any policy recommendation emerging from this research should take into account that improving corporate governance entails the consideration of both private and public interests. Controlling shareholders will not be inclined to cooperate with such a change unless the incremental benefits (acting as regular shareholders) outweigh the loss of their private benefits of control. The evidence reported here on the ROA-governance nexus will hopefully be taken into account by insiders. Less apparent are the benefits from higher q. Historically, stock issuance has been almost negligible in Argentina; so, a topic for future research is whether stock prices and returns play any role at all in enhancing access to the market and bank debt.

But corporate governance is, at the same time, a public policy issue in that uninformed minority shareholders should be legally protected against expropriation. Raising awareness among investors and businesses about improving corporate governance is a first, obvious step that should be taken by the authorities to stimulate a cultural change in this area. Likewise, our poor TDI scores suggest that disclosure requirements frequently found in other emerging and developed markets should be put in place. Nevertheless, legal reforms that are not supported to some extent by the very companies that must apply these rules may not come to fruition; the mixed and rather disappointing outcome of the 2001 reforms in Argentina is a case in point. In addition, a compulsory, full-fledged regime of strict governance provisions may be self-defeating as long as some companies are able ultimately to decide to delist, and delisting is another chronic problem of the Argentine Stock Exchange that forms part of the future research agenda. This conclusion arises from the observation that implementing a proper governance framework is costly and time consuming, and some expected benefits may not readily materialize. Thus, a balance between the adequate protection of minority shareholders and the incentive structure of controlling shareholders should be sought in designing corporate governance reforms.

Notes

1. See La Porta et al. (1998) and Claessens et al. (1999).

2. See Baker, Powell, and Veit (2002) for a survey and Bebczuk (2003) for a textbook presentation.

3. See, for example, Miller and Rock (1985).

4. See Jensen (1986).

5. See Fernández Baribiera (2002) and Bebczuk (1997).

6. See Bebczuk, Fanelli, and Pradelli (2002).

7. See OECD (1999); Fremond and Capaul (2002); COSRA (2000); Klapper and Love (2002); Standard & Poor's (2002); Gompers, Ishii, and Metrick (2003); Black, Jang, and Kim (2003); Drobetz, Schillhofer, and Zimmermann (2003).

8. Questionnaires were sent out in early March 2004, and, after many reminders, only nine responses were obtained as of November 2004.

9. See, for example, Black, Jang, and Kim (2003).

10. The only exception is that they must disclose changes involving more than 5 percent of capital, but, even in these cases, they are not required to present information on owners who do not participate in the particular transactions.

11. The decision not to go back further in time arises from the fact that our governance and ownership indicators reflect the situation as of 2003–04. Though these variables change slowly over time (and thus we are assuming that they are valid for the whole period 2000–03), we are not certain that they are an adequate representation of the 1990s.

12. See Weill (2003) and Bebczuk (2003).

13. In fact, the investor relations officers (*responsables de relaciones con el mercado*) of only three companies responded to our phone calls after two reminders over a two-week period. To facilitate participation, the survey was narrowed to only three questions: (1) Has the company issued or subscribed to a code of best practices on corporate governance? (2) Does the external auditor provide any additional paid service to the company? and (3) Does the company inform its controlling and minority shareholders about the rationale and amount of the remuneration to the top management and the board, distinguishing the fixed and variable components and the form of payment (cash, shares, options)?

14. With the exception of the one share–one vote rule, which is voluntarily included by 66 percent of companies in their charters, the remaining items are present in at most three out of the 65 companies.

15. The new index ranges from 0 to 3, and its mean value is 0.93, with a correlation of 0.4 with the TDI. We also tested other components for the index, including the one share–one vote dummy, whether the chief executive officer and the chairman of the board are the same person, and whether the chief executive officer or any director is, at the same time, a direct controlling shareholder of the company. However, the results lose statistical significance when any of these variables was added to the index. Given that these variables are usually associated with good governance, these results call for additional work regarding the role these variables actually play in corporate governance and performance.

16. The questions had to do with general opinions on corporate governance, the functioning of boards and top management, disclosure, and minority shareholder protection.

17. The correlation of the TDI and the grade obtained through the questionnaire is positive and statistically significant (0.29). Obviously, the sample is too small to draw definite conclusions, but this positive association reinforces our confidence in the informative content of the TDI.

18. Note that the median trading intensity is 0.44, indicating that many stocks listed in Argentina are quite illiquid.

19. This is why we discard one additional instrument, a dummy for companies held by pension funds. Pension funds, as minority shareholders, should naturally be inclined toward good governance companies, but because they mostly follow long-term, buy-and-hold strategies, a positive relationship between this instrument and the ROA is probably present.

20. Note that the usable sample drops from 65 to 46 observations for the ROA and q, respectively. Because the TDI remains significant after this change, these regressions provide an additional robustness check for governance.

21. It must be noted that, due to multicollinearity, the regressions do not include the ownership variables, but rather their interactions with the TDI.

22. The source of dividend data is IAMC (2002) and the Buenos Aires Stock Exchange. García Zamora (2002) investigates dividend policies in Argentina in the 1990s.

23. As explained in endnote 11, we are not certain that corporate and ownership characteristics in 2003–04 are representative of the 1990s.

24. Actually, absent the costs of bankruptcy, firms find debt attractive as an insurance device because it enables more risk sharing with creditors instead of forcing shareholders to absorb an expected negative shock entirely by themselves.

25. ADR issuance may also indicate low financial constraints because being listed in more regulated foreign markets represents a positive signal.

26. Of course, this does not mean that endogeneity should be overlooked. Even without knowing the direction and magnitude of the bias, it should be remembered that endogeneity in any single regressor may cause other regressors to show bias in the estimates unless no correlation exists among the whole set of independent variables.

27. Assets and the ROA are excluded from this regression due to the ensuing multicollinearity.

References

Allayannis, G., G. Brown, and L. F. Klapper. 2003. "Capital Structure and Financial Risk: Evidence from Foreign Debt Use in East Asia." *Journal of Finance* 58 (6): 2667–2710.

Allen, F., and R. Michaely. 1995. "Dividend Policy." In *Finance*, Vol. 9 of *Handbooks in Operations Research and Management Science*, ed. R. A. Jarrow, V. Maksimovic, and W. T. Ziemba, 793–837. Amsterdam: Elsevier Science.

Angrist, J., and A. Krueger. 2001. "Instrumental Variables and the Search for Identification: From Supply and Demand to Natural Experiments." NBER Working Paper 8456, National Bureau of Economic Research, Cambridge, MA.

Baker, K., G. Powell, and T. Veit. 2002. "Revisiting the Dividend Puzzle: Do All of the Pieces Now Fit?" *Review of Financial Economics* 11 (4): 241–61.

Bebczuk, R. N. 1997. "Is the Argentine Stock Market Efficient?: Some Empirical Tests." University of Illinois at Urbana-Champaign, Champaign, IL.

———. 2003. *Asymmetric Information in Financial Markets*. Cambridge: Cambridge University Press.

Bebczuk, R. N., J. Fanelli, and J. Pradelli. 2002. "Financial Constraints Facing Firms in Argentina." Research Network Working Paper R-453, Research Department, Inter-American Development Bank, Washington, DC.

Black, B. S., H. Jang, and W. Kim. 2006. "Does Corporate Governance Predict Firms' Market Values?: Evidence from Korea." *Journal of Law, Economics, and Organization* 22 (2): 366–413.

Black, F. 1976. "The Dividend Puzzle." *Journal of Portfolio Management* 2 (2): 5–8.

Caprio, G., and R. Levine. 2002. "Corporate Governance in Finance: Concepts and International Observations." Unpublished working paper, World Bank, Washington, DC.

Chordia, T., S. Huh, and A. Subrahmanyam. 2003. "The Cross-Section of Expected Trading Activity." Unpublished working paper, Anderson School, University of California–Los Angeles, Los Angeles.

Claessens, S., S. Djankov, J. P. H. Fan, and L. H. P. Lang. 1999. "Expropriation of Minority Shareholders: Evidence from East Asia." Policy Research Working Paper 2208, World Bank, Washington, DC.

Claessens, S., S. Djankov, and T. Nenova. 2000. "Corporate Risk around the World." Policy Research Working Paper 2271, World Bank, Washington, DC.

Claessens, S., D. Klingebiel, and S. L. Schmukler. 2002. "The Future of Stock Exchanges in Emerging Economies: Evolution and Prospects." In *Brookings-Wharton Papers on Financial Services 2002*, ed. Robert E. Litan and Richard Herring, 167–212. Washington, DC: Brookings Institution Press.

COSRA (Council of Securities Regulators of the Americas). 2000. "Report on Corporate Governance Practices." Unpublished working paper, Council of Securities Regulators of the Americas, no location.

Drobetz, W., A. Schillhofer, and H. Zimmermann. 2003. "Corporate Governance and Firm Performance: Evidence from Germany." Unpublished working paper, University of Basel, Basel, Switzerland, http://www.cofar.uni-mainz.de/dgf2003/paper/paper146.pdf.

Dyck, A., and L. Zingales. 2002. "Private Benefits of Control: An International Comparison." NBER Working Paper 8711, National Bureau of Economic Research, Cambridge, MA.

Faccio, M., L. H. P. Lang, and L. Young. 2001. "Dividends and Expropriation." *American Economic Review* 91 (1): 54–78.

Fama, E., and K. French. 2001. "Disappearing Dividends: Changing Firm Characteristics or Lower Propensity to Pay?" *Journal of Financial Economics* 60 (1): 3–43.

Fernández Baribiera, A. 2002. "Estacionalidad en la Bolsa argentina: El efecto 'fin de semana.'" Unpublished working paper, Universidad Rovira-i-Virgili, Tarragona, Spain.

Fremond, O., and M. Capaul. 2002. "The State of Corporate Governance. Experience from Country Assessments." Policy Research Working Paper 2858, World Bank, Washington, DC.

Friedman, E., S. Johnson, and T. Mitton. 2003. "Propping and Tunneling." NBER Working Paper 9949, National Bureau of Economic Research, Cambridge, MA.

García Zamora, F. 2002. "Determinantes de la política de dividendos en efectivo en Argentina, 1991–2001." Thesis, postgraduate specialization in capital markets, Universidad Nacional de Buenos Aires, Buenos Aires.

Gertler, M., and R. G. Hubbard. 1988. "Financial Factors in Business Fluctuations." NBER Working Paper 2758, National Bureau of Economic Research, Cambridge, MA.

Gobert, K. 2001. "Capital Structure and Risk Management." CIRANO Scientific Series 2001s–51, Centre for Interuniversity Research and Analysis on Organisations, Quebec.

Gompers, P. A., J. L. Ishii, and A. Metrick. 2003 "Corporate Governance and Equity Prices." *Quarterly Journal of Economics* 118 (1): 107–55.

IAMC (Instituto Argentino de Mercado de Capitales). 2002. "Política de distribución de dividendos en efectivo en Argentina: Decisiones empresariales y mercado accionario." Working paper, Instituto Argentino de Mercado de Capitales, Buenos Aires.

Isaksson, M., and M. Lubrano. 2003. "White Paper on Corporate Governance in Latin America." Unpublished working paper, Organisation for Economic Co-operation and Development, Paris.

Jensen, M. C. 1986. "Agency Cost of Free Cash Flow, Corporate Finance, and Takeovers." *American Economic Review* 76 (2): 323–29.

Jensen, M. C., and W. H. Meckling. 1976. "Theory of the Firm: Managerial Behavior, Agency Costs, and Ownership Structure." *Journal of Financial Economics* 3 (4): 305–60.

Johnson, S., P. Boone, A. Breach, and E. Friedman. 2000. "Corporate Governance in the Asian Financial Crisis." *Journal of Financial Economics* 58 (1–2): 141–86.

Klapper, L. F., and I. Love. 2002. "Corporate Governance, Investor Protection, and Performance in Emerging Markets." Policy Research Working Paper 2818, World Bank, Washington, DC.

La Porta, R., F. López-de-Silanes, and A. Shleifer. 1999. "Corporate Ownership around the World." *Journal of Finance* 54 (2): 471–517.

La Porta, R., F. López-de-Silanes, A. Shleifer, and R. W. Vishny. 1997. "Legal Determinants of External Finance." *Journal of Finance* 52 (3): 1113–55.

———. 1998. "Agency Problems and Dividend Policies around the World." NBER Working Paper 6594, National Bureau of Economic Research, Cambridge, MA.

———. 2002. "Investor Protection and Corporate Valuation." *Journal of Finance* 57 (3): 1147–70.

Lintner, J. 1956. "Distribution of Incomes of Corporations among Dividends, Retained Earnings, and Taxes." *American Economic Review* 46 (2): 97–113.

Miller, M. H., and F. Modigliani. 1961. "Dividend Policy, Growth, and the Valuation of Shares." *Journal of Business* 34 (4): 411–33.

Miller, M. H., and K. Rock. 1985. "Dividend Policy under Asymmetric Information." *Journal of Finance* 40 (4): 1031–51.

Morck, R., A. Shleifer, and R. W. Vishny. 1988. "Management Ownership and Market Valuation: An Empirical Analysis." *Journal of Financial Economics* 20 (1): 293–315.

Odean, T. 1999. "Do Investors Trade Too Much?" *American Economic Review* 89 (5): 1279–98.

OECD (Organisation for Economic Co-operation and Development). 1999. *Principles of Corporate Governance*. Paris: Organisation for Economic Co-operation and Development.

Petersen, M., and R. Rajan. 1994. "The Benefits of Lending Relationships: Evidence from Small Business Data." *Journal of Finance* 49 (1): 3–37.

Standard & Poor's. 2002. "Standard & Poor's Corporate Governance Scores: Criteria, Methodology, and Definitions." Governance Services, Standard & Poor's, McGraw-Hill, New York, http://www2.standardandpoors.com/spf/pdf/products/CGSCriteria.pdf.

Titman, S., J. Wei, and F. Xie. 2003. "Capital Investments and Stock Returns." NBER Working Paper 9951, National Bureau of Economic Research, Cambridge, MA.

Weill, L. 2003. "Leverage and Corporate Performance: A Frontier Efficiency Analysis." Unpublished working paper, Université Robert Schuman, Strasbourg.

3

Corporate Governance and Value in Brazil (and in Chile)

*Ricardo P. C. Leal and André L. Carvalhal-da-Silva**

Introduction

Do better corporate governance practices lead to a lower cost of capital and a greater market valuation? This chapter presents evidence that this is the case in Brazil and that efforts by regulators, stock exchanges, multilateral organizations, and others to improve corporate governance practices do pay off. The chapter also discusses the reasons why better corporate governance practices may not be a panacea for all firms. There are many ways to represent corporate governance. One of them is through the relationship between the concentration of cash flow rights (voting and nonvoting shares) and control rights (voting shares), the so-called separation (or wedge) of voting and cash flow rights of major shareholders. Cash flow and control rights, however, may be only part of the story. Good corporate governance practices may also be represented by indexes based on charter measures and company practices. These indexes consider many different

* The authors wish to thank Daniel Karrer and Letícia Torres for their excellent research assistance. The authors additionally wish to acknowledge grants received from the Inter-American Development Bank and the National Scientific and Technological Development Council of Brazil, as well as a previous grant from the Carlos Chagas Filho Rio de Janeiro State Foundation for Research Support. The authors wish to thank the Coppead Graduate School of Business of the Federal University of Rio de Janeiro for additional support. Comments from Alberto Chong, Maximiliano González, Florencio López-de-Silanes, Jairo Procianoy, and Winston Fritsch are greatly appreciated.

aspects of corporate governance and may gauge the quality of *overall* corporate governance practices more accurately. This chapter develops a corporate governance index (CGI) or score. The CGI includes information from a very representative sample of Brazilian public firms, and it consists of items that may be objectively assessed without the need for qualitative evaluations. The design of the score is intended to be objective because response rates may be quite low in subjective questionnaires, although respondents may be able to provide valuable information. Another goal has been to obtain the largest sample possible.

This approach stands in contrast to qualitative surveys that evaluate corporate governance practices; these surveys are becoming more common. For example, Credit Lyonnais Securities Asia uses a questionnaire that is filled out by its analysts and that involves qualitative evaluations on their part or on the part of respondents. Similarly, the Brazilian Institute of Corporate Governance (IBGC) conducts biannual corporate governance surveys, but the sample is limited and may suffer from the usual survey biases and low response rates. Durnev and Kim (2005) and Patel, Balic, and Bwakira (2002) report on a transparency and disclosure index computed by Standard & Poor's using 98 0 or 1 questions. Durnev and Kim (2005) consider the Credit Lyonnais Securities Asia index as partially subjective, while they consider Standard & Poor's index as largely objective. Brown and Caylor (2006) build a governance score for U.S. firms from the Institutional Shareholder Services database. Gompers, Ishii, and Metrick (2003) and Bebchuk, Cohen, and Ferrell (2004) use a corporate governance index built from provisions followed by the Investor Responsibility Research Center. Bauer, Günster, and Otten (2004) use the Deminor ratings of about 300 items related to corporate governance practices for companies included in the FTSE Eurotop 300 index. Black, Jang, and Kim (2006) use a subset of 38 objective questions from a survey conducted by the Korean Stock Exchange; they leave out all subjective questions.

Alternatively, some authors prefer to compute their own indexes. Barontini and Siciliano (2003) define a number of dummies representing the risk of expropriation that depend on the existence of a controlling shareholder, the share of voting rights of large outside shareholders, and the existence of either pyramids or nonvoting shares. Their dummies are a reduced version of our index. What we do is also methodologically similar to what La Porta et al. (1998) and Gompers, Ishii, and Metrick (2003) have done. Like Black, Jang, and Kim (2006), this chapter includes only features that may be objectively assessed without the need to interview or survey interested parties. This chapter also provides a short time series of the index it presents; obtaining such information retroactively is not an option with subjective surveys or the use of current Web site information.

This chapter investigates the relationship of corporate valuation and performance with the corporate governance measures it sets forth. More concentrated control (voting rights) may be associated with the expropriation of external shareholders and poor corporate governance practices. This is sometimes called managerial entrenchment. More concentrated cash flow rights may be associated with an alignment of the interests of controlling shareholders with those of external shareholders, possibly leading to better corporate governance practices. This is sometimes labeled managerial incentives. The separation between voting and cash flow rights is large in Latin America, and it is usually achieved through the combined use of indirect control structures and nonvoting shares, thereby allowing a reduced investment by controlling shareholders in the total capital of the company without a loss of control.

Finally, Chilean corporate governance data from Lefort and Walker (2005) are used in a brief comparative analysis of the markets in Brazil and Chile. The objective of this section of the chapter is to put the results in a regional context. Chile was chosen instead of Argentina or Mexico because of the differences between Chile and Brazil, because the Argentine market is much smaller than the markets in the other large Latin American economies, and because comparable studies of Mexico have not been available.[1] Brazil represents a large Latin American economy, while Chile, though smaller, has had a more stable economy over the last 20 years. The legal systems in the two countries have the same origin, but they differ greatly in investor protection. La Porta et al. (1998) have created an antidirector rights index to measure the degree of shareholder protection in 49 countries, including Brazil and Chile. The index is the sum of six dummies that assume the value of 1 if a given form of shareholder protection exists. Brazil and Chile present different levels of antidirector rights within the region. The value of the index is 2 for Brazil and 5 for Chile.[2] Argentina scored 4, and Mexico 1 in La Porta et al. (1998). The large difference between Brazil and Chile is the motivation behind the selection of Chile; it provides the chapter with a truer Latin American context.

This chapter contributes to the existing literature by presenting a case study of a French civil law developing country (Brazil), which is compared to another country (Chile) at a similar stage of development, with a similar quality of law enforcement, and with a legal system of similar origin, but with a different level of legal investor protection. High concentration levels in voting rights are found in Brazil, and these are leveraged by the widespread use of indirect control structures and nonvoting shares. Nonvoting shares make up the majority of the shares traded in the secondary market. They are different from U.S. preferred shares because they pay no fixed dividends and because they dominate the secondary market, while, in the United States, common stock dominates trading in the market.

In addition, control was concentrated between 1998 and 2002, the period under examination. The chapter shows that a worst-to-best improvement in the CGI in 2002 would have led to a 0.38 increase in Tobin's q, which represents a 95 percent worst-to-best increase in the market value of equity for a company with the average leverage and Tobin's q ratios. An increase of 1 point in the CGI would have led to a 6.8 percent increase in the stock price of the average firm; this result seems to be robust. On the other hand, no significant relationship is found between the dividend payout and the CGI, which suggests that the payout is endogenously determined. A scale factor appears to affect the impact of corporate governance on value; larger firms benefit the most. In the comparative analysis with Chile, because there are no major differences in legal origin and judiciary quality, it has been concluded that the key difference lies in investor protection, largely due to the almost exclusive use of voting shares by Chilean firms, while Brazilian law allowed two-thirds of the shares in equity capital to be non-voting. This level has now been reduced to 50 percent, however, for firms that have gone public since 2001.

This chapter offers a positive answer to the question of whether good corporate governance practices lead to a greater market valuation and a lower cost of capital in Brazil. The chapter is divided into seven sections. The next section reviews some of the relevant literature on the association between corporate valuation and governance and presents the chapter's working hypotheses. The subsequent section presents the data, the methodology for building a corporate governance practices index for Brazil, a review of the supporting literature for the index components, and a discussion of the evidence derived from the application of the index questionnaire. The following section presents the empirical analysis, including the ownership concentration tabulations and the results on the relationship between corporate governance practices and value, as well as initial robustness tests. The section after that presents the endogeneity tests and additional robustness checks. The penultimate section compares the chapter's findings with those reported elsewhere for Chile, and the final section concludes and presents policy implications.

A Brief Review of the Literature and Working Hypotheses

Recent studies suggest that the Berle and Means (1932) model of widely dispersed ownership is uncommon even in developed countries. Large shareholders control a significant number of firms in the wealthier countries as well. La Porta, López-de-Silanes, and Shleifer (1999) identified the ultimate owners of cash flow and voting rights of firms in 27 developed countries. There are systematic differences among countries in the structure and enforcement of laws, such as the historical origin of the laws. La Porta, López-de-Silanes, and Shleifer find that relatively few firms are widely held except in economies with good shareholder protection; most firms are controlled by families or by the state. Controlling shareholders typically have control rights that considerably exceed their cash flow rights, mainly because of the use of pyramids.

Recent research highlights the importance of corporate governance in developed and emerging markets and suggests there are empirical relationships between governance and corporate performance. Results indicate that better corporate governance is associated with better performance and higher corporate valuation. La Porta et al. (1998, 2000a, 2002) evaluate the influence that is exercised on corporate valuation by investor protection and ownership by the controlling shareholders. They conclude that better shareholder protection is associated with a higher valuation of corporate assets and with more developed and valuable financial markets. When shareholder rights are more well protected by the law, outside investors are willing to pay more for financial assets such as equity and debt.

Gompers, Ishii, and Metrick (2003) compute a corporate governance index for 1,500 U.S. companies consisting of 24 antitakeover provisions and shareholder rights that have been compiled by the Investor Responsibility Research Center and that may be objectively assessed. Each index item is a dummy variable, and the index is the simple sum of these variables. Gompers, Ishii, and Metrick find that better shareholder rights are associated with greater corporate valuation and that this association increased in the 1990s. They also find that pro-shareholder governance practices are positively related to profits and sales growth and negatively related to capital expenditures and the amount of acquisitions. Their results are confirmed by Brown and Caylor (2006), among others, who find that firms with better governance practices are worth more, perform better, are less risky and volatile, and pay out more dividends. Bebchuk, Cohen, and Ferrell (2004) use a subset of six provisions from the 24 employed by Gompers, Ishii, and Metrick as an entrenchment index and conclude that entrenchment is negatively associated with firm value, while the remaining 18 provisions are not associated with firm value.

Using a different sample and approach, Claessens, Djankov, and Lang (2000) have performed a trace on East Asian corporations to discover ultimate ownership and control. In particular, they have examined the extent of the deviations from the one share–one vote rule, the use of pyramiding and cross holding, the presence of single and multiple controlling owners, and the presence of controlling shareholders as top managers of companies. Their study shows that most East Asian firms are controlled by a single shareholder that often turns out to be a family. Pyramidal and cross-holding structures are common. In contrast, the use of dual-class shares is limited. The authors have also documented a significant separation in ultimate ownership and control, which is most pronounced among family-controlled firms and smaller firms. In a similar study, Faccio and Lang (2002) analyzed ultimate ownership and control in Europe and reported that families are the most frequent type of controlling shareholders and that there is a significant separation in ownership and control, mainly through the use of pyramids and cross holdings.

Claessens et al. (2002) separate the effects of control and cash flow ownership on the market valuation of firms in several East Asian countries and find that more concentrated control adversely affects valuation, while cash flow ownership affects valuation positively. Wiwattanakantang (2001) investigates the effects of controlling shareholders on corporate performance in Thailand. Her results indicate that the presence of controlling shareholders is associated with better performance when this presence is assessed by accounting measures such as return on assets (ROA) and the ratio of sales to assets. Because most firms in her sample do not implement mechanisms to separate voting rights from cash flow rights, controlling shareholders might be self-constrained and not extract private benefits.

The measures of corporate performance used in these and other studies include the ROA, the dividend payout, and proxies for Tobin's q. Himmelberg, Hubbard, and Palia (1999), Black, Jang, and Kim (2006), and Klapper and Love (2004), among others, argue that there may be an endogeneity problem when performance measures are correlated with proxies for good governance practices, such as the concentration of control and cash flow rights or a governance practices index. Klapper and Love (2004) give the example of firms with good growth potential. To finance growth, insiders may decide in favor of costly better governance practices, which might please investors and lead to a rise in the firm's Tobin's q, as well as a simultaneous improvement in the corporate governance practices index. Thus, at a given point, there might be a positive correlation between Tobin's q and the governance practices index. Himmelberg, Hubbard, and Palia (1999) provide other examples. In standard cross-sectional analysis, it is difficult to determine whether there is causality between performance and governance practices or whether they are simply being affected by unobserved heterogeneity, that is, firm-specific common factors that are not observed or measured by the analyst. A more detailed discussion of the way different authors have dealt with this problem is presented elsewhere below.

Shleifer and Vishny (1997) state that corporate governance in Italy must be more like corporate governance in the rest of the world than corporate governance in Germany, Japan, or the United States. Barontini and Siciliano (2003) test if the risk of expropriation was associated with stock returns and Tobin's q in a sample of public Italian firms between 1991 and 2000. They use dummies to represent the risk of expropriation, and their dummies are associated with the proportion of voting rights by controlling shareholders and the stock ownership of large outside shareholders, as well as with the presence of pyramids and nonvoting shares. These researchers find no relationship between stock returns and the risk of expropriation and conclude that this is consistent with the actions of rational investors who discount stock prices in anticipation of expropriation, as discussed by Jensen and Meckling (1976). They also find that Tobin's q is lower among companies that present a higher risk of expropriation, particularly if these are holding companies or are controlled by the state or by families.

The literature documents that ownership concentration is associated with both costs and benefits. The presence of controlling shareholders may be harmful to a firm because the interests of these shareholders may not align with those of noncontrolling shareholders.[3] However, the presence of controlling shareholders may not always be detrimental to a firm. Large shareholders may mitigate the free rider problem of monitoring a management team and thereby reduce agency costs. La Porta, López-de-Silanes, and Shleifer (1999) argue that, in countries where the law and law enforcement do not offer sufficient protection to outside investors, concentrated ownership may mitigate shareholder conflicts.

Within the early literature that focused largely on shareholder-manager conflicts, Jensen and Meckling (1976) and Morck, Shleifer, and Vishny (1988) provided important early contributions for understanding the relationship between ownership structures and corporate valuation. Jensen and Meckling (1976) concluded that concentrated ownership is beneficial to corporate valuation because large investors are better at monitoring managers. Morck, Shleifer, and Vishny (1988) distinguish between the negative control effects and the positive incentive effects of ownership concentration. They suggest that the absence of separation between ownership and control reduces conflicts of interest and increases the value for shareholders.

Recent research suggests that greater cash flow rights are associated with greater valuation (the incentive effect).[4] In contrast, the concentration of control rights and the separation of voting rights from cash flow rights have a negative effect on firm value (the entrenchment effect). This recent literature focuses on the conflicts between controlling shareholders and outside shareholders. When large investors control a corporation, their policies may result in the expropriation of the wealth of outside shareholders. Such companies are not attractive to outside shareholders, and their shares may present lower market valuations.

Dispersed ownership is rare in Brazil, and the inside-outside shareholder conflict is considered the most relevant issue. Thus, the above review of the impact of ownership and governance practices on value leads to the following hypotheses:

- Hypothesis 1: A higher concentration of voting rights among controlling shareholders is associated with lower corporate valuation and worse performance.
- Hypothesis 2: A higher cash flow ownership by controlling shareholders is associated with higher corporate valuation and better performance.
- Hypothesis 3: A greater separation between voting rights and cash flow rights by controlling shareholders is associated with lower corporate valuation and worse performance.
- Hypothesis 4: Better corporate governance practices are associated with higher corporate valuation and better performance.

A Governance Practices Index for Brazil

This chapter presents an index based on information that may be objectively obtained from public sources, such as the mandatory filings with the Brazilian Securities Commission (CVM) and the annual and periodic reports of companies. The index is structured according to manuals of best practice, particularly the code of best practices of the IBGC. The Organisation for Economic Co-operation and Development code of best practices and the CVM code of best practices are used as well. These codes provide the framework for selecting the items to be measured in the index. It has been decided that the number of items should be neither too small to capture the multivariate nature of corporate governance nor too large to render data gathering difficult, time consuming, and costly.

A set of 24 questions has been developed. If the answer to any given question is yes, this is interpreted as a pro-shareholder provision or action and assigned a value of 1. Negative answers are assigned a null value. The index is the simple sum of the values assigned to the answers. Although the relative impact or importance of each question is not assessed, an unweighted index is easier to reproduce and less subjective than a weighted index. Indexes constructed in other studies have also followed this method, beginning with La Porta et al. (1998) and proceeding with Gompers, Ishii, and Metrick (2003), Black, Jang, and Kim (2006), and Barontini and Siciliano (2003), among others. Klapper and Love (2004) use a similar method to adapt the Credit Lyonnais Securities Asia index for their study. This chapter will consider subindexes, as well as a partial index obtained through the deletion of questions that do not greatly differentiate companies.

Agrawal and Knoeber (1996) recognize that mechanisms to control agency problems, such as board composition and block shareholding, are interdependent. Correlations between any one of these mechanisms and performance may be spurious because they may be compensated for or offset by some other mechanism that is not considered. The method used in this chapter does not ignore this substitution effect, also described by John and Senbet (1998), because the existence of alternative mechanisms is simultaneously and additively considered.

The inclusion of two questions was initially contemplated to determine if companies had level 2 or level 3 American depositary receipts (ADRs) listed in the United States or if they belonged to the *Novo Mercado* (New Market) trading lists of Bovespa, the São Paulo Stock Exchange.[5] These questions were omitted, however, because of their redundancy with many other questions that have been retained, such as questions on the use of international accounting standards. In any case, Doidge (2004) and Doidge, Karolyi, and Stulz (2004) provide evidence that foreign firms that list in the United States present, respectively, lower control premiums and greater value. The present analysis uses two separate control dummies for ADRs and the Novo Mercado.

This section presents the data sources, the criteria for selecting index questions, and selected supporting literature for each item included; it then discusses the empirical findings on the answers to each question.

Data Sources

The sample of public Brazilian firms is drawn from the universe of companies listed at Bovespa. The sample includes both financial and nonfinancial institutions, but does not include companies with incomplete or unavailable information, a negative book value of assets, or a negative book value of common equity, or firms that did not trade. The final sample consists of firms that represent most of the capitalization of the market.[6]

The questionnaire is answered using information from the INFOinvest database (http://www.infoinvest.com.br). This database is freely available except for the most recent filings, quarter and semiannual filings, and a few other items; a subscription to the database provided full access to all information. Data on annual filings were obtained for 1998, 2000, and 2002. Publicly traded companies are required to provide information about the previous calendar year by the end of April of each year. These filings must supply, among other data, information about equity capital and ultimate ownership if the holding is greater than 5 percent. Market and accounting information comes from the Economática database (http://www.economatica.com), which is available by subscription and which contains time series data on companies and company financial statements.

Index Components

Table 3.1 shows the questionnaire that has been used. Questions were included if they could be objectively answered through access to the INFOinvest database, CVM filings, annual or periodic company reports, and Web sites. Many of the questions included in the Credit Lyonnais Securities Asia index, for example, require that analysts make qualitative assessments or interview company officers and directors. This type of procedure has been avoided to include the largest possible number of firms in the sample.[7] Of course, time and cost concerns have also been issues.

Based on the IBGC's code of best practices, our 24 questions are grouped in table 3.1 according to four dimensions: disclosure; board composition and functioning; ethics and conflicts of interest; and shareholders' rights. This organization has turned out to be very similar to others in the literature, such as that in Black, Jang, and Kim (2006). These dimensions define the subindexes used in the tests in this chapter, but bear no influence on the weighting of individual questions in the index. The criteria and sources used to answer each question are outlined in table 3.1.

Table 3.1 Index Questions Applied to Brazilian Companies

Number	*Question (remarks about what has really been done)*
Dimension: disclosure	
1	Does the company's annual report, Web site, or public disclosure include information about potential conflicts of interest such as related party transactions? (*We verified if the annual report contained a section on related party transactions.*)
2	Does the company specify in its charter, annual reports, or other means any sanctions against management in the case of violations of desired corporate governance practices? (*We verified if the corporate charter included any sanctions.*)
3	Does the company produce its legally required financial reports by the required date? (*We verified if the company published its legally required reports up to April 30 of each year, which is the legal limit date.*)
4	Does the company use an international accounting standard (the International Accounting Standards Board or the U.S. Generally Accepted Accounting Principles)?
5	Does the company use one of the leading global auditing firms? (*The leading companies considered were PricewaterhouseCoopers, Coopers & Lybrand, Arthur Andersen, KPMG, Ernst & Young, and Deloitte Touche Tohmatsu.*)
6	Does the company disclose on its Web site or in its annual report compensation information for the chief executive officer and board members? (*We verified in the annual filings with the CVM if any compensation information was disclosed, even if not by individual executives.*)
Dimension: board composition and functioning	
7	Are the chairman of the board and the chief executive officer different persons? (*We verified if the name of the chairman and the chief executive officer were the same in the annual CVM filings.*)
8	Does the company have monitoring committees such as a compensation, nominations, or audit committee? (*We verified the existence of such committees in the corporate charter.*)
9	Is the board clearly made up of outside and possibly independent directors? (*We verified if directors were key executives in the company.*)
10	Is the board size between five and nine members, as recommended in the IBGC code of best practices? (*The size of the board was obtained from the annual filings with the CVM.*)
11	Do board members serve consecutive one-year terms, as recommended in the IBGC code of best practices? (*We verified the term for directors in the corporate charter.*)

(continued)

Table 3.1 Index Questions Applied to Brazilian Companies *(continued)*

Number	*Question (remarks about what has really been done)*
Dimension: ethics and conflicts of interest	
12	Is there a permanent fiscal board? (*We verified if the fiscal board was permanent according to the corporate charter.*)
13	Is the company free of any ongoing inquiries at CVM regarding governance malpractice? (*We verified on the CVM Web site if the company was listed among those being investigated.*)
14	Is the company free of any CVM convictions or fining for governance malpractice or other securities law violations in the last five years? (*We verified on the CVM Web site if the company was listed among those convicted or fined.*)
15	Does the company submit to arbitration in place of regular legal procedures in the case of corporate governance malpractice? (*We verified if the corporate charter privileges arbitration over regular legal proceedings.*)
16	Do ultimate controlling shareholders, considering shareholder agreements, own less than 50 percent of the voting shares? (*We computed this percentage from the annual filings with the CVM; we considered 50 percent as the threshold of control.*)
17	Is the percentage of nonvoting shares in total capital less than 20 percent? (*We computed this information from the number of shares in the annual CVM filings.*)
18	Is the ratio of the cash flow rights to the voting rights of ultimate controlling shareholders greater than 1? (*We computed this information using the procedure described in this chapter; the threshold for control was 50 percent.*)
Dimension: shareholder rights	
19	Does the company charter facilitate the process of voting for all shareholders beyond what is legally required? (*We compared the relevant contents of the corporate charter, if any exist, with the legal requirements at the time.*)
20	Does the company charter grant additional voting rights beyond what is legally required? (*We compared the relevant contents of the corporate charter, if any exist, with the legal requirements at the time.*)
21	Does the company grant tag-along rights beyond what is legally required? (*We compared the relevant contents of the corporate charter, if any exist, with the legal requirements at the time: 80 percent for voting shares and no tag-along rights for nonvoting shares.*)

(continued)

Table 3.1 Index Questions Applied to Brazilian Companies *(continued)*

Number	*Question (remarks about what has really been done)*
22	Are pyramid structures that decrease control concentration present? (*We used the annual filings to verify if there were indirect control structures and if they reduce the control concentration of the ultimate controlling shareholder.*)
23	Do shareholder agreements that decrease control concentration exist? (*We used the annual filings to verify if there were shareholder agreements and the terms of the agreements to check if they reduce the control concentration of the ultimate controlling shareholder.*)
24	Is the free-float greater than or equal to what is required in Bovespa's level 1 trading list (25 percent)? (*We verified in the annual CVM filings if the declared free-float was greater than 25 percent.*)

Source: Compiled by the authors.

Note: Each question corresponds to a yes or no answer. If the answer is yes, then the value of 1 is attributed to the question; otherwise, the value is 0. The index is the sum of the points for the questions. The maximum index value is 24. Index dimensions are simply for presentation purposes, and there is no weighting among questions. All questions are answered using public information disclosed by listed companies, not by means of potentially subjective interviews. Sources of information are, for example, company filings, charters, and annual reports made available through INFOinvest (http://www.infoinvest.com.br).

A preliminary list of questions was submitted to a number of practitioner panels in Rio de Janeiro and in São Paulo. The panels consisted of lawyers, controlling shareholders, representatives of IBGC, Bovespa, institutional investors, and CVM officers. These panels helped in refining the questions that were included in the final version of the questionnaire. Not all practices prescribed in best practice codes or in listing requirements are fully supported by the empirical academic literature, nor are they all free of contradiction or of measurement problems. In any case, it was decided to proceed with the questions listed in table 3.1.

The substitution effect described by John and Senbet (1998) is the idea that different corporate governance mechanisms are not independent of each other. Agrawal and Knoeber (1996) identify seven alternative, but not mutually exclusive mechanisms of agency control: shareholdings of insiders, shareholdings of institutions, shareholdings of outsiders, the use of outside directors, debt policy, the labor market for executives, and the market for corporate control. When the internally defined mechanisms (insider shareholding, the use of outside directors, debt policy, and reliance on the external labor market) are optimally set, there should be no effect on the value of corporations in a cross-sectional analysis. The index used in this chapter accounts for two of these dimensions simultaneously (insider shareholding and the use of outside directors) and uses leverage as a control variable. In Brazil, there are no takeovers because control, as is shown hereafter, is very concentrated and not really traded in stock exchanges. Meanwhile, the number of public firms per industry may be too small in relative terms to implement a meaningful proxy for the labor market for executives in any specific industry.

The remainder of this section provides a brief review of the literature associated with each of the four dimensions used for grouping questions. To keep the number of citations low, a limited number of survey papers are used and cited to support the inclusion of specific questions or sets of questions. Thus, not all papers provide evidence in support of each question in itself, but rather review the literature. A brief discussion of the findings for each of the dimensions in this section is also presented. For reasons of space, the percentages of yes answers to each question in each year are reported only in the text, but not in the tables. Full tabulations are available upon request.

Disclosure questions. The first set of six questions in table 3.1 is listed under the disclosure dimension. This set of questions deals with related party transactions, company sanctions against governance malpractice, compensation disclosure, the auditors, and accounting practices.

Greater disclosure in general leads to more value. Doidge, Karolyi, and Stulz (2004) and Gledson de Carvalho and Pennacchi (2005) present evidence about listing in the United States and at Bovespa's Novo Mercado, respectively. Firms that issue ADRs must meet a number of requirements that make them disclose more information and therefore become more transparent. Klapper and Love (2004) find that an ADR dummy is positively and significantly related to a governance index. Disclosing the pay of a chief executive officer is a good governance practice given the monitoring function of boards. Hermalin and Weisbach (2003) state that firms with weaker governance structures tend to pay chief executive officers more. However, in time, chief executive officers may acquire more leverage over boards, particularly if the officers are successful. Shleifer and Vishny (1997) maintain that there is a weak, but positive relationship between executive pay and performance.

The selection of an auditor with a global reputation may convey better disclosure practices. For instance, Michaely and Shaw (1995) find that more prestigious auditors are associated with U.S. initial public offerings that are less risky and that perform better in the long run. Coffee (2003) presents a thorough legal and economic discussion about the role of external auditors. Newman, Patterson, and Smith (2005) show that investment levels and outside shareholding are greater in countries where penalties for auditor failures and insider fund diversion are stiffer. Kohlbeck and Mayhew (2004) provide evidence that weak corporate governance practices are associated with more frequent related party transactions.

The answers to the questions in the disclosure dimension reveal that most firms include factual information about related party transactions in their annual reports; in most cases, they disclose related party transactions in a specific chapter of the explanatory notes. Companies often disclose transactions and their value, but they do not provide many details. Additionally, most companies do not specify any sanctions in their charters against management for corporate governance malpractice. About 30 percent of companies use international accounting standards, and about 75 percent use one of the leading global auditing firms. Most companies disclose information about the compensation of their chief executive officers and directors. However, because highly paid corporate officers see detailed disclosure of their compensation as a threat to their families and their own personal safety, the disclosure usually reports on the types of compensation schemes used and on the total values paid to chief officers and directors, without specifying amounts and compensation packages for each individual.

Board composition and operation. Becht, Bolton, and Röell (2003) and Hermalin and Weisbach (2003) state that the empirical work in this area is partially based on practical and policy insights rather than on theory-based hypotheses. The evidence regarding the link between board characteristics and performance does not always support the existence of a relationship, particularly in the United Kingdom and the United States. For example, Weir and Laing (2001) report that there is no direct effect of governance structure on performance, with an exception for board committees. Brown and Caylor (2006) find that the main board characteristics studied in the literature (independence, director compensation, and audit committees) do not explain performance in the United States. For Brazil, Leal and Oliveira (2002) review board practices and report that most firms do not adhere to best practice recommendations, while Da Silveira, Barros, and Famá (2003) find that, if the chief executive officer and the chairman of the board are the same person, firm value is significantly reduced. Becht, Bolton, and Röell (2003) present evidence that boards play a role in critical situations, while Klapper and Love (2004) include various board composition and operation dummies in their study, which finds a positive relationship between governance practices and value. Black, Jang, and Kim (2006) conclude that the proportion of outside directors is positively and significantly associated with corporate value in the Republic of Korea.

Through experiments, Gillette, Noe, and Rebello (2003) find that boards with outsider representation, even if the outsiders are not a majority, lead to the rejection of insider favored projects and the acceptance of institutionally preferred projects. A majority of outsiders on a board improves the results. Xie, Davidson, and DaDalt (2003) find that the composition and the qualifications of board and committee members are associated with lower management compensation. Hermalin and Weisbach (2003) believe that the composition of the board may not be important on a day-to-day basis, but that it is instrumental for infrequent and crucial situations. They present evidence that board composition and size are important in chief executive officer turnover, takeovers, and chief executive officer compensation issues.

Shleifer and Vishny (1997) argue that board effectiveness is a controversial issue and that boards may take too much time to act and be dominated by managers. Hermalin and Weisbach (2003) believe that board size proxies for a board's activity, explaining why smaller board sizes are better than larger boards that may be plagued by free rider and monitoring problems. The optimal board size is an open question, although the authors of this chapter adhere to a size within the five to nine member recommendation of the IBGC. John and Senbet (1998) report empirical evidence showing that the presence of monitoring committees (audit, nomination, and compensation committees) is positively related to factors associated with the benefits of monitoring. Klein (2002) shows that independent audit committees reduce the likelihood of irregularities in management earnings, improving transparency. Finally, the fiscal board is an optional device included in Brazilian corporate law. This device, which may resemble the U.S.–style audit committee, is formed upon the request of minority shareholders. However, the fiscal board is formed to ensure that the rights of minority shareholders are respected and their voices heard; it performs only a superficial role in the supervision of a company's financial reporting and control structure and provides virtually no monitoring or understanding of audit processes.[8]

The board questions described in this chapter have revealed that, in 36 percent of the cases in 2002, the chairman of the board and the chief executive officer were the same person. Most companies do not use committees, and 70 percent of boards are do not clearly consist of a majority of outside directors. About 37 percent of the boards do not fit the IBGC's recommended board size of five to nine members. In most boards, directors do not serve consecutive one-year terms, and most companies do not have a fiscal board mandated by minority shareholders.

Ethics and conflicts of interest. Eisenberg (1998) states that obedience to legal and ethical principles is consistent with maximization, even if greater gains might have been achieved by acting unlawfully or unethically, because law and ethics are channels through which maximization must flow. In line with this argument, two questions have been included about inquiries and convictions by the CVM. A question has also been asked about whether the company submits to a more rapid and less expensive dispute resolution system of arbitration instead of the usual legal proceedings, which are slow and expensive and offer countless opportunities for delay and appeals.

The questionnaire included three questions about the concentration of control; the questions relate to conflicts of interests between controlling and outside shareholders. There is a large literature on conflicts of interest, and the introduction to this chapter reviews some of this literature and the main implications for this chapter. Morck, Shleifer, and Vishny (1988) find that, in the United States, profitability first rises and then falls as the concentration of ownership increases. The rise is consistent with the incentive hypothesis, but, after a while, there is too much voting power concentration (entrenchment), which leads to the fall in corporate value due to a greater likelihood of expropriation. Claessens et al. (2002) find evidence for this relationship in Asia, while Lins (2003) finds stronger evidence for entrenchment than for incentives in 18 emerging markets. Leal, Carvalhal-da-Silva, and Valadares (2000) discover some evidence for entrenchment in Brazil. Shleifer and Vishny (1997) also review empirical evidence for the United States and believe that the ability of controlling shareholders to take advantage of minority shareholders is greater if the former have superior voting rights, if the concentration of their voting rights is greater than the percentage of their cash flow rights, or if they use indirect control structures or nonvoting shares. Shleifer and Vishny (1997) also comment that monitoring by large minority shareholders is effective only in countries with good investor protection. In countries with poor investment protection, only majority ownership would be effective. Lins (2003) maintains that the presence of large nonmanagerial block holders mitigates the negative effect of control concentration on value, particularly in countries with poor legal protection.

In the six questions under the ethics and conflicts of interest dimension of the index, most companies are not under investigation by the CVM and have not been convicted by the CVM or the judiciary on charges of violations of securities law. This appears to be largely due to the low quality of law enforcement in Brazil and does not necessarily represent good behavior on the part of Brazilian companies. This is probably also the reason why most companies refuse to submit to arbitration courts. While arbitration decisions are more rapid and are final, court decisions take a long time and offer many possibilities for appeals. According to stock exchange officers, controlling shareholders also believe that arbitration may be biased in favor of minority shareholders.

In 75 percent of the companies, controlling shareholders own more than 50 percent of the voting shares, and the percentage of nonvoting shares is greater than 20 percent in nearly 80 percent of the firms. Consequently, in almost 90 percent of cases, there is control leverage; the proportion of voting shares relative to the proportion of total capital indirectly held by the largest shareholder is greater than 1 because of indirect control structures and nonvoting shares.

Shareholder rights. Shleifer and Vishny (1997) state that providing minority shareholders with the ability and incentives to vote for the board of directors, as well as ensuring the ease of minority shareholders in access to voting, is a common governance arrangement for granting minority shareholders a voice because their investment is sunk in the firm. This also applies to inferior voting rights. When voting is concentrated, it is easy for controlling shareholders to be heard and to monitor management. Consequently, a question is included about shared control and agreements among major shareholders, because shareholder agreements may be good or bad for minority shareholders. We specifically ask if the terms of existing agreements are beneficial to minority shareholders. Shleifer and Vishny (1997) present evidence on the private benefits of control that materialize through large control premiums. Nenova (2001) reports high control premiums for Brazil during a period in which tag-along rights were removed from the law.[9] When these rights were reinstated, the control premiums decreased. Questions are thus included about voting procedures, voting rights, and tag-along rights that exceed legal requirements. Becht, Bolton, and Röell (2003) find that indirect ownership structures, particularly if they are coupled with the presence of nonvoting shares, may create strong incentives for the expropriation of minority shareholders. For instance, Claessens et al. (2002), Lins (2003), and Leal, Carvalhal-da-Silva, and Valadares (2000), respectively, find evidence that these structures are negatively related to value in Asian countries, emerging markets, and Brazil. One question about the presence of indirect control structures has thus been included. Finally, Becht, Bolton, and Röell (2003) list evidence that liquidity is positively associated with firm value and negatively associated with ownership concentration. Thus, a question is included on whether the free-float is greater than 25 percent, the minimum required for Bovespa's level 1 trading list.

The results for the shareholder rights dimension reveal that more than 90 percent of the companies do not facilitate voting by all shareholders beyond what is legally required and that nearly 90 percent of the companies do not grant any voting rights beyond what is legally required. Most companies do not grant better tag-along rights than what is mandated in the law. All of these numbers have decreased (improved) a little since 1998. Some indirect control structures actually dilute control instead of increasing it. This is the situation in about 20 percent of the cases. However, most shareholder agreements do not reduce control concentration. About 30 percent of companies offer insufficient liquidity to shareholders.

The next section discusses the overall characteristics of the data and of the CGI built from the questionnaire. It also presents an initial analysis of the relationship among corporate governance practices, value, and performance.

Empirical Results

Ownership Measures

Direct shareholding and indirect shareholding are analyzed. Direct shareholders are those who own shares in the public company itself. Considered here are all shareholders possessing 5 percent or more of the voting capital because this is the threshold for the mandatory identification of shareholders in Brazil. Indirect shareholding represents the stockholders who ultimately own the company. This is determined by accounting for the ownership of voting shares involved in control rights and the ownership of voting and nonvoting shares involved in cash flow rights. The ultimate percentage ownership is computed differently for cash flow and control rights. For example, if a shareholder has 51 percent of the total capital of company B, which owns 80 percent of the total capital of company A, the shareholder ultimately owns 40.8 percent of the total capital of company A (51 percent, times 80 percent). Assuming that all shares have the same voting rights, this shareholder controls 51 percent of company A (the minimum between 51 percent and 80 percent). The computation of ultimate control ownership uses the weakest-link method commonly employed in the literature. The ultimate control ownership is the sum of an ultimate shareholder's indirect control percentage or percentages (if there is more than one control chain) and the shareholder's direct control holdings, if any. This procedure is similar to the one used by La Porta, López-de-Silanes, and Shleifer (1999) and Claessens, Djankov, and Lang (2000), among others. In addition, to calculate ultimate ownership percentages for control and cash flow rights, it is necessary to adjust the percentages according to the terms of existing shareholder agreements. The conditions in each agreement are considered to lead to adjustments in the cash flow and voting rights percentages for the entire controlling block.

This ownership analysis is possible because mandatory annual filings with the regulatory authority show the shareholding composition of parent companies, when these exist, even if they are not public. Thus, shareholding composition is analyzed backwards through public and nonpublic parent corporations until it is possible to classify the ultimate owners into one of the following groups: individuals, institutional investors (banks, insurance companies, pension funds, foundations, or investment funds), foreigners (either individuals or entities), and the government. This is done for the filings relative to 1998, 2000, and 2002.

Results for ownership percentages in Brazil may be unusual relative to those in other countries. The use of nonvoting shares is rampant. The law still allows companies that went public before 2001 to maintain two-thirds of their shares as nonvoting shares, while the current legal maximum is 50 percent for companies that went public after 2001. More than 90 percent of trading volume is in nonvoting shares, while the voting shares of a dual-class company trade little, if they trade at all. Thus, it is not surprising that direct control ownership percentages are high. Few companies have only voting shares. Saito (2003) presents evidence that the price differential between voting and nonvoting stocks is negative because of the low liquidity of voting stocks.

Table 3.2 Direct and Indirect Shareholding Composition of Brazilian Companies, 1998–2002

		Direct ownership (%)			*Ultimate ownership (%)*		
Year	*Number*	*Voting*	*Cash flow*	*Voting over cash flow*	*Voting*	*Cash flow*	*Voting over cash flow*
Major shareholder							
1998	240	69	47	1.47	66	33	2.00
2000	238	70	47	1.49	65	37	1.77
2002	214	71	50	1.42	68	34	2.00
Three largest shareholders							
1998	240	87	59	1.47	83	50	1.66
2000	238	88	60	1.47	84	50	1.68
2002	214	89	60	1.48	85	51	1.67

Source: Compiled by the authors.

Note: The table shows median percentage direct and indirect shareholding concentration of Brazilian companies listed on the São Paulo Stock Exchange. The ratio of voting to cash flow is the median percentage of the concentration of voting rights divided by the median percentage of the concentration of cash flow rights. See the text for additional details.

Table 3.2 shows the ownership results. As expected, ownership is highly concentrated. The largest shareholder has a median of 71 percent (50 percent) of the voting (cash flow) rights in direct ownership and 68 percent (34 percent) of the voting (cash flow) rights indirectly, indicating that the use of nonvoting shares and indirect control structures leads to a large separation (wedge) in voting and cash flow rights, with a median of two times. It is interesting to note that the very high median direct ownership of the largest controlling shareholder in Brazil seems to be much higher than the figures reported in the ownership examples in La Porta, López-de-Silanes, and Shleifer (1999) and Claessens, Djankov, and Lang (2000) and that the direct control percentage of the largest direct shareholder is larger than the control percentage of the largest ultimate shareholder. This occurs in all but one of the ownership map examples displayed in Valadares (2002) and Valadares and Leal (2000) for 1996. As noted above, the inordinate use of nonvoting shares in Brazil appears to explain this phenomenon.

An example of an ownership structure that is more in line with the international evidence occurs when there is more than one control chain. Suppose company A is owned by companies B and C, which have

30 percent and 25 percent of the voting rights, respectively. Company B is then owned by family F with 50 percent of the votes, and company C is also owned by family F with 60 percent of the votes. In the chain from the family to B and on to A, the family owns 30 percent of A. In the other chain, the family owns 25 percent of A. Their ultimate ownership of A is 55 percent. In Brazil, the most common type of ownership structure is one in which there already is a shareholder who directly controls more than 50 percent of the votes. Then, ultimate shareholders own a smaller percentage of the firms higher up in the chain. Because the weakest link method is used (that is, the smallest percentage in the chain is the control percentage of the ultimate shareholder), it is quite common to see percentages of indirect ultimate control ownership that are less than the percentages of direct control ownership.

The point is illustrated in the ownership map in figure 3.1. For Companhia Energética de Pernambuco (CELPE), an energy utility, there is a single direct controlling shareholder, the privately held company Guaraniana, with 94.9 percent of the voting rights (V) and 85.1 percent of the

Figure 3.1 Example of Ownership Structure: CELPE

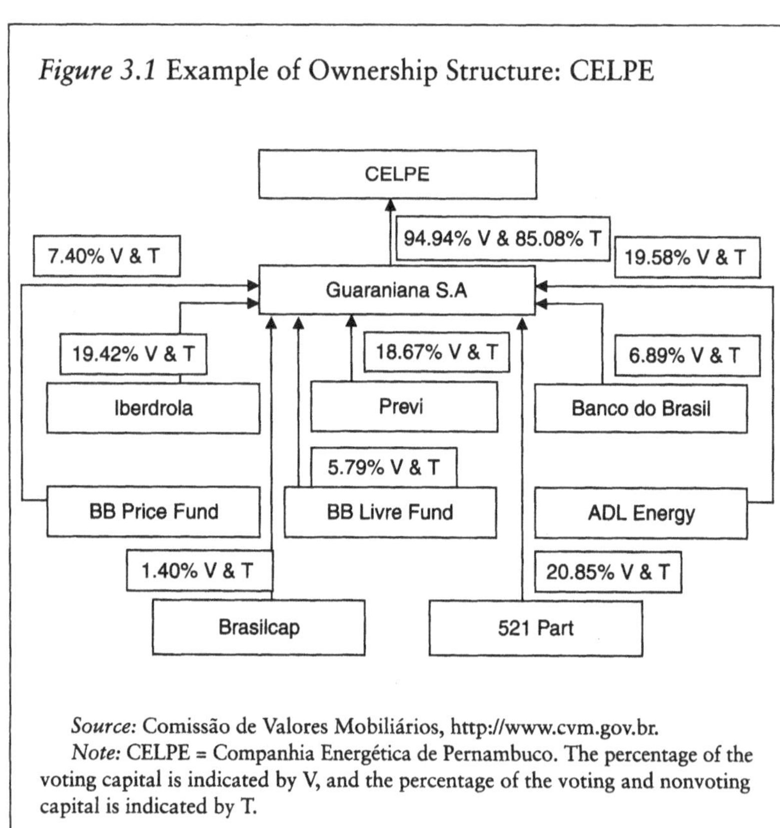

Source: Comissão de Valores Mobiliários, http://www.cvm.gov.br.
Note: CELPE = Companhia Energética de Pernambuco. The percentage of the voting capital is indicated by V, and the percentage of the voting and nonvoting capital is indicated by T.

total capital (T). Indirectly, the largest shareholder is 521 Part, a holding company, with 20.9 percent of the votes. The research presented here does not aim to classify firms as widely held, and 50 percent is used as a cutoff to identify the nature of the ultimate controlling shareholders. This cutoff percentage is usually lower in other studies, such as 20 percent in La Porta, López-de-Silanes, and Shleifer (1999). The cutoff does not affect the ownership percentages presented here.

Voting rights concentration has slightly increased over time. A more detailed analysis of ownership is presented in Valadares and Leal (2000) for 1996, Leal, Carvalhal-da-Silva, and Valadares (2000) for 1998, and Carvalhal-da-Silva and Leal (2004) for 2002. The 1996 data in Valadares and Leal (2000) were hand collected and are not available in the database used here; these authors did not adjust for shareholder agreements nor did they include government-owned companies.

Table 3.3 shows other ownership characteristics of our sample. Ultimate foreign ownership hovers between 25 percent and 29 percent. Ultimate government ownership, as well as institutional ownership, stays between 8 percent and 9 percent of the total number of firms. About 75 percent of the firms present an indirect control structure, and 20 percent of the firms have agreements among their largest shareholders. Voting shares have typically represented a little less than 50 percent of the total number of shares, while outstanding free-floating shares are about 50 percent of total shares. The proximity of these last two percentages is not a coincidence. Most shares that trade in the stock exchange are nonvoting shares anyway. About 90 percent of trading volume at the Bovespa Stock Exchange have involved nonvoting shares in the last few years.

Table 3.3 Ownership Characteristics of the 1998, 2000, and 2002 Samples (percent)

Year	*FOR*	*GOV*	*INST*	*PYR*	*AGR*	*VOTE*	*FREE*
1998	28.8	8.8	8.3	75.4	20.0	47.3	50.7
2000	28.4	8.9	8.5	77.5	19.5	46.9	50.3
2002	24.9	8.0	8.9	75.2	21.5	46.3	49.0

Source: Compiled by the authors from company filings with the CVM.

Note: The ultimate ownership by foreigners (FOR), institutions (INST, banks, insurance companies, pension funds, foundations, or investment funds), and the government (GOV) is represented after considering indirect control structures and shareholder agreements. The remaining balance is owned by families. The percentage of companies with indirect control structures (PYR) and shareholder agreements (AGR) is also indicated. Vote (VOTE) is the percentage of voting shares in the total capital. Free (free-float or FREE) is the percentage of shares outstanding, voting and nonvoting, available for trading in the market.

Value, the CGI, and Control Variables

Researchers have employed Tobin's q to measure the discount in market values resulting from expropriation.[10] Tobin's q is constructed by dividing the market value of assets by the replacement cost of assets. DaDalt, Donaldson, and Garner (2003) assert that Tobin's original intent was to measure the firm's propensity to invest. However, q has been used as a general measure of the relative value of firms, and the original intent is not inconsistent with our own purposes in measuring the relative market value of firms.

An estimate of the numerator of Tobin's q is the book value of assets, minus the book value of common equity, plus the market value of common equity. The denominator is the book value of assets. Other forms of computing q are described in DaDalt, Donaldson, and Garner (2003). These authors find that simpler computations of q should be preferred over more complex estimates, particularly if data availability is a concern, which is our case. In our robustness tests, we used the ratio of price to book (P/B), the ratio of price to sales (P/S), and the ratio of price to cash flow (P/CF), as defined in the annex, as alternate proxies for relative firm market value.

To estimate Tobin's q, we used the market value of equity computed by Economática, which uses the market price of the most liquid stock (be it voting or nonvoting), times the total number of shares (voting and nonvoting). In Brazil, the most liquid shares are often the nonvoting shares. Voting shares are held by controlling shareholders and are rarely traded in the market. One may think that the equity market value we used may show a control discount because it largely reflects the market prices of nonvoting shares. However, the case is actually the opposite. While there are control premiums in Brazil, these premiums do not show strongly in daily market prices, but in private control transfer transactions that are not enacted in the stock exchange.[11] However, as Saito (2003) shows, the most liquid shares (the nonvoting) usually trade at premiums over the voting shares on a day-to-day basis in the market. There is a liquidity discount applied on most voting shares in the Brazilian exchanges. Thus, our proxy for Tobin's q and relative market value is not affected by a control discount. We also have no reason to believe that the use of book values to compute Tobin's q is affected by inflation any more than it would be in any other country; this proxy has been used because inflation rates in Brazil have been relatively low since 1995.

Table 3.4 shows descriptive statistics on our variables. For brevity, we present the statistics computed for each firm-year. Thus, the observations for the same firm in 1998, 2000, and 2002 are considered different observations. The median Tobin's q is 0.87; the median P/B is 0.55; and the median dividend payout is 24 percent. Most Brazilian firms have traded below book value for a long time. The P/B for the entire market

Table 3.4 Descriptive Statistics on All Variables

Variable	*Mean*	*Median*	*Standard deviation*	*Minimum*	*Maximum*
Performance measures					
Q	0.91	0.87	0.40	0.07	4.77
Payout	31%	24%	47%	0%	460%
P/B	0.95	0.55	2.14	-5.85	26.20
P/S	1.25	0.37	5.03	0.00	62.72
P/CF	5.72	1.75	47.17	-227.89	604.03
Governance and ownership measures					
CGI	10	10	2	4	19
1VDIR	70%	70%	22%	9%	100%
1TDIR	50%	48%	26%	3%	100%
1V/TDIR	1.68	1.40	0.76	0.72	10.29
3VDIR	83%	88%	18%	18%	100%
3TDIR	61%	60%	25%	8%	100%
3V/TDIR	1.58	1.34	0.70	0.83	10.29
5VDIR	85%	90%	16%	18%	100%
5TDIR	63%	64%	24%	9%	100%
5V/TDIR	1.56	1.32	0.69	0.83	10.29
1VIND	65%	66%	26%	6%	100%
1TIND	41%	34%	27%	1%	100%
1V/TIND	2.81	1.72	4.89	0.84	56.94
3VIND	78%	84%	21%	18%	100%
3TIND	51%	50%	26%	2%	100%
3V/TIND	2.16	1.59	2.73	0.62	46.32
5VIND	82%	88%	19%	18%	100%
5TIND	55%	53%	26%	4%	100%
5V/TIND	1.90	1.54	1.30	0.83	15.37
FOR	0.28	0.00	0.45	0.00	1.00
GOV	0.09	0.00	0.28	0.00	1.00
INST	0.09	0.00	0.28	0.00	1.00
PYR	0.76	1.00	0.43	0.00	1.00
AGR	0.20	0.00	0.40	0.00	1.00
ADR	0.20	0.00	0.40	0.00	1.00
NM	0.14	0.00	0.35	0.00	1.00
FREE	48%	50%	26%	0%	100%
VOTE	55%	47%	23%	27%	100%

(continued)

Table 3.4 Descriptive Statistics on All Variables *(continued)*

Variable	*Mean*	*Median*	*Standard deviation*	*Minimum*	*Maximum*
Control variables					
CA/TA	38%	36%	21%	0%	91%
Growth	20%	15%	40%	-86%	778%
Leverage	60%	59%	26%	1%	270%
ROA	10%	10%	9%	-41%	38%
Size	13.52	13.59	1.70	8.96	18.62
Volatility	86%	70%	62%	10%	520%

Source: Compiled by the authors.

Note: The averages pool the values for all firm-years used, that is, the values for the same firm in 1998, 2000, and 2002 are considered as three different observations. See the annex for a definition of each variable.

has fluctuated between 0.5 and 1.6 between 1993 and 2002, according to Standard & Poor's (2003) for firms included in the Standard & Poor's–International Finance Corporation Global Brazil index (70 or so, usually among the largest). Low liquidity, a series of economic crises, volatility, and high real interest rates have kept stock prices depressed for a long time. Thus, Brazil's Tobin's q is also low relative to that in other emerging markets, and it offers the lowest ROA of 14 emerging markets studied by Klapper and Love (2004). All profitable Brazilian firms in a given year must pay at least 25 percent of tax-adjusted net income to shareholders, and most pay only this minimum. It is not surprising that the median dividend payout is 24 percent of unadjusted net income.

The average CGI is 10 of 24 possible points, ranging between 4 and 19. As we have seen already, there is a high concentration of voting rights, and the value of the median indirect wedge between voting rights and cash flow rights is 1.72 for the largest shareholder and 1.54 for the five largest shareholders. We also highlight the median for some of our control variables: 59 percent for leverage, 15 percent for sales growth per year, and 10 percent for the ROA. The average for the ADR and the Novo Mercado dummies shows that 20 percent of the firms have ADR programs, while 14 are listed in Bovespa's Novo Mercado.

In table 3.5, we show the progress of the CGI over time. The number of companies with a score above 16, the upper third of potential scores, went from zero in 1998 and 2000 to three in 2002. All three are listed in the Novo Mercado. This indicates that the score distribution is becoming slightly more skewed to the right, with a few outlying firms achieving better levels of corporate governance practice. This trend is slowly moving

Table 3.5 Score Distribution for the CGI and Four Subindexes, 1998, 2000, and 2002

Year	*Minimum*	*First quartile*	*Median*	*Third quartile*	*Maximum*	*Number in upper third score*
CGI						
1998	4	8	10	11	15	0
2000	5	9	10	11	16	0
2002	5	9	10	12	19	3
Disclosure						
1998	1	3	4	4	5	43
2000	0	3	4	4	6	50
2002	1	3	4	5	6	55
Board practices						
1998	0	1	2	3	5	5
2000	0	1	2	3	5	4
2002	0	1	2	3	6	12
Ethics and conflicts of interest						
1998	0	2	2	3	5	1
2000	0	2	2	3	5	3
2002	0	2	2	3	5	5
Shareholder rights						
1998	0	1	2	2	5	2
2000	0	1	2	2	5	1
2002	0	1	2	2	6	2

Source: Compiled by the authors.

Note: The CGI score may range from 0 to 24. Each subindex score may range from 0 to 6. The upper third of potential scores started at above 16 for the CGI and above 4 for the subindexes.

the sample to higher scores for corporate governance. Even though the median is constant at 10 points, both the minimum and the maximum have gone up, as well as the first and the third quartiles, demonstrating that there is a modest general improvement in the corporate governance practices captured by our index. When we examine the subindexes, we notice that Brazilian firms score better in disclosure, although they are below Standard & Poor's disclosure index average for emerging markets reported by Patel, Balic, and Bwakira (2002). The number of firms in the upper third of the possible score for this subindex is by far the largest. On the opposite end are shareholder rights. This subindex shows the lowest number of firms in the upper third of the score range. The other two subindexes, board practices and ethics and conflicts of interest, have registered some improvement as well. These figures indicate that Brazilian firms may have a long way to go in terms of the quality of their corporate governance practices.[12]

Figures 3.2 and 3.3 illustrate the relationships between the CGI and Tobin's q and the CGI and firm size. Both figures suggest that there is a positive relationship between the CGI and these variables. In fact, firm size concerns us in a particular way in our ensuing analysis. Table 3.6 shows the correlations among selected variables. The correlations between the CGI and the indirect voting rights and cash flow rights are negative. Better governance practices are inversely associated with ownership concentration. Curiously, the correlation between the CGI and the wedge is positive, but very low. We would like at least some of the control variables to be strongly correlated with the governance variables and to be weakly correlated with Tobin's q if they are to be candidates for instrumental variables in our robustness checks. That seems to be the case judged by the evidence of the correlations. The GGI is negatively related to volatility and positively related to size. Actually, the two largest correlations in the table

Figure 3.2 CGI and Tobin's q in 2002

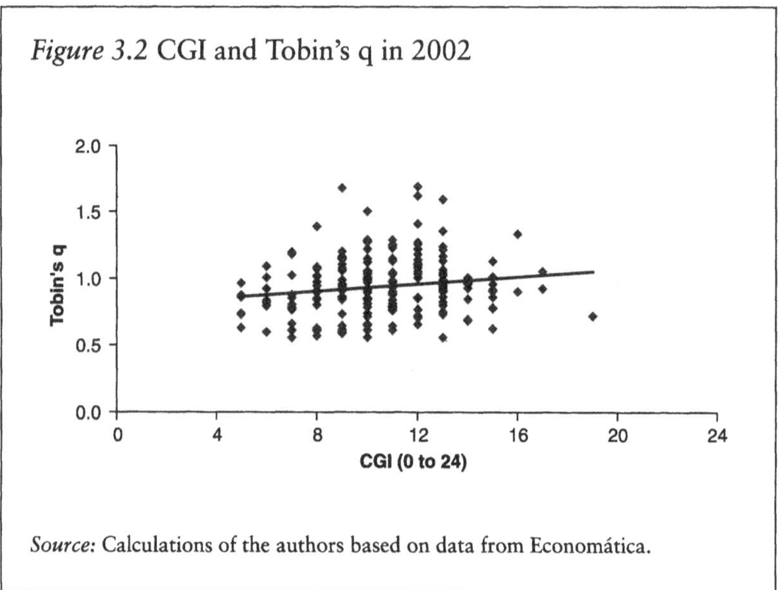

Source: Calculations of the authors based on data from Economática.

Figure 3.3 The CGI and the Log of Asset Size in 2002

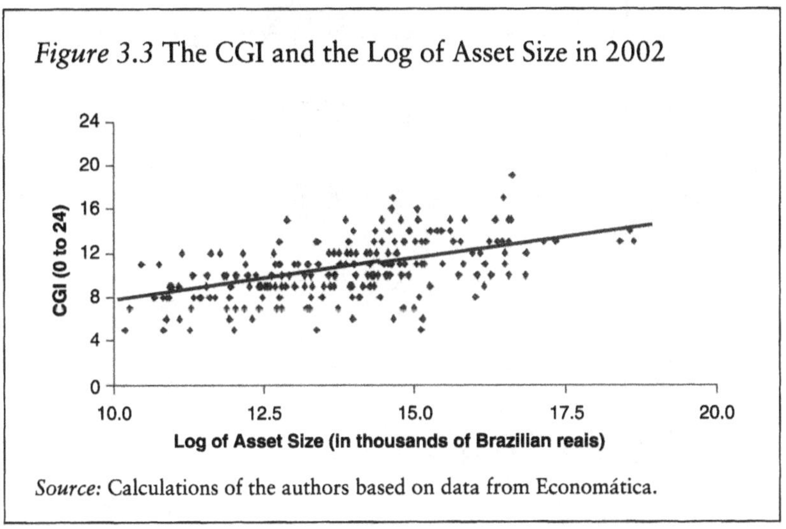

Source: Calculations of the authors based on data from Economática.

are those between size and the CGI (0.50) and between concentrations of voting shares and concentrations of nonvoting shares (0.74).

We use four control variables. We expect leverage to be positively related to governance because more well-governed and more transparent firms may use more debt, and debt may mitigate agency conflicts. In Brazil, debt financing is scarce and expensive because the federal government takes most of the savings available in the market. It is reasonable to expect that larger and more transparent firms are in a better position to use more debt than are other firms. Table 3.6 shows a positive correlation between leverage and the CGI. We expect riskier firms to rely on poorer governance practices because greater risk may lead to more concentration in control and greater expropriation of minority shareholders. We find a negative correlation between volatility and the CGI. Growing firms may find greater need for external finance and may benefit from improving their corporate governance practices. We find a positive, but low correlation between our proxy for growth and the CGI. We have also used the ROA as a proxy for growth and profitability in some of our models and find a positive relationship between the ROA and the CGI.

Klapper and Love (2004), Durnev and Kim (2005), and Black, Jang, and Kim (2006) investigate whether their control variables are determinants of corporate governance practices. If governance is determined by their control variables, they believe that, when the variables are included in a model of performance as a function of governance and governance turns out to be significant, then this would represent a control for endogeneity. Klapper and Love deal with the problem using control variables such as size, past growth, capital intensity, an ADR dummy, legal system effectiveness measures, and an interaction term between the legal system

Table 3.6 Correlation among Selected Variables

	Variable	2	3	4	5	6	7	8	9	10	11	12	13	14	*Size*
1	Q	–.11	.44	.17	–0.3	.03	.02	.17	.03	–.11	.09	.09	–.01	.13	.10
2	Payout		–.02	.03	–.02	–.01	.00	.04	.00	–.06	–.17	–.06	–.07	.04	.05
3	P/B			–.03	.04	.07	.00	–.02	–.01	–.02	.07	.24	–.02	–.12	–.03
4	CGI				–.36	–.22	.11	.04	.12	.09	.13	–.22	.06	.19	.50
5	1 VIND					.74	–.10	.07	–.13	.07	–.04	.07	–.03	–.14	–.07
6	1 TIND						–.38	.25	–.04	.07	.00	.00	.01	–.05	.02
7	1 V/TIND							–.11	–.01	–.06	.05	.07	.05	.00	.02
8	FOR								–.19	–.19	.02	–.07	–.03	.26	.15
9	INST									–.09	.05	–.03	.00	–.01	.07
10	GOV										–.01	–.07	–.03	–.06	.28
11	Leverage											–.12	.04	.18	.20
12	Volatility												–.03	–.28	–.31
13	Growth													.00	.11
14	ROA														.25

Source: Complied by the authors.

Note: The correlations are for the pooled values for all firm-years used, that is, the values for the same firm in 1998, 2000, and 2002 are considered as three different observations. See the annex for definitions of the variables.

and the existence of ADRs. They also state that unobserved country effects account for a large variation in firm-level governance rankings. Himmelberg, Hubbard, and Palia (1999) maintain that it is likely unobserved factors may still affect value and corporate governance practices even if one uses an extensive list of control variables.

Table 3.7 presents our ordinary least squares (OLS) analysis of the relationship between our control variables and the corporate governance variables. We have also included two dummies for listings in Bovespa's Novo Mercado (NM) and for the existence of ADR programs. None of the variables maintains a consistent significant association with all corporate governance variables for every year. We find it difficult to use these variables as joint determinants of the CGI, other governance variables, and corporate value. The ADR dummy is negatively and significantly related to the ultimate voting rights percentage for the largest shareholder and to the wedge between voting rights and cash flow rights. Only size is positively and significantly related to the CGI for the three years. The ADR and the Novo Mercado dummies are positively and significantly related to the CGI in 2002.

We expect that, at least, the inclusion of size may help control for endogeneity. Actually, we build an instrumental variable based on size in our robustness checks. We maintain the other variables in our empirical models as well. We return to the endogeneity problem in the section on robustness checks, but, first, we present our empirical exercises with a set of models using ownership data, the CGI, and control variables.

Multivariate Regression Analysis

Market valuation. We have first analyzed value as a function of our ownership measures and the CGI. We run our regressions separately for each year, 1998, 2000, and 2002. Table 3.8 presents our results for Tobin's q for 2002. The results for 1998 and 2000 are practically the same, and we have therefore omitted them. Model 1 includes only the CGI and the control variables. For a 1 unit increase in the CGI, q goes up by 2.3 percent. This corresponds to an increase of 5.75 percent in the share value of a company with the average q and leverage of the sample. Volatility and ROA are positively related to q as well. Models 2, 3, and 4 omit the CGI and include the largest ultimate shareholder's percentage of voting rights, the percentage of cash flow rights, and the wedge, respectively. None is significant. Model 5 includes these three ownership variables together, but there is no significance here either. Models 6, 7, and 8 include these three ownership variables and the CGI. Still, the CGI is significant and positively related to q. For a 1 unit CGI score change, q would increase by between 2.7 percent and 3.1 percent, depending on the model. Model 9 includes the ADR and Novo Mercado dummies; there is no tangible effect. Some of our control variables are significant and present the expected

Table 3.7 Control and Corporate Governance Variables

	2002			2000			1998		
	Coefficient	*t*	*p*	*Coefficient*	*t*	*p*	*Coefficient*	*t*	*p*
1VIND on									
Intercept	**0.5492**	3.1453	0.0019	**0.6269**	3.6651	0.0003	**0.7764**	5.0333	0.0000
Volatility	0.0367	1.1972	0.2326	0.0225	0.6577	0.5114	−0.0178	−0.6298	0.5295
Growth	−0.0098	−0.3039	0.7615	−0.0488	−0.9151	0.3611	−0.0333	−0.5409	0.5891
ROA	−0.2576	−1.3013	0.1946	−0.1486	−0.7130	0.4766	**−0.7655**	−3.5741	0.0004
Size	0.0082	0.6536	0.5141	0.0021	0.1740	0.8620	0.0016	0.1372	0.8910
Leverage	0.0289	0.4448	0.6569	0.0253	0.3512	0.7258	−0.1085	−1.5548	0.1214
ADR	**−0.0982**	−2.0602	0.0406	−0.0563	−1.2088	0.2280	**−0.1143**	−2.3034	0.0221
NM	0.0173	0.3141	0.7538						
Adj R^2	0.0507			0.0208			0.0596		
F	1.5716		0.1455	0.8112		0.5621	3.5233		0.0023
1V/TIND on									
Intercept	0.0541	0.2948	0.7685	0.2167	1.1985	0.2320	0.4000	2.5243	0.0123
Volatility	0.0434	1.3486	0.1789	−0.0151	−0.4182	0.6762	−0.0303	−1.0452	0.2970
Growth	0.0025	0.0753	0.9401	−0.0776	−1.3749	0.1705	0.1042	1.6498	0.1003
ROA	−0.1088	−0.5234	0.6013	−0.0891	−0.4046	0.6862	**−0.4372**	−1.9869	0.0481
Size	**0.0290**	2.2046	0.0286	0.0199	1.5611	0.1199	0.0115	0.9852	0.3255
Leverage	−0.0053	−0.0776	0.9382	−0.0124	−0.1626	0.8710	**−0.1639**	−2.2863	0.0231
ADR	**−0.1485**	−2.9652	0.0034	**−0.1235**	−2.5102	0.0128	**−0.1583**	−3.1057	0.0021

(continued)

Table 3.7 Control and Corporate Governance Variables *(continued)*

	2002			*2000*			*1998*		
	Coefficient	*t*	*p*	*Coefficient*	*t*	*p*	*Coefficient*	*t*	*p*
1V/TIND on									
NM	−0.0565	−0.9751	0.3307						
Adj R^2	0.0327			0.0110			0.0566		
F	2.0302		0.0528	1.4353		0.2020	3.3890		0.0032
CGI on									
Intercept	**3.4090**	2.3429	0.0201	**2.3473**	1.8240	0.0694	1.4960	1.3545	0.1769
Volatility	**−0.4714**	−1.8459	0.0663	−0.2565	−0.9959	0.3204	0.0048	0.0239	0.9810
Growth	0.0223	0.0835	0.9336	0.4183	1.0415	0.2987	−0.4118	−0.9353	0.3506
ROA	1.3926	0.8442	0.3995	0.3700	0.2360	0.8137	**2.8961**	1.8884	0.0602
Size	**0.4807**	4.6098	0.0000	**0.5601**	6.1782	0.0000	**0.5857**	7.2202	0.0000
Leverage	0.3174	0.5868	0.5579	0.2673	0.4935	0.6221	0.6773	1.3556	0.1766
ADR	**0.7716**	1.9417	0.0535	0.3071	0.8765	0.3817	0.5002	1.4077	0.1606
NM	**1.4673**	3.1899	0.0016			—	—	—	—
Adj R^2	0.3198			0.2259		—	0.2351	—	—
F	15.3033		0.0000	12.4265		0.0000	13.2403	—	0.0000

Source: Compiled by the authors.

Note: OLS regressions of control variables and the indirect voting rights percentages of the largest shareholder, the wedge, and the CGI. The Novo Mercado (NM) dummy appears only in 2002 because this listing category did not exist in 2000 and 1998. All variables are defined in the Appendix.

Significant coefficients up to the 10% level are shown in boldface.

Table 3.8 OLS Regressions of Tobin's q on Corporate Governance Measures, 2002

Independent variable	*Dependent variable = Tobin's q*								
	(1)	*(2)*	*(3)*	*(4)*	*(5)*	*(6)*	*(7)*	*(8)*	*(9)*
Constant	0.2185	0.1823	0.2080	0.2532	0.2320	0.1194	−0.0897	−0.1199	0.2213
	(0.4007)	(0.5024)	(0.4264)	(0.3321)	(0.3995)	(0.6669)	(0.7265)	(0.6533)	(0.5070)
CGI	*0.0228**					*0.0311***	*0.0265***	*0.0273***	*0.0254**
	(0.0837)					*(0.0280)*	*(0.0407)*	*(0.0367)*	*(0.0635)*
1VIND		0.1040			−0.0569	0.0404	−0.0105	0.0071	−0.0324
		(0.3590)			(0.7467)	(0.8225)	(0.9493)	(0.9666)	(0.9609)
1TIND			0.1558		0.2087	0.2013	0.2105	0.1891	−0.5667
			(0.1422)		(0.2402)	(0.2526)	(0.1925)	(0.2605)	(0.4213)
1V/TIND				−0.0021	0.0020	0.0009	−0.0013	−0.0017	−0.0176
				(0.7223)	(0.7680)	(0.8945)	(0.8287)	(0.7880)	(0.4175)
(1VIND)2									0.1327
									(0.7844)
(1TIND)2									0.6367
									(0.2622)
(1V/TIND)2									0.0002
									(0.5440)
Leverage							*0.6121****	*0.6000****	*0.5997****
							(0.0000)	*(0.0000)*	*(0.0000)*
Dummy foreigner								0.0343	0.0380
								(0.6281)	(0.6111)

(continued)

Table 3.8 OLS Regressions of Tobin's q on Corporate Governance Measures, 2002 *(continued)*

Independent variable	*Dependent variable = Tobin's q*								
	(1)	*(2)*	*(3)*	*(4)*	*(5)*	*(6)*	*(7)*	*(8)*	*(9)*
Dummy government								−0.0693	−0.0483
								(0.5332)	(0.6697)
Dummy institutional								−0.0126	−0.0017
								(0.9010)	(0.9866)
Dummy ADR									0.0994
									(0.1920)
Dummy NM									0.0225
									(0.8045)
Volatility	*0.2369****	*0.2206****	*0.2172****	*0.2257****	*0.2160****	*0.2297****	*0.1900****	*0.1913****	*0.1818****
	(0.0000)	*(0.0000)*	*(0.0000)*	*(0.0000)*	*(0.0000)*	*(0.0000)*	*(0.0001)*	*(0.0001)*	*(0.0002)*
Growth	−0.0702	−0.0688	−0.0704	−0.0688	−0.0719	−0.0713	−0.0529	−0.0534	−0.0417
	(0.1811)	(0.1921)	(0.1805)	(0.1928)	(0.1747)	(0.1740)	(0.2719)	(0.2716)	(0.3967)
ROA	*0.5865**	*0.6376***	*0.6249**	*0.6100**	*0.6125**	*0.6115**	*0.8004****	*0.7346***	*0.7495***
	(0.0686)	*(0.0500)*	*(0.0529)*	*(0.0599)*	*(0.0606)*	*(0.0586)*	*(0.0075)*	*(0.0178)*	*(0.0163)*
Size	0.0207	0.0362**	0.0348**	0.0364**	0.0340*	0.0136	0.0062	0.0086	−0.0059
	(0.2950)	*(0.0423)*	*(0.0500)*	*(0.0422)*	*(0.0593)*	(0.4974)	(0.7356)	(0.6617)	(0.7896)
F-statistic	51,978	47,154	50,093	45,561	35,676	37,933	84,203	63,200	46,514
	(0.0002)	(0.0004)	(0.0002)	(0.0006)	(0.0012)	(0.0004)	(0.0000)	(0.0000)	(0.0000)
Adjusted R2	0.0897	0.0802	0.0860	0.0770	0.0778	0.0950	0.2387	0.2306	0.2257

Source: Compiled by the authors.

Note: The columns show the results for each model, 1–9. All variables are defined in the annex. P-values are shown in parentheses.

* significant at 10 percent

** significant at 5 percent

*** significant at 1 percent

signs. Despite their significance, the CGI is always significant. For the range of coefficients in table 3.8, the stock price would go up from 5.75 percent to 7.75 percent for each 1 point increase in the CGI score. This is a statistically and economically significant result. We find support for the positive relationship of overall governance practices and value in this set of models. Our overall corporate governance practices measure includes ownership-related questions. However, we do not find any evidence that indirect control and holdings of cash flow rights by the largest shareholder influence value.

We have divided our index into four groups of six questions each. The groups represent disclosure practices, board functioning and composition, ethics and conflicts of interest, and shareholder rights. In table 3.9, we reproduce model 8 in table 3.8 for 2002, but, this time, using each of the four groups of the index separately; our intention is to verify which subindexes matter most. Our findings show that the results are largely dominated by our disclosure subindex. This should come as no surprise. Firms scored higher in disclosure, and the disclosure scoring is more discriminating among firms than are the remaining portions of the index related to other aspects of corporate governance practices. While a 1 point rise in the overall CGI has an impact of 2.73 percent on Tobin's q, which is about the same magnitude for the corporate governance subindexes of the CGI, a 1 point increase in the disclosure subindex has an impact of 7.24 percent on Tobin's q. In Brazil, the largest impact so far comes from disclosure, probably because the use of best practice corporate governance is still limited.

It is possible that some of our disclosure questions are related to company size, particularly questions 4 and 5, which inquire about whether the auditors are with one of the big six auditing companies and whether the company uses international accounting standards. We have computed the correlation of the answers for each question with our proxy for company size. We do not show the detailed results here, but questions 4 and 5, as we suspected, present the two largest correlation coefficients, at 0.53 and 0.51, respectively. No other correlation coefficient was larger than 0.35, and most were close to zero. We proceeded to compute a reduced version of the CGI by excluding questions 4 and 5. The result is shown in model 6 in table 3.9. The CGI coefficient is of the same order of magnitude as in model 8 in table 3.8; however, the CGI coefficient is no longer significant. Company size, as we discuss elsewhere below, is a factor in terms of the impact of good corporate governance practices. We have also determined whether the removal of additional questions according to their correlation to company size would substantially affect our results. We have excluded all questions with correlations above 0.25 (questions 1, 4, 5, 7–9, 12, and 20). The results are essentially the same as the results found after the removal of questions 4 and 5 only; they are not reported here.

Table 3.9 OLS Regressions of Tobin's q on Corporate Governance Subindexes, 2002

Group	*(1)*	*(2)*	*(3)*	*(4)*	*(5)*	*(6)*	*(7)*
Constant	−0.0264 (0.9200)	−0.0100 (0.9699)	−0.1263 (0.6805)	−0.0337 (0.8989)	−0.1199 (0.6533)	−0.1451 (0.5999)	0.5175 (0.0983)
Disclosure	*0.0724*** *(0.0294)*						
Board		0.0236 (0.3282)					
Conflicts			0.0275 (0.5036)				
Shareholder rights				0.0327 (0.2730)			
CGI					*0.0273*** *(0.0367)*		
CGI reduced						0.0210 (0.1368)	
Prin 1							*0.1239**** *(0.0008)*
Prin 2							0.0012 (0.9717)
Prin 3							*−0.0549** *(0.0748)*

(continued)

Table 3.9 OLS Regressions of Tobin's q on Corporate Governance Subindexes, 2002 *(continued)*

Group	*(1)*	*(2)*	*(3)*	*(4)*	*(5)*	*(6)*	*(7)*
Prin 4							*0.0675*** *(0.0234)*
Prin 5							−0.0182 (0.5739)
Prin 6							−0.0197 (0.5308)
1VIND	−0.0891 (0.5871)	−0.0733 (0.6586)	0.0058 (0.9780)	−0.08678 (0.6003)	0.0071 (0.9666)	−0.0134 (0.9377)	0.1439 (0.4446)
1TIND	0.2325 (0.1680)	0.2060 (0.2245)	0.1311 (0.5086)	0.2458 (0.1592)	0.1891 (0.2605)	0.1889 (0.2639)	0.0574 (0.7864)
1V/TIND	−0.0003 (0.9610)	−0.0010 (0.8676)	−0.0014 (0.8296)	−0.0008 (0.8979)	−0.0017 (0.7880)	−0.0012 (0.8486)	−0.0066 (0.3135)
Leverage	*0.6350**** *(0.0000)*	*0.6035**** *(0.0000)*	*0.61099**** *(0.0000)*	*0.6016**** *(0.0000)*	*0.6000**** *(0.0000)*	*0.5993**** *(0.0000)*	*0.6083**** *(0.0000)*
Dummy foreigner	0.0355 (0.6168)	0.0193 (0.7886)	0.0329 (0.6487)	0.0355 (0.6210)	0.0343 (0.6281)	0.0370 (0.6055)	−0.0486 (0.5266)
Dummy government	−0.0340 (0.7610)	−0.0839 (0.4622)	−0.0697 (0.5363)	−0.0471 (0.6769)	−0.0693 (0.5332)	−0.0712 (0.5247)	−0.1378 (0.2509)

(continued)

Table 3.9 OLS Regressions of Tobin's q on Corporate Governance Subindexes, 2002 *(continued)*

Group	*(1)*	*(2)*	*(3)*	*(4)*	*(5)*	*(6)*	*(7)*
Dummy institutional	−0.0021	−0.0273	−0.0074	0.0057	−0.0126	−0.0075	−0.0738
	(0.9832)	(0.7924)	(0.9424)	(0.9562)	(0.9010)	(0.9414)	(0.4726)
Volatility	*0.1826****	*0.1824****	*0.1799****	*0.1846****	*0.1913****	*0.1878****	*0.1640****
	(0.0001)	*(0.0001)*	*(0.0002)*	*(0.0001)*	*(0.0001)*	*(0.0001)*	*(0.0005)*
Growth	−0.0425	−0.0583	−0.0499	−0.0560	−0.0534	−0.0552	−0.0452
	(0.3830)	(0.2362)	(0.3115)	(0.2529)	(0.2716)	(0.2586)	(0.3553)
ROA	*0.6717***	*0.7294***	*0.7551***	*0.7870***	*0.7346***	*0.7459***	*0.7639***
	(0.0309)	*(0.0198)*	*(0.0159)*	*(0.0123)*	*(0.0178)*	*(0.0167)*	*(0.0134)*
Size	0.0042	0.0217	0.0264	0.0209	0.0086	0.0178	−0.0155
	(0.8374)	(0.2422)	(0.1433)	(0.2622)	(0.6617)	(0.3418)	(0.4622)
F-statistic	63,642	59,313	58,738	59,591	63,200	60,739	53,889
	(0.0000)	(0.0000)	(0.0000)	(0.0000)	(0.0000)	(0.0000)	(0.0000)
Adjusted R^2	0.2321	0.2174	0.2154	0.2184	0.2306	0.2223	0.2594

Source: Compiled by the authors.

Note: The columns show the results for each model, 1–7. All variables are defined in the annex. P-values are shown in parentheses.

* significant at 10 percent

** significant at 5 percent

*** significant at 1 percent

As yet another initial robustness check, we have obtained the principal components for the set of 24 questions for each firm for 2002. We have selected those principal components that show an eigenvalue greater than 1 (10 components) and that explained 5 percent or more of the variance, resulting in six principal components. We then performed our analysis once again using these six principal components. The results are shown in model 7 in table 3.9. In the annex, we define each of the six principal components, and we provide their correlation with the original variables and the rationale for their interpretation. Principal components 1, 2, and 4 are positively related to Tobin's q, but only components 1 and 4 are significant. Principal component 1 was named one share–one vote and involves the use of nonvoting shares to separate the control rights from the cash flow rights. It shows the largest positive coefficient and the strongest significance. Principal component 4 has the second largest positive coefficient and significance level; it is named disclosure supervision; it involves the use of international accounting standards, board size, and the presence of a fiscal board. Principal component 2, named board independence, does not show a significant relationship with Tobin's q.

The three remaining principal components show negative coefficients with Tobin's q. Only principal component 3, named malpractice free, which covers whether a firm is free of corporate governance malpractice inquiries and convictions, is marginally significant at the 10 percent level. Because the number of firms actually under inquiry or found to have been guilty of malpractice by the authorities in the last five years is small, it is possible that the negative sign may be interpreted as a market judgment for companies that exhibit poor practices, but are not under investigation. Principal components 5 (shareholder rights enforcement) and 6 (related party transactions potential) show no significant relationship with Tobin's q.

Our principal component analysis has shown that the largest coefficients involve a coincidence of controlling shareholder interests (control rights) with minority shareholder rights (cash flow rights) through parsimonious use of nonvoting shares and the ability of minority shareholders to supervise disclosure. Of course, principal components are labeled according to the analyst's subjective interpretation. Nevertheless, we believe that our principal component analysis favors our conclusion (up to this point) that good corporate governance practices and narrow separation between control and cash flow rights lead to greater corporate valuations.

Dividend payout. In addition to the relationship between ownership and corporate valuation, recent literature also studies the effect of corporate governance on the dividend payout. La Porta et al. (2000b) suggest that dividend policies may address agency problems between corporate insiders and outside shareholders. Firms in countries with better investor protection show higher dividend payouts than firms in countries with poor investor protection. The agency perspective of dividends asserts that cash payments to shareholders may help reduce agency problems. Fluck (1998) and Myers (2002) present theoretical agency models of dividend behavior whereby managers pay dividends to avoid disciplining action by shareholders. Additionally, Jensen (1986) sees expected, continuing dividend payments as a good use of cash, which might otherwise have been wasted in value-reducing projects.

The presence of large shareholders, a substantial concentration of voting rights, and a low concentration of cash flow rights may be harmful to the firm because the large shareholders may then expropriate minority shareholders by, for example, adopting low dividend payout strategies. On the other hand, when controlling shareholders have large stakes in cash flow rights, they have an incentive to pay a greater fraction of net income as dividends. By the same token, it is reasonable to expect that firms with better governance practices may also show a higher dividend payout as a costly sign of those practices. Thus, the dividend payout, as suggested in the literature, is another governance practice that should be examined, as we do in this chapter. In our robustness tests, we do not assume that the dividend payout is caused by corporate governance practices, and we consider it simultaneously with value and governance practices. In this section, however, we analyze it as a dependent variable.

Table 3.10 presents our results for the dividend payout in 2002. For the sake of brevity, we omit the results for 1998 and 2000. The CGI is positively related to the dividend payout for all models in 1998 and 2000, but that is not the case in 2002. For all years and models, the relationship between the CGI and the dividend payout is not significant. This is consistent with the findings of Black, Jang, and Kim (2006) for Korea. We have included one new control variable—current assets over total assets—to account for liquidity. More liquid firms may pay more dividends. Many of our control variables are significantly and positively related to the dividend payout, such as liquidity, size, and the ROA. Leverage is negatively and significantly related to the dividend payout. The larger shareholder percentage of ultimate control and cash flow rights, when examined alone, presents a significant and negative relationship with the dividend payout at the 10 percent and 5 percent levels, respectively, indicating a larger payout when there is less concentration of control and more separation between control rights and cash flow rights. We find no significant evidence that the dividend payout is influenced by the identity of the controlling shareholder. When we consider the ownership variables jointly with overall corporate governance practices, we find no significant relationship between the dividend payout and these corporate governance variables. Because of the nature of the dividend payout—there is a minimum mandatory payout of 25 percent of net income computed for tax purposes—and its potential use in mitigating conflicts of interest, it is quite possible that it is endogenously determined and that it is not adequately represented by the models in table 3.10. We also run regressions of the

Table 3.10 OLS Regressions of the Dividend Payout on Corporate Governance Measures, 2002

Independent variable	*Dependent variable = dividend payout*							
	(1)	*(2)*	*(3)*	*(4)*	*(5)*	*(6)*	*(7)*	*(8)*
Constant	–492,372	–401,497	–445,075	–511,422	–441,803	–411,779	–347,463	–377,839
	(0.0134)	(0.0467)	(0.0231)	(0.0091)	(0.0296)	(0.0489)	(0.0934)	(0.0699)
CGI	0.1061					–0.5641	–0.4316	–0.4597
	(0. 9027)					(0.5410)	(0.6353)	(0.6146)
1VIND		*–12.4990**			–6.5398	–8.2664	–67,475	–100,914
		(0.0878)			(0.5628)	(0.4787)	(0.5575)	(0.3906)
1TIND			*–14.4733***		–61,690	–61,099	–63,958	–29,114
			(0.0347)		(0.5885)	(0.5926)	(0.5696)	(0.8024)
1V/TIND				*0.7300**	0.5608	0.5746	0.6398	0.6402
				(0.0608)	(0.2003)	(0.1908)	(0.1399)	(0.1418)
Leverage							*–18.2930****	*–17.0541***
							(0.0074)	*(0.0147)*
Dummy foreigner								–47,246
								(0.3413)
Dummy government								–35,267
								(0.6595)
Dummy institutional								–110,538
								(0.1168)

(continued)

Table 3.10 OLS Regressions of the Dividend Payout on Corporate Governance Measures, 2002 *(continued)*

Independent variable	*Dependent variable = dividend payout*							
	(1)	*(2)*	*(3)*	*(4)*	*(5)*	*(6)*	*(7)*	*(8)*
Volatility	−0.7289	−0.3153	−0.1066	−10,118	−0.4172	−0.7088	0.4701	0.4530
	(0.8252)	(0.9226)	(0.9737)	(0.7542)	(0.8979)	(0.8295)	(0.8857)	(0.8900)
Current assets to total assets	*33.8491****	*33.4845****	*33.5070****	*36.1554****	*35.4220****	*34.4247****	*34.2450****	*32.5916****
	(0.0012)	(0.0011)	(0 .0011)	(0.0005)	(0.0006)	(0.0011)	(0.0010)	(0.0025)
Growth	0.4242	0.3219	0.4948	0.1596	0.1962	0.1857	−0.3639	−0.7478
	(0.9011)	(0.9243)	(0.8835)	(0.9624)	(0.9538)	(0.9564)	(0.9134)	(0.8238)
ROA	*76.1068****	*72.8532****	*74.8262****	*74.1207****	*72.1804****	*72.7963****	*67.2575****	*70.9753****
	(0.0006)	(0.0009)	(0.0006)	(0.0007)	(0.0010)	(0.0010)	(0.0020)	(0.0016)
Size	3.5343***	3.5636***	3.6994***	3.5788***	3.6092***	3.9376***	4.1522***	4.5918***
	(0.0087)	*(0.0040)*	*(0.0027)*	*(0.0038)*	*(0.0036)*	*(0.0036)*	*(0.0019)*	*(0.0010)*
F-statistic	80,586	86,603	89,844	87,863	69,409	61,926	64,777	51,931
	(0.0000)	(0.0000)	(0.0000)	(0.0000)	(0.0000)	(0.0000)	(0.0000)	(0.0000)
Adjusted R2	0.1659	0.1775	0.1836	0.1799	0.1824	0.1799	0.2046	0.2038

Source: Compiled by the authors.

Note: The columns show the results for each model, 1–8. All variables are defined in the annex. P-values are shown in parentheses.

* significant at 10 percent

** significant at 5 percent

*** significant at 1 percent

dividend payout on our corporate governance subindexes and find no significance for any of them.[13]

In our computation of the dividend payout, we have not considered stock repurchases because they differ greatly in Brazil from the U.S. equivalents. First of all, repurchases may generate capital gains, which are taxed at 20 percent, while dividends are not taxed. So, taking only taxation into consideration, stock repurchases do not maximize the wealth of shareholders, and extra dividends would be a better alternative. The motivations for stock repurchases may also be quite different. Possibly, they may be used for delisting or for the expropriation of minority shareholders. For instance, repurchases may be a way to pay controlling shareholders a dividend even when a company has no profits, or they may be a way to reduce the number of outside shareholders with the company's cash, concentrating the equity position of controlling shareholders and facilitating a future sale of the company associated with an ongoing private move by the new controlling shareholders.[14]

Before 1997, Brazilian corporate law granted tag-along rights to all minority voting shareholders when the intent of a repurchase was a delisting or a transfer of control. These rights were deleted from the law in May 1997 to facilitate privatizations. Minority shareholders would have no right to sue to receive the same amount for their shares if control were transferred. Tag-along rights were reinstated in 2001 through the corporate law reform. In February 1999, CVM introduced a new regulation to mandate greater disclosure of stock repurchases; this step was taken because of abuses in these types of transactions, particularly when the motivation was to take a company private. Many privatized companies, as well as other companies acquired or controlled by foreigners, went private to avoid the costs of keeping the company public and of the greater transparency. The reader is reminded that real interest rates have been high, and equity fundraising in the domestic capital market has been quite modest.

Disclosure and data on repurchases are limited. Announcements are made to Bovespa or to the CVM depending on the period and type of repurchase, but no announcement about the completion of a bid is made. No data are readily available on the actual result of a bid. Procianoy and Moreira (2004) report that, based on the announcement information published by companies, repurchase bids average about 7.1 percent of the stock outstanding. They also report that there are no wealth effects on the announcement day. Saito (2002) presents evidence that minority shareholders of firms that repurchased stocks experience a significantly lower market valuation when the separation of control rights and cash flow rights is greater, while we have not found any significance in the same period for the overall sample of listed companies. Finally, the number of stock repurchase offers is not large. Procianoy and Moreira (2004) analyze offers from 48 companies in the 1997–98 period, many with a motivation toward delisting, while Saito (2002) has examined offers from 30 firms in the 1994–99 period. Data on the offers, particularly on the actual percentage of outstanding shares that were bought, are not readily available and would have to be hand collected. If our omission of repurchases introduces any bias, Saito's (2002) findings suggest that it would be toward making our findings for the separation of control and cash flow rights significant, thereby confirming our hypothesis.

Individual question analysis. We close this section with an analysis of each question alone and then with all the other questions simultaneously to determine the impact in the CGI on Tobin's q and the dividend payout. We include all control variables in the analysis. Each question admits only a zero or 1 answer and therefore provides a dummy variable for the specific subject addressed. We highlight that different governance practices are substitutes for each other and that they therefore may behave differently when studied in isolation or together with other practices. Our results are summarized in table 3.11.

Five questions show individual significance at the 5 percent level for Tobin's q. The two largest coefficients belong to disclosure questions. Question 1 inquires about substantial disclosure of related party transactions, and question 5 about the use of leading global auditing firms. When we control for the remaining questions, only question 5 remains significant. Two questions about the board composition show individual significance: board independence and board size. Only board size remains significant after controlling for the remaining questions. Da Silveira, Barros, and Famá (2003) find a nonlinear relationship between the square of the number of directors on the board with Tobin's q, suggesting an optimal size for the board. Curiously, our dummy for the use of the recommended board size shows a negative impact on performance. Question 22, about using pyramids to *decrease* control concentration, is positively related to value. Our individual question analysis shows that disclosure and the use of indirect control structures dominate the positive impact of corporate governance practices on Tobin's q.

Our analysis for the dividend payout shows less consistency. Two questions show significance individually, but, when we control for the remaining questions, three different questions show significance. The three questions showing significance when we control for the other questions address the existence of committees (with a positive sign), board size, and additional voting rights (these last with a negative sign). The opposite signs reveal an inconsistent impact of individual CGI components on the dividend payout. We have already stressed that the dividend payout may be endogenously determined as a potential corporate governance practice in itself. We will address this issue more extensively when we perform our endogeneity checks.

Table 3.11 OLS Regressions of Tobin's q and the Dividend Payout on the CGI, 2002

	Tobin's q		*Dividend payout*	
Question	*Alone*	*With other items*	*Alone*	*With other items*
1	*0.2816**	0.2158	*-18.7461**	-169,525
	(0.0620)	(0.1673)	*(0.0730)*	(0.2116)
2	0.0297	0.0572	-111,637	-126,829
	(0.8148)	(0.6746)	(0.1993)	(0.1285)
3	0.0359	0.0291	66,198	81,206
	(0.7688)	(0.8185)	(0.4278)	(0.1828)
4	0.0756	0.0151	-47,835	-73,493
	(0.2873)	(0.8492)	(0.3451)	(0.3596)
5	*0.2298****	*0.1945***	13,279	15,336
	(0.0027)	*(0.0179)*	(0.8011)	(0.2007)
6	-0.0305	-0.0761	13,099	54,206
	(0.6981)	(0.3575)	(0.8068)	(0.7868)
7	0.0932	0.0394	-63,358	-110,054
	(0.1466)	(0.5961)	(0.1525)	(0.3469)
8	0.0266	0.0003	32,047	*0.7778***
	(0.7593)	(0.9976)	(0.5910)	*(0.0369)*
8	*0.1190**	0.0723	61,157	110,703
	(0.0571)	(0.3261)	(0.1625)	(0.9001)
10	*-0.1267***	*-0.1359***	-58,492	*-4.2860***
	(0.0296)	*(0.0259)*	(0.1414)	*(0.0320)*
11	-0.0084	-0.0639	-52,828	-456,534
	(0.8943)	(0.3501)	(0.2220)	(0.3096)
12	*0.1760***	0.1118	10,466	16,216
	(0.0422)	(0.2396)	(0.8619)	(0.3378)
13	0.1225	0.1648	60,771	80,046
	(0.3607)	(0.3098)	(0.5116)	(0.8068)
14	0.1099	-0.0965	61,323	-41,452
	(0.6456)	(0.7336)	(0.7079)	(0.4803)
15	0.0172	-0.0298	-145,189	41,419
	(0.9181)	(0.8798)	(0.2169)	(0.8339)
16	0.0585	-0.0526	72,419	-0.2092
	(0.5836)	(0.6444)	(0.3265)	(0.7637)
17	-0.0158	-0.0226	-38,641	27,915
	(0.8326)	(0.7918)	(0.4484)	(0.9797)
18	0.0469	0.1315	-99,579	-96,407
	(0.6425)	(0.2219)	(0.1476)	(0.6388)

(continued)

Table 3.11 OLS Regressions of Tobin's q and the Dividend Payout on the CGI, 2002 *(continued)*

	Tobin's q		*Dividend payout*	
Question	*Alone*	*With other items*	*Alone*	*With other items*
19	-0.1201 (0.3258)	-0.2032 (0.1316)	*-17.3284*** *(0.0374)*	-224,958 (0.1999)
20	0.0173 (0.8511)	0.0324 (0.7415)	-47,630 (0.4555)	*-5.9470*** *(0.0172)*
21	0.0579 (0.4875)	0.0926 (0.3131)	-47,823 (0.4145)	-15,479 (0.3894)
22	*0.1749**** *(0.0027)*	*0.1537*** *(0.0140)*	22,383 (0.5812)	34,041 (0.8117)
23	0.0276 (0.6982)	-0.0293 (0.6922)	52,773 (0.2749)	63,222 (0.4369)
24	*-0.1321** *(0.0910)*	-0.0919 (0.2687)	17,943 (0.7390)	28,669 (0.2206)

Source: Compiled by the authors.

Note: All regressions include the control variables defined in the annex. The questions are shown in table 3.1. P-values are shown in parentheses.

* significant at 10 percent

** significant at 5 percent

*** significant at 1 percent

We conclude from all the previous exercises that value seems to be determined by overall good corporate governance practices. Our results are significant statistically and economically, but we still need to verify if they stand the endogeneity tests and additional robustness checks. So far, disclosure seems to be a practice that has the greatest impact in Brazil. However, our factor analysis test has revealed that limiting the use of non-voting shares and reducing the ability of controlling shareholders to take advantage of related party transactions also influence value. Our findings for the dividend payout are mostly not significant and not consistent when the CGI is a dependent variable, but suggest that dividends are larger when there is more control concentration. We now turn to our endogeneity checks and additional robustness checks.

Extensions and Additional Robustness Checks

In this section, we discuss alternate empirical implementations and potential problems that may affect our results. We begin by checking if additional variables, such as a quadratic version of our ownership variables, are related to corporate value. We also check if the results are different in the absence of outliers, and we experiment with other definitions of our firm value proxy. We proceed to verify if our results are affected by endogeneity through a panel data analysis and the use of a simultaneous equation system with a size dummy instrumental variable. We also use a reduced version of the CGI in which we drop the questions that present little variation among firms. We close discussing potential survivorship bias.

Alternative Implementations of the Multivariate Model

We have reproduced the analysis in table 3.8 with the squares of the voting and cash flow rights concentration variables, plus the square of the wedge, to control for a potential nonlinear relationship of ownership and Tobin's q. Our results do not change with the inclusion of these variables, and they are not significant in any models except for the dividend payout in 1998. In table 3.8, we show the coefficients with the quadratic variables in model 9 and in 2002. We do not show this analysis for the remaining years and for the dividend payout.

We have considered the P/B as an alternative measure of relative firm value. We have reproduced the analysis for model 8 in table 3.8, as well as the analysis in table 3.9, replacing Tobin's q with P/B. In table 3.6, one can see that the P/B is not correlated with the CGI and that it shows a 0.44 correlation with q. Possibly, the P/B reflects other factors, such as risk, and may not be a very good proxy for relative firm value. In fact, Rodrigues and Leal (2003) show that low P/B (value) stocks are riskier than high P/B stocks in Brazil.

Our analysis in table 3.12 shows that the P/B is not significantly related to the CGI and its subindexes, but the coefficients with the disclosure subindex and with the CGI are positive. Interestingly, the P/B is significantly and positively related to the concentration of cash flow rights and negatively, but not significantly related to the concentration of voting rights. It is also positively and marginally significantly related to principal component 1, which we have named one share–one vote. The P/B seems to be a proxy for risk as well, and it is negatively related to performance (ROA). If the P/B were our proxy of choice for relative value, our findings in table 3.8 would be weakened, but the hypothesized signs would be maintained.

We have also used the P/S and the P/CF as proxies for market value. We have reproduced all the models in table 3.8 for these variables. We do not show these results here.[15] All CGI coefficients are positive, but not significant. We have also found positive coefficients for the principal components that show positive and significant coefficients in our initial analysis. If these variables were our proxies of choice for relative value,

Table 3.12 OLS Regressions of the P/B on Corporate Governance Measures, 2002

Measures	*(1)*	*(2)*	*(3)*	*(4)*	*(5)*	*(6)*	*(7)*
Constant	−190,379 (0.0452)	−188,438 (0.0488)	−126,720 (0.2481)	−191,134 (0.0455)	−198,209 (0.0409)	−184,175 (0.0653)	−60,055 (0.6007)
Disclosure	16,730 (0.1612)						
Board		0.2219 (0.7978)					
Conflicts			−16,826 (0.2524)				
Shareholder rights				0.4581 (0.6679)			
CGI					0.2411 (0.6083)		
CGI reduced						0.0952 (0.8509)	
Prin 1							2.5136* *(0.0616)*
Prin 2							−14,512 (0.2381)
Prin 3							0.0439 (0.9689)

(continued)

Table 3.12 OLS Regressions of the P/B on Corporate Governance Measures, 2002 *(continued)*

Measures	*(1)*	*(2)*	*(3)*	*(4)*	*(5)*	*(6)*	*(7)*
Prin 4							0.7607
							(0.4848)
Prin 5							−0.6931
							(0.5597)
Prin 6							−11,352
							(0.3264)
1VIND	−63,787	−61,239	−115,332	−62,757	−54,190	−65,081	−71,478
	(0.2813)	(0.3037)	(0.1267)	(0.2914)	(0.3770)	(0.2915)	(0.3021)
1TIND	*10.4145**	97,205	*13.8773***	*10.3062**	95,680	97,139	*13.0025**
	(0.0870)	(0.1106)	*(0.0500)*	*(0.1000)*	(0.1160)	(0.1109)	*(0.0961)*
1V/TIND	0.0387	0.0262	0.0693	0.0281	0.0209	0.0316	−0.0598
	(0.8620)	(0.9067)	(0.7586)	(0.9001)	(0.9257)	(0.8879)	(0.8022)
Leverage	−0.0385	−0.6411	−0.4635	−0.7093	−0.6673	−0.4966	−0.6948
	(0.9915)	(0.8597)	(0.8976)	(0.8450)	(0.8536)	(0.8911)	(0.8485)
Dummy	−18,722	−21,416	−24,314	−19,491	−20,041	−21,152	−39,794
foreigner	(0.4640)	(0.4067)	(0.3456)	(0.4499)	(0.4350)	(0.4118)	(0.1591)
Dummy	−29,647	−383,199	−32,343	−34,118	−36,913	−36,002	−56,553
government	(0.4621)	(0.3494)	(0.4217)	(0.4002)	(0.3588)	(0.3715)	(0.2000)
Dummy	−23,865	−27,235	−26,831	−23,439	−25,837	−25,650	−38,666
institutional	(0.5132)	(0.4646)	(0.4631)	(0.5262)	(0.4808)	(0.4842)	(0.3063)

(continued)

Table 3.12 OLS Regressions of the P/B on Corporate Governance Measures, 2002 *(continued)*

Measures	*(1)*	*(2)*	*(3)*	*(4)*	*(5)*	*(6)*	*(7)*
Volatility	*10.0053****	*9.9444****	*9.8137****	*9.9943****	*10.0210****	*9.8644****	*9.5041****
	(0.0000)	*(0.0000)*	*(0.0000)*	*(0.0000)*	*(0.0000)*	*(0.0000)*	*(0.0000)*
Growth	–18,147	–21,139	–22,905	–21,039	–20,677	–20,617	–23,361
	(0.3017)	(0.2312)	(0.1938)	(0.2314)	(0.2389)	(0.2407)	(0.1939)
ROA	*–22.3466***	*–20.7410**	*–20.9152**	*–20.0252**	*–20.6847**	*–20.5401**	*–20.0055**
	(0.0461)	*(0.0641)*	*(0.0607)*	*(0.0748)*	*(0.0642)*	*(0.0661)*	*(0.0770)*
Size	0.7164	*1.1815**	*1.2065**	*1.1493**	10,684	*1.2607**	0.3234
	(0.3308)	*(0.0765)*	*(0.0615)*	*(0.0859)*	(0.1341)	*(0.0628)*	(0.6758)
F-statistic	48,998	46,960	48,294	47,086	47,170	46,927	36,942
	(0.0000)	(0.0000)	(0.0000)	(0.0000)	(0.0000)	(0.0000)	(0.0000)
Adjusted R^2	0.1801	0.1723	0.1775	0.1728	0.1732	0.1722	0.1770

Source: Compiled by the authors.
Note: The columns show the results for each model, 1–7. All variables are defined in the annex. P-values are shown in parentheses.
* significant at 10 percent
** significant at 5 percent
*** significant at 1 percent

our findings in table 3.8 would be weakened, but the hypothesized signs would be maintained.

We proceed to check for the effect of outliers. We regress Tobin's q, the dividend payout ratio, and the P/B on the CGI alone and a constant term and delete the observations for which the Studentized residual exceeds ±1.96, as has been done by Black, Jang, and Kim (2006). Table 3.13 shows that our main result for Tobin's q does not qualitatively change, although the coefficient and its significance drop. Seven outliers have been removed in the Tobin's q analysis. An examination of the removed outliers does not reveal any particular patterns.

Endogeneity Checks

Claessens et al. (2002) address the issue of reverse causality by dismissing it as unlikely. They consider ownership changes and the impact of these changes on corporate value and believe that the changes are slow relative to value changes. Our analysis in table 3.2 supports this view. Ownership percentages increase slightly over time and remain high. We doubt that our results are affected by endogeneity in the case of ownership concentration, given the magnitude of this concentration. The CGI is also stable. In any case, we proceed to check for endogeneity.

Himmelberg, Hubbard, and Palia (1999) affirm that panel data in a firm fixed effects model might deal with the presence of endogeneity despite the use of control variables. Their argument is put forward in a very simple way. If corporate governance practices, be they ownership concentration measures or the CGI, are described by a linear relationship such as:

$$G_{i,t} = \beta_1 x_{i,t} + \gamma_1 u_i + e_{i,t}, \tag{3.1}$$

where $G_{i,t}$ are the governance practices of firm i in time t; $x_{i,t}$ is a vector of observed control variables, and u_i represents time invariant unobserved factors. Because these factors are fixed firm effects, Himmelberg, Hubbard, and Palia claim that using panel data analysis with fixed firm effects might identify if the relationship between corporate governance and firm value is endogenous. The firm value equation is represented as:

$$Q_{i,t} = \alpha G_{i,t} + \beta_2 x_{i,t} + \gamma_2 u_i + v_{i,t}, \tag{3.2}$$

where $Q_{i,t}$ is the firm relative value, such as in Tobin's q. However, the model represented in table 3.8 takes the form of equation 3.3 in most empirical tests, including our own.

$$Q_{i,t} = a_1 G_{i,t} + a_2 x_{i,t} + \varepsilon_{i,t}. \tag{3.3}$$

Table 3.13 OLS Regressions of Tobin's q, Dividend Payout, and the P/B, 2002

	Tobin's q		*Dividend payout*		*P/B*	
Measures	*All data*	*Without outliers*	*All data*	*Without outliers*	*All data*	*Without outliers*
Constant	−0.1199	0.2215	−377,839	−431,012	−198,209	−200,296
	(0.6533)	(0.1441)	(0.0699)	(0.0021)	(0.0409)	(0.0429)
CGI	*0.0273***	*0.0126**	−0.4597	−0.2238	0.2411	0.2180
	(0.0367)	*(0.0869)*	(0.6146)	(0.7190)	(0.6083)	(0.6482)
1VIND	0.0071	0.0340	−100,914	−53,273	−54,190	−49,746
	(0.9666)	(0.7221)	(0.3906)	(0.4996)	(0.3770)	(0.4277)
1TIND	0.1891	−0.0817	−29,114	22,350	95,680	95,280
	(0.2605)	(0.3964)	(0.8024)	(0.7703)	(0.1160)	(0.1283)
1V/TIND	−0.0017	−0.0030	0.6402	*0.9397****	0.0209	0.0178
	(0.7880)	(0.3876)	(0.1418)	*(0.0010)*	(0.9257)	(0.9375)
Leverage	*0.6000****	*0.5540****	*−17.0541***	*−14.0579****	−0.6673	−0.4192
	(0.0000)	*(0.0000)*	*(0.0147)*	*(0.0024)*	(0.8536)	(0.9096)
Dummy foreigner	0.0343	0.0657	−47,246	−33,352	−20,041	−21,522
	(0.6281)	(0.1025)	(0.3413)	(0.3116)	(0.4350)	(0.4143)
Dummy government	−0.0693	0.0022	−35,267	−69,823	−36,913	−37,736
	(0.5332)	(0.9718)	(0.6595)	(0.1992)	(0.3588)	(0.3574)
Dummy institutional	−0.0126	0.0263	−110,538	*−8.0705**	−25,837	−26,819
	(0.9010)	(0.6479)	(0.1168)	*(0.0853)*	(0.4808)	(0.4723)

(continued)

Table 3.13 OLS Regressions of Tobin's q, Dividend Payout, and the P/B, 2002 *(continued)*

	Tobin's q		*Dividend payout*		*P/B*	
Measures	*All data*	*Without outliers*	*All data*	*Without outliers*	*All data*	*Without outliers*
Volatility	*0.1913****	0.0106	0.4530	0.9543	*10.0210****	*10.1348****
	(0.0001)	(0.7101)	(0.8900)	(0.6535)	*(0.0000)*	*(0.0000)*
Growth	-0.0534	-0.0107	-0.7478	-10,058	-20,677	-20,931
	(0.2716)	(0.6936)	(0.8238)	(0.6442)	(0.2389)	(0.2395)
ROA	*0.7346***	*0.8425****	*70.9753****	*51.4791****	*-20.6847**	*-20.3081**
	(0.0178)	*(0.0000)*	*(0.0016)*	*(0.0007)*	*(0.0642)*	*(0.0748)*
Size	0.0086	0.0085	*4.5918****	*3.8882****	10,684	10,704
	(0.6617)	(0.4403)	*(0.0010)*	*(0.0000)*	(0.1341)	(0.1423)
Current assets to total assets			*32.5916****	*32.8335****		
			(0.0025)	*(0.0000)*		
F-statistic	63,200	101,818	51,931	84,128	47,170	46,712
	(0.0000)	(0.0000)	(0.0000)	(0.0000)	(0.0000)	(0.0000)
Adjusted R^2	0.2306	0.3485	0.2038	0.3285	0.1732	0.1755

Source: Compiled by the authors.

Note: We treat observations as outliers and drop them from the sample if a Studentized residual obtained by regressing the dependent variable on the CGI and a constant term exceeds ± 1.96. This method identifies seven outliers for Tobin's q, 16 for the dividend payout, and six for the P/B. All variables are defined in the annex. P-values are shown in parentheses.

* significant at 10 percent

** significant at 5 percent

*** significant at 1 percent

This equation will only be a valid representation of the corporate governance practices and value relationship if the correlation between G and ε is zero, which occurs only if the coefficients of the unobserved variables in equations 3.1 and 3.2 are null. Himmelberg, Hubbard, and Palia maintain that this is very unlikely. They model unobserved firm heterogeneity by assuming that the omitted firm effects are fixed in time and use the fixed firm effects panel data analysis to verify the behavior of their cross-sectional coefficients.

We follow the same procedure and use a reduced version of our index, with 15 questions, including those that are more discriminating among firms, and perform a balanced panel data analysis for every year from 1998 to 2002. We include the same control variables. We find that the coefficients in the fixed firm effects model are no longer significant, although they remain positive. These results suggest that our findings in the cross-sectional model may be endogenous. Our results are not reported here, but are available in a companion paper.[16]

Himmelberg, Hubbard, and Palia believe that the endogeneity suggested by our panel data analysis imposes the need for more structure to identify the impact of corporate governance variables on firm value. They use size as an instrumental variable. Their proxies for size are nonlinearly related to corporate governance practices, but are not strongly related to firm value when their corporate governance variables are present. The same is true in our analysis. In table 3.7, size is positively and significantly related to the CGI. In table 3.8 size is not related to Tobin's q when the CGI is included in the model. This is exactly the property we would expect from an instrumental variable. In our case, it should directly predict the CGI, but only indirectly predict firm value through the CGI.

Black, Jang, and Kim (2006) use a size dummy induced by a peculiar Korean regulation that requires certain governance practices only for firms larger than a predefined asset size. Even though Brazil does not have this type of regulation, the results are similar in practice, as the correlation between size and the CGI suggests. We believe that there is a scale factor that renders the adoption of better corporate governance practices easier and more advantageous for larger firms. We remind the reader that the credit and capital markets in Brazil are very small relative to the country's gross domestic product and that the government absorbs most savings through treasury securities. External financing is expensive, scarce, and available mainly only to larger firms. An illustration of this scale factor is the cost of short-term credit. While the average interest rate for working capital loans with an average maturity of 305 days was 35 percent per year in July 2004, the rate for vendor credit was 21 percent, according to Brazilian Central Bank statistics. Vendor credit is a typical form of loan made to suppliers of large Brazilian and multinational firms that guarantee these loans and are the ultimate debtors. Thus, our belief in the existence of this scale factor. Another reason for this scale factor would be the large fixed costs reported in the Brazilian literature to keep a company public and listed.[17] We have decided to use a size dummy that is equal to 1 if the firm is in the top size quartile and zero otherwise. We have also experimented with other definitions of this size dummy.

A system of simultaneous equations is estimated via three-stage least squares. Tobin's q and dividend payout measures may be included in this specification, as well as our size dummy instrumental variable. The endogenous model may be represented using the circular notation of Hermalin and Weisbach (2003), combined with the simultaneous equation notation used by Agrawal and Knoeber (1996).

$$c_j = \alpha + \sum_{i \neq j} \phi_i c_i + \sum_{i=1}^{N} \varphi_i X_i + \varepsilon \tag{3.4}$$

Equation 3.4 represents the kind of test performed in our table 3.8 and by many others, such as Klapper and Love (2004), with c as a vector of governance practices measures, such as the CGI or ownership percentages, and X as a vector of control variables that are associated with governance practices as well. Such equations, one for each governance practice measure, may be included in a simultaneous equation system, as in Agrawal and Knoeber (1996), whereby the firm value or performance equation is represented by equation 3.5. If the coefficients of c in equation 3.5, simultaneously determined, are still significant, this will be an indication that the net effect of alternate governance practices is significant over the value of the firm.

$$Q_i = \alpha + \sum \beta_i c_i + \sum_{i=1}^{N} \lambda_i X_i + \xi \tag{3.5}$$

The results of our simultaneous equations analysis are shown in table 3.14 for the year 2002 alone. The results for the other years are essentially the same.[18] With the size dummy instrumental variable, the coefficient for the impact of the CGI on Tobin's q is even larger than the one found in our multiple regression study. The coefficient of Tobin's q in the CGI equation, however, is not significant. The size dummy behaves as expected. It helps predict the CGI, but it is not related to Tobin's q in the presence of the CGI. We have repeated the analysis for the dividend payout and confirmed what we have already suspected from our analysis in table 3.10: the dividend payout is unrelated to the CGI and, quite possibly, should be considered as an additional corporate governance practice indicator, simultaneously determined with other items in the CGI.

We have experimented with size dummies defined as 1 for firms in the top decile, top third, and top half of the sample. We have also computed the correlations between all our size dummies and the ADR and the Novo Mercado (NM) dummies. Correlations are below 0.30 for the NM dummy and below 0.50 for the ADR dummy. Finally, we have included the ADR, the NM, and an ADR*NM interaction in our simultaneous equations

Table 3.14 Three-Stage Least Squares Regressions on Corporate Governance Measures, 2002

	Tobin's q			*Dividend payout*	
Measures	*CGI*	*q*	*Measures*	*CGI*	*Payout*
Constant	52,102	−0.1596	Constant	−102,166	121,016
	(0.3853)	(0.2976)		(0.8204)	(0.7725)
q	208,764		Payout	0.7377	
	(0.2114)			(0.6221)	
CGI		*0.0401******	CGI		13,760
		(0.0001)			(0.6784)
1VIND	−14,760	0.0487	1VIND	10,042	−14,634
	(0.7201)	(0.7607)		(0.9332)	(0.9259)
1TIND	−38,434	0.1838	1TIND	49,815	−65,704
	(0.4647)	(0.2644)		(0.6939)	(0.5602)
1V/TIND	0.0473	−0.0021	1V/TIND	−0.2138	0.3094
	(0.7399)	(0.7255)		(0.7221)	(0.4632)
Leverage	−123,519	*0.5940******	Leverage	144,805	*−19.5771******
	(0.2506)	*(0.0000)*		(0.6126)	*(0.0039)*
Dummy foreigner	−0.8465	0.0378	Dummy foreigner	47,397	−61,001
	(0.6354)	(0.5912)		(0.6469)	(0.1974)

(continued)

Table 3.14 Three-Stage Least Squares Regressions on Corporate Governance Measures, 2002 *(continued)*

	Tobin's q			*Dividend payout*	
Measures	*CGI*	*q*	*Measures*	*CGI*	*Payout*
Dummy government	15,020	−0.0724	Dummy government	86,724	−110,689
	(0.5345)	(0.5158)		(0.6066)	(0.1381)
Dummy institutional	0.2517	−0.0143	Dummy institutional	102,587	*−13.7483***
	(0.9137)	(0.8883)		(0.6239)	*(0.0459)*
Volatility	−42,123	*0.1973****	Volatility	0.2910	−0.2372
	(0.1345)	*(0.0000)*		(0.9268)	(0.9501)
Growth	11,147	−0.0533	Growth	0.6152	−0.8243
	(0.4089)	(0.2587)		(0.8163)	(0.7967)
ROA	−149,528	*0.7284***	ROA	−679,316	*90.4811****
	(0.3247)	*(0.0147)*		(0.6328)	*(0.0000)*
Size dummy	*0.5609****	0.0025	Size	−106,634	*14.6172***
	(0.0002)	(0.9858)	Dummy	(0.6759)	*(0.0129)*
Adjusted R^2	0.0000	0.2269	Adjusted R^2	0.0000	0.1670

Source: Compiled by the authors.

Note: Some nonsignificant control variables have been omitted to save space. All variables are defined in the annex. P-values are shown in parentheses.

* significant at 10 percent
** significant at 5 percent
*** significant at 1 percent

analysis with all size dummies. None of these variables is significant in any model. The results obtained with this new formulation are consistent with the previous ones presented in table 3.8. It is worth noting that the coefficients for the top decile, top quartile, and top third largest firms in the sample are lower with the inclusion of the dummies for ADR, NM, and their interaction at 0.0161, 0.0257, and 0.0250, respectively. The dummy for the top half of the largest firms in the sample does not work as an instrumental variable because q becomes significantly and negatively correlated with the CGI when we use it. Finally, we have repeated the panel data analysis with the size dummies, but there is no change in the results.

As in Black, Jang, and Kim (2006) for Korea, we have concluded, after checking for endogeneity, that our evidence supports a causal relationship between corporate governance practices and firm value. We also present evidence that this relationship is exogenous in the presence of a scale factor, represented by a size dummy, which is robust to most definitions we have used. The impact of an increase in the CGI is larger for larger firms.

Discussion of Potential Biases

The number of public corporations in Brazil has increased over the last 10 years. There were 844 public corporations in January 1995, and, in April 2004, there were 928. The maximum number in the period was 1,046 in January 1998. Gledson de Carvalho (2000) demonstrates that this rise in the number of public companies in 1998 was an illusion. He shows that many of the corporations created in this period were state-owned corporations and syndicates related to the privatization program, corporations that became public to issue ADRs, securitization and leasing companies, and corporations that issued less than US$1 million. He deletes these companies and shows that the number of public corporations in Brazil has declined. However, after this combined privatization and ADR phase, and a subsequent decline in the number of pubic companies, the number of companies stabilized and increased. We do not believe that the dynamics of the number of public companies in Brazil introduces any biases into our results because, in most cases, these companies have not been listed or did not have any market liquidity that allowed for the computation of some of the variables we need in our research.

The number of Bovespa listed firms has been decreasing in Brazil. It started at 545 companies, and the number stood at 364 in March 2004. Gledson de Carvalho (2000) reports that the costs of keeping a company listed and public are cited by 88 percent of surveyed respondents as the main obstacles preventing companies from becoming or remaining public. Among these costs, the largest burdens are publication costs, mandated overhead, external auditors, and the shareholder services department. The law makes public corporations publish their financial statements in major newspapers, as well as in the official registry of the state or county where they are incorporated. Many of these official publications charge exorbitant prices, thereby representing a de facto tax on public companies levied by states and counties. Another reason for delisting is acquisition by foreigners. Siffert Filho (1998) shows an increase in ownership by foreigners in Brazil. Our table 3.3 shows a decline in foreign ownership of listed companies. Many companies that have delisted have been acquired by foreign investors that see no advantage in incurring the costs of keeping the subsidiary public in Brazil. Given this combination of circumstances, we believe that the companies in our sample are survivors. Their governance practices are probably better than those of companies that have delisted or have remained private. Therefore, our results are representative of currently listed companies in Brazil, though they most likely overstate the quality and importance of corporate governance practices for other public Brazilian companies that are not listed or that are listed and have not been included in the sample.

Our discussion assumes that there are no demand issues, that is, there is money inside and outside the country for stock investment, and that prices are fair, that is, the market is efficient. Obviously, we may not safely make these representations. Liquidity has always been an issue in the Brazilian market, as stated elsewhere in this chapter. Thus, market prices may not reflect all relevant information and may not be a fair representation of corporate value. Along the same lines, we have briefly mentioned that public sector debt may crowd out private sector securities, reducing the potential demand for new issues of corporate securities. Our work does not address these issues, and they may represent important limitations on the significance of our results and on the desire for better governance practices.

To counter argue, we should say that stock issuance in Brazil has experienced a renaissance since 2004 and that, at the same time, the number of ADR programs has been drastically reduced. The introduction of the Novo Mercado in Brazil and of the Sarbanes Oxley law in the United States may have offered substitute arrangements for some Brazilian companies. While issuance in the United States has become more costly and the risk of litigation greater, the Brazilian market has offered a way for companies to adhere to better governance practices under a certification label (the Novo Mercado listing) and to enjoy capital at lower cost without the need to borrow on the better reputation of developed markets. Of course, this is all recent, and the long-term effects are still unknown.

Comparative Analysis with Chile

In this section, we provide a brief comparative analysis using the results obtained through a similar study on Chile. Our intention is to put our findings in context in Latin America. While Chile shows many similarities with Brazil, there are also some key differences, namely, Chile has a smaller and more stable economy, and it may offer better shareholder protection. Other differences emerge in the ensuing paragraphs.

In the small sample of Brazilian and Chilean companies used by Klapper and Love (2004), relative market valuations of companies are low, while the CGI level is high, suggesting a weak relationship between market value and governance in these countries. However, our own findings and those of Lefort and Walker (2005) suggest the opposite for much larger samples. Patel, Balic, and Bwakira (2002) report an average firm-level Standard & Poor's transparency and disclosure score of 32 percent for Brazil and Chile in 2000, which is low relative to an average of 43 percent for emerging Asian markets and to the 55 percent score of South Africa, the highest-ranking emerging market. They find that the Standard & Poor's index is negatively correlated with large shareholdings and positively correlated with the P/B in Brazil. They include 30 Brazilian firms and 19 Chilean firms.

Klapper and Love (2004) have noted that there is a large variation in Credit Lyonnais Securities Asia's measure of the quality of governance practices within specific countries. However, Brazil and Chile present, respectively, the third highest and the highest within-country homogeneity in the firm-level governance index computed by Credit Lyonnais Securities Asia. These authors also note that Brazil and Chile present low relative market valuations, while showing relatively high firm-level governance indicators. These results, nevertheless, should be taken with caution because the number of companies covered in that study in Brazil (24) and Chile (13) is small, including mostly companies that have listed ADRs in the United States and are therefore very similar in terms of their governance practices. Durnev and Kim (2005) have included 30 Brazilian firms and 15 Chilean firms in their sample, with similar results. Our study has advanced this research by verifying if better governance practices bring benefits to a much larger sample of firms in Brazil. Lefort and Walker (2005) have done the same for Chile. This brief comparative analysis with Chile uses findings from the latter authors and our own. We also use the World Bank's Corporate Governance Country Assessment for Chile from 2003.

The legal systems in Brazil and Chile share a similar origin and traditions, but this should have no bearing on our analysis. We assume that the quality of the legal system is the same in Brazil and Chile. Klapper and Love (2004) report that the legality index for each country is about the same and that the judicial efficiency index for the two countries is not far apart, though it is higher in Chile.[19] Similar ratings are reported by Durnev and Kim (2005). We have also verified that the disclosure quality is about the same according to Standard & Poor's ratings. Our reading of the World Bank's (2003) assessment has led us to conclude the same.

As in Brazil, cross holdings are not allowed, and indirect control structures are very common in Chile; however, nonvoting shares are unusual, while they dominate the Brazilian stock market. Chilean economic groups control 70 percent of listed companies and 90 percent of their assets, while group affiliation and conglomerates are not important in Brazil. Control concentration is also high in Chile, but larger in Brazil. The five largest shareholders indirectly control 57 percent in Chile and 89 percent, on average, in Brazil. Control concentration has been increasing in the two countries.

Lefort and Walker (2005) have used a 67-item questionnaire that had to be partly answered by firm representatives to compute their corporate governance score. Their response ratio was 29 percent. However, the companies that responded tended to be larger, representing 42 percent of Chilean market capitalization, and these may be the companies with the best corporate governance practices. This experience shows the problems with this methodology, which we tried to avoid. Lefort and Walker were well aware of this drawback and broadened their response ratio by answering about one-third of the questions themselves on the basis of public information, thus increasing their sample size to 106 companies and 76 percent of market capitalization. This also suggests that data availability is probably better in Brazil than in Chile, as our reading of the World Bank's (2003) assessment also seems to indicate.

The overall unweighted average company score in Chile was 58 percent, while ours was 42 percent of the maximum score value used in each country. Although the questionnaires used by Lefort and Walker (2005) and by ourselves are not directly comparable, it is possible that Chilean firms actually offer better protection to investors than do Brazilian firms, as has also been previously suggested elsewhere. As in Brazil, Chilean companies score higher in disclosure than in other areas of corporate governance practices. In terms of board functioning and composition, Chilean boards are also dominated by insiders and rarely use committees. In what Lefort and Walker (2005) have classified as shareholder rights, Chilean companies scored well, at 60 percent, while Brazilian companies scored 33 percent, on average. This is the most distinctive category for the two countries in the subgroups that make up each questionnaire used. In the World Bank's (2003) assessment of Chile, we have noticed that some practices seem better in Chile, while others do not. There is no clear superiority in Chilean practices, with the notable exception of the use of nonvoting shares.

Lefort and Walker (2000, 2005) find that firm affiliation to groups tends to decrease the value of the firms, but this is mitigated when there is little separation between control and cash flow rights and when pension funds are present as minority shareholders. In our study, we find that the ultimate control of institutional investors bears no impact on firm value.

They find that the relationship between ownership and the separation of control and cash flow rights is nonlinear, while we essentially find no significant relationship even for quadratic versions of these variables. Probably, because ownership concentration is so much higher in Brazil, it does not discriminate firm value well among firms.

In Chile, there is a minimum dividend payment of 30 percent that is instituted by law, similar to the minimum of 25 percent in Brazil. The payout ratio averaged 36 percent in 2002, close to the 31 percent average in Brazil. In Chile, payout ratios are larger in firms affiliated with conglomerates and where pension funds are present as minority shareholders. Like us, Lefort and Walker find that payout ratios increase with greater separation between the control and cash flow rights up to an inflection point of 70 percent of voting rights in the case of Chile. This decrease in the payout for high concentration values is consistent with our findings in table 3.10. In our endogeneity checks, we find no significant relationship between payout and corporate governance proxies in the presence of the CGI in Brazil, while they maintain a significant relationship with ownership variables in Chile, even when their CGI is absent. The Chilean authors find little in terms of the impact of their CGI on corporate value.

The Chilean results seem to confirm previous findings that investor protection is better in Chile than in Brazil even though the two countries are comparable in terms of the quality of their judiciary. The Chilean practice of one share–one vote and other shareholder rights seems to be the key difference in governance practices between the two countries. In general, the findings in Lefort and Walker (2005) confirm the Brazilian findings that market values are higher when corporate governance practices are better and when controlling shareholders are less entrenched. They also point to an important policy recommendation: nonvoting shares should be banned by regulators. In our opinion, these shares have been among the key factors that explain inadequate investor protection in Brazil.

Conclusion and Policy Implications

Do good corporate governance practices pay in Brazil? Our answer is yes. We have built a corporate governance practices index from a set of 24 objective questions. Our intent has been to stay clear of questionnaires that would require responses from analysts or company officers and directors. The response rates of those sorts of questionnaires may be quite low; the results may be biased to represent companies with better governance practices; and the surveys are costly to repeat on an annual basis. Besides, it would not be possible or reliable to use answers from previous periods. Finally, these types of questionnaires have already been used in the IBCG studies. Our goal has been to produce a questionnaire that we might answer ourselves using publicly available data. This has allowed us to build a short time series for our CGI for the 1998–2002 period. It has also allowed us to have a very large sample of firms, and it has provided us with an instrument that may be used in the next few years to gauge the evolution of corporate governance practices in Brazil.

The answers to our questionnaire reveal that most companies do not specify any sanctions against management relating to corporate governance malpractice. Companies disclose related party transactions in explanatory notes, but provide only general information about the compensation of chief officers and directors. About 30 percent of the companies use international accounting standards, and about 75 percent use one of the leading global auditing firms. Board practices are worse than those in the larger markets. The chairman of the board and the chief executive officer are the same person in about one-third of the companies. In most companies, boards do not use committees and are not made up of a majority of outside directors; directors do not serve consecutive one-year terms; and the firms do not have minority shareholder mandated fiscal boards. About 37 percent of the boards are not the size recommended by the IBGC. The number of companies under investigation or convicted by securities authorities is very small, but this is not an indication of good corporate behavior and is almost certainly due to the low levels of law enforcement in Brazil. This is probably also the reason companies do not submit to arbitration courts. While arbitration decisions are arrived at more quickly and are final, court decisions take a long time, and there are many possibilities for appeals. Most companies do not facilitate voting by all shareholders and do not grant any additional voting rights and tag-along rights beyond what is legally required. About 30 percent of the companies offer insufficient liquidity to their shareholders. Our overall corporate governance practices analysis shows a modest general improvement in firm practices captured by our index in the 1998–2002 period. We also show that Brazilian firms score much better in the disclosure dimension of our index than in the other dimensions of board practices, ethics and conflicts of interest, and shareholder rights.

In our study of voting and cash flow rights, we find, as expected, high concentrations. The percentage of indirect control rights for the five largest shareholders increased from 1998 to 2002, approaching a median of 90 percent in 2002. There was an increase in the proportion of cash flow rights in the same period, reaching a median of 54 percent in 2002. Because 75 percent of the firms sampled have indirect control structures, entrenchment in Brazil is considerable. There is widespread use of nonvoting shares as well. The Brazilian economy has been one of the riskiest among the large emerging markets, and the Brazilian stock market is very volatile. Greater risk favors a greater concentration of control, as well as the use of mechanisms to leverage control. Finally, we show that the separation between control rights and cash flow rights is more pronounced for the largest shareholder when this shareholder is considered alone than it is when other large shareholders are also considered.

In our regression analysis, we have used proxies for leverage, growth, risk, size, and profitability, as well as other control variables. We have first related these variables to our corporate governance practices variables. Most of them do not maintain any significant and consistent relationship with the CGI over the years. Only size is significant for every year. We have included these variables in a set of models, using Tobin's q as our proxy for firm value. We find that the CGI shows a positive and significant relationship with Tobin's q. A 1 point increase in the 24-point CGI leads to a 2.3 to 3.1 percent increase in Tobin's q, depending on the model used. A 1 point increase in the CGI score leads to a 5.75 to 7.75 percent increase in the value of the company's shares, as measured by Tobin's q, for a company with the average sample q and leverage. A minimum to maximum increase in the CGI for 2002 leads to a 95 percent increase in the share value of the average company. Good corporate governance practices may lead to a substantial increase in value and a reduction in the cost of capital for Brazilian firms. This result is robust to a number of different formulations and does not seem to be plagued by endogeneity. We control for endogeneity using a size dummy instrumental variable and three-stage least squares simultaneous equations, which reveal that there is a scale factor; the impact of better corporate governance practices is greater for larger firms in the upper-size quartile.

We also find that disclosure has a much larger impact on corporate value than do other corporate governance practices, such as board composition and voting procedures. This last result may be due to the low score of most firms in the questions pertaining to corporate governance practices in general, while their median disclosure score is much higher. Better disclosure practices were introduced in the mid-1970s through a new corporate law and have been perfected since then, while better corporate governance practices are a recent issue in Brazil; little was introduced in the new corporations law passed in 2001. Most new measures have been included in pension fund regulation and private contracting, as in the Novo Mercado. In a principal component analysis, we find that factors named one share–one vote and disclosure supervision had a large impact on Tobin's q, emphasizing the importance of aligning control and cash flow rights and of oversight.

We do not find a significant relationship between our ownership concentration variables and value. In most models, ultimate voting rights percentages of the largest shareholder and the wedge are negatively related to Tobin's q, while the total capital percentages are positively related. However, these relationships have never shown strong significance except for one model in one year. We do not find evidence for entrenchment and incentives as measured by the concentration percentages of the largest shareholder. However, as stated above, few firms abide by the one share–one vote rule. One reason for this surprising result may be the high concentration percentages of ownership by the largest shareholders. We do not find any significant evidence that the dividend payout is caused by corporate governance practices; this should probably be included as one of the corporate governance practices determined simultaneously with other measures. Dividends seem to be greater when control is more concentrated.

Investors in countries with poor legal protection, such as in Latin America, discount the prices of firms to compensate for expropriation. However, lower stock prices may not raise the demand for stocks sufficiently in these countries, thereby keeping the supply of outside equity limited.[20] It would be reasonable to assume that outside equity financing would increase if the risk of expropriation were reduced through better legal protection and better corporate governance practices. Our comparison with Chile reveals that Chile scores better in investor protection because of shareholder rights, by and large because of Brazil's predominant use of nonvoting shares, while the levels of disclosure and the quality of the judiciary in Chile are similar to those in Brazil.

One of the authors of this chapter has been asked to comment on a recent statement by the Brazilian Association of Public Companies about good corporate governance practices. The association essentially represents controlling shareholders, given the ownership structure of Brazilian companies depicted here. The document of the association is mostly generic and bland; however, when the association comments on the issuance of new shares, it uses stronger language and states that companies should use whatever securities are legally allowed in Brazil without adopting *dogmatic* positions regarding nonvoting stocks. (The emphasis is ours.) We are obviously not surprised by this statement, coming from such an association, but heartily disagree. We take precisely the kind of *dogmatic* view they try to avoid. Brazilian regulators have always been indulgent about nonvoting shares, and our market is dominated by them, but the market exhibits poor investor protection levels. We believe that it is time for bolder actions so as to inhibit the issuance of nonvoting shares. Our comparative analysis with Chile also suggests that this is the case.

There are initiatives in Brazil and in other Latin American markets to improve corporate governance practices. One key policy question is whether such practices pay off. Our analysis indicates they do. The very high concentration levels of voting rights and the widespread use of indirect control structures and nonvoting shares may deter most firms from adopting better corporate governance practices in Brazil. However, a small number of companies have improved their practices and are benefiting from a lower cost of capital. In fact, the Brazilian primary stock market experienced a renaissance in 2004; many strong brand-name private companies in cosmetics, airlines, logistics, energy, apparel, health care, insurance, and other industries went public by listing in the Novo Mercado. It is too early to say if this is a trend, but it is a good sign.

According to Morck and Yeung (2004), dividends are taxed each time they are paid in the United States. So, in a chain of firms in a pyramid, dividends are taxed every time they are paid in the chain so that when they are paid to ultimate shareholders at the apex of the pyramid, they have been taxed many times, creating a disincentive for pyramids. The United States was also once plagued by control pyramids, but introduced this taxation system in the 1930s precisely to fight them. Legislation banning pyramids from utility companies was also introduced in the United States at the same time. Both measures represent interesting policy issues. In Brazil, as we have discussed, dividends are not taxed at all. Therefore, dividends may be paid as many times as necessary, facilitating the transfer of earnings among firms in a single indirect control structure or group; this is an incentive for tunneling. Public utilities are regulated by independent agencies in Brazil. Given the nature of their business and their nearly monopolistic status in many cases, banning indirect control structures might be considered by authorities in the various regulated public services industries according to industry characteristics and market competition. Morck and Yeung also suggest that raising competition through globalization may undermine the value of political connections, thereby reducing the attractiveness of control pyramids.

Obviously, policy makers should encourage a greater number of firms to adopt better corporate governance practices. Our evidence of a scale factor shows that better incentives should be devised for smaller public and listed firms, as well as for nonpublic, family-controlled firms. Another general suggestion is to proceed, at least gradually, toward the elimination of nonvoting shares in Brazil. The recent change in the corporate law lowering the maximum amount of nonvoting shares issued and outstanding from 67 percent to 50 percent is a step in the right direction, but a long way from the ideal. However, some measures, such as the initiative of the National Development Bank to reduce the cost of debt among firms that commit to adopting better governance practices, have been left aside since the Lula administration took office (but are being quietly putting back into place). Considering the size of its financing operations, estimated at US$20 billion in 2004, we believe that this bank may be instrumental in improving corporate governance practices in Brazil, particularly because other sources of long-term financing are scarce and expensive. The bank should take an active role in promoting better corporate governance practices, and it should put its points for governance system in practice. Regulatory limits on asset allocation among institutional investors, particularly pension funds, should motivate acquisitions only among new issues that list in the Novo Mercado and provide higher ceilings for holdings of voting shares. The steady improvement of corporate governance practices depends on the permanent vigilance of the Securities Commission and on perfecting and enforcing corporate laws. The resources and oversight of the commission have been insufficient according to some of its own past chief commissioners. Lowering the costs firms incur to become more transparent and to adopt better corporate governance is another key line of action for policy makers, particularly if it is to become viable for smaller corporations to raise funds in Brazilian capital markets. One of these measures might be to lower the hidden taxes represented by the high cost of publication in official state registers. It is obvious that improving the legal process in the judiciary is a prerequisite for the development of the Brazilian corporate securities market. A substantial reduction in the cost of capital may await firms that improve corporate governance practices. The recent movement among strong brand-name companies that are going public to list in the Novo Mercado is evidence.

Annex 3.1 Variable Definitions

Variable	*Definition*
1TDIR	Percentage of total capital (voting and nonvoting) owned directly by the largest shareholder
1TIND	Percentage of total capital (voting and nonvoting) owned indirectly by the largest shareholder
1V/TDIR	Ratio (wedge) of the percentage of voting capital to total capital owned directly by the largest shareholder
1V/TIND	Ratio (wedge) of the percentage of voting capital to total capital owned indirectly by the largest shareholder
1VDIR	Percentage of voting capital owned directly by the largest shareholder
1VIND	Percentage of voting capital owned indirectly by the largest shareholder
3TDIR	Percentage of total capital (voting and nonvoting) owned directly by the three largest shareholders
3TIND	Percentage of total capital (voting and nonvoting) owned indirectly by the three largest shareholders
3V/TDIR	Ratio (wedge) of the percentage of voting capital to total capital owned directly by the three largest shareholders
3V/TIND	Ratio (wedge) of the percentage of voting capital to total capital owned indirectly by the three largest shareholders
3VDIR	Percentage of voting capital owned directly by the three largest shareholders
3VIND	Percentage of voting capital owned indirectly by the three largest shareholders
5TDIR	Percentage of total capital (voting and nonvoting) owned directly by the five largest shareholders
5TIND	Percentage of total capital (voting and nonvoting) owned indirectly by the five largest shareholders
5V/TDIR	Ratio (wedge) of the percentage of voting capital to total capital owned directly by the five largest shareholders
5V/TIND	Ratio (wedge) of the percentage of voting capital to total capital owned indirectly by the five largest shareholders
5VDIR	Percentage of voting capital owned directly by the five largest shareholders
5VIND	Percentage of voting capital owned indirectly by the five largest shareholders
ADR	1 if the firm has issued level 1, 2, or 3 ADRs; 0 otherwise

(continued)

Annex 3.1 Variable Definitions *(continued)*

Variable	*Definition*
AGR	Dummy indicating the presence of a shareholder agreement
CA/TA	Ratio of currents assets to total assets at year-end
CGI	Corporate governance index, scaled to a value between 0 and 24, taking into account 24 different aspects of the corporate governance structure of the company according to table 3.1
CGI reduced	CGI without questions 4 and 5 in table 3.1, which may be correlated to company size
FOR	Dummy indicating that the largest ultimate shareholder is a foreign investor
FREE	Percentage of outstanding shares available for trading
GOV	Dummy indicating that the largest ultimate shareholder is the government
Growth	Average annual growth of sales over the previous three years ending on the day of measurement of Tobin's q
INST	Dummy indicating that the largest ultimate shareholder is an institutional investor
Leverage	Ratio of total (nonequity) liabilities to total assets at year-end
NM	1 if firm is listed in levels 1, 2, or Novo Mercado at the São Paulo Stock Exchange; 0 otherwise
P/B	The market value of stock, divided by the book value of stock
Payout	The ratio of cash and stock dividends to net income with year-end values
P/S	The market value of equity divided by net sales
P/CF	The market value of equity, divided by earnings before interest, taxes, depreciation, and amortization
Prin 1	Principal component 1. Principal components extracted from the 24 questions that showed eigenvalues greater than 1 and that explained 5 percent or more of the questions variance. After a Varimax rotation, this factor showed absolute correlation values greater than 50 percent with questions 17 (0.80), 18 (0.78), and 24 (–0.68) in table 3.1. These have to do with the lesser use of nonvoting shares to leverage control over cash flow rights and the free-float (question 24). We called this factor one share–one vote. It is reasonable that the free-float is negatively correlated with the factor because nonvoting shares are the most liquid shares in Brazil. If they are not used and control is concentrated, than the free-float is less.

(continued)

Annex 3.1 Variable Definitions *(continued)*

Variable	*Definition*
Prin 2	Principal component 2. Same extraction criteria as Prin 1. After a Varimax rotation, this factor showed absolute correlation values greater than 50 percent with questions 7 (0.83) and 9 (0.74) in table 3.1. These have to do with the board's independence. We called this factor board independence.
Prin 3	Principal component 3. Same extraction criteria as Prin 1. After a Varimax rotation, this factor showed absolute correlation values greater than 50 percent with questions 13 (0.85) and 14 (0.81) in table 3.1. These have to do with freedom from corporate governance malpractice inquiries, and convictions. We called this factor malpractice free.
Prin 4	Principal component 4. Same extraction criteria as Prin 1. After a Varimax rotation, this factor showed absolute correlation values greater than 50 percent with questions 4 (0.50), 10 (–0.63), and 12 (0.71) in table 3.1. These have to do with using international accounting standards, board size, and presence of a fiscal board. Smaller companies tend to have smaller boards, no fiscal boards, and no international accounting standards usage; thus, the negative correlation of this question with this factor. We called this factor disclosure supervision.
Prin 5	Principal component 5. Same extraction criteria as Prin 1. After a Varimax rotation, this factor showed absolute correlation values greater than 50 percent with questions 11 (0.63), 15 (0.57), and 21 (0.75) in table 3.1. These have to do with board member terms, use of arbitration, and generous tag-along rights. We called this factor shareholder rights enforcement.
Prin 6	Principal component 6. Same extraction criteria as Prin 1. After a Varimax rotation, this factor showed absolute correlation values greater than 50 percent with questions 1 (0.71), 5 (0.61), and 22 (0.60) in table 3.1. These have to do with disclosure of related party transactions, auditor quality, and pyramids. We called this factor related party transactions potential.
PYR	Dummy indicating the presence of a pyramid (indirect structure). La Porta, López-de-Silanes, and Shleifer (1999) define a pyramid as a control structure whereby a public company is in the control chain of another public company. We use the term more loosely and call any indirect control structure a pyramid.

(continued)

Annex 3.1 Variable Definitions *(continued)*

Variable	*Definition*
ROA	Ratio of operating income to total assets (return on assets) at year-end
Size	Firm size, measured according to the natural logarithm of the book value of total assets in thousands of Brazilian reais at year-end
Size dummy	Equal to 1 if the firm size is in the top quartile; 0 otherwise. We also experimented with size dummies for the top decile, top third, and top half firm size in the sample. Firm size is defined as in Size above.
Tobin's q	Ratio of the market value to the book value of assets. The market value of assets is computed as the market value of equity, plus the book value of assets, minus the book value of equity at year-end values. The numerator, market value of equity, has been computed directly by Economática as the market price of the most liquid stock type (voting or nonvoting), times the total number of shares (voting and nonvoting).
Volatility	Annualized standard deviation of daily Brazilian currency stock returns in the year ending on the day of measurement of Tobin's q
VOTE	Percentage of voting capital to total capital

Source: Compiled by the authors.

Notes

1. At the end of 2002, the last year for which this chapter's governance scores have been computed, Argentina's market capitalization was US$17 billion, Brazil's was US$127 billion, Chile's was US$50 billion, and Mexico's was $103 billion, according to the World Federation of Exchanges. Gross domestic product at the end of 2003 was US$130 in Argentina, US$492 billion in Brazil, US$72 billion in Chile, and US$626 billion in Mexico, according to the World Bank (2003).

2. The index is recalculated here because there was a misconception involving the dual shares dummy reported in La Porta et al. (1998) for Brazil. The so-called Brazilian preferred shares are actually nonvoting shares that do not possess the characteristics of preferred shares in the United States.

3. See Shleifer and Vishny (1997); La Porta et al. (1998, 2000a, 2002).

4. See Shleifer and Vishny (1997); La Porta et al. (1998, 2000a, 2002); Claessens et al. (2002).

5. Bovespa created two new trading lists for existing firms in December 2000 called the level 1 list and the level 2 list. The term Novo Mercado is also used to refer to the trading list for companies that adhere essentially to the level 2 requirements and issue only voting shares when they first list. The level 1 requirements involve better disclosure and liquidity. The level 2 requirements are much more

demanding and include all the level 1 requirements, plus accounting that follows international standards; tag-along rights; voting rights for nonvoting shares in some cases, such as mergers and acquisitions; a unified one-year term for board members; and submission to an arbitrage court. In September 2004, Bovespa had 358 listed firms, of which only five were on the level 2 trading list, 31 on the level 1 trading list, and four in the Novo Mercado. Voluntary adherence to better governance and disclosure practices has been slow, although there is some precarious empirical evidence that such adherence may have a positive impact on corporate value; see Gledson de Carvalho (2000). For additional details, see http://www.bovespa.com.br.

6. The average daily trading volume was US$272.7 million in 2003. The 10 largest market capitalization companies accounted for approximately 47 percent of the market capitalization and 51.2 percent of the trading volume. This chapter's sample of about 250 firms each year accounts for more than 90 percent of the market capitalization.

7. For example, the latest IBGC survey started with a sample of 285 firms, and about 1,500 questionnaires were mailed. Responses totaled 110 questionnaires, representing 70 firms.

8. See IBGC (2003).

9. Tag-along rights basically relate to the minimum proportion of the price paid to controlling shareholders that is to be paid to minority voting shareholders during acquisitions.

10. See Morck, Shleifer, and Vishny (1988); La Porta et al. (2002).

11. See Nenova (2001); Valadares (2002).

12. In a related paper, we detail how we used a reduced CGI with the 15 most discriminating questions computed for every year between 1998 and 2002. The result is the same trends described above. There is a modest improvement in corporate governance practices, in particular, a rise in the number of firms with much better practices than most. See Carvalhal-da-Silva and Leal (2005) for details.

13. The analysis is available upon request.

14. We thank Professor Jairo Procianoy for a discussion on share repurchases and the use of this means to expropriate minority shareholders.

15. The results are available upon request.

16. See Carvalhal-da-Silva and Leal (2005).

17. See Gledson de Carvalho (2000).

18. The other results are available upon request.

19. The legality index has been computed by Berkowitz, Pistor, and Richard (2003). The judicial efficiency index has been obtained from the International Country Risk Guide for 2000. See PRS Group (2004).

20. See Shleifer and Wolfenzon (2002).

References

Agrawal, A., and C. Knoeber. 1996. "Firm Performance and Mechanisms to Control Agency Problems between Managers and Shareholders." *Journal of Financial and Quantitative Analysis* 31 (3): 377–97.

Barontini, R., and G. Siciliano. 2003. "Equity Prices and the Risk of Expropriation: An Analysis of the Italian Stock Market." ECGI Finance Working Paper 24, European Corporate Governance Institute, Brussels, http://ssrn.com/abstract=443220.

Bauer, R., N. Günster, and R. Otten. 2004. "Empirical Evidence on Corporate Governance in Europe: The Effect on Stock Returns, Firm Value, and Performance." *Journal of Asset Management* 5 (2): 91–104.

Bebchuk, L. A., A. Cohen, and A. Ferrell. 2004. "What Matters in Corporate Governance?" Harvard Law School John M. Olin Discussion Paper 491, Harvard Law School, Cambridge, MA, http://ssrn.com/abstract=593423.

Becht, M., P. Bolton, and A. Röell. 2003. "Corporate Governance and Control." In *Corporate Finance*, ed. G. M. Constantinides, M. Harris, and R. Stulz, 1–109. Vol. 1A of *Handbook of the Economics of Finance*. Vol. 21 of *Handbooks in Economics*. New York: Elsevier North Holland.

Berkowitz, D., K. Pistor, and J. Richard. 2003. "Economic Development, Legality, and the Transplant Effect." *European Economic Review* 47 (1): 165–95.

Berle, A., and G. Means. 1932. *The Modern Corporation and Private Property*. New York: Macmillan.

Black, B. S., H. Jang, and W. Kim. 2006. "Does Corporate Governance Predict Firms' Market Values?: Evidence from Korea." *Journal of Law, Economics, and Organization* 22 (2): 366–413.

Brown, L. D., and M. L. Caylor. 2006. "Corporate Governance and Firm Performance." *Journal of Accounting and Public Policy* 25 (4): 409–34.

Carvalhal-da-Silva, A. L., and R. P. C. Leal. 2004. "Corporate Governance, Market Valuation, and Dividend Policy in Brazil." *Frontiers in Financial Economics* 1 (1): 1–16.

———. 2005. "Corporate Governance Index: Firm Valuation and Performance in Brazil." *Revista Brasileira de Finanças* 3 (1): 1–18.

Claessens, S., S. Djankov, J. P. H. Fan, and L. H. P. Lang. 2002. "Disentangling the Incentive and Entrenchment Effects of Large Shareholdings." *Journal of Finance* 57 (6): 2741–71.

Claessens, S., S. Djankov, and L. H. P. Lang. 2000. "The Separation of Ownership and Control in East Asian Corporations." *Journal of Financial Economics* 58 (1–2): 81–112.

Coffee, J. C., Jr. 2003. "What Caused Enron?: A Capsule Social and Economic History of the 1990s." Columbia Law and Economics Working Paper 214, Columbia University Law School, New York, http://ssrn.com/abstract=373581.

DaDalt, P. J., J. Donaldson, and J. Garner. 2003. "Will Any Q Do?" *Journal of Financial Research* 26 (4): 535–51.

Da Silveira, A. M., L. A. B. C. Barros, and R. Famá. 2003. "Estrutura de governança e valor das companhias abertas brasileiras." *Revista de Administração de Empresas* 43 (3): 50–64.

Doidge, C. 2004. "U.S. Cross-Listings and the Private Benefits of Control: Evidence from Dual-Class Firms." *Journal of Financial Economics* 72 (3): 519–53.

Doidge, C., G. A. Karolyi, and R. M. Stulz. 2004. "Why Are Foreign Firms Listed in the U.S. Worth More?" *Journal of Financial Economics* 71 (1): 205–38.

Durnev, A., and E. H. Kim. 2005. "To Steal or Not to Steal: Firm Attributes, Legal Environment, and Valuation." *Journal of Finance* 60 (3): 1461–93.

Eisenberg, M. 1998. "Corporate Conduct That Does Not Maximize Shareholder Gain: Legal Conduct, Ethical Conduct, the Penumbra Effect, Reciprocity, the Prisoner's Dilemma, Sheep's Clothing, Social Conduct, and Disclosure." *Stetson Law Review* 28 (1): 1–27.

Faccio, M., and L. H. P. Lang. 2002. "The Ultimate Ownership of Western European Corporations." *Journal of Financial Economics* 65 (3): 365–95.

Fluck, Z. 1998. "Optimal Financial Contracting: Debt Versus Outside Equity." *Review of Financial Studies* 11 (2): 383–418.

Gillette, A., T. Noe, and M. Rebello. 2003. "Corporate Board Composition, Protocols, and Voting Behavior: Experimental Evidence." *Journal of Finance* 58 (5): 1997–2032.

Gledson de Carvalho, A. 2000. "Ascensão e Declínio do Mercados de Capitais no Brasil: A Experiência dos Anos 90." *Economia Aplicada* 4 (3): 595–632.

Gledson de Carvalho, A., and G. G. Pennacchi. 2005. "Can Voluntary Market Reforms Promote Efficient Corporate Governance?: Evidence from Firms' Migration to Premium Markets in Brazil." University of São Paulo Working Paper, January 25, University of São Paulo, São Paulo, http://ssrn.com/abstract=678282.

Gompers, P. A, J. L. Ishii, and A. Metrick. 2003. "Corporate Governance and Equity Prices." *Quarterly Journal of Economics* 118 (1): 107–55.

Hermalin, B. E., and M. S. Weisbach. 2003. "Boards of Directors as an Endogenously Determined Institution: A Survey of the Economic Literature." *Economic Policy Review* 9 (1): 7–26.

Himmelberg, C. P., R. G. Hubbard, and D. Palia. 1999. "Understanding the Determinants of Managerial Ownership and the Link between Ownership and Performance." *Journal of Financial Economics* 53 (3): 353–84.

IBGC (Brazilian Institute of Corporate Governance). 2003. *Newsletter*, March–April, Brazilian Institute of Corporate Governance, São Paulo.

Jensen, M. C. 1986. "Agency Costs of Free Cash Flow, Corporate Finance, and Takeovers." *American Economic Review* 76 (2): 323–29.

Jensen, M. C., and W. H. Meckling. 1976. "Theory of the Firm: Managerial Behavior, Agency Costs, and Ownership Structure." *Journal of Financial Economics* 3 (4): 305–60.

John, K., and L. Senbet. 1998. "Corporate Governance and Board Effectiveness." *Journal of Banking and Finance* 22 (4): 371–403.

Klapper, L. F., and I. Love. 2004. "Corporate Governance, Investor Protection, and Performance in Emerging Markets." *Journal of Corporate Finance* 10 (5): 703–28.

Klein, A. 2002. "Audit Committee, Board of Directors Characteristics, and Earnings Management." *Journal of Accounting and Economics* 33 (3): 375–400.

Kohlbeck, M. J., and B. W. Mayhew. 2004. "Related Party Transactions." Unpublished working paper, University of Wisconsin, Madison, WI, http://ssrn.com/abstract=592582.

La Porta, R., F. López-de-Silanes, and A. Shleifer. 1999. "Corporate Ownership around the World." *Journal of Finance* 54 (2): 471–517.

La Porta, R., F. López-de-Silanes, A. Shleifer, and R. W. Vishny. 1998. "Law and Finance." *Journal of Political Economy* 106 (6): 1113–55.

———. 2000a. "Investor Protection and Corporate Governance". *Journal of Financial Economics* 58 (1–2): 3–27.

———. 2000b. "Agency Problems and Dividend Policies around the World." *Journal of Finance* 55 (1): 1–33.

———. 2002. "Investor Protection and Corporate Valuation." *Journal of Finance* 57 (3): 1147–70.

Leal, R. P. C., A. L. Carvalhal-da-Silva, and S. Valadares. 2000. "Ownership, Control, and Corporate Valuation of Brazilian Companies." Paper presented at the Bovespa, CVM, and IBGC Latin American Corporate Governance Roundtable, São Paulo, April 26–28, http://www.oecd.org/dataoecd/56/25/1921869.pdf.

Leal, R. P. C., and C. L. Oliveira. 2002. "An Evaluation of Board Practices in Brazil." *Corporate Governance* 2 (3): 21–25.

Lefort, F., and E. Walker. 2000. "Ownership and Capital Structure of Chilean Conglomerates: Facts and Hypotheses of Governance." *Abante* 3 (1): 3–27.

———. 2005. "The Effect of Corporate Governance Practices on Company Market Valuation and Payout Policy in Chile." Research Network Working Paper R-515, Research Department, Inter-American Development Bank, Washington, DC.

Lins, K. 2003. "Equity Ownership and Firm Value in Emerging Markets." *Journal of Financial and Quantitative Analysis* 38 (1): 159–84.

Michaely, R., and W. Shaw. 1995. "Does the Choice of Auditor Convey Quality in an Initial Public Offering?" *Financial Management* 24 (4): 15–30.

Morck, R., A. Shleifer, and R. W. Vishny. 1988. "Management Ownership and Market Valuation: An Empirical Analysis." *Journal of Financial Economics* 20 (1): 293–315.

Morck, R., and B. Yeung. 2004. "Special Issues Relating to Corporate Governance and Family Control." Policy Research Working Paper 3406, World Bank, Washington, DC.

Myers, S. 2000. "Outside Equity." *Journal of Finance* 55 (3): 1005–37.

Nenova, T. 2001. "Control Values and Changes in Corporate Law in Brazil." Paper prepared for the European Financial Management Association Meetings, London, June 26–29, 2002, http://ssrn.com/abstract=294064.

Newman, P., E. Patterson, and R. Smith. 2005. "The Role of Auditing in Investor Protection." *Accounting Review* 80 (1): 289–313.

Patel, S., A. Balic, and L. Bwakira. 2002. "Measuring Transparency and Disclosure at Firm-Level in Emerging Markets." *Emerging Markets Review* 3 (4): 325–37.

Procianoy, J. L., and L. F. Moreira. 2004. "Open Market Stock Repurchases at Bovespa." Paper presented at the Fourth Brazilian Finance Society Meeting, Rio de Janeiro, July.

PRS Group. 2004. *International Country Risk Guide* 25 (3). East Syracuse, NY: Political Risk Services.

Rodrigues, M. A., and R. P. C. Leal. 2003. "O modelo de três fatores de Famá e French no Brasil." In *Gestão de Riscos no Brasil*, ed. A. Duarte, Jr. and G. Varga. Rio de Janeiro: Financial Consultoria.

Saito, R. 2002. "Share Repurchase Rules and Expropriation of Minority Shareholders: Evidence from Brazil." Working paper, Brazil Fundação Getúlio Vargas Business School, São Paulo, http://ssrn.com/abstract=602005.

———. 2003. "Determinants of the Differential Pricing between Voting and Non-Voting Shares in Brazil." *Brazilian Review of Econometrics* 23 (1): 77–109.

Shleifer, A., and R. W. Vishny. 1997. "A Survey of Corporate Governance." *Journal of Finance* 52 (2): 737–83.

Shleifer, A., and D. Wolfenzon. 2002. "Investor Protection and Equity Markets." *Journal of Financial Economics* 66 (1): 3–27.

Siffert Filho, N. 1998. "Governança Corporativa: Padrões Internacionais e Evidências Empíricas no Brasil nos Anos 90." *Revista do BNDES* 9: 123–46.

Standard & Poor's. 2003. *Global Stock Markets Factbook*. New York: Standard & Poor's.

Valadares, S. 2002. "Estimativa de Valor de Controle no Brasil." In *Finanças Aplicadas ao Brasil*, ed. M. Bonomo. Rio de Janeiro: FGV Editora.

Valadares, S., and R. Leal. 2000. "Ownership and Control Structure of Brazilian Companies." *Abante* 3 (1): 29–56, http://ssrn.com/abstract=213409.

Weir, C., and D. Laing. 2001. "Governance Structures, Director Independence, and Corporate Performance in the UK." *European Business Review* 13 (2): 86–95.

Wiwattanakantang, Y. 2001. "Controlling Shareholders and Corporate Value: Evidence from Thailand." *Pacific Basin Finance Journal* 9 (4): 323–62.

World Bank. 2003. "Report on the Observance of Standards and Codes (ROSC): Corporate Governance Country Assessment, Chile." Report, World Bank, Washington, DC, http://www.worldbank.org/ifa/rosc_chlcg.pdf.

Xie, B., W. Davidson, and P. J. DaDalt. 2003. "Earnings Management and Corporate Governance: The Role of the Board and the Audit Committee." *Journal of Corporate Finance* 9 (3): 295–316.

4

Corporate Governance, Market Valuation, and Payout Policy in Chile

*Fernando Lefort and Eduardo Walker**

Introduction

The growing interest in corporate governance practices around the world has reached Latin America both from positive and normative perspectives. In the case of Chile, the large, controversial control premiums transferred during acquisitions of controlling stakes in several flagship Chilean companies by foreign firms have triggered legal reform and raised investor awareness of the related problems. Despite this recent interest and the development advances in Chilean capital markets relative to markets in other countries of the region, corporate governance in Chile is far from perfect. Although recent studies such as Klapper and Love (2004) and Lefort and Walker (2003a) provide some approximate indicators, a major difficulty remains in that we do not have a precise measure of the relative strength of our governance mechanisms or of their importance in explaining firm value and performance.

A standard framework for analyzing corporate governance practices is provided by the principles of the Organisation for Economic Co-operation and Development. These principles acknowledge the importance not only of legal protection, but also of other mechanisms of corporate governance.

* We have benefited from comments by Florencio López-de-Silanes, Alberto Chong, Claudio Raddatz, and Lorenzo Preve. We thank Ronald Espinosa and Katherine Villalobos for their valuable research assistance.

The principles are classified according to five categories that encompass shareholder rights, board responsibilities, and the disclosure of information, among other concerns. Based on an analysis of the Chilean legal framework, the opinions of market participants, and conglomerate structure, Lefort and Walker (2003b) show that, according to a preliminary review of corporate governance practices in Chile, there is adequate compliance with 11 of the 16 principles of the Organisation for Economic Co-operation and Development examined, for a compliance rate of 69 percent. In addition, Klapper and Love (2004) construct corporate governance indexes (CGIs) using information produced by Credit Lyonnais Securities Asia for a list of 25 emerging economies. They find that, using a sample of 12 Chilean firms, Chile scores one of the highest values in the sample considered (61.6 percent). However, these authors also find that the two Latin American economies considered (Brazil and Chile) present the lowest correlation between firm performance and governance quality. These are not the only studies showing that Chile scores well in corporate governance measures. Using the La Porta, López-de-Silanes, and Shleifer (1999) antidirector rights index, Chile would score 5 on a 6 point scale.

Because Chile scores well in corporate governance measures relative to other emerging economies and because of the precocious development of its capital market (fueled in part by the early reform of its pension system) relative to most Latin American economies, the study of the effect of corporate governance measures on corporate performance in Chile is a subject of interest for the region.

In particular, the Chilean case presents at least three attractive features that render such a study especially relevant in terms of policy recommendations for countries in the region. First, the corporate structure in Chile is characterized by highly concentrated ownership, the widespread use of pyramids to separate cash flow rights and control rights, and opaque ultimate ownership identification. Second, from the legal point of view, the civil origin of the Chilean system is characterized by a lack of self-regulation practices in capital markets, although an amendment to the law on the securities market and the law on corporations has recently been passed with the intention of improving corporate governance in Chile. Finally, the Chilean capital market is relatively developed, with more than two decades of substantial participation by institutional investors.

Accordingly, this chapter reports on the results of two main initiatives. First, we have built an extensive database at the firm level comprising standard corporate governance charter measures. The database includes two different types of data. The first type is drawn from a corporate governance survey of principal executives and board members of more than 100 listed companies in Chile. Through this survey, we have been able to gather more than 60 binary-type parameters measuring transparency, accountability, and other aspects of corporate governance as of the year 2003. The second type of data is drawn from a panel of several quantitative variables measuring ownership structure, the separation of cash flow rights and control rights, payout policy, and market valuation, plus a list of firm-specific characteristics. This second type of data was collected annually for the period 1990–2002 for all companies listed on Chilean stock markets. For this purpose, we have carefully identified conglomerate structures in Chile and built consolidated financial statements at the conglomerate level.

Second, we have performed panel data regression analysis to estimate the impact of these corporate governance variables on corporate valuation and payout policy in Chile. This is in line with the surge in empirical research on corporate governance following the seminal work of La Porta, López-de-Silanes, Shleifer, and Vishny (in various combinations) during the 1990s. The original research investigated whether specific legal arrangements relating to investor protection in different countries affected capital market development. The focus of this chapter is a related question. Here, we ask whether corporate governance practices at the firm level within a single country affect the market valuation of these firms. This question is crucial in assessing the potential benefits for firms of changing their own practices, even though they may not affect the rules in their country. As more empirical studies attempt to address this question, our understanding of the difficulties involved in the task improves. Even if firm-level corporate governance practices correlate with share prices, we may not be sure that these practices cause investors to value firms more highly. Alternative explanations related to different forms of endogeneity and omitted variable bias are also consistent with such empirical findings.

In this chapter, we perform regression analysis of measures of firm performance and payout policy on corporate governance indicators at the firm level and a series of control variables. We carefully check that our results are not due to omitted variable bias or to particular specification and samples through an extensive robustness check. We also control for reverse causality using two features of the Chilean law on corporations that provide an exogenous instrument for some of the corporate governance practices of Chilean firms. In summary, we find that firms that present higher coincidence between cash flow rights and control rights tend to be consistently more valued by the market. We interpret this result as an indication that potential conflicts of interest between controllers and minority shareholders are penalized by the Chilean capital market.

The structure of the chapter is as follows. In the next section, we describe the Chilean capital market and its institutional environment. The following section provides a conceptual framework for the working hypotheses of the chapter. The subsequent section describes the extensive process of data gathering and compilation. The section thereafter analyzes empirically the effect of agency problems on firm market valuation and payout policy, and the penultimate section examines the statistical relationship between good corporate governance practices and company value in Chile. The final section concludes.

Capital Markets and the Institutional Environment: An Overview

The Chilean capital market is characterized by high market capitalization and low turnover. By 2002, approximately 250 different stocks were traded on the Santiago Stock Exchange, with a total market value of nearly US$60 billion, or 85 percent of the country's gross domestic product. However, the turnover ratio is low; it has fallen to 7.5 percent of market capitalization. Capital issues have also declined since 1997, averaging US$1.2 billion per annum over the last five years; there was only US$270 million in capital issues in 2001, or 3 percent of fixed capital formation. Delistings have increased, and, since 1997, there have been only two new listings in the stock market, confirming a declining trend in the importance of the stock market as a source of funds for companies. For the 60 most highly traded stocks, 68 percent of the equity is held by controlling shareholders. The concentration level is even higher in the case of less highly traded stocks. The free-float is therefore around 32 percent in the case of the most highly traded stocks and 14 percent overall. However, about 25 percent of the free-float is held by domestic pension funds that trade their holdings infrequently. Another 25 percent of market value not held by controlling shareholders is held for depositary receipts. Thus, only about 10 to 15 percent of issued stocks are generally traded on the domestic stock exchange.

Groups are the predominant form of corporate structure in Chile. Lefort and Walker (2000a) show that around 70 percent of listed nonfinancial companies in Chile belong to one of approximately 50 conglomerates controlling, as a group, 91 percent of the assets of listed nonfinancial companies in the country. There is no clear declining trend in these figures. Cross holdings are prohibited in Chile, and dual-class shares, although allowed, are seldom used by Chilean corporations. By far, the most common way of separating control rights from cash flow rights in Chilean conglomerates is through simple pyramid schemes. The 1986 banking law imposed restrictions on related lending and prohibited banks from owning shares of corporations. These regulations have notably decreased the importance of banks for conglomerates.

On the other hand, institutional investors are important in Chilean securities markets. The main institutional investors are pension fund managers, who have more than US$35 billion in assets, and insurance companies, which manage US$12 billion in assets. Although pension funds have been allowed to invest in equity only since 1985, the value of their stock holdings during the 1990s reached a peak of more than 30 percent of the total market value of pension funds. Because the Chilean pension fund system is mandatory and of the defined contribution type, several capital market regulations have pursued the development of an adequate capital market wherein pension funds might safely and efficiently channel retirement savings. In addition, the authorities have developed appropriate supervision institutions that control compliance with this regulatory framework.

The securities market law and the corporations law comprise the legal framework governing capital markets and the actions of companies listed in Chile. The main body of both the corporations law and the securities law was written in 1981. They were both amended in 1989 and more deeply in 1994. More recently, both laws were amended by the corporate governance law of 2000. In 2001, the securities market law was again amended. Although the Chilean legal system follows the tradition of French civil law, the securities market law and the corporations law were written and reformed on the basis of their counterparts in the United States. However, as the Chilean judiciary does not enjoy the same flexibility as exists under common law, some tension arises between the spirit of the law and its application. In addition, sharp differences in ownership concentration, market liquidity, and law enforcement between Chile and the United States persist, and convergence is not evident.

Three main supervisory entities overlook different aspects of financial markets in Chile: the Securities and Insurance Commission (SVS), the Commission on Banks and Financial Institutions, and the Commission on Pension Fund Managers. The Central Bank also participates actively in the regulatory and supervisory process within the financial system, especially on issues regarding international transactions and foreign market participants. The main supervisory entity, the SVS, was created in 1980 as an autonomous public organization linked to the Chilean Finance Ministry. It regulates all issuers of securities, the stock exchanges, the insurance industry, and all capital market participants, with the exception of pension fund managers and banks. The chairman (*superintendente*) is chosen by the president. More than 200 people work at the SVS, and recently the SVS received a budget increase to enhance its enforcement capacity.

Self-regulation is not important in Chilean capital markets. Regulations are imposed by the appropriate authorities, in the civil law tradition. Public corporations must be registered with the securities registrar administered by the SVS. In Chile, all shares are registered. At the moment of the initial public offering, a public corporation must sell at least 10 percent of its registered shares. As a continuing obligation, listed companies must provide all relevant information to the SVS in a timely fashion and prepare quarterly financial statements, which must be externally audited in December. The stock exchanges impose no additional requirements on listed companies. However, they may stop transactions at any time provided that there is reasonable suspicion of the existence of relevant information not disclosed to the market. The stock exchange must inform the SVS of this step within 24 hours, and transactions may be suspended for up to five days.

The SVS has taken the lead in recent reforms promoting minority shareholder protection and more disclosure. In December 2000, the securities market law and the corporations law were amended. The amendment, known as the corporate governance reform, introduced changes in five areas of the law. First, the market for control was regulated, requiring transactions involving changes of control to be performed through a tender offer under a version of the equal opportunity rule. Second, the regulator increased the information and disclosure requirements for listed corporations, especially in the case of transactions with related parties. Third, large listed corporations were required to form a committee with a majority of board members not related to the controlling shareholder; the functions of this committee were specified by law. Fourth, share repurchases were allowed in order to implement stock option packages as an incentive to executives. Fifth, equal treatment of foreign shareholders was guaranteed by law, especially in matters regarding voting procedures. The amendments included a transitional rule that allowed firms to postpone for three years the adoption of the new regulations on changes in control. Most large companies filed for the transitional rule. Additionally, the SVS is promoting the adoption of a best practices code for corporate governance and the creation of an institute of directors.

Conceptual Framework and Working Hypotheses

Conglomerates, Corporate Governance, and Company Valuation

It is well known now that, contrary to popular belief, the standard Bearle and Means (1936) firm, which is characterized by dispersed ownership, is a rare phenomenon in most economies.[1] In fact, most firms in emerging economies are linked in some way or another to an economic group or conglomerate that exercises tight control over the firm and owns a large fraction of the firm's shares.

As a consequence, a growing literature in corporate governance and corporate strategy has shifted its focus away from the standard agency problem between managers and dispersed shareholders in favor of examining the relationship between minority and majority shareholders. This is especially relevant in the case of emerging economies such as Chile. In particular, it has been argued that concentrated structures or economic groups are prone to carry inefficient investments and generate minority shareholder expropriation. This is so especially when the controlling shareholders of these groups exercise their control through complex mechanisms such as pyramid schemes, cross holdings, and dual-class shares. In such cases, the agency problem is exacerbated because, on the one hand, ownership concentration insulates the controller from the market for corporate control, and on the other hand, control is exercised by a shareholder who holds a relatively small fraction of the cash flow rights.[2]

Interestingly, many of the studies on this issue recognize that one of the most salient characteristics of conglomerates in emerging economies is that they are persistent in time and able to adapt to most changing situations. Khanna and Palepu (1999a, 1999b) on Chile and India and Lefort and Walker (2000a) on Chile have shown that conglomerates have been able to grow and increase their scope and self-intermediation practices even during times of fierce economic reform and deregulation. This kind of evidence has supported a more favorable view of conglomerates in emerging economies, suggesting that economic groups are a natural and efficient way for firms to deal with imperfect capital markets, poor institutions, corruption, and other imperfections that plague emerging economies.[3] In this context, economic groups arise to fill voids left by (or to take advantage of) poor institutions. In particular, internal capital markets, that is, the allocation of funds by a headquarters to the various business units of a conglomerate, create value in a credit-constrained world.[4] Other financial synergies arise because of the option available to conglomerates to liquidate the assets of specific units in response to a general downturn[5] and because of risk diversification that might be valuable to investors in economies with imperfect capital markets. Operational synergies are also generated through conglomeration. These might be related to economies of scale and scope in product and factor markets arising because of poor basic services such as power provision or postal delivery. Groups may enjoy an additional advantage in settings where consumer protection is poor and group branding provides an advantage. One of the reasons cited most often for the presence of conglomerates in emerging markets is the advantage they create in dealing with a corrupt government, a highly regulated economy, and a poor judiciary system.[6]

We now have a better understanding of the ownership and control structures of firms in most emerging economies, and we have at least two competing conceptual frameworks for explaining the costs and benefits of conglomerates in emerging markets. It is not surprising, then, that an empirical literature has developed to try to ascertain whether affiliation with a conglomerate constitutes good news for investors. Some of the most important contributions in the attempt to explain the performance of business groups in emerging markets include Khanna and Palepu (1999a, 1999b), who find that group affiliation improves firm economic performance in Chile and India. They also find that the degree of diversification of the conglomerate helps enhance performance only after the diversification has reached a certain threshold. In addition, Khanna and Palepu (1999c) find that, in Chile and India, the performance of groups has improved following economic reform, indicating that part of the benefits of affiliation are not related to the poor economic environment. Khanna and Rivkin (2001) look at firms in 18 emerging economies and find that affiliated firms perform better in six countries, worse in three, and equally well in five. They also find that the returns on firms belonging to a single conglomerate tend to move more closely relative to those of other firms. Claessens, Djankov, and Klapper

(2000) find that East Asian group structures are used to diversify risks, while Claessens, Djankov, and Lang (2000) show that East Asian firms affiliated with conglomerates present a 4 percent average value discount and that this discount arises in firms in which the owners have more voting rights than cash flow rights. Thomsen and Pedersen (2001) look at the 435 largest European companies and find that ownership concentration shows a nonlinear relationship with performance whereby too much concentration reduces performance. Lefort and Walker (2003a) find preliminary evidence for Chile that firm affiliation with a group tends to decrease firm value and that this effect is partially reduced when there is little separation between cash flow rights and control rights.

Klapper and Love (2004) use data on more than 400 companies in 25 emerging economies to show that good corporate governance practices are highly correlated with the market valuation of firms. Their study also indicates the importance of legal protection. It turns out that, although firm-level corporate governance practices tend to be worse in countries with poor legal protection, they make a more important difference in terms of individual market valuation. Similar results for a developed economy such as the United States are provided by Gompers, Ishii, and Metrick (2003).

Corporate Governance and Payout Policy

The major objective of adequate corporate governance practices is the satisfactory compensation of company shareholders. Under the assumptions of the original Modigliani-Miller irrelevance theorems, dividend policies are irrelevant for company value and shareholder wealth. However, under asymmetric information, there are several hypotheses that may be raised to relate corporate governance practices and payout policy in the context of the agency problem inherent to a modern corporation. On the one hand, La Porta, López-de-Silanes, and Shleifer (1999) have argued that a specific dividend policy is the result of the pressure exercised by minority shareholders to force insiders to pay cash. Under this view, more investor protection should be associated with a more generous payout policy to shareholders. On the other hand, La Porta, López-de-Silanes, and Shleifer (1999) argue that the association might react the other way around in that insiders would pay high dividends to obtain a good reputation. High dividends would thus act as a compensatory policy at the firm level. In this case, more and better shareholder rights will reduce the need to establish a good reputation; this implies lower dividend levels. This family of theories on dividend policies is sometimes called rent-seeking theory.[7]

More traditional theories of the relevance of dividend policies under asymmetric information emphasize the signaling importance of payout policies with respect to future cash flows in a company. An example of this line of thought is provided by Bharati, Gupta, and Nanisetty (1998), who show how dividend policies may be used by insiders to give signals to the market regarding the company's prospects of future profits. A related theory of dividend policy determinants is the catering theory, which revolves around the presence of uninformed investors and the existence of dividend-driven stock premiums.[8]

In the context of an emerging economy that presents high ownership concentration and extensive use of conglomerates and pyramid structures, such as the case of Chile, the rent-seeking theory of the effect of agency problems on payout policies seems to be especially relevant. Large and controlling shareholders have the incentive and the power to extract private benefits of control at the expense of minority shareholders because the controlling shareholders receive the full benefits, but only bear a fraction of the cost. In this situation, a dividend payment guarantees equal treatment to all shareholders. Gugler and Yurtoglu (2002) hypothesize that, under the rent-seeking view of dividend payments, an increase in dividends implies that there is less cash available for expropriation and therefore an abnormally positive return. Their results support this hypothesis since dividend reductions in companies with higher ownership concentration generate larger negative wealth effects.

Other papers have tested the rent-seeking hypothesis about dividends. Faccio, Lang, and Young (2001) and Gugler and Yurtoglu (2002), following La Porta et al. (2000), test this hypothesis on companies in Asia and Western Europe, including Finland and Germany. In general, the evidence is supportive of the hypothesis indicating that firms with strong controlling shareholders tend to exhibit lower payout ratios. This effect is mitigated if there is a second blockholder in the company.

Data Sources and Corporate Governance Measures

Data Sources

We have used several data sources. Complete accounting and financial information is provided on the Fecus Plus database prepared by the Santiago Stock Exchange for all listed companies. In some cases, it has been necessary to contact firms directly or to use other public records to complete missing information. The Fecus Plus database also provides information on main shareholders, board members, and a set of corporate features and policies. Some historical market information for listed companies has been obtained through Economática or directly from the Santiago Stock Exchange. The SVS provides data on corporate actions and the material information reported to the SVS. We have also used the *Diario Oficial* (Official Gazette) database to identify the investment companies used by ultimate conglomerate owners to control firms. This is an important input in the conglomerate consolidation procedure.

In addition, we sent a questionnaire on corporate governance practices to officers and board members of more than 200 companies listed on stock markets in Chile. The questionnaire consists of 67 questions and has been adapted for the Chilean market from the Credit Lyonnais Securities Asia questionnaire used by Klapper and Love (2004).

Ownership and Control Structures of Listed Chilean Firms

A crucial aspect of corporate governance mechanisms in Chile is the ownership structure. Conglomeration and the widespread use of pyramids to separate cash flow rights from control rights constitute important measures of the incentive structure and the likelihood of agency costs. We have revised and expanded the Lefort and Walker (2000a) database with an eye to the universe of Chilean corporations registered with SVS in 1990–2002. Our final database comprises almost 200 public companies that were listed for at least one year during that period. We have analyzed the balance sheets and shareholder identification information submitted by these firms to the SVS. We have used this information, along with the Diario Oficial database, to undertake a detailed analysis of the direct and indirect holdings of groups in each corporation to replicate the ownership chains that characterize Chilean conglomerates. Through this procedure, we have reproduced consolidated economic balance sheets at the group level, allowing us to avoid double counting among related investments. We have also constructed market value balance sheets at the individual firm level. These calculations are essential for producing correct measurements of the economic performance and value of firms and for constructing measures of the separation between cash flow rights and control rights.

The first step in building ownership chains consists of identifying the corporations associated with specific conglomerates. We use the definition of groups found in Lefort and Walker (2000a) and apply it to the years 1991–93, 1995–97, and 1999–2003. In this procedure, we consider a list of 50 economic groups that are diverse in terms of size, number of public companies controlled, identity of the controlling shareholder, and other dimensions. In using this definition, we exclude groups that are only comprised of closed (that is, nonpublic) companies that are not consolidated within any public company. It may well be the case that a group in our sample has only two public companies. Obviously, in some instances, we have not been able to consolidate the nonpublic companies belonging to the groups in the sample. Despite this, our study adds a considerable amount of new information on conglomerates in Chile.

The second step in the consolidation procedure is the identification of all links among companies controlled by a group. In most cases, these companies are linked through pyramid schemes that must be properly identified to avoid the double counting of group assets. As Lefort and Walker (2000a) show, pyramid schemes are the most common method used to achieve control by Chilean conglomerates because cross holdings are forbidden by law and dual-class shares are relatively rare. To determine the investments of minority and controlling shareholders in subsidiary and parent companies, we have used the information about the 12 most important stockholders provided to the SVS by corporations. We have used public information in the Diario Oficial to identify the owners of investment companies among the 12 largest shareholders of each corporation and to associate them with the different groups. In some cases, it is possible that we have underestimated the stakes of controlling shareholders because some of the group holdings may be realized through investment vehicles that do not appear among the 12 largest shareholders. However, considering that the 12th-largest shareholder holds, on average, less than 1 percent of total shares and that the 12 largest investors usually hold at least 80 percent of company shares, it is unlikely that this may introduce a substantial bias.

Through this tedious procedure, we have been able to compute several entries in consolidated balance sheets such as the direct and indirect investments of controlling shareholders in parent companies and subsidiaries. In both cases, the specific investment vehicles used by group members must be identified through the official company registrations in the Diario Oficial. A more detailed explanation may be viewed in Lefort and Walker (2000a).

Tables 4.1–4.3 summarize the data on Chilean conglomerates for selected years. Chilean economic groups directly control more than 70 percent of listed Chilean companies, corresponding to 90 percent of the assets of these groups. This proportion has been stable for more than 13 years, but the capital structure of Chilean companies has been changing (see table 4.2). By 1990, listed companies controlled by economic groups showed ratios of debt to assets of nearly 26 percent. Because of rising equity prices, this ratio fell to 18 percent in 1994. By 2002, the ratios had increased to an average of 45 percent because of both the decrease in equity prices after the Asian crisis of 1997–98 and the absolute increase in debt issues. Firms not affiliated with conglomerates present much lower debt ratios. By 2002, their debt ratios were 12 percentage points lower than those of affiliated companies.

Table 4.3 shows the control structure of Chilean companies. The control to total equity columns show the proportion of total equity directly and indirectly owned by controlling shareholders. These ratios increased from 52 percent to 58 percent in the case of affiliated firms and decreased in the case of nonaffiliated firms. The figures have been calculated taking into account the consolidated holdings of equity through direct ownership and pyramid structures. It is clear that the percentage of consolidated equity held by controlling shareholders is much larger than needed strictly to exercise the control. Lefort and Walker (2000a) show that, on average, Chilean economic groups reside on 2.5 layers of listed companies; less than 20 percent of consolidated equity therefore represents a majority in every layer of the pyramid. The other columns measure the ratio of external funds (debt, plus minority shareholders) to the equity of controlling shareholders. This relationship gives an idea of the leverage of control exercised by those in control of the company at the consolidated level.

Table 4.1 The Importance of Chilean Conglomerates

	1990		*1994*		*1998*		*2002*	
Conglomerates	*Assets (US$ millions)*	*Relative size (%)*	*Assets (US$ millions)*	*Relative size (%)*	*Assets (US$ millions)*	*Relative size (%)*	*Assets (US$ millions)*	*Relative size (%)*
Largest	4,617	22.0	9,454	14.0	16,220	23.0	11,306	20.5
5 largest	9,264	44.0	34,018	51.0	37,704	54.0	26,304	47.6
10 largest	16,784	79.0	46,316	69.0	49,357	70.0	37,008	67.0
20 largest	18,784	88.0	54,259	81.0	57,570	82.0	46,655	84.5
All conglomerates	19,422	91.0	57,973	87.0	63,957	91.0	49,729	90.0
Nonaffiliated	1,841	9.0	8,879	13.0	6,059	9.0	5,511	10.0
Total	**21,263**	**100.0**	**66,852**	**100.0**	**70,017**	**100.0**	**55,241**	**100.0**

Source: Compiled by the authors.

Table 4.2 The Capital Structure of Chilean Conglomerates

	1990		1994		1998		2002	
Conglomerates	*Debt/ assets*	*Equity/ assets*	*Debt/ assets*	*Equity/ assets*	*Debt/ assets*	*Equity/ assets*	*Debt/ assets*	*Equity/ assets*
Largest	27.3	72.7	14.0	86.0	53.2	46.8	58.1	41.9
5 largest	26.6	73.4	14.7	85.3	46.0	54.0	52.9	47.1
10 largest	26.6	73.4	17.9	82.1	44.9	55.1	55.1	44.9
20 largest	25.4	74.6	18.2	81.8	45.7	54.3	54.8	45.2
All conglomerates	25.9	74.1	18.5	81.5	46.7	53.3	54.7	45.3
Nonaffiliated	22.5	77.5	11.1	88.9	42.7	57.3	43.4	56.6
Total	**25.6**	**74.4**	**17.6**	**82.4**	**46.4**	**53.6**	**53.6**	**46.4**

Source: Compiled by the authors.

In the empirical analysis in the next section, we use the inverse of this measure as an indicator of the degree of coincidence between cash flow rights and control rights, under the assumption that the controlling shareholders hold 100 percent of the controlling rights.

Dividend Policies and Payout Ratios in Chile

To measure the effect of corporate governance practices and investor protection on dividends, we have calculated annual payout ratios for more than 200 listed companies from 1994 to 2002. The data have been obtained from the Fecus Plus database and supplemented with data from Economática. We have used the ratio between dividend payments (including noncash payments) in year t and after-tax earnings in year $t - 1$ as an indicator of the dividend policy of each company. We have relied on this traditional measure even though dividends may often be paid out of earnings in other years.

In Chile, the law establishes a minimum dividend requirement of 30 percent of annual earnings. This compensatory measure is meant to protect minority shareholders;[10] it suggests that controlling shareholders enjoy less freedom in determining and applying dividend policies. In theory, a company might pay less than 30 percent of earnings if shareholders have unanimously approved such a step.[11] However, a company may also pay less than 30 percent by simply declaring the amount of the dividend and postponing the payment.[12] Hence, despite the legal restriction, it is possible to observe effective payout ratios of less than 30 percent of earnings.

Payout ratios in Chile were more than 53 percent in 1994, but steadily declined to 36 percent in 2002 (see table 4.4). There is a wide dispersion among the payout ratios in our sample; some companies paid out more than 150 percent of the previous year's earnings. Negative ratios generally indicate that a company paid dividends even though the previous year's earnings had been negative. Companies affiliated with a conglomerate have, on average, higher payout ratios than do nonaffiliated firms (see table 4.5).

Table 4.3 The Control Structure of Chilean Conglomerates

	1990		*1994*		*1998*		*2002*	
Conglomerates	*Control/ total equity*	*External/ control*	*Control/ total equity*	*External/ control*	*Control/ total equity*	*External/ control*	*Control/ total equity*	*External/ control*
Largest	55.4	1.5	63.7	0.8	18.4	10.6	49.1	3.9
5 largest	52.5	1.6	52.4	1.2	53.0	2.5	57.1	2.7
10 largest	52.9	1.6	53.2	1.3	56.0	2.2	60.2	2.7
20 largest	52.1	1.6	52.8	1.3	56.1	2.3	59.0	2.7
All conglomerates	52.3	1.6	53.6	1.3	57.0	2.3	58.8	2.8
Nonaffiliated	85.3	0.5	98.0	0.1	93.5	0.9	62.8	1.8
Total	**55.2**	**1.4**	**60.0**	**1.0**	**60.4**	**2.1**	**59.3**	**2.6**

Source: Compiled by the authors.

Table 4.4 Payout Ratios by Year

	1994	*1995*	*1996*	*1997*	*1998*	*1999*	*2000*	*2001*	*2002*
Mean	0.536	0.496	0.447	0.380	0.348	0.321	0.367	0.347	0.366
Standard deviation	0.374	0.327	0.346	0.347	0.334	0.337	0.375	0.337	0.447
Maximum	1.538	1.447	1.203	1.369	1.261	1.283	1.383	1.193	1.579
Minimum	0.000	0.000	–0.309	–0.380	–0.214	–0.571	–0.046	–0.608	–0.850

Source: Compiled by the authors.

Table 4.5 Payout Ratios by Conglomerate Affiliation

	All companies	*Affiliated companies*	*Nonaffiliated companies*
Mean	0.391	0.428	0.314
Standard deviation	0.366	0.366	0.353
Maximum	1.579	1.538	1.579
Minimum	–0.850	–0.850	–0.776

Source: Compiled by the authors.

Agency Problems

Corporate governance mainly involves dealing with agency problems inside the firm. In highly concentrated Chilean firms, agency problems generally take the form of conflicts of interest between controlling shareholders and minority shareholders. In this chapter, we explore several dimensions of this relationship and its impact on firm valuation and payout policies.

Several of the theories discussed elsewhere above maintain that agency problems between controlling shareholders and minority shareholders are more severe in firms affiliated with conglomerate structures. However, the effect of affiliation on firm valuation is not clear; this is demonstrated by the competing hypotheses. For instance, after controlling for the separation of rights, affiliation with a conglomerate in emerging economies may be value enhancing because of internal capital markets, information sharing, and other synergies. Following Lefort and Walker (2000a), we have identified more than 50 conglomerate structures operating in the Chilean economy between 1990 and 2002 and constructed a dummy variable taking a value of 1 if a company is affiliated with any such structures in any given year.

A key indicator of the potential existence of agency problems is the degree of separation between the cash flow rights accrued by a controlling shareholder and the control rights this shareholder is exercising. In measuring the separation between cash flow rights and control rights at the firm level, we take into account the direct and indirect holdings of controlling shareholders and the existence of dual-class shares. Following agency theory, we hypothesize that a higher separation is associated with a lower valuation and lower payout. We have constructed two different indicators of the degree of coincidence between cash flow rights and control rights under the assumption that the largest shareholder effectively controls all company assets.[13] We analyze the validity of this assumption elsewhere below. First, we measure separation as the ratio between the equity directly and indirectly owned by the largest shareholder and the total consolidated assets under the control of the company. This ratio captures the relative proportions of the cash flows accrued by the controlling shareholders and the total cash flows potentially generated by the company, including debt payments. The second measure considers only the ratio between the cash flows of the controlling shareholders and the cash flows of all shareholders. In both cases, the assumption of total effective control by the controlling shareholders means that the percentage of cash flow rights is a direct indicator of coincidence. Perfect coincidence is achieved as these variables approach 1.

Institutional investors have had an important role in helping to develop Chilean capital markets.[14] Specifically, pension fund managers may buy the shares of Chilean companies that reach specific levels of ownership dispersion and are approved as investment vehicles by the Risk Classification Commission. Hence, the presence of pension funds as shareholders of a company is an indication that the firm is less risky and that its governance mechanisms are more mature. In addition, once pension funds reach a given level of ownership in a company, they may elect a board member and become an active minority shareholder. Under the assumption that important institutional investors improve governance, their presence may improve performance. They may also be seen as a second important set of shareholders.[15]

Corporate Governance Practices

Corporate governance has many more dimensions than merely affiliation with a conglomerate and the degree of coincidence between cash flow rights and control rights. To complement our measures on those issues, we have conducted a survey on corporate governance practices at the firm level through a 67-item questionnaire for principal officers and board members of more than 200 listed companies in Chile. The survey was conducted between May and September 2004. Questions referred to firm practices as of the end of 2003.

The response rate was moderate to low. We received 59 completed questionnaires, representing less than 30 percent of the firms contacted (see table 4.6). The low response rate was expected given the type of survey we were conducting. Nonetheless, the companies that answered the questionnaire tended to be the largest in terms of market capitalization, accounting for 42 percent of total market capitalization in Chile. Around one-third of the questions in the survey could be directly completed using public information available from company financial statements and annual reports or information made public by the SVS. We have compiled information through these mechanisms for an additional 47 firms, achieving a total coverage of 106 companies, amounting to 76 percent of total market capitalization in Chile.

The questionnaire was divided into sections on the following four areas: (1) general principles, (2) officers and the board, (3) shareholders, and (4) disclosure and information. Most questions could be answered by a

Table 4.6 Questionnaire on Corporate Governance Practices, 2003, Distribution

Sample	*Number of firms*	*% of firms contacted*	*% of total listed firms*	*% of total market capitalization*
Companies contacted	206	100.0	76.3	98
Filled questionnaires	59	28.6	21.9	42
Direct sources	47	22.8	17.4	34
Total	106	51.5	39.3	76

Source: Compiled by the authors.

simple yes or no. For all of these questions (approximately 55), we used an indicator variable that took the value of 1 whenever the answer could be associated with best practices and 0 otherwise. In many cases, the answer was in fact "don't know/no answer." This was the case, for instance, for companies for which the questionnaires were filled using sources other than officers or board members. Indeed, one-third of the questions could not be answered using public information as detailed above. We then normalized each answer using a value between 0 and 7. A score of 7 would correspond to questions where all respondents received a 1 in the indicator regardless of the size of the company. We then averaged the results for each section. This procedure implicitly considers that each question has the same relative importance in measuring the quality of a company's corporate governance practices. This assumption is not necessarily true. The average results must therefore be interpreted with care.

Table 4.7 shows that, by 2003, Chilean companies were scoring relatively well in corporate governance practices, obtaining an overall score (unweighted) of 4.12 out of 7. Not surprisingly, the worst results were in the first category, general principles (2.63). Most Chilean companies do not have a code or a mission statement that gives any explicit importance to governance practices. The best scores were in the category disclosure and information (5.14). Chilean companies adequately disclose information on control, ownership, and related party transactions. The weakest aspects of information disclosure are promptness and the lack of announced targets with respect to future company performance.

The second category in the questionnaire involved officers and the board. The average score was 4.54. The weakest aspect revealed in this category was the low participation of independent directors on company boards and the absence of special committees such as audit and governance committees. According to corporation law in most Latin American countries, boards are the main decision-making bodies of companies, and

Table 4.7 Questionnaire on Corporate Governance Practices, 2003, Summary of Results

Category	*Number of questions*	*Average score*
Aboout general principles	7	2.63
About officers and the board	26	4.54
About shareholders	20	4.18
About disclosure and information	14	5.14
Total, average	67	4.12

Source: Compiled by the authors.

Note: Higher score means better corporate governance practices. The highest possible score is 7.

board members owe their loyalty and duty to all shareholders. However, as a consequence of the high ownership concentration in most firms in the region, boards tend to be much weaker in Latin American countries than in the United Kingdom or the United States and constitute a poor mechanism for governance. In general, boards in Latin America mainly serve as advisers to controlling shareholders because they contain few independent board members and few if any functioning committees. Lefort and Walker (2000a) have also examined board composition and operation in Chile and reach similar conclusions regarding the scarcity of truly independent directors in corporations.

In areas related to shareholder rights, Chilean companies scored relatively well (4.18). This was the case in regard to the application of the one share–one vote rule, the general voting rights of minority shareholders, and the absence of formal sanctions applied by the SVS on board members and officers.

To ascertain empirically the importance of corporate governance practices in the market valuation and payout policies of Chilean firms, we have focused on a subset of the questionnaire. We have selected 20 questions according to the following three criteria: (1) they had been answered directly or indirectly by most companies in the sample; (2) they capture a relevant feature of corporate governance practices in an emerging economy such as Chile; and (3) they may be answered by a simple yes or no. Table 4.8 summarizes the results for this subset of 20 questions that comprise our simple CGI for Chile.

The questions on the CGI are grouped into four categories: disclosure, board operation and independence, shareholder rights, and conflicts of interest. The table presents the questions and the original number of each question in the full-length questionnaire. The CGI has a maximum score of 20, but the average score of the 106 companies surveyed was 11.3, indicating only mediocre performance. Not surprisingly, the worst areas on the survey were board operation and conflict of interest. We detected a low level of board involvement in committees. Less than 5 percent of the largest firms in the country have a corporate governance committee, and only 14 percent have compensation or nomination committees. In only 21 percent of the companies is the chairman of the board an independent and unaffiliated board member. On 70 percent of the boards of the largest Chilean companies, there are board members who are also executives or board members of other companies in the same group, indicating a high degree of board intermingling and a lack of independence among board members. This result is consistent with the findings of Lefort and Walker (2000a) and indicates a high likelihood of conflict of interest at the group level.

On the other hand, large Chilean firms score relatively well in disclosure and shareholder rights. Chilean legislation, especially the law on corporations approved in 2000, is largely responsible for the rigorous disclosure of related party transactions by listed Chilean companies.

Table 4.8 Index on Corporate Governance Practices, Chile, 2003

Question number	*Original question number*	*Question*	*Number of yes*	*Number of no*	*No answers*	*Average score*
Disclosure						4.46
1	67	Does the company disclose related party transactions and/or conflicts of interest of managers and directors on the board?	106	0	0	100.0%
2	2	Does the company's annual report include a section devoted to the company's performance in implementing corporate governance principles?	12	93	1	11.4%
3	55	Has the company been sanctioned for failure to publish timely company reports in the last three years?	2	102	2	98.1%
4	54	Are accounts presented according to IGAAP?	51	55	0	48.1%
5	61	Is the external auditing company internationally recognized?	101	5	0	95.3%
6	25	Does the company disclose board compensation and benefits?	98	7	1	93.3%
Board functioning and independence						2.28
7	18	Does the company have a corporate governance committee?	5	100	1	4.8%
8	16	Does the company have an audit committee?	76	30	0	71.7%
9	14	Is the chairman of the board an independent, nonaffiliated director?	17	63	26	21.3%

(continued)

Table 4.8 Index on Corporate Governance Practices, Chile, 2003 *(continued)*

Question number	*Original question number*	*Question*	*Number of yes*	*Number of no*	*No answers*	*Average score*
10	9	Does the board have five to nine members?	22	84	0	20.8%
11	21	Are there any other committees in the board (that is compensation, nomination, and so on)?	15	87	4	14.7%
12	30	Has there been any sanction to the board or management for violations of securities and/or corporations laws in the last three years?	5	101	0	95.3%
Shareholder rights						2.61
13	34	Does each share have one vote?	100	6	0	94.3%
14	38	Do shareholders have to be present in the meeting to vote?	30	75	1	71.4%
15	41	Can shareholders ask management to include items in the list of topics to be dealt with during the shareholders' meetings?	83	17	6	83.0%
16	7	Is the company listed on a major foreign stock exchange?	13	93	0	12.3%
Conflict of interest						1.92
17	28	Are any board members also board members/executives of firms belonging to the same economic group?	68	30	8	30.6%
18	33	Is senior management remuneration tied to the value of company shares?	5	101	0	4.7%

(continued)

Table 4.8 Index on Corporate Governance Practices, Chile, 2003 *(continued)*

Question number	*Original question number*	*Question*	*Number of yes*	*Number of no*	*No answers*	*Average score*
19	42	Does the company disclose its ownership structure (that is the ownership by large shareholders)?	102	3	1	97.1%
20	12	Do the chairman of the board and the chief executive officer belong to the same family/controlling group?	26	39	41	60.0%

Source: Compiled by the authors.

The Effects of Agency Problems on the Market Valuation of Firms

Empirical research on corporate governance greatly increased in the wake of the seminal work of La Porta, López-de-Silanes, Shleifer, and Vishny during the 1990s. The original research investigated whether specific legal arrangements on investor protection in various countries affected the development of capital markets. This chapter focuses on a related question. We ask whether corporate governance practices at the firm level within a single country affect the market valuation of the firms. This question is crucial in assessing the potential benefits for firms of a change in their own practices, even though they may not affect the rules in their country. As clearly queried by Black, Jang, and Kim (2006): to what extent may a firm increase its market value by upgrading its corporate governance practices and to what extent is a firm tied to its home country's rules and reputation?

As an increasing number of empirical studies try to respond to this question, our understanding of the difficulties involved in the task improves. Even if firm-level corporate governance practices correlate with share prices, we cannot be sure that these practices cause investors to value firms more highly. Alternative explanations involving different forms of endogeneity and omitted variable bias are also consistent with the empirical findings.

In this section, we perform regression analyses of the measures of firm performance and payout policy on corporate governance indicators at the firm level and a series of control variables. Among the indicators of firm performance, we consider firm market valuation using Tobin's q and the ratio of the market to book value, the return on assets (ROA), and the ratio of dividends to earnings. The empirical model tries to capture the hypotheses discussed elsewhere above regarding company control structure, the extent of the agency problem at the firm level, and company market value.

The empirical model is therefore of the type:

$$y_{it} = \alpha + \beta_1(dgroup_{it}) + \beta_2(concent_{it}) + \beta_3(coincid_{it}) + ZF_{it}\cdot\Gamma_1 + ZG_{it}\cdot\Gamma_2 + \varepsilon_{it}, \quad (4.1)$$

where y is a firm performance and value indicator such as Tobin's q, the ROA, and the dividend payout ratio; *dgroup* is the affiliation to a conglomerate dummy; *coincid* is the degree of coincidence between cash flow rights and control rights at the firm level; *concent* is the ownership concentration at the firm level; *ZF* is a set of control variables at the firm level, including Tobin's q in the payout equation, and time and industry dummies; and *ZG* is a set of control variables at the group level.

For estimation purposes, we consider three different samples because of restrictions on data availability. First, we use annual panel data comprising all listed companies with a fair amount of trading (around 200) over a time horizon of 13 years (1990–2002). On average, this database supplies more than 1,800 firm-year observations, allowing robust estimates relying on different estimation procedures to be obtained on the relationship between agency problems and the market valuation of firms. Second, we construct a similar annual panel for the period 1994–2002 because no information on dividend payments was available for the period prior to 1994. This panel provides more than 1,100 firm-firm observations. Finally, in the next section, we analyze a cross-sectional sample of 106 large companies for the year 2003. Although this is a smaller database, we use it to capture the effect of other dimensions of corporate governance practices on firm valuation and payout policies. We also use it to provide estimates of the impact of corporate governance practices at the firm level on company valuation that are robust to the endogeneity problem. We use the CGI and its components for this purpose.

Econometric Concerns

Endogeneity. A key concern in this type of study is the potential endogeneity problem as discussed by Klapper and Love (2004) and Black, Jang, and Kim (2006), among others. In the context of this chapter, the endogeneity problem would arise, for instance, if firms with high market valuation tended to adopt good governance practices to improve the prices of their shares. In that case, part of the correlation captured in the regressions would reflect reverse causality. Black, Jang, and Kim (2006) refer to a slightly different type of endogeneity as optimal differences, which occurs when firms endogenously and optimally choose different governance practices in the sense of Demsetz and Lehn (1985).[16]

A related problem of spurious correlation might arise because of omitted variable bias. In equilibrium, corporate governance likely correlates with various economic variables. A study that omits some economic variables that predict both governance and share price might wrongly conclude that governance is directly associated with share price. This problem may be described by the observation that corporate governance practices at the firm level may be determined by the contracting environment of firms. For instance, firms with more tangible assets or more growth opportunities would want to improve corporate governance mechanisms to raise external financing. In such a situation, they may decide to reduce, for instance, the separation between control rights and cash flow rights or transfer control to other, perhaps foreign companies. Hence, if we do not adequately control for these variables, the governance factors will capture the effect of the contracting environment on the market value of firms.

Panel data estimation. The use of a panel database increases the number of observations, but introduces potential biases into the estimation. To account for unobservable individual effects, we provide fixed and random effects estimates, in addition to the traditional pooled least squares. Moreover, we also provide estimators consistent with generalized least squares heteroskedasticity in case observations of different companies present different variances. We also perform Hausman tests of specification to choose the best estimations.

Censored data. Traditionally, payout ratio data are censored at zero because companies do not pay negative dividends even if they were willing to. In addition, Chilean legislation requires companies to pay dividends of at least 30 percent of the profits from the previous year. Hence, we have estimated panel Tobit regressions in the case of payout ratios because of the censored nature of the dependent variable and have computed Hausman tests to evaluate the importance of the censoring problem.

Empirical Results on Agency Problems and Firm Valuation

In the first part of the empirical analysis, we want to explore the information contained in the panel data regarding the effect of agency conflicts at the firm level on market valuation and payout ratios. We take the lack of coincidence between cash flow rights and control rights as an indicator of conflict of interest and potential agency problems and, thus, as a proxy for bad corporate governance practices at the company level. In the next subsection, we complement our analysis by considering indicator variables of the quality of corporate governance that have been constructed from index variables derived from the questionnaire described elsewhere above.

To construct our proxy for the potential existence of agency problems, we calculate the market value of the consolidated equity held by the controlling shareholders of each company. We then divide this value by the market value of assets calculated as the sum of the market value of total equity, plus debt. As explained elsewhere above, this ratio indicates the percentage accruing to the controlling shareholders of each dollar of assets created by the company. We take this variable as an indicator of the coincidence between cash flow rights and control rights and we call it *Coincid.* We also compute a simple measure of ownership concentration as the fraction of total equity held by the three largest shareholders (*concent*).

To measure firm valuation, we consider three variables. Following most of the empirical literature, we use Tobin's q measured as the ratio between the sum of the market value of equity and the book value of debt on the one hand and the book value of assets on the other. We also calculate the ratio of the market to book value of equity and the ROA.

From a long list of control variables, we have selected a group affiliation dummy, a pension fund dummy, debt-equity ratios (at market value), the log of firm size, investment ratios, the available cash flow, the average traded volume, time dummies, and 11 industry dummies. Tables 4.9 and 4.10 explain the construction of these variables and summarize the related descriptive statistics, including cross correlations.

Table 4.9 Descriptive Statistics on the Main Variables

	Tobin's q	*MB Ratio*	*ROA*	*Concent*	*Coincid*	*DGroup*	*Dafp*	*LAEC*	*DE Ratio*	*Cash*	*Invest*	*Volume*
All sample (1990–2002)												
Number of observations	1851	1820	2500	2495	1980	3081	3081	2014	1960	1899	2030	1,102
Mean	1.30	1.47	5.9%	59.0%	38.0%	0.52	0.39	17.46	1.07	20.4%	6.1%	130,983
Median	1.08	1.12	5.4%	61.1%	34.5%	1.00	0.00	17.58	0.40	15.7%	2.3%	3,497
Maximum	5.00	7.40	47.0%	100.0%	99.7%	1.00	1.00	22.97	47.83	99.9%	98.0%	14,400,000
Minimum	0.40	0.04	–73.5%	0.0%	0.1%	0.00	0.00	6.82	0.00	–37.0%	–39.1%	0
Standard deviation	0.73	1.15	8.9%	24.9%	21.5%	0.50	0.49	2.11	2.77	19.7%	18.5%	678,779
1990												
Number of observations	109	108	145	141	119	237	237	122	118	0	0	0
Mean	1.15	1.29	7.7%	53.9%	34.8%	0.41	0.16	16.15	1.03	—	—	—
Median	0.99	1.00	6.3%	54.4%	32.5%	0.00	0.00	16.38	0.42	—	—	—
Maximum	5.00	7.03	47.0%	99.8%	91.3%	1.00	1.00	20.52	10.15	—	—	—
Minimum	0.44	0.15	–31.4%	2.2%	2.2%	0.00	0.00	8.71	0.00	—	—	—
Standard deviation	0.62	1.12	10.2%	26.7%	21.3%	0.49	0.36	2.10	1.82	—	—	—

(continued)

Table 4.9 Descriptive Statistics on the Main Variables *(continued)*

	Tobin's q	*MB Ratio*	*ROA*	*Concent*	*Coincid*	*DGroup*	*Dafp*	*LAEC*	*DE Ratio*	*Cash*	*Invest*	*Volume*
1991												
Number of observations	115	112	152	147	124	237	237	126	123	122	130	0
Mean	1.60	1.96	8.7%	56.9%	41.9%	0.44	0.20	16.79	0.45	27.5%	6.3%	—
Median	1.40	1.57	7.2%	57.2%	43.0%	0.00	0.00	16.93	0.25	22.2%	2.1%	—
Maximum	4.04	6.71	35.9%	99.8%	96.3%	1.00	1.00	21.06	4.08	97.3%	90.1%	—
Minimum	0.46	0.21	–19.3%	2.2%	2.2%	0.00	0.00	8.34	0.00	–3.9%	–33.2%	—
Standard deviation	0.84	1.38	9.7%	26.2%	21.7%	0.50	0.40	2.07	0.69	24.5%	17.8%	—
1992												
Number of observations	113	111	169	164	124	237	237	126	123	128	135	0
Mean	1.55	1.90	8.7%	58.3%	41.1%	0.48	0.27	17.02	0.52	28.6%	12.4%	—
Median	1.44	1.63	8.1%	59.6%	40.1%	0.00	0.00	17.13	0.26	23.7%	5.1%	—
Maximum	3.80	5.40	41.5%	100.0%	91.7%	1.00	1.00	21.24	13.57	99.9%	98.0%	—
Minimum	0.55	0.41	–26.1%	2.4%	2.4%	0.00	0.00	8.34	0.00	–20.8%	–32.8%	—
Standard deviation	0.74	1.17	9.9%	26.3%	20.9%	0.50	0.44	2.01	1.29	24.3%	24.1%	—

(continued)

Table 4.9 Descriptive Statistics on the Main Variables *(continued)*

	Tobin's q	*MB Ratio*	ROA	*Concent*	*Coincid*	*DGroup*	*Dafp*	LAEC	*DE Ratio*	*Cash*	*Invest*	*Volume*
1993												
Number of observations	116	114	179	180	125	237	237	126	124	137	147	0
Mean	1.64	2.02	8.0%	59.1%	41.2%	0.50	0.32	17.28	0.57	25.6%	8.8%	—
Median	1.41	1.61	7.3%	60.0%	39.3%	1.00	0.00	17.28	0.22	24.5%	6.1%	—
Maximum	4.10	6.49	34.1%	100.0%	92.9%	1.00	1.00	21.72	18.54	89.4%	83.0%	—
Minimum	0.44	0.14	–17.5%	2.4%	2.4%	0.00	0.00	8.34	0.00	–32.9%	–36.7%	—
Standard deviation	0.87	1.40	8.7%	25.7%	21.0%	0.50	0.47	2.08	1.76	21.1%	16.7%	—
1994												
Number of observations	*111*	*109*	*181*	*181*	*126*	*237*	*237*	*128*	*124*	*152*	*148*	92
Mean	*1.75*	*2.17*	*6.5%*	*57.9%*	*42.4%*	*0.51*	*0.41*	*17.32*	*1.00*	*24.9%*	*7.5%*	81,422
Median	1.56	1.86	6.7%	61.1%	40.4%	1.00	0.00	17.55	0.20	22.7%	3.3%	2,495
Maximum	4.66	6.84	41.2%	99.8%	96.4%	1.00	1.00	21.99	47.83	98.7%	88.0%	2,286,086
Minimum	0.43	0.36	–73.5%	2.3%	1.7%	0.00	0.00	6.82	0.00	–30.0%	–30.0%	0
Standard deviation	0.87	1.33	10.5%	24.2%	21.8%	0.50	0.49	2.52	4.67	20.6%	19.2%	294,279

(continued)

Table 4.9 Descriptive Statistics on the Main Variables *(continued)*

	Tobin's q	*MB Ratio*	*ROA*	*Concent*	*Coincid*	*DGroup*	*Dafp*	*LAEC*	*DE Ratio*	*Cash*	*Invest*	*Volume*
1995												
Number of observations	115	112	192	193	126	237	237	127	124	155	161	96
Mean	1.71	2.05	7.1%	58.1%	41.8%	0.52	0.43	17.71	0.39	24.3%	8.3%	301,793
Median	1.57	1.83	5.9%	61.1%	40.9%	1.00	0.00	17.83	0.23	21.1%	4.5%	4,128
Maximum	4.92	7.40	37.3%	100.0%	97.7%	1.00	1.00	21.93	3.91	88.3%	81.4%	14,400,000
Minimum	0.52	0.37	–35.9%	2.2%	2.2%	0.00	0.00	8.38	0.00	–28.9%	–38.3%	0
Standard deviation	0.83	1.20	8.7%	25.0%	22.1%	0.50	0.50	2.12	0.51	19.4%	18.7%	1,542,535
1996												
Number of observations	120	116	202	203	126	237	237	128	123	174	178	101
Mean	1.43	1.59	6.8%	58.4%	39.8%	0.55	0.47	17.62	0.79	22.1%	10.2%	177,948
Median	1.20	1.37	6.2%	60.6%	36.7%	1.00	0.00	17.66	0.36	21.5%	5.6%	2,879
Maximum	4.67	6.27	33.9%	100.0%	98.0%	1.00	1.00	22.97	35.55	75.8%	86.9%	8,008,483
Minimum	0.40	0.04	–35.8%	2.4%	0.4%	0.00	0.00	8.74	0.00	–37.0%	–24.3%	0
Standard deviation	0.80	1.07	8.1%	24.5%	22.4%	0.50	0.50	2.18	3.21	19.7%	19.2%	897,931

(continued)

Table 4.9 Descriptive Statistics on the Main Variables *(continued)*

	Tobin's q	*MB Ratio*	*ROA*	*Concent*	*Coincid*	*DGroup*	*Dafp*	*LAEC*	*DE Ratio*	*Cash*	*Invest*	*Volume*
1997												
Number of observations	173	171	211	211	183	237	237	186	181	164	183	144
Mean	1.22	1.33	5.6%	58.9%	37.5%	0.56	0.48	17.71	0.96	22.1%	9.6%	110,663
Median	1.00	0.99	4.9%	61.3%	33.9%	1.00	0.00	17.75	0.46	19.2%	5.0%	7,623
Maximum	3.93	6.08	27.5%	99.8%	95.8%	1.00	1.00	22.30	21.63	92.2%	93.9%	3,997,243
Minimum	0.42	0.06	−38.7%	2.4%	1.0%	0.00	0.00	8.43	0.00	−35.2%	−23.6%	0
Standard deviation	0.63	1.00	8.1%	24.9%	21.0%	0.50	0.50	1.93	2.17	19.8%	19.9%	498,631
1998												
Number of observations	173	171	212	211	183	237	237	186	181	169	192	136
Mean	1.22	1.33	4.7%	58.9%	37.5%	0.56	0.48	17.71	0.96	19.5%	6.4%	119,914
Median	1.00	0.99	4.7%	61.3%	33.9%	1.00	0.00	17.75	0.46	17.8%	3.6%	7,175
Maximum	3.93	6.08	31.1%	99.8%	95.8%	1.00	1.00	22.30	21.63	90.5%	79.4%	4,845,584
Minimum	0.42	0.06	−42.8%	2.4%	1.0%	0.00	0.00	8.43	0.00	−27.3%	−38.6%	0
Standard deviation	0.63	1.00	8.6%	24.9%	21.0%	0.50	0.50	1.93	2.17	19.6%	18.0%	522,536

(continued)

Table 4.9 Descriptive Statistics on the Main Variables *(continued)*

	Tobin's q	*MB Ratio*	*ROA*	*Concent*	*Coincid*	*DGroup*	*Dafp*	*LAEC*	*DE Ratio*	*Cash*	*Invest*	*Volume*
1999												
Number of observations	172	169	216	213	186	237	237	189	184	165	185	122
Mean	1.05	1.03	4.0%	60.7%	35.1%	0.57	0.48	17.56	1.37	17.5%	2.1%	148,478
Median	0.88	0.77	3.8%	62.7%	31.0%	1.00	0.00	17.63	0.72	16.4%	0.3%	3,024
Maximum	4.46	5.98	29.5%	100.0%	98.0%	1.00	1.00	22.45	26.37	80.4%	94.3%	4,475,889
Minimum	0.41	0.07	–20.9%	2.4%	2.4%	0.00	0.00	8.44	0.00	–33.7%	–39.1%	0
Standard deviation	0.61	0.84	7.7%	24.0%	21.2%	0.50	0.50	1.96	2.53	19.0%	16.3%	619,599
2000												
Number of observations	175	173	220	215	185	237	237	188	184	161	190	128
Mean	1.11	1.17	4.1%	61.1%	36.6%	0.57	0.48	17.71	1.36	19.2%	2.3%	90,781
Median	0.95	0.91	3.6%	63.1%	33.3%	1.00	0.00	17.76	0.58	18.1%	–1.1%	2,633
Maximum	3.55	4.68	28.5%	100.0%	98.0%	1.00	1.00	22.86	22.87	69.2%	95.1%	3,840,981
Minimum	0.42	0.07	–24.2%	0.5%	0.2%	0.00	0.00	8.45	0.00	–23.0%	–36.1%	0
Standard deviation	0.59	0.91	7.2%	24.3%	21.0%	0.50	0.50	2.04	2.66	16.8%	17.1%	421,632

(continued)

Table 4.9 Descriptive Statistics on the Main Variables *(continued)*

	Tobin's q	*MB Ratio*	*ROA*	*Concent*	*Coincid*	*DGroup*	*Dafp*	*LAEC*	*DE Ratio*	*Cash*	*Invest*	*Volume*
2001												
Number of observation.	178	176	216	222	186	237	237	189	185	190	199	141
Mean	1.02	1.05	3.7%	61.5%	35.1%	0.56	0.48	17.74	1.72	11.4%	3.7%	109,526
Median	0.88	0.79	4.3%	62.9%	31.6%	1.00	0.00	17.75	0.61	8.4%	–0.5%	3,077
Maximum	3.72	4.73	29.8%	100.0%	98.0%	1.00	1.00	22.82	28.18	90.7%	82.6%	4,402,062
Minimum	0.40	0.04	–46.8%	2.6%	2.6%	0.00	0.00	8.46	0.00	0.4%	–36.6%	0
Standard deviation	0.53	0.88	8.4%	24.2%	21.4%	0.50	0.50	2.09	3.49	13.5%	17.6%	463,807
2002												
Number of observations	181	178	205	214	187	237	237	193	186	182	182	142
Mean	1.07	1.15	4.2%	60.3%	34.4%	0.56	0.48	17.82	1.84	9.9%	–0.7%	87,934
Median	0.94	0.87	4.4%	61.3%	30.7%	1.00	0.00	17.83	0.73	7.9%	–1.4%	2,321
Maximum	3.27	5.77	28.2%	100.0%	99.7%	1.00	1.00	22.89	39.88	61.4%	57.0%	2,363,277
Minimum	0.40	0.04	–54.9%	0.0%	0.1%	0.00	0.00	11.68	0.00	0.1%	39.1%	0
Standard deviation	0.52	0.98	8.6%	24.0%	21.9%	0.50	0.50	2.06	4.19	8.7%	13.6%	349,906

Source: Compiled by the authors.

Table 4.10 Correlation Matrix of the Main Variables

	Tobin's q	*MB Ratio*	*ROA*	*Concent*	*Coincid*	*DGroup*	*Dafp*	*LAEC*	*DE Ratio*	*Cash*	*Invest*	*Volume*
Tobin's q	1											
MB Ratio	0.94*	1										
ROA	0.33*	0.40*	1									
Concent	–0.13*	–0.11*	0.02	1								
Coincid	0.20*	0.22*	0.15*	0.69*	1							
DGroup	–0.01	0.02	0.13*	–0.15*	–0.11*	1						
Dafp	0.13*	0.18*	0.25*	–0.11*	–0.04	0.39*	1					
LAEC	0.08*	0.14*	0.17*	–0.07*	–0.10*	0.46*	0.55*	1				
DE Ratio	–0.24*	–0.28*	–0.17*	0.10*	–0.35*	0.01	–0.11*	0.01	1			
Cash	0.32*	0.37*	0.64*	0.01	0.17*	0.05*	0.20*	0.05*	–0.13*	1		
Invest	0.15*	0.17*	0.21*	–0.03	0.04	0.08*	0.14*	0.17*	–0.11*	0.25*	1	
Volume	–0.07*	–0.07*	–0.07*	–0.18*	–0.18*	0.12*	–0.03	0.14*	0.05	–0.03	0.05	1

Source: Compiled by the authors.
*statistically significant at 10 percent

We want to study the effect of agency problems on the firm, including on firm value. A simple look at the correlation matrix of the variables, presented in table 4.10, shows that a higher ownership concentration is negatively correlated with firm valuation and that a higher coincidence between cash flow rights and control rights is positively correlated with firm valuation. Although group affiliation is not correlated with the proxies for the market valuation of firms, affiliation is positively correlated with the ROA of firms. Figure 4.1 supplements the evidence through scatter plots of the relationships that indicate the results are not likely caused by a few outliers.

However, as discussed elsewhere above, the correlations do not necessarily indicate causality. This is because of potential endogenous relations and omitted variable bias. We tackle the second problem by running multiple regressions using the set of control variables. Table 4.11 presents this first set of results using standard ordinary least squares (OLS) pooled multivariate regressions. We have tried several specifications to see whether our results are robust. We have found that the inclusion of a large set of control variables does not alter the preliminary results. In all specifications, firm valuation is negatively and significantly correlated with ownership concentration and positively and significantly correlated with the degree of coincidence of cash flow rights and control rights. We have also found that changing the set of control variables does not affect the signs and significance of these coefficients.

These results tend to support the hypothesis that agency problems, characterized by a lesser degree of coincidence of cash flow rights and control rights in the hands of controlling shareholders, are penalized by the market. If we hold ownership concentration constant, more aligned incentives increase company value. On the other hand, if we hold the relation between cash flow rights and control rights constant, an increase in ownership concentration may be associated with more power in the hands of controlling shareholders and, potentially, more agency conflicts between controlling and minority shareholders. However, the negative coefficient in the ownership concentration value might also be related to liquidity problems. We explore this possibility elsewhere below using a measure of turnover.

There is another important result regarding corporate governance practices and firm valuation. We find that the presence of pension funds as minority shareholders increases the market value of listed companies. This result is robust across different estimation procedures. This means that, for a given level of separation between cash flow rights and control rights, institutional investors tend to mitigate agency problems between controlling and minority shareholders.

The results indicate that, under this type of model specification, group affiliation does not significantly affect firm value. Both the time dummies and the industry dummies are statistically significant as a

Figure 4.1 Ownership Concentration and the Coincidence of Control and Cash Flow Rights

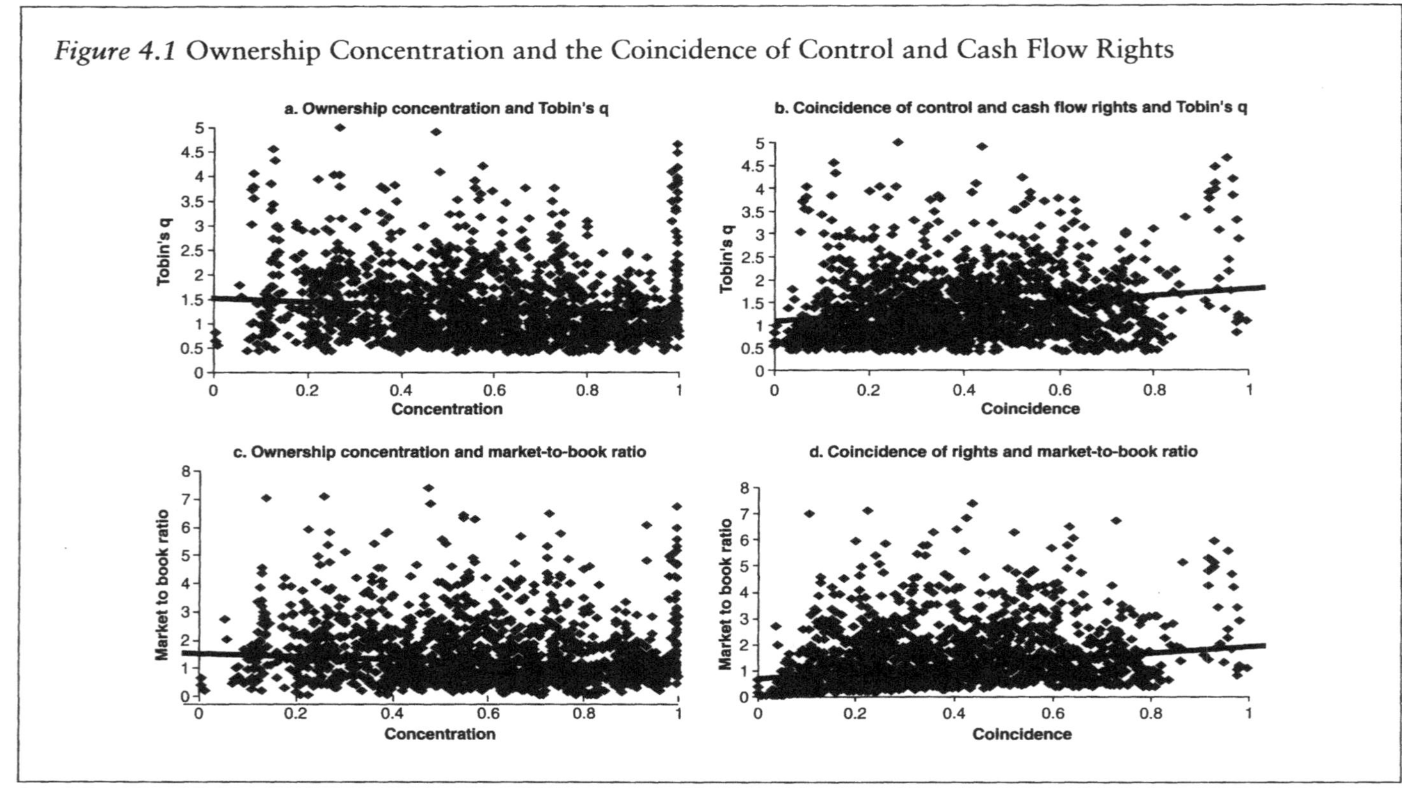

Figure 4.1 Continued

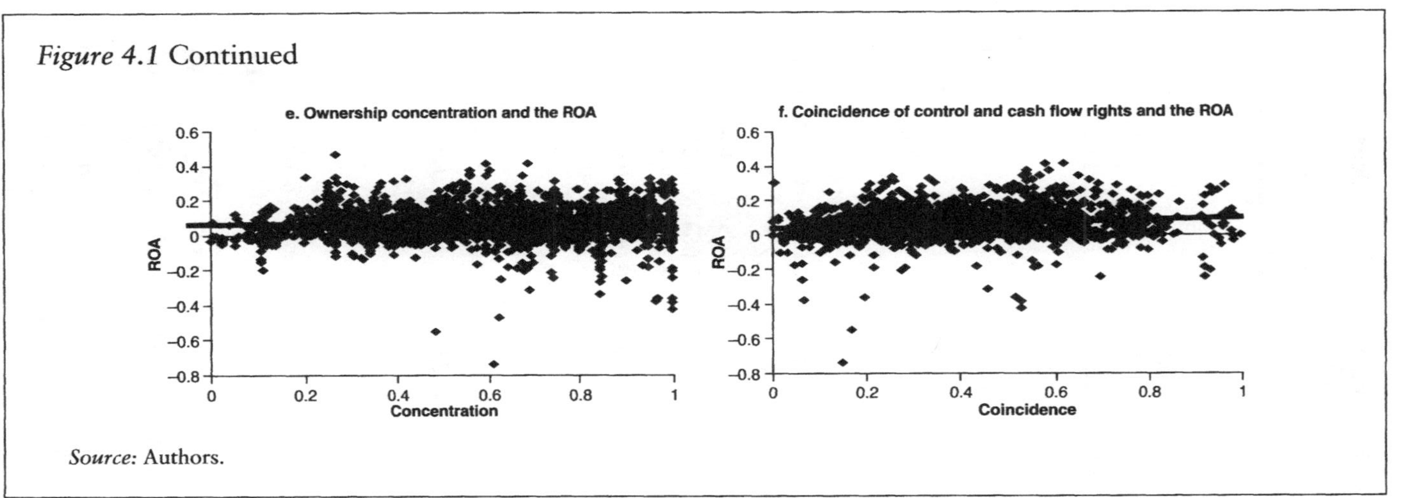

Source: Authors.

Table 4.11 OLS Pooled Regressions for the Coincidence of Cash Flow and Control Rights on Tobin's q

	(1)	*(2)*	*(3)*	*(4)*	*(5)*	*(6)*
Concent	–0.330		–1.431			–1.404
	–4.8		*–13.0*			*–12.5*
	0.0%		*0.0%*			*0.0%*
Coincid		0.266	1.755			1.728
		3.0	*12.4*			*12.1*
		0.2%	*0.0%*			*0.0%*
DGroup				0.049		–0.017
				1.2		*–0.4*
				21.7%		*66.0%*
Dafp					0.145	0.081
					3.6	*2.1*
					0.0%	*3.8%*
LAEC	0.052	0.065	0.051	0.056	0 .043	0.043
	5.4	*6.7*	*5.4*	*5.2*	*4.0*	*3.9*
	0.0%	*0.0%*	*0.0%*	*0.0%*	*0.0%*	*0.0%*
DE Ratio	–0.061	–0.053	0.015	–0.063	–0.058	0.017
	–7.5	*–6.1*	*1.6*	*–7.8*	*–7.1*	*1.7*
	0.0%	*0.0%*	*11.7%*	*0.0%*	*0.0%*	*8.3%*
Cash	0.953	0.903	0.790	0.945	0.920	0.781
	10.1	*9.5*	*8.8*	*10.0*	*9.8*	*8.6*
	0.0%	*0.0%*	*0.0%*	*0.0%*	*0.0%*	*0.0%*
Invest	0.117	0.125	0.076	0.127	0.128	0.078
	1.3	*1.4*	*0.9*	*1.4*	*1.4*	*0.9*
	20.1%	*17.1%*	*37.9%*	*16.7%*	*16.3%*	*37.0%*
Industry dummies	*Yes*	*Yes*	*Yes*	*Yes*	*Yes*	*Yes*
Time dummies	*Yes*	*Yes*	*Yes*	*Yes*	*Yes*	*Yes*
Number of observations	*1413*	*1418*	*1413*	*1418*	*1418*	*1413*
F(29, 1383)	*33.8*	*33.0*	*41.7*	*32.5*	*33.2*	*39.1*
Prob > F	*0.0%*	*0.0%*	*0.0%*	*0.0%*	*0.0%*	*0.0%*
R-squared	*0.388*	*0.381*	*0.449*	*0.378*	*0.383*	*0.450*
Adj R-squared	*0.376*	*0.370*	*0.438*	*0.366*	*0.371*	*0.439*
Root MSE	*0.568*	*0.571*	*0.540*	*0.572*	*0.570*	*0.539*

Source: Compiled by the authors.

Note: The figure is based on annual data on 177 firm from 1990 to 2002.

group in all specifications where they are included. Also, we find that larger firms have a higher Tobin's q, indicating higher market valuation, while more indebted firms present lower market valuation after controlling for other factors. Both coefficients are statistically significant in most specifications.

Robustness Checks

Tables 4.12 and 4.13 present additional results that confirm the robustness of the findings. In table 4.12, we replicate the last regression in table 4.11 using different measures of firm valuation. The evidence shows it is highly unlikely our previous results are due to spurious correlations arising from measurement errors in the construction of Tobin's q and the concentration and coincidence variables. The table shows that the results hold when we substitute Tobin's q with the market-to-book ratio or a firm's ROA. In table 4.13, we show cross-sectional regressions for each of the 12 years included in the sample. Again, the coefficient on concentration is negative and significant, while the coefficient on coincidence is positive and significant in each of the 12 cross-sections.

Additional tests for robustness are presented in table 4.14, where we show the results for different econometric methods. Among other tests, we run fixed-effect panel regressions to account for potential unobservable firm effects that might be correlated with ownership concentration and rights coincidence and thereby bias our previous results. The coefficients obtained are similar to those already obtained; they almost certainly rule out the possibility that the results are due to omitted variable biases.

We also check for the existence of nonlinearities in the relationship among concentration, coincidence, and valuation. We find that the introduction of these variables squared does not substantially change the results. We find an inverse U-shaped relation for concentration, but no significant nonlinear relationship between coincidence and value after we control for ownership concentration. The results are presented in table 4.15.

Endogeneity

Because of all these safeguards, we are confident that our results are not induced by omitted variable bias. However, we must still tackle the potentially endogenous nature of the correlations obtained. Ownership concentration and the degree of coincidence between cash flow rights and control rights might both be endogenously determined by the market valuation or performance of a firm.

The positive coefficient obtained for the coincidence between cash flow rights and control rights may also be explained by reverse causation. Endogeneity of this type would imply that, for a given level of control rights, the owners of a firm with a high Tobin's q are more likely to

Table 4.12 OLS Pooled Regressions for the Coincidence of Cash Flow and Control Rights on Firm Value and Performance

	Tobin's q	*Market-to-book ratio*	*ROA*
Concent	−1.404	−1.772	−0.040
	−12.5	*−9.6*	*−3.9*
	0.0%	*0.0%*	*0.0%*
Coincid	1.728	2.348	0.070
	12.1	*10.0*	*5.5*
	0.0%	*0.0%*	*0.0%*
DGroup	−0.017	−0.043	0.011
	−0.4	*−0.7*	*2.9*
	66.0%	*48.7%*	*0.4%*
Dafp	0.081	0.111	0.014
	2.1	*1.7*	*3.8*
	3.8%	*8.3%*	*0.0%*
LAEC	0.043	0.109	−0.001
	3.9	*6.1*	*−1.0*
	0.0%	*0.0%*	*29.7%*
DE Ratio	0.017	−0.026	−0.003
	1.7	*−1.5*	*−3.6*
	8.3%	*13.0%*	*0.0%*
Cash	0.781	1.551	0.257
	8.6	*10.4*	*30.7*
	0.0%	*0.0%*	*0.0%*
Invest	0.078	0.161	−0.015
	0.9	*1.1*	*−1.8*
	37.0%	*25.5%*	*6.6%*
Industry dummies	*Yes*	*Yes*	*Yes*
Time dummies	*Yes*	*Yes*	*Yes*
Number of observations	*1413*	*1401*	*1467*
F(29, 1383)	*39.1*	*37.7*	*62.3*
Prob > F	*0.0%*	*0.0%*	*0.0%*
R-squared	*0.450*	*0.443*	*0.557*
Adj R-squared	*0.439*	*0.432*	*0.548*
Root MSE	*0.539*	*0.875*	*0.051*

Source: Compiled by the authors.

Note: The figure is based on annual data on 177 firms from 1990 to 2002.

Table 4.13 OLS Cross-Sectional Regressions for the Coincidence of Cash Flow and Control Rights on Tobin's q

	1991	*1992*	*1993*	*1994*	*1995*	*1996*	*1997*	*1998*	*1999*	*2000*	*2001*	*2002*
Concent	–2.967	–2.174	–2.938	–2.731	–3.829	–1.742	–1.153	–1.121	–0.877	–0.825	–1.055	–0.965
	–3.0	*–3.6*	*–4.2*	*–3.6*	*–3.2*	*–2.1*	*–4.5*	*–4.3*	*–2.1*	*–2.8*	*–3.7*	*–3.8*
	0.3%	*0.1%*	*0.0%*	*0.1%*	*0.2%*	*3.8%*	*0.0%*	*0.0%*	*3.4%*	*0.6%*	*0.0%*	*0.0%*
Coincid	3.099	2.126	3.157	3.284	4.546	2.259	1.427	1.241	1.543	1.216	1.313	1.515
	2.5	*2.9*	*3.7*	*3.6*	*3.1*	*2.1*	*4.2*	*3.5*	*2.7*	*2.9*	*3.7*	*4.6*
	1.5%	*0.5%*	*0.0%*	*0.1%*	*0.2%*	*3.6%*	*0.0%*	*0.1%*	*0.8%*	*0.5%*	*0.0%*	*0.0%*
DGroup	–0.070	–0.187	–0.244	0.376	0.119	–0.078	0.019	–0.014	–0.040	0.048	–0.078	0.024
	–0.3	*–1.0*	*–1.2*	*1.8*	*0.6*	*–0.5*	*0.2*	*–0.2*	*–0.4*	*0.5*	*–0.8*	*0.3*
	76.8%	*32.0%*	*24.9%*	*7.4%*	*55.8%*	*65.0%*	*83.2%*	*87.8%*	*71.7%*	*63.0%*	*41.3%*	*79.2%*
Dafp	0.239	0.054	0.223	0.127	0.213	–0.084	–0.074	–0.029	–0.029	0.046	0.037	0.100
	1.1	*0.3*	*1.1*	*0.6*	*1.1*	*–0.5*	*–0.8*	*-0.3*	*–0.2*	*0.4*	*0.3*	*1.0*
	29.6%	*77.2%*	*28.0%*	*56.7%*	*28.0%*	*62.6%*	*42.6%*	*75.7%*	*81.2%*	*66.8%*	*73.2%*	*32.7%*
LAEC	0.068	0.053	0.091	0.084	–0.043	0.076	0.014	0.032	–0.001	0.022	0.030	0.031
	1.0	*1.0*	*1.6*	*1.6*	*–0.8*	*1.6*	*0.5*	*1.2*	*0.0*	*0.8*	*1.1*	*1.2*
	30.0%	*31.0%*	*10.9%*	*11.7%*	*42.4%*	*11.3%*	*63.3%*	*24.9%*	*98.2%*	*45.0%*	*26.7%*	*22.7%*
DE Ratio	0.203	0.124	0.130	0.180	0.651	–0.146	–0.023	–0.019	0.024	0.008	0.013	0.007
	0.9	*1.9*	*2.4*	*2.3*	*1.8*	*–0.7*	*–1.3*	*–1.0*	*0.4*	*0.2*	*0.6*	*0.4*
	38.1%	*5.6%*	*1.8%*	*2.4%*	*7.6%*	*49.1%*	*21.3%*	*31.6%*	*71.4%*	*86.0%*	*55.8%*	*70.9%*

(*continued*)

Table 4.13 OLS Cross-Sectional Regressions for the Coincidence of Cash Flow and Control Rights on Tobin's q *(continued)*

	1991	*1992*	*1993*	*1994*	*1995*	*1996*	*1997*	*1998*	*1999*	*2000*	*2001*	*2002*
Cash	1.672	1.203	1.744	1.500	0.878	0.155	1.115	0.883	0.250	0.672	–0.264	0.236
	3.7	*3.1*	*3.4*	*3.3*	*2.1*	*0.4*	*5.0*	*4.1*	*0.9*	*2.5*	*–0.8*	*0.4*
	0.0%	*0.2%*	*0.1%*	*0.2%*	*4.2%*	*68.1%*	*0.0%*	*0.0%*	*37.4%*	*1.5%*	*41.6%*	*69.0%*
Invest	–0.251	–0.020	0.168	0.106	–0.238	–0.089	0.048	0.259	–0.252	0.100	0.229	0.246
	–0.4	*–0.1*	*0.3*	*0.3*	*–0.6*	*–0.2*	*0.2*	*1.2*	*–0.9*	*0.4*	*1.0*	*0.8*
	69.2%	*95.1%*	*74.3%*	*79.8%*	*56.9%*	*81.8%*	*83.8%*	*22.4%*	*35.1%*	*69.3%*	*34.4%*	*43.6%*
Industry dummies	*Yes*	*Yes*	*Yes*	*Yes*	*Yes*	*Yes*	*Yes*	*Yes*	*Yes*	*Yes*	*Yes*	*Yes*
Number of observations	*97*	*96*	*97*	*93*	*99*	*104*	*132*	*136*	*132*	*131*	*153*	*143*
F	*3.2*	*3.8*	*4.8*	*5.3*	*3.8*	*3.9*	*8.8*	*8.4*	*3.0*	*4.4*	*3.7*	*4.1*
Prob > F	*0.0%*	*0.0%*	*0.0%*	*0.0%*	*0.0%*	*0.0%*	*0.0%*	*0.0%*	*0.0%*	*0.0%*	*0.0%*	*0.0%*
R-squared	*0.421*	*0.469*	*0.524*	*0.563*	*0.463*	*0.449*	*0.584*	*0.564*	*0.320*	*0.412*	*0.330*	*0.372*
Adj R-squared	*0.287*	*0.345*	*0.414*	*0.457*	*0.343*	*0.332*	*0.517*	*0.497*	*0.212*	*0.317*	*0.240*	*0.280*
Root MSE	*0.718*	*0.590*	*0.672*	*0.652*	*0.657*	*0.607*	*0.388*	*0.402*	*0.470*	*0.429*	*0.466*	*0.438*

Source: Compiled by the authors.

Table 4.14 Panel Regressions for the Coincidence of Cash Flow and Control Rights on Tobin's q

	OLS	*GLS het. corr.*	*Random effects*	*Fixed effects*	*A-B dynamic panel*
Tobin's q (-1)					0.108
					5.3
					0.0%
Concent	–1.404	–1.224	–1.913	–2.046	–1.321
	–12.5	–18.8	–14.3	–13.9	-6.9
	0.0%	0.0%	0.0%	0.0%	0.0%
Coincid	1.728	1.702	2.770	3.056	1.668
	12.1	19.4	17.3	17.6	7.0
	0.0%	0.0%	0.0%	0.0%	0.0%
DGroup	–0.017	–0.010	–0.225	–0.445	–0.088
	–0.4	–0.5	-2.7	–2.1	–0.3
	66.0%	62.5%	0.7%	3.3%	79.6%
Dafp	0.081	0.078	–0.105	–0.154	
	2.1	4.0	–2.1	–2.7	
	3.8%	0.0%	3.7%	0.7%	
LAEC	0.043	0.056	0.146	0.244	0.768
	3.9	8.3	7.7	9.4	24.5
	0.0%	0.0%	0.0%	0.0%	0.0%
DE Ratio	0.017	0.026	0.021	0.021	0.018
	1.7	0.0	2.5	2.4	2.4
	8.3%	0.0%	1.3%	1.5%	1.6%
Cash	0.781	0.789	0.762	0.790	0.116
	8.6	14.1	9.2	9.1	1.7
	0.0%	0.0%	0.0%	0.0%	8.1%
Invest	0.078	–0.002	0.033	–0.004	–0.134
	0.9	–0.1	0.5	–0.1	-3.0
	37.0%	96.1%	62.5%	95.1%	0.2%
Industry dummies	Yes		No	No	No

(*continued*)

Table 4.14 Panel Regressions for the Coincidence of Cash Flow and Control Rights on Tobin's q *(continued)*

	OLS	*GLS het. corr.*	*Random effects*	*Fixed effects*	*A-B dynamic panel*
Time dummies	Yes		Yes	Yes	No
Number of observations	1,413	1,413	1,413	1,413	1,413
Number of groups		177	177	177	177
F(29, 1383)	39.1			82.5	
Prob> F	0.0%			0.0%	
Wald chi2		3215.8	1833.9		1415.0
Prob > chi2		0.0%	0.0%		0.0%
Adj R-squared	0.439				
Root MSE	0.539				

Source: Compiled by the authors.
Note: The figure is based on annual data on 177 firms from 1990 to 2002.

increase their rights over the cash flows of the firm and thereby raise the degree of coincidence between cash flow rights and control rights. In this case, there might still be a causal connection between coincidence and firm value, but the OLS coefficient would overstate it. Furthermore, if an endogenous relationship of the type predicted by Demsetz's hypothesis is present, one could not infer that other firms would be able to improve their market values by increasing the degree of coincidence between rights even if there is a causal relationship between coincidence and valuation in the case of some firms.

It might also be argued that the controlling shareholders of companies more valued by the market would also tend to raise the concentration of their holdings. This would be the situation if they increased the ownership concentration through a pyramid scheme without necessarily increasing the coincidence between their cash flow rights and their control rights. However, because the coefficient on concentration is negative, the reverse causality correlation would run in the opposite direction in this case and, hence, would not reinforce the direct effect.

To solve the endogeneity problems adequately, we should find suitable instruments for running some type of instrumental variable or simultaneous equations model. A suitable instrument should ideally be exogenous and should not be influenced by the dependent variable of interest. It

Table 4.15 OLS Pooled Regressions for the Coincidence of Cash Flow and Control Rights on Tobin's q: Nonlinear Relationships

	(1)	(2)	(3)	(4)	(6)
Concent	–1.788	—	–1.295	–3.057	–3.262
	–5.7	—	*–11.0*	*–9.7*	*–7.7*
	0.0%	—	*0.0%*	*0.0%*	*0.0%*
Concent2	1.314	—	—	1.447	1.595
	4.8	—	—	*5.6*	*4.8*
	0.0%	—	—	*0.0%*	*0.0%*
Coincid	—	–1.716	0.682	1.760	2.098
	—	*–5.2*	*1.7*	*12.4*	*4.3*
	—	*0.0%*	*8.2%*	*0.0%*	*0.0%*
Coincid2	—	2.240	1.050	—	–0.336
	—	*6.3*	*2.9*	—	*–0.7*
	—	*0.0%*	*0.4%*	—	*46.8%*
Controls	*Yes*	*Yes*	*Yes*	*Yes*	*Yes*
Industry dummies	*Yes*	*Yes*	*Yes*	*Yes*	*Yes*
Time dummies	*Yes*	*Yes*	*Yes*	*Yes*	*Yes*
Number of observations	*1,413*	*1,418*	*1,413*	*1,413*	*1,413*
F(29, 1383)	*32.1*	*32.5*	*38.3*	*39.6*	*38.4*
Prob > F	*0.0%*	*0.0%*	*0.0%*	*0.0%*	*0.0%*
R-squared	*0.402*	*0.405*	*0.454*	*0.463*	*0.463*
Adj R-squared	*0.390*	*0.392*	*0.442*	*0.451*	*0.451*
Root MSE	*0.562*	*0.560*	*0.538*	*0.533*	*0.533*

Source: Compiled by the authors.
Note: The figure is based on annual data on 177 firms from 1990 to 2002.

should be strongly correlated with the independent variable about which there is a suspicion of endogeneity (*conc* and *coincid*), and it should predict the dependent variable not directly, but indirectly through its effect on the independent variable. Given these restrictions, it would be difficult to obtain suitable instruments unless some restrictive assumptions are made or an exogenous condition on corporate governance practices is imposed on firms. The last regression in table 4.14 is intended to solve the endogeneity problem under certain restrictive assumptions. For this purpose, we run an Arellano and Bond dynamic panel general method of moments regression. This econometric procedure addresses unobserved firm-specific effects and the potential endogeneity of the explanatory variables under the assumption that there is no second-order serial correlation on the error term. The estimated coefficients are similar to those obtained previously, but a Sargan test of the validity of the instruments (lagged values of the control variables) largely rejects the null hypothesis.

Because the concentration and coincidence measures present much less time series variation than the firm valuation and performance variables, we conjecture that the endogeneity problem is unlikely to be important in this case. However, we directly tackle the endogeneity problem using an instrument related to control concentration. In the previous analysis, we used a measure of ownership concentration and of the coincidence of cash flow rights and control rights. Rule 67 of the Chilean corporations law establishes that major company decisions must be taken with the support of two-thirds of the voting rights. It might be argued, then, that effective control requires two-thirds of the voting rights. Figures 4.2 and 4.3 show the relationship between a control dummy variable and the coincidence between cash flow rights and control rights. Notice that, although both variables are related, the relationship is not obvious. For instance, a controlling shareholder may have control of two-thirds of the votes in a holding company that owns two-thirds of the shares of a firm. The control concentration dummy for the firm would be 1, although, even in a zero debt case, the coincidence between cash flow rights and control rights would

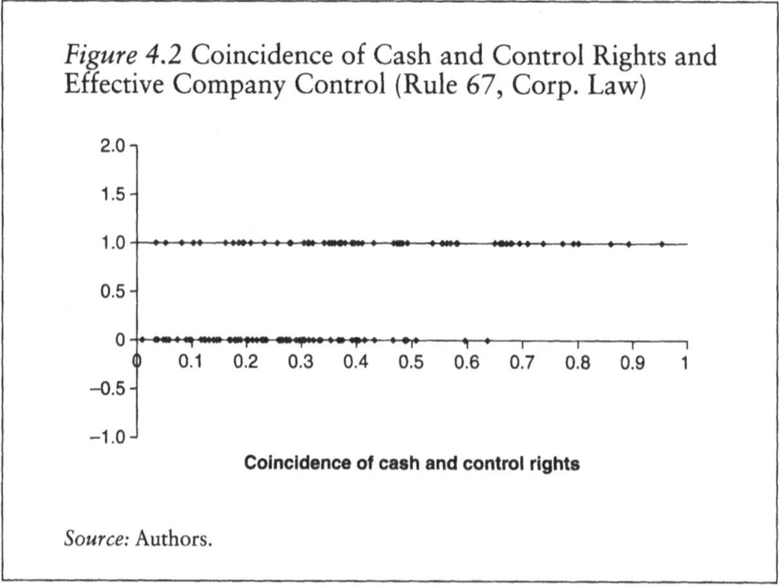

Figure 4.2 Coincidence of Cash and Control Rights and Effective Company Control (Rule 67, Corp. Law)

Source: Authors.

Figure 4.3 Tobin's q and Ownership Concentration

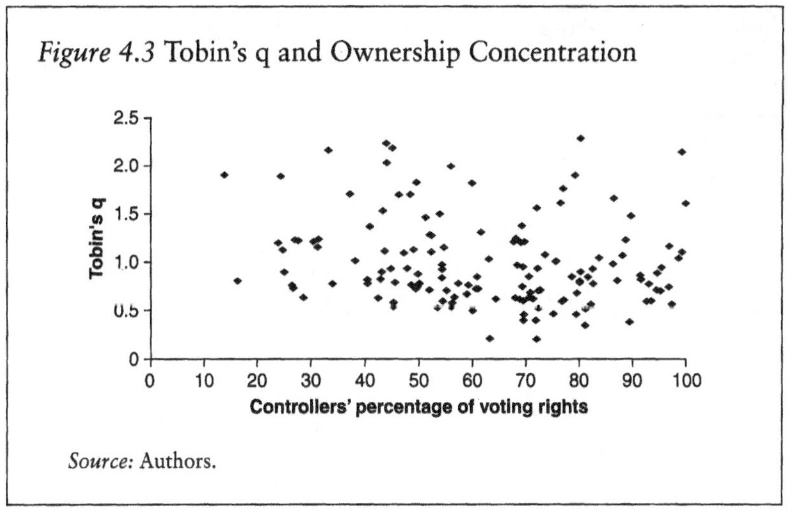

Source: Authors.

be only four-ninths. Figure 4.2 shows that, in any case, the degree of coincidence tends to be higher in firms that surpass the two-thirds threshold. Figure 4.3 shows that there is no obvious clustering of firms around the two-thirds threshold and that company market value does not respond in an evident way to the threshold.

In the following analysis, we therefore use a dummy variable that takes the value of 1 whenever the controlling shareholder of a firm directly or indirectly holds more than two-thirds of the voting rights as an instrument for the coincidence of the cash flow rights and control rights variables. Table 4.16 presents OLS regressions of Tobin's q on this dummy, the coincidence variable and a series of control variables under different specifications. The results are straightforward. When we include the dummy variable in our standard specification, the results obtained previously do not change. Lower ownership concentration and higher coincidence are still related to higher valuation. We then run a first-stage OLS regression of the degree of coincidence on the concentration dummy and a series of controls. We find that, as expected, firms showing a control concentration of more than two-thirds present higher coincidence. A hypothesis for this result is that, as a company reaches such a level of concentration in voting rights, it becomes difficult for the controlling shareholder to attract external investors to separate cash flow rights and control rights.

We then run a second-stage regression of Tobin's q on all control variables and the instrumented coincidence variable. As shown in table 4.16, the two-stage least squares regressions indicate that, after controlling for endogeneity and omitted variable bias, the coefficient on the degree of coincidence remains positive, although the economic and statistical significance is notably reduced. Table 4.16 shows that the results hold for a

Table 4.16 Two-Stage Least Squares Estimation of Instrumental Variables for Coincidence of Cash Flow and Control Rights on Tobin's q

	(1990–2002)			*(1994–2002)*		
		IV Estimation			*IV Estimation*	
	OLS	*First stage*	*Second stage*	*OLS*	*First stage*	*Second stage*
Dep. variable	*Tobin's q*	*Coincid*	*Tobin's q*	*Tobin's q*	*Coincid*	*Tobin's q*
Dconc	0.074	0.254			0.216	
	1.4	*31.5*			*21.6*	
	15.9%	*0.0%*			*0.0%*	
Concent	−1.524		−0.430	−0.978		−0.269
	−10.8		*−3.8*	*−9.7*		*−2.5*
	0.0%		*0.0%*	*0.0%*		*1.3%*
Coincid	1.727		0.301	1.309		0.234
	12.1		*1.4*	*10.2*		*1.0*
	0.0%		*16.7%*	*0.0%*		*31.4%*
DGroup	−0.013	0.005	0.012	−0.001	0.000	0.013
	−0.3	*0.5*	*0.3*	*0.0*	*0.0*	*0.4*
	73.8%	*59.5%*	*76.3%*	*98.2%*	*98.4%*	*72.0%*
Volume				0.000	0.000	0.000
				−3.2	*−3.0*	*−3.1*
				0.1%	*0.3%*	*0.2%*
Dafp	0.080	0.014	0.123	0.101	0.017	0.140
	2.1	*1.4*	*3.0*	*2.8*	*1.5*	*3.7*
	4.0%	*15.6%*	*0.3%*	*0.5%*	*14.3%*	*0.0%*
LAEC	0.045	0.005	0.037	0.032	−0.006	0.027
	4.1	*2.0*	*3.2*	*3.1*	*−1.8*	*2.4*
	0.0%	*4.9%*	*0.1%*	*0.2%*	*7.4%*	*1.5%*
DE Ratio	0.017	−0.033	−0.046	0.002	−0.040	−0.039
	1.7	*−20.3*	*−4.3*	*0.2*	*−18.0*	*−3.5*
	9.0%	*0.0%*	*0.0%*	*84.8%*	*0.0%*	*0.1%*
Cash	0.793	0.145	0.911	0.585	0.086	0.666
	8.7	*6.4*	*9.4*	*6.7*	*3.0*	*7.2*
	0.0%	*0.0%*	*0.0%*	*0.0%*	*0.3%*	*0.0%*

(continued)

Table 4.16 Two-Stage Least Squares Estimation of Instrumental Variables *(continued)*

	(1990–2002)			*(1994–2002)*		
		IV Estimation			*IV Estimation*	
	OLS	*First stage*	*Second stage*	*OLS*	*First stage*	*Second stage*
Dep. variable	*Tobin's q*	*Coincid*	*Tobin's q*	*Tobin's q*	*Coincid*	*Tobin's q*
Invest	0.078	0.011	0.116	0.256	0.024	0.305
	0.9	*0.5*	*1.3*	*3.1*	*0.9*	*3.5*
	36.8%	*61.9%*	*20.5%*	*0.2%*	*38.2%*	*0.1%*
Industry dummies	Yes	Yes	Yes	Yes	Yes	Yes
Time dummies	Yes	Yes	Yes	Yes	Yes	Yes
Number of observations	*1,413*	*1,481*	*1,413*	*915*	*928*	*915*
F(29, 1383)	*37.9*	*58.6*	*30.9*	*41.3*	*41.8*	*33.5*
Prob > F	*0.0%*	*0.0%*	*0.0%*	*0.0%*	*0.0%*	*0.0%*
R-squared	*0.451*	*0.531*	*0.393*	*0.557*	*0.547*	*0.505*
Adj R-squared	*0.439*	*0.522*	*0.380*	*0.543*	*0.534*	*0.490*
Root MSE	*0.539*	*0.141*	*0.567*	*0.393*	*0.133*	*0.415*

Source: Compiled by the authors.

Note: The instrument in the first stage is the concentration dummy. The regressions in columns 1, 2, and 3 use data corresponding to the period 1990–2002, while the remaining columns correspond to 1994–2002.

similar set of regressions run for a smaller sample of firms after controlling for traded volumes.

Dividend Payout Ratios

Tables 4.17 and 4.18 present the results for the regressions using the dividend payout ratio as the explanatory variable. The regressions are structured similarly to the regressions for Tobin's q. In the case of dividend payout ratios, we find inverse U-shaped relationships similar to the one obtained for the German case by Gugler and Yurtoglu (2003). The results are the following. First, firms affiliated with conglomerates, firms with pension funds as minority shareholders, and larger firms present higher payout ratios. Second, more debt implies lower dividends. Third, the separation of cash flow rights and control rights affects payout ratios in a nonlinear way.

Table 4.17 Dividend Payout and Coincidence of Cash Flow and Control Rights: Generalized Least Squares

	Dependent variable: Dividend pay-out ratio				
Group	0.080		0.077	0.077	0.109
	0.1%		*0.1%*	*0.1%*	*6.2%*
Coincidence		−0.083	−0.050	−0.030	0.010
		19.9%	*44.2%*	*63.8%*	*91.3%*
Coincidence*Group					−0.058
					58.5%
Pension Fund				0.100	0.103
				0.0%	*0.0%*
Tobin's q	0.155	0.150	0.155	0.143	0.140
	0.0%	*0.0%*	*0.0%*	*0.1%*	*0.0%*
Tobin's q*Group					−0.001
					99.0%
Cash flow	0.578	0.552	0.581	0.564	0.715
	1.7%	*2.3%*	*1.6%*	*1.9%*	*3.2%*
Cash flow*Group					−0.235
					48.3%
Assets	−0.002	0.004	−0.002	−0.013	−0.011
	79.8%	*50.4%*	*71.6%*	*5.8%*	*10.7%*
Debt	−0.387	−0.452	−0.417	−0.381	−0.357
	0.0%	*0.0%*	*0.0%*	*0.0%*	*0.0%*
Time dummies	Yes	Yes	Yes	Yes	Yes
Industry dummies	Yes	Yes	Yes	Yes	Yes
Wald test	412.25	398.12	413.06	436.21	420.65
p	*0.0%*	*0.0%*	*0.0%*	*0.0%*	*0.0%*
Number of companies	178	178	178	178	177
Number of observations	1,117	1,117	1,117	1,117	1,085

Source: Compiled by the authors.

Note: The table shows the results of generalized least squares regressions corrected for heteroskedasticity.

Similar to the German case, we find that there is a holding threshold at around 45 percent where the effect of higher controlling shareholder participation changes the sign of the marginal effect of separation on payout ratios. We find that, for low values of the coincidence variable, increases

Table 4.18 Dividend Payout, Coincidence of Cash Flow and Control Rights, and the Panel Tobit

	Dependent variable: Dividend pay-out ratio				
	Random effects	*Fixed effects*	*Generalized least squares*	*Panel Tobit LC = 0*[a]	*Panel Tobit LC = 0.3*[a]
Group	0.201	0.137	0.230	0.244	0.330
	6.0%	*37.2%*	*0.0%*	*8.9%*	*2.6%*
Coincidence	0.969	1.239	1.108	1.445	1.504
	2.2%	*1.8%*	*0.0%*	*0.9%*	*0.7%*
(Coincidence)2	–1.157	–1.473	–1.177	–1.653	–1.676
	1.1%	*0.9%*	*0.0%*	*0.5%*	*0.4%*
Coincidence* group	–0.683	–1.245	–0.832	–1.064	–1.169
	15.1%	*2.9%*	*0.3%*	*8.3%*	*5.8%*
(Coincidence)2* group	0.694	1.232	0.805	1.037	1.176
	19.1%	*5.8%*	*1.3%*	*12.1%*	*7.9%*
Tobin's q	0.045	–0.112	0.112	–0.047	0.029
	35.5%	*8.7%*	*0.0%*	*44.6%*	*63.2%*
Tobin's q* group	–0.025	0.007	0.031	–0.021	–0.043
	62.8%	*91.8%*	*28.5%*	*73.5%*	*47.2%*
Cash flow	0.409	0.210	0.595	0.762	0.363
	17.5%	*49.7%*	*0.1%*	*4.3%*	*31.7%*
Cash flow* group	–0.123	–0.039	–0.077	–0.291	–0.258
	68.6%	*90.1%*	*70.9%*	*43.4%*	*46.8%*
Assets	0.000	0.053	–0.003	0.042	–0.002
	97.1%	*9.3%*	*52.3%*	*0.1%*	*90.6%*
Debt	–0.396	–0.456	–0.333	–0.665	–0.478
	0.0%	*0.0%*	*0.0%*	*0.0%*	*0.0%*
Pension fund	0.110	0.017	0.099	0.133	0.173
	0.8%	*89.2%*	*0.0%*	*0.5%*	*0.4%*
Time dummies	*Yes*	*Yes*	*Yes*	*Yes*	*Yes*
Industry dummies	*Yes*	*No*	*Yes*	*Yes*	*Yes*
Alpha	0.418564	0.420593	0.470804	0.436994	0.448524
Alpha*group	0.308586	–0.011778	0.371893	0.309425	0.334579

(continued)

Table 4.18 Dividend Payout, Coincidence of Cash Flow and Control Rights, and the Panel Tobit *(continued)*

	Dependent variable : Dividend pay-out ratio				
	Random effects	*Fixed effects*	*Generalized least squares*	*Panel Tobit LC = 0*[a]	*Panel Tobit LC = 0.3*[a]
Wald test	168.5		1368.6	221.0	167.4
p	*0.0%*		0.0%	0.0%	0.0%
F test		3.9			
p		0			
Sigma ui	*19.2%*			*30.1%*	0.251
Sigma e	*25.1%*			*28.4%*	0.260
Number of companies	177	177	177	177	177
Number of observations	1,085	1,085	1,085	1,085	1,085

Source: Compiled by the authors.
Note: The table is based on annual data on from 1994 to 2002.
a. LC = left censoring.

in ownership concentration, as expected, increase the payout ratios. However, when concentration in terms of equity reaches more than 70 percent of the shares owned by the controlling shareholder, payout ratios start to decrease. The result may be related to tax incentives. As we discuss elsewhere above, once controlling shareholders have achieved such a high level of ownership, they may do almost anything without opposition, and there may be less expensive ways (in terms of taxes) of getting their money back.

Do Governance Practices Affect Market Valuation and Payout Policy?

Correlations With the Market Valuation of Firms

In this section, we focus on cross-sectional data for the year 2003 to include other dimensions of corporate governance in the empirical analysis. We include in the analysis the corporate governance indicator variables constructed on the basis of the questionnaire and summarized in the CGI described elsewhere above. As explained, we have divided the CGI into four parts: disclosure, board practices, shareholder rights, and conflict of interest. In addition, we consider a dummy variable that takes the value of 1 whenever we must fill in the answers to the questionnaire without company assistance, and we consider separately the pension fund dummy.

One might expect the different measures of corporate governance to be highly correlated. In table 4.19, we look at the correlations between the control variables used in the previous regressions and the corporate governance indicators. In general, the CGI and the subindexes are positively correlated among themselves and with market valuation. The subindex of shareholder rights is the exception and presents a negative, but low correlation with the other subindexes. Firm size is positively correlated with good corporate governance practices and less potential for agency problems, while the opposite is true for debt.

In table 4.20, we present multivariate Logit regressions between the CGI components and the control variables. Larger firms, less indebted firms, firms with more growth opportunities, and firms with larger available cash flows tend to show better corporate governance practices.

Finally, we look at the effect of better corporate governance practices on market valuation, as measured by the CGI and its components. The regressions presented in table 4.21 are estimated over a cross-sectional sample of 85 companies for the year 2003. The results are not encouraging. We find that, after controlling for the list of control variables, only the subindex on conflict of interest appears to be statistically significant in explaining firm value, and only a few questions have individual significance in the regressions. The overall index is not significant, and the subindex on shareholder rights, although significant, appears with a negative sign in the regressions. The lack of explanatory power may be attributed to the limited sample used because most of the variables that are significant in the previous panel data regressions are statistically insignificant in these cross-sectional regressions. In addition, the high correlation observed among the different measures of corporate governance and the control variables may imply multicollinearity in the regressions and, hence, low individual explanatory power.

Controlling for Endogeneity

Of course, even the positive and significant coefficient on the indicator of conflict of interest may be due to endogeneity through reverse causality. Without knowing whether this is the case, we are unable to affirm that these types of better corporate governance practices at the firm level are valued by the market. Following Black, Jang, and Kim (2006), we look for exogenous determinants of corporate governance practices not directly caused by firm market valuation. Similar to the case of the Republic of Korea, corporations law in Chile requires that all firms with market

Table 4.19 Pairwise Correlations of Key Variables

	Tobin's q	*Separation*	*Disclosure*	*Board*	*Share.*	*Conflict*	*CGI*	*Assets*	*Debt*	*Pension fund*
Tobin's q	100.0									
Separation	27.9	100.0								
Disclosure	–0.5	4.6	100.0							
Board	8.9	–3.3	28.9	100.0						
Shareholders	–0.6	–2.1	–14.8	5.8	100.0					
Conflict	16.7	5.1	23.8	34.3	–11.2	100.0				
CGI	6.7	0.5	61.9	76.1	19.9	66.9	100.0			
Assets	8.8	–18.5	11.7	10.7	25.7	–17.3	9.5	100.0		
Debt	–45.8	–71.9	–4.9	–9.6	10.8	–17.9	–10.6	23.3	100.0	
Pension fund	19.2	1.3	–0.3	4.7	3.7	–14.3	–7.8	47.5	3.3	100.0

Source: Compiled by the authors.
Note: Data are for the year 2003.

Table 4.20 Ordered Logit Regressions of Corporate Governance Subindexes on Control Variables

	CGI	*Disclosure*	*Board*	*Share*	*Conflict*[a]
Assets	0.294	0.208	0.283	0.320	–0.016
	0.9%	9.4%	1.5%	0.7%	
Debt	–1.631	–0.866	–1.685	0.182	–1.740
	5.6%	37.4%	6.7%	83.8%	
ROA	1.254	2.900	2.249	–1.733	-0.162
	42.6%	14.1%	22.8%	34.2%	
Liquidity	–2.758	–2.891	–1.546	2.255	–2.371
	13.7%	18.3%	44.3%	27.2%	
Industry dummies	Yes	Yes	Yes	Yes	Yes
Number of observations	100	100	100	100	100
LR chi2(14)	24.98	24.16	25	20.2	35.46
P Value	0.0347	0.0438	0.0346	0.1241	0.0013
Pseudo R2	0.0601	0.1107	0.0928	0.085	0.1683

Source: Compiled by the authors.
Note: Data are for the year 2003.
a. Convergence not achieved.

capitalization above US$45 million form an audit committee on which a majority is represented by independent directors.[17] Presumably, firms with market capitalization above this value will tend to have better corporate governance practices to be sure that they comply with the law. Figure 4.4 shows that, in fact, firms above this threshold have audit committees, while smaller firms do not. As a simple way to look at the validity of this instrument, figure 4.5 shows that there is no apparent relationship between this size threshold and the market valuation of firms.

The last two columns of table 4.21 show two-stage least squares regressions using the size dummy as an instrument for the CGI index in a regression of Tobin's q on the agency problem variables and the set of control variables. The results show that the second-stage coefficient of conflict of interest on Tobin's q remains positive and similar in value to the one obtained in an OLS regression indicating no evidence of endogeneity in an important way. However, the result is only significant at the 15 percent level.

Table 4.21 Corporate Governance Practices and the Market Valuation of Firms

							IV Estimation	
	OLS Tobin's q	*OLS Tobin's q*	*OLS Tobin's q*	*OLS Tobin's q*	*OLS Tobin's q*	*OLS Tobin's q*	*First-stage conflict*	*Second-stage Tobin's q*
Dsize							0.367	
							18.3%	
Source	–0.218	0.022	0.032	–0.067	–0.032	0.026	0.497	–0.050
	6.6%	*82.7%*	*74.9%*	*52.1%*	*73.5%*	*79.8%*	*0.7%*	*81.3%*
Disclosure	0.049	0.031						
	45.2%	*64.0%*						
Board	–0.009		0.016					
	86.2%		*74.6%*					
Shareholders	–0.168			–0.126				
	0.5%			*3.4%*				
Conflict	0.188				0.154			0.192
	0.4%				*1.5%*			*14.8%*
CGI						0.008		
						71.9%		
Concent	–0.749	–0.768	–0.743	–0.764	–0.717	–0.750	–0.133	–0.708
	1.6%	*2.2%*	*2.7%*	*1.8%*	*2.5%*	*2.5%*	*83.2%*	*4.1%*
Coincid	0.898	0.846	0.835	0.906	0.822	0.836	–0.007	0.816
	0.2%	*0.7%*	*0.9%*	*0.3%*	*0.7%*	*0.9%*	*99.0%*	*1.1%*

(continued)

Table 4.21 Corporate Governance Practices and the Market Valuation of Firms (*continued*)

							IV Estimation	
	OLS Tobin's q	*OLS Tobin's q*	*OLS Tobin's q*	*OLS Tobin's q*	*OLS Tobin's q*	*OLS Tobin's q*	*First-stage conflict*	*Second-stage Tobin's q*
DGroup	–0.018	–0.101	–0.103	–0.085	–0.055	–0.101	–0.354	–0.044
	84.7%	*31.7%*	*30.6%*	*38.4%*	*57.2%*	*31.6%*	*7.0%*	*78.0%*
DAFP	0.091	0.210	0.216	0.152	0.194	0.217	0.134	0.188
	43.7%	*8.7%*	*7.6%*	*21.0%*	*9.6%*	*7.4%*	*55.7%*	*16.3%*
LAEC	0.027	0.009	0.009	0.029	0.006	0.008	–0.034	0.005
	37.5%	*77.2%*	*77.2%*	*36.6%*	*84.1%*	*80.1%*	*66.5%*	*88.6%*
DE Ratio	–0.002	–0.012	–0.014	–0.007	–0.013	–0.013	0.014	–0.013
	86.0%	*41.7%*	*35.2%*	*64.5%*	*33.9%*	*35.4%*	*63.0%*	*35.9%*
Cash	0.825	0.752	0.618	1.725	–0.287	0.567	7.180	–0.542
	70.7%	*74.3%*	*79.1%*	*44.6%*	*89.8%*	*81.0%*	*10.2%*	*87.8%*
Industry dummies	Yes	Yes	Yes	Yes	Yes	Yes	Yes	Yes
Number of observations	*85*	*85*	*85*	*85*	*85*	*85*	*85*	*85*
F(29, 1383)	*3.0*	*2.3*	*2.3*	*2.7*	*2.8*	*2.3*	*2.4*	*2.3*
Prob > F	*0.0%*	*0.8%*	*0.8%*	*0.2%*	*0.1%*	*0.8%*	*0.4%*	*0.8%*
R^2	*0.517*	*0.398*	*0.397*	*0.436*	*0.449*	*0.397*	*0.416*	*0.398*
Adj R^2	*0.345*	*0.222*	*0.220*	*0.272*	*0.288*	*0.221*	*0.245*	*0.222*
Root MSE	*0.330*	*0.359*	*0.360*	*0.348*	*0.344*	*0.360*	*0.680*	*0.359*

Source: Compiled by the authors.

Figure 4.4 Audit Committees and the Size of Equity in Firms (Art. Sobis, Corp. Law)

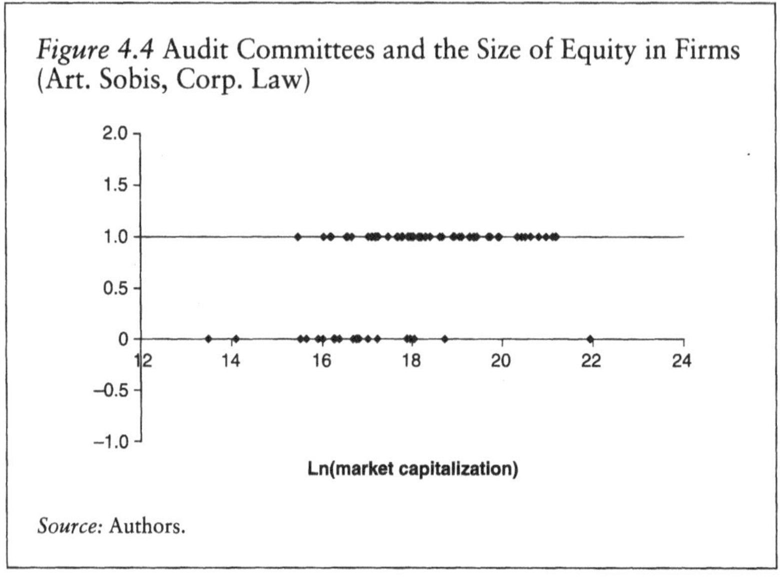

Source: Authors.

Figure 4.5 Tobin's q and the Size of Equity in Firms

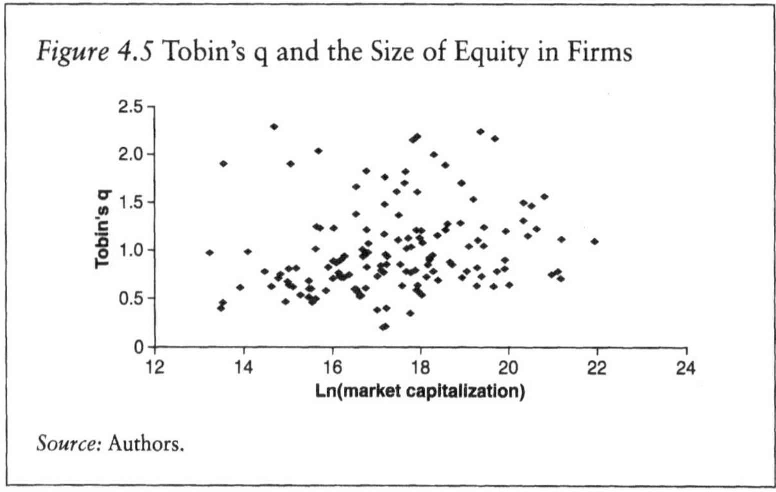

Source: Authors.

Conclusions

Recent studies comparing corporate governance practices at the country level have shown that Chilean companies present standards comparable to those of emerging economies with higher levels of capital market development and higher per capita income. In general, large Chilean companies have been characterized by corporate governance standards above those of other economies in Latin America.

The results of this chapter support two complementary sets of conclusions. First, we have looked at specific aspects of corporate governance practices in companies and find that Chilean companies are especially good in the areas of transparency and information disclosure. Among other reasons, this result may be related to early reforms in the securities market law and the corporations law in the context of the process of the privatization of pension funds. There are also indications that more recent legal reforms in Chile that seek to follow what is considered the world's best corporate governance practices have also played a role. Because Chile shares largely the same legal and political traditions with other countries in the region, the relatively better standards achieved by Chilean companies mean that adequate legal reform is important in shaping corporate governance practices at the firm level. Institutional investors, investors in American depositary receipts, and creditors are important stakeholders in Chilean firms, and they understand that good corporate governance practices are valuable. They are crucial players in translating better corporate governance practices into better access to capital among firms.

The worst aspects of Chilean corporate governance practices are related to conflicts of interest between controlling and minority shareholders. The results obtained through our questionnaires are consistent with the widespread use in Chile of pyramids as a way to separate cash flow rights and control rights. Pyramids seem to be an efficient way for economic groups to exercise control over a wide variety of productive assets and to establish internal capital markets that compensate for relatively poorly developed formal markets. However, the use of pyramids may exacerbate agency problems and be detrimental to the market value of companies and to the level of economic development of the country.

In this chapter, we try to shed light on this issue by performing regression analyses of measures of firm market valuation, performance, and payout policy on corporate governance indicators at the firm level and a series of control variables. We carefully check that our results are not due to omitted variable bias or to particular specification and samples through an extensive robustness check. We also control for reverse causality using two features of the Chilean corporations law that provide an exogenous instrument for some of the corporate governance practices of Chilean firms.

In summary, we find that firms presenting a higher coincidence between cash flow rights and control rights tend to be consistently more valued by the market. We interpret this result as an indication that potential conflicts of interest between controlling and minority shareholders are penalized by the Chilean capital market. We also consistently find that firms scoring poorly on indicators of conflict of interest are less valued by the market. Hence, the shares of firms presenting agency problems tend to be traded in the market at a discount, indicating that a reduction in conflicts of interest and agency problems improves the conditions for firms to access portfolio capital.

Notes

1. See La Porta et al. (2000).

2. See Bebchuk (1999); Wolfenzon (1999). Relevant papers analyzing the effect of conglomeration on corporate governance and firm performance in emerging economies include Khanna and Palepu (1999a, 1999b); Ghemawat and Khanna (1998); Lefort and Walker (2000a, 2000b); Leal, Carvalhal-da-Silva, and Valadares (2000) on Brazil; Khanna and Palepu (1999a, 1999b, 1999c) on India; Claessens, Fan, and Lang (1999); and Claessens, Djankov, and Lang (2000) on Chile and most East Asian economies.

3. See Khanna and Palepu (1997).

4. See Stein (1997).

5. See Shleifer and Vishny (1992).

6. See Khanna and Palepu (1997).

7. See Gugler and Yurtoglu (2002).

8. See Baker and Wurgler (2002).

9. This assumption is realistic because there is only one Chilean company (Soquimich, but only since 2000) that is not tightly controlled by a single family, business group, or other company.

10. See La Porta et al. (1997).

11. Corporations law, rule 79.

12. Corporations law, rule 84 establishes that, if dividends are postponed, the amount eventually paid must be adjusted for inflation and include interest.

13. Rule 67 of the corporations law establishes that major company decisions require the support of two-thirds of the voting shares during a shareholders meeting. The rule also establishes a mandatory tender offer requirement whenever a shareholder would reach the two-thirds threshold through an acquisition.

14. See Walker and Lefort (2000a).

15. See Gugler and Yurtoglu (2002).

16. Black, Jang, and Kim (2006) offer an alternative explanation for the potential correlation: quality signaling. The idea is that firms may adopt good governance rules to signal their good behavior. In this case, the signals rather than the governance practices of the firms would affect the prices of shares.

17. Rule 50 bis, corporations law.

References

Agosín, M., and E. Pastén. 2001. "Corporate Governance in Chile." Paper presented at the Meeting on Corporate Governance in Developing Countries and Emerging Economics sponsored by the Development Centre of the Organisation for Economic Co-operation and Development and the European Bank for Reconstruction and Development, Paris, April 23–24.

Agrawal, A., and C. Knoeber. 1996. "Firm Performance and Mechanisms to Control Agency Problems between Managers and Shareholders." *Journal of Financial and Quantitative Analysis* 31 (3): 377–97.

Baker, M. P., and J. A. Wurgler. 2002. "Market Timing and Capital Structure." *Journal of Finance* 57 (1): 1–32.

Bebchuk, L. A. 1999. "The Rent Protection Theory of Corporate Ownership and Control." Unpublished working paper, Harvard Law School, Cambridge, MA.

Bebchuk, L. A., A. Cohen, and A. Ferrell. 2004. "What Matters in Corporate Governance?" Harvard Law School John M. Olin Discussion Paper 491, Harvard Law School, Cambridge, MA, http://ssrn.com/abstract=593423.

Becht, M., P. Bolton, and A. Röell. 2002. "Corporate Governance and Control." NBER Working Paper 9371, National Bureau of Economic Research, Cambridge, MA.

Beck, T., R. Levine, and N. Loayza. 2000. "Finance and the Sources of Growth." *Journal of Financial Economics* 58 (1–2): 261–300.

Berglöf, E., and E.-L. von Thadden. 1999. "The Changing Corporate Governance Paradigm: Implications for Transition and Developing Countries." Paper presented at the annual World Bank Conference on Development Economics, Washington, DC, April 28–30.

Berle, A., and G. Means. 1932. *The Modern Corporation and Private Property*. New York: Macmillan.

Bharati, R., M. Gupta, and P. Nanisetty. 1998. "Are Dividends Smoothed Signals of Earnings Asymmetry?" *International Journal of Business* 3 (2): 1–18.

Black, B. S., 1992. "Agents Watching Agents: The Promise of Institutional Investor Voice." *UCLA Law Review* 39 (4): 811–93.

Black, B. S., H. Jang, and W. Kim. 2006. "Does Corporate Governance Predict Firms' Market Values?: Evidence from Korea." *Journal of Law, Economics, and Organization* 22 (2): 366–413.

Brown, L. D., and M. L. Caylor. 2004. "Corporate Governance and Firm Performance." Unpublished working paper, School of Accountancy, Georgia State University, Atlanta, http://ssrn.com/abstract=586423.

Claessens, S., S. Djankov, and L. F. Klapper. 2000. "The Role and Functioning of Business Groups in East Asia and Chile." *Abante* 3 (1): 91–107.

Claessens, S., S. Djankov, and L. H. P. Lang. 2000. "The Separation of Ownership and Control in East Asian Corporations." *Journal of Financial Economics* 58 (1–2): 81–112.

Claessens, S., J. P. H. Fan, and L. H. P. Lang. 1999. "The Cost of Group Affiliation: Evidence from East Asia." Unpublished working paper, World Bank, Washington, DC.

Coffee, J. C., Jr. 1999. "The Future as History: The Prospects for Global Convergence in Corporate Governance and Its Implications." *Northwestern University Law Review* 93 (3): 631–707.

Demsetz, H. 1983. "The Structure of Ownership and the Theory of the Firm." *Journal of Law and Economics* 26 (2): 375–90.

Demsetz, H., and K. Lehn. 1985. "The Structure of Corporate Ownership: Causes and Consequences." *Journal of Political Economy* 93 (6): 1155–77.

Durnev, A., and E. H. Kim. 2005. "To Steal or Not to Steal: Firm Attributes, Legal Environment, and Valuation." *Journal of Finance* 60 (3): 1461–93.

Faccio, M., and L. H. P. Lang. 2002. "The Ultimate Ownership of Western European Corporations." *Journal of Financial Economics* 65 (3): 365–95.

Faccio, M., L. H. P. Lang, and L. Young. 2001. "Dividends and Expropriation." *American Economic Review* 91 (1): 54–78.

Fama, E., and M. Jensen. 1983. "Separation of Ownership and Control." *Journal of Law and Economics* 26 (2): 301–25.

Franks, J., and C. Mayer. 1994. "The Ownership and Control of German Corporations." Unpublished working paper, London Business School, London.

Gálvez, J., and J. Tybout. 1985. "Microeconomic Adjustments in Chile during 1977–81: The Importance of Being a Grupo." *World Development* 13 (8): 969–94.

Ghemawat, P., and T. Khanna. 1998. "The Nature of Diversified Business Groups: A Research Design and Two Case Studies." *Journal of Industrial Economics* 46 (1): 35–61.

Gillette, A., T. Noe, and M. Rebello. 2003. "Corporate Board Composition, Protocols, and Voting Behavior: Experimental Evidence." *Journal of Finance* 58 (5): 1997–2032.

Glaeser, E., S. Johnson, and A. Shleifer. 2000. "Coase Versus the Coasians." Unpublished working paper, Harvard University, Cambridge, MA.

Gompers, P. A., J. L. Ishii, and A. Metrick. 2003. "Corporate Governance and Equity Prices." *Quarterly Journal of Economics* 118 (1): 107–55.

Grossman, S. J., and O. D. Hart. 1986. "The Costs and Benefits of Ownership: A Theory of Vertical and Lateral Integration." *Journal of Political Economy* 94 (4): 691–719.

Gugler, K., and B. B. Yurtoglu. 2002. "Average Q, Marginal Q, and the Relation between Ownership and Performance." *Economics Letters* 78 (3): 379–84.

———. 2003. "Corporate Governance and Dividend Pay-out Policy in Germany. *European Economic Review* 47 (2): 731–58.

Hayashi, F. 1982. "Tobin's Marginal Q and Average Q: A Neoclassical Interpretation." *Econometrica* 50 (1): 213–24.

Hermalin, B. E., and M. S. Weisbach. 2003. "Boards of Directors as an Endogenously Determined Institution: A Survey of the Economic Literature." *Economic Policy Review* 9 (1): 7–26.

Hoshi, T., A. Kashyap, and D. Scharfstein. 1991. "Corporate Structure, Liquidity, and Investment: Evidence from Japanese Industrial Groups." *Quarterly Journal of Economics* 106 (1): 33–60.

Iglesias-Palau, A. 2000. "Pension Reform and Corporate Governance: Impact in Chile." *Abante* 3 (1): 109–41.

Jensen, M. C. 1986. "Agency Cost of Free Cash Flow, Corporate Finance, and Takeovers." *American Economic Review* 76 (2): 323–29.

Jensen, M. C., and W. H. Meckling. 1976. "Theory of the Firm: Managerial Behavior, Agency Costs, and Ownership Structure." *Journal of Financial Economics* 3 (4): 305–60.

Jensen, M., and K. J. Murphy. 1990. "Performance Pay and Top Management Incentives." *Journal of Political Economy* 98 (2): 225–64.

Khanna, T., and K. G. Palepu. 1997. "Why Focused Strategies May Be Wrong for Emerging Markets." *Harvard Business Review* 75 (4): 41–51.

———. 1999a. "Is Group Affiliation Profitable in Emerging Markets?: An Analysis of Diversified Indian Business Groups." *Journal of Finance* 55 (2): 867–91.

———. 1999b. "The Future of Business Groups in Emerging Markets: Long Run Evidence From Chile." Working Paper 99–077, Harvard Business School, Cambridge, MA.

———. 1999c. "Policy Shocks, Market Intermediaries, and Corporate Strategy: The Evolution of Business Groups in Chile and India." *Journal of Economics and Management Strategy* 8 (2): 271–310.

Khanna, T., and J. Rivkin. 2001. "Estimating the Performance Effects of Business Groups in Emerging Markets." *Strategic Management Journal* 22 (1): 45–74.

Khanna, T., and Y. Yafeh. 2000. "Business Groups and Sharing around the World." Unpublished working paper, Harvard Business School, Cambridge, MA.

Klapper, L. F., and I. Love. 2004. "Corporate Governance, Investor Protection, and Performance in Emerging Markets." *Journal of Corporate Finance* 10 (5): 703–28.

Klein, A. 2002. "Audit Committee, Board of Directors Characteristics, and Earnings Management." *Journal of Accounting and Economics* 33 (3): 375–400.

La Porta, R., F. López-de-Silanes, and A. Shleifer. 1999. "Corporate Ownership around the World." *Journal of Finance* 54 (2): 471–517.

La Porta, R., F. López-de-Silanes, A. Shleifer, and R. W. Vishny. 1996. "Law and Finance." NBER Working Paper 5661, National Bureau of Economic Research, Cambridge, MA.

———. 1997. "Legal Determinants of External Finance." *Journal of Finance* 52 (3): 1131–50.

———. 2000. "Agency Problems and Dividend Policies around the World." *Journal of Finance* 55 (1): 1–33.

Leal, R. P. C., A. L. Carvalhal-da-Silva, and S. Valadares. 2000. "Ownership, Control, and Corporate Valuation of Brazilian Companies." Paper presented at the Bovespa, CVM, and IBGC Latin American Corporate Governance Roundtable, São Paulo, April 26–28, http://www.oecd.org/dataoecd/56/25/1921869.pdf.

Lefort, F., and E. Walker. 2000a. "Ownership and Capital Structure of Chilean Conglomerates: Facts and Hypotheses of Governance." *Abante* 3 (1): 3–27.

———. 2000b. "Corporate Governance: A Challenge for Latin America." *Abante* 2 (2): 99–111.

———. 2001. "Gobierno Corporativo, Protección a Accionistas Minoritarios y Tomas de Control." Documentos de Discusión 1 (May), Superintendency of Securities and Insurance, Santiago, Chile.

———. 2003a. "Economic Performance of Conglomerates: Evidence from Chile." Unpublished working paper, Business School, Pontificia Universidad Católica de Chile, Santiago, Chile.

———. 2003b. "Chilean Financial Markets and Corporate Structure." Unpublished working paper, Business School, Pontificia Universidad Católica de Chile, Santiago, Chile.

Majluf, N., N. Abarca, D. Rodriguez, and L. A. Fuentes. 1998. "Governance and Ownership Structure in Chilean Economic Groups." *Abante* 1 (1): 111–39.

Morck, R., A. Shleifer, and R. W. Vishny. 1988. "Management Ownership and Market Valuation: An Empirical Analysis." *Journal of Financial Economics* 20 (1): 293–315.

Myers, S. 2000. "Outside Equity." *Journal of Finance* 55 (3): 1005–37.

Myers, S., and N. Majluf. 1984. "Corporate Financing and Investment Decisions when Firms Have Information That Investors Do Not Have." *Journal of Financial Economics* 13 (2): 187–221.

Paredes, R., and J. M. Sánchez. 1995. "Organización Industrial y Grupos Económicos: El caso de Chile." Unpublished working paper, Programa de Postgrado en Economía, Ilades–Georgetown University, Santiago, Chile.

Parisi, F., R. Godoy, and A. Parisi. 2000. "Gobierno Corporativo en Chile: Evidencia." Unpublished working paper, Facultad de Ciencias Económicas y Administrativas, Universidad de Chile, Santiago, Chile.

Scharfstein, D. 1998. "The Dark Side of Internal Capital Markets II: Evidence from Diversified Conglomerates." Unpublished working paper, Sloan School of Management, Massachusetts Institute of Technology, Cambridge, MA.

Scharfstein, D., and J. C. Stein. 1997. "The Dark Side of Internal Capital Markets: Divisional Rent Seeking and Inefficient Investment." NBER Working Paper 5969, National Bureau of Economic Research, Cambridge, MA.

Shleifer, A., and R. W. Vishny. 1992. "Pervasive Shortages under Socialism." *RAND Journal of Economics* 23 (2): 237–46.

Shleifer, A., and D. Wolfenzon. 2002. "Investor Protection and Equity Markets." *Journal of Financial Economics* 66 (1): 3–27.

Stein, J. C. 1997. "Internal Capital Markets and the Competition for Corporate Resources." *Journal of Finance* 52 (1): 111–33.

Stulz, R. M. 1988. "Managerial Control of Voting Rights: Financing Policies and the Market for Corporate Control." *Journal of Financial Economics* 20: 25–54.

Thomsen, S., and T. Pedersen. 2001. "The Causal Relationship between Insider Ownership, Owner Identity, and Market Valuation among the Largest European Companies." Working Paper 15, Department of International Economics and Management, Copenhagen Business School, Copenhagen.

Wolfenzon, D. 1999. "A Theory of Pyramidal Structures." Unpublished working paper, Harvard University, Cambridge, MA.

Xie, B., W. Davidson, and P. J. DaDalt. 2003. "Earnings Management and Corporate Governance: The Role of the Board and the Audit Committee." *Journal of Corporate Finance* 9 (3): 295–316.

Zingales, L. 1997. "Corporate Governance." NBER Working Paper 6309, National Bureau of Economic Research, Cambridge, MA.

5

Corporate Governance and Firm Valuation in Colombia

*Luis H. Gutiérrez and Carlos Pombo**

Introduction

The analysis of corporate governance systems has attracted attention in recent years. Some studies have examined the connection between ownership structures and performance, while, more recently, others have focused on the relationship between corporate governance indexes (CGIs) at the firm level and the market valuation and performance of firms. In the first set of papers, researchers have tested two opposite effects of ownership upon performance. On the one hand, large blockholders who have good information on their firms have incentives to monitor managers and then to minimize problems of management entrenchment. This monitoring effect is positive. On the other hand, the incentives of large blockholders may be at odds with those of minority shareholders. Some of these incentives may be empire building, excessive risk taking, and the like. This has been called the tunneling effect, which is, of course, negative for a firm's valuation and performance.

* We wish to thank Alberto Chong, Florencio López-de-Silanes, and seminar participants at Research Network meetings of the Inter-American Development Bank for their valuable comments and suggestions. We are especially grateful to Jorge Restrepo, president of the Banco Agrario de Colombia and former president of Fabricato, who helped us to established direct communication with company chief executive officers for the follow-up on the survey on corporate governance practices. We are especially indebted to Rodrigo Taborda, who provided the basic measures of stockholder cash flow rights and voting rights, and Roberto Fortich for his research assistance. All errors are ours.

In the second set of papers, researchers have examined firm-level corporate governance mechanisms; most have focused on cross-country analyses wherein the emphasis is on the effect upon governance of the legal systems across countries. La Porta, López-de-Silanes, and Shleifer (1999) argue that investor protection tends to be greater when the legal environment is stronger, and, therefore, the willingness of an investor to invest tends to increase. They test whether corporate governance helps explain a firm's valuation and performance and find a strong positive association.

This chapter addresses both types of research for the Colombian context. This is the first time such an approach has been taken on Colombia. The chapter starts by reporting results that link different ownership and control measures and separation ratios with a firm's value and performance for a set of 108 nonfinancial firms that traded their stock from 1998 to 2002. After controlling for a variety of control variables, we have found evidence that large blockholders exert a positive influence on a firm's valuation and performance, which validates the monitoring approach. However, we have also found that this relation is not monotonic, implying that, when the separation of control and ownership tends to increase, a negative effect is exerted on a firm's valuation.

To analyze the effects of corporate best practices on a firm's performance and valuation, we report the results of a survey of corporate governance practices conducted in 2004 among 43 Colombian nonfinancial companies. For 10 additional companies, the survey questionnaire was filled out based on official documentation, such as company reports on general shareholder meetings and the minutes of meetings of boards of directors filed at the Financial Superintendence (Superintendencia Financiera de Colombia), until recently the Superintendence of Securities (Superintendencia de Valores, SVAL). We have fashioned a CGI that includes information on six different criteria: independence, accountability, fairness, responsibility, transparency, and discipline. The measurement outcomes suggest that the implementation of good governance in Colombian firms has been slow and poor. The average CGI is less than half the maximum attainable value. The Colombian stock market is underdeveloped and needs to be strengthened and improved. In fact, during the period under analysis, the market shrank in terms of the number of firms that were trading shares. This chapter, then, tries to address the question of whether better governance practices lead to better (accounting) performance. We have used standard ordinary least squares (OLS) and corrected for endogeneity, but the results are not robust. Performance is not explained by good governance practices. This is the first attempt that has been made to verify such a hypothesis for the case of Colombia; thus, despite the outcome, the study helps broaden the understanding of corporate practices in emerging markets.

The next section describes the data set of stockholder stakes that we have used, as well as the methodology we have followed in measuring integrated ownership as a proxy for investor voting rights. It also presents an explanation of the final working panel of firms, which matches up ownership statistics and indicators with firm market valuation and performance indicators. The subsequent section presents the core results on the corporate ownership and control statistics for the sample of companies that traded shares during 1998–2002, as well as an analysis of ultimate ownership. The following section shows the main results on corporate best practices based on a survey carried out during the third quarter of 2004, which is the first survey performed in Colombia according to the Credit Lyonnais Security Asia (CLSA) format. The penultimate section reports on the econometric analysis of corporate control and ownership, alongside firm valuation and performance. It includes a statistical analysis on the determinants of our CGI. The last section summarizes the main results of our study and highlights the policy implications for better corporate governance practices in future.

Data and Methodology

The data on corporate shareholders used in this study have been derived from two sources, the SVAL and the Superintendence of Commercial Companies (Superintendencia de Sociedades, SSOC). These two institutions are responsible for inspecting and overseeing equity-issuing corporations and larger unlisted firms, respectively. The SVAL ownership database is based on national equity registry forms, which record information on a company's top 20 shareholders. Filling out this form is mandatory for all equity issuers who are under the oversight of the SVAL, and the form must be updated on a yearly basis. The form also records the names of board members, the number of outstanding shares, the number of preferred dividend shares, and the nominal value of each type of share. Corporate law in Colombia, according to the commercial code, forbids dual shares and any other kind of legal deviations from the one share–one vote rule.

We have assembled a comprehensive data set of shareholder records for 233 real sector companies that were listed during 1996–2002. This database has been used for the study by Gutiérrez, Pombo, and Taborda (2007) on ownership and control among the largest listed nonfinancial Colombian corporations. The existence of a panel data set on ownership improves the analysis because we are able to capture the dynamics of ownership, an element not usually included in international studies on corporate control.[1] At most, this database provides first or second property layers. To complete each company's second, third, and higher ownership layers, we have assembled a data set of information on shareholders of unlisted firms that appeared as major shareholders of a listed corporation and were affiliated with a business group. This information is found in the SSOC records of the largest stakeholders for open, but not public corporations, as well as partnership distributions for limited liability and all other legal firm types. Thus, we have been able to gather complementary ownership information for about 431 unlisted firms for 1996–2002.

Annex 5.1 describes schematically the structure of the ownership data set. The top of the figure shows that listed firms are included in the analysis of ownership and control. This group of firms is referred to as the SVAL data set. The largest shareholders may be an individual, a family, a listed firm, an unlisted firm, a nonprofit organization, a holding investment or trust fund, or other legal contractual entity allowed by law.[2] If the shareholder is a firm, it may be listed or unlisted. In the first case, a second layer is added from the SVAL data set, and, in the second case, the original information is supplemented by information from the SSOC or the SSOC data set; the process is continued until a third layer is completed for most listed companies.

From the shareholders ownership data set, a sample of 108 companies has been extracted, the stocks of which were traded at least once during 1998–2002. This means that all Colombian companies that traded their stocks during that period have been included, as were the year(s) in which their stock was actually traded, while those years in which their stocks were not traded have been excluded. This was done for the following reasons. First, companies may issue several types of securities, such as stocks, bonds, and commercial papers. However, stocks are the only securities that have variable returns depending on how well a firm is managed and how well its corporate governance is conducted. Bonds and other types of fixed return securities may be assimilated with bank loans. Second, reliable data for the (average) annual market prices of stocks are almost nonexistent or are difficult to obtain for years other than the period selected. Because one of the objectives of this study is to test how measures of the valuation of firms (such as the Tobin's q) are related to ownership and other control variables, it has been essential to obtain stock market prices; this was only possible for firms that satisfied the trading and year criteria. Third, the data have been restricted to the year(s) in which the stocks were actually traded at least once, meaning that the complete panel is unbalanced. The rationale for doing this stems from a desire to study how the relationships of shareholder interests evolved during the period among firms that traded their stocks during all five years relative to firms that traded for four or fewer years.

Definitions of Ownership and Control

This subsection discusses conceptual and methodological issues revolving around the measurement of cash flow rights and voting rights, which are central for the analysis of the ownership of firms and the separation between the types of rights. The study of ultimate ownership or controlling shareholders begins with the fundamental question about who actually owns a firm: the investor who has greater direct stakes or the investor who is able to exercise greater control rights. The corporate finance view is based on the delegation problem within the principal agent framework relative to shareholders and company executives. Following Grossman and Hart (1982), the literature has concluded that the owners are those who are in control of the firm.

Studies of ownership and control have followed two complementary approaches to identify and measure the ultimate controlling shareholders. The first follows the La Porta, López-de-Silanes, and Shleifer (1999) methodology, which defines a firm's ultimate controlling shareholder as those shareholders whose direct and indirect voting rights exceed 20 percent. According to this methodology, under a one share–one vote rule, if a shareholder has a direct stake in a company, then the shareholder must add controlling power through indirect ownership along the property chain. Thus, the ratio of cash flow rights to voting rights is less than or equal to 1, meaning that one dollar of direct investment will provide $(1+x)$ voting rights if there is any indirect ownership.

The second approach is based on consideration of the portfolio of a company's direct investments. This approach relies on an input-output methodology to compute integrated ownership stakes as the sum of direct and indirect ownership. It has been used in several case studies on Japan and continental Europe, where the structure of business groups is more complex than the structures in the United Kingdom or the United States because of the existence of cross-shareholdings, rings, pyramidal cascades, interlocks with financial institutions, and the high concentration levels of voting and direct ownership stakes.[3] This methodology defines cash flow rights as direct ownership and voting rights as integrated ownership.

The integrated ownership formula is provided in the paper by Baldone, Brioschi, and Paleari (1997), which defines integrated ownership as the sum of percentage shares of total equity a shareholder i holds in firm j directly, through cross-shareholdings, and indirectly. This definition in matrix algebra is equivalent to the following equation:

$$\mathbf{Y} = \underbrace{\mathbf{A}}_{\text{Direct Ownership}} + \underbrace{\mathbf{YA}}_{\text{Indirect Ownership}} - \underbrace{\mathbf{D}(\mathbf{Y})\mathbf{A}}_{\text{Reciprocal or cross-shareholding ownership}}, \quad (5.1)$$

where A is the matrix of direct equity held by firm i in firm j, $\mathbf{D}(\mathbf{Y})$ stands for the diagonal elements of $\mathbf{Y}$, and $\mathbf{I}$ is an $(N \times N)$ identity matrix. The solution for $\mathbf{Y}$ in equation (5.1) is the following:

$$\mathbf{Y} = \left(\mathbf{D}(\mathbf{I}-\mathbf{A})^{-1}\right)^{-1}\mathbf{A}(\mathbf{I}-\mathbf{A})^{-1}. \quad (5.2)$$

We have used equation 5.2 to estimate the integrated ownership of all affiliated firms in our sample.[4] Lastly, the direct ownership of firms has been estimated through concentration ratios (CR) for the largest shareholder (CR_1), the sum of the two largest shareholders (CR_2), and so on, as desired. The concentration ratio at the r level for a total of N individuals is given by the following equation:

$$CR_r = \frac{\sum_{i=1}^{r} a_{ij}}{\sum_{i=1}^{N} a_{ij}} \quad \text{and} \quad r < N. \tag{5.3}$$

Valuation and Performance Measures

This study focuses on firms listed during the period 1998 to 2002 for which we have been able to compute valuation measures such as Tobin's q. The estimation of Tobin's q follows Black, Jang, and Kim (2003), who defined Tobin's q as the ratio of the market value of assets to the book value of assets. As in the case of the firms in the Republic of Korea examined in that study, Colombian accounting and tax regulations require that all firms update their book values yearly. The use of the book value of assets is therefore close to the replacement cost. The market value of assets has been estimated as the sum of the book value of debt, the book value of preferred stocks, and the market value of common stock. In turn, the yearly market value of common stocks has been calculated as the product of the average market price and the number of common stocks. The book value of liabilities has been taken as the book value of debt.[5]

Unfortunately, the market value of firms cannot be obtained if firms are not listed, if they delist, or if they do not trade their stocks. Because two of the samples in this chapter are composed of firms that fall into one or more of these categories, two accounting performance measures have also been estimated, such as the return on assets (ROA) and the return on equity (ROE), following standard definitions. The financial data are taken from company balance sheets and income statements reported to the SVAL or the SSOC. When a firm is delisted from the stock exchange, it has to report to the SSOC if the company fulfills the threshold in sales or size that is required by law.[6] All delisted cases in the study sample of the 108 trading stock companies have records at the SSOC, and thus the financial variables could be chained for the whole period.

Corporate Ownership and Control

Ownership Statistics

It is well known that corporate ownership and control are highly concentrated in Colombia. This fact has been linked to the formation of conglomerates and business groups from the 1950s to the late 1970s, when vertical control provided the incentive for the control of productive chains from upstream to downstream industries. Most of these groups started as family businesses and then became corporate groups with strategic investments in their core businesses. Gutiérrez, Pombo, and Taborda (2007) show that there are four relevant characteristics of corporate ownership and control for the entire sample of listed companies during the 1996–2002 period:

- Corporate ownership is highly concentrated. The four largest shareholders have more than 51 percent of the cash flow rights in almost all companies. Under the one share–one vote rule, this represents the exercise of private control by the largest shareholders. Moreover, for affiliated companies, the largest voting blocks belong to the same business groups.
- Ownership concentration has increased. The frequency distribution of concentration ratios for the top four voting blocks (CR4) became left skewed from 1996 to 2002. On average, the four largest shareholders had more than 80 percent of cash flow rights in 45 percent of the sample firms in 2002. This number was around 32 percent in 1996.
- There are low separation ratios within the largest voting blocks, among the top four voting blocks, and at the level of ultimate owner. Nonetheless, in some cases, there is evidence of full separation at the level of controlling shareholders.
- Investment firms play a central role as controlling shareholders.

In this subsection, we want to test if the above patterns hold for the sample of 108 trading stock companies. Table 5.1 reports the main results of the measurements of direct ownership stakes for the total sample and time period. The study sample represents 60 percent of the total listed companies for which ownership data were collected. These numbers are similar to those in the first characteristic mentioned above. In fact, the concentration ratios are high, implying that control over a company is exercised within the top four voting blocks. On average, the largest shareholder has 30 percent of the cash flow rights, while the top four have 60 percent. Ownership concentration increased across the two periods. The median of the largest stake rose 6 points, while the median rose 5 percentage points across the top four shareholders. Together, these companies exhibit low liquidity according to the trading indicator, which measures the percentage of days in which stocks were traded over a year's working days. Half of these companies traded less than 3 percent of the days, while the average traded 16 percent and 19 percent during 1996–99 and 2000–02, respectively.

These numbers suggest that there was a change in the distribution of ownership concentration over the period. Figures 5.1 and 5.2 depict

Table 5.1 Ownership Statistics on the Sample of Stock Trading Companies

Indicator/statistic	*1996–99*	*2000–02*
Sample firms	90	83
Total listed firms	148	133
Coverage	0.6064	0.6216
Share top 20 shareholders		
N	90	83
Mean	0.7336	0.7537
Median	0.8104	0.8340
75th percentile	0.9290	0.9586
25th percentile	0.5776	0.6017
Standard deviation	0.2355	0.2381
Interquantile range	0.3514	0.3568
Share largest shareholder: CR1		
N	90	83
Mean	0.3106	0.3476
Median	0.2509	0.3172
75th percentile	0.4396	0.4836
25th percentile	0.1372	0.1678
Standard deviation	0.2164	0.2185
Interquantile range	0.3024	0.3158
Share top four shareholders: CR4		
N	90	83
Mean	0.5902	0.6171
Median	0.5877	0.6331
75th percentile	0.7912	0.8092
25th percentile	0.3975	0.4327
Standard deviation	0.2469	0.2546
Interquantile range	0.3937	0.3765
Trading		
N	42	58
Mean	0.1596	0.1952
Median	0.0250	0.0350
75th percentile	0.1184	0.2442
25th percentile	0.0100	0.0133
Standard deviation	0.2742	0.2920
Interquantile range	0.1084	0.2309

Source: Calculations of the authors based on a data set newly assembled from SVAL national equity registry forms.

Note: The direct stakes are equal to direct voting rights under the one share–one vote rule. The firm sample excludes financial institutions, utilities, and livestock funds. The trading stock variable has been calculated from 1998.

Figure 5.1 Histogram of the Top Four Shareholders (CR4), 1996

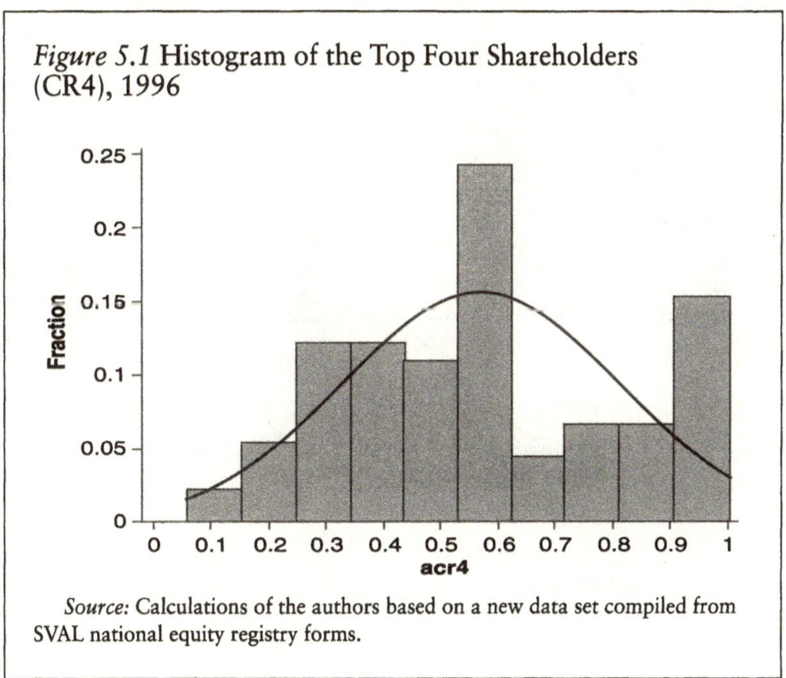

Source: Calculations of the authors based on a new data set compiled from SVAL national equity registry forms.

and contrast the change in the distribution of ownership concentration at the CR4 level between 1996 and 2002. The histograms show that the CR4 distribution became left skewed, meaning that there was a higher concentration within firms. In 1996, there were two peaks in the frequency distribution at the 0.55–0.65 and 0.9–1.0 bins. At the first peak, at around 25 percent of the firms in the sample, the four largest shareholders had on average control of 60 percent of the voting rights. The second peak indicates that, in 15 percent of the firms, the top four shareholders had more than 90 percent of the voting rights. In 2002, the four largest stakes had direct voting rights at above 90 percent in 20 percent of the firms and at between 70 and 80 percent in 15 percent of the firms. Thus, structural changes took place within the largest voting blocks across trading firms.

Breaking down these measurements by economic sector, as shown in table 5.2, one finds similar patterns for ownership structure, where the mean (median) of the top four owners of direct stakes is above 51 percent, with the exception of firms in agriculture and livestock activities, where the mean (median) is around 0.34 (0.35) for the entire period. The most concentrated corporations are located in manufacturing, where the mean (median) increased from 0.62 (0.63) to 0.66 (0.68), and health and personal services, where the mean (median) decreased slightly from 0.85 (0.93) to 0.83 (0.87) over the two subperiods.[7]

Figure 5.2 Histogram of the Top Four Shareholders (CR4), 2002

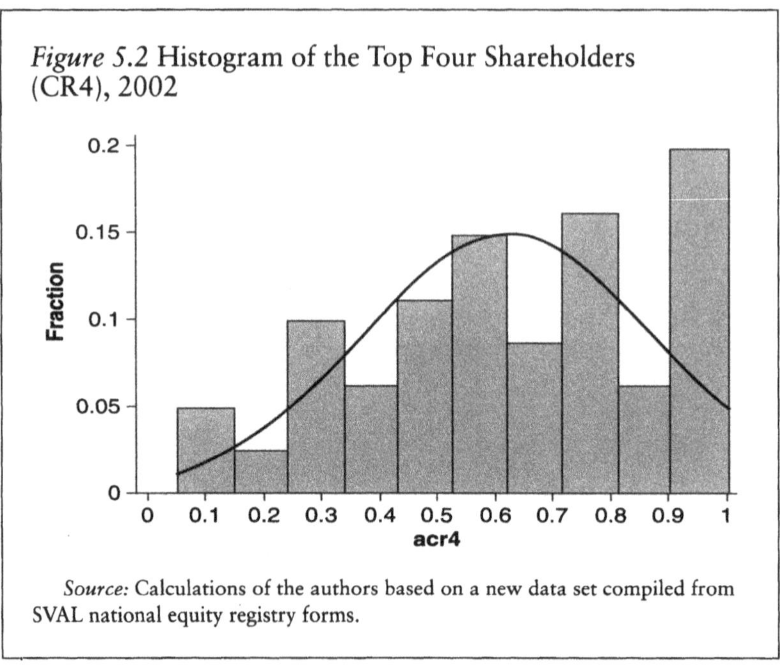

Source: Calculations of the authors based on a new data set compiled from SVAL national equity registry forms.

The Separation Between Ownership and Control

Berle and Means (1932) stressed the difference between ownership and control. In their work, they estimated the separation of ownership and control among the 200 largest U.S. corporations. For them, it was clear that:

> Since direction over the activities of a corporation is exercised through the board of directors, we may say for practical purposes that control lies in the hands of the individual or group who have the actual power to select the board of directors (or its majority), either by mobilizing the legal right to choose them—"controlling" a majority of the votes directly or through some legal device—or by exerting pressure which influences their choice. (p. 69)

However, subsequent corporate research for many years focused only on the structure of corporate ownership, setting aside the overwhelming differences between control and ownership. In the United States, the main early works were conducted by Demsetz and Lehn (1985) and Morck, Shleifer, and Vishny (1988), who used corporate ownership estimates to test whether such measures had any bearing on a corporation's profitability. Prowse (1992) conducted similar research on Japanese corporations.

Table 5.2 Direct Ownership Stakes in the Sample, by Industry

	Largest voting block (CR1)		*Top four voting blocks (CR4)*	
ISIC[a]	*1996–99*	*2000–02*	*1996–99*	*2000–02*
1 Agriculture, hunting, forestry, and fishing				
N	5	5	5	5
mean	0.1507	0.1934	0.3223	0.3672
median	0.1227	0.1629	0.3029	0.4073
2 Mining and quarrying				
N	2	2	2	2
mean	0.2713	0.3642	0.5979	0.6301
median	0.2713	0.3642	0.5979	0.6301
3 Manufacturing				
N	48	43	48	43
mean	0.3295	0.3784	0.6203	0.6555
median	0.2838	0.3566	0.6273	0.6799
5 Construction				
N	4	3	4	3
mean	0.1940	0.1944	0.4956	0.4490
median	0.1950	0.1874	0.5591	0.4975
6 Wholesale, retail trade, restaurants, and lodging services				
N	9	7	9	7
mean	0.3256	0.3281	0.6207	0.6420
median	0.2976	0.3015	0.6389	0.6862
7 Transport, storage, and communication				
N	6	6	6	6
mean	0.2487	0.3620	0.6189	0.6839
median	0.1930	0.2857	0.6018	0.6737
8 Financing, insurance, real estate				
N	10	11	10	11
mean	0.2306	0.2269	0.4434	0.4636
median	0.1909	0.1905	0.3990	0.4033
9 Community, social, and personal services				
N	5	5	5	5
mean	0.5894	0.5634	0.8546	0.8328
median	0.5558	0.5173	0.9372	0.8707

(continued)

Table 5.2 Direct Ownership Stakes in the Sample, by Industry *(continued)*

	Largest voting block (CR1)		*Top four voting blocks (CR4)*	
ISIC[a]	*1996–99*	*2000–02*	*1996–99*	*2000–02*
10 Other nonclassified business activities				
N	2		2	—
mean	0.3026		0.5174	—
median	0.3026		0.5174	—

Source: Calculations of the authors based on a new data set compiled from SVAL national equity registry forms.

Note: — = not available.

a. ISIC = International Standard Industrial Classification.

More recently, La Porta, López-de-Silanes, and Shleifer (1999) returned to the seminal analyses of Berle and Means by looking at what they called ultimate owners. In their words "a corporation has a controlling shareholder (ultimate owner) if this shareholder's direct and indirect voting rights in the firm exceed 20 percent" (p. 476). That percentage was estimated following links in votes along a chain of control.

Claessens, Djankov, and Lang (2000) and Claessens et al. (2002) also studied the separation of ownership and control for almost 3,000 East Asian corporations. They used a slightly different measure than La Porta, López-de-Silanes, and Shleifer (1999) and estimated the separation ratio in the following terms: Suppose that a family owns 11 percent of the stock of firm B. We then say that the family controls 11 percent of firm B, the weakest link on the chain of control rights. In contrast, we say that the family owns about 2 percent of the cash-flow rights of firm B, the product of the two ownership stakes along the chain.

In both studies, researchers used different cutoff points to determine effective control either at 10 or 20 percent.

The separation of ownership and control in this chapter follows the portfolio or input-output methodology that yields not only the ultimate owner, as in La Porta, López-de-Silanes, and Shleifer (1999), but also any blocks of selected ultimate owners.[8] Gutiérrez, Pombo, and Taborda (2007) provide a thoroughly detailed explanation of the methodology and present general estimates for a sample of about 148 Colombian companies, some of which will be used here in testing the hypothesis.

The measurement of voting rights under the portfolio view relies on the concept of a shareholder's integrated ownership (direct, plus indirect), while cash flow is associated with direct ownership. In terms of control, the former provides indirect votes, and the latter provides direct votes. Through this approach, one may define different separation levels as concentration ratios are being measured. The ratio of cash flow rights to voting rights of the largest, the two largest, the four largest, and the n-largest shareholders are defined as *SR1*, *SR2*, *SR4*, and *SRn*. Thus, the separation ratios are defined from an interval between 0 and 1 by construction. One says that there is a complete separation if this ratio approaches 0, meaning that the controlling shareholder is an investor who is able to control a company without having much direct equity in the firm, but through investments along the company's ownership chain.

Table 5.3 displays the results regarding the measurements of the separation ratio for the four largest shareholders (SR4) under the 20 percent cutoff level, at which, in most cases, the ultimate owner belongs to these voting blocks. The measurement has been applied to the 108 stock trading firms that form the study sample of companies for which the market value may be proxied using Tobin's q. Two timespans are considered: before and after the year 2000.

Several facts are visible from the table. First, the separation ratios are low, meaning that they are close to 1. This result goes in the same direction as those presented in Gutiérrez, Pombo, and Taborda (2007) for all listed nonfinancial firms in Colombia. The mean (median) of the separation

Table 5.3 Separation between Cash Flow Rights and Voting Rights *averages per period*

International standard industrial classification	*N*	*Mean*	*Median*	*P25*
		1996–99		
Agriculture, hunting, forestry, and fishing	5	0.9181	0.8967	0.8954
Mining and quarrying	2	0.7816	0.7816	0.5633
Manufacturing	48	0.8732	0.9753	0.7570
Construction	4	0.9745	1.0000	0.9345
Wholesale, retail trade, restaurants, and lodging services	9	0.9263	0.9666	0.8639
Transport, storage, and communication	6	0.7919	0.8098	0.6219
Financing, insurance, and real estate	10	0.8786	0.9850	0.8580
Community, social, and personal sevices	5	0.9913	1.0000	1.0000
Other nonclassified business activities	2	0.9592	0.9592	0.9184
Total sample	90	0.8885	0.9803	0.8187
Total listed firms	148	0.7697	0.8409	0.8378

(continued)

Table 5.3 Separation between Cash Flow Rights and Voting Rights *averages per period (continued)*

International standard industrial classification	N	*Mean*	*Median*	*P25*
	2000–02			
Agriculture, hunting, forestry, and fishing	5	0.8877	0.8857	0.8586
Mining and quarrying	2	0.8090	0.8090	0.6179
Manufacturing	43	0.8650	0.9592	0.7446
Construction	3	0.9807	1.0000	0.9420
Wholesale, retail trade, restaurants, and lodging services	7	0.8876	0.9237	0.7701
Transport, storage, and communication	6	0.8258	0.8367	0.6979
Financing, insurance, and real estate	11	0.8528	0.9038	0.7862
Community, social, and personal sevices	5	0.9747	1.0000	1.0000
Other nonclassified business activities				
Total sample	83	0.8711	0.9421	0.7719
Total listed firms	133	0.7398	0.8134	0.7573

Source: Calculations of the authors based on a new data set compiled from the SVAL national equity registry forms.

Note: The separation ratio is the ratio between direct ownership and integrated ownership. The table shows the results for the top four voting blocks by industry group.

ratios for the four largest shareholders (SR4) is 0.88 (0.98) and 0.87 (0.94) for each of the two periods, respectively. The numbers for the whole sample of listed firms are lower in more than 10 basic points. The mean (median) of the SR4 in each period is 0.77 (0.84) and 0.74 (0.81), respectively. This outcome implies that firm control is exerted through direct ownership. Corporate structure thus follows a strong owner-management (private) bias. In other words, owners command and control boards and appoint chief executive officers. Second, the control levels proxied by these separation ratios remain constant across the two periods. Third, the concentration of voting is greater in construction, manufacturing, and health and personal services. The SR4 mean for construction firms is around 0.97, for manufacturing 0.87, and for health 0.98 for both periods. Financial and insurance companies, composed of holding investment or trust funds, play the role of ultimate controlling shareholders within business groups. Voting concentration decreased slightly in the two periods, from 0.88 to 0.85; so, these ultimate owners are still strategically the same.

The overall ratios tend to be slightly higher in Colombia (0.88, 0.87) than those found in other studies. Although we show the SR4 ratios here, they do not differ significantly from the largest voting block ratio (SR1), for which the means are 0.92 and 0.93 for each of the two periods. For instance, Chapelle (2004) reports a 0.80 separation ratio for the largest voting block for 135 listed Belgian firms in 1995. Claessens, Djankov, and Lang (2000) report an overall average ultimate controlling shareholder separation ratio of 0.74 for 2,611 publicly traded East Asian corporations in 1997, with a ratio of 0.88 for Hong Kong (China), 0.90 for the Philippines, and 0.94 for Thailand. In addition, La Porta, López-de-Silanes, and Shleifer (1999) find that, in Argentina and Mexico, the ultimate controlling shareholders need approximately 19.6 percent and 16.5 percent of the cash flow, respectively, to obtain 20 percent of the voting rights. High equity concentration is therefore associated with low separation ratios and induces a strong control bias toward owners; there is no need for additional voting leverage through indirect ownership investments.

Table 5.4 reports on the ultimate owner analysis of our study sample of 108 stock trading companies for the years 1996 and 2002, which are the starting and ending years of the working panel. The results make our findings concerning the separation ratios more robust. First, controlling shareholders have, on average, a 32 percent share of cash flow rights and a share of around 34 percent in voting rights in these two years. In 1996, widely held companies represented 32 percent of the ultimate owners. This means that 68 percent of the companies had ultimate owners. The latter number increased to 86 percent in 2002 because widely held corporations decreased their participation as ultimate owners.

Second, domestic corporations are the main type of controlling shareholders. Most of these firms are unlisted, nonpublic corporations. They increased their participation from 26 percent to 33 percent as ultimate owners over the period.

Third, investment firms play a central role as a controlling voting block. As shown by Gutiérrez, Pombo, and Taborda (2007), investment firms play a central role not only as controlling shareholders of affiliated corporations, but also in entire business groups. Usually, family owners are hidden behind these investment firms and trust fund contracts.

Fourth, financial institutions play a limited role as controlling shareholders. While regulations prohibit banks from having direct stakes in real sector companies, banks participate through subsidiary firms such as trust funds, investment banks, and insurance companies. For both years, though, financial institutions represent less than 9 percent of the controlling owners. This finding is consistent with the figures reported in La Porta, López-de-Silanes, and Shleifer (1999) and Claessens, Djankov, and Lang (2000).

The finding regarding the role of families as ultimate owners deserves a special explanation. At first glance, table 5.4 seems to show that the weight

Table 5.4 Ultimate Shareholders and the Separation between Ownership and Control

Type	Number of corporations	Part %	Cash-flow rights	Voting rights	Separation ratio		
					Mean	Minimum	Maximum
Total sample 1996							
Family	5	5.5	0.341	0.341	1	1	1
Investment firms	14	15.4	0.297	0.330	0.885	0	0.906
Trust funds	3	3.3	0.254	0.254	1.000	0.999	1.000
Financial institutions	8	8.8	0.256	0.291	0.877	0.601	0.895
Domestic corporations	24	26.4	0.434	0.473	0.879	0.402	0.895
Limited liability	1	1.1	0.133	0.133	1	1	1
Widely held	29	31.9	0.179	0.186	0.930	0	0.991
Foreign firm	4	4.4	0.368	0.368	1	1	1
State	1	1.1	0.797	0.797	1	1	1
Miscellaneous	2	2.2	0.430	0.430	1	1	1
Total sample	91	100	0.303	0.323	0.917	0	1
Total sample 2002							
Family	3	3.8	0.405	0.405	1	1	1
Investment firms	19	24.1	0.268	0.286	0.935	0.587	1
Trust funds	4	5.1	0.355	0.356	0.994	0.976	1
Financial institutions	4	5.1	0.354	0.354	1	1	1
Domestic corporations	26	32.9	0.399	0.441	0.873	0.089	1
Limited liability	1	1.3	0.500	0.500	1	1	1
Widely held	11	13.9	0.198	0.252	0.921	0.181	1
Foreign firm	5	6.3	0.325	0.325	1.000	0.999	1
State	3	3.8	0.493	0.493	0.999	0.996	1
Miscellaneous	3	3.8	0.246	0.330	0.720	0.160	1
Total sample	79	100	0.329	0.358	0.921	0.089	1

Sources: Calculations of the authors based on a new data set compiled from SVAL national equity registry forms and shareholder information from SSOC files.

Note: Control is defined at the 20 percent cutoff.

of families was less than 6 percent in 1996 and that it decreased during the period to 4 percent in 2002. This finding is the opposite of what has been found in international studies of corporate control in emerging markets. For instance, the study of La Porta, López-de-Silanes, and Shleifer (1999) reports that firms controlled by families represent 65 percent of Argentine corporations and 100 percent of Mexican large- and medium-size publicly traded firms. Claessens, Djankov, and Lang (2000) report similar results. In particular, using the 20 percent cutoff, firms controlled by families represent an average of 58 percent of the East Asian corporations studied. Indonesia has the highest rate, at 71.5 percent, and the Philippines has the lowest rate, at 45 percent. The exception is Japan, where approximately 10 percent of firms are controlled by families.

A closer look at the data and the ownership layers for Colombia shows, however, that families are hidden behind some legal types of firms such as investment firms, fiduciary contracts, and the so-called *sociedades en comandita* (*sociétés en commandite*).[9] If all investment firms, trust fund contracts, and around 50 percent of limited partnerships, as well as unlisted corporations, are classified as family controlled, it may be seen that they represent 38 percent of the total sample in 1996 and 50 percent in 2002. These numbers are more than twice the numbers commonly observed for continental Europe (18 percent), but still significantly lower than the levels in Argentina and Mexico, though similar to countries such as the Philippines.

Lastly, investment firms, widely held companies, and domestic corporations show the higher separation ratios (closer to 0) for both years within the sample of stock trading firms. These results are in accordance with the findings for holding firms as described in detail in Gutiérrez, Pombo, and Taborda (2007). A strong evidence for voting leverage is the fact that there are cases where the separation ratio of controlling shareholders is 0 according to the minimum values recorded within investment firms in 1996, or the 0.08 within domestic corporations in 2002. This means that, in some companies, there are ultimate owners who have low cash flow rights, but nonetheless have the greatest voting right levels. This is a strong outcome that reinforces the previous results and constitutes evidence of the real voting power leverage that takes place within affiliated companies.

Corporate Best Practices

Corporate best practices represent market signals that firms send regarding investor protection, payout policies, rulings by boards of directors, managerial strategies, and accountability. According to Jensen (1993), four mechanisms of corporate governance are worth studying in this context. The first is legal and regulatory mechanisms; the second is internal; the third is external; and the fourth is product-market competition.[10] However, it is evident that, for most emerging economies, the third and fourth mechanisms are less valuable because the main mechanism of the third group—takeovers—is almost nonexistent given the high degree of control among the largest shareholder(s), while, for the fourth group, one assumes that, in the case of the agency problems of management entrenchment and in the case of ownership concentration, firms are efficient in the market structure within which they compete. Thus, only the mechanisms belonging to the first two groups are viable.

Although a country's legal system is a given and is the same for all firms, firms with good governance in weak legal systems, as is the case in Colombia, would try to differentiate themselves from badly governed ones by doing more than is required by the legal system. In more global, interrelated capital markets, firms that wish to obtain capital in external markets need to adopt internationally recognized corporate governance standards, which are usually stricter than those imposed by domestic legal regimes. Regarding the second group of mechanisms, the main mechanisms are the board of directors, executive compensation and ownership, minority privileges, and the like.

Research on corporate governance has been mostly conducted on mechanisms such as ownership and boards of directors. More recent research has turned to surveys to obtain information regarding the way firms use the different governance mechanisms included in groups one and two. The information has come primarily through reports by specialized international entities such as CLSA, Deminor, Standard & Poor's, and others that calculate indexes of corporate governance rankings. For instance, Klapper and Love (2004) have used the CLSA ranking as a proxy for firm-level corporate governance in 495 companies across 14 emerging economies. They address the question of how firm-level performance is explained by the index. In a cross-country study on 859 firms in 27 countries, Durnev and Kim (2005) also use the CLSA ranking as a proxy for corporate governance and complement it with the Standard & Poor's measure of corporate disclosure practices (as a proxy for firm disclosure) to test whether the index might explain a firm's performance.

Black, Jang, and Kim (2006) have constructed an index of corporate governance for a (large) sample of listed Korean firms from a questionnaire designed by the Korean Stock Exchange. In this case, the authors took the survey results and proceeded to design the index. Black (2001) used a corporate governance ranking developed by a Russian investment bank to test whether the ranking was correlated with firm value. The ranking ranges from 0 to 60, with 60 the worst corporate ranking.

Finally, Gompers, Ishii, and Metrick (2003) constructed an index of corporate governance for a sample of U.S. firms based on antitakeover defense provisions along the lines of the third group of governance mechanisms outlined above.

The CGI

The questionnaire used in this chapter follows the CLSA format. Some key differences exist, however. First, the questionnaire used here was sent directly to company chief executive officers, while, in the case of the CLSA, a CLSA team of financial analysts responded to the forms themselves. Second, the questionnaire used here initially consisted of 67 questions organized around four criteria: general principles, senior management and the board, shareholders, and disclosure. The second criterion consisted of 25 questions, and the third 20, with 11 for each of the other two. Unlike the CLSA, no ex ante weight was assigned to any criterion. However, the questionnaire was subject to revision and refinements after answers were received, and some questions were deleted. Third, the way the questions are posed differs. For instance, the CLSA posed some questions in this manner: "Is it true that there has been no controversy . . . ?" A yes answer was then assigned a value of 1 and a no answer a value of 0. In our case, some questions have been posed in this manner: "Has the board received any complaints from shareholders in the last three years?" It is clear that a yes answer must receive a lower valuation than a no answer. For all other questions, a yes answer is interpreted as an action in favor of shareholders and is assigned a value of 1.

Some refinements were made to reduce subjectivity and obtain a more robust index. Some questions were deleted because they had no bearing in the context of the corporate legal framework in Colombia.[11] To reduce subjectivity further, other questions were deleted due to the low or null variability of the answers; otherwise, it would have been difficult to determine the answers that unambiguously indicated better governance. Some questions overlapped. Questions were bundled as much as possible around the same criteria established by the CLSA. Hence, there were six criteria: discipline (4 questions), accountability (2), responsibility (3), independence (4), transparency (13), and fairness (5). Because of the refinements, a greater number of questions covered transparency, while few covered accountability. After the final refinements, there were six subindexes, each one standardized to have a value between 0 and 100/6. The sum of the results for the subindexes gives the overall CGI.[12]

The Company Sample

The number of nonfinancial companies registered as issuers of any sort of securities was about 104 in 2004. The questionnaires were sent to 99 companies belonging to various industries that were listed in the second half of 2004. The selection of firms was motivated by considerations such as size measured by sales or assets, importance within a business group, and weight within the Colombian stock market. Five companies refused to answer the questionnaire, arguing that the information was confidential, a response that is at odds with being a publicly traded company. Thirty-nine of the surveyed companies responded to the questionnaire. To obtain a higher number of companies in the final sample, it was necessary to fill out the questionnaires for 10 companies that did not respond. The criteria for the selection of these extra companies revolved around whether the information would be publicly and nonpublicly available and of high quality. Ten companies met the criteria, resulting in a total sample of 49 companies. However, three companies belonged to regulated industries, and, for another three, the financial statements were unobtainable. Therefore, the index is based on a final sample of 43 nonfinancial companies.

Survey Results

Table 5.5 summarizes the main results of the measurement of the CGI for Colombia for 2004. Three main outcomes are worth mentioning. First, the implementation of corporate governance practices has been poor among the sample of surveyed companies according to the median of the index. Half of the sample recorded a result below 47 of 100 possible points. Second, independence and discipline are practices that do not seem to be implemented by firms in this sample because the averages (medians) are only about 40 (25) percent of the maximum attainable. Third, the responsibility component recorded the highest median, around 67 percent of the maximum attainable. This result may be associated more with legal compliance rather than a voluntary best practice. Colombia belongs to the group of Latin American countries that have issued a commercial code following the German tradition. This means that many practices are already regulated, in contrast to other jurisdictional systems where the regulation of many commercial practices is covered by the civil code. Two of the three questions involved practices mandated by law. This explains the relatively high number of positive answers.

This outcome, although it resulted from a different survey structure, is in line with the outcomes of previous corporate best practices surveys carried out in the country. For instance, the Confederation of Chambers of Commerce undertook, in 2001, the first survey of leading corporate governance indicators for 20 listed Colombian companies. Their overall CGI scored

Table 5.5 Descriptive Statistics on the CGI and Subcomponents

	Firms	*Mean*	*Standard deviation*	*Minimum*	*Maximum*	*Median*
Discipline	43	6.88	4.63	0.00	16.67	4.17
Accountability	43	10.08	3.43	8.33	16.67	8.33
Responsibility	43	8.66	4.25	0.00	16.67	11.11
Independence	43	6.30	3.07	0.00	12.50	4.17
Transparency	43	8.77	2.42	2.56	12.82	8.97
Fairness	43	8.76	3.99	0.00	16.67	6.67
CGI	43	49.44	9.61	34.47	69.21	47.41

Source: Calculations of the authors based on their corporate governance survey.

3.4 of an 8.5 maximum points registered as the benchmark by the highest scoring country.[13] Hence, Colombian companies show an important lag in adopting and implementing good principles of corporate governance.

Ownership, Control, and Firm Valuation

Two of the most important features of modern corporations in most economies are the separation of ownership and control and the concentration of equity among shareholders. This has been supported by many studies since the influential work of Claessens, Djankov, and Lang (2000), who provide comprehensive evidence that modern corporations around the world exhibit high degrees of ownership concentration and a strong separation between cash flow rights and control rights. For the case of Colombia, according to the novel evidence analyzed in Gutiérrez, Pombo, and Taborda (2007), the same patterns hold. This applies also for the subsample of stock trading companies discussed in the section on Corporate Ownership and Control.

Agency problems arise in these structures. In particular, research concerns are now addressing the divergence of interests between large blockholders and minority shareholders. Large shareholders may transfer a firm's resources through self-dealing transactions and obtain private benefits from control. This kind of conduct, known as tunneling, seeks private benefits from corporate control.[14]

From a different perspective, some authors have argued that large blockholders may have a positive effect on a firm's valuation and performance. For instance, Shleifer and Vishny (1986) argue that, based on the assumption that large shareholders are disconnected from management, a large shareholder would have an incentive to carry out some monitoring activity on the incumbent management. Hence, some degree of ownership concentration might improve the control over management and so increase firm value. This second type of large blockholder behavior represents the monitoring of management view, which clearly must have a positive effect.

Furthermore, it has also been documented that, in addition to the fact that most firms are owned by large shareholders, they belong to business groups as well.[15] This dimension of ownership may deepen the agency problem of tunneling outlined above. Therefore, from a theoretical perspective, there are no expected unambiguous effects that should dominate. It will depend on whether the monitoring effect outweighs the tunneling or rent-extraction effect.

Working Hypotheses

This subsection presents the main hypotheses related to the effects of block ownership on firm valuation and performance. In particular, we want to test if private monitoring of the largest voting blocks positively affects firm valuation and performance. The evidence of high ownership concentration and voting leverage through pyramids and cross-shareholdings in Colombian corporations leads to the following working hypotheses:

- *Hypothesis 1:* Greater cash flow rights (direct ownership) and direct voting rights by the four largest controlling shareholders are associated with higher corporate valuation and better performance.
- *Hypothesis 2:* Greater separation between voting rights and cash flow rights by controlling shareholders is associated with lower corporate valuation and worse performance.
- *Hypothesis 3:* Affiliated firms with one or several controlling shareholders display higher valuation and better performance than do nonaffiliated firms.

The regression equations try to capture the corporate governance mechanisms, while controlling for firm ownership, control, characteristics, business group affiliation, firm investment opportunities, and leverage. The econometric specification follows a general two-way error component model with a matrix dimension of $i \times t$:

$$Y_{it} = B_0 + B_k \mathbf{X}_{it} + \varphi_k \mathbf{Z}_{it} + (\alpha_i + \lambda_t + \varepsilon_{it}), \tag{5.4}$$

where X = financial indicators of solvency, liquidity, and operative efficiency; firm characteristics such as business group affiliation, size, foreign investor, listing history, and industry dummy; Z = ownership variables such as cash flow rights, voting rights, and separation ratios. If α_i and λ_t are both 0, then the specification in (5.4) becomes a pooled-OLS regression. The data set is an unbalanced panel form by firm-year observations for the 1998–2002 period.

To assess the relationship between the CGI and firm attributes, each firm's corporate governance score is run on growth opportunities, firm size, business group affiliation, and other firm-specific control variables. The estimating cross-sectional equation is as follows:

$$\mathrm{CGI}_i = \alpha + \beta_1 \mathrm{GO}_i + \beta_2 \mathrm{Size}_i + \beta_3 \mathrm{BGA}_i + \sum_{k=1}^{K} \delta_k \mathrm{X}_{k,i} + \varepsilon_i. \tag{5.5}$$

As Durnev and Kim (2005) point out, one must be cautious in drawing inferences from the results of this equation because of the potential problems of endogeneity between firm valuation and corporate governance outcomes.

Variable Statistics

Table 5.6 presents descriptive statistics for the variables used in one of the econometric regressions. Panel A lists the statistics for the period

Table 5.6 Descriptive Statistics, 1998–2002

a. Main variables

Variable	*Observations*	*Mean*	*Std*	*Minimum*	*Maximum*	*Median*
Tobin's q	344	0.819	0.38	0.09	2.39	0.756
MTBR	343	0.748	0.64	–0.07	3.98	0.626
MTS	336	2.171	3.29	0.00	17.84	0.848
ROA	342	0.024	0.07	–0.21	0.19	0.024
ROE	349	0.009	0.16	–0.91	0.57	0.030
CR4	347	0.59	0.24	0.05	1.00	0.60
Voting Rights4	353	0.71	0.33	0.06	2.14	0.72
Separation Ratio4	353	0.87	0.16	0.34	1.00	0.95
Dif1	354	0.13	0.21	–0.98	1.15	0.02
Dif2	354	0.62	0.48	0.00	1.00	1
Dif3	354	0.31	0.46	0.00	1.00	0.00
Wedge10	353	0.23	0.42	0.00	1.00	0
Ln-sales	354	10.97	1.86	5.33	15.29	11.26
Growth-sales	338	0.46	6.76	–0.63	124.23	0.02
PPE-Sales ratio	354	1.12	1.71	0.00	16.64	0.51
Debt-Ratio	354	0.34	0.24	0.00	1.96	0.29
Trading	354	0.17	0.28	0.00	0.99	0.03
Bursatil	354	3.93	2.79	0.00	10.00	3.33
Lyears	354	21.30	20.66	1.00	74.00	13.50
BGA	354	0.73	0.45	0.00	1.00	1
Rdummy	354	0.50	0.50	0.00	1.00	1
Fowner	354	0.26	0.44	0.00	1.00	0

b. Year to year evolution of some variables

Year	*Firms*	*Tobin's q*	*Grsales*	*Trading*	*Cr4*	*Dif1*
1998	97	0.945	–0.017	0.133	0.593	0.136
1999	81	0.838	1.597	0.170	0.593	0.119
2000	69	0.777	0.150	0.156	0.577	0.116
2001	57	0.716	0.242	0.196	0.598	0.141
2002	50	0.723	0.241	0.240	0.619	0.117

Sources: Calculations of the authors. All variables have been derived from each firm's financial reports recorded as SVAL and SSOC data sets. Ownership information has been taken from a new data set compiled from SVAL national equity registry forms and shareholder information from SSOC files.

Note: The table shows the descriptive statistics of the main variables used in the econometric section of the chapter. See annex 5.2 for a description.

1998–2002 for the Colombian nonfinancial companies that had their stock traded for at least one year during that period. Besides the ownership and control variables that are analyzed in the first section, there are several features worth highlighting. The first one refers to the Trading and Bursatil variables. The former shows the average percentage of days a stock was traded in a year. It is about 0.17, which means that, on average, shares were not traded much. The Bursatil variable measures how many stocks were traded for a given company in terms of days and numbers of shares. This variable is a proxy for the liquidity of common stocks. Ten is the maximum level, and 0 is the minimum according to the Colombian Stock Exchange definition. The average is less than 4, which confirms the low liquidity of the stocks of listed Colombian firms during that period.

A second feature is depicted in panel B. On the one hand, there is a declining trend in the number of firms that traded their stocks. In 1998, there were 97 nonfinancial firms that traded their stocks on the stock exchanges. That number decreased to 81 the following year, and, in 2002, there were only 50 firms, a decrease of 47 firms in only a few years and a reduction of about 45 percent of companies in an already tiny market. But, on the other hand, there was an increase in stock trading; trading increased from a low of 0.13 to 0.24. This may be explained by two opposing forces: stocks with a very low likelihood of being traded quit the market or the firms (stocks) that remained in the market were the most active. Apparently, both forces were in effect. A standard test of the equality of means of the two groups of firms (not presented), whereby one group is formed by firms affiliated with a business group, and the other by nonaffiliated firms, shows that, statistically, both means are quite different. Therefore, the variable trading might have increased because nonaffiliated firms chose to remove their stocks from the stock exchanges.

The last feature is the declining trend is Tobin's q, which moved from a value close to 1 in 1998 to 0.72 in 2002, a very large reduction in firm valuation. A common critique of the measurement of Tobin's q ratios in emerging markets is that one is assuming the capital asset pricing model holds as the equilibrium returns on risky assets. It may be true that the observed prices are disequilibrium prices due to frictions on local capital markets where few players influence average prices, which are explained by the power that the largest shareholders exert over corporations and business groups. The empirical question revolves around the behavior on the supply side in capital markets. For the period under analysis, figure 5.3 plots the Colombian Index Fund (the Indice General Bolsa de Colombia) and the country's net capital flows. It is clear from the figure that part of the cycle of the Indice General Bolsa de Colombia is explained by the resources coming from direct foreign investment, repatriated capital, and foreign loans to the Colombian private sector.[16] The correlation coefficient for the entire period is 50 percent, and, if we exclude 2002, the correlation climbs to 82 percent.

Figure 5.3 The Colombian Index Fund and Net Capital Flows

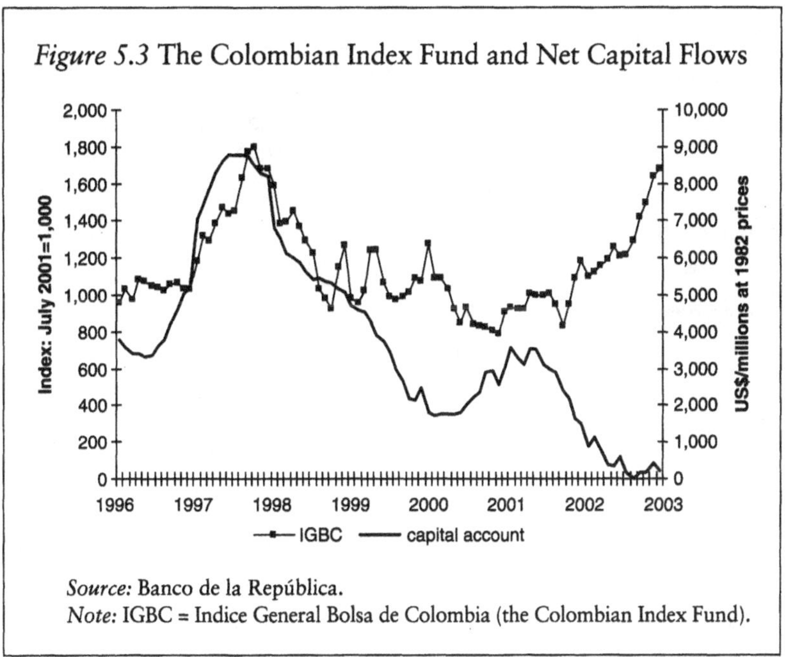

Source: Banco de la República.
Note: IGBC = Indice General Bolsa de Colombia (the Colombian Index Fund).

Econometric Results

This subsection reports on the econometric analysis of the determinants of firm valuation and performance for the sample of 108 stock trading companies that reported a transaction at least once during 1998–2002. The regressions follow the estimating equation in (5.4) for firm valuation and performance measures: Tobin's q, the market-to-book ratio, the ROE, and the ROA. Table 5.7 reports on the valuation regressions.[17] The results of regression equations (1), (3), and (4) in table 5.7 clearly validate hypothesis 1, that greater cash flow rights (direct ownership) and direct voting rights by the four largest controlling shareholders are associated with higher corporate valuation.

Regardless of the variable of ownership or control used, the stakes of the four largest shareholders are positive and are associated with higher firm valuation at significance levels of 10 percent or greater. In all cases, the coefficients are similar, ranging from a low of 0.66 to a high of 0.73, which shows the robustness of the results. The magnitude of the coefficients also shows that the effects are economically very significant. For instance, on average, a 10 percent increase in the CR4 increases Tobin's q by 7 percent. Nonetheless, the relationship is clearly nonmonotonic because, in all specifications, increases in the direct stakes of ownership are negatively associated and are significant with firm valuation. Thus, although the positive effect of ownership over firm value is validated, there

Table 5.7 Valuation Regressions

Independent variable	*a: Tobin's q*				*b: MTBR*	
	Eq. 1	*Eq. 2*	*Eq. 3*	*Eq. 4*	*Eq. 5*	*Eq. 6*
CR_4	0.7283		0.7001	0.6579	0.8663	0.8413
	(2.13)		*(2.05)*	*(1.90)*	(1.38)	(1.35)
Squared-CR_4	–0.6290		–0.6514	–0.6094	–1.0137	–1.0376
	(–2.10)		*(–2.17)*	*(–2.01)*	*(–1.88)*	*(–1.90)*
Voting $rights_4$		0.1469				
		(1.97)				
Squared-voting $rights_4$		–0.2593 *(–2.07)*				
DIF1			0.1861	0.1689		0.1811
			(1.86)	*(1.65)*		(0.94)
Ln-(Sales)	–0.0234	–0.0171	–0.0267	–0.1447	0.0013	–0.0020
	(–1.39)	(–1.00)	(–1.55)	*(–1.90)*	(0.04)	(–0.06)
Squared-Ln (sales)				0.0056		
				(1.57)		
Growth-Sales	0.0031	0.0028	0.0030	0.0026	0.0039	0.0037
	(1.55)	(1.48)	(1.51)	(1.32)	(1.38)	(1.33)
Debt-Ratio	0.7939	0.7379	0.7895	0.7952	0.3634	0.3595
	(8.51)	*(7.52)*	*(8.45)*	*(8.56)*	(1.44)	(1.43)
PPE-sales ratio	–0.0350	–0.0338	–0.0349	–0.0375	–0.0690	–0.0691
	(–2.85)	*(–2.84)*	*(–2.85)*	*(–3.13)*	*(–2.69)*	*(–2.69)*
BGA	0.2105	0.1758	0.1809	0.1903	0.1019	0.0738
	(3.65)	(3.08)	(2.95)	(3.07)	(0.98)	(0.67)
Foreign-owner	–0.0841	–0.0870	–0.0703	–0.0765	–0.2486	–0.2355
	(–1.52)	*(–1.64)*	(–1.26)	(–1.37)	*(–2.41)*	*(–2.24)*
LYEARS	–0.0036	–0.0033	–0.0035	–0.0037	–0.0085	–0.0084
	(–3.84)	*(–3.77)*	*(–3.74)*	*(–3.93)*	(–4.98)	(–4.89)
Rdummy	0.0378	–0.0441	0.0361	0.0448	0.1119	0.1104
	(1.21)	(1.38)	(1.16)	(1.44)	*(1.67)*	*(1.63)*
Constant	0.7517	0.7438	0.8284	1.4419	0.7709	0.8459
Industry dummy	yes	yes	yes	yes	yes	yes

(continued)

Table 5.7 Valuation Regressions *(continued)*

Independent variable	*a: Tobin's q*				*b: MTBR*	
	Eq. 1	*Eq. 2*	*Eq. 3*	*Eq. 4*	*Eq. 5*	*Eq. 6*
Regression statistics						
R^2	0.4931	0.4671	0.4973	0.5006	0.3404	0.3417
Observations	321	328	321	321	321	321
F-test	22.53	16.75	21.68	20.81	9.70	9.61
Prob > F	[0.0000]	[0.0000]	[0.0000]	[0.0000]	[0.0000]	[0.0000]

Source: Compiled by the authors.

Note: The variable definitions are provided in annex 5.2. We regress our valuation measures against standard controls, including cash flow rights and voting rights as the most relevant variables. The dependent variable in panel A is Tobin's q and in panel B the market-to-book ratio (MTBR). All regressions are corrected by White-Hubert robust standard errors. T-statistics are in parentheses. Italics mean the coefficients are significant at the 10 and 5 percent level. P-values are in brackets.

are thresholds beyond which firm value starts to decline. The net effect of direct ownership and direct ownership squared is still positive and is around 0.65 percent.[18]

The same results follow using voting rights instead of cash flow rights. The same applies to the market-to-book ratio equations, although CR4 is no longer significant. In both cases, the monotonic effect of ownership is stronger (equations 2, 5, and 6).

Hypothesis 2 is not validated because the proxy that measures the separation of ownership and control (Dif1) is positive and significantly related to firm valuation. This outcome is a consequence of the low separation ratios observed across Colombian corporations. Thus, ultimate owners exert direct and private control over managers because they have sufficient direct and indirect control, and they are thereby able to minimize the delegation problem in manager decisions commonly observed in widely held corporations.

Two findings in regression equations (1) to (6) merit further comment. The first refers to the positive association found between a firm's affiliation with a business group and firm value. The coefficients are similar and economically significant, which strongly validates hypothesis 3, whereby affiliated firms with one or several controlling shareholders display higher valuation than do nonaffiliated firms. The second finding concerns a firm's listing experience (LYEARS), which is statistically significant in all regressions and negatively associated with firm value. On average, an additional year as a listed company implies that Tobin's q is reduced by 0.3 percent, and the market-to-book ratio is reduced by 0.8 percent.

At first glance, this result seems counterintuitive. However, Black, Jang, and Kim (2006) and other authors take listed years as a proxy for age. Black, Jang, and Kim conclude that more recently listed firms are likely to be more rapidly growing. This implies that a firm shows growth opportunities, and investors therefore realize that the stocks of these firms are growth stocks rather than fixed-income stocks.

Other control variables turned out to be significant in the model. The debt-to-asset ratio was positively associated with firm value in all regressions and is statistically significant with Tobin's q. In particular, a 10 percent increase in the ratio will boost Tobin's q by 7.9 percent. A similar result has been found in other studies (such as Black, Jang, and Kim 2006); this is a consequence of the fact that the leverage is used as a device to discipline the incentives that managers have to expand firm size and obtain private benefits. Debt must be paid out of the cash flow the firm generates. On the other hand, others believe the leverage may generate the opposite incentives among managers or owners given the existence of corporate governance mechanisms. If managers want to retain control and increase the firm's size, they are forced to issue debt because issuing stock will dilute their control.

Disciplinary corporate governance devices such as the threat of takeover also lead owners to increase leverage. In the Colombian case, owners have been afraid of losing control given the weak legal framework and have historically only traded a small amount of the shares of their firms in the stock exchanges. They have expanded firm size and retained control via leverage.

The expected negative correlation between capital intensity—the ratio of property, plant, and equipment to sales—and firm valuation is validated. Capital intensity measures the alleviation of agency problems because such assets are easily monitored and provide good collateral.[19] Thus, the negative sign means that the stock market values the intangibles of the firm more than the attributes represented by book values.

On the other hand, a negative association between firm size, measured by sales, and Tobin's q was always expected, and, in some of the regressions, the association is statistically significant. Larger firms are assimilated to mature industries that have lower growth opportunities and, so, lower market valuation. The moving average of sales growth in the past three years has also had the expected positive sign, but in none of the specifications was it statistically significant, and the economic magnitude of the coefficient was poor.

The presence of foreign ownership had the opposite of the expected sign. This regressor was statistically significant with the market-to-book ratio. A plausible explanation of this result is the structure of our sample of companies; the most valuable ones were firms affiliated with local conglomerates in which the weight of foreign investment was marginal or the foreign investment did not represent corporate control during the period under analysis.

Table 5.8 has the same format as table 5.7, but the dependent variables are the ROE and the ROA as proxies for firm performance. To achieve the maximum degree of freedom in the regression equations, the sample has been expanded by including, whenever possible, more years for each individual firm. This procedure renders a panel as balanced as possible because, for each firm, there are financial data for the entire period. The ownership structure was kept constant, which is a reasonable assumption on a short-run basis. Thus, the scope of this exercise is to study how the accounting performance of firms evolved during a longer period regardless of whether the stocks of the firms were traded. To accomplish this, a dummy variable (stock traded) was included that takes a value of 1 if a firm traded its stocks in a year and 0 otherwise.[20] The analysis of the ROA and the ROE also permits the inclusion of companies that issued long-term bonds and companies for which the market price was not recorded because they were not traded in common stocks.

The results are in the same direction as the valuation regressions. First, hypothesis 1 is again verified. The cash flow rights held by the four largest blockholders are positively associated with a firm's ROA or ROE and negatively associated, as expected, with its square. The effect is higher when one controls by fixed effects. A 10 percent increase in cash flow rights boosts the ROA by 6.4 percent, while the effect is offset by its square by 4.7 percent. Regarding the ROE regressions, hypothesis 1 alone is verified by the estimations of the feasible generalized least squares, whereby a 10 percent increase in cash flow implies, on average, a 1.9 percent increase in the ROE, but its square reduces this effect by 1.7 percent. Hence, the overall effect is positive, and variables are significant at 5 percent.

Second, hypothesis 2 is now verified. The regressions include three additional measures of separation between control and ownership besides Dif1, as suggested in Claessens et al. (2002). One is Dif2, which is a dummy variable equal to 1 if control exceeds ownership and 0 otherwise. Dif3, another dummy variable, takes the value of 1 if control is greater than ownership and if this difference is greater than the median separation in firms where control and ownership differ (for the top four owners); it is 0 otherwise. Wedge10 is a dummy variable equal to 1 if the control rights of the largest shareholder exceed the cash flow rights by at least 10 percent and 0 otherwise.

For both the ROA and the ROE, the separation proxies are negatively related, which verifies that, as a firm's wedge between control and ownership stakes increases, the firm's returns fall. On average, if a firm's wedge increases by 10 percent, then the ROA falls by 2.1 percent, and the ROE falls by 7 percent. Hence, greater separation implies additional monitoring costs between managers and stakeholders.

Third, hypothesis 3 is again verified. The affiliation to business groups boosts firm performance. Three specifications control for whether or not a firm's stocks were traded during a year. One would expect that, because

Table 5.8 Performance Regressions

	a: ROA			*b: ROE*	
Independent variable	*Pooled OLS Eq.1*	*FGLS Eq. 2*	*FE Eq. 3*	*Pooled OLS Eq. 4*	*FGLS Eq. 5*
CR_4		0.1290	0.6161		0.1913
		(2.75)	*(2.57)*		*(3.28)*
Squared-CR_4		–0.1175	–0.4717		–0.1712
		(–2.89)	*(–2.36)*		*(–3.68)*
Voting $rights_4$	0.0273			0.029	
	(1.69)			(0.77)	
Squared-voting $rights_4$	–0.0763			–0.098	
	(–2.38)			(–1.53)	
Wedge10	–0.0312			–0.075	
	(–2.81)			*(–2.60)*	
DIF2					–0.0706
					(–6,93)
DIF3		–0.0104			
		(–1.61)			
Ln (Sales)	0.0108	0.0131	–0.0028	0.015	0.0103
	(3.32)	*(7.74)*	*(–0.34)*	*(2.19)*	*(3,57)*
Growth-sales	0.0007	0.0003	0.0012	0.001	0.0032
	(1.23)	(0.54)	*(2.2)*	(0.90)	(1,07)
Debt-ratio	–0.1289	–0.1700	–0.0834	–0.272	0.0183
	(–6.04)	*(–14.47)*	*(–6.42)*	*(–4.15)*	(1,36)
PPE-sales ratio	–0.0070	–0.0002	–0.0001	–0.013	0.0000
	(–2.60)	*(–2.47)*	(–0.29)	*(–2.13)*	(–0,04)
Foreign-owner	–0.0319	–0.0544	–0.0664	–0.076	–0.0570
	(–3.30)	*(–8.48)*	(–0.84)	*(–3.44)*	*(–7,38)*
BGA	0.0200	0.0159		0.014	0.1214
	(1.96)	*(2.60)*		(0.56)	*(8,98)*
LYEARS	–0.0002	–0.0002	0.0027	0.000	–0.0003
	(–1.01)	*(–1.75)*	(1.03)	(0.71)	(–1.53)

(continued)

Table 5.8 Performance Regressions *(continued)*

	a: ROA			*b: ROE*	
Independent variable	*Pooled OLS Eq.1*	*FGLS Eq. 2*	*FE Eq. 3*	*Pooled OLS Eq. 4*	*FGLS Eq. 5*
Rdummy	–0.0231	–0.0329	–0.0265	–0.030	–0.0428
	(–3.60)	*(–9.40)*	*(–2.27)*	*(–1.97)*	*(–8,56)*
Stocks-traded		0.0070	0.0295		0.0383
		(1.54)	*(2.07)*		*(4,08)*
Constant	(–1.31)	–0.0521	–0.1573		–0.1351
Industry dummy	yes	yes		yes	yes
Regression statistics					
R^2	0.4657		0.1652	0.3269	
Num observations	325	455	455	332	455
F-test	12.04		6.6		
Prob > F	[0.0000]		[0.0000]		
Wald chi2		1163			725.5
Prob > chi2		[0.0000]			[0.0000]

Source: Compiled by the authors.

Note: The variable definitions are described in annex 5.2. We regress our performance measures against standard controls, including cash flow rights and voting rights as the most relevant variables. The dependent variable in panel A is the ROA and, in panel B, the ROE. FGLS = feasible generalized least squares. FE = fixed effects. All regressions are corrected by White-Hubert robust standard errors. T-statistics are in parentheses. Italics mean that coefficients are significant at the 10 and 5 percent levels. P-values are in brackets.

public firms are more closely scrutinized by regulators and private investors, they would be more risk averse, and, so, their performance might be better. The stock-traded dummy has the expected positive relationship with both accounting measures, and, in most cases, there is a strong statistical significance validating this conjecture. Listing experience and leverage are still negatively related, and both indicators maintain the same pattern found in the Tobin's q regressions.

Summing up, for both performance indicators and after controlling for unobserved heterogeneity, the positive effect of ownership by the largest shareholders on performance is confirmed, but the relationship is not monotone. These results show that firm performance falls whenever there is a separation between ownership and control. The positive effect of firm affiliation with an economic conglomerate is also confirmed. The conjecture that firms behave better when they are held more accountable is also validated.

The next step in the analysis focuses on the CGI determinants. The estimating sample consists of 43 firms that responded to the 2004 questionnaire on corporate governance practices. The objective is to evaluate the relationship between the CGI and control variables associated with firm characteristics as specified in equation (5.4). Table 5.9 presents the main results.

The table merits comment. First, the growth in sales over the previous three years meant that there was a consistent significant positive relation with the CGI. On average, a 1 percent increase in the rate of growth in sales during the previous three years raised the CGI by 11 points.

Second, firm size is also positively associated in all specifications, but it turned out not to be statistically significant. Furthermore, variables such as business group affiliation or type of security issued (that is, stocks versus bonds) were very sensitive to the inclusion of other control variables, changing signs in most cases or displaying the wrong sign. The lack of robustness of business group affiliation as a control variable reflects that, despite the importance of affiliation for firm valuation or profitability, the decision to implement good corporate governance practices is more an individual choice rather than an overarching demand of holding companies. Also, this outcome may reflect that an incipient process of corporate governance has taken place within holding companies. Thus, it may not yet be possible to capture a peer-group effect.

Regression equations (4) and (5) in the table include two additional variables that turned out to be robust regressors. The first is CGC, which is a dummy variable that takes a value of 1 if the firm has voluntarily issued a code of good corporate governance practices and 0 otherwise. The second is Bursatil, a variable that measures the level and intensity of stock trading. Two insights are noteworthy. The coefficients of these two variables are high and positively associated with the CGI, meaning that firms that issued a corporate governance code actually showed better scores for their governance practices. It also means that firms that traded most of their stocks also had better governance practices. In other words, as companies become more public, they ease the implementation and adoption of codes of corporate governance.

Lastly, the goodness of fit of the model is low according to R^2 statistics. On average, the model explains at most 35 percent of the CGI.

In the literature, there is a general concern regarding the endogeneity problem in estimating equations on the CGI. For example, Klapper and Love (2004) have raised a concern about the likely endogeneity of corporate governance practices. To address this problem and given that their governance data show no time variation, as is the case here, they suggest

Table 5.9 Cross-Sectional Regressions, Dependent Variable: CGI

Independent variable	*Eq. 1*	*Eq. 2*	*Eq. 3*	*Eq. 4*	*Eq. 5*
Ln (Sales)	1.7361	1.6234	2.0266	0.7156	0.9654
	(1.27)	(0.94)	(1.21)	(0.45)	(0.51)
Growth-Sales	11.3	14.0	14.0	11.9	10.2
	(2.49)	*(2.33)*	*(2.34)*	*(2.48)*	*(1.69)*
LYEARS		–0.0198	–0.0211	–0.0149	–0.1578
		(–0.30)	(–0.31)	(–0.23)	(–1.59)
BG-Affiliation		–1.9378	–2.8750	–4.0695	–4.2839
		(–0.50)	(–0.76)	(–1.26)	(–1.22)
Tsecurity		3.2114	3.5951	3.4570	–1.7744
		(0.97)	(1.08)	(1.16)	(–0.42)
CG-Code				8.1638	
				(2.64)	
Debt-Ratio		2.3910	2.8430	5.3520	6.3740
		(0.23)	(0.28)	(0.64)	(0.65)
PPE-sales ratio		2.4730	2.0750	1.7780	0.4454
		(1.59)	(1.20)	(1.14)	(0.22)
Members			–0.5515	–0.7473	–0.8376
			(–0.99)	(–1.15)	(–1.23)
Bursatil					1.7780
					(1.86)
Constant	26.9	25.1	26.4	40.4	44.3
Regression statistics					
R^2	0.1034	0.1797	0.1976	0.3457	0.2631
Observations	43	43	43	43	43
F-test	3.9900	1.6600	1.7000	6.3000	3.1800
Prob > F	[0.0263]	[0.1507]	[0.1334]	[0.0000]	[0.0071]

Source: Compiled by the authors.

Note: The variable definitions are described in annex 5.2. All regressions are corrected by White-Hubert robust standard errors. T-statistics are in parentheses. Italics mean that the regression coefficients are significant at the 10 and 5 percent levels. P-values are in brackets.

that one must control for the endogeneity problem by using variables such as size, growth opportunities, and the rate of investment. The above regressions do not include any performance or valuation variable on the right-hand side. The specification reduces the endogeneity problem, but this does not mean the problem has been eliminated.[21]

Final Remarks and Policy Implications

This chapter reports on an in-depth analysis of the separation of ownership and control in the real sector for a sample of listed companies that traded their stocks at least once during the 1998–2002 period. It provides evidence of direct measures of voting rights at the ultimate shareholder level following the modern approach of recent studies of corporate ownership and control undertaken on East Asian and European countries.

There are four main conclusions from the measurement analysis of control rights and cash flow rights. First, equity concentration is high within Colombian corporations that effectively trade stocks or show some float trading on the stock exchange. Furthermore, concentration has risen mainly among the four largest shareholders of firms. The stake of the four largest shareholders is about 60 percent, matching the power level of the largest blocks observed in countries such as Austria, Belgium, Italy, and Spain according to the numbers reported in the Becht (1997) study of control in corporate Europe. Our study also finds that ownership concentration rose about 5 percent from 1996 to 2002, though no single voting block has a 51 percent absolute direct control under a one share–one vote regime. In particular, the median of the concentration ratios for the top four shareholders increased from 58 percent to 63 percent between 1996 and 2002, and the share of firms where the top four voting blocks control between 90 percent and 100 percent of a company increased from 15 percent to 20 percent during those years.

Second, the separation between cash flow rights and voting rights ratios is low. On average, the figure for the top four voting blocks was 0.88 for the entire period. The separation decreases slightly, that is, it approaches closer to 1, if the measurement is restricted to controlling shareholders. In particular, the separation ratio for ultimate owners averaged 0.91, which is similar to the numbers reported for some East Asian markets such as Hong Kong (China) (0.88) and Thailand (0.94). This constitutes strong evidence that corporate control is subject to a privately owned bias, whereby controlling voting blocks effectively set firm management policies.

Third, the composition of ultimate owners shows that investment firms play a strategic role as controlling shareholders. They increased their weight as ultimate owners from 15 to 24 percent during the period under analysis. In contrast, widely held firms drastically reduced their weight as ultimate owners by 18 points, from 32 to 14 percent of the sample. This result is a direct consequence of the rise in equity concentration. Indeed, families (natural persons) are behind most of these holding investment firms and most of the nonpublic or unlisted corporations that show up as controlling shareholders. Hence, families constitute the main type of ultimate owners, as has been shown in studies for other emerging markets as well.

On the other hand, our study provides answers to the following questions regarding the effects of corporate control on firm valuation and performance. To what extent is valuation and performance driven by ownership and control? Do firms affiliated with business groups perform better and show better valuation than unaffiliated firms? Does the implementation of good corporate governance lead to better accounting performance?

The answer to the first two questions is positive. We have found evidence that the cash flow rights of the largest shareholders are positively associated with better firm valuation and performance, but that the relationship is not monotonic. We have also found that the wedge or separation between cash flow rights and voting rights has a negative effect only on firm performance. The evidence is strong that affiliated firms also enjoy better market valuation and show better performance. More research must be conducted to disentangle a plausible explanation. One may hypothesize that, because the Colombian legal and regulatory framework is weak according to international standards, investors may fear expropriation via tunneling effects or management entrenchments. Because ownership has historically been highly concentrated, they have realized that the second concern is not viable in the country, and, because firms have expanded via high levels of leverage, investors may tend to trust only firms affiliated with large, politically influential business groups.

Our study has not found evidence that firms with better standards of corporate governance enjoy better performance, despite recent efforts by authorities and regulators to promote better governance practices. The results of the survey have proved illuminating. The most important observation is that, on average, firms have been reluctant or slow to implement good practices. This result partially confirms other findings in surveys conducted by the government and chambers of commerce about the inadequate adoption of good governance rules by Colombian firms.

What may explain this conduct? The answer is complex. We may begin to understand by examining the way domestic firms have traditionally financed their need for capital. In the exposition of the motives behind a bill on capital markets presented to the Colombian Congress in 2004, the Ministry of Finance reported that only large Colombian firms have made use of bonds and other types of securities to finance their need for capital, and, even for these firms, the amount collected by this type of financing has not represented, on average, more than 5 percent of total financing. Medium and small firms do not make use of capital markets when they look for financing. Forty-three percent of the financing of large firms has consisted of reimbursements from company profits and loans from suppliers. The remainder has come from financial obligations, mainly bank loans. This clearly shows that listed Colombian firms, usually the largest ones, have not been and may not be interested in implementing better governance practices. Funds may be obtained through other sources rather than reliance on good practices, although, it may be argued, at higher prices. Nor is it surprising that most of the firms listed in local stock exchanges belong to business groups, and it is also not surprising that investors acknowledge this by paying a small premium for the stocks of such companies because these firms have traditionally faced fewer financial constraints.

New SVAL regulations, as well as a congressional bill on capital markets, will have little, if any, influence on companies adopting better corporate governance practices. It is overwhelmingly evident in all studies on the subject that firms with better governance standards achieve, on average, better valuation and performance, and, so, the attempts of the Colombian government to encourage the adoption of good practices by Colombian firms are understandable. The government is seeking better protection for investors, more disclosure of relevant and timely information, and better information systems. To this end, it has proposed putting a limit on the number of members of boards of directors, ensuring that minority shareholders have a greater presence and voice on boards of directors, and increasing the number of independents on boards of directors. These types of proposals follow general recommendations found in the seminal papers of La Porta et al. (1997, 2000, 2002) and have been adopted in many countries around the world.

However, the proposals have not addressed the two main trends in Colombian stock exchanges in recent years: listed firms (that trade stocks) have been decreasing in number, and more and more of the firms remaining active on the stock market belong to business groups. Criticisms are frequently heard that business groups are the root of all problems, but the research presented here indicates that investors value such groups. Business groups have represented the response, as in other emerging markets in Latin America, to the lack of capital market institutions; despite the insider dominance within such groups, they do not seem to do harm to their own shareholders.[22] Hence, these are still challenging issues on the agenda for reforming and deepening the capital market in Colombia.

Annex 5.1 Ownership Data Structure

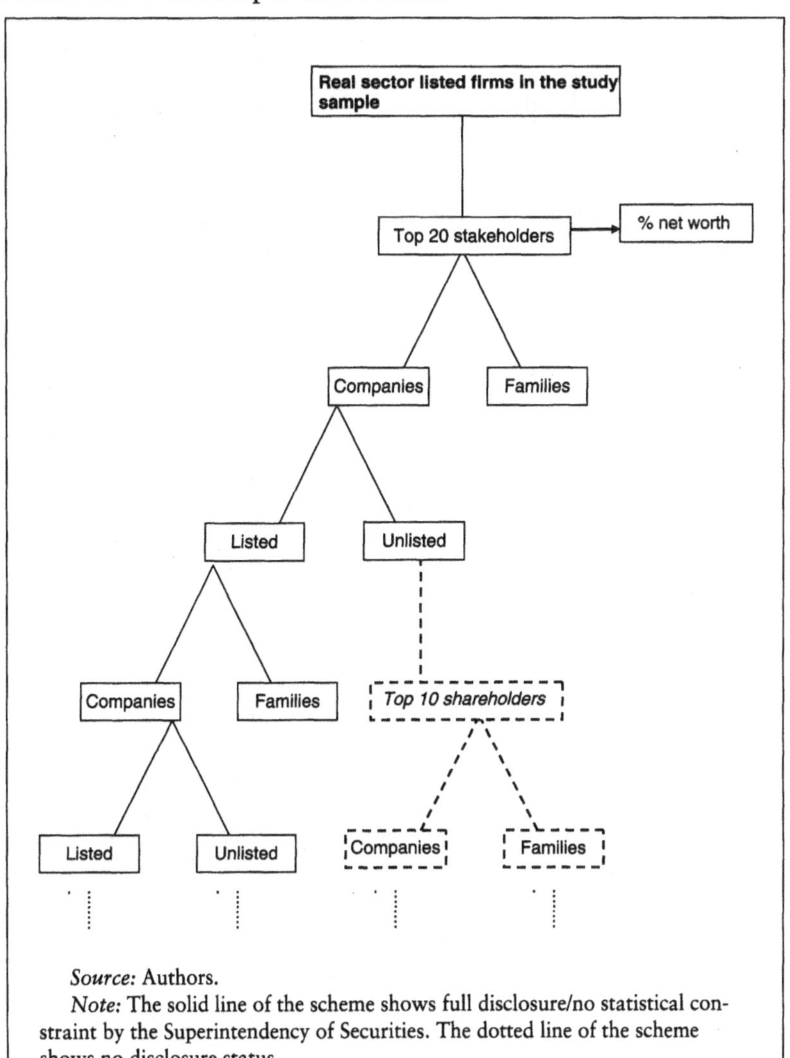

Source: Authors.

Note: The solid line of the scheme shows full disclosure/no statistical constraint by the Superintendency of Securities. The dotted line of the scheme shows no disclosure status.

Annex 5.2 Variable Definitions

Variable	*Description*
Tobin's q	Tobin's q was estimated as the ratio of market value of assets to book value of assets. Market value of assets is the sum of the book value of debt, book value of preferred stock (if any), and market value of common stocks.
MTBR	Market-to-book ratio is the market value of common stock, divided by the book value of common stock.
MTS	Market-to-sale ratio is the ratio of market stock of common stock to operational income.
ROA	is total profits before tax, divided by total assets.
ROE	is total profits before tax, divided by book value of equity.
Total debt	is the book value of total liabilities in Colombian pesos.
Total assets	is the book value of total assets in Colombian pesos.
CR4	is the sum of the direct ownership of the four largest shareholders.
Square-CR4	is the square of CR4.
Voting rights	is the percentage of control that the four largest shareholders have in the firm. The methodology is explained in detail in Gutiérrez and Pombo (2006).
Square-voting rights	is the square of voting rights.
Dif1	is the difference between the voting rights and CR4.
Dif2	is a dummy variable that takes the value of 1 if control rights exceed cash flow rights and 0 otherwise.
Dif3	is a dummy variable that takes the value of 1 if ownership stakes exceeds control rights of a given number of chosen shareholders and if this difference is above the median separation and 0 otherwise.

(continued)

Annex 5.2 Variable Definitions *(continued)*

Variable	*Description*
Wedge10	is a dummy variable that takes the value of 1 if control rights of the largest shareholder exceed cash flow rights at least in 10 percent.
LnSales	is the natural logarithm of operational income in Colombian pesos of 1998.
SqLnSales	is the square of LnSales.
Growth-sales	is the average of the previous three years of annual growth rates of operational income in Colombian pesos of 1998.
Debt-ratio	is leverage measured as total debt, divided by total assets.
PPE-sales rattio	is the book value of property, plant, and equipment, divided by operational income.
Trading	shows the ratio of the number of days a firm's stocks were traded during a year to the total days the stock exchange was open.
Bursatil	is a liquidity variables estimated by the Financial Superintendency that takes into account number of days the stock is traded, the monetary volume of trade, and the number of shares that are traded.
Business group affiliation	is a dummy variable that takes a value of 1 if the firm is affiliated to a business group and 0 otherwise.
Fowner	is a dummy variable that takes a value of 1 if among the first four largest shareholders there is a foreign owner and 0 otherwise.
Lyears	is the number of years the firm has been listed in the RNVI of Financial Superintendency.
Rdummy	is a dummy variable that takes the value of 1 for the years 1998 and 1999 and 0 otherwise.

Source: Compiled by the authors.
Note: The value series are at constant 1998 prices.

Notes

1. We have excluded all companies subject to special regulations such as public utilities, financial intermediaries, educational institutions, and livestock funds because their performance might be affected by regulations or state ownership participation, which means that the results would not be comparable. The listing status criterion refers to whether a listed firm was still listed at the end of 2002 or had canceled its equity registry and been delisted.

2. For instance, there are inheritance and estate taxes.

3. For instance, see the studies of Flath (1992), Baldone, Brioschi, and Paleari (1997), and Barca and Becht (2001). This last applies the matrix formula of Baldone, Brioschi, and Paleari to analyze corporate structure and voting blocks in European conglomerates in seven countries.

4. The complete derivation is presented and analyzed in Gutiérrez, Pombo, and Taborda (2007). A common critique of this methodology is the way voting rights are counted. Because cross-shareholdings may be double counted, integrated ownership statistics might overestimate the concentration of voting rights when the ultimate owner, such as a holding, cannot be fully traced down the ownership chain. An interesting refinement of this methodology occurs in the analysis of systems where there are no deviations from the one share–one vote rule. With simple majority rule, a shareholder with direct shares above 50 percent of the total will exert total company control. For details, see Becht (1997) and Chapelle (2004).

5. Researchers have suggested that, for emerging economies, Tobin's q may not be a good indicator of firm value because of measurement problems. They have proposed related value measures. The first such measure is the market-to-book ratio, which is defined as the ratio between the market value of common stock (as defined in the text) and the book value of common stock; the latter is estimated as the book value of assets, minus the book value of liabilities, minus the book value of preferred stock. The second measure is the market-to-sales ratio, which is the market value of common stock divided by sales.

6. The SSOC oversees all commercial firms with assets or annual earnings of at least 20,000 legal minimum salaries or around US$2.3 million. From 1995 to 2000, an average of 9,000 firms reported data to the SSOC.

7. The health system in Colombia consists of two types of private health care providers. One type is the so-called health promotion companies, which belong to the mandatory health program. The prices of these are regulated, and they receive cross-subsidies from the social security system. Their main source of income is the social security deductions from all workers in the country with formal labor contracts. The second type of provider is prepaid medical companies, the Colombian equivalent of health maintenance organizations in the United States, which work through direct contracts that are not price regulated. The main regulation that these companies face is a quality service regulation that is similar to that in any industry required to comply with safe product regulations. The companies in the sample used in this chapter are prepaid medical companies and private clinics.

8. See Brioschi, Buzzachi, and Colombo (1989); Ellerman (1991); Chapelle and Szafarz (2005); Chapelle (2004).

9. Corporate law in Colombia follows the French system. The *sociétés en commandite* are firms with two types of partnerships: passive ones (*les commanditaires*) and active ones (*les commandites*). The former delegate control over the latter and are accountable for the firm's liabilities. There are two types of such companies: simple (limited liability) and *par actions* (incorporated).

10. A slightly different classification of mechanisms is found in Agrawal and Knoeber (1996). These are the shareholdings of insiders, institutions, and large

blockholders; the use of outside directors; debt policy; the managerial labor market; and the market for corporate control.

11. One example is worth mentioning. In Colombia, the election of external auditors is the responsibility of the general assembly of shareholders and, so, is not delegated to the board or a committee. There was a question regarding the existence of a selection committee for external auditors. Hence, this question and others closely related to it did not make any sense and were eliminated.

12. To obtain each standardized subindex, the raw subindex was multiplied by 16.6; although this method introduces a subjective weighting, it is a common procedure. See Black, Jang, and Kim (2006).

13. The countries selected were Belgium, Colombia, France, Germany, the Netherlands, the United Kingdom, and the United States.

14. For details, see Johnson et al. (2000); Bertrand, Mehta, and Mullainathan (2002); Holderness (2003).

15. See, for example, Barca and Becht (2001); Denis and McConnell (2003); Holderness (2003); Chang and Choi (1988); Ghemawat and Khanna (1998); Khanna and Palepu (2000a, 2000b); Bianco and Casavola (1999); Khanna and Rivkin (2001); Bae, Kang, and Kim (2002).

16. These flows include current public sector capital income and spending, as well as treasury operations between public institutions and the Central Bank (Banco de la República). These flows account for 30 percent of total net capital flows. The Indice General Bolsa de Colombia was chained with the previous indexes of the Bogotá Stock Exchange and the Medellín Stock Exchange. The original Indice General Bolsa de Colombia base was 1,000 on July 5, 2001.

17. There should be no significant collinearities in the regressions because the correlations among independent variables are low.

18. The reading of the regression coefficients here is in terms of slope magnitudes, according to the tradition in economics, rather than the expression of the effects in terms of standard deviations, which are commonly found nowadays in papers on applied corporate finance.

19. See Khanna (2005).

20. The fact that a firm's stocks were not traded in a given year does not mean that the firm's securities were not listed.

21. Indeed, we run several instrumental variable or simultaneous equation models between the CGI and the ROA. In general, the results are not at all robust. For more details on these results, see Gutiérrez and Pombo (2006).

22. See Berglöf and von Thadden (1999).

References

Agrawal, A., and C. R. Knoeber. 1996. "Firm Performance and Mechanisms to Control Agency Problems between Managers and Shareholders." *Journal of Financial and Quantitative Analysis* 31 (3): 377–97.

Bae, K.-H., J.-K. Kang, and J. Kim. 2002. "Tunneling or Value Added?: Evidence from Mergers by Korean Business Groups." *Journal of Finance* 57 (6): 2695–2740.

Baldone, S., F. Brioschi, and S. Paleari. 1997. "Ownership Measures among Firms Connected by Cross-Shareholdings and a Further Analogy with Input-Output Theory." Paper presented at the 4th Japanese Association of Financial Econometrics and Engineering "International Conference on Investments and Derivatives," Tokyo, July 30–31.

Barca, F., and M. Becht, eds. 2001. *The Control of Corporate Europe*. New York: Oxford University Press.

Becht, M. 1997. *Strong Blockholders, Weak Owners, and the Need for European Mandatory Disclosure*. Vol. 1 of *The Separation of Ownership and Control: A Survey of 7 European Countries*. Brussels: European Corporate Governance Institute.

Becht, M., and A. Röell. 1999. "Blockholdings in Europe: An International Comparison." *European Economic Review* 43 (4–6): 1049–56.

Becht, M., and C. Mayer. 2001. "Introduction." In *The Control of Corporate Europe*, ed. F. Barca and M. Becht, 1–45. New York: Oxford University Press.

Berglöf, E., and E.-L. von Thadden. 1999. "The Changing Corporate Governance Paradigm: Implications for Transition and Developing Countries." Paper presented at the annual World Bank Conference on Development Economics, Washington, DC, April 28–30.

Berle, A., and G. Means. 1932. *The Modern Corporation and Private Property*. New York: Macmillan.

Bertrand, M., P. Mehta, and S. Mullainathan. 2002. "Ferreting Out Tunneling: An Application to Indian Business Groups." *Quarterly Journal of Economics* 117 (1): 121–48.

Bianco, M., and P. Casavola. 1999. "Italian Corporate Governance: Effects on Financial Structure and Firm Performance." *European Economic Review* 43 (4–6): 1057–69.

Black, B. S. 2001. "The Corporate Governance Behavior and Market Value of Russian Firms." *Emerging Market Review* 2 (1): 89–108.

Black, B. S., H. Jang, and W. Kim. 2006. "Does Corporate Governance Predict Firms' Market Values?: Evidence from Korea." *Journal of Law, Economics, and Organization* 22 (2): 366–413.

Brioschi, F., L. Buzzachi, and M. G. Colombo. 1989. "Risk Capital Financing and the Separation of Ownership and Control in Business Groups." *Journal of Banking and Finance* 13 (4–5): 747–72.

Chang, S. J., and U. Choi. 1988. "Strategy, Structure, and Performance of Korean Business Groups: A Transactions Cost Approach." *Journal of Industrial Economics* 37 (2): 141–58.

Chapelle, A. 2004. "Separation between Ownership and Control: Where Do We Stand?" Unpublished working paper, Université Libre de Bruxelles, Brussels.

Chapelle, A., and A. Szafarz. 2005. "Controlling Firms through the Majority Voting Rule." *Physica A* 355: 509–29.

Claessens, S., S. Djankov, J. P. H. Fan, and L. H. P. Lang. 2002. "Disentangling the Incentive and Entrenchment Effects of Large Shareholdings." *Journal of Finance* 57 (6): 2741–71.

Claessens, S., S. Djankov, and L. F. Klapper. 2000. "The Role and Functioning of Business Groups in East Asia and Chile." *Abante* 3 (1): 91–107.

Claessens, S., S. Djankov, and L. H. P. Lang. 2000. "The Separation of Ownership and Control in East Asian Corporations." *Journal of Financial Economics* 58 (1–2): 81–112.

De Jong, A. 2002. "The Disciplining Role of Leverage in Dutch Firms." *European Finance Review* 6 (1): 31–62.

Demsetz, H., and K. Lehn. 1985. "The Structure of Corporate Ownership: Causes and Consequences." *Journal of Political Economy* 93 (6): 1155–77.

Demsetz, H., and B. Villalonga. 2001. "Ownership Structure and Corporate Performance." *Journal of Corporate Finance* 7 (3): 209–33.

Denis, D. K., and J. J. McConnell. 2003. "International Corporate Governance." *Journal of Financial and Quantitative Analysis* 38 (1): 1–36.

Durnev, A., and E. H. Kim. 2005. "To Steal or Not to Steal: Firm Attributes, Legal Environment, and Valuation." *Journal of Finance* 60 (3): 1461–93.

Ellerman, D. 1991. "Cross-Ownership of Corporations: A New Application of Input-Output Theory." *Metroeconomica* 42 (1): 33–46.

Flath, D. 1992. "Horizontal Shareholding Interlocks." *Managerial and Decision Economics* 13 (1): 75–77.

Ghemawat, P., and T. Khanna. 1998. "The Nature of Diversified Business Groups: A Research Design and Two Case Studies." *Journal of Industrial Economics* 46 (1): 35–61.

Gibson, M. S. 2003. "Is Corporate Governance Ineffective in Emerging Markets?" *Journal of Financial and Quantitative Analysis* 38 (1): 231–50.

Gompers, P. A., J. L. Ishii, and A. Metrick. 2003. "Corporate Governance and Equity Prices." *Quarterly Journal of Economics* 118 (1): 107–55.

Grossman, S. J., and O. D. Hart. 1982. "Corporate Financial Structure and Managerial Incentives." In *Economics of Information and Uncertainty, ed.* J. J. McCall, 107–40. *Chicago: University of Chicago Press.*

———. 1986. "The Costs and Benefits of Ownership: A Theory of Vertical and Lateral Integration." *Journal of Political Economy* 94 (4): 691–719.

Gutiérrez, L. H., and C. Pombo. 2006. "Corporate Valuation and Governance: Evidence from Colombia." Research Network Working Paper R-518, Research Department, Inter-American Development Bank, Washington, DC.

Gutiérrez, L. H., C. Pombo, and R. Taborda. 2007. "Corporate Ownership and Control in Colombian Corporations." *Quarterly Review of Economics and Finance* Forthcoming.

Himmelberg, C. P., R. G. Hubbard, and D. Palia. 1999. "Understanding the Determinants of Managerial Ownership and the Link between Ownership and Performance." *Journal of Financial Economics* 53 (3): 353–84.

Holderness, C. G. 2003. "A Survey of Blockholders and Corporate Control." *Economic Policy Review* 9: 51–64.

Jensen, M. C. 1993. "The Modern·Industrial Revolution, Exit, and the Failure of Internal Control Systems." *Journal of Finance* 48 (3): 831–80.

Johnson, S., R. La Porta, F. López-de-Silanes, and A. Shleifer. 2000. "Tunneling." *American Economic Review Papers and Proceedings* 90 (2): 22–27.

Khanna, A. 2005. "Managerial Ownership and Firm Value: Agency Problems of Empire Building and Overvalued Equity." Butler University Working Paper, May, Butler University, Indianapolis.

Khanna, T., and K. Palepu. 2000a. "Is Group Affiliation Profitable in Emerging Markets?: An Analysis of Diversified Indian Business Groups." *Journal of Finance* 55 (2): 867–91.

———. 2000b. "The Future of Business Groups in Emerging Markets: Long-Run Evidence from Chile." *Academy of Management Journal* 43 (3): 268–85.

Khanna, T., and J. Rivkin. 2001. "Estimating the Performance Effects of Business Groups in Emerging Markets." *Strategic Management Journal* 22 (1): 45–74.

Klapper, L. F., and I. Love. 2004. "Corporate Governance, Investor Protection, and Performance in Emerging Markets." *Journal of Corporate Finance* 10 (5): 703–28.

La Porta, R., F. López-de-Silanes, and A. Shleifer. 1999. "Corporate Ownership around the World." *Journal of Finance* 54 (2): 471–517.

La Porta, R., F. López-de-Silanes, A. Shleifer, and R. W. Vishny. 1997. "Legal Determinants of External Finance." *Journal of Finance* 52 (3): 1131–50.

———. 2000. "Investor Protection and Corporate Governance." *Journal of Financial Economics* 58 (1–2): 3–27.

———. 2002. "Investor Protection and Corporate Valuation." *Journal of Finance* 57 (3): 1147–70.

McKinsey & Company. 2000. *Investor Opinion Survey*. June Report. New York: McKinsey & Company.

Morck, R., A. Shleifer, and R. W. Vishny. 1988. "Management Ownership and Market Valuation: An Empirical Analysis." *Journal of Financial Economics* 20 (1): 293–315.

Prowse, S. D. 1992. "The Structure of Corporate Ownership in Japan." *Journal of Finance* 47 (3): 1121–40.

Shleifer, A., and R. W. Vishny. 1986. "Large Shareholders and Corporate Control." *Journal of Political Economy* 94 (3): 461–88.

6

Corporate Governance and Firm Value in Mexico

Alberto Chong and Florencio López-de-Silanes

Introduction

Throughout the world, the role of the state is being redefined to accommodate the needs of a market economy. Institution building is becoming widely accepted as the principal means of fulfilling this role. As in other emerging markets, the policy process in Mexico has gone beyond macroeconomic stability, and the next decade should be critically focused on institution building. This includes the development of financial institutions such as banks and stock exchanges, the strengthening of the legal infrastructure supporting business, and the creation of regulatory mechanisms compatible with best world practices.

There is now a large cross-country literature that shows the importance of investor protection for the development of capital markets, firm valuation, and more efficient investment allocation, among other benefits.[1] Investor protection allows firms to gain access to the external funding needed to undertake investments at lower costs. This literature is rooted in the agency model and goes beyond the simple Modigliani-Miller framework wherein the size of capital markets is determined only by the cash flows that accrue to investors.[2] Due to the separation between ownership and control, securities entitle investors to exercise certain control rights that may have a large effect on their access to finance. The legal approach may explain why some countries have much larger capital markets than others because legal protections for investors differ enormously from country to country.

An analysis of the history of Mexico's capital markets provides confirmation for many aspects of the legal approach to finance. The first goal of this chapter is to look at the evolution of Mexico's capital markets and shareholder protections in the last 30 years and offer a comparison of the status of investors in Mexico and in the rest of the world. The establishment of self-sustainable capital markets has gained particular importance among some sectors in Mexico as a result of the country's increasing rate of integration into the global economy. It is clear to some that, without self-sustainable capital markets, local firms will face difficulties in surviving in the long run because they will not be able to secure the funding needed to reach the appropriate scale for international competition. As the chapter shows, the last 10 years have brought about a series of reforms to improve corporate governance in Mexico, but there is still substantial ground to cover if the country is to reach the upward-moving level of shareholder protections generated because of recent corporate governance scandals all over the world.

In the environment of intense competition brought about by the North American Free Trade Agreement (NAFTA) and the absence of wholesale legal reform, some Mexican firms have started to offer better protections on their own to try to bring in external capital on better terms. For this reason, the second goal of this chapter is to provide a first set of empirical results on corporate governance at the firm level in Mexico. The econometric estimates show that better firm-level corporate governance practices are linked to higher valuations, better performance, and more dividends disbursed to investors. This approach follows the recent evidence supplied by Gompers, Ishii, and Metrick (2003), Klapper and Love (2002), and Black, Jang, and Kim (2006a), who have provided similar results for other countries.

The evidence gathered in this chapter shows that the legal environment in Mexico poses serious problems for the access to capital by corporations. Nonetheless, those firms that have started to use the available differentiating tools are rewarded by the market through lower costs for capital as they offer better returns to investors. Overall, the country-level and firm-level evidence on Mexico is supportive of the growing literature, arguing that only through the development of efficient institutions and investor security may firms secure what they require to achieve sustainable long-run access to finance.

The chapter is organized as follows. The next two sections analyze the development of Mexico's capital markets and investor protections over the last 25 or 30 years. Through the use of comparative statistics from other papers,[3] we are able to follow the development of corporate governance in recent times and assess the relatively low shareholder protection environment that has characterized most of this period. As a result of a long history of poor investor protection, Mexico shows some of the smallest and least well-developed stock markets in the world. This has been accompanied by high levels of ownership concentration and a recent effort among large firms to migrate securities by issuing them abroad to raise capital.

The subsequent section presents a set of new data and results that constitute the core of the chapter and supplements previous marketwide analyses. This section examines the firm-level data specifically gathered for this study. In 2000, the Mexican private sector and market authorities created the first code of corporate governance in Latin America. This code compels all publicly traded firms to disclose a list of their corporate governance practices at the end of their annual reports. We have collected these data and matched them with firm-level characteristics to analyze the link between corporate governance practices and firm valuations and performance. The results show that better corporate governance leads to improved valuations, better operational performance, and higher levels of dividend payout ratios. As in other papers deploying firm-level data on governance, endogeneity is a potential concern. We undertake several steps to address this problem, and our results persist.

Finally, the last two sections conclude with ideas on how to capitalize the new laws approved in December 2005 for publicly listed firms and how to push forward the development of Mexico's local markets through a combination of market mechanisms that align incentives, as well as corporate law and judicial reforms.

Capital Markets in the Last 30 Years

Mexico's capital markets have shown dynamism over the last three decades, but their performance has not matched that of the economy. Today, the Mexican Stock Exchange is among the smallest in the world relative to the size of the economy. A series of economic and political changes and several rounds of reforms have still left the markets without the capacity to sustain the required levels of investment that Mexican firms need to face a globalized economy. In this section, we review the recent history of the evolution of the Mexican Stock Exchange and trace some of the milestones to understand the current situation.

The first Mexican shares in mining companies were negotiated in 1850. The Mexican Stock Exchange formally opened up its doors in Mexico City in 1895, during a period of economic growth and relative political stability under President Porfirio Diaz. In 1905, the stock market was quoting around 60 mining firms, 30 industrial firms, and 20 banks. But it was not until 1933 that modern stock trading began in Mexico through the creation of the National Banking and Stock Market Commission (Comisión Nacional Bancaria y de Valores), an internal regulatory body.

In the years following World War II, two other stock exchanges were created, one in Monterrey (1950) and one in Guadalajara (1960). These markets never did well, and the central place of the original stock exchange was consolidated. Until the mid-1970s, with a few, rare exceptions, the stock market did not represent an important source of financing for firms. Most financing was provided by banks, other financial institutions, some of which were run by the government, and a few international loans and placements for the benefit of the largest companies.

The Birth of the Modern Stock Exchange and the Initial Collapse (1975–87)

The last 30 years of the life of the stock market may be divided into three periods. The first period began in 1975, when the markets started to consolidate with the help of the new stock market law of that year and the incorporation of the two other exchanges into the one in Mexico City.[4] The approach of the 1975 law was different from that embodied in the stock market regulations in the United States, where a system based on truthful and complete revelation of information by the stock issuer and its advisors is the basis for the authorization to issue titles and for the penalties that may be applied. In the case of Mexico, the 1975 law continued to follow the old pre–Great Depression merit scheme, whereby the regulator decides if a firm may issue securities based on his review of the firm's characteristics and healthy financial practices. The merit system that remained in place in Mexico, as in other countries, is less conducive to disclosure to the public, as the regulator is the actor who decides. Although the general philosophy of the law did not change, the regulation did establish the basic framework that defined the various market participants and authorities and their respective responsibilities and obligations within a unified body of law.

Assisted by the new law, which fostered the institutionalization of brokerage firms, and the oil boom of the late 1970s, the stock market price index had risen almost sixfold by mid-1979. But the bonanza was short lived. After the 1979 crash, the economy encountered additional troubles that culminated in the nationalization of commercial banks in 1982. As figure 6.1 shows, market capitalization, which stood at over 10 percent of gross domestic product (GDP) in 1978, collapsed to about 1 or 2 percent of GDP from 1982 until around 1987.

Another indicator of the activity in the market that does not depend on pricing and valuation—which one may expect to be of concern, given the ups and downs in the economy during those years—is the number of listed domestic companies per million people. As figure 6.2 shows, Mexico's stock market was free-falling beginning in the late 1970s. By 1986, the number of listed companies had almost halved, dropping from about four to around two firms per million people. Figures 6.3 and 6.4 depict the similar trend in trading volume, characterized by low volumes except during economic crises.

Figure 6.1 Ratio of Market Capitalization to GDP

Sources: World Bank 2005; Comisión Nacional Bancaria y de Valores de México, various years.

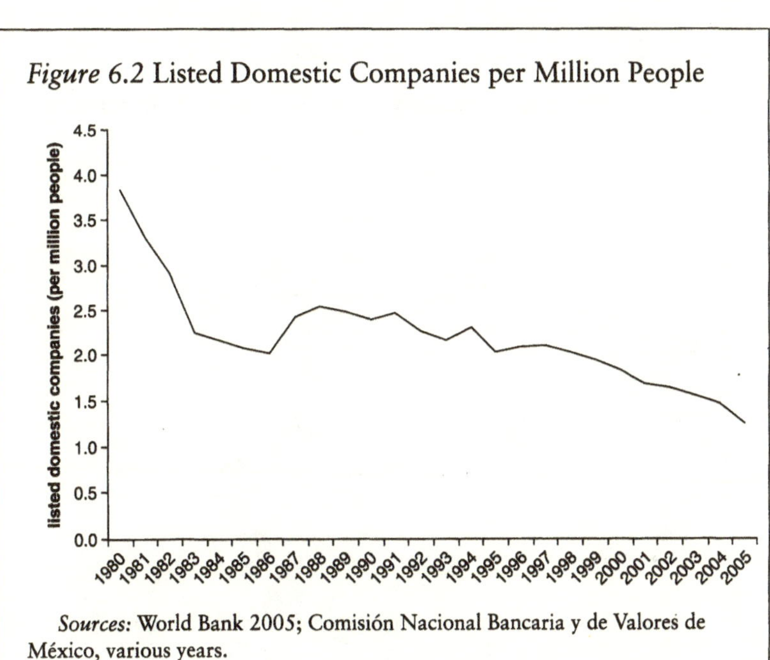

Figure 6.2 Listed Domestic Companies per Million People

Sources: World Bank 2005; Comisión Nacional Bancaria y de Valores de México, various years.

Figure 6.3 Ratio of Trading Volume to GDP

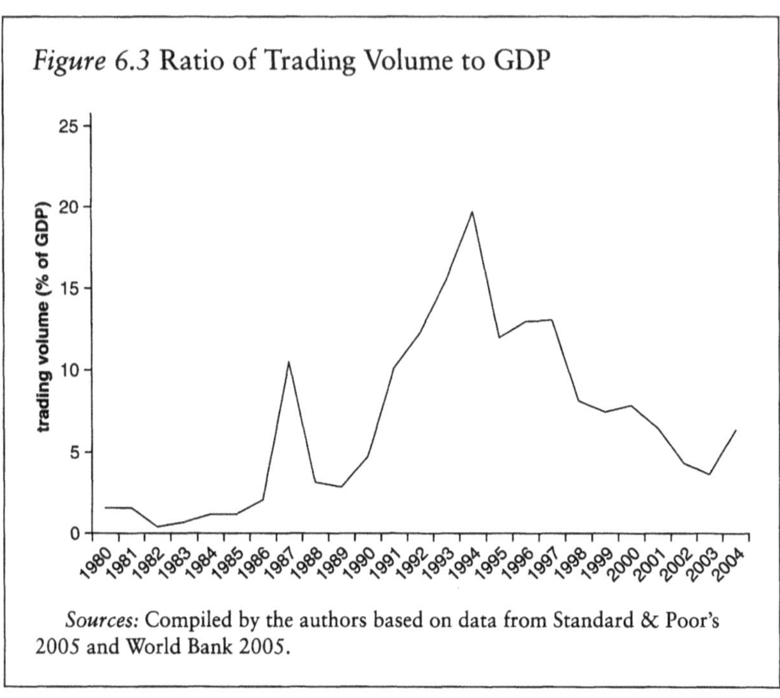

Sources: Compiled by the authors based on data from Standard & Poor's 2005 and World Bank 2005.

Figure 6.4 Ratio of Trading Volume to Market Capitalization

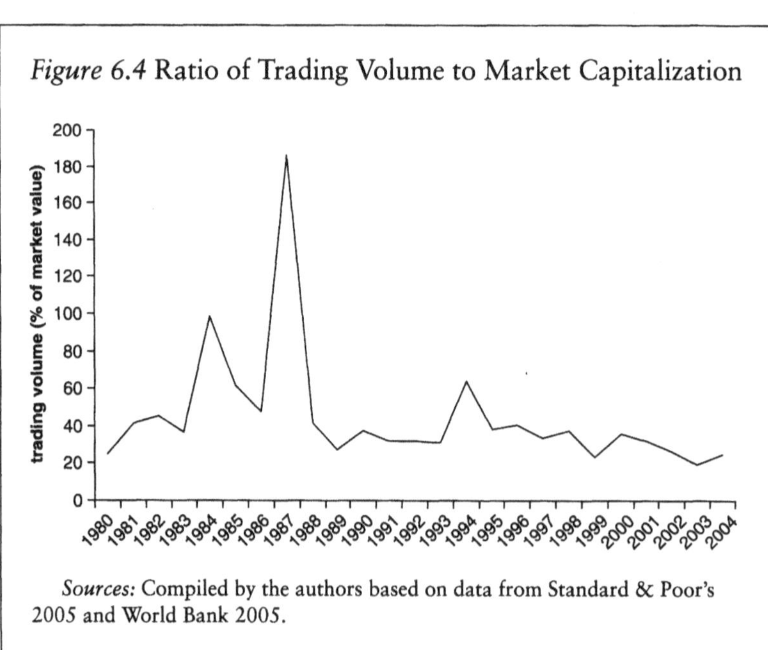

Sources: Compiled by the authors based on data from Standard & Poor's 2005 and World Bank 2005.

Authorities and officials were concerned about this trend and undertook a series of measures to try to revitalize the markets. Unfortunately, the tone of the first wave of measures was one of intervention and manipulation, rather than improved disclosure or fundamental legal changes to allow increased market participation. Direct government intervention in the market basically occurred through Nacional Financiera, S.A. (Nafinsa), one of the largest development banks. During the 1980s, Nafinsa was instrumental in creating several funds to promote investment in Mexican securities by institutional investors via the Stock Market Promotion Trust (Fideicomiso de Promoción Bursatil) and by foreigners via the Mexico Fund (Fondo México). It also provided liquidity to the market through the Support Fund (Fondo de Apoyo). The rules of operation of these funds were anything but clear, and their participation, although helpful at times, increased uncertainty and worries among market participants.

The Spurt: Stabilization and the North American Free Trade Agreement (1987–97)

The decade from 1987 to 1997 represented the golden age of Mexican capital markets. Although the development of the Mexican Stock Exchange during those years markedly contrasts with that in other periods, overall activity still never reached the levels in comparable emerging market economies.

Starting in 1987, reforms took hold in the country and helped the market out of its quagmire. Comprehensive economic stabilization and privatization programs were the main ingredients of a macroeconomic package that transformed the rules of the game. The reforms were accompanied by a series of fundamental changes in the investment climate in Mexico, including new mechanisms designed around stringent regulations that had been in place for decades. Unlike in previous years, the authorities started to work on mechanisms and legal changes that would provide investors with more security. One of the most important measures was the publication of new regulations on foreign direct investment that enormously enhanced the flexibility of the restrictions faced by foreigners in investing in the country. Additional financial liberalization included stronger disclosure rules for financial information by publicly traded firms and fresh regulations on insider trading that were contained in the new 1989 law on the stock exchange.

The role of Nafinsa was also restructured in 1989. Nafinsa was transformed from a market maker and liquidity provider, with close to one-third of total market capitalization, to a much simpler unit that divested itself of most of its holdings, which amounted to only about 5 percent of stock market capitalization in 1994.[5] Nafinsa was also instrumental in facilitating foreign investment on the stock exchange. The old regulations did not allow foreign investors to exercise control over certain kinds of corporations or to hold more than a certain percentage of shares. To circumvent these rules, Nafinsa began issuing certificates of ordinary share participation (certificados de participación ordinaria), which, de facto, cut the link between cash flow rights and voting rights. These certificates could now be owned by foreigners; several companies represented on the stock exchange started to issue nonvoting shares to replicate the scheme. In the early 1990s, Mexico also tried to promote the incorporation of small- and medium-size firms into the markets by opening up a new market, the mercado intermedio, for these companies.

Figures 6.1 and 6.3 show that there was a surge in market activity. The economic and regulatory measures, plus a series of large privatizations through the stock market in the early 1990s and NAFTA in 1994, provided the additional fuel. In 1986, total market capitalization and trading volume were less than 3 percent of GDP. The numbers started climbing and peaked in 1993–94. In 1993, the ratio of market capitalization to GDP had reached 50 percent, while trading volume reached close to 20 percent of GDP in 1994. The Tequila crisis took a toll on the market, but, until 1997, the value of all publicly traded securities as a proportion of GDP was still in the 30 percent range, while trading volume hovered around 15 percent of GDP. Figure 6.5 provides additional evidence on the change in Mexican securities markets. According to Martinez and

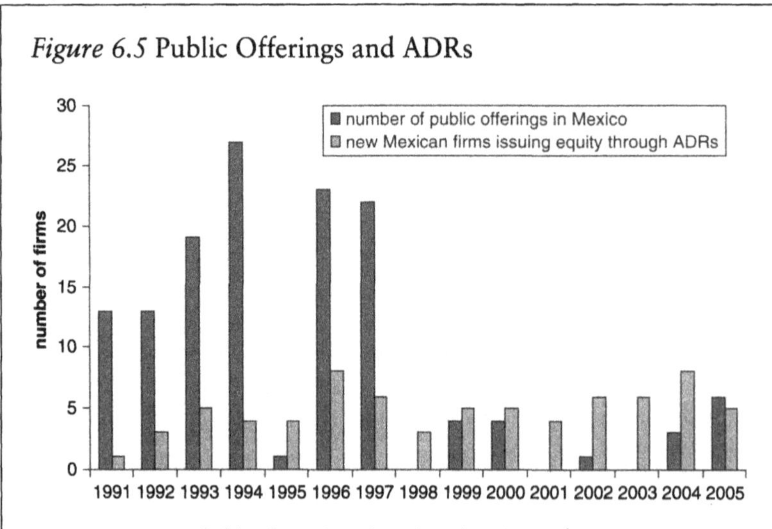

Sources: Compiled by the authors based on data from Martinez and Werner 2002; Comisión Nacional Bancaria y de Valores de México, vaious, and Bank of New York 2005.

Werner (2002), until about 1997, even after the Tequila crisis, the number of public offerings in the domestic market and through American depositary receipts (ADRs) in the United States was quite substantial.

Unfortunately, a deeper look at the evidence shows that the surge lacked some of the fundamentals required to make it sustainable. Although there was a numerical increase in market capitalization and trading volume relative to GDP, part of the increase was caused by improved valuations, possibly due to the significantly enhanced economic and market conditions generated by reform. Figure 6.6 shows that, before 1990, the average price to book value of equity was below 1 and that it jumped to a mean of about 2 during the following years. Figures 6.2 and 6.4 shed additional light on this issue. The breadth of the market indicators, such as the number of listed firms per million people and the ratio of trading volume to market capitalization, did not follow the growth one should expect from a sustainable take-off. In fact, these figures show a downward trend. The ratio of trading to capitalization, shown in figure 6.4, remained stagnant, with the exception of the years of turmoil. Similarly, the number of listed firms started the glorious decade at 2.5 per million people and ended at 2 per million. Figure 6.5 shows that there was a large number of primary and secondary public offerings; however, there was also a large number of delistings. Overall, as figure 6.2 shows, the number of companies listed was declining.

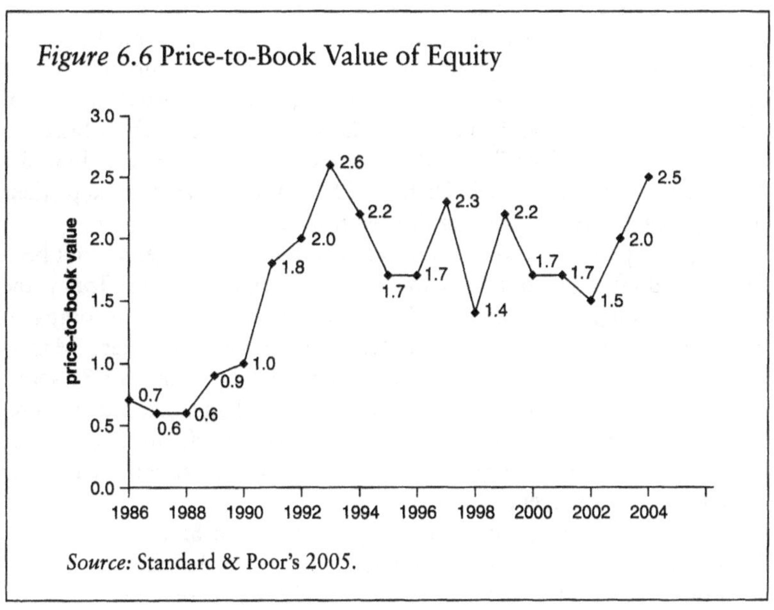

Figure 6.6 Price-to-Book Value of Equity

Source: Standard & Poor's 2005.

Despite the growth in some development indicators during the glorious decade, the Mexican Stock Exchange was still among the smallest markets in the world in proportion to the national economy. Data from La Porta et al. (1997, 1998) show that, among 49 countries, Mexico ranked 30th in terms of market capitalization relative to GDP, 45th with respect to the number of listed firms per million people, and 43rd in the number of initial pubic offerings (IPOs) per million people in an average year in the mid-1990s.

Back to the Same Place (1997–2006)

Unfortunately, there has been even more decline in market penetration since 1997. Figures 6.1 through 6.5 show the similarly discouraging downward trend. The ratio of market capitalization to GDP has averaged around 25 percent for most of the period; the number of firms has continued to drop steadily, reaching 1.25 per million people in 2005; and trade volume relative to GDP and market capitalization has approached the pre-1987 levels. Local firms no longer use the Mexican Stock Exchange for new equity issues.

As figure 6.5 shows, there has been only a handful of IPOs in Mexico since 1997. In 2004 and 2005, the markets seemed to recover from the dry spell a little, with three and six listings, respectively. But the steady number of delistings has taken a toll on the market. There were 15 delistings in 2000 alone. In 2005, four delistings had already occurred by November, and there were 21 more as a result of revisions made based on the lack of compliance by firms on regulations on information disclosure. By the end of that process, the Mexican Stock Exchange had 132 listed firms. Not only is the market small compared to those in countries such as Brazil or Spain, with 357 and 2,071 listed securities, respectively, but its liquidity levels are constantly falling. Of the 132 securities that have kept their listing, only 35 are classified as actively traded.

Despite a period of growth and stability, the stock market has not been able to solidify a position as a source of financing for firms. Today, the market is among the smallest and least liquid in the world, even compared to those in less-developed nations in Latin America and elsewhere. Market relevance indicators have been systematically falling. In the last 30 years, equity financing through the Mexican Stock Exchange has never represented more than 3.5 percent of all financing in the nonfinancial corporate sector. If we take out the peak years of 1993–94, the number has never gone beyond 1.7 percent.[6]

Overall, our review of activity on the Mexican Stock Exchange in the last 30 years finds signs of underachievement in building on the few growth opportunities that have appeared during these years. Mexico's economy has certainly gone through pronounced business cycles, but the remarkable inability of the stock exchange to act as a relevant source of finance for firms is a puzzle, which we now address.

What Explains the Poor Performance of Capital Markets?

The previous section shows that capital markets have not developed at an adequate pace to sustain business growth in Mexico. Our review finds evidence of growth and collapse, but mostly stagnation, over the last three decades. The data reveal low market penetration throughout the period. Several hypotheses have been advanced to explain this phenomena.

The first candidate is economic and political stability. The data do indicate that there is an important relationship between the macroeconomic and political stability of the country and stock market swings. In the 1970s and the first half of the 1980s, an earlier pattern of macroeconomic instability, large government deficits, and economic imbalances continued. In such an environment, domestic savings were hardly sufficient to finance firms. Currency devaluations triggered significant capital flight and uncertainty in company investment programs.

As in other countries, investment opportunities are closely linked to economic and political cycles. Nonetheless, the relatively more stable economic environment and transition to democracy that has characterized Mexico since 1987 has not been reflected in a consolidation in capital markets so as to provide a serious source of financing. In the last 15 years, a package of economic reforms has been implemented in Mexico that has reduced the role of the state in the economy and helped the country participate actively in NAFTA, which was regarded as a large shock to investment opportunities. These events might have triggered more rapid growth in capital markets, but the data show that this has not occurred.

In the rest of this section, we take a look at the fundamentals of investor protection in a global context in an attempt to understand better Mexico's lackluster capital markets and other characteristics of Mexican companies.

Shareholder Protection in 1995

The letter of the law. An alternative explanation for the near absence of institutional investors and the persistently narrow capital markets in Mexico involves structural deficiencies. The legal approach to finance holds that better investor protection should translate into a lower cost of capital and more access to finance. La Porta et al. (1997, 1998) have assembled a data set covering legal rules pertaining to the rights of investors and the quality of the enforcement of these rules in 49 countries.

Laws tend not to be written from scratch, but rather to be transplanted—voluntarily or coincidentally—from a few legal families or traditions. In general, commercial laws follow two broad traditions: common law and civil law. Mexico, like most of Latin America, belongs to the civil law family, and scholars classify it as a French civil law nation because the biggest influence on the country's commercial code is the Napoleonic Code.

There are numerous differences among laws on companies in different countries. But, for the purpose of understanding the status of minority investors that are facing a decision whether or not to invest in a firm, it seems relevant to focus on basic rules that scholars believe essential for corporate governance. Annex 6.1 and annex 6.2 provide detailed descriptions of all the variables used in this chapter, and table 6.1 presents the evidence on shareholder rights for the cross-section of 49 countries included in the original La Porta et al. (1998) paper. The table only includes a few countries that are useful for comparison, as well as the figures on the mean for the common law and civil law families of laws. The table is explained in more detail elsewhere below.

Shareholders have residual rights over the cash flows of firms. The right to vote is the shareholders' main source of power. This right to vote in the general meeting to elect directors and make major corporate decisions guarantees shareholders that management will channel the firm's cash flows to shareholders through the payment of dividends rather than divert the funds to pay themselves higher compensation, undertake poor acquisitions, or take other measures not in the interest of shareholders. Therefore, voting rights and the rights that support voting mechanisms are the defining features of equity.

Institutional investors and those associations that sell them analysis of corporate practices around the world pay close attention to these measures because they constitute some of the main tools they have for monitoring firms and ensuring that returns flow to them. Table 6.2 shows excerpts from the analyses of such institutions. It is a vivid example of the difficulties faced by investors trying to control management behavior in Mexico. The table is explained in more detail elsewhere below.

Investors are more well protected when corporations are subject to one share–one vote rules because this ensures that dividend rights are tightly linked to voting rights.[7] There are many ways out of the one share–one vote principle, including caps on the number of votes a shareholder may cast and the issuance of nonvoting shares, low- and high-voting shares, or shares tied to votes that increase over time. In fact, only 11 countries in the sample of 49 nations of La Porta et al. (1998) impose genuine one share–one vote rules. As the previous section mentions, although Mexico's regulations initially did not allow the issuance of shares without voting rights, the need to circumvent foreign investment regulations led, in 1989, to a reform of securities laws that allowed firms to issue nonvoting and

Table 6.1 Indexes of Shareholder Rights in 1995

a. Country	*Proxy by mail allowed*	*Shares not blocked*	*Cumulative voting*	*Capital to call a meeting*	*Preemptive rights*	*Oppressed minority*	*Antidirector rights*
Common law origin							
Malaysia	0	1	0	10%	1	1	4
New Zealand	1	1	0	5%	0	1	4
United Kingdom	1	1	0	10%	1	1	5
United States	1	1	1	10%	0	1	5
Mean common law	0.39	1	0.28	9%	0.44	0.94	4.00
Civil law origin							
Chile	0	1	1	10%	1	1	5
Korea, Rep. of	0	0	0	5%	0	1	2
Mexico	0	0	0	33%	1	0	1
Spain	0	0	1	5%	1	1	4
Mean civil law	0.06	0.55	0.26	12%	0.58	0.29	2.41
World average	0.18	0.71	0.27	11%	0.53	0.53	3.00

(continued)

Table 6.1 Indexes of Shareholder Rights in 1995 *(continued)*

b. Country	*Efficiency of judicial system*	*Rule of law*	*Corruption*	*Court formalism to collect bounced check*	*Accounting standards*
Common law origin					
Malaysia	9.00	6.78	7.38	2.34	76
New Zealand	10.00	10.00	10.00	1.58	70
United Kingdom	10.00	8.57	9.10	2.58	78
United States	10.00	10.00	8.63	2.62	71
Mean common law	8.15	6.46	7.06	2.76	69.62
Civil law origin					
Chile	7.25	7.02	5.30	4.57	52
Korea, Rep. of	6.00	5.35	5.3	3.37	62
Mexico	6.00	5.35	4.77	4.71	60
Spain	6.25	7.8	7.38	5.25	64
Mean civil law	7.38	7.07	6.80	4.48	56.89
World average	7.67	6.85	6.90	3.53	60.93

Sources: La Porta et al. 1997, 1998; Djankov et al. 2003.

Note: This table classifies countries by legal origin. Definitions for each of the variables may be found in annex 6.1. There is also extensive explanation in the text. Data are available in both panels for 49 countries except for the "Court formalism to collect bounced check," in panel b, which is available for 109 countries.

Table 6.2 Indexes of Shareholder Rights in 2005

Country	*Vote by mail*	*Shares not deposited*	*Cumulative voting*	*Capital to call meeting (%)*	*Preemptive rights*	*Oppressed minority*	*Antidirector index*
Common law origin							
Malaysia	1	1	0	10	1	1.0	5.0
New Zealand	0	1	0	5	1	1.0	4.0
United Kingdom	1	1	0	10	1	1.0	5.0
United States	1	1	0		0	1.0	3.0
Mean common law	0.81	1.00	0.10	9	0.52	0.95	4.29
Civil law origin							
Chile	0	1	1	10	1	0.0	4.0
Korea, Rep. of	1	0	1	3	0	0.5	3.5
Mexico	0	1	0	10	1	0.0	3.0
Spain	1	0	1	5	1	1.0	2.0
Mean civil law	0.16	0.47	0.31	10	0.86	0.29	2.88
World average	0.33	0.68	0.28	10	0.79	0.49	3.39

Source: Djankov et al. 2006.

Note: This table classifies countries by legal origin. Definitions for each of the variables may be found in annex 6.1. The text contains additional explanation. Data are available for 72 countries.

limited-voting shares. The privatization of Telefonos de México in 1991 was when the use of limited voting shares came into its own. Since then, about one in four IPOs have involved restricted shares. In 2005, about 17 percent of public companies in Mexico listed restricted shares. The market capitalization of shares with restricted voting rights is close to a third of the value of the market. It is also interesting that, in close to 80 percent of the cases of firms with restricted shares, these are the only shares that the firm has listed.

Following La Porta et al. (1998), the columns of table 6.1, panel a, provide various measures of the strength of laws that protect minority shareholders against oppression by managers or dominant shareholders. These measures paint a picture of how easy it is for investors to exercise any voting rights they may have.

A colorful way to examine these rights is to assume the role of an investor in a U.K. firm and then become an investor in a Mexican corporation. Shareholders in the United Kingdom receive proxy statements in advance of a shareholders meeting. The statements contain detailed information on the items to be discussed at the meeting. The shareholders do not need to show up in person at the meeting; they may mail their proxy vote instead. The shares of investors who have indicated they will participate in a shareholders meeting do not need to be deposited in the days prior to the meeting, because the freedom to trade shares before shareholders meetings is an important right for people who may want to form alliances to challenge management proposals. Our hypothetical investors each have the right to call an extraordinary shareholders meeting to consider a resolution if they own 10 percent of the share capital. They are also protected against the issuance of shares at favorable prices to other parties, such as associates of the controlling shareholders, because of the existence of preemptive rights. Finally, U.K. investors who feel they have been hurt by the decisions of the majority may seek redress through the courts. If the court believes that oppression has indeed taken place, it may order the firm to remedy the matter at issue. In the United Kingdom, directors may be chosen one at a time or in a slate through a majority vote, which does not entitle shareholders to have proportional representation or cumulative voting for directors. Out of the six antidirector rights shown in this table, this is the only one that shareholders in U.K. corporations do not have.

Based on the regulations applicable to firms in Mexico in 1995, as in the United Kingdom, not all shares are endowed with the same right to vote. However, unlike in the United Kingdom, investors in Mexico are not usually sent detailed information about the agenda when they are notified of forthcoming shareholders meetings. (For example, see table 6.3.) Only by going to the meeting will they know what is discussed. In fact, attending the meeting—or designating someone to do so in their place—is the only way in which they may vote; proxy by mail is not allowed. Furthermore, announcing that they intend to vote their shares will cause the shares to be blocked, making it impossible for them to trade the shares in the days surrounding the meeting. At the meeting, shareholders vote on the slate of directors proposed by management and are not allowed proportional representation on the board. Investors in Mexican firms that are not publicly traded must have at least 33 percent of share capital to have a resolution considered by the extraordinary shareholders meeting. Fortunately, investors in Mexico do have a preemptive right that prevents dilution. Regrettably, they do not have any legal recourse against the decisions of the majority if the minority claims oppression. To summarize, table 6.1 paints a very bleak picture of shareholder rights in Mexico in 1995.

A convenient way of summarizing shareholder rights is to aggregate the antidirector rights shown in table 6.1, panel a, into an index by adding 1 if the corporation law protects minority shareholders and 0 otherwise. For the case of the percentage of share capital needed to call an extraordinary

Table 6.3 Sample Management Proposals for Vote at Annual General Meetings

PROPOSAL No. 1: Amend statutes
Status: Nonroutine Sponsor: Management Opposition: None known Proxy materials contained no information on this agenda item. Most likely it is intended to restate the company's capital stock in its statutes.
PROPOSAL No. 2: Approve financial statements
Status: Routine Sponsor: Management Opposition: None known
PROPOSAL No. 3: Set dividend
Status: Routine Sponsor: Management Opposition: None known Management is asking shareholders to approve a dividend of 0.08 pesos per share. It is not clear from materials furnished by the company whether this is full dividend or a fourth-quarter payment.
PROPOSAL No. 4: Authorize share repurchase
Status: Routine Sponsor: Management Opposition: None known Management is asking for shareholder authorization to repurchase its shares. It gives no reason, time limit, or maximum or minimum amount for the proposal.

(continued)

Table 6.3 Sample Management Proposals for Vote at Annual General Meetings *(continued)*

PROPOSAL No. 5: Pro-forma ratification of board actions, elect directors, and appoint shareholder representative

Status: Routine

Sponsor: Management

Opposition: None known

The proposal wants shareholders to approve any board candidates who might be standing for election or reelection. As is common in Mexico, the company does not include information identifying the nominees in its proxy statement. If directors are to be elected, their names will be announced at the annual meeting.

Shareholders are asked to approve the fees for the directors, their alternates, and the stockholders examiners. The amounts are not disclosed in the proxy materials.

PROPOSAL No. 6: Appoint auditors and set their fees

Status: Routine

Sponsor: Management

Opposition: None known

Shareholders are asked to approve the appointment of independent auditors and their fees. Management has not published the names of the authors, but will announce these and the proposed fees at the annual meeting itself.

Source: Compiled by the authors based on communications with associations advising institutional investors.

shareholders meeting, we give a 1 to those countries where this percentage is at or below the world median of 10 percent. When we add up the six scores on antidirector rights scores, the United Kingdom has a score of 5, while Mexico's score is only 1. The table also shows that the difference in protection afforded by U.K. and Mexican laws may be rooted in a more general pattern of difference among laws across legal origins. The average common law country in the sample has a total score of 4.0, while the average civil law country only reaches 2.65. But legal origin is not destiny: countries such as Chile and Spain, for example, show very high shareholder rights scores, although they belong to the French civil law family.

A vivid illustration of the poor shareholder protection environment in Mexico depicted in table 6.1 is offered in table 6.2, which includes the opinions of various institutions that advise institutional investors around the world. As the table illustrates, associations such as the Investor Responsibility Research Center and Institutional Shareholders Services argue that the corporate practices of Mexican firms are not best practices.[8]

The enforcement of laws. Legal rules are only one element of investor protection; the enforcement of these rules may be equally or even more important. For this reason, table 6.1, panel b, presents several categories to describe the quality of the enforcement of laws in Mexico and other countries. The first three columns of measures are subjective indexes collected by private credit-risk agencies that average the responses of investors in each country about the legal environment. The numbers are averages of these responses for the 1980s and up to 1995 for the original 49 countries of La Porta et al. (1998), where a higher number means a better environment on a scale of 0 to 10. The first two of these proxies pertain to law enforcement, while the last one captures the government's general attitude toward business. The fourth column of the table panel has an additional measure of the efficiency of the legal system as proxied by the degree of cumbersomeness of the civil procedure in each country for the court collection of a small claim, such as a bounced check. In this case, as opposed to the previous columns, a higher number means more proceduralism or less efficiency in civil procedure.[9] Finally, the last column of the table panel shows data on the quality of the accounting standards in publicly traded firms in different countries. Accounting is central to corporate governance because it may be difficult to assess management performance without reliable accounting standards.[10]

The picture painted in table 6.1, panel b, is pretty bleak for Mexico across all measures. Compared with virtually all countries in the table, Mexico has weak legal institutions and accounting standards. Mexico's scores for all enforcement variables are below the world's average, the common law average, and even the civil law average, with the exception of accounting standards. In fact, Mexico ranks in the lowest 20 percent of countries in each of these measures.

These results do not support the conclusion that the quality of law enforcement substitutes or compensates for the quality of laws in Mexico. An investor in Mexico is poorly protected by both the laws and the system that enforces the laws. Poor enforcement and poor accounting standards aggravate rather than cure the difficulties faced by investors in Mexican corporations.

The Evolution of Shareholder Protection from 1995 to 2005

Shareholder rights in corporate law. Almost a decade has passed since the initial calculation of shareholder protections undertaken by La Porta et al. (1997, 1998). The wave of corporate governance scandals during the East Asian crisis and then the Russian crisis and the poor corporate governance practices of firms that have been shockingly revealed in Europe and the United States lately have propelled investor protection to the headlines of newspapers and the top of the policy agenda in many countries. For these reasons, it is important to take a look at the more recent evolution of investor protection in Mexico and other countries.

In the rest of this section, we review the newer evidence from various sources that paints a fuller picture of the state of shareholder protection in Mexico and elsewhere. We also analyze several of the reforms that have been undertaken in Mexico to try to catch up with an increasingly upward-moving target in corporate governance best practices.

The first natural candidate for our interest is the new calculation of shareholder rights undertaken by Djankov et al. (2006) and outlined in table 6.2. The number of countries included in the sample has increased from 49 to 72, representing more than 99 percent of the world's market capitalization. The revised index relies on the same basic dimension of corporate law as the previous index, but defines the variables with more precision by eliminating enabling clauses from actual shareholder protections. It also focuses on the impact of the law on publicly traded firms when there are different regulations that apply to these firms relative to firms not publicly traded.

Table 6.2 shows that the level of protection in the average country in the world has increased from 3 to 3.4, consistent with the view that corporate governance scandals have triggered some reforms. But the differences between the level of shareholder protections between common and civil law countries remains virtually intact.

For the case of Mexico, the revised index in table 6.2 shows an aggregate score of 3, versus 1 in 1995. These numbers should not be interpreted as evidence of large reforms during the period in Mexican corporate law (ley general de sociedades mercantiles). In fact, there has been no significant reform of corporate law for more than 25 years. The improvement in the index in the case of Mexico arises from the change in the definition of securities needed to be deposited (by which we do not count the indeval deposit as relevant) and the fact that, as of 2001, shareholders with 10 percent of the capital in a publicly traded corporation may call for an extraordinary shareholders meeting, versus the 33 percent of capital needed for firms not publicly traded, which is the threshold still contained in the corporate law.

Securities law in 2005 (before the December 2005 new law). The change in the index hints at the area in which Mexico has shown substantial legal improvement: securities law. The reality that enforcement of good conduct through market mechanisms and litigation of private contracts is costly constitutes the analytical foundation for the benefits of securities law. Securities law may complement corporate law and tort law and provide additional incentives to keep market issuers from taking advantage of investors, thus reducing the cost of contracting and resolving disputes and encouraging the search for external financing.

In Mexico, securities regulation has been the most active area of investor protection reform. A series of measures has improved transparency and shareholder rights for publicly traded firms. A new law on securities markets was passed in 2001, followed by additional small changes that culminated in yet another new law, which was approved in December 2005 after several rounds of negotiations that took more than a year.

The 2001 law consolidated the early advances in information disclosure that had been undertaken in 1997,[11] and it set the tone for a new vision of securities regulation. Until 2001, as explained elsewhere above, Mexico followed a regulation based on merit rather than the revelation of information. The most important change of the 2001 law was to adopt the sunlight or disclosure scheme, first typified in the securities acts of 1933 and 1934 in the United States. Under the information disclosure approach, the main goal of the regulator is to ensure that investors have access to all relevant information about the securities at the appropriate time. For efficiency reasons, the lowest-cost providers of information, that is, the issuers, the distributors, and the accountants, should collect and disclose the information and be liable if there are omissions.[12] In an efficient securities law, this strategy is reflected in disclosure requirements and liability standards that make it cheaper for investors to recover damages when information is wrong or omitted. The switch to an information-based scheme also meant that several areas of disclosure that used to be only part of the initial prospectus in Mexico (that is, the ownership of large shareholders, related party transactions, the main risks, officers of the business, adherence to the code of best corporate practices) became part of periodic disclosures.

There are three other areas that saw a large improvement as a result of the 2001 law. First, minority shareholder protections were improved because lower ownership thresholds, ranging from 10 to 20 percent of shares, were required to allow shareholders to take actions against potential abuses. Second, there was further movement toward one share–one vote through a new restriction on restricted-voting shares to up to 25 percent of capital. Third, the corporate governance mechanisms directed at related party transactions improved because of clearer rules for analyzing such transactions, including the requirement to establish an audit committee with a majority of independent directors, enhanced rules covering abuses of privileged information by corporate insiders, and the adoption of several of the board structure mechanisms that were only proposed as corporate best practices in the code of best practices of 1999.

In 2002, additional protections for minority shareholders were added to address the case of changes in corporate control. The new rules, prompted by a series of abuses, allow minority investors to share equally in the profits obtained from such control changes.[13] Several other measures supplemented and simplified the regulatory framework, such as the 2003

"Circular Unica para Emisoras," which put together in a single document all the regulations that needed to be followed by issuing companies.

Clearly, securities regulations cover many aspects of the regulation of the behavior of market participants. But, across all these areas, a common central theme is the creation of a system that provides incentives so that issuers do not abuse their information advantages and cheat investors. This objective may be achieved by empowering supervisory bodies, improving disclosure, and strengthening liability standards to facilitate private enforcement against those who take advantage of investors.

For this reason and with the aim of establishing specific measures for investor protection in securities laws, one may find a focus on the promoter problem useful. This problem involves numerous agency conflicts between prospective investors in an IPO and the promoter or issuer who offers the shares for sale. La Porta, López-de-Silanes, and Shleifer (2006) have collected data covering three groups of measures in the context of an IPO. Table 6.4 shows these measures for a few countries, including Mexico.[14] The first two columns of the table contain an index of compulsory disclosures of potential conflicts of interests in an IPO and an index of the liability standards in cases against the issuers, directors, distributors, and accountants involved in the offering. The last column reports an index of the characteristics and investigative and sanction powers of the regulator

Table 6.4 Indexes of Securities Laws, December 2000

Country	*Disclosure requirements*	*Liability standards*	*Public enforcement*
Common law origin			
Malaysia	0.92	0.66	0.77
New Zealand	0.67	0.44	0.33
United States	1.00	1.00	0.90
United Kingdom	0.83	0.66	0.68
Mean common law	0.78	0.58	0.62
Civil law origin			
Chile	0.58	0.33	0.60
Korea, Rep. of	0.75	0.66	0.25
Mexico	0.58	0.11	0.35
Spain	0.50	0.66	0.33
Mean civil law	0.54	0.32	0.39
World average	0.60	0.41	0.52

Source: La Porta, López-de-Silanes, and Shleifer 2006.

Note: The table classifies countries according to legal origin. Data are available for 49 countries. Definitions for each of the variables may be found in annex 6.1. See the text for a description of the indexes.

or public enforcer. All indexes are standardized to fall between 0 and 1, whereby higher numbers mean higher standards.

The information we have on Mexico shows that most of the work on the modernization of securities regulations has taken place in the area of disclosure. Although, before the 2001 law, the publication of a prospectus for investors was not compulsory, Mexico did require that an IPO be accompanied by disclosures on the aggregate compensation of all officers and directors, as well as on their individual ownership in the firm. Similarly, the regulations required disclosure on the terms of material contracts outside the ordinary course of business, as well as on transactions in which related parties had an interest. Missing from the disclosure requirement were any disclosures shareholders might provide. Given these characteristics, Mexico managed to be in the middle of the pack on the disclosure ladder, close to countries such as Chile and Spain. But, as table 6.4 shows, the disclosure strength is far superior in other nations of the same legal family, such as the Republic of Korea, and in most of the common law countries.

Liability standards for participants in IPOs in Mexico are, for the most part, at the lowest level in the world. When we compare the data on Mexico to the data on the rest of the world, it is clear that more work needs to be done in Mexico on raising the liability standards faced by issuers, directors, and underwriters. Investors are unable to recover losses from any of these parties because of the extremely difficult requirement of proof at the level of intent or gross negligence. Only in the case of accountants participating in IPOs is the standard somewhat lowered to require only proof of negligence. This contrasts sharply with the situation in the United States, where investors need merely prove that the prospectus contains misleading information, or in countries such as Korea, Malaysia, Spain, or the United Kingdom, where investors are required to show only that they have relied on the prospectus or that their losses have been caused by the misleading information.

Finally, in terms of the characteristics and powers of the public enforcement entity, Mexico fares better. Nonetheless, the regulatory body is rather weak in comparison to the typical body elsewhere in the world. Rule-making powers and the ability to impose criminal sanctions on accountants involved in IPOs and the directors and officers of the issuers are the most important abilities possessed by the National Banking and Stock Market Commission. The main areas that explain the lower score in this regard are the lack of independence and focus of the regulatory body and the body's limited investigative abilities and power to deter participants from engaging in certain actions or to order them to remedy violations.

The differences between common law and civil law countries in the investor protection supplied through securities law are significant in both public enforcement and private enforcement. In the areas of disclosure and public enforcement, the differences between Mexico and the average civil law country are quite small, but, in the area of liability standards, Mexico's regulations rank near the bottom. Investors in only five other countries in the La Porta, López-de-Silanes, and Schleifer (2006) sample of 49 countries face as many difficulties in recovering damages.

The cross-country data in table 6.4 pertain to the regulations in place on December 2000 and therefore may not do justice to the situation in Mexico because it misses the changes introduced by the stock market law of 2001. On the one hand, it is probably better to use the old regulations to understand the 25 years of data analyzed here. On the other hand, even if we were to incorporate the changes introduced by the 2001 law, the score would only increase substantially in the area of disclosure. The powers of the regulatory body have remained intact in terms of independence, but have been increased somewhat because the National Banking and Stock Market Commission now has more authority to investigate market abuses. Liability standards remain at the old, worryingly low levels. This should not be interpreted as meaning that the changes have not improved the environment, but some of the main ones have been more closely tied to the area of corporate governance in related party transactions, which is reflected in the next set of measures that take a more comprehensive approach toward self-dealing transactions.

Regulations on self-dealing transactions in 2005 (before the December 2005 new law). The discrepancies between corporate law and securities law indicate the difficulties involved in reforming corporate governance. The government has more direct ways to reinforce or modify securities law, while reforming the commercial code involves intense interactions with Congress, which are more problematic. One may think that, by reforming securities law, we may bypass this road block, but, in fact, for a large set of situations where investor protections are essential, the regime that is put in place draws from both corporate law and securities law, as well as from other regulatory regimes, including even civil procedure (that is, rules of evidence and so on). For this reason, a more comprehensive approach is needed to evaluate the environment for corporate governance.

Djankov et al. (2006) undertake such an analysis. They focus on what is likely the most frequent abuse by controlling shareholders: conflicts of interest or self-dealing transactions. These transactions, which include executive compensation and loans, transfer pricing, targeted repurchases, corporate opportunities, and the purchase and sale of assets, among others, are, in fact, one of the main objects of decades of legal doctrine and regulation in most countries. A comparative analysis on Mexico and other countries in this arena would probably give us a most comprehensive picture on the battery of measures available at all levels of law and regulation to protect investors against self-dealing transactions.

Somewhat like IPOs, self-dealing transactions may be monitored using public and private enforcement mechanisms. Public enforcement has become a center of attention, as evidenced by the recent U.S. Sarbanes-Oxley Act, which includes higher fines and prison terms for those found guilty of abuses. There has also been an increase in measures that facilitate private enforcement; several countries have enhanced their corporate disclosure standards and approval procedures, and a few have also tried to facilitate private litigation aimed at redressing unfair transactions.

Table 6.5 presents summary data on the measurement of the regulation of a classic transaction with potential conflicts of interest: the same controlling shareholder is on both sides of an asset purchase. The table classifies measures according to three different groups: (1) actions that may be taken before the transaction occurs, (2) actions that may be taken after the transaction has occurred, and (3) public enforcement measures. The table shows the numbers for a few countries relevant for a comparison with Mexico, as well as the averages for the 72 nations covered in the study by Djankov et al. (2006) on the scope of the regulations in force.

Table 6.5 Indexes of Anti–Self-Dealing Regulations

Country	*Ex ante private control*	*Ex post private control*	*Anti–self-dealing index*	*Public enforcement*
Common law origin				
Malaysia	1.00	0.90	0.95	1.00
New Zealand	1.00	0.90	0.95	0.00
United Kingdom	1.00	0.85	0.93	0.00
United States	0.33	0.97	0.65	0.00
Mean common law	0.58	0.76	0.67	0.27
Civil law origin				
Chile	0.50	0.75	0.63	1.00
Korea, Rep. of	0.25	0.67	0.46	0.50
Mexico	0.19	0.16	0.18	0.50
Spain	0.22	0.52	0.37	0.75
Mean civil law	0.31	0.44	0.37	0.42
World average	0.39	0.53	0.46	0.38

Source: Djankov et al. 2006.

Note: The table classifies countries by legal origin. Data are available on 72 countries. Definitions for each of the variables may be found in annex 6.1. See the text for a fuller explanation.

The easiest way to clarify these data is to contrast the regulations in Mexico with those in a few other countries. The first column shows the data for ex ante measures against self-dealing. These measures keep track of compliance with approval requirements and mandatory disclosures that need to occur before a transaction may take place. As a result of the new approach adopted in 2001, board members who do not have an interest need to approve the transaction. Shareholders may not find this particularly protective of their interests given that the majority election rules for choosing directors allow the controlling shareholder to dominate the board. The controlling shareholder needs to tell the board that there is a conflict of interest involved in this transaction, and the firm has the obligation to disclose to the public the type of transaction, the amount, and the parties involved. No independent review of the transaction needs to take place before the transaction actually happens.

As table 6.5 shows, Mexico has a low level of ex ante scrutiny, ranking 29th among the 72 countries in the sample. Although the level of ex ante disclosures has improved in Mexico, bringing the country closer to the world mean, the lack of a truly disinterested approval mechanism is still evident.

Once the transaction has occurred, the annual report only needs to include information on the nature and the amount of the transaction. Shareholders would have a hard time obtaining standing to sue because the 2001 Mexican regulations, although improved, only grant this right through a derivative suit by shareholders who are able to put together at least 15 percent of the shares. Shareholders rarely use this option because the chances of winning are pretty slim. First, it requires high levels of ownership to be able to request a court to appoint an inspector to look into the company's affairs. Second, the approving body of directors is only liable if they are shown to have acted on bad faith or with gross negligence, while the controlling shareholder is not liable at all because he did not vote with the directors. Third, although the plaintiff may examine the defendant and nonparties without seeking the approval of the judge for the questions, the rules of evidence do not provide for full access to evidence and witnesses. Finally, rescission of the transaction is generally unavailable.

While Mexico's ex ante disclosures were close to the world mean, the lack of additional disclosure following a transaction contrasts with the requirements in most countries. This explains why Mexico's post-disclosure score is in the lowest quartile of the world. The existing regulatory framework makes it extremely difficult to prove wrongdoing. Overall, the fewer than average ex post disclosures and the difficulties in seeking redress mean that Mexico has one of the five lowest scores in terms of ex post anti–self-dealing tools. The other four countries in this group are Jordan, Panama, the Russian Federation, and República Bolivariana de Venezuela. If we look at the aggregate anti–self-dealing index, Mexico ranks 64th among the 72 countries in the sample. Despite the recent progress, the data in table 6.5 seem to suggest that there is a lot more room to improve effective shareholder protections.

The last column of table 6.5 shows the penalties imposed by the public regulatory body on those who have been found to self-deal. Mexico gives fines and 12 years of prison for those directors found liable, but not for controlling shareholders. The penalties are among the highest in the world, but no record of actual application to a case along the lines described has yet been reported. The risk is that, as in many other countries, the existing penalties are hardly a deterrent if it is virtually impossible to prove wrongdoing.

Table 6.5 also contains data on some countries where the regulations differ from those in Mexico. In the United Kingdom, for example, related party transactions are reviewed by independent financial experts and approved by disinterested shareholders. Extensive disclosures take place both before and after the approval process for the transaction. Establishing liability, although costly, is relatively easier in the United Kingdom than in Mexico because of lower ownership requirements, a lower threshold in the evidence requirements, and substantial access to evidence. The score ranks the United Kingdom among the highest countries in the sample.

Chile is another example of a country with substantially higher scores in the index than Mexico. Chile is an interesting example because of the many characteristics it shares with Mexico, particularly the fact that it has the same civil law tradition. In Chile, as table 6.5 shows, the ex ante and ex post disclosure standards are at the highest possible levels in the world in terms of the requirements of both the firm and the party exhibiting the conflict of interest. Similarly, standing to sue is gained with a lower share ownership in Chile, and the liability standards are restricted to questions of negligence. Chile's ranking is superior to that of Mexico and close to that of the United States.

Pension Funds: The Consequences of Poor Investor Protection

Ultimately, the question whether legal institutions matter is fundamentally empirical. If avoiding poor investor protection were cheap and simple to accomplish, we would observe no clear patterns of ownership or access to external financing among firms as firms would not be affected by differences in legal institutions across countries. Accordingly, in this section, we examine two types of evidence regarding the influence of legal institutions on external financing: ownership concentration and the size and breadth of capital markets. Table 6.6 summarizes the results.

Ownership concentration and lack of institutional investors. If legal institutions matter, as the previous sections suggest, ownership concentration should be greater in countries with poor investor protection than it is in countries with strong protections for investors. There are at least two reasons for this. First, agency problems may call for large-scale shareholders to monitor managers and thus prevent or minimize expropriation. Second, minority shareholders may be unwilling to pay high prices for securities in countries with weak legal protections; meanwhile, entrepreneurs will be more reluctant to offer shares at discounted prices, thus resulting in higher ownership concentration, as well as smaller and narrower markets for external equity.[15]

The first striking result shown in table 6.6, in the last column, is the fact that, in the world as a whole, dispersed ownership is a myth. In a typical top 10 firm, 45 percent of the common shares are held by the three largest shareholders.[16] A second key result is the finding that the countries with weaker investor protection show larger share ownership concentration. In particular, countries in the French legal family, such as Chile, Mexico, and Spain in the table, show an average ownership concentration of 55 percent. This is over 10 percent more than the average common law country and more than the other two legal families in the civil law tradition. Statistically, this number is significantly higher than the mean for the rest of the world and for the mean for each of the other three legal families individually.

Table 6.6 Market Outcomes

Country	*Market capitalization to GDP*	*Listed firms per million population*	*IPOs to GDP*	*Block premium (%)*	*Ownership concentration (%)*
Common law origin					
Malaysia	148.4	34.6	6.18	5	54
New Zealand	40.1	36.9	0.06	4	48
United Kingdom	157.7	33.1	11.27	0	19
United States	142.1	22.8	5.47	2	20
Mean common law	85.5	32.6	3.7	4	44
Civil law origin					
Chile	89.7	16.7	0.51	15	45
Korea, Rep. of	54.1	29.4	5.32	17	23
Mexico	21.9	1.7	0.22	47	64
Spain	79.9	45.9	2.41	2	51
Mean civil law	48.6	25.7	2.54	14	49
World average	59.4	27.7	2.97	11	47

Sources: La Porta et al. 1998; Dyck and Zingales 2004.

Note: The table classifies countries by legal origin. Data are available on 72 countries. Definitions for each of the variables may be found in annex 6.1. See the text for a fuller explanation.

Like the rest of the French legal origin, Mexico has highly concentrated ownership. With the exception of Chile, which has strong shareholder rights, all Latin American countries in the sample show ownership concentration that is greater than the world mean. After Colombia and Greece (68 percent), Mexico has the third highest level of ownership concentration in the world (67 percent). In sum, these data indicate that Mexico has unusually high ownership concentration, possibly as an adaptation to its weak legal protections.

Large-scale concentration comes at a cost because it creates another agency problem: the expropriation of the stakes of minority shareholders by large-scale shareholders. Some indirect evidence for differences in the ease of expropriating from small investors becomes available through an examination of the block premium, which is shown in table 6.6, column 4. This variable, derived from Dyck and Zingales (2004), represents the median premium paid for control in corporate control transactions in each country. In theoretical work, the premium has been interpreted as a measure of the private benefits of control. As the table shows, the premium is higher in weak protection countries, such as Mexico. In fact, Mexico's premium of 47 percent is the second highest control premium in the world after the 49 percent of Brazil. An additional cost of heavily concentrated ownership arises from the fact that core investors are not diversified. For these reasons, high ownership concentration is costly for the development of capital markets and for large shareholders.

Unlike in other countries, such as Chile, institutional investors are not significant players in capital markets in Mexico. Part of the reason is the relatively recent restructuring of the pension fund system. Although the reform of the pension fund system began in 1993, it was almost four years before money started to flow into the capitalization accounts of individuals.[17] Since 1997, the capitalization of pension funds (administradores de fondos de ahorro para el retiro) has been increasing; it surpassed 5 percent as a share of GDP in 2000. That year, pension funds invested close to 90 percent of their funds in government bonds. Although investment regulations have been very restrictive for most of the period, the law only required the funds to place 65 percent of their investments in government bonds at that time. For this reason, it is likely that the portfolio composition observed among the funds is due more to the lack of appropriate private instruments. In the last five years, the growth of the private bond market has provided an escape valve that has been used thoroughly by institutional investors. Nonetheless, as of December 2005, less than 9 percent of the assets of all institutional investors (including pension funds) had been invested in private bonds, while another 10 percent was in stocks. Close to 60 percent of the investments of institutional investors were still in government bonds. It seems clear that a combination of investment restrictions and poor investor protections is rendering private sector titles unattractive.[18] The large benefits of the participation of institutional investors in capital markets have not yet materialized in Mexico, and this has helped maintain ownership concentration ratios at among the highest in the world.

The size and breadth of local capital markets. Several interesting patterns emerge from an examination of the categories of external equity financing through the stock market. Table 6.6 uses three measures of equity financing developed in the literature. The first measure is the 1999–2003 ratio of equity finance (that is, stock market capitalization) to GDP in each country. A measure of the development of capital markets that does not have a valuation component and that offers information about market breadth is the number of firms listed in the stock market standardized across countries by comparing it with the number of people living in each country. The average of this number for 1999 to 2003 is shown in the second column. A third potential indicator of the size of local capital markets is the average ratio of the equity issued by newly listed firms in a country as a proportion of GDP. The averages for the 1996–2000 values for several countries are shown in the third column of the table.

The data bear the same message as the information on ownership patterns. First, access to external equity financing is more limited in countries such as Mexico and other civil law countries. But the data on Mexico are alarming even within the civil law tradition. Specifically, the ratio of external capital to GDP in Mexico is roughly half the civil law mean and one-fourth the mean in Chile and Spain. Stock market capitalization in Mexico is several orders of magnitude smaller than that in the average country in the common law tradition and between one-seventh and one-eighth of that in countries such as Malaysia or the United States.

The story is very similar if one looks at the information on the other two measures of the development of markets that is shown in table 6.6, columns 2 and 3. The ratio of listed domestic firms to total population is between 10 and 15 times lower in Mexico relative to the world mean and the ratios for Chile and the United States. Finally, the ratio of IPOs to GDP in Mexico is only half that in Chile, but roughly 12 times less than the world mean and the ratio in Spain and 20 times lower than the ratio in the United States. Institutional investors and public funds find very little choice among companies if they wish to diversify their local portfolios in Mexico. Moreover, the numbers are not getting any larger.

Dividend payments. The fact that institutional investors are not attracted by the market becomes a little puzzling if we compare data on the dividend payout policies of Mexican firms to the corresponding data on firms in other countries. The median Mexican firm pays higher dividends than the median firm in the world. It has been argued that institutional investors care disproportionately about dividends because they may be required to hold stocks that pay dividends or they may be able only to use money from these payments. Dividend payout policies have always been rather confusing in finance. There are two agency models on dividends that might explain firm dividend payments. The first one may be called the outcome model; in this case, dividends are the result of effective pressure exercised by minority shareholders to force corporate insiders to disgorge cash. Under this view, stronger minority shareholder rights should be associated with higher dividends. An alternative model of dividends is the substitute model, which says that insiders choose to pay dividends to establish a reputation for the decent treatment of minority shareholders so that firms may subsequently raise equity financing. Under this view, stronger minority shareholder rights would reduce the need to establish a reputation and, so, should be associated with lower dividends.

La Porta et al. (2000a) compare these models using a cross-section of 4,000 companies in 33 countries. The companies rely on different levels of shareholder protection and, therefore, different levels of minority shareholder rights. Mexican firms are included in the sample. The study findings on dividend payouts and other indicators support the outcome agency model of dividends explained above. Stronger minority shareholder rights are associated with higher dividend payouts in the cross-section of countries. In this case, too, Mexican firms, are found to pay dividends above the world median. While the median ratios of dividends to cash flow and dividends to earnings are 11.8 and 30 percent for the world sample, respectively, the figures are 19.5 and 46.5 percent for the median Mexican firm. The Mexican ratios are even higher than those of the median firm in the United Kingdom and the United States.[19]

This evidence suggests that the attractiveness of higher than average dividends among Mexican firms is not sufficient to entice institutional investors. It is possible that investors consider the potential for expropriation to be much greater in a country with higher dividend ratios. In any case, the evidence suggests that there is an urgent need to change the legal infrastructure to attract institutional investors and pension funds.

Enforcement. The overall levels of disclosure in the initial offerings and periodical filings of listed companies have substantially improved in Mexico since 1998. The higher disclosure requirements have also allowed public authorities to improve enforcement.

Before the series of reforms to improve the quality and timeliness of disclosures to shareholders and markets, it was fairly common for issuers to submit their periodical reports after the due dates. Starting in 1998, in addition to the economic fines that had always been imposed, the National Banking and Stock Market Commission began to count late reporting as a relevant event, thereby requiring firms to submit an explanation for the delay. The following year, a penalty started to be imposed for late filings without reasonable prior justification. As a result of these changes, the number of sanctions for late filing declined from close to 250 in 1987 to around five per year since 2003.

Enhanced rules on transparency have also allowed the regulators to start imposing sanctions for abuses of insider information and violations of minority shareholder rights. Starting in 2003, the regulating commission has been publishing a list of offenders and the fines in these areas. In the past three years, 13 firms and individuals have been fined for such violations.

However, the judicial arm of the enforcement effort has not improved at the same pace. Court efficiency indicators have not substantially changed over the last decade. This represents a serious obstacle to the quality of enforcement, which now generally relies on the public regulatory body to act. More importantly, enforcement among small firms outside the markets depends on the courts. These topics are addressed in the section on policy recommendations.

Migration, cross-listings, and acquisitions. Several authors have argued that there is an important movement toward functional convergence in corporate governance whereby firms around the world are adopting U.S.–type mechanisms to protect investors. The growth in the number of foreign firms issuing ADRs or cross-listing in U.S. markets reflects this trend. An ADR is equivalent to listing a foreign company's securities on an exchange that protects shareholders, mainly through stricter disclosure requirements. Such a listing in New York, supported in part by the threat of delisting, raises the level of shareholder protection.

The data in figure 6.5 shows that Mexican companies have been issuing ADRs in the United States throughout the boom and bust years on the local market.

The recent literature appears to show that cross-listing improves access to external capital markets. Lins, Strickland, and Zenner (2005) find that the sensitivity of investment to cash flow falls when an ADR is issued by a company from a country with a weak legal system and a less well-developed capital market. Reese and Weisbach (2002) show that companies in French and Scandinavian civil law countries are more likely to list ADRs on an organized exchange in the United States. This means that ADRs seem to be used as a partial substitute for weak legal institutions because they commit firms to exhibit at least greater disclosure. In the data in the latter study, Mexico emerges as the country with the highest percentage of locally listed firms cross-listing in the United States. Figure 6.7 shows that close to 38 percent of all Mexican firms that are listed on the Mexican Stock Exchange have some listing in U.S. stock markets. The percentage of Mexican firms that have ADRs is among the highest, reaching close to 15 percent. In fact, the boom in Mexican ADRs started as soon as regulations on foreign direct investment were eased in 1989. This supports the

Figure 6.7 Firm Migration by Legal System and in Mexico

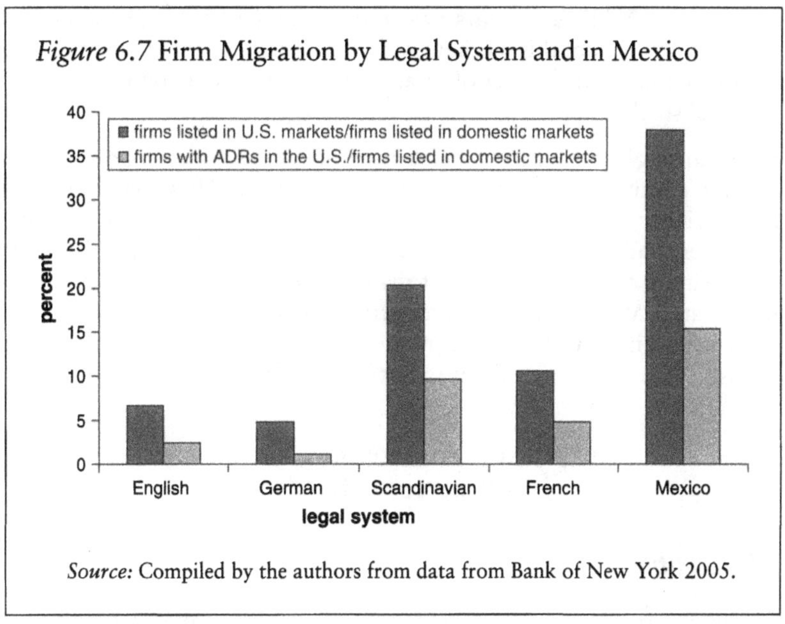

Source: Compiled by the authors from data from Bank of New York 2005.

view that, in the current environment of weak investor protection, firms have been trying to find alternative ways to access external capital markets and secure capital at lower cost.[20]

Listing abroad is apparently a good solution for companies that are able to jump across the river. But the literature has also pointed out the potential negative externalities on local markets of the migration of a large firm through ADRs. Domowitz, Glen, and Madhavan (1998) analyze the early Mexican data on cross-listings and find that there is a fall in liquidity and an increase in price volatility in the local market among companies that are open to foreign investors. This is consistent with a flight of foreign investors from the local market and may partly explain the increasingly lower liquidity levels in Mexico indicated in figures 6.3 and 6.4. In the last five years, the value traded by Mexican firms in foreign markets has been 5 to 10 times greater than the value traded in the Mexican Stock Exchange.

Another way of opting into a more protective legal regime is by being acquired by a company already operating within such a regime. When a U.S. company acquires a Mexican firm, the chance that investors will be legally expropriated diminishes. In a friendly acquisition, the controlling shareholders of the Mexican company may be compensated for the benefits they lose, making it more likely that they will acquiesce. Such acquisitions enhance efficiency because the wasteful expropriation is replaced by publicly shared profits and dividends. Some of the acquisitions in the countries of NAFTA in years past reflect this particular phenomenon. A clear drawback of this mechanism for accessing capital at lower rates is the reduction in the number of local firms and the reduction in the size of the local stock market.

So, what might firms do? A quick reaction to the evidence presented so far is to continue to call for wholesale legal reform. However, improving the efficiency of the judicial system and asserting the rule of law are slow processes, and firms need capital today to face the challenge of foreign competitors. So, what else might managers do to try to access funds at lower rates? Might firms unilaterally try to improve their governance standards? And, if so, would this translate into higher valuations and cheaper funds? This is the topic examined in the rest of the paper.

Corporate Governance, Valuation, and Investor Returns

The Sample

The literature on corporate governance has established that laws and regulations affect the valuation of firms and dividend payout ratios.[21] In this section, we follow the approach used in recent papers to determine if the variation in firm-level governance practices is also associated with firm valuation, performance, and dividend payments.[22] For this purpose, we have collected firm-level financial data and calculated a set of indexes on corporate governance practices for Mexican corporations during 2002–05.

There were 159 companies listed on the Mexican Stock Exchange in 2002. To obtain historical financial data for all these companies, we put together the information in several data sets. Our main data source is Bloomberg, from which we were able to obtain the main financial and operations data. The coverage from Bloomberg was not sufficient to meet the goals of the project because Bloomberg did not include an extensive history for all firms and did not cover all firms across sizes, and we also wanted to examine firms that had issued bonds rather than shares. Moreover, some companies were missing from the data because of suspensions, delisting, or lack of trading activity. To solve all these potentially important selection and survivorship biases, we added historical and financial information from the annual reports of each company. The annual reports contained general information on the firms, financials, administrative standards, and shareholders, as well as information on the market behavior of equity prices. Using these various sources, we obtained complete financial information for 150 companies listed in fiscal year 2002/03.

Table 6.7 provides the main financial characteristics of the firms in our sample. To avoid the sometimes large year-to-year variations in profitability and performance ratios, the table provides data for the average of two

Table 6.7 Descriptive Statistics

Variable	*Observations*	*Mean*	*Median*	*Standard deviation*	*Minimum*	*Maximum*
Tobin's q	108	0.943	0.86	0.361	0.372	2.280
Price-to-book ratio	102	0.901	0.75	0.604	0.036	2.518
ROA	139	2.312	2.27	5.701	-12.762	17.814
ROE	135	6.353	6.98	11.703	-25.895	34.515
Dividend payout	120	14.375	0.00	23.649	0.000	106.067
Log (net sales)	145	5.373	5.62	2.413	-6.623	9.328
Financial leverage	140	2.853	2.18	2.497	1.005	15.742
Debt to assets	143	52.393	53.92	20.571	0.498	95.592
Sales growth	137	2.710	2.93	23.077	-99.733	71.429
Income to sales	141	4.799	4.12	20.783	-105.772	74.979
Lagged income to sales	98	5.10	0.06	9.6	-31.1	36.4
Size (top 10%)	150	0.09	0.00	0.292	0.000	1.000
Located in Mexico City	150	0.591	1.00	0.493	0.000	1.000
Equity listing	150	0.840	1.00	0.368	0.000	1.000
CGI	150	0.783	0.81	0.132	0.273	0.982
Board composition	150	0.667	0.67	0.194	0.111	1.000
Board structure	150	0.693	0.80	0.258	0.000	1.000
Board functions	150	0.890	0.92	0.150	0.167	1.000
Duties of board members	150	0.903	0.89	0.099	0.714	1.000
Evaluation and compensation committee	150	0.530	0.50	0.364	0.000	1.000
Audit committee	150	0.842	0.89	0.162	0.143	1.000
Finance and planning committee	150	0.712	1.00	0.422	0.000	1.000
Shareholders meeting	150	0.779	0.75	0.167	0.375	1.000

Source: Compiled by the authors.

Note: The table shows descriptive statistics on the main variables used in the empirical section of the chapter. All variables have been taken from each firm's annual financial report, the corporate governance code of best practices, and each firm's general statement. Detailed definitions of each variable are provided in annex 6.2. All reports are available on the Mexican Stock Exchange Web site, http://www.bmv.com.mx/.

fiscal years, 2003/04 and 2004/05. As the table shows, this is a period of relatively positive growth. The average firm shows an income-to-sales ratio of almost 5 percent and average sales growth of almost 3 percent. The return on assets (ROA) and the return on equity (ROE) for the mean firm is 2.3 and 6.3 percent, respectively. Past profitability was also growing during 1997–2002 at a similar 5 percent rate, as measured by lagged income to sales. The average Mexican firm with listed securities showed a debt-to-assets ratio of close to 50 percent, which is pretty standard.

We use five outcome variables in this paper. The first are valuation measures. We rely on the classic valuation measure, Tobin's q, found in the initial studies in governance, as well as in more recent papers.[23] But we supplement it with the price-to-book multiple for robustness. As table 6.7 shows, valuation multiples for the average company are 0.943 and 0.901 when we calculate Tobin's q and the price-to-book ratios. The maximum valuation measures reach between 2.2 and 2.5, respectively. As alternative outcome measures, we also use the ROA and the ROE as proxies for operating performance.[24] For our sample, the average ROA is 2.3 percent, while the mean ROE is three times as large, at 6.4 percent. Firms are disbursing positive dividends, on average, at a mean dividend payout ratio of 14.4 percent.

As the table also shows, 84 percent of the sample had listed stock, while the remaining companies had only public bond issues. Close to 60 percent of firms in our sample have headquarters in Mexico City.

We analyze below the relationship between various corporate governance indicators and measures of valuation, performance, and dividend payouts. But before doing this, let us explain the origin and configuration of the data on corporate governance practices we have put together.

Data on Corporate Governance Practices

The second database on corporate governance practices has been obtained from the annual governance reports that all firms must present to the Mexican Stock Exchange when they present their annual reports. These reports are required by the Committee on Best Corporate Practices that was created to pool forces from the private (*Consejo Coordinador Empresarial*) and the public sectors. The committee was formed by a multidisciplinary group, including academics, controlling shareholders of large and small corporations, managers, and representatives of the accounting, finance, and legal professions.

In 1999, the committee published a code of best practices that included a series of recommendations on what was regarded at the time as good corporate governance practices. The recommendations fell into four main areas: (1) disclosure of information related to the administrative structure, the objectives, and operations of the various board committees; (2) the existence of adequate channels for timely disclosure and the existence of good quality financial information; (3) the adequacy of communications between management and board members; and (4) the protection of shareholder rights, as well as the related disclosure and communication mechanisms.

Mexico was concerned about corporate governance mainly as a result of the lack of growth in domestic markets and the damaging experience in East Asia, where economies were emerging from the 1997–98 crisis. This was the first reform effort undertaken in Latin America and one of the first in the world; it came before the U.S. corporate governance scandals. At the time, only the United Kingdom and a few other countries had adopted such an approach to try to foster more transparency in the market and establish a mechanism that facilitated the transmission of information to investors.

The philosophical principle underlying the code is that the disclosure of information about corporate governance practices and investor protections by firms allows the market to perceive the differences among the policies followed by various companies. This information should allow shareholders to distinguish those firms that support investor protections, in turn making the shareholders more willing to give the companies funds. In the end, those firms with better practices should find that their access to capital is easier and costs less because they provide a more certain environment for investors.

The adoption in Mexico of the principles of the code of best practices, as in most other countries, is voluntary, but the disclosure by each firm in the stock exchange is compulsory. Starting with fiscal year 2000/01, all publicly traded firms on the Mexican Stock Exchange have had to declare, in their annual reports to shareholders, the rules they follow in the code and the rules they do not follow. They may also explain why they do not follow the rules they have elected not to follow and describe any alternate mechanisms they may have adopted for the protection of investors. All firms with publicly traded securities, both equity and debt, must disclose the information.

Disclosure about the list of corporate governance practices consists of mandatory answers to 55 questions. Although firms are not required to meet the recommendations of the code, the fact that all firms with publicly traded securities must make the disclosures has been useful for investors. We should also mention that, although the answers are provided by the firms themselves, analysts and market participants may request specific additional information about these issues and monitor the accuracy of the provided information. The reputation loss from a deviation from truthful answers might be substantial, because the nature of the information requested is verifiable by market participants and is published as part of the annual reports of the firms, which are approved by the boards of directors.

From the corporate governance questionnaire, we have constructed a firm-level corporate governance index (CGI) by adding 1 point for every response to the questionnaire indicating that the company meets a recommendation of the code. We have standardized the CGI to lie between 0 and 1 by dividing the number of positive answers by the total number of questions in the questionnaire. Table 6.7 shows the main descriptive statistics of our CGI for the 150 firms in our sample. Our CGI is the average of the indexes for the two years (2003 and 2004) for which we have disaggregated company data. The mean company in Mexico met 78.4 percent of all the recommendations in the code. The best firm showed a 98.2 percent rate of compliance, while the worst firm met less than 30 percent of the code recommendations. In 2004, close to 90 firms of the 150 in our sample met more than 80 percent of the code recommendations. Another 35 firms met between 70 and 80 percent of the code, bringing the accumulated share of firms showing more than 70 percent compliance to 83 percent of the sample.

Although we do not have firm-by-firm disaggregated data for previous years, figure 6.8 shows the share of recommendations met by the average company in the market, according to the National Banking and Stock Market Commission.[25] Compliance has increased over time. In 2000, the

Figure 6.8 Share of Recommendations of the Code of Best Practices Met by the Average Firm

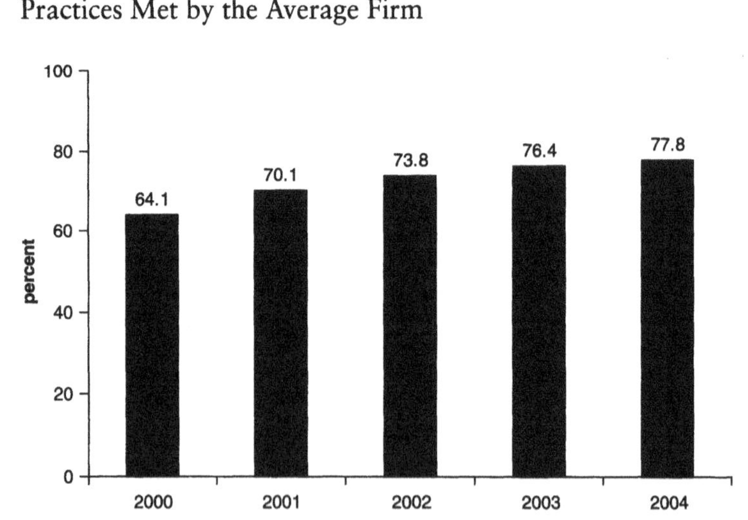

Source: Compiled by the authors from data from Comisión Nacional Bancaria y de Valores de México 2004.

Note: The figure shows the average level of compliance with all of the recommendations of the code of best practices by all firms with publicly traded equity and bonds listed on the Mexican Stock Exchange. The number of firms changes each year according to new listings and delistings.

first year of the code, the mean firm followed 64 percent of the principles, while, the following year, the number jumped to 70 percent. The period 2002–04 saw smaller increases, so that the total compliance was close to 77 percent at the end of the period. Compliance increased only 1 percent from 2003 to 2004, suggesting a slowdown in the changes in corporate practices.

Figure 6.9 shows the cumulative density of the CGI. It reveals that there is a peak around the 80 percent level of recommendations met in 2004. The seemingly large initial jump from 2000 to 2001 might mean that some firms may have been confused about the exact meaning of the questions the first year, or that the code introduced some pressure for firms to change quickly.

As table 6.7 shows, 84 percent of the firms in our sample are equity issuers, while the rest are involved in public bonds trading on the Mexican Stock Exchange. Both sorts of firms are required to supply answers in their annual reports to the corporate governance questions. In 2004, equity issuers, which tend to be larger, older firms, met an average of 81 percent of the code recommendations, while firms with publicly traded bonds met only 65 percent.

Figure 6.10 indicates differences in compliance with the code between firms issuing equity (publicly traded stocks) and those issuing public debt

Figure 6.9 CGI Density, 2003 and 2004

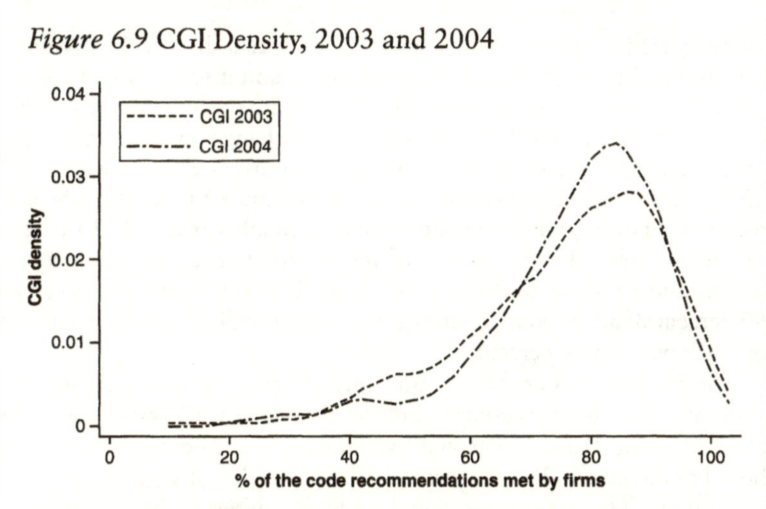

Source: Compiled by the authors from data from Comisión Nacional Bancaria y de Valores de México 2004.

Note: The horizontal axis represents the percent of the recommendations of the code of best practices met by firms. The vertical axis measures the density function, which shows the proportion of firms meeting each percentage range of the principles of the code.

Figure 6.10 Distribution of Compliance with the Code of Best Practices

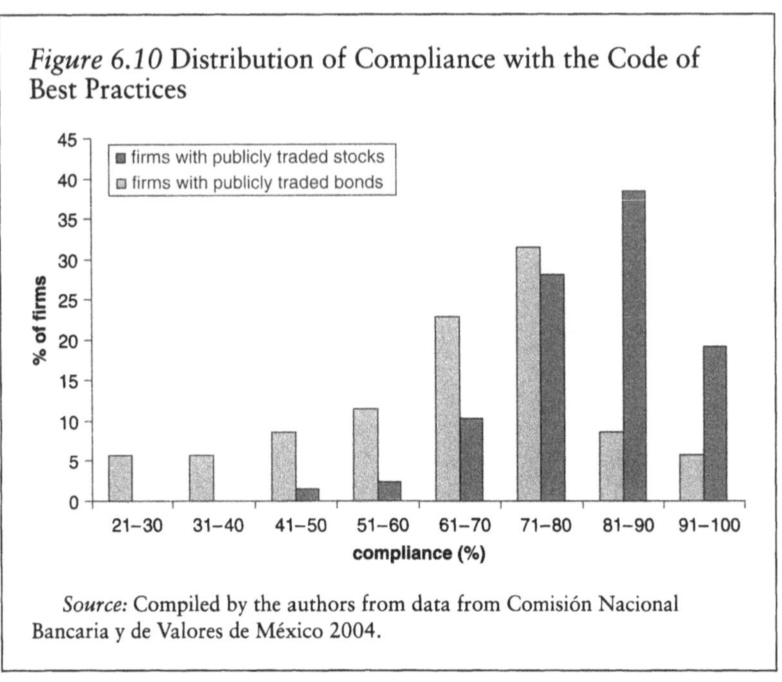

Source: Compiled by the authors from data from Comisión Nacional Bancaria y de Valores de México 2004.

(publicly traded bonds) in the market. Debt issuers show a slightly flatter distribution in compliance and a lower mean and median rate of compliance. Debt issuers tend to be smaller firms that have only recently started to use the public credit market because of changes in the regulations. These changes have produced a boom, as discussed elsewhere above. In 2004, 56 percent of equity issuers met more than 80 percent of the code recommendations, while the corresponding number was only 15 percent for debt issuers. The lower tail of the distribution among debt issuers is also thicker: close to 30 percent of public bond issuers met less than 60 percent of all recommendations; the corresponding number for issuers of stock was only 4 percent.

The 55 questions of the questionnaire are grouped into eight sections, from which we have created subindexes that have also been standardized to lie between 0 and 1. The eight subindexes are (1) composition of the board of directors, (2) board functions and the general structure of board committees, (3) board operational rules, (4) duties of board members, (5) structure and functions of the evaluation and compensation committee, (6) structure and functions of the audit committee, (7) structure and functions of the finance and planning committee, and (8) shareholder meetings and protection of shareholder rights. The bottom of table 6.7 shows the percentage of questions in each category that are met by the mean company in our sample. These numbers range from 53 percent for questions on the committee of evaluation and compensation to 90.3 percent for questions on the duties of board members.

Table 6.8 goes into finer detail on the data we have gathered. It shows the percentage of firms that meet each specific recommendation for the years 2003 and 2004 separately. The bottom of the table shows that

Table 6.8 The Corporate Governance Code of Best Practices

Number	*Question*	*2003*	*2004*
Board composition			
1	The board of directors has between 5 and 15 members	90.8	91.1
2	Board members do not have substitutes	24.8	26.0
3	Only preestablished substitute directors may take the place of an actual board member	86.5	64.4
4	Actual board member suggests the substitute	67.4	42.5
5	Independent directors and owner directors jointly represent at least 40 percent of the board	89.4	87.0
6	Independent directors represent at least 20 percent of the total board	90.1	89.0
7	The classification of directors as independent, owner, and related is included in the annual report	58.9	63.0
8	The annual report indicates the category to which each owner director belongs	52.5	54.1
9	The annual report indicates the positions and functions of each board member	66.0	65.8
Mean		69.6	64.8
Board functions and committee structure			
10	The board performs the functions of evaluation and remuneration, auditing, and finance and planning through one or various intermediate governance bodies	79.4	82.2
11	Substitute directors are not part of board committees	60.3	61.6
12	Board committees have between 3 and 7 members	80.1	82.9
13	In addition to his/her board duties, each independent director participates in at least one committee	46.8	45.2
14	An independent director chairs the audit committee	79.4	81.5
Mean		69.2	70.7
Board operation			
15	The board meets at least 4 times a year	95.7	96.6
16	The board defines long-term strategies at least once a year	93.6	93.2

(continued)

Table 6.8 The Corporate Governance Code of Best Practices *(continued)*

Number	*Question*	*2003*	*2004*
17	At least 25 percent of the directors may call a board meeting	90.1	89.7
18	Directors have access, at least 5 business days prior to the meeting, to all relevant information for the decisions to be taken according to the agenda for the meeting	84.4	83.6
19	A mechanism is established to enable directors to adequately assess the proposal related to confidential strategic matters	77.3	79.5
20	First-time directors are given adequate information on their responsibilities and duties, as well as data related to the corporation and its business environment	92.9	90.4
Mean		89.0	88.8
Duties of board members			
21	Disclose to the chairman and secretary of the board any situation that may result in a conflict of interest and refrain from participating in such matters	97.2	97.9
22	Use of the assets and services of the corporation only for matters related to it and clearly define the policies that would apply for the use of such assets for personal matters	97.2	98.6
23	There are specific policies that regulate private use of the assets of the firm	65.2	63.0
24	Dedication of the necessary time and attention to the performance of their duties, assisting in at least 70 percent of the meetings (not applicable to the alternate directors)	97.2	95.2
25	Maintain absolute confidentiality on all information that may affect the operation of the corporation, as well as of the deliberations that take place at the board meetings	100.0	100.0
26	Directors and their alternate directors, if any, must keep mutually informed in relation to the matters discussed in the board meetings they attend	81.6	74.7
27	Participate in the board of directors with opinions, recommendations, and suggestions that derive from the analysis of the corporation's operations	97.2	99.3
Mean		90.8	89.8

(continued)

Table 6.8 The Corporate Governance Code of Best Practices *(continued)*

Number	*Question*	*2003*	*2004*
Compensation and evaluation committee			
28	The board should be supported by reviewing the terms and conditions by which the chief executive officer and the high-ranking officers are being hired, as well as the possible payments in case of separation from the corporation; such terms and conditions should follow the general guidelines approved by the board	63.1	63.4
29	The annual report presented by the board of directors discloses the policies adopted and the terms and conditions of the remuneration package of the directors, the chief executive officer, and the corporation's high-ranking officers	43.3	43.2
Mean		53.2	53.3
Audit committee			
30	For the financial statements, external audit, and any other external review, the board should not hire any accountant firm the income of which for fees for all the services rendered to the corporation represent more than 20 percent of its total income	92.2	92.5
31	To ensure objectivity in the audit report, a rotation mechanism of the partner in charge of the preparation of the audit report should be recommended to the board; it is suggested that this rotation be made at least every six years	88.7	96.6
32	The person who signs the audit report in the annual financial statements of the corporation should not be the same person who acts as the statutory auditor; nonetheless, both persons may be partners of the same firm	86.5	90.4
33	The committee should ensure that the professional profile of the statutory auditor enables him/her to adequately perform the assigned duties; it is also recommended that the annual report presented by the board of directors disclose relevant information regarding the professional profile of the statutory auditor	51.8	50.7
34	The company should have an internal audit department	87.2	90.4

(continued)

Table 6.8 The Corporate Governance Code of Best Practices *(continued)*

Number	*Question*	*2003*	*2004*
35	The committee should submit to the approval of the board of directors the accounting policies used in the preparation of the financial information	73.0	77.4
36	The board is assured that the mid-term financial information is prepared with the same criteria, policies, and practices as the annual financial information; in the process, the board may obtain support from the internal auditor, the external auditor, and the statutory auditor of the corporation	82.3	83.6
37	There is an internal monitoring system	97.9	97.9
38	The committee should submit for board approval the general guidelines of the internal monitoring system	77.3	78.8
39	The committee should assist the board by evaluating the effectiveness of the internal monitoring system and by giving an opinion on the financial and operational checks	77.3	78.1
40	The external auditors should validate the effectiveness of the internal monitoring system and present a report on the system	85.8	84.2
41	The committee should ensure the existence of mechanisms that allow the board to determine if the corporation duly complies with all applicable laws and regulations	83.0	84.9
42	The board revises the applicable laws and regulations at least once a year and holds a review on the matter at least once a year	94.3	95.9
43	The board is informed about the legal situation	92.9	92.5
Mean		83.6	85.3
Finance and planning committee			
44	The committee should submit to the board of directors an evaluation of the feasibility of the main investments and financing transactions of the corporation, and the same should be in line with existing policies	69.5	74.0
45	The committee should periodically evaluate the strategic position of the corporation in terms of the strategic plan	68.8	72.6
46	The committee should assist the board in reviewing the consistency of the investment and financing policies with the strategic plan of the corporation	68.8	71.2

(continued)

Table 6.8 The Corporate Governance Code of Best Practices *(continued)*

Number	*Question*	*2003*	*2004*
47	The committee should assist the board in reviewing the financial projections of the corporation, while assuring their consistency with the strategic plan	68.8	71.2
Mean		69.0	72.3
Shareholders meeting			
48	It is suggested that an item referred to as general matters not be included in the agenda	92.9	93.2
49	It is suggested that the grouping of matters related to different topics within a single item should be avoided; the latter has the purpose of allowing stockholders to vote each item separately, in addition to providing them with information on all topics to be discussed at the meeting	98.6	98.6
50	The company should make available, 15 days prior to the day of the meeting, all information on each item of the shareholders meeting agenda	96.5	95.9
51	The shareholders with enough information and voting alternatives have the power to twist the voting according to their interests	66.7	64.4
52	The company should include the proposals of members to be appointed to the board of directors and a brief professional profile of each candidate as part of the information delivered to the shareholders	50.4	52.7
53	The information disclosed includes the relevant issues of the work of the intermediate governance bodies	51.8	58.9
54	The board of directors should include in its annual report to the shareholders meeting the relevant aspects involved in the tasks performed by each intermediate governance body, make available to the shareholders the reports of each governance body submitted to the board, together with all other material for the meeting, with the exception of information the confidentiality of which may affect the competitiveness of the corporation; in addition, it is recommended that the names of the members of each intermediate governance body be included in the annual report	66.0	71.2

(continued)

Table 6.8 The Corporate Governance Code of Best Practices *(continued)*

Number	*Question*	*2003*	*2004*
55	To keep communication channels open with shareholders and potential investors, each corporation should have in place policies and mechanisms and designate responsible parties to inform these investors	95.7	96.6
Mean		77.3	78.9
All firms with publicly traded securities		78.4	78.5
Firms with publicly traded bonds		65.4	65.6
Firms with publicly traded stocks		80.3	80.8

Source: Compiled by the authors based on information provided by the Comisión Nacional Bancaria y de Valores de México.

Note: The table shows the percentage of listed firms that answered yes to each of the questions on the corporate governance code of best practices developed by the National Banking and Stock Market Commission. The table includes data on the 150 firms in our sample. See the text for additional information.

compliance with the recommendations of the code of best practices was increasing. In 2004, corporations with publicly traded securities met 78.5 percent of all code recommendations, while the number had only been 78.4 percent a year earlier. The table lumps equity and debt issuers together, but the paragraphs below describing the data in the table point out the main differences between these groups.

An analysis of the specific questions in each of these categories reveals several interesting corporate governance patterns among Mexican corporations. There are three areas of the code that deal with the board's functions, structure, and operations. In terms of board composition, Mexican firms have substantially reduced the size of their boards over the last 10 years. Today, more than 91 percent of firms that issue either equity or debt have boards with between 5 and 15 members. It is also the case that, in 98 percent of the firms that issue equity, at least 20 percent of the members of the board are independent. The number is only 40 percent for firms issuing debt, and this explains the low overall average in the table. While these are clear advances from what the classic board of a Mexican firm looked like 10 years ago, firms are still not communicating the information about board members clearly to their shareholders. Only between 50 and 65 percent of firms specify in their annual reports the classification of directors as independent, owner, and related. This number reaches 65–70 percent for firms issuing equity and only 15 to 30 percent for firms issuing debt. Another area where more progress may be needed is substitute board members. In Mexico, board members have the right to nominate a substitute who may take their place at the meetings. Only a quarter of firms have adopted a structure without substitute directors. In fact, in 63 percent of occasions, only a previously established substitute may take the place of the actual board member. These are not best corporate governance practices because actual directors might become detached from their functions if the substitute is the one doing the work or going to the meetings.

The second area of the code deals with the functions of the board and the general structure of the specialized board committees. As in the previous area, most boards have shrunk the size of committees, and close to 90 percent of the firms issuing equity, but only 55 of those issuing debt meet the 3-to-7 target size of the code. Importantly, more than 80 percent of boards have established specialized committees to deal with management evaluation and compensation, auditing, and financial planning. An independent director is the chair of the audit committee among 90 percent of equity issuers, but only in 35 percent of the firms issuing public bonds. The operation or internal working of the board is one of the areas where most firms follow the suggested principles, with close to 90 percent of all issuers meeting the targets in terms of number of meetings per year, devoting time to the strategy of the firm, ease in calling a meeting, and training of first-time directors. It is in the area of access to relevant information in a timely fashion where the percentage of firms falls to about 80 percent.

The forth area of the questionnaire surveys the duties of directors. Close to 90 percent of firms meet all principles. In basically all firms, board members are said to report conflicts of interest and abstain from voting, to only use the assets of the firm's business, to keep confidentiality, and to dedicate the appropriate time to their jobs as board members. The only two questions where the number of firms responding yes falls to 60–70 percent are those that ask about the existence of specific policies for the personal use of the firm's assets and the communication between the board member and his or her substitute. The picture painted by this subindex is one of strong boards of directors with clearly defined duties that deal with conflicts of interest. This is probably one of the areas that is harder to verify objectively by market participants, and thus we want to make sure our results in the econometric work do not depend crucially on these answers.

The next three areas of the questionnaire deal with the specific functions and inner working of specialized committees. The questions on the compensation and evaluation committee find one of the largest deficiencies in corporate governance practices. More than half the listed companies do not reveal the policies used in this area, and 40 percent of firms declare that they do not have such a committee or, if they do, it does not deal with the issues of the evaluation of compensation packages for high-level executives. The numbers for debt issuers are only about 10 percent below those of equity issuers. This is clearly an area where there is a lot of room to grow for both kinds of firms. Most firms meet best corporate governance practices, as specified in the code, as regards the audit committee, which was the object of substantial changes in regulations over the last five years. In the vast majority of firms, the external auditor is different from the *comisario*, who is supposed to represent an additional check as he has the duty to report problems to shareholders. Curiously, only half the firms disclose the profile of the comisario in the annual report. In more than 90 percent of cases, firms limit the income of the external auditor and require audit partner rotation every six years. Most firms have internal audit and monitoring systems, but the board has a role in setting up and approving these policies in only 75–80 percent of cases. The third committee that is the subject of specific recommendations in the code has the function of supervising firm investment policies and planning. The numbers show that the boards of close to 30 percent of firms do not analyze these sorts of issues in a systematic manner or through a specific committee. The numbers are remarkably similar for equity and bond holders. This is one of the board functions that has permeated through to relatively few Mexican companies.

The final area of the code deals with shareholder rights. As previous studies have shown, corporations rarely deviate from the package of shareholder rights that is mandated by laws and regulations. Therefore, this area of the code is mostly devoted to issues revolving around the flow of information to shareholders and the way shareholder meetings are conducted. Mainly as a result of regulations, there has been a substantial change in the way firms disclose meeting agendas. Today, the old practice of grouping various issues under a vague agenda point or including an agenda item for various issues has virtually disappeared among stock issuers and among 80–90 percent of firms trading in public bonds. But the rest of the numbers in the section reveal a couple of deficiencies. Only half the firms include information on proposed board members among the information given to shareholders. Additionally, in only 57 percent of cases does the information include relevant issues about specialized board committees. Not surprisingly, only two in three firms say that their shareholders have sufficient information and voting alternatives to be able to instruct others to vote on their behalf. The data show that the average Mexican corporation does not provide complete, timely information so that shareholders may consider relevant issues and facilitate their voting in the meetings.

It is worth mentioning that the practices of bond issuers trails substantially those of equity issuers in the areas of board composition and structure. In these two areas, the number of bond issuers meeting all recommendations is only half that of equity issuers. The differences between the two groups are negligible only in the duties of board members, the audit committee, and the finance committee. In the rest of the categories, equity issuers meet all requirements in 10 to 15 percent more of the cases.

Econometric Results

The previous section provided a first look at the main corporate governance and financial characteristics of publicly listed corporations in Mexico. The goal of the rest of this section is to examine the relationship among firm-level governance measures, valuation, performance, and dividend payout ratios. It is possible that certain types of firms, for example those that will need to raise capital in the future, are more likely to adopt better corporate governance. Endogeneity is certainly a concern in other papers on this area of firm-level practices.[26]

Several potential sources of endogeneity are at play in these data. First and foremost, unobserved future growth opportunities might lead controlling shareholders and managers to improve their levels of disclosure and minority protections to be able to raise capital at lower cost. This means that our valuation measures are likely also to be influenced by anticipated future growth prospects. A second source of endogeneity might arise from the intrinsic nature of the firm, its assets, or cash flows. Firms with large free cash flows would cause investors to worry about potential expropriation, and such firms may thus adopt better corporate governance measures to keep investors content.[27] Similarly, investors may find it more difficult to monitor firms with lower tangible assets and might thus require better governance practices.[28] It might also be argued that the size or age of a firm might affect corporate practices. The operations of a small firm might be more easily understood and monitored, while larger firms or firms in multiple industries would exhibit potentially larger agency problems and would thus tend to adopt better corporate governance.

In this chapter, we follow the approach used in similar studies to try to disentangle the corporate governance effect on performance and valuation measures by controlling for various company characteristics likely to be associated with higher growth prospects, higher needs of monitoring due to the nature of the firm's assets and cash flows, and firm size. At the end of the section, we also use instrumental variable methods to provide additional robustness to our initial results.

Because of endogeneity concerns, it is important to establish the association between firm characteristics and our measures of governance. In table 6.9, we analyze these relationships to establish patterns that help us identify important company traits that we should take into account in the subsequent econometric work. Table 6.9 shows pairwise correlations among our aggregate CGI, valuation and performance measures, and company characteristics for the cross-section of 150 firms in our sample.

Four sets of results emerge from the table. First, the initial column of correlations between the CGI and the rest of the variables shows that firms with better corporate governance have higher valuations, as measured by

Table 6.9 Correlation Matrix of the Main Variables

Variable	*CGI*	*Tobin's q*	*Price-to-book ratio*	*ROA*	*ROE*	*Dividend payout*	*Log (net sales)*	*Financial leverage*	*Debt to assets*	*Sales growth*	*Income to sales*	*Lagged income to sales*	*Located in Mexico City*	*ADR holder*	*Size (top 10%)*
Tobin's q	0.2309														
	0.0162														
Price-to-book	0.1834	0.8667													
ratio	0.0651	0.0000													
ROA	0.0880	0.4139	0.4015												
	0.3030	0.0000	0.0000												
ROE	−0.0136	0.4533	0.3652	0.8602											
	0.8760	0.0000	0.0003	0.0000											
Dividend	0.1024	0.2708	0.2334	0.3387	0.2988										
payout	0.2655	0.0079	0.0286	0.0002	0.0015										
Log (net sales)	0.2947	0.3753	0.2969	0.2092	0.1719	0.3015									
	0.0003	0.0001	0.0026	0.0134	0.0463	0.0008									
Financial	−0.1972	0.0080	0.0273	−0.1035	0.2619	−0.0850	−0.0402								
leverage	0.0195	0.9354	0.7864	0.2307	0.0022	0.3666	0.6374								
Debt to assets	−0.0992	0.0051	−0.1257	−0.1700	0.1815	−0.0923	0.1768	0.7276							
	0.2385	0.9582	0.2103	0.0455	0.0351	0.3202	0.0347	0.0000							
Sales growth	0.0417	0.2713	0.2682	0.2965	0.4357	0.0739	0.3808	0.1144	0.1658						
	0.6289	0.0053	0.0082	0.0006	0.0000	0.4347	0.0000	0.1916	0.0546						

(continued)

Table 6.9 Correlation Matrix of the Main Variables *(continued)*

Variable	*CGI*	*Tobin's q*	*Price-to-book ratio*	*ROA*	*ROE*	*Dividend payout*	*Log (net sales)*	*Financial leverage*	*Debt to assets*	*Sales growth*	*Income to sales*	*Lagged income to sales*	*Located in Mexico City*	*ADR holder*	*Size (top 10%)*
Income to	−0.1585	0.1577	0.1653	0.5583	0.6184	0.0867	−0.0471	0.3443	0.1121	0.3295					
sales	0.0605	0.1047	0.1002	0.0000	0.0000	0.3546	0.5790	0.0000	0.1856	0.0001					
Lagged income	−0.0688	0.2817	0.1574	0.5175	0.4710	0.2767	0.1860	−0.2186	−0.3323	0.0591	0.4397				
to sales	0.5011	0.0068	0.1478	0.0000	0.0000	0.0104	0.0682	0.0323	0.0009	0.5692	0.0000				
Located in	0.1467	0.2112	0.2390	−0.0259	0.0465	−0.0153	0.0653	0.0908	0.0688	0.0212	0.1300	0.0236			
Mexico City	0.0741	0.0282	0.0155	0.7623	0.5924	0.8681	0.4353	0.2858	0.4145	0.8057	0.1245	0.8175			
ADR issuer	0.2283	0.0084	0.1147	0.0984	0.0130	0.2015	0.3237	−0.1145	−0.0745	0.0339	−0.1758	0.0180	0.0678		
	0.0050	0.9310	0.2508	0.2490	0.8813	0.0273	0.0001	0.1781	0.3762	0.6943	0.0371	0.8603	0.4115		
Size (top 10%)	0.0561	0.2095	0.1090	0.1082	0.1625	0.1044	0.3993	0.1323	0.1675	0.0643	0.1279	0.1565	0.0342	0.1100	
	0.4953	0.0295	0.2753	0.2047	0.0597	0.2567	0.0000	0.1190	0.0456	0.4553	0.1307	0.1238	0.6786	0.1802	
Equity listing	0.4499			−0.0468	−0.2003	0.1427	0.1670	−0.3774	−0.3273	−0.1182	−0.2553		−0.0157	0.1905	0.0775
	0.0000	1.0000	1.0000	0.5841	0.0198	0.1201	0.0447	0.0000	0.0001	0.1690	0.0022	1.0000	0.8491	0.0196	0.3458

Source: Compiled by the authors.

Note: The table presents the pairwise correlation matrix of the main variables used in the empirical section of the paper. P-values are shown below the correlation coefficients.

Tobin's q and the price-to-book value, but not higher performance in the form of the ROA and the ROE. Firms with better corporate governance practices tend to be larger in terms of sales and domiciled in Mexico City and to have issued equity locally and abroad in the form of ADRs. These results are consistent with the view that firms entering the U.S. market have higher levels of corporate governance, probably because they have to meet higher international requirements. We should also be aware that a contrasting phenomenon may be taking place in that firms showing better governance to begin with are able to raise capital internationally. Importantly, current growth rates and lagged profitability are not significantly correlated to our CGI. Lagged profitability has, in fact, a negative correlation with our index. This should help alleviate some concerns about the main source of potential endogeneity here. In terms of cash flow or asset characteristics that may explain higher corporate governance, we do not observe a clear pattern of association between our CGI and industries that might, a priori, be regarded as having higher free cash flows or intangible assets (results not included in the table).

Overall, the data in the first column do not show signs of serious endogeneity problems, with the exception of firm size, but, to disentangle the true effect of corporate governance on valuation, performance, and dividend payments, we control for several company characteristics in the regressions that follow.

The second set of results in table 6.9 explores the relationship among the dependent variables in the regression work. The two valuation measures and the two profitability measures show a correlation of 0.86. The correlations between valuation and profitability measures are also very high, ranging from 0.36 to 0.45, and are all statistically significant at 1 percent. The table also highlights that it is the most valuable and more profitable firms that have the highest dividend payouts. Overall, these series of correlations show that our future dependent variables all move together very strongly.

In terms of predictors of other variables correlated with our outcome measures, we may observe three basic patterns. First, larger firms and those with higher sales growth have higher Tobin's qs and price-to-book ratios, as well as higher measures of performance. But it is only the firms with larger sales and those with the highest past growth that pay more dividends now. There is really no clear pattern among measures of indebtedness, valuation, performance, or dividend payout. Finally, there is some evidence that firms located in Mexico City have higher valuation multiples, but not those that have issued ADRs. Neither of these two types of firms has higher profitability, as proxied by the ROA and the ROE. The only finding worth mentioning is the fact that firms that only have public debt are more profitable, that is, they show higher ROE and income-to-sales ratios than firms that only have a local equity listing.

Making use of the patterns shown in table 6.9, the econometric work in the following tables controls for various company characteristics that might be determinants of valuation and performance. Tables 6.10–6.12 show the results of regressing each of our five dependent variables on the CGI and other company and industry controls. All regressions control for key company characteristics that theory predicts should have an impact on valuation or performance measures. In each regression, we include a measure of indebtedness, a size control, a measure of profitability (except where the dependent variable is performance), and a measure of growth, either current or lagged.[29]

We also take into account the potential endogeneity problems emerging because of the nature of firm assets or cash flows that arise from differences across industries. Tables 6.10–6.12 present the results of industry-level fixed effects regressions. To try to proxy for the differences in assets and cash flows, we use a fairly detailed industry breakdown. The industry classifications in our sample is Bloomberg's industry group-level classification, which is similar to a 2-digit Standard Industrial Classification coding. Finally, all regressions present robust standard errors.

The regressions shown in these tables use the average of the two years for which we have data (2002–03 and 2003–04). Thus, there is one observation per firm in the regressions. This approach has several advantages. It eliminates the high volatility of yearly financials and helps avoid problems with standard errors. But it also has the disadvantage of not exploiting the information of a panel. We have also run alternative econometric specifications for each year separately and for a panel regression with two years of observations per firm and adding year dummies in the specification. The results do not significantly change; so, we only present the average regressions.[30]

Table 6.10 presents the valuation results. Table 6.10, panel a, uses Tobin's q as the dependent variable, while the price-to-book value is the outcome variable in panel b. As table 6.9 shows, these two measures are highly correlated, but we still use both to provide a robustness check. Several results are worth mentioning. First, the only company characteristic that is related to valuation is size. Bigger firms tend to have higher valuation multiples, but significance at 10 percent is only reached in two of the six specifications in each case. According to the theory, sales growth is positively associated with higher valuation, but statistical significance is not reached. Neither of the two measures of indebtedness is statistically related to Tobin's q or price-to-book ratios in our sample.

The aggregate CGI shows up positive and significant in all Tobin's q regressions and in half of those with price-to-book ratios. The economic impact of the index is large: a two standard deviation increase in the CGI increases Tobin's q by between 0.16 and 0.21, or between 16 and 23 percent above the mean Tobin's q of 0.94 for the sample. The same two standard deviation jump increases the price-to-book multiples by between 0.19 and 0.23, or a 21 and 26 percent above the mean 0.90 price-to-book ratio. Figures 6.11 and 6.12 show the partial regression plot of the CGI, Tobin's q,

Table 6.10 Valuation Regressions

	(1)	(2)	(3)	(4)	(5)	(6)
a. Tobin's q						
CG index	1.010	1.025	0.991	0.792	0.855	0.973
	(0.432)**	(0.370)***	(0.437)**	(0.423)*	(0.385)**	(0.465)**
Log (net sales)	0.042	0.033	0.061	0.032	0.029	0.066
	(0.024)*	(0.025)	(0.036)*	(0.026)	(0.026)	(0.041)
Financial leverage	0.014	0.003	0.021			
	(0.017)	(0.014)	(0.017)			
Debt to assets				−0.000	−0.000	−0.001
				(0.003)	(0.003)	(0.004)
Sales growth	0.001			0.003		
	(0.002)			(0.003)		
Income to sales		0.005			0.004	
		(0.002)*			(0.003)	
Lagged income to sales			0.007			0.005
			(0.587)			(0.607)
Constant	−0.172	−0.119	−0.343	0.120	0.074	−0.248
	(0.374)	(0.309)	('0.453)	(0.330)	(0.286)	(0.420)
Observations	102	105	90	104	107	91
Number of industries	31	31	30	31	31	31
R^2	0.17	0.20	0.21	0.15	0.15	0.21
Log likelihood	−9.90	−6.03	−2.64	−11.86	−9.92	−2.54
Rho	0.30	0.31	0.26	0.29	0.30	0.24
b. Price-to-book ratio						
CGI	1.175	1.088	0.903	1.050	1.082	0.930
	(0.663)*	(0.620)*	(0.711)	(0.655)	(0.632)*	(0.712)
Log (net sales)	0.038	0.066	0.030	0.050	0.076	0.051
	(0.034)	(0.039)*	(0.056)	(0.033)	(0.036)**	(0.051)
Financial leverage	0.040	0.012	0.035			
	(0.023)*	(0.024)	(0.034)			
Debt to assets				−0.001	−0.003	−0.004
				(0.005)	(0.005)	(0.006)
Sales growth	0.004			0.003		
	(0.004)			(0.004)		
Income to sales		0.003			0.003	
		(0.004)			(0.004)	

(continued)

Table 6.10 Valuation Regressions *(continued)*

	(1)	(2)	(3)	(4)	(5)	(6)
Lagged income to sales			0.001			0.007
			(0.939)			(0.789)
Constant	-0.394	-0.394	-0.156	-0.222	-0.277	0.026
	(0.538)	(0.497)	(0.703)	(0.504)	(0.502)	(0.684)
Observations	96	100	85	96	100	85
Number of industries	31	31	30	31	31	30
R^2	0.13	0.11	0.10	0.11	0.12	0.10
Log likelihood	-50.92	-60.56	-43.08	-51.69	-60.21	-42.90
Rho	0.42	0.37	0.52	0.40	0.35	0.50

Source: Compiled by the authors.

Note: The table shows industry-level fixed effects regressions of the firms included in the sample. The valuation measures are regressed against standard controls. The CGI is included as the interest variable. The dependent variable in the first is Tobin's q and, in the second panel, the price-to-book ratio. All variables are described in annex 6.2. Robust standard errors are shown in parentheses.

* significant at 10 percent

** significant at 5 percent

*** significant at 1 percent

and price-to-book for the first regression in table 6.10, panels a and b, respectively. The results are robust to outliers, as the graphs show.

The results on the impact of corporate governance practices on valuation are large and significant. They support the results in Klapper and Love (2002), Black, Jang, and Kim (2006a), and other papers cited in this chapter. In fact, we would expect valuation measures to be the prime variable that would capture the effect of improved corporate governance. According to the model in La Porta et al. (2000a), improved valuations as a result of better corporate governance are caused by the higher confidence among investors that controlling shareholders will not expropriate the cash flows of the firm. Investors are thus more willing to provide capital to such firms at lower cost, which is reflected in higher valuation multiples for firms with better governance practices.

Table 6.11 has the same format of the previous table, but the dependent variables here are the ROA and the ROE as proxies for operating performance. As in the previous table, larger firms in terms of sales have higher performance, and, in two of the four specifications in each panel, this relationship is statistically significant. In the case of the ROA, both financial leverage and the debt-to-assets ratio come in negative, but, again, this is only significant for two of the four regressions. Current sales growth

Figure 6.11 Partial Regression Plot of the CGI and Tobin's q

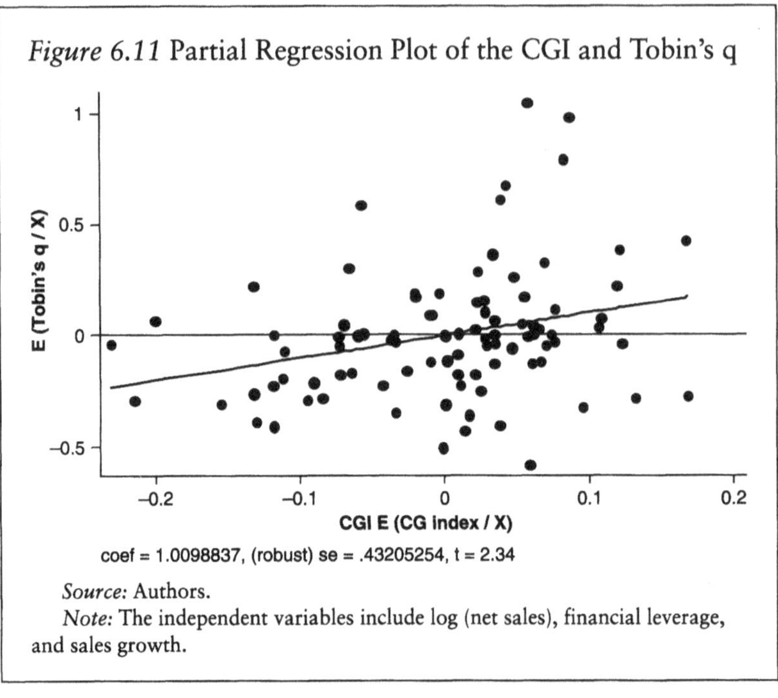

Source: Authors.
Note: The independent variables include log (net sales), financial leverage, and sales growth.

Figure 6.12 Partial Regression Plot of the CGI and the Price-to-Book Ratio

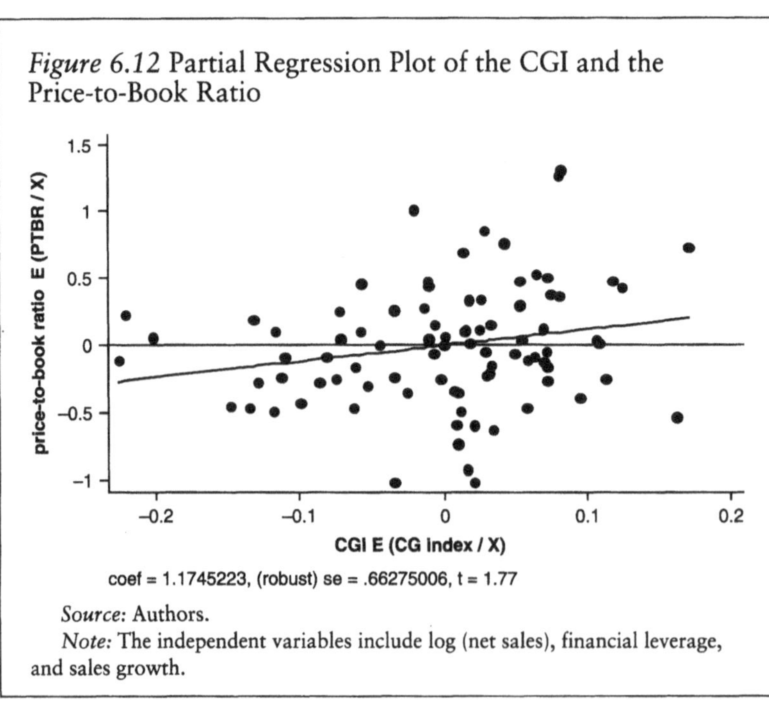

Source: Authors.
Note: The independent variables include log (net sales), financial leverage, and sales growth.

and lagged profitability do come in positive and are strongly associated with higher performance in both panels.

We would expect the first-order impact of corporate governance to be captured by the valuation measures used in table 6.10. Nonetheless, an argument may be made that better governed firms are better run, probably because of the existence of better mechanisms to face changing conditions or new opportunities. These firms would then be thought of as able to turn a higher return per dollar. The logic behind a positive association between performance and governance has to rely on some form of market inefficiency because investors underestimate the higher agency costs associated with poor governance practices. Some recent papers have tested this hypothesis for other countries and have found a positive effect of governance on operating performance.[31] An additional incentive for us to add this analysis is because operating performance measures allow us to include in our analysis all firms that have publicly traded bonds on the market.[32] The results on the association between our CGI and the ROA are positive and significant in all four regressions, while, for the ROE, they only reach significance in one specification. In the case of the ROA, the economic significance is also large: an increase by two standard deviations leads to an increase in the ROA to 75 percent above the mean ROA of

Table 6.11 Performance Regressions

	(1)	*(2)*	*(3)*	*(4)*
a. ROA				
CGI	7.368	12.898	7.615	12.099
	(4.434)*	(5.826)**	(4.501)*	(5.840)**
Log (net sales)	0.555	0.490	0.742	0.522
	(0.301)*	(0.480)	(0.341)**	(0.507)
Financial leverage	-0.488	-0.045		
	(0.213)**	(0.354)		
Debt to assets			-0.085	-0.028
			(0.034)**	(0.059)
Sales growth	0.089		0.063	
	(0.021)***		(0.031)**	
Lagged income to sales		0.231		0.219
		(9.237)**		(9.654)**
Constant	-5.328	-12.100	-3.457	-10.316
	(3.893)	(6.475)*	(4.369)	(6.253)
Observations	128	94	131	95
Number of industries	31	31	32	31

(continued)

Table 6.11 Performance Regressions *(continued)*

	(1)	*(2)*	*(3)*	*(4)*
R^2	0.23	0.31	0.23	0.31
Log likelihood	-358.23	-253.62	-372.61	-256.35
Rho	0.44	0.49	0.39	0.47
b. ROE				
CGI	13.005	20.076	12.491	19.174
	(9.353)	(11.282)*	(9.160)	(11.494)
Log (net sales)	1.334	1.168	1.383	1.006
	(0.621)**	(0.962)	(0.629)**	(1.070)
Financial leverage	0.311	0.151		
	(0.510)	(1.172)		
Debt to assets			0.012	0.052
			(0.060)	(0.119)
Sales growth	0.217		0.219	
	(0.055)***		(0.056)***	
Lagged income to sales		0.411		0.439
		(18.749)**		(21.251)**
Constant	-13.055	-20.342	-12.602	-20.978
	(8.414)	(12.417)	(8.629)	(11.810)*
Observations	126	92	127	92
Number of industries	30	30	31	30
R^2	0.25	0.27	0.25	0.27
Log likelihood	-441.44	-312.16	-444.78	-311.89
Rho	0.39	0.48	0.39	0.48

Source: Compiled by the authors.

Note: The table shows industry-level fixed effects regressions of the firms included in the sample. The performance measures are regressed against standard controls and include the CGI as the interest variable. The dependent variable in the first panel is the ROA and, in the second panel, the ROE. All variables are described in annex 6.2. Robust standard errors are shown in parentheses.

* significant at 10 percent

** significant at 5 percent

*** significant at 1 percent

2.53 points for the running sample. In the case of the ROE, a similar two standard deviation jump in governance leads to only a 48 to 70 percent increase above the mean.

Table 6.12 offers the same kind of analysis as tables 6.10 and 6.11, but for dividend payout ratios. Following the outcome agency model of dividend payments specified in La Porta et al. (2002), firms with stronger governance practices should be associated with higher dividend payouts.

Table 6.12 Dividend Regressions

Dividend payout	*(1)*	*(2)*	*(3)*	*(4)*	*(5)*	*(6)*
CGI	93.726	23.243	65.213	74.107	22.644	57.726
	(42.878)**	(38.593)	(49.781)	(40.993)*	(37.873)	(51.364)
Log (net sales)	10.488	8.238	7.306	10.272	8.865	7.308
	(2.987)***	(2.857)***	(3.570)**	(2.882)***	(2.827)***	(3.856)*
Financial leverage	4.418	−0.875	13.457			
	(2.785)	(2.301)	(4.590)***			
Debt to assets				−0.029	−0.227	0.683
				(0.251)	(0.248)	(0.354)*
Sales growth	0.401			0.335		
	(0.288)			(0.282)		
Income to sales		0.436			0.426	
		(0.215)**			(0.213)**	
Lagged income to sales			0.272			0.255
			(80.760)***			(87.564)***
Constant	−157.051	−70.945	−148.821	−125.754	−63.837	−147.088
	(49.259)***	(41.501)*	(59.755)**	(47.175)***	(41.207)	(62.708)**
Observations	109	113	84	112	116	85
Pseudo R^2	0.12	0.10	0.15	0.11	0.11	0.14

Source: Compiled by the authors.

Note: The table shows Tobit regressions, including industry-level dummies of the firms in the sample. Dividend measures have been regressed against standard controls and include the CGI as the interest variable. The dependent variable is the dividend payout. All variables are described in annex 6.2. Robust standard errors are shown in parentheses.

* significant at 10 percent

** significant at 5 percent

The results of the Tobit regressions in the table support this view: stronger firm-level governance practices are associated with higher dividend payouts that are statistically significant in two of the six specifications. To provide a magnitude of the effect, a two standard deviation increase in the CGI is reflected in an increase in the dividend payout ratio of between 5.4 and 21.7 percentage points, equivalent to a 36 to 144 percent increase in the mean ratio. As with figures 6.11 and 6.12, figures 6.13 and 6.14 show that the results are robust to potential concerns about outliers.

Overall, the results in tables 6.10–6.12 show a positive and significant impact of firm-level corporate governance measures on valuation, operating performance, and dividend payouts. In line with the evidence on other countries from other studies, these results support the view that firms that provide a better package of governance measures are more appreciated by the markets and distribute more profits to their shareholders.

Robustness checks

Although the regressions in the tables control for several variables capturing other firm characteristics that might be associated with higher valuations, as well as with better corporate governance, one may still be concerned about endogeneity. As indicated in most papers in the literature on firm-level governance, it is difficult to find a perfect set of instruments. Table 6.13

Figure 6.13 Partial Regression Plot of the CGI and the ROA

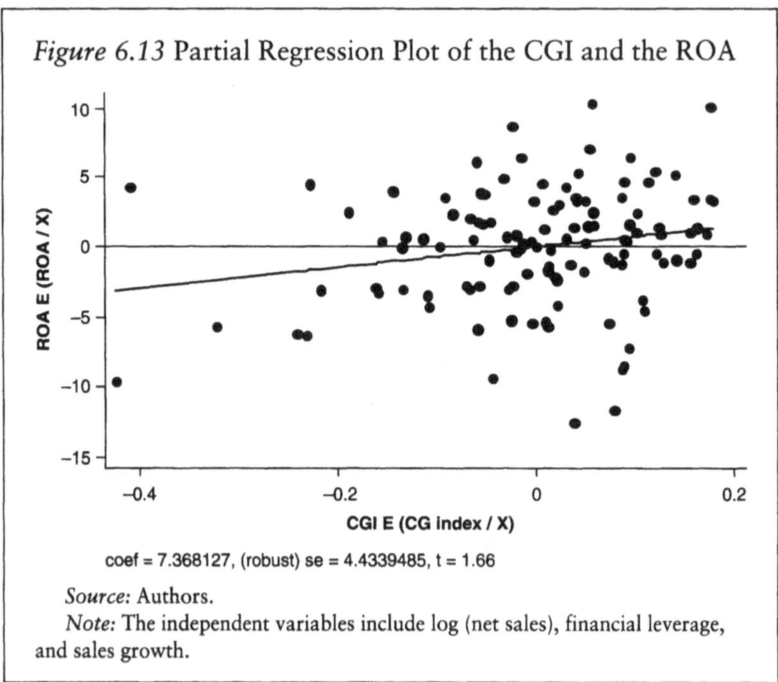

Source: Authors.
Note: The independent variables include log (net sales), financial leverage, and sales growth.

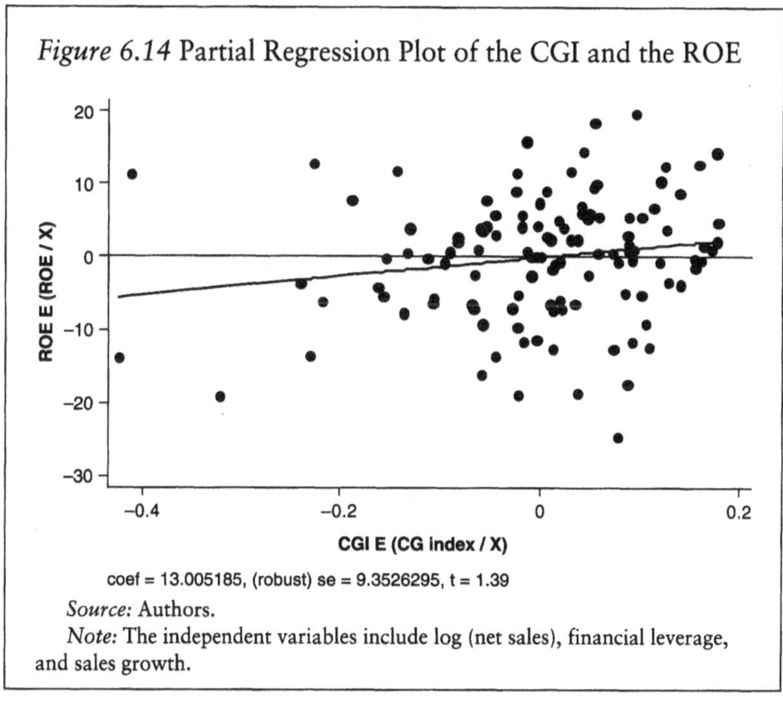

Figure 6.14 Partial Regression Plot of the CGI and the ROE

Source: Authors.

Note: The independent variables include log (net sales), financial leverage, and sales growth.

represents our attempt to deal with this issue through instrumental variables. The table uses three instruments that might arguably be said to have some exogenous variation on governance practices. The first instrument is a dummy for the location of the firm's headquarters. The distribution of headquarters in Mexico has certainly been impacted by the search for political connections. But since the adoption of NAFTA and even before, several firms and industrial sectors have chosen for other reasons to locate outside Mexico City in the north or in other regional capitals. About 60 percent of the firms in our sample are headquartered in Mexico City.

The second instrument is a size dummy for the top decile of firms in terms of assets. We have argued in the previous section that size is a potential determinant of corporate governance because, for example, bigger firms are more difficult to monitor or their higher visibility as top corporations makes them more prone to adopt better governance practices.

Our third instrument is a dummy equal to 1 for those firms that have equity issues and 0 for those that have public bonds on the market. Close to 16 percent of the firms in our sample are bond issuers alone. These firms are typically new entrants into the market and are familiar with a different world of scrutiny and market pressures than long-time stock issuers. We may only use this instrument on the subset of regressions of operating performance and dividend payments.

Table 6.13 Instrumental Variable Regressions

a. Valuation regressions	*Tobin's q*			*Price-to-book ratio*		
CGI	3.429	3.100	3.316	5.596	7.545	8.747
	(2.024)*	(1.851)*	(2.147)	(3.315)*	(4.749)	(6.760)
Log (net sales)	0.039	0.017	0.076	0.020	−0.012	0.009
	(0.030)	(0.034)	(0.038)*	(0.052)	(0.081)	(0.096)
Financial leverage	0.039	0.009	0.035	0.087	0.041	0.098
	(0.039)	(0.026)	(0.040)	(0.061)	(0.063)	(0.108)
Sales growth	−0.001			−0.002		
	(0.003)			(0.006)		
Income to sales		0.006			0.004	
		(0.003)*			(0.007)	
Lagged income to sales			0.004 (0.585)			0.004 (1.546)
Constant	−2.189	−1.727	−2.349	−3.995	−5.243	−6.520
	(1.679)	(1.428)	(1.838)	(2.749)	(3.654)	(5.592)
Observations	95	98	83	88	92	78
Number of industries	31	31	30	31	31	30
R^2 overall	0.09	0.12	0.18	0.04	0.03	0.03
F test	2.11	2.33	2.15	1.21	0.92	0.53

b. Performance regressions	*ROA*		*ROE*	
CGI	19.370	16.848	45.336	163.476
	(9.655)**	(162.571)	(20.438)**	(912.525)
Log (net sales)	0.272	0.501	0.811	1.816
	(0.327)	(0.574)	(0.644)	(4.377)
Financial leverage	−0.399 (0.230)*	−0.018 (1.176)	0.321 (0.460)	1.126 (6.383)
Sales growth	0.087		0.215	
	(0.028)***		(0.057)***	
Income to sales				
Lagged income to sales		0.228 (12.559)*		0.285 (83.352)

(continued)

Table 6.13 Instrumental Variable Regressions *(continued)*

b. Performance regressions	ROA		ROE	
Constant	−13.579	−15.437	−35.689	−142.795
	(7.257)*	(137.360)	(15.496)**	(779.293)
Observations	122	94	123	92
Number of industries	31	31	30	30
R^2 overall	0.11	0.26	0.08	0.05
F test	5.76	5.55	6.97	1.34

c. Dividend regressions	*Dividend payout*	
CGI	201.662	289.307
	(136.052)	(219.096)
Log (net sales)	9.514	7.288
	(2.820)***	(4.001)*
Financial leverage	3.705	0.783
	(3.218)	(0.008)
Sales growth	0.316	
	(0.316)	
Income to sales		0.466
		(0.506)
Constant	-239.088	-290.529
	(116.731)**	(0.084)***
Observations	109	113
Wald chi^2	28.36	22.61

Source: Compiled by the authors.

Note: The table shows instrumental variable regressions, including industry-level dummies of the firms in the sample. The dependent variables have been regressed against standard controls and include the instrumented CGI. All variables are described in annex 6.2. See the text for additional details. Robust standard errors are shown in parentheses.

* significant at 10 percent

** significant at 5 percent

*** significant at 1 percent

Although there are some plausible arguments for the use of these instruments, they are admittedly not perfect. Statistically, as shown in table 6.9, the correlation between these measures and our CGI is high and significant. Meanwhile, they show a mixed correlation pattern with valuation, operating performance, and dividend payout measures.

The results of the table, although weaker than the results of other tables, also show a positive pattern of association between our CGI and all outcome measures. In close to half the specifications, statistical significance is reached. The magnitude of the coefficients and their economic impact more than double for all measures.

The results in the previous sections should be encouraging for firms trying to improve their access to capital at lower cost. The evidence is much more on the side of positive effects than on lack of impact. The next section brakes down the CGI into its components to see if it may be worthwhile to concentrate on improving some measures.

The Impact of Various Areas of Firm-Level Governance

Given the positive effects of firm-level corporate governance variables, corporations seeking to benefit may wish to know if there are specific areas where they should be concentrating their efforts. This may be particularly important if one believes firms have only limited room to change structures that are likely to be sustained by a long tradition favoring strong insiders with large discretionary powers.

Table 6.14 highlights the correlations among our CGI, its components, and our outcome measures. To the initial eight components of the index, we have added an area called board of directors. This groups the initial three areas of the index that have to do with the board. It is clear from table 6.14, first, that all subindexes are highly and statistically significantly correlated with each other. The only exception is the relationship between the duties of board members, board composition, and the committee of evaluation and compensation. But, by and large, the data suggest that firms tending to perform well in one category also tend to perform well in the rest of the categories or subindexes. Second, although the first column shows that there is a significant positive correlation between the aggregate index of governance and valuation measures, this is not the case for most of the subindexes on their own. Only the subindexes of the audit committee and the finance and planning committee show an independent positive correlation with valuation measures. In the case of measures of performance and dividends, neither the aggregate nor the independent components achieve a significant positive correlation.

Table 6.15 takes a closer look at the same question in a multivariate setting. The table presents the same sort of regressions as the ones run in other tables, but we only show one of the specifications of controls across our five outcome measures.[33] Although all subindexes have a positive impact on valuation and performance, only a few are statistically significant on their own. There is no clear pattern on what works best. In terms of valuation, it seems that the impact of the audit committee and the finance committee are the most significant, along with the duties of board members. Meanwhile, the board of directors subindexes work best for operating performance and dividends in general.

Table 6.14 Correlation Matrix of Dependent Variables, the CGI, and the CGI Components

Variable	*CGI*	*Administrative board*	*Board composition*	*Board structure*	*Board operations*	*Board member duties*	*Evaluation and compensation committee*	*Audit committee*	*Finance and planning committee*	*Shareholders meetings*	*Tobin's q*	*Price-to-book ratio*	ROA	ROE
Administrative board	0.696													
	0.000													
Board composition	0.696	0.496												
	0.000	0.000												
Board structure	0.757	0.589	0.534											
	0.000	0.000	0.000											
Board operations	0.605	0.906	0.395	0.420										
	0.000	0.000	0.000	0.000										
Board member duties	0.304	0.188	0.099	0.138	0.197									
	0.000	0.021	0.228	0.091	0.016									
Compensation and evaluation committee	0.646	0.335	0.296	0.479	0.297	0.258								
	0.000	0.000	0.000	0.000	0.000	0.001								
Audit committee	0.825	0.518	0.490	0.539	0.451	0.161	0.396							
	0.000	0.000	0.000	0.000	0.000	0.049	0.000							
Finance and planning committee	0.601	0.306	0.176	0.313	0.230	0.098	0.567	0.399						
	0.000	0.000	0.032	0.000	0.005	0.235	0.000	0.000						

(continued)

Table 6.14 Correlation Matrix of Dependent Variables, the CGI, and the CGI Components *(continued)*

Variable	*CGI*	*Administrative board*	*Board composition*	*Board structure*	*Board operations*	*Board member duties*	*Evaluation and compensation committee*	*Audit committee*	*Finance and planning committee*	*Shareholders meetings*	*Tobin's q*	*Price-to-book ratio*	*ROA*	*ROE*
Shareholders meetings	0.697	0.397	0.413	0.506	0.363	0.197	0.381	0.499	0.269					
	0.000	0.000	0.000	0.000	0.000	0.016	0.000	0.000	0.001					
Tobin's q	0.231	0.057	0.131	0.033	0.071	0.229	0.081	0.177	0.191	0.145				
	0.016	0.560	0.176	0.733	0.465	0.017	0.403	0.067	0.048	0.133				
Price-to-book ratio	0.183	0.118	0.050	0.018	0.071	0.145	0.138	0.156	0.165	0.136	0.867			
	0.065	0.236	0.620	0.856	0.477	0.146	0.168	0.117	0.098	0.173	0.000			
ROA	0.088	0.099	0.026	0.129	0.108	0.034	0.109	0.053	0.065	-0.004	0.414	0.402		
	0.303	0.248	0.761	0.130	0.207	0.694	0.202	0.535	0.444	0.960	0.000	0.000		
ROE	-0.014	0.032	-0.117	-0.042	0.079	0.037	0.101	-0.037	0.084	-0.051	0.453	0.365	0.860	
	0.876	0.717	0.176	0.628	0.360	0.667	0.246	0.668	0.331	0.560	0.000	0.000	0.000	
Dividend payout	0.102	0.007	0.158	0.105	0.063	0.062	0.032	0.080	-0.040	0.059	0.271	0.233	0.339	0.299
	0.266	0.940	0.085	0.254	0.497	0.503	0.730	0.388	0.665	0.523	0.008	0.029	0.000	0.002

Source: Compiled by the authors.

Note: The table presents the pairwise correlation matrix of the dependent variables used in the regressions, the CGI, and the CGI components. The variables are described in annex 6.2. P-values are shown below the correlation coefficients.

Table 6.15 Regressions for Corporate Governance Subindexes

Variable	*Tobin's q*	*Price-to-book ratio*	*ROA*	*ROE*	*Dividend payout*
CGI	1.010	1.175	7.368	13.005	93.726
	(0.432)**	(0.663)*	(4.434)*	(9.353)	(42.878)**
Administrative board	0.605	1.619	8.698	17.580	53.442
Aggregate (all 3 below)	(0.575)	(0.868)*	(4.160)**	(9.527)*	(43.745)
Board composition	0.358	0.360	3.770	5.430	76.031
	(0.246)	(0.405)	(3.172)	(5.995)	(28.685)***
Board structure	−0.137	−0.385	4.747	8.535	23.797
	(0.216)	(0.340)	(2.197)**	(4.782)*	(20.794)
Board operation	0.599	1.029	8.528	17.021	64.080
	(0.382)	(0.630)	(3.584)**	(8.230)**	(37.694)*
Board member duties	0.780	0.875	4.863	6.662	91.951
	(0.418)*	(0.610)	(5.391)	(10.458)	(51.153)*
Compensation and evaluation committee	0.120	0.167	2.131	5.009	22.506
	(0.090)	(0.156)	(1.360)	(2.868)*	(12.677)*
Audit committee	0.922	0.664	1.814	0.440	47.971
	(0.458)**	(0.737)	(4.455)	(9.027)	(38.369)
Finance and planning committee	0.183	0.280	1.396	2.324	8.289
	(0.086)*	(0.125)**	(1.216)	(2.418)	(10.505)
Shareholders meetings	0.414	0.714	2.555	7.930	33.978
	(0.259)	(0.467)	(3.362)	(6.415)	(29.647)

Source: Compiled by the authors.

Note: The table shows regression coefficients taken from industry fixed effects models and controlling by log (net sales), financial leverage, and sales growth. For the case of the dividend payout ratio, a Tobit model has been run controlling for all the above and industrial sector dummies. Robust standard errors are shown in parentheses.

* significant at 10 percent

** significant at 5 percent

*** significant at 1 percent

Reforms for Deepening Financial Markets

The previous sections have two broad implications. First, they show that the most well-developed financial markets are protected by regulations and laws. However, they do not tell us what the best form of regulation is, which may well include self-regulation, as well as government regulation.

Still, totally unregulated financial markets do not work well, presumably because they allow corporate insiders to expropriate too much from outside investors. One dramatic illustration of this phenomenon is the evidence presented on cross-listing for Mexican firms in figures 6.5 and 6.7: the most sought-after place for listing by Mexican publicly held companies happens to be New York—a heavily regulated exchange in terms of disclosure and the protection of minority shareholders—rather than Mexico City.

Second, better firm-level corporate governance practices within Mexico have real benefits in terms of valuation, performance, and greater disgorgement of profits. The analysis in the previous pages suggests that the objective of both kinds of measures should be to protect the rights of outside investors. As the empirical research shows, a result of such changes would be to expand a country's financial markets, facilitate the external financing of new firms, move away from concentrated ownership, and improve the efficiency of investment allocations.

What may be done to achieve this goal, and what are the obstacles? This analysis raises a number of questions for firm-level and countrywide legal reforms. How might a policy maker try to improve markets? What might a firm do in a poor legal environment? We address these questions below.

Improvements in investor protection would require rather radical changes in the legal system or unilateral internal company-level governance changes. Securities and company laws would need to be amended, and the regulatory and judicial mechanisms to enforce investor rights would need to be radically enhanced. But effective legal reform in Mexico, as in many other countries, faces tremendous political obstacles. Perhaps the most important barriers arise from controlling shareholders at the top of large corporations. Under the status quo, firms may finance their own investment projects through internal cash flows, as well as relationships with captive banks or banks that are closely tied to the firms. But this opposition may also be supported by opposition from labor interests, which are also receiving rents through the existing arrangements.

Further Legal Reform

As the evidence in this chapter demonstrates, the law and its enforcement are a good predictor of the development of capital markets. Although the market-based mechanisms outlined above may help foster the growth of external funding, they have limitations. Firms might adopt improved protections through nonstandard contracts, but, when violations occur, enforcement of the contracts may be more difficult in weak legal systems. For these reasons, additional countrywide reforms are necessary. The strategy for reform should not aim at creating an ideal set of rules and then seeking to establish enforcement, but rather at enacting rules that may be enforced within existing structures.

Mexico's success in passing a new securities law that substantially increases the level of disclosure and improves corporate governance requirements for listed firms should be complemented through a revamping of the current law on limited companies (ley de sociedades anónimas) of the commercial code. In some instances, this might require refining existing principles to make them more applicable. In other cases, it might be necessary legally to recognize rights that are easily enforceable. The reform of Mexican corporation law may not need to follow the U.S.-type mechanisms that rely heavily on the judicial system by means of derivative or class-action suits. Instead, it might be better for Mexico if reformers respond to the characteristics of the legal system and apply more automatic principles.

Judicial reform is another key ingredient in this agenda. Without a serious restructuring of the rules of civil procedure, among other items, the inefficient judicial system will mean that all companies will be at a significant disadvantage in facing international competition for resources. Judicial reform along the lines suggested in López-de-Silanes (2002) should be pushed forward.

One government measure that may be more politically feasible to implement through Congress is the improvement of corporate governance practices among firms in which the state participates. Despite widespread privatization in Mexico, there are still close to 150 state-controlled enterprises. These firms might set an example for private firms by adopting better investor protections. Most of the state-run firms in Mexico are large public utilities or are involved in natural resources. External funding is at least as important for them as it is for private firms because of the substantial reduction in government expenditures. These firms require higher levels of investment to meet the demand from the growing private sector. It is therefore imperative for them to find mechanisms to fund their projects through capital markets. The reform of corporate charters and improved investor protection would also alleviate the government budget constraint. The adoption of the code of best practices outlined above might provide a quick and easy way for these state-controlled firms substantially to transform themselves and secure access to funds at better rates.

Market-Based Mechanisms

Slow and difficult as it is, real legal reform is needed in Mexico. But it is necessary to complement legal reform through market-based mechanisms that push firms to improve their firm-level governance practices unilaterally. The evidence on the benefits of firm-level measures corroborates the importance of supporting the establishment of such mechanisms.

Market-based mechanisms should be designed to act as temporary substitutes for or a complement to the reform of laws and regulations. Like the corporate governance code, these measures should be public measures and should facilitate competition and ratings, making it possible for the firms to adhere to them to access capital at lower cost. At the same time, such mechanisms should also have the objective of enhancing awareness and extending the influence of the concept of better corporate governance practices. The code is a substantial step forward in the creation of a culture of investor protection because it allows investors to distinguish firms that do have effective corporate governance mechanisms in place and to reward firms that offer better protection by assigning to them higher valuation multiples or lower costs for capital.

Enhanced disclosure requirements may not be sufficient to push firms to engage in unilateral changes. An additional, desirable complementary measure would involve restricting institutional investors to investment in companies that meet minimum corporate governance standards. These standards may be determined in relation to the code of best practices or through an independent best practice commission, for example. This recommendation is based purely on sensible reasons, as well as on the need to create an incentive for firms to support better investor protection. A similar idea has been implemented in Chile, another civil law country in the French tradition. In Chile, a commission has drafted a long list of minimum requirements that issuers of securities must meet before they may receive investment by institutional investors.

The adoption of market-based measures would constitute a useful first step in Mexico because this would facilitate the unilateral movement for better firm-level changes in governance and create a precedent for more legal reform.

Conclusions and Policy Implications

In this chapter, we have provided an analysis of the evolution of capital markets, laws governing investor protection, the quality of enforcement of these laws, and their effect on the availability of external financing in Mexico over the last two decades.

Our review of the country-level evidence shows that the legal environment faced by corporations in Mexico has improved, though it still poses serious problems for the access to capital by corporations. After a series of financial crises and corporate governance scandals around the world, several countries have engaged in governance reforms and raised the bar of international best practices. In these conditions, Mexican firms have started to act unilaterally by seeking capital abroad through cross-listings that may bond them to a more protective legal environment, selling part of their nonessential assets to foreigners, and looking for alliances through foreign capital participation. Additionally, the introduction of the code of best corporate governance practices in 1999 has allowed firms to adopt better firm-level governance measures unilaterally.

The main contribution of this report is to present a new data set on corporate governance practices at the firm-level in Mexico and test the impact of these practices on valuation, operating performance, and dividend payout ratios. The results at the firm-level demonstrate that the firms that have started to use the available differentiating tools to improve their corporate governance are recognized by the market through lower costs for capital even as they are able to provide better returns to their investors.

Based on Mexico's evolution and a cross-country comparison, the last section of the chapter has outlined the possibilities of legal reform and the use of additional market-based incentives to push individual firms to increase investor protection and thus deepen Mexican financial markets.

Overall, the country- and firm-level evidence on Mexico supports the growing literature arguing that only through the development of efficient institutions and the security of investors may firms secure the foundations for sustainable long-run access to finance.

Annex 6.1 Variable Definitions

Variable	*Description*	*Sources*
Legal origin	Identifies the legal origin of the company law or commercial code of each country. Equals 1 if the origin is common law, 2 if the origin is the French commercial code, and 3 if the origin is the German commercial code.	La Porta et al. (1998), collected from "Foreign Law Encyclopedia of Commercial Laws of the World"
Proxy by mail allowed	Equals 1 if the company law or commercial code allows shareholders to mail their proxy vote to the firm and 0 otherwise.	La Porta et al. (1998)
Vote by mail	Equals 1 if the law explicitly mandates or sets as a default rule that: (1) proxy solicitations paid by the company include a proxy form allowing shareholders to vote on the items on the agenda, (2) a proxy form to vote on the items on the agenda accompanies the notice of the meeting, or (3) shareholders vote by mail on the items on the agenda (that is, a postal ballot); 0 otherwise.	Djankov et al. (2006)
Shares not blocked	Equals 1 if the company law or commercial code does not allow firms to require that shareholders deposit their shares prior to a general shareholders meeting, thus preventing them from selling those shares for a number of days and 0 otherwise.	La Porta et al. (1998)
Shares not deposited	Equals 1 if the law does not require or explicitly permit companies to require shareholders to deposit with the company or another firm any of their shares prior to a general shareholders meeting.	Djankov et al. (2006)
Cumulative voting or proportional representation	Equals 1 if the company law or commercial code allows shareholders to cast all their votes for one candidate standing for election to the board of directors (cumulative voting) or if the company law or commercial code allows a mechanism of proportional representation in the board by which minority interests may name a proportional number of directors to the board; 0 otherwise.	La Porta et al. (1998); Djankov et al. (2006)

(continued)

Annex 6.1 Variable Definitions (*continued*)

Variable	*Description*	*Sources*
Capital to call a meeting	The minimum percentage of ownership of share capital that entitles a shareholder to call for an extraordinary shareholders meeting; it ranges from 1 to 33 percent.	La Porta et al. (1998); Djankov et al. (2006)
Preemptive rights	Equals 1 if the company law or commercial code grants shareholders the first opportunity to buy new issues of stock and if this right may only be waved by a vote of shareholders; 0 otherwise.	La Porta et al. (1998); Djankov et al. (2006)
Oppressed minorities	Equals 1 if the company law or commercial code grants minority shareholders either a judicial venue to challenge the decisions of management or of the assembly or the right to step out of the company by requiring the company to purchase their shares when they object to certain fundamental changes, such as mergers, asset dispositions, and changes in the articles of incorporation. The variable equals 0 otherwise. Minority shareholders are defined as those shareholders who own 10 percent of share capital or less.	La Porta et al. (1998); Djankov et al. (2006)
Antidirectors rights index	An index aggregating the shareholder rights that we have labeled antidirector rights. The index is formed by adding 1 if: (1) the country allows shareholders to mail their proxy vote to the firm, (2) shareholders are not required to deposit their shares prior to the general shareholders meeting, (3) cumulative voting or proportional representation of minorities on the board of directors is allowed, (4) an oppressed minorities mechanism is in place, (5) the minimum percentage of share capital that entitles a shareholder to call for an extraordinary shareholders meeting is less than or equal to 10 percent (the sample median), or (6) shareholders have preemptive rights that may only be waved by a vote of shareholders. The index ranges from 0 to 6.	La Porta et al. (1998); Djankov et al. (2006)

(continued)

Annex 6.1 Variable Definitions (*continued*)

Variable	*Description*	*Sources*
Disclosure requirements index	The index of disclosure equals the arithmetic mean of (1) prospect, (2) compensation, (3) shareholders, (4) insider ownership, (5) contracts irregular, (6) and transactions.	La Porta, López-de-Silanes, and Shleifer (2006)
Liability standards index	The index of liability standards equals the arithmetic mean of (1) liability standard for the issuer and its directors, (2) liability standard for distributors, and (3) liability standard for accountants.	La Porta, López-de-Silanes, and Shleifer (2006)
Public enforcement index	The index of public enforcement equals the arithmetic mean of (1) supervisor characteristics index, (2) rule-making power index, (3) investigative powers index, (4) orders index, and (5) criminal index.	La Porta, López-de-Silanes, and Shleifer (2006)
Ex ante private control of self-dealing	Index of ex ante control of self-dealing transactions: average of approval by disinterested shareholders and ex ante disclosure.	Djankov et al. (2006)
Ex post private control of self-dealing	Index of ex post control over self-dealing transactions: average of disclosure in periodic filings and ease of proving wrongdoing. Ranges from 0 to 1.	Djankov et al. (2006)
Anti–self-dealing index	Average of ex ante and ex post private control of self-dealing.	Djankov et al. (2006)
Public enforcement of self-dealing	Index of public enforcement. Ranges from 0 to 1. One-quarter point when each of the following sanctions is available: (1) fines for the approving body, (2) jail sentences for the approving body, (3) fines for Mr. James, and (4) jail sentence for Mr. James.	Djankov et al. (2006)

(*continued*)

Annex 6.1 Variable Definitions (*continued*)

Variable	*Description*	*Sources*
Efficiency of judicial system	Assessment of the efficiency and integrity of the legal environment as it affects business, particularly foreign firms, produced by the country-risk rating agency Business International Corporation. It may be taken to represent investors' assessments of conditions in the country in question. Average between 1980 and 1983. Scale from 0 to 10; lower scores mean lower efficiency levels. "Foreign Law Encyclopedia of Commercial Laws of the World."	La Porta et al. (1998)
Rule of law	Assessment of the law and order tradition in the country produced by the country-risk rating agency International Country Risk. Average of the months of April and October of the monthly index between 1982 and 1995. Scale from 0 to 10, with lower scores for less tradition for law and order. (We have changed the scale from its original range of 0 to 6.)	La Porta et al. (1998)
Corruption	International Country Risk's assessment of the corruption in government. Lower scores indicate that high government officials are likely to demand special payments and that illegal payments are generally expected throughout lower levels of government in the form of bribes connected with import and export licenses, exchange controls, tax assessment, policy protection, or loans. Average of the months of April and October of the monthly index between 1982 and 1995. Scale from 0 to 10, with lower scores for higher levels of corruption. (We have changed the scale from its original range of 0 to 6.)	La Porta et al. (1998)
Accounting standards	Index created by examining and rating the 1990 annual reports of companies according to their inclusion or omission of 90 items. These items fall into seven categories (general information, income statements, balance sheets, fund flow statements, accounting standards, stock data, and special items). A minimum of three companies in each country have been studied. The companies represent a cross-section of various industry groups, whereby industrial companies numbered 70 percent, while financial companies represented the remaining 30 percent.	La Porta et al. (1998)

(continued)

Annex 6.1 Variable Definitions (*continued*)

Variable	*Description*	*Sources*
Court formalism to collect a bounced check	The index measures substantive and procedural statutory intervention in judicial cases at lower-level civil trial courts and is formed by adding up the following indexes: (1) professionals versus laymen, (2) written versus oral elements, (3) legal justification, (4) statutory regulation of evidence, (5) control of superior review, (6) engagement formalities, and (7) independent procedural actions. The index ranges from 0 to 7, where 7 means a higher level of control or intervention in the judicial process.	Djankov et al. (2003)
Stock market capitalization to GDP	Ratio of the market capitalization (also known as market value, which is the share price, times the number of shares outstanding) of listed domestic companies (the domestically incorporated companies listed on the country's stock exchanges at the end of the year) divided by GDP (in millions).	La Porta et al. (1998) for table 6.6; World Bank (2005) for figure 6.1
Listed firms per million population	The ratio of the listed domestic companies are the domestically incorporated companies listed on the country's stock exchanges at the end of the year—this does not include investment companies, mutual funds, or other collective investment vehicles—to its population (in millions).	La Porta et al. (1998) for table 6.6; World Bank (2005) for figure 6.2
IPOs to GDP	Average of the ratio of the equity issued by newly listed firms in a given country (in thousands) to its gross domestic product (in millions) over the period 1996–2000.	La Porta, López-de-Silanes, and Shleifer (2006)
Block premium	The block premium is computed taking the difference between the price per share paid for the control block and the exchange price two days after the announcement of the control transaction, divided by the exchange price and multiplied by the ratio of the proportion of cash flow rights represented in the controlling block. We use the country sample median.	La Porta, López-de-Silanes, and Shleifer (2006), taken from Dyck and Zingales (2004)

(*continued*)

Annex 6.1 Variable Definitions (*continued*)

Variable	*Description*	*Sources*
Ownership concentration	Average percentage of common shares not owned by the top three shareholders in the ten largest nonfinancial, privately owned domestic firms in a given country. A firm is considered privately owned if the state is not a known shareholder.	La Porta, López-de-Silanes, and Shleifer (1999); Hartland-Peel (1996) for Kenya; Bloomberg and various annual reports for Ecuador, Jordan, and Uruguay
Trading volume to GDP	Total trading volume divided by the country's GDP (expressed in 2001 US$) of a certain country in a given year.	World Bank (2005)
Trading volume to market capitalization	Total trading volume, divided by the country's total market capitalization (expressed in 2001 US$) of a certain country in a given year.	Standard & Poor's (2005); World Bank (2005)
Number of public offerings in Mexico	Number of total public offerings registered in the Mexican Stock Exchange.	World Bank (2005); Martinez and Werner (2002); Mexican Stock Exchange
Mexican firms issuing equity abroad	Total number of Mexican firms issuing equities in external financial markets.	Martinez and Werner (2002)

(*continued*)

Annex 6.1 Variable Definitions (*continued*)

Variable	*Description*	*Sources*
New Mexican firms issuing equity through ADRs	Number of Mexican firms incorporated each year in U.S. stock markets through the issuance of ADRs.	Bank of New York (2005)
Firms listed in U.S. markets relative to firms listed in domestic markets	Quotient of the number of firms listed in U.S. markets and the number of firms listed in domestic markets.	Bank of New York (2005); Standard & Poor's (2005)
Firms with ADRs in the United States relative to firms listed in domestic markets	Quotient of the number of firms with ADRs in the United States and the number of firms listed in domestic markets.	Bank of New York (2005); Standard & Poor's (2005)
Price-to-book value of equity	Quotient between the market value of equity and the book value of equity.	Standard and Poor's (2005)
Dividend yield	Dividend yield measured in percentage points.	Standard and Poor's (2005)

Source: Compiled by the authors.

Note: This table describes the variables collected for the 49 countries included in the chapter. The first column gives the name of the variable. The second column describes the variable and gives the range of possible values. The third column provides the sources from which the variable has been collected.

Annex 6.2 Variable Definitions

Tobin's q	Defined as the market value of equity (actual shares outstanding, times the closing price of the period), plus total liabilities divided by total assets.
Price to book ratio	Ratio between the market value of equity and the book value of equity.
ROA	Ratio between net income and total assets. Expressed in percentage points.
ROE	Ratio between net income and the book value of equity (total assets, minus total liabilities). Expressed in percentage points.
Dividend payout	Ratio between the dividends paid and net income. Expressed in percentage points.
Log (net sales)	Natural logarithm of net sales, expressed in US$ millions.
Financial leverage	Ratio between the total assets and the book value of equity.
Debt to assets	Ratio between total debt and total assets. Expressed in percentage points.
Sales growth	Percentage change in net sales.
Income to sales	Ratio between net income and net sales. Expressed in percentage points.
Lagged income to sales	Mean of the ratio between net income and net sales for the period 1997–2001. Expressed in percentage points.
Size (top 10%)	Dummy variable that takes the value of 1 if the company is in the top 10% of the total asset distribution and 0 otherwise.
Located in Mexico City	Dummy variable that takes the value of 1 if the company is legally located in Mexico City and 0 otherwise.
Equity	Dummy variable that takes the value of 1 if the company has an equity trading in the stock market and 0 if it has bonds trading.
CGI	Mean of the CGI for the years 2003 and 2004. This variable is between 0 and 1 and represents the accomplishment of the corporate governance principles stated in the questionnaire that all listed companies must present to the Mexican Stock Exchange every year.

Source: Compiled by the authors.

Note: This table describes the variables used in the empirical section of the paper. All variables have been taken from each firm's annual financial report, the corporate governance code of best practices, and each firm's general statement. All reports are available in the Mexican Stock Exchange Web site, http://www.bmv.com.mx/.

Notes

1. See Claessens et al. (2002); Kumar, Rajan, and Zingales (2001); La Porta, López-de-Silanes, and Shleifer (1999, 2006); La Porta et al. (1997, 1998, 2000a, 2000b, 2002); Wurgler (2000).

2. See Modigliani and Miller (1958).

3. See La Porta et al. (1997, 1998); La Porta, López-de-Silanes, and Shleifer (2006).

4. Heyman (1998, 1999) and Martinez and Werner (2002) present good accounts and descriptions of the evolution of the stock market in recent years.

5. See Martinez and Werner (2002).

6. This is an extrapolation of the authors from the 1991–2001 data in Martinez and Werner (2002).

7. See Grossman and Hart (1986); Harris and Raviv (1988).

8. Babatz (1998) has more examples.

9. This column shows numbers for a sample of 109 countries. The data are found in Djankov et al. (2003).

10. The index of accounting standards is provided by the Center for International Financial Analysis and Research based on an examination of company reports of firms in each country. It is available for 41 countries in the sample.

11. See Familiar Calderón (2003).

12. This would arise from a structure such as the one described in Grossman and Hart (1980).

13. "Reglas Generales Aplicables a las Adqusiciones de Valores que deban ser Reveladas y de Ofertas Publicas de Compra de Valores" (ruling of the National Banking and Stock Market Commission in April 2002).

14. The La Porta, López-de-Silanes, and Shleifer (2006) sample is the 49 countries with the largest stock market capitalization in 1993 (the original sample in La Porta et al. 1998).

15. Ownership concentration per se may be efficient because, if large-scale shareholders are monitoring management, then the agency problem between management and shareholders is reduced; see Jensen and Meckling (1976) and Shleifer and Vishny (1986).

16. To measure ownership concentration, a 1998 study assembled data on the 10 largest publicly traded, nonfinancial private domestic firms in each of 45 countries. For each country, the study measured ownership concentration as the median percentage owned by the three largest shareholders in each firm; see La Porta et al. (1998).

17. For a detailed account of these reforms, see Gonzalez-Anaya and Maruffo (2001).

18. Pension funds were not able to invest in equity financing until 2003.

19. The differences among countries described in this section are supported by regression results on all of these outcome variables, which include the indexes of investor protection, legal enforcement, and control for country characteristics.

20. Siegel (2005) offers evidence that, in the case of Mexico, the bonding between a good reputation and the use of ADRs may be more important than the legal aspects. Some Mexican issuers have exploited the weak legal enforcement by the Securities and Exchange Commission in the United States against cross-listings.

21. See La Porta et al. (2000a, 2000b); Daines (2001).

22. See Gompers, Ishii, and Metrick (2003); Klapper and Love (2002); Black, Jang, and Kim (2006a).

23. See Demsetz and Lehn (1985); Morck, Shleifer, and Vishny (1988); La Porta et al. (2002); Gompers, Ishii, and Metrick (2003).

24. As in other papers, such as Klapper and Love (2002), we do not use returns as a proxy for performance, given the volatility of returns, particularly in emerging markets.

25. The number of companies used here is not the 150 companies in our sample because the commission data include all firms with publicly listed securities in a given year. For example, in 2004, 159 firms had listed securities.

26. See Gompers, Ishii, and Metrick (2003); Klapper and Love (2002).

27. See Jensen (1986).

28. See Klapper and Love (2002).

29. We have also tried other financial control measures, and these produced the same sort of results.

30. In alternative specifications, we have also used the lagged CGI. Results are also robust for this alternative. We are currently working on collecting the data of the CGI for the previous three years of information and plan to expand the specifications into a panel across the five years of data.

31. See Gompers, Ishii, and Metrick (2003), Klapper and Love (2002), and other papers cited in this chapter.

32. We have not used returns as a measure of performance due to the high volatility of this variable in emerging markets, including Mexico. See elsewhere above.

33. Similar results are obtained for the other specifications.

References

American Bar Association. 1989. *Multinational Commercial Insolvency*. Chicago: American Bar Association.

———. 1993. *Multinational Commercial Insolvency*. Chicago: American Bar Association.

Babatz, G., 1998. "Agency Problems, Ownership Structure, and Voting Structure under Law Corporate Governance Rules: The Case of Mexico." PhD Thesis, Harvard University, Cambridge, MA.

Bank of New York. 2005. "Information on American Depositary Receipts." Bank of New York, http://www.bankofny.com/.

Beck, T., R. Levine, and N. Loayza. 2000. "Finance and the Sources of Growth." *Journal of Financial Economics* 58 (1–2): 261–300.

Berglöf, E., and E.-L. von Thadden. 1999. "The Changing Corporate Governance Paradigm: Implications for Transition and Developing Countries." Paper presented at the annual World Bank Conference on Development Economics, Washington, DC, April 28–30.

Black, B. S., H. Jang, and W. Kim. 2006a. "Does Corporate Governance Predict Firms' Market Values?: Evidence from Korea." *Journal of Law, Economics and Organization* 22 (2): 366–413.

———. 2006b. "Predicting Firms' Corporate Governance Choices: Evidence from Korea." *Journal of Corporate Finance* 12 (3): 660–91.

Carlin, W., and C. Mayer. 1999. "Finance, Investment, and Growth." Unpublished working paper, University College, London.

Claessens, S., S. Djankov, J. P. H. Fan, and L. H. P. Lang. 2002. "Disentangling the Incentive and Entrenchment Effects of Large Shareholdings." *Journal of Finance* 57 (6): 2741–71.

Coffee, J. C., Jr. 1999. "The Future as History: The Prospects for Global Convergence in Corporate Governance and Its Implications." *Northwestern University Law Review* 93 (3): 631–707.

Comisión Nacional Bancaria y de Valores de México. Various. "Sanctions Imposed on Market Participants." http://www.cnbv.gob.mx.

Daines, R. 2001. "Does Delaware Law Improve Firm Value?" *Journal of Financial Economics* 62 (3): 525–58.

Davis Arzac, J. 2004. "Innovando para un major mercado." Paper presented at the "XV Annual Stock Market Convention," Mexico City, November 15.

Demirgüç-Kunt, A., and V. Maksimovic. 1998. "Law, Finance, and Firm Growth." *Journal of Finance* 53 (6): 2107–37.

Demsetz, H., and K. Lehn. 1985. "The Structure of Corporate Ownership: Causes and Consequences." *Journal of Political Economy* 93 (6): 1155–77.

Diamond, D. W. 1989. "Reputation Acquisition in Debt Markets." *Journal of Political Economy* 97 (4): 828–62.

———. 1991. "Debt Maturity Structure and Liquidity Risk." *Quarterly Journal of Economics* 106 (3): 709–37.

Djankov, S., R. La Porta, F. López-de-Silanes, and A. Shleifer. 2003. "Courts." *Quarterly Journal of Economics* 118 (2): 453–517.

———. 2006. "The Law and Economics of Self-Dealing." Unpublished working paper, November 13, World Bank, Washington, DC.

Domowitz, I., J. Glen, and A. Madhavan. 1998. "International Cross-Listing and Order Flow Migration: Evidence from an Emerging Market." *Journal of Finance* 53 (6): 2001–27.

Dyck, A., and L. Zingales. 2004. "Private Benefits of Control: An International Comparison." *Journal of Finance* 59 (2): 537–600.

Easterbrook, F., and D. Fischel. 1991. *The Economic Structure of Corporate Law.* Cambridge, MA: Harvard University Press.

Familiar Calderón, J. 2003. "Gobierno Corporativo en México: Evolución, Avances, y Retos." Paper presented to the Inter-American Development Bank, "Second Meeting of the Regional Forum on Corporate Governance and the Financial Sector," Washington, DC, November 14.

Glaeser, E., S. Johnson, and A. Shleifer. 2000. "Coase Versus the Coasians." Unpublished working paper, Harvard University, Cambridge, MA.

Gomes, A. 1996. "The Dynamics of Stock Prices, Manager Ownership, and Private Benefits of Control." Unpublished working paper, Harvard University, Cambridge, MA.

Gompers, P. A., J. L. Ishii, and A. Metrick. 2003 "Corporate Governance and Equity Prices." *Quarterly Journal of Economics* 118 (1): 107–55.

Gonzalez-Anaya, J. A., and G. M. Maruffo. 2001. "Financial Market Performance in Mexico." Paper prepared for the Stanford Center for International Development "Mexican Credit Conference," Stanford University, Stanford, CA, October 5–6.

Grossman, S. J., and O. D. Hart. 1980. "Takeover Bids, the Free-Rider Problem, and the Theory of the Corporation." *Bell Journal of Economics* 11 (1): 42–64.

———. 1986. "The Costs and Benefits of Ownership: A Theory of Vertical and Lateral Integration." *Journal of Political Economy* 94 (4): 691–719.

Harris, M., and A. Raviv. 1988. "Corporate Governance: Voting Rights and Majority Rules." *Journal of Financial Economics* 20 (1–2): 203–35.

Hart, O. D. 1999. "Different Approaches to Bankruptcy." Unpublished working paper, Harvard University, Cambridge, MA.

Hart, O. D., R. La Porta, F. López-de-Silanes, and J. Moore. 1997. "A New Bankruptcy Procedure That Uses Multiple Auctions." *European Economic Review* 41 (3–5): 461–73.

Hartland-Peel, C. 1996. *African Equities: A Guide to Markets and Companies.* London: Euromoney Publications.

Hellwig, M. 1999. "On the Economics and Politics of Corporate Finance and Corporate Control." Unpublished working paper, University of Mannheim, Mannheim.

Heyman, T. 1998. *Inversion en la Globalizacion: Analisis y Administración de las nuevas inversions Mexicanas.* Mexico City: Editorial Milenio.

———. 1999. *Investing in Mexico: Mexican Economy and Financial Markets.* Mexico City: Editorial Milenio.

Hirschman, A. 1963. *Journeys toward Progress.* New York: Twentieth Century Fund.

IRRC (Investor Responsibility Research Center). 1994. *Proxy Voting Guide.* Washington, DC: Global Shareholder Service, Investor Responsibility Research Center.

ISS (Institutional Shareholder Services, Inc.). 1994. *Proxy Voting Guidelines.* Washington, DC: Global Proxy Services, Institutional Shareholder Services, Inc.

Jensen, M. C. 1986. "Agency Costs of Free Cash Flow, Corporate Finance, and Takeovers." *American Economic Review* 76 (2): 323–29.

Jensen, M. C., and W. H. Meckling. 1976. "Theory of the Firm: Managerial Behavior, Agency Costs, and Ownership Structure." *Journal of Financial Economics* 3 (4): 305–60.

Johnson, S. 1999. "Does Investor Protection Matter?: Evidence from Germany's Neuer Markt." Unpublished working paper, Massachusetts Institute of Technology, Cambridge, MA.

Johnson, S., P. Boone, A. Breach, and E. Friedman. 2000. "Corporate Governance in the Asian Financial Crisis." *Journal of Financial Economics* 58 (1–2): 141–86.

King, R., and R. Levine. 1993. "Finance and Growth: Schumpeter Might Be Right." *Quarterly Journal of Economics* 108 (3): 717–38.

Klapper, L. F., and I. Love. 2002. "Corporate Governance, Investor Protection, and Performance in Emerging Markets." Policy Research Working Paper 2818, World Bank, Washington, DC.

Kumar, K. B., R. G. Rajan, and L. Zingales. 2001. "What Determines Firm Size?" CEPR Discussion Paper 2211, Center for Economic Policy Research, London.

La Porta, R., F. López-de-Silanes, and A. Shleifer. 1999. "Corporate Ownership around the World." *Journal of Finance* 54 (2): 471–517.

———. 2006. "What Works in Securities Laws?" *Journal of Finance* 61 (1): 1–32.

La Porta, R., F. López-de-Silanes, A. Shleifer, and R. W. Vishny. 1997. "Legal Determinants of External Finance." *Journal of Finance* 52 (3): 1131–50.

———. 1998. "Law and Finance." *Journal of Political Economy* 106 (6): 1113–55.

———. 2000a. "Agency Problems and Dividend Policies around the World." *Journal of Finance* 55 (1): 1–33.

———. 2000b. "Investor Protection and Corporate Governance." *Journal of Financial Economics* 58 (1–2): 3–27.

———. 2002. "Investor Protection and Corporate Valuation." *Journal of Finance* 57 (3): 1147–70.

Levine, R. 1999. "Law, Finance, and Economic Growth." *Journal of Financial Intermediation* 8 (1–2): 8–35.

Levine, R., and S. Zervos. 1998. "Stock Markets, Banks, and Economic Growth." *American Economic Review* 88 (3): 537–58.

Lins, K. V., D. Strickland, and M. Zenner. 2005. "Do Non-US Firms Issue Equity on US Stock Exchanges to Relax Capital Constraints?" *Journal of Financial and Quantitative Analysis* 40 (1): 109–33.

López-de-Silanes, F. 2002. "The Politics of Legal Reform." *Economia* 2 (2): 91–152.

Martinez, L., and A. Werner. 2002. "Capital Markets in Mexico: Recent Developments and Future Challenges." Paper prepared for the Banco de México Seminar on "Estabilidad Macroeconomica, Mercados Financieros, y Desarollo Economico," Mexico City, November 12–13.

McCraw, T. K. 1984. *Prophets of Regulation*. Cambridge, MA: Belknap Press of Harvard University.

Modigliani, F., and M. Miller. 1958. "The Cost of Capital, Corporation Finance, and the Theory of Investment." *American Economic Review* 48 (3): 261–97.

Morck, R., A. Shleifer, and R. W. Vishny. 1988. "Management Ownership and Market Valuation: An Empirical Analysis." *Journal of Financial Economics* 20 (1): 293–315.

Rajan, R., and L. Zingales. 1995. "What Do We Know about Capital Structure: Some Evidence from International Data." *Journal of Finance* 50 (5): 1421–60.

———. 1998. "Financial Dependence and Growth." *American Economic Review* 88 (3): 559–86.

Reese, W. A., Jr., and M. S. Weisbach. 2002. "Protection of Minority Shareholder Interests, Cross-Listings in the United States, and Subsequent Equity Offerings." *Journal of Financial Economics* 66 (1): 65–104.

Reynolds, T., and A. Flores. 1989. *Foreign Law: Current Sources of Basic Legislation in Jurisdictions of the World*. Littleton, CO: Rothman and Co.

Secretaria de Hacienda y Credito Publico. 2005. "Reform of the System of Pensions of Workers of the State (ISSSTE)." Secretaria de Hacienda y Credito Publico, Mexico City.

Shleifer, A., and R. W. Vishny. 1986. "Large Shareholders and Corporate Control." *Journal of Political Economy* 94 (3): 461–88.

Siegel, J. 2005. "Can Foreign Firms Bond Themselves Effectively by Renting U.S. Securities Laws?" *Journal of Financial Economics* 75 (2): 319–59.

Standard & Poor's. 2005. *Global Stock Markets Factbook*. New York: McGraw-Hill.

Vishny, P. H. 1994. *Guide to International Commerce Law*. New York: McGraw-Hill.

Vittas, D., and A. Iglesias. 1992. "The Rationale and Performance of Personal Pension Plans in Chile." Policy Research Working Paper 867, World Bank, Washington, DC.

White, M. 1993. "The Costs of Corporate Bankruptcy: The U.S.–European Comparison." Unpublished working paper, Department of Economics, University of Michigan, Ann Arbor, MI.

World Bank. Various. *World Development Indicators*. Washington, DC: World Bank.

Wurgler, J. 2000. "Financial Markets and the Allocation of Capital." *Journal of Financial Economics* 58 (1–2): 187–214.

7

CEO and Director Turnover in República Bolivariana de Venezuela

Urbi Garay and Maximiliano González[*]

Introduction

Firms in emerging economies are sometimes unable to fund even superb projects because investors are afraid they will not get their money back. This expropriation risk is the essence of corporate governance, and the empirical evidence shows that there are great differences among corporate governance mechanisms around the world. This is particularly illustrated by La Porta et al. (2000a).

Although the whole range of corporate governance mechanisms has been studied in depth for the case of the United States and other developed economies,[1] not much work has been done for the rest of the world, especially the emerging markets. A recent exception is Gibson (2003), who reports that poorly performing managers in eight emerging markets are more likely to be replaced, leading him to the conclusion that corporate governance mechanisms in these emerging economies are effective.[2] This finding is important because a necessary condition for any corporate governance system is to ensure that poorly performing managers are more likely to be removed from their positions than well-performing managers.

* Comments by Florencio López-de-Silanes, Alberto Chong, Enrique Kawamura, Carlos Molina, Renato Baunmann, and Guillermo Zamarripa have been particularly helpful. Rafael García, Millie Honik, and Daniel Ruiz have provided excellent research support. The usual disclaimer applies.

The aim of this study is to continue the effort to achieve a better understanding of corporate governance structures and mechanisms outside the United States and the rest of the developed world by looking at a specific emerging economy: República Bolivariana de Venezuela. We first build a corporate governance index (CGI) for publicly listed companies in this market using standard corporate governance measures contained in a questionnaire adapted from Klapper and Love (2002). The overall results indicate that República Bolivariana de Venezuela would be located within the average for the 14 emerging markets reported by these two authors, and the results also show that public companies in that country exhibit relatively low corporate governance scores, especially in the categories of general principles and of officers and the board of directors. The scores on shareholders and on disclosure and information are relatively better. We then conduct a number of nonparametric tests and regression analyses to test the relation between this CGI and its subcomponents and a set of three alternative measures of value (Tobin's q, the price-to-book ratio, and dividend payout). In general, we find a positive relation between the CGI and our value measures.

In this environment of relatively low corporate governance scores, together with an underdeveloped financial market, a weak legal system, poor law enforcement, and high ownership concentration,[3] we then address the question of whether the existing corporate governance system works in República Bolivariana de Venezuela. This is important because all these issues are present in many Latin American countries and emerging markets around the world; therefore, República Bolivariana de Venezuela becomes an ideal case study on how the governance system works in this type of environment. Moreover, the Venezuelan commercial code (código de comercio) makes the board of directors responsible for the management of the firm.

More specifically, we would like to answer the following two questions in this chapter. First, are poorly performing managers more likely to be removed than well-performing managers? Second, is the role of the board to monitor the chief executive officer (CEO) or to serve as an advisor? This contribution is important because, to the best of our knowledge, this is the first country-specific analysis of how firm performance affects the likelihood of CEO and director turnover in a specific Latin American country.[4]

To this end, we have collected detailed data from 51 Venezuelan firms from 1984 to 2002 and constructed an unbalanced panel (878 observations) to study the extent to which the likelihood of CEO and director turnover is explained by the financial performance of firms. After controlling for CEO characteristics, board characteristics, ownership, firm characteristics, and time periods, we find that, for this sample of Venezuelan firms, bad financial performance significantly increases the likelihood of CEO and director turnover. The empirical evidence is also consistent with the idea that directors in República Bolivariana de Venezuela play a mainly advisory role rather than monitoring the CEO, as we show hereafter.

The remainder of this study is organized as follows. In the next section, we present an overview of the Venezuelan economy, the Venezuelan stock market, and the legal framework of the country's capital markets. We also present the results of a survey we have conducted on corporate governance practices in the country and try to relate results from the questionnaire to measures of value. In the following section, we describe the database used to examine how performance affects the likelihood of CEO and director turnover in República Bolivariana de Venezuela. In the section thereafter, we develop the empirical analysis to test our hypotheses and review some of the literature on the subject. In the penultimate section, we present a set of robustness checks on the results we have obtained. Finally, in the last section, we discuss our findings and conclude.

Institutional Characteristics

An Overview of the Economy and Stock Market

The Venezuelan economy is characterized by the preeminence of oil, which accounts for about one-third of gross domestic product (GDP) and half of government revenue and represents the main source of foreign currency. Because the oil industry is owned by the state, the government has considerable influence on the economy. By the.end of 2004, GDP was expected to reach US$100 billion, the fourth largest in Latin America.

The Caracas Stock Exchange (BVC, Bolsa de Valores de Caracas) was founded in 1947.[5] Before that date, stock trades were performed over the counter. By the end of 2004, 57 companies were listed on the BVC, less than half of which trade regularly. Moreover, the BVC has experienced a severe decline in traded volumes since the mid-1990s as a result of a declining economy, the migration of stocks to U.S. markets in the form of American depositary receipts (ADRs), the takeovers to which a number of firms have been subjected (with a concomitant reduction in the number of shares available for trade), and an increasing country risk that has frightened investors, particularly foreign investors.[6] In fact, daily trading volume has decreased from the equivalent of US$25 million to US$30 million in 1997 to less than US$1 million by 2000, and it has not recovered since then.[7] The BVC has survived during this period thanks to the growing trade in government debt securities. Stock prices, measured by the Indice Bursátil Caracas, have also been depressed during the past decade and have not recovered to the highest-ever levels experienced, in dollar terms, in 1991. According to the International Finance Corporation, the market value of the Venezuelan stock market was US$7 billion in 2000, or only about 6 percent of GDP.

Capital issues have decreased dramatically during the past five years, while the economy entered a severe recession. No new listing of companies has taken place in recent years, and a small number of companies have delisted; bond issues by listed companies have also decreased. This trend has accentuated the importance of bank loans as the main source of funding for Venezuelan companies, although total bank loans as a percentage of GDP have also declined.[8] The fact that a new pension funds law has still not been approved by Congress has not helped the market attract the much-needed presence of long-term funds for investment in various capital market instruments issued by local corporations.

As in most countries in Latin America, groups represent the typical corporate structure in República Bolivariana de Venezuela.[9] Dahlquist et al. (2003) document that, by 1997, 62 percent of the total market capitalization of the BVC was held by insiders. Today, that number is higher because a number of takeovers and mergers have occurred, most notably AES–Electricidad de Caracas, Polar-Mavesa, and a number of bank mergers.

The Legal Framework of the Capital Market

The institutional setting in República Bolivariana de Venezuela, as in most developing economies, differs a great deal from those in advanced economies, especially the United States.[10] The country's legal origin is French civil law, which is generally considered to have the weakest investor protection among all types of civil law systems; in any case, capital markets are less well developed.[11]

The commercial code and the securities market law (ley de mercado de capitales) represent the umbrella under which capital markets and listed companies operate in República Bolivariana de Venezuela. The commercial code was enacted in 1955, while the securities market law was enacted in 1975 and amended in 1998.

The securities market law regulates the public offer of stocks and other medium- and long-term financial instruments, except for those issued by the government or those regulated by the banking law (ley general de bancos y otros institutos de crédito) and the national savings and loans law (ley del sistema nacional de ahorro y préstamo). The main supervisory entity of the Venezuelan capital markets, the National Securities Commission (CNV, Comisión Nacional de Valores), was created under the securities market law of 1975; it is affiliated with the Finance Ministry.[12] The president of the CNV is appointed by the president of the country for four years and may be reelected. The CNV has four directors, who are also appointed by the president, for three years; they may be reelected as well.

Public corporations must be registered with the Securities Registrar (Registro Nacional de Valores) administered by the CNV. Listed companies must also provide all relevant information to the CNV in a timely fashion and produce financial statements, which must be externally audited. The stock exchange may stop transactions at any time, provided there is reasonable suspicion of the existence of relevant information not revealed to the market. The stock exchange must inform the CNV within 24 hours, and transactions may remain suspended for up to five days.

The securities market law requires companies registered with the CNV to be administered by a board of directors composed of at least five members who will remain in their positions for at least one year and who may be reelected. Any group of stockholders representing at least 20 percent of a company's stocks has the right to elect at least one member of the board of directors. According to terms of Resolution 49–2001 of March 2001, the CNV regulates the process whereby minority shareholders may elect members of the board of directors.

The commercial code mandates that companies regulated by the CNV have two commissioners (*comisarios*), who are elected by shareholders in the general meeting to supervise the work of and the financial statements presented by the board of directors to stockholders at the annual meeting. The commissioners must also have unlimited access to all the operations of the company. With the explicit intention of protecting minority shareholders, the securities market law requires public companies to distribute to shareholders at least 50 percent of the net income obtained during the fiscal year, of which at least 25 percent must be in the form of cash dividends. Companies with accumulated losses from previous years may be exempted from this requirement until they fill the deficit.

The CNV has additionally enacted a number of recent reforms with the intention of protecting minority shareholders and promoting greater disclosure. For example, during the hostile takeover bid of Electricidad de Caracas by AES Corporation, the CNV required the latter company to purchase all the shares that were submitted during the public acquisition offer, even though AES Corporation only needed 51 percent of the shares to control the company, thus benefiting minority shareholders. In terms of disclosure, recent decisions by the CNV require listed companies to abide by international accounting standards.

To assess institutional differences among countries, La Porta et al. (1997) have constructed two variables to assess the legal protection afforded an individual shareholder in different countries around the world. The first of these variables is called antidirector rights,[13] and the second is the perceived quality of the country's legal system and law enforcement, which they call rule of law.[14] As shown in table 7.1, an individual investor is less well protected in República Bolivariana de Venezuela than in the average Latin American country, based on the antidirector rights index, and much less well protected than in the United States. In terms of the rule of law,

Table 7.1 Institutional Variables

Variable	*Venezuela, R. B. de*	*Latin America*	*United States*
Antidirector rights	1.00	1.89	5.00
Rule of law	6.37	5.03	10.00
Domestic firms to population (millions)	4.28	7.48	30.11
Initial public offerings to population (millions)	0.00	0.08	3.11
Debt to GDP	0.10	0.29	0.81
External capitalization to GDP	0.08	0.27	0.58

Source: La Porta et al. 1997.

Note: The table compares the antidirector rights index, the rule of law index, the ratio of listed domestic firms to the country's population, the ratio of initial public offerings to the country's population, the ratio of the bank debt outstanding in the private sector to GDP in 1994, and the ratio of minority shareholder capitalization to GDP for República Bolivariana de Venezuela, the Latin America average, and the United States.

the index for República Bolivariana de Venezuela is slightly higher than that for the average Latin America country, but is still substantially below the U.S. index.

The other four variables in table 7.1 represent proxies for the size and depth of the capital market and attempt to measure the effect of legal protection on the development of each of the capital markets considered. The first variable is the ratio of domestic firms listed in the stock exchange of a country to its population (in millions) for 1996. República Bolivariana de Venezuela falls very far from the U.S. standard and below the Latin America average (excluding Chile and Ecuador, which are outlying examples at the higher end for the Latin America sample, with index values of 19.92 and 13.18, respectively; including them, the index would go down to 4.89).[15] This is initial evidence that lower levels of protection are related to the existence of fewer public companies.

The second variable is the ratio of the initial public offerings of equity to the country's population (in millions) for 1996. In this period, there were no initial public offerings of Venezuelan companies, which is the typical case in Latin America. Both the Venezuelan and the Latin American averages are well below that of the United States, which confirms the conclusion of La Porta et al. (1997) that legal protection and law enforcement are positively related to the development of capital markets.

The third variable is the ratio of all bank debt in the private sector to GDP in 1994; the ratio for República Bolivariana de Venezuela is 0.10, which is lower than the Latin American average of 0.29 and much lower than the U.S. average of 0.81.

Finally, we present the ratio of the stock market capitalization held by minority shareholders to GDP for 1994. In this last case, the Venezuelan ratio is 0.08, which is considerably lower than the U.S. ratio of 0.58 and the Latin American ratio of 0.27 (taking out Chile, which is a sample outlier, with an index of 0.8; adding Chile, the regional index would fall to 0.18).

Unfortunately, none of these four variables have shown an improvement during the past few years, despite the recent reforms by the CNV to promote minority shareholder protection and more disclosure.[16] Other factors, such as political uncertainty and an economic collapse in 2002 and 2003, may partially explain these results.

Taken together, the statistics on República Bolivariana de Venezuela are generally lower in both legal protection and market development than those of the other countries in Latin America and well below the numbers for the United States. These statistics give us the opportunity in this research to contrast two different environments—República Bolivariana de Venezuela and the United States—and to analyze the relationship between firm financial performance and CEO and director turnover in a small and underdeveloped capital market. The conclusions drawn from this study may be important for other Latin American countries as well.

Corporate Governance Practices

In this section, we present the results of a questionnaire on corporate governance practices in public financial and public nonfinancial firms in República Bolivariana de Venezuela. The questionnaire allows us to place our study in context by showing the current state of corporate governance practices in the country. The results also lead us to suggest, in the last section of the chapter, a set of policy recommendations that should be adopted by regulators to improve corporate governance practices.

We sent the questionnaire to each of the 57 companies listed on the BVC at the beginning of 2004. The survey represents an adaptation of the Credit Lyonnais Securities Asia (2001) questionnaire presented in Klapper and Love (2002); that questionnaire has here been adapted for the Venezuelan and Chilean (as presented in Lefort and Walker 2005) stock markets. The questionnaires were sent to each company's CEOs and were answered mainly by the legal officers of each of the firms, although a number of questionnaires were also answered directly by the CEO, by the assistant to the board of directors, or by another firm director.[17]

Given that the number of companies listed on the BVC is small, we need to have a relatively high response rate for our results to be meaningful. To this end, we contacted each of the 44 companies that had not answered the questionnaires when we first sent them. We were able to collect answers through direct interviews with 19 of these firms between December 2004 and January 2005. This brought the total number of completed questionnaires to 31, representing 54 percent of the firms listed on the BVC. Firms that answered the questionnaire accounted for approximately 87 percent of the total market capitalization of the BVC (see table 7.2).

As in Klapper and Love (2002) and Lefort and Walker (2005), the questionnaire contains four sections or subindexes: (1) general principles, (2) officers and the board, (3) shareholders, and (4) disclosure and information. The questionnaire consists of 71 questions, 62 of which are of the yes-or-no type.[18] A yes answer adds 1 point to the corporate governance score if it indicates a better corporate governance practice. We have normalized each answer between 0 and 7 to make our results comparable to those of Lefort and Walker (2005), and then we have calculated a simple average of the results for each of the sections.

The outcome is presented in table 7.3, which shows that Venezuelan public companies exhibit relatively low corporate governance scores, especially in the categories of general principles and of officers and the board. The scores on shareholders and on disclosure and information are relatively better. Overall results would give Venezuelan firms a score of 3.79 out of 7, which is equivalent to 54 points out of 100. Mean results for the 14 emerging markets considered in Klapper and Lover (2002) yielded a very similar score of 54.11. Scores for the two Latin American countries considered in that paper were 57.26 (Brazil) and 61.63 (Chile).[19]

Regarding general principles, on which the results are similar to those found by Lefort and Walker (2005) for Chile, Venezuelan companies generally do not adhere to an international code of conduct. However, more than half of the companies that answered the questionnaire acknowledged having issued a mission statement that explicitly places a priority on good corporate governance. They include in their annual reports a section devoted to the company's performance in implementing corporate governance principles, and they have a code of conduct with corporate governance principles. We suspect, though, that some of these numbers overestimate the reality.

The second section of the questionnaire covers officers and the board. The average score for this section was 3.92. For almost half the companies

Table 7.2 Questionnaire Response

Sample	*Number of firms*	*Total listed firms (%)*	*Share of total market capitalization (%)*
Firms contacted	57	100	100
Questionnaire responses	31	54.4	87

Source: Compiled by the authors, including from data from Datastream (Infor), http://www.datastream.net.

Table 7.3 Questionnaire on Corporate Governance: Open Questions

No.	*Question*	*Mean*	*Median*	*Minimum*	*Maximum*
About general principles					
6	What percentage of the company's shares are traded on the stock market?	25.6%	10.5%	0%	100%
About officers and the board					
9	How many principal members are on the board of directors?	8.5	8.0	4	18
17	How many members of the board of directors are also members of the audit committee? (Only for companies that acknowledged having an audit committee.)	3.5	3.0	0	8
About shareholders					
38	What percentage of the company's stock is necessary to call an extraordinary shareholders meeting?	38%	20%	20%	80%
52	What percentage of the company's stock is directly or indirectly controlled by the controlling shareholder?	48.1%	53.0%	23%	100%
53	How many groups of blockholders possess at least 10% of the firm's equity?	2.2	2.0	0	5
54	How many groups of blockholders possess at least 20% of the firm's equity?	1.4	1.0	0	3
57	How many principal members of the board of directors represent the controlling shareholder?	3.2	20	0	10

Source: Compiled by the authors.

surveyed, the CEO was also the chairman of the board and belonged to the same family or control group. More than half the companies acknowledged having independent board members, and the majority have an audit committee, but only a few have a corporate governance committee. Although companies in República Bolivariana de Venezuela are legally obliged to inform the CNV of management and director compensation and shareholdings, a number of them admit that they have not disclosed this information. None of the directors or managers of the companies surveyed has been sanctioned by the regulator during the past three years, and only one of the companies ties management remuneration to the value of the company's shares. This is not surprising, given the illiquidity of the local stock market.

The average score for the section on shareholders was 3.78. For all but one of the firms, each share equals one vote, and multiple voting shares are not allowed. Shareholders do not have to be present at the general shareholders meeting to vote as long as they send a proxy. Minority shareholders are described as those shareholders representing at least 20 percent of the shares of the company, according to the capital markets law. Minority shareholders have benefited from recent decisions by the CNV regarding tag-along rights to sell shares at the same price received by the controller when the company is sold, as was the case in the AES hostile acquisition of Electricidad de Caracas in 2000 mentioned elsewhere above.

Finally, Venezuelan companies score relatively well in the section on disclosure and information. Most of the companies answering the questionnaire publish their semiannual and annual reports within two months of the end of the half-year and of the quarter, respectively. The majority of firms present their accounts according to international Generally Accepted Accounting Principles and are audited by an internationally recognized external auditing firm. Companies are also obliged to disclose ownership information, executive and director compensation, and related party transactions to the CNV. On the other hand, results and other announcements are generally not updated promptly; companies typically do not disclose ultimate ownership information; external auditors are not elected by the firm's audit committee; and external auditors are hired for consulting purposes.

In the annex at the end of the chapter, we present nonparametric tests and regression analysis on the relation between the measures of corporate value (Tobin's q, the price-to-book ratio, and dividend payout) and the CGI and subindexes.

Data

Table 7.4 presents the definitions of the variables used to study the effectiveness of corporate governance mechanisms in República Bolivariana de

Venezuela by evaluating whether CEO and director turnover is related to corporate performance in that country.

To achieve this goal, we have constructed a panel data set. The initial sample includes all the public companies that were traded on the BVC during the period 1984–2002. This represented 89 companies in various economic sectors in 1984, but it had decreased to 59 companies by 2002.[20] After excluding all companies without public annual financial proxies and information on the board of directors (the names of CEOs and principal directors) and firms with less than nine years of historical data, the sample was reduced to 51 firms and 878 observations (see table 7.5, panel a). CEO turnover was measured by comparing the name of each CEO in year *t–1* to the name of the CEO in year *t*. If the name changed, we record a CEO turnover for year *t*. We follow the same procedure to account for director turnover.[21] We have thus recorded a total of

Table 7.4 Variable Descriptions

Variable	*Description*
Turnover	
CEOTUR	Equals 1 if there is a change in CEO for each firm *i* and for each year *t*.
LCEOTUR	One-year lagged CEOTUR.
DIRTUR	Equals 1 if there is a change in a director for each firm *i* and for each year *t*.
LDIRTUR	One-year lagged DIRTUR.
BODITU	Fraction of the board that turned over at firm *i* in year *t*. NUMDIR, divided by BOASIZ in year *t*–1.
FORCED	Equals 1 if there is a change in CEO for each firm *i* and for each year *t* and if the departing CEO does not remain on the board.
NEWCEO	Equals 1 if there is a change in CEO for each firm *i* and for each year *t* and the incoming CEO was not previously in the board.
Board and CEO characteristics	
BOASIZ	Size of the board of directors (number of members) for each firm *i* and for each year *t*.
GRADIR	Fraction of the board of directors that is considered to be family related (same last name) to the CEO or to the chairman of the board for each firm *i* and for each year *t*.

(continued)

Table 7.4 Variable Descriptions *(continued)*

Variable	*Description*
INSDIR	Fraction of the board of directors that is considered to be insiders for each firm *i* and for each year *t*. Directors are classified as insiders if they hold any managerial position in the firm according to the firm's annual report. If CEOs or chairmen of the board were replaced, but remained on the board of directors, they are classified as inside directors.
OUTDIR	Fraction of the board of directors that is considered to be outsiders for each firm *i* and for each year *t*. Directors are classified as outsiders if they are neither inside directors nor gray directors.
INDEPE	Coefficient of independence in the board of directors for each firm *i* and for year *t*. The variable is calculated as the arithmetic difference between OUTDIR and INSDIR.
LPCHAIN	Lagged value of the percentage change in board independence for firm *i* in year *t*.
CEOTEN	Number of years that the CEO has remained in office for each firm *i* and for each year *t*.
MEDITE	Median number of years that the directors of the board have remained appointed for each firm *i* and for each year *t*.
DIRTEN	Average number of years that the directors of the board have remained appointed for each firm *i* and for each year *t*.
CEOAGE	Years of age of the CEO of firm *i* in year *t*. *Source:* Venezuelan electoral body (Consejo Nacional Electoral) database or the firm's human resources department.
CEOCHA	Equals 1 if the CEO is also the chairman of the board for each firm *i* in year *t*.
Performance	
ROA	Return on assets. The variable is calculated as the ratio of earnings before interest and taxes to end-of-year total assets for each firm *i* and for each year *t*.
LROA	One-year lagged ROA.

(continued)

Table 7.4 Variable Descriptions *(continued)*

Variable	*Description*
ROAA	Return on assets adjusted by industry. The variable is calculated for each firm *i* and for each year *t* as the ratio of earnings before interest and taxes to end-of-year total assets, less the median ROA for all firms that belong to the same industry for year *t*. Firms have been classified in the following three industries: manufacturing, financial, and services and others.
LROAA	One-year lagged ROAA.
ROE	Return on equity. The variable is calculated for each firm *i* and for each year *t* as the ratio of earnings before interest and taxes to end-of-year total equity.
LROE	One-year lagged ROE.
ROEA	Return on equity adjusted by industry. The variable is calculated for each firm *i* and for each year *t* as the ratio of earnings before interest and taxes to end-of-year total equity, less the median ROE for all firms that belong to the same industry for year *t*. Firms have been classified in the following three industries: manufacturing, financial, and services and others.
LROEA	One-year lagged ROEA.
NEGAINC	Equals 1 if firm *i* reported a negative net income in year *t*.
LNEGAINC	One-year lagged NEGAINC.
Other variables	
FSIZE	Natural logarithm of each firm *i*'s year-end total assets in each year *t*.
FSIZEB	Year-end book value of assets, reported in U.S. dollars, using each year's average exchange rate. The source of the average exchange rate, bolívar to U.S. dollar, is the Venezuelan Central Bank's Web page (http://www.bcv.gov.ve).
OWNCON	Fraction of the book value of firm *i* held by the major stockholder during each year *t* in the sample. *Source:* Ownership reports and legally certified stockholders minutes all taken from the CNV.

(continued)

Table 7.4 Variable Descriptions *(continued)*

Variable	*Description*
BLOHOL	Number of shareholders with more than 20 percent of the book value of firm *i* during each year *t* in the sample. *Source:* Ownership reports and legally certified stockholders minutes, all taken from the CNV.
ADRUSA	Dummy variable that takes the value of 1 if firm *i* in year *t* has ADRs trading in the United States and 0 otherwise.
YEACON	Number of years since the incorporation of each firm *i* in year *t*.
CASTR	Leverage ratio measured as the ratio of year-end total debt to total assets.
PERIOD2	Equals 1 if the observation *it* was taken from year 1991 to 1996 (inclusive) and 0 otherwise.
INVTA	Changes in fixed assets, divided by total assets for each firm *i* and for each year *t*.
PPTTOSALES	Fixed assets, divided by total sales for each firm *i* and for each year *t*.
Tobin's q	The variable is computed as the ratio of the market value to the book value of assets. Market value is the market value of equity, plus the book value of assets, minus the book value of equity. They have all been computed for the end of 2004.
Price-to-book	Market value, divided by book value at the end of 2004. Market value and book value have been obtained from Economática (http://www.economatica.com) and Datastream (Infor at http://www.datastream.net).
Dividend payout	Cash and stock dividends, divided by net income. Data correspond to 2003. They are all computed at year-end values and have been obtained from BVC (2003).
Volatility	Annualized standard deviation of monthly stock returns for the three years previous to the computation of Tobin's q. For a number of firms, no monthly stock returns have been recorded for some months because shares did not trade. Data have been obtained from Economática (http://www.economatica.com), Datastream (Infor at http://www.datastream.net), and BVC (2003).

(continued)

Table 7.4 Variable Descriptions *(continued)*

Variable	*Description*
Leverage	Nonequity liabilities, divided by total assets at the end of 2004. Data have been obtained from Economática (http://www.economatica.com) and the financial proxies of the firms.
Size	Natural logarithm of the book value of total assets in millions of Venezuelan bolívars at the end of 2004. Data have been obtained from Economática (http://www.economatica.com) and the financial proxies of the firms.
ROA2	Operating income, divided by total assets at the end of 2004. Data have been obtained from Economática (http://www.economatica.com) and the financial proxies of firms.
Growth	Average annual growth of sales between the end of 2000 and the end of 2004. Data have been obtained from Economática (http://www.economatica.com), BVC (2003), and the financial proxies of firms.

Sources: Compiled by the authors. The source of the information on those variables for which a source has not been explicitly identified in the table is the annual financial proxies and investor relations offices of the firms.

131 CEO turnovers and 946 director turnovers during our sample period (see table 7.5, panel a).

Regarding industries, as shown in table 7.5, panel b, we have grouped our sample into three economic sectors: manufacturing (51 percent), financial (33 percent), and services and others (16 percent). Finally, table 7.5, panel c, shows the percentage coverage of our sample for each year.

Although the size of the sample may seem small relative to the studies that have been done in the United States and other developed economies, it is not small relative to the number of firms on the BVC because the firms in the sample represent close to 70 percent, on average, of the total number of firms listed and close to 95 percent (in each year studied) in terms of market capitalization.

Summary Statistics

Table 7.6 shows the mean, median, and standard deviation of selected variables. The first panel shows the number of CEO and director turnovers, *CEOTUR*, which varies through the years from only 2 yearly turnovers in 1984 and 1990 to 11 turnovers in 1996. The variation is similar in the other years in the sample, but it is not shown in the table. In

Table 7.5 Database Description

a. Distribution of sample observations

Number of firms	*Years in sample*	*Firm-year observations*	CEO *turnovers (number)*	*Director turnovers (number)*
33	19	627	90	629
2	18	36	9	45
4	17	68	9	87
2	16	32	3	33
1	15	15	0	11
1	13	13	0	5
2	12	24	6	43
4	11	44	10	71
1	10	10	2	12
1	9	9	2	10
51		878	131	946

b. Distribution of sector

Sector	*Number of firms*	*Percentage*	*Observations*	*Percentage*
Manufacturing	26	50.98	446	50.80
Financial	17	33.33	291	33.14
Service and others	8	15.69	141	16.06
Total	51	100.00	878	100.00

c. Coverage

Year	*Sample firms*	*Total firms*	*Coverage (%)*
1984	40	89	44.94
1985	41	83	49.40
1986	41	83	49.40
1987	41	78	52.56
1988	42	74	56.76
1989	43	75	57.33
1990	44	76	57.89
1991	46	76	60.53

(continued)

Table 7.5 Database Description *(continued)*

c. Coverage

Year	*Sample firms*	*Total firms*	*Coverage (%)*
1992	49	72	68.06
1993	51	54	94.44
1994	51	54	94.44
1995	51	57	89.47
1996	51	57	89.47
1997	51	62	82.26
1998	51	73	69.86
1999	51	63	80.95
2000	49	67	73.13
2001	45	63	71.43
2002	41	59	69.49

Sources: BVC, various; annual financial proxies.

Note: The database used in this study is composed of 878 firm-year observations of a sample of 51 firms listed on the BVC from 1984 to 2002.

a related recent finding, Kaplan and Minton (2006) analyze a sample of large U.S. firms and discover that annual CEO turnover for the period 1992–2005 is 14.9 percent and increases to 16.5 percent for the period 1998–2005.

In the case of director turnover, *DIRTUR*, the number of turnovers increases substantially, from a minimum of 22 turnovers in 1984 and 1990 to a maximum of 65 turnovers in 2002. In terms of board characteristics, the second panel shows that the average size of the board of directors, *BOASIZ*, in República Bolivariana de Venezuela is around 8 members,[22] which is smaller than in the United States,[23] and remains fairly stable throughout the years in the sample. The maximum board size in the whole sample is 14, and the minimum is 5. The fraction of the board that is classified as outsiders in the annual financial reports, *OUTDIR*, is around 53 percent and remains stable during these years; for U.S. firms the fraction is 45.6 percent, less than what we find here.

In terms of board independence, *INDEPE*, which is calculated as *OUTDIR*, minus *INSDIR* (fraction of the board of directors that is accounted for by insiders), we observe a positive independence, on average, in each year, that is, the average board of directors in República Bolivariana de Venezuela tends to have more outsiders than insiders. However, we suspect that this proportion tends to be lower because it is difficult to determine if a given director is truly an outsider. The median CEO tenure, *CEOTEN*, decreased substantially in the sample. In 1984, the median *CEOTEN* was eight years, and, in 2002, it was approximately three years. A similar

Table 7.6 Summary Statistics for Selected Variables

a. Turnover

	1984	1987	1990	1993	1996	1999	2002
CEOTUR	2	8	2	7	11	7	8
DIRTUR	22	31	22	62	58	44	65

b. Board and CEO characteristics

	1984			1987			1990			1993			1996			1999			2002		
	Mean	Median	S.D.	Mean	Median	S.D.	Mean	Median	S.D.	Mean	Median	S.D.	Mean	Median	S.D.	Mean	Median	S.D.	Mean	Median	S.D.
BOASIZ	7.78	7.00	1.66	7.83	8.00	1.56	8.02	8.00	1.80	8.18	8.00	1.75	8.10	8.00	1.59	8.16	8.00	2.00	8.24	8.00	2.01
OUTDIR	0.53	0.57	0.40	0.54	0.57	0.17	0.55	0.57	0.18	0.53	0.55	0.17	0.54	0.56	0.19	0.53	0.57	0.18	0.54	0.57	0.17
INDEPE	0.13	0.14	0.30	0.15	0.14	0.31	0.15	0.20	0.32	0.12	0.13	0.31	0.15	0.14	0.33	0.11	0.18	0.36	0.15	0.20	0.34
CEOTEN	11.90	8.00	10.06	10.12	6.00	10.94	10.89	7.00	10.45	9.08	4.00	10.69	7.69	4.00	9.66	7.24	4.00	8.91	6.85	3.00	8.64
DIRTEN	10.14	9.95	4.17	10.14	10.14	4.66	10.75	11.11	4.52	8.97	8.14	5.36	7.79	7.80	4.70	8.74	8.18	5.07	7.55	6.83	4.58
CEOAGE	53.50	53.50	10.94	56.83	56.00	10.54	55.91	56.50	9.34	55.63	56.00	11.75	53.78	54.00	11.59	58.22	57.00	9.17	52.27	51.00	9.90

c. Performance

	1984			1987			1990			1993			1996			1999			2002		
	Mean	Median	S.D.	Mean	Median	S.D.	Mean	Median	S.D.	Mean	Median	S.D.	Mean	Median	S.D.	Mean	Median	S.D.	Mean	Median	S.D.
ROA	0.04	0.02	0.07	0.06	0.05	0.06	0.04	0.03	0.08	0.04	0.03	0.07	0.10	0.09	0.15	−0.02	0.02	0.14	0.00	0.02	0.19
ROE	0.12	0.13	0.18	0.21	0.20	0.10	0.13	0.17	0.29	0.12	0.13	0.19	0.19	0.30	0.74	−0.04	0.06	0.37	0.01	0.14	0.59

(continued)

Table 7.6 Summary Statistics for Selected Variables *(continued)*

d. Others	1984			1987			1990			1993			1996			1999			2002		
	Mean	Median	S.D.	Mean	Median	S.D.	Mean	Median	S.D.	Mean	Median	S.D.	Mean	Median	S.D.	Mean	Median	S.D.	Mean	Median	S.D.
FSIZEB	6.91	6.72	1.64	7.50	7.49	1.76	8.44	8.59	1.93	9.40	9.59	1.79	10.53	10.84	2.22	11.33	11.02	2.11	11.84	11.66	2.25
OWNCON	0.45	0.49	0.25	0.46	0.49	0.25	0.51	0.50	0.25	0.56	0.57	0.26	0.58	0.63	0.26	0.63	0.66	0.24	0.60	0.65	0.24
YEACON	39.18	32.50	21.79	41.22	35.00	22.37	42.45	37.00	22.90	45.80	41.00	22.49	48.80	44.00	22.49	51.80	47.00	22.49	55.39	50.00	22.43

Source: Compiled by the authors from the annual financial proxies and investor relations offices of the firms.
Note: The table reports the mean, median, and standard deviation (S.D.) on a set of select variables. Definitions of the variables are provided in table 7.4.

phenomenon is reported in Kaplan and Minton (2006), who show that average CEO tenure in the United States has decreased from seven to six years in the period 1998–2005.

Also, the median director tenure, *DIRTEN*, decreased in the sample from 10 years in 1984 to a little more than 7 in 2002. Finally, the CEO age remained fairly stable at around 55 years, on average.

The third panel presents two accounting measures of firm performance: return on assets (*ROA*), and return on equity (*ROE*). These ratios have been deteriorating since 1984. The average *ROA* and *ROE* were negative in 1999. These statistics lead to the question of whether declining corporate performance is related to increasing CEO and director turnover.

Other variables reported in table 7.6, panel d, are firm size (book value of assets); *FSIZEB*, reported in U.S. dollars using each year's average exchange rate; and ownership concentration, *OWNCON*, which is the fraction of book value held by the major stockholder of the firm. This variable shows that firms in the sample tend to have highly concentrated ownership, which is consistent with the findings of Dahlquist et al. (2003) and the arguments given in Lefort and Walker (2005) on ownership concentration in Latin America. Finally, table 7.6 shows that, for 1984, the firms in the sample had been in operation for an average of around 39 years (*YEACON*).

Empirical Analysis on CEO and Director Turnover

In this section, we concentrate on two hypotheses. The first is directly drawn from the corporate governance literature.[24]

> *Hypothesis 1:* A CEO whose firm performs poorly will have a greater probability of being replaced than a CEO whose firm has performed well.

Our second hypothesis is drawn from the Venezuelan commercial code, which states that boards of directors are responsible for the management of firms. Therefore, we investigate whether or not director turnover is also associated with poor firm financial performance, specifically:

> *Hypothesis 2:* Director turnover will be greater when firm performance is poor.

These hypotheses are fundamental in corroborating whether the corporate governance *system* in República Bolivariana de Venezuela is able to remove poorly performing managers and directors. In what follows, we seek evidence that will help us answer these two questions: First, is the CEO at risk of losing his or her job when poor corporate performance occurs? Second, are directors monitors of the CEO, or are they also removed when corporate performance deteriorates?

Hypothesis 1 has already been tested in the United States. For instance, Coughlan and Schmidt (1985), Furtado and Rozeff (1987), Weisbach (1988), Warner, Watts, and Wruck (1988), Morck, Shleifer, and Vishny (1988), Gilson (1989), Kaplan and Reishus (1990), Jensen and Murphy (1990), Martin and McConnell (1991), Denis and Denis (1995), Denis, Denis, and Sarin (1997), and more recently, Huson, Parrino, and Starks (2001) have all found empirical evidence in the United States supporting Hypothesis 1.

Also, using international data sets, Kaplan (1994a), Kaplan and Minton (1994), and Kang and Shivdasani (1995) have found evidence in Japan supporting Hypothesis 1; Volpin (2002) and Brunello, Graziano, and Parigi (2000) have found support in Italy; Kaplan (1994b) has found support in Germany; and Renneboog (2000) confirms this hypothesis in Belgium.

Dahya, McConnell, and Travlos (2002) find that, after the Cadbury Committee's recommendations were put into effect in the United Kingdom, CEO turnover sensitivity to performance increased significantly. More recently, Gibson (2003) has found support for this hypothesis in a study of 1,200 firms in eight emerging economies. However, to the best of our knowledge, no published studies testing Hypothesis 1 in any Latin American country in particular have been conducted to this date.

In contrast to the large amount of work done to test Hypothesis 1, Hypothesis 2 has received much less attention. Among the few existing studies, Coles and Hoi (2003) find that directors of firms who opt out of Pennsylvania Senate bill 1310 (a bill to give more security to directors in the case of takeovers) are significantly more likely to keep their board seats and obtain new board appointments. This finding is consistent with Gilson (1990), who reports an increase in director turnover in firms experiencing financial distress. Harford (2003) finds that the overwhelming majority of outside directors are replaced after a merger or acquisition. Fich and Shivdasani (2006) find that busy directors (directors who hold three or more board seats) are more likely to depart boards following poor performance. Finally, Farrell and Whidbee (2000) and Yermack (2004) also document a connection between CEO turnover and changes in the board of directors. To our knowledge, our work is the first time Hypothesis 2 is tested in any Latin American country.

The empirical analysis follows four steps. First, we present evidence using a univariate test of the relationship between corporate performance and CEO and director turnover. Second, we explore, using a *Logit* regression model, the relationship between the likelihood of CEO turnover (*CEOTUR*) and corporate performance; this result provides direct evidence to test Hypothesis 1. Third, we use a *Poisson* regression model to determine the relationship between the number of director turnovers (*NUMDIR*) and corporate performance. Finally, we investigate the relationship between director turnover and corporate performance, but, this time, we use an ordinary least squares (OLS) regression model and, as a dependent variable, the fraction of director turnovers (*BODITU*). These results will provide evidence to test Hypothesis 2.

CEO and Director Turnover, a Univariate Approach

We first approximate the relationship between corporate performance and CEO and board of director turnover to determine the pooled sample correlations between our proxies of performance and the CEO and director turnover variables.

We use only accounting performance measures for this and the other tests in this chapter for two reasons. First, many of the firms in our sample did not trade frequently during the sample period, and, therefore, the use of any market performance variable reduces significantly the number of observations. The relative illiquidity of emerging stock markets has already been documented by a number of authors.[25] Also, according to Domowitz, Glen, and Madhavan (2001), transaction costs in emerging markets are significantly higher than those in developed markets. In fact, in the case of the Venezuelan stock market, transaction costs are found to be among the highest in the region.[26] As Gibson (2003) contends, these factors, taken together with the documented inefficiencies of stock markets in developing countries and, in particular, in the Venezuelan stock market,[27] render stock market returns a noisy signal of firm performance in emerging stock markets.

Second, it may be argued that accounting performance results accrue strictly on the current CEO, whereas market performance measures also reflect the impact of market factors outside the CEO's control and the expected productivity of a new CEO.[28] On the econometric side, Bhagat and Jefferis (2002) show that regressions based on cash flow estimates such as ours are more robust to variations in specifications on how performance is measured. Also, Murphy and Zimmerman (1993) find that accounting-based performance measures have predictive power.

In table 7.7, we present the correlation matrix for the pooled data set. The turnover variables *CEOTUR*, *DIRTUR*, and *BODITU* have the correct expected correlation sign (negative) with all our performance measures (*ROA*, *ROAA*, *LROA*, *LROAA*, *ROE*, *ROEA*, *LROE*, and *LROEA*) and a positive sign, as expected, for *NEGINC* and *LNEGAINC*. In terms of significance, almost all correlation coefficients show significance levels in the 1 to 10 percent range. The variable *BODITU*, which also measures director turnover, but in relative terms (the fraction of the board that turned over), is also significant in all cases. In general, we are not able to infer causality using these correlation coefficients; however, we may state that these coefficients show a strong (linear) association between the financial performance measures and the turnover variables.

Table 7.7 Correlation Matrix for the Pooled Turnover and Performance Variables

Performance variables	*CEOTUR*	*Turnover variables, DIRTUR*	*BODITU*
ROA	-0.1132***	-0.1991***	-0.1571***
ROAA	-0.1077***	-0.1948***	-0.1512***
LROA	-0.1127***	-0.1311***	-0.1188***
LROAA	-0.1043***	-0.1237***	-0.1113***
ROE	-0.0667**	-0.0858**	-0.0580*
ROEA	-0.0685**	-0.0981***	-0.0685**
LROE	-0.1289***	-0.1421***	-0.1475***
LROEA	-0.1401***	-0.1552***	-0.1623***
NEGINC	0.1237***	0.1385***	0.1439***
LNEGINC	0.1396***	0.1729***	0.1844***

Source: Compiled by the authors from the annual financial proxies and investor relations offices of the firms.

Note: The total sample consists of 878 firm-year observations of 51 firms listed on the BVC from 1984 to 2002. Correlations are calculated pooling all observations in the sample. See table 7.4 for the description of all the variables. The coefficients reported are the pairwise correlation coefficients.

* significant at 10 percent

** significant at 5 percent

*** significant at 1 percent

In the next two subsections, we explore further the relationship between CEO and director turnover and corporate performance.

CEO Turnover, a Logit Approach

The model we use in this test is a Logit regression; this model estimates the likelihood of CEO turnover given a set of regressors. The multivariable logistic response function is given by the equation:

$$E\{Y_{it}\} = \frac{e^{\beta' X_{it}}}{1 + e^{\beta' X_{it}}}. \tag{7.1}$$

The log-likelihood function is given by the equation:[29]

$$L(\beta) = \sum_{i=1}^{N}\sum_{t=1}^{T} Y_{it}(\beta' X_{it}) - \sum_{i=1}^{N}\sum_{t=1}^{T} \ln\left[1 + e^{\beta' X_{it}}\right]. \tag{7.2}$$

Using maximum likelihood estimator procedures, we obtain the vector $\hat{\beta}$, which maximizes (7.2). After regressing CEO turnover with the proxies for performance and controlling for CEO characteristics, board characteristics, blockholding ownership, firm characteristics, and time period, we are able to test Hypothesis 1 directly. We report the results of our panel data regressions in table 7.8 using random- and fixed-effects specifications. Following Bhagat and Jefferis (2002), Himmelberg, Hubbard, and Palia (1999), and Hermalin and Weisbach (1991), we argue that the use of panel data regressions with lagged performance variables allows us to control, at least to some extent, for possible biases and inconsistencies due to the joint endogeneity between CEO turnover and a firm's performance.

Although we have used a fixed-effects specification so that we might take explicitly into consideration the unobserved heterogeneity that exists among the firms in our sample, we also report the results using the random-effects specification to measure the robustness of our estimated coefficients.[30]

As table 7.8 shows, the relation between CEO turnover and firm performance is negative when we use *LROAA* (lag value of the ratio of earnings, before interest and taxes, to total assets, less the median value of the ratio for all firms in the same industry) and *LROEA* (lag value of the ratio of earnings, before interest and taxes, to total equity, less the median value of the ratio for all firms in the same industry) as the performance measure and positive when we use *LNEGINC* (lag value of *NEGAINC*, which takes the value of 1 if firm i reports a negative net income in year t) as the performance measure.

In terms of statistical significance, the coefficients for *LROAA* and *LNEGINC* are significant at the 1 and 5 percent levels when random- and fixed-effects specifications are used, respectively; for these two performance measures the z-statistics are robust to various model specifications.[31] For example, in the first model, we interpret the slope coefficient of *LROAA* for the random-effects model (–2.2922) as follows. If *LROAA* is reduced by 1 percent, while the other coefficients in the model remain constant, the probability that a CEO turnover occurs (*CEOTUR* = *1*) increases by 10.1 percent ($\approx e^{-2.2922}$). In none of the models we study is *LROEA* statistically significant, although the sign is consistently negative. Recent research in the United States using a sample of large firms for the period 1998–2005 reported that a firm's ROA one standard deviation worse than the industry's ROA causes a 5.3 percent increase in the likelihood of CEO turnover.[32]

Contrary to our expectations, the coefficient of *CEOAGE* is negatively related and statistically significant to CEO turnover in all model specifications. We may interpret this result by arguing that relatively old CEOs are less likely to leave the firm due to poor firm performance than relatively young CEOs in our sample of Venezuelan companies. This might be regarded as evidence of CEO entrenchment as they get older. Moreover, the coefficient of the dummy variable *CEOCHA* that takes the value of 1 when the *CEO* is also the chairman of the board is also negative (proxy

Table 7.8 Panel Data Logit Regression on CEO Turnover

Variables	*Random effects (1)*	*Fixed effects (2)*	*Random effects (3)*	*Fixed effects (4)*	*Random effects (5)*	*Fixed effects (6)*
Intercept	2.0692***		1.9402***		1.6714**	
	z = 2.73		z = 2.56		z = 2.04	
LROAA	−2.2922***	−2.4041**				
	z = −2.66	z = −1.96				
LROEA			−0.2537	−0.0195		
			z = −1.32	z = −0.11		
LNEGINC					1.0135***	0.8293**
					z = 3.48	z = 2.41
CEOAGE	−0.0449***	−0.0583***	−0.0463***	−0.0618***	−0.0435**	−0.0572***
	z = −2.57	z = −3.58	z = −2.62	z = −3.79	z = −2.45	z = −3.50
CEOCHA	−0.3201	−1.0372***	−0.2695	−1.0168**	−0.3097	−1.0595**
	z = −1.11	z = −2.57	z = −0.93	z = −2.52	z = −1.09	z = −2.56
LDIRTUR	−0.2724***	−0.3370***	−0.2674***	−0.3263***	−0.2898***	−0.3417***
	z = −3.13	z = −4.67	z = −2.97	z = −4.56	z = −3.21	z = 4.70
LPCHAIN	0.2149*	0.1308	0.1773	0.1234	0.2296**	0.1513
	z = 1.75	z = 0.88	z = 1.30	z = 0.84	z = 1.97	z = 1.03
MEDITE	−0.2198***	−0.2446***	−0.2120***	−0.2487***	−0.2119***	−0.2489***
	z = −3.86	z = −5.64	z = −3.64	z = −5.71	z = −3.84	z = −5.70

(*continued*)

Table 7.8 Panel Data Logit Regression on CEO Turnover *(continued)*

Variables	*Random effects (1)*	*Fixed effects (2)*	*Random effects (3)*	*Fixed effects (4)*	*Random effects (5)*	*Fixed effects (6)*
BLOHOL	−0.1370	0.1699	−0.1199	0.1550	−0.0941	0.1644
	z = −0.74	z = 0.70	z = −0.63	z = 0.64	z = −0.51	z = 0.68
FSIZE	0.0990**	0.1487*	0.1044**	0.1459*	0.0986**	0.1088
	z = 1.98	z = 1.82	z = 2.06	z = 1.81	z = 1.97	z = 1.32
CASTR	−0.7067	1.4310**	−0.6551	1.4748**	−0.6235	1.0543
	z = 1.39	z = 2.04	z = −1.28	z = 2.13	z = −1.26	z = 1.44
PERIOD2	0.0070	0.2189	0.0405	0.2557	0.0757	0.2653
	z = 0.04	z = 0.90	z = 0.23	z = 1.06	z = 0.44	z = 1.09
Observations	827	737	827	737	827	737
Wald Chi^2 (10)	120.16***		116.82***		105.70***	
LR Chi (10)		118.16***		114.28***		120.04***
Hausman	24.22***		18.10*		15.99*	

Source: Compiled by the authors from the annual financial proxies and investor relations offices of the firms.

Note: The total sample consists of 878 firm-year observations of 51 firms listed on the BVC from 1984 to 2002. The dependent variable is CEOTUR. The performance variables are LROAA, LROEA, and LNEGINC. We control for CEO characteristics using CEOAGE and CEOCHA. We control for board characteristics using LDIRTUR, LPCHAIN, and MEDITE. We control for blockholding ownership using BLOHOL. We control for firm characteristics using FSIZE and CASTR. We control for time periods using PERIOD2. Definitions of the variables are given in table 7.4.

* significant at 10 percent
** significant at 5 percent
*** significant at 1 percent

for CEO power) in all model specifications and statistically significant at the 5 percent level for the fixed-effects models.

To control for board characteristics, we use the lag value of director turnover (*LDIRTUR*), the percentage change in board independence (*LPCHAIN*), and the median board tenure (*MEDITE*). Table 7.8 shows a negative and significant coefficient at the 1 percent level for *LDIRTUR* for all model specifications. This indicates that changes in the board of directors negatively affect the probability of CEO turnover for this sample of Venezuelan firms. For the coefficient of *LPCHAIN*, we find positive coefficients in all model specifications (an increase in board independence increases the probability of CEO turnover); however, the coefficients are statistically significant only in models 1 and 5 (at the 10 and 5 percent level). The last variable used to control for board characteristics is *MEDITU*, which shows a negative and significant coefficient (at the 1 percent level) for all model specifications. This seems to indicate that the longer the board members are in office, the less likely the CEO will be removed due to bad corporate performance. This might also be interpreted as preliminary evidence of CEO entrenchment.[33]

To control for ownership concentration, we use the number of shareholders with more than 20 percent of the book value of the firm, or blockholders (*BLOHOL*). The coefficient for this variable is not significant in any of the model specifications. We also use (not reported in table 7.8) the ownership concentration of the major shareholder (*OWNCON*), but the coefficient is not statistically significant either. The explanation for these results is twofold. First, as we note in table 7.6, the ownership structure of Venezuelan firms is highly concentrated; so, there is little *between-firm* variability. Second, the ownership concentration remains stable during the sample year for each firm; so, there is also little *within-firm* variability.

To control for the characteristics of firms, we use the natural logarithm of a firm's assets, *FSIZE*, and the leverage ratio of debt to assets, *CASTR*. We find that size is positively related to *CEOTUR*. In our sample, the CEO of a relatively large firm is statistically more likely to leave the firm after a period of bad performance than the CEO of a relatively smaller firm; however, the statistical significance of the coefficient is sensitive to changes in the model specification (fixed versus random effects). For the *CASTR* variable, the signs and the significance of the coefficients are also sensitive to the model specification.

We control for time periods using the variable *PERIOD2*, which is a dummy variable that takes the value of 1 if the observation is taken from year 1991 to 1996 (inclusive) and 0 otherwise. We include this variable to determine whether CEO turnover is influenced by the banking crisis in República Bolivariana de Venezuela in 1994, whereby approximately half the banking system went bankrupt, and many Venezuelan firms experienced financial problems. The coefficient shown in table 7.8 indicates no statistical relation between this time period and CEO turnover.

The Hausman test for the random-effects model shows that we fail to reject the hypothesis that the observed firm characteristics are correlated to our set of regressors at the 1 percent significance level in model (1) and at the 10 percent level in models (3) and (5). The first response to this would be to conclude that the random-effects assumptions do not hold and that we should focus our conclusions on fixed-effects models (2), (4), and (6).[34] However, as we may see in table 7.8, models (2) and (6) also show a strong negative and statistically significant relation between the probability of CEO turnover and firm performance, although this is not the case for model (4).

We conclude this subsection by confirming that we find empirical support for Hypothesis 1 in República Bolivariana de Venezuela. There is evidence that CEO turnover is negatively related to firm performance after controlling for CEO characteristics, board of directors characteristics, ownership characteristics, firm characteristics, and for the time period 1991–96.[35]

Director Turnovers, a Poisson Approach

The first model we use to test Hypothesis 2 is the Poisson regression model.[36] This model is appropriate for analyzing director turnover for at least one reason: the dependent variable, *DIRTUR*, is a count variable with values *0, 1, 2, . . . , n*, where *DIRTUR* = *0* (no director turnover) is a natural outcome of the Poisson process. This statistical model is a generalization of the Poisson distribution, where events occur randomly and independently in time. Consider the Poisson parameter λ with the following specification:

$$\ln \lambda = X_{it}'\beta, \tag{7.3}$$

where X is a vector of regressors that describes the characteristics of an observation unit (firm) i in a given time period t. Denote $DIRTUR_{it}$ as the observed unit count for firm i and time t. In this case:

$$E\{DIRTUR_{it}|X_{it}\} = \lambda. \tag{7.4}$$

Note that the zero problem, that is $DIRTUR_{it} = 0$, is a natural outcome of the Poisson distribution, and the only assumption we need to make is the time independence of observations. The Poisson probability density function is given by the following equation:

$$\Pr\{DIRTUR_{it}\} = \frac{e^{-\lambda_{it}}\lambda_{it}^{DIRTUR_{it}}}{DIRTUR_{it}!}. \tag{7.5}$$

Substituting (7.3) into (7.5) and taking logs in both sides gives the following equation:

$$\ln(\Pr\{DIRTUR_{it}\}) = \ln(-DIRTUR_{it}! - e^{X'_{it}\beta} + DIRTUR_{it}X'_{it}\beta). \qquad (7.6)$$

Summing for a sample of N firms over T periods, the log likelihood function for the Poisson model is given by the next equation:

$$L(\beta) = \sum_{i=1}^{N}\sum_{t=1}^{T}(-DIRTUR_{it}! - e^{X'_{it}\beta} + DIRTUR_{it}X'_{it}\beta). \qquad (7.7)$$

Hausman, Hall, and Griliches (1984) have shown that this function is globally concave, as long as X is a full column rank and $e^{X_{it}\beta}$ does not go to zero for all X_{it}.

As argued elsewhere above, in a cross-sectional investigation such as ours, it is necessary to include firm-specific fixed effects to take into consideration the unobserved heterogeneity of our sample. We are able to show that (7.7) takes the form of this equation:

$$L(\beta) = C - \sum_{i=1}^{N}\sum_{t=1}^{T} DIRTUR_{it} \ln\left[\sum_{t=1}^{T}\left(e^{-(X_{it} - X_{is})\beta}\right)\right] \qquad (7.8)$$

after we have included the firm-specific effect into the model.[37] Equation (7.8) ignores the variations among firms and only studies the within-firm variation; this omission substantially reduces the variability of our sample. We present, however, the results using both model specifications.

In table 7.9, we report the results of these regressions. In the table, all performance measures show the correct signs and are statistically significant,[38] except in model (4), where the z-value of *LROEA* is –1.52 (p-value 0.129). These results confirm the inverse relationship between corporate performance and director turnovers found in the univariate test. In addition, the control variables show a significant effect on the median director tenure (*MEDITE*), the lag value of CEO turnover (*LCEOTUR*), size (*FSIZE*), and *PERIOD2*. *MEDITE* is negative, suggesting that the longer the director stays on the board, the harder it is to observe a director turnover due to poor firm performance. This also reflects a possible entrenchment effect on the board. *LCEOTUR* is negative, suggesting that, when a new CEO is appointed (replacing the CEO involved in the turnover), there is also a change on the board; we should therefore observe a few changes in the board of directors one year after a new CEO has taken charge. This is consistent, on the one hand, with the hypothesis that the CEO may also wish to remake the board with directors of his or her own choosing and, on the other hand, with the fact that, in República Bolivariana de Venezuela, directors are considered by law to have administrative responsibilities.[39]

Table 7.9 Panel Data Poisson Regression on the Number of Director Turnovers

Variables	*Random effects (1)*	*Fixed effects (2)*	*Random effects (3)*	*Fixed effects (4)*	*Random effects (5)*	*Fixed effects (6)*
Intercept	0.4791		0.4698		0.3593	
	z = 1.50		z = 1.46		z = 1.03	
LROAA	−0.9112**	−0.7396**				
	z = −2.22	z = −2.42				
LROEA			−0.0894**	−0.0636		
			z = −2.35	z = −1.52		
LNEGINC					0.4595***	0.4087***
					z = 2.81	z = 3.96
MEDITE	−0.1972***	−0.1734***	−0.1947***	−0.1747***	−0.1848***	−0.1691***
	z = −8.05	z = −14.06	z = −7.78	z = −14.09	z = −7.14	z = −13.69
CEOCHA	0.0213	−0.1446	0.0374	−0.1506	0.0201	−0.1572
	z = 0.19	z = −1.22	z = 0.34	z = −1.26	z = 0.17	z = −1.30
LCEOTUR	−0.5927**	−0.6423***	−0.5567**	−0.6226***	−0.5871**	−0.6422***
	z = −2.42	z = −6.28	z = −2.28	z = −6.10	z = −2.41	z = −6.27
BLOHOL	−0.0557	−0.0400	−0.0438	0.0382	−0.0308	0.0414
	z = −0.84	z = −0.54	z = −0.67	z = 0.51	z = −0.51	z = 0.56
ADRUSA	0.2223*	0.1896	0.2682**	0.2378	0.1624	0.1778
	z = 1.76	z = 1.07	z = 2.21	z = 1.35	z = 1.19	z = 1.00

(continued)

Table 7.9 Panel Data Poisson Regression on the Number of Director Turnovers *(continued)*

Variables	*Random effects (1)*	*Fixed effects (2)*	*Random effects (3)*	*Fixed effects (4)*	*Random effects (5)*	*Fixed effects (6)*
FSIZE	0.07330***	0.1121***	0.0719***	0.1066***	0.0725***	0.0920***
	z = 3.89	z = 4.12	z = 3.93	z = 3.92	z = 3.84	z = 3.35
CASTR	0.0223	0.3676*	-0.0181	0.3252	-0.0185	0.1979
	z = 0.09	z = 1.89	z = -0.07	z = 1.62	z = -0.08	z = 0.98
PERIOD2	0.1991**	0.2447***	0.2082**	0.2527***	0.2064**	0.2553***
	z = 2.08	z = 3.45	z = 2.21	z = 3.57	z = 2.15	z = 3.59
Observations	827	827	827	827	827	827
Wald Chi (9)	171.59***	299.74***	172.84***	297.86***	247.13***	315.23***
Hausman	119.54***		1126.88***		60.88***	

Source: Compiled by the authors from the annual financial proxies and investor relations offices of the firms.

Note: The total sample consists of 878 firm-year observations of 51 firms listed on the BVC from 1984 to 2002. We perform a Poisson regression using DIRTUR as a dependent variable. The performance variables are LROAA, LROEA, and LNEGINC. We control for board characteristics using MEDITE and CEOCHA. We control for CEO characteristics using LCEOTUR. We control for blockholding ownership using BLOHOL and ADRUSA. We control for firm characteristics using FSIZE and CASTR. We control for time periods using PERIOD2. Definitions of the variables are given in table 7.4.

* significant at 10 percent

** significant at 5 percent

*** significant at 1 percent

FSIZE is positive, showing that, in bigger firms (with presumably bigger boards), we observe more director turnovers. Finally, *PERIOD2* is positive and significant, indicating that, in this period (1991–96 inclusive), there were unusual director turnovers. This result is probably a consequence of the Venezuelan banking crisis, during which half the banking system had to be restructured, and many directors had to leave their firms.

Table 7.9 also shows a positive sign in the coefficient of *ADRUSA* (a dummy variable that takes the value of 1 if the firm has issued ADRs in the United States), suggesting that firms change directors (presumably, for more independent directors) before going to the U.S. market. However, this coefficient is statistically significant at the 10 and 5 percent levels only in models (1) and (3), respectively. The other control variables, *CEOCHA*, *CASTR*, and *BLOHOL*, show no statistical significance in any of the models.

In the three models presented in table 7.9, we find the presence of serial correlation in the random-effects models (all Hausman tests are statistically significant at the 1 percent level), but this problem is not uncommon in panel data analysis.[40] However, the main results are similar when we include firm-specific fixed effects.[41]

These results leave us to conclude that Hypothesis 2 may not be rejected; that is, performance seems to affect director turnover. In the next subsection, we investigate whether or not these results still hold when we change the turnover measure for directors.

Director Turnovers, OLS Approach

Here, we perform an OLS estimation of the percentage turnover of the board (*BODITU*) as a dependent variable. This model may be written as:

$$Y_i = \beta' X_i + \varepsilon_i. \tag{7.9}$$

Also, we need to assume here that $E\{\varepsilon_i\} = 0$ and

$$E\{\varepsilon_i \varepsilon_j\} = \frac{\sigma_{ij}}{1-\rho_i \rho_j} \begin{pmatrix} 1 & \rho_j & \cdots & \rho_j^{T-1} \\ \rho_i & 1 & \cdots & \rho_j^{T-2} \\ \cdot & \cdot & \cdot & \cdot \\ \cdot & \cdot & \cdot & \cdot \\ \cdot & \cdot & \cdot & \cdot \\ \rho_i^{T-1} & \rho_i^{T-2} & \cdots & 1 \end{pmatrix}. \tag{7.10}$$

Here, we also assume that $e_{it} = \rho_i e_{i,t-1} + v_{it}$ for $i = 1, 2, \ldots, N$, where $E\{v_{it}\} = 0$, $E\{v_{it}\, v_{jt}\} = \sigma_{it}$ and $E\{v_{it}\, v_j\} = 0$ for $t \neq s$.

In table 7.10, we report the results for this model. As the table shows, the coefficients of all performance measures have the correct sign and are statistically significant. This confirms the inverse relationship between corporate performance and director turnover found using the Poisson regression model and the univariate test. Also, the control variables display similar behavior as we report for the Poisson approach. Contrary to the Poisson approach, however, we do not find serial correlation in the random-effects models. (Hausman tests were not statistically significant in any of the models.) This finding explains the similarities of the performance coefficient estimates when we use random- or fixed-effects models.[42]

The univariate test, the Poisson regression, and the OLS regression provide strong evidence in favor of Hypothesis 2, that is, performance affects the departure of directors in this Venezuelan sample. The empirical evidence shows that the poorer the firm performance, the higher the incidence of director turnovers, which is consistent with Yermack (2004) and Farrell and Whidbee (2000), who found similar results in the United States, a very different context in terms of market development and legal framework.

Robustness Checks

In this section, we present a set of robustness checks on our results. We group the tests into the following categories: lagged values of performance measures, macroeconomic controls, ownership structure, endogeneity problem, and forced turnover.

Lagged Values of Performance Measures

We run three additional sets of regressions (not shown).[43] The first uses the second lag of our performance proxies instead of the first lag. The coefficient of the lag value of *LROAA* (that is, the second lag), the lag value of *LROEA*, and the lag value of *LNEGINC* are –1.930618 (z = –2.958), –0.3169111 (z = –2.150), and 0.3557117 (z = 1.056), respectively, for the random-effects models. Note that the signs of the coefficient are all correct and statistically significant, except for *LNEGINC*, and they are even higher than those reported using the first lag (see table 7.8). However, for the fixed-effects models, although the sign is still correct, the estimated coefficients are not statistically significant.

For the second set of regressions, we have included the first and the second lag for each of the performance measures. In all cases, the signs are correct for the random- and fixed-effects models, and at least one of the coefficients is statistically significant. For example, the coefficients

Table 7.10 Panel Data OLS Regression on the Percentage of Director Turnovers

Variables	*Random effects (1)*	*Fixed effects (2)*	*Random effects (3)*	*Fixed effects (4)*	*Random effects (5)*	*Fixed effects (6)*
Intercept	0.1890***	0.1749	0.1779***	0.0808	0.1476***	0.1523*
	z = 4.13	t = 0.84	z = 3.92	t = 0.91	z = 3.09	t = 1.69
LROAA	–0.1794*	–0.1755**				
	z = –1.74	t = –2.20				
LROEA			–0.0422**	–0.0327**		
			z = –2.05	t = –1.97		
LNEGINC					0.1492***	0.1390***
					z = 3.99	t = 4.75
MEDITE	–0.0172***	–0.0176***	–0.0170***	–0.0177***	–0.0166***	–0.0175***
	z = –6.36	t = –8.59	z = –6.38	t = –8.60	z = –6.44	t = –8.61
CEOCHA	0.0357*	–0.0063	0.0354	–0.0033	0.0372**	–0.0028
	z = 1.87	t = –0.20	z = 1.85	t = –0.11	z = 2.05	t = –0.09
LCEOTUR	–0.0707**	–0.1069***	–0.0687**	–0.1030***	–0.0794**	–0.1085***
	z = –2.09	t = –4.13	z = –2.00	t = –3.99	z = –2.32	t = –4.21
BLOHOL	–0.0026	0.0084	–0.0020	0.0091	0.0041	0.0024
	z = –0.28	t = 0.47	z = –0.23	t = 0.51	z = 0.47	t = 0.12
ADRUSA	0.0009	0.0143	0.0015	0.0210	–0.0202	–0.0139
	z = 0.04	t = 0.34	z = 0.07	t = 0.51	z = –0.83	t = 0.34

(continued)

Table 7.10 Panel Data OLS Regression on the Percentage of Director Turnovers *(continued)*

Variables	*Random effects (1)*	*Fixed effects (2)*	*Random effects (3)*	*Fixed effects (4)*	*Random effects (5)*	*Fixed effects (6)*
FSIZE	0.0111***	0.0200***	0.0115***	0.0194***	0.0117***	0.0140**
	z = 2.97	t = 3.10	z = 3.01	t = 3.01	z = 3.17	t = 2.18
CASTR	-0.0566	0.0202	-0.0514	0.0108	-0.0541	-0.0367
	z = -1.22	t = 0.36	z = -1.14	t = 0.19	z = -1.20	t = -0.65
PERIOD2	0.0223	0.0220	0.0244	0.0237	0.0283*	0.0272
	z = 1.40	t = 1.23	z = 1.53	t = 1.33	z = 1.90	t = 1.54
Observations	827	827	827	827	827	827
Wald Chi^2 (9)	78.13***		73.42***		109.59***	
F(9,767)		12.82***		12.70***		15.09***
R^2 (overall)		0.1192		0.1237		0.1618
Hausman	10.46		7.26		3.26	

Source: Compiled by the authors from the annual financial proxies and investor relations offices of the firms.

Note: The total sample consists of 878 firm-year observations of 51 firms listed on the BVC from 1984 to 2002. We perform an OLS regression using BODITU as a dependent variable. The performance variables are LROAA, LROEA, and LNEGINC. We control for board characteristics using MEDITE and CEOCHA. We control for CEO characteristics using LCEOTUR. We control for blockholding ownership using OWNERS and ADRUSA. We control for firm characteristics using FSIZE and CASTR. We control for time periods using PERIOD2. Definitions of the variables are given in table 7.4.

* significant at 10 percent

** significant at 5 percent

*** significant at 1 percent

of *LROAA* (first lag) and its second lag in the random-effects model are -2.047963 (z = -3.081) and -1.440506 (z = -2.191), respectively.

For the third set of regressions, we take the arithmetic average of the first and the second lag values for each performance measure. For both the random- and fixed-effects models, the signs of the coefficients are correct and significant. The coefficient of the average lag of the *ROAA* is -3.545955 (z = -3.261) and -3.152654 (z = -1.805) for the random- and fixed-effects models, respectively.

These analyses confirm that the model reported in table 7.8 is robust in terms of the lag value chosen.

Macroeconomic Controls

Although we control for industry-wide shocks by adjusting our performance measures according to industry, an aggregate macroeconomic shock might have difference effects across industries and across firms. Because the Venezuelan economy is highly dependent on oil, we include two macroeconomic controls: the annual variation of GDP in real terms, but without oil, and the annual variation of the national income from oil, also in real terms.

The regression results (not shown)[44] do not change significantly from those reported in tables 7.8, 7.9, and 7.10. The annual variation of national income from oil is never significant, and the annual variation of the gross national product in real terms, but without oil is only significant at the 10 percent level in the regression where the dependent variable is *CEOTUR*.

Ownership Structure

We use three variables to measure the impact of ownership concentration in the relationship between turnover and performance: *OWNCON*, *BLOHOL*, and *ADRUSA*. We run a set of eight regressions (all possible combinations among these three variables, including using none of them), and the results do not change significantly.[45]

The empirical implication of this variable is not clear from the theoretical point of view.[46] On the one hand, we might have a positive relation with turnover, arguing that the higher the concentration, the better the monitoring of the CEO. Therefore a better monitoring history might explain higher turnover because of poor firm performance when ownership concentration is high; we would thus expect a negative sign for the firm performance proxy and a positive sign for the ownership proxy. On the other hand, a high concentration might also mean that the firm's owner appoints a puppet CEO to extract rents from minority shareholders; therefore, we would expect no relation between turnover and performance and a negative coefficient for ownership (that is, more ownership concentration means less CEO turnover).

Also, as we argue elsewhere above, the low *between-firm* variability and *within-firm* variability in each of these three variables might explain the lack of statistical power. (They are not statistically significant in any of our regression model.) For example, only 13 firms in República Bolivariana de Venezuela issued ADRs; only six firms were considered widely held at the 20 percent level (meaning that no single shareholder or group held more than 20 percent of the firm shares); and only two firms were considered widely held at the 10 percent level (Banco de Venezuela in 1986–99 and Banco Provincial in 1984–93). This shows the high ownership concentration in our sample; moreover, ultimate ownership is fully identified in only 32 of the 51 firms in our sample (individuals, families, or business groups). It is therefore possible that ownership concentration is even higher if pyramidal ownership were considered in greater detail.[47] This demonstrates low *between-firm* variability, which might have an important impact on the power of the ownership variables in our statistical test.

Although, in our sample, 31 firms experienced drastic changes in ownership structure, once the change had occurred, the ownership structure tended to remain stable throughout the period under analysis. Moreover, in 20 firms the ownership structure remained almost unchanged for the whole sample period. This demonstrates low *within-firm* variability, which might be reducing the statistical power of our ownership variables.

Endogeneity Problem

The variable *CEOTUR* and each of the performance measures are likely to be endogenous. This is a serious problem because it violates the crucial assumption that regressors are either nonstochastic or, if they are stochastic, they are distributed independently of the stochastic disturbance term. Therefore, the estimated coefficients are not only biased, but are also inconsistent.

We deal with this problem in two ways. First, because *CEOTUR*, *ROAA*, *ROEA*, and *NEGINC* are likely to be endogenous, we use the lag value of the performance measures in our results—reported in tables 7.8, 7.9, and 7.10—and not the current value (although the results are similar if the current values are used). Also, the main results are unaltered when we use panel data fixed-effects specifications, which are known to alleviate endogeneity problems.[48] However, we recognize that the use of lag performance variables and fixed-effects specifications do not necessarily eliminate the potentially spurious relation between CEO turnover (and director turnover) and firm performance. For this reason, to alleviate our endogeneity concerns, we perform an instrumental variable analysis as a measure of the robustness of our results.

One of the main problems in the instrumental variable analysis is finding a truly exogenous variable (instrument) that affects performance, but not the probability of CEO and director turnover. Ideally, we want to find an exogenous event such as a change in legislation, for example, that has affected all firms in the sample. However, for the period 1984–2002, we are not able to find major changes in corporate law that may be used as an exogenous shock. (The current commercial code in República Bolivariana de Venezuela was approved by Congress in 1955.) Another problem is the limitation of our data set in terms of the number of variables.

We perform a two-stage estimation using *INVTA* (changes in fixed assets, divided by total assets) and *PPTTOSALES* (fixed assets, divided by total sales) as instrumental variables.[49] The first variable attempts to measure the rate of investment,[50] which is likely to affect the current level of industry-adjusted (but not lagged) ROA, but there is no intuitive reason to assume that this rate of investment affects CEO and director turnover as well. The second variable aims to measure a firm's collateral value,[51] but it might also be considered a measure of firm efficiency in terms of the amount of fixed assets needed to produce a unit of sale. This variable should affect (negatively) the performance coefficient, but not, at least intuitively, CEO and director turnover.[52]

The results indicate (not shown)[53] that the relationship between CEO and director turnover and performance becomes more negative and more statistically significant. For example, when the dependent variable is *CEOTUR* and the performance variable generated by the two-stage process is the industry-adjusted ROA, the estimated coefficients are more negative (–13.8045 versus –2.2922, see table 7.8) and more statistically significant ($z = -4.80$ versus $z = -2.66$, see table 7.8). For *DIRTUR*, *BODITU*, and the other performance measures, the results are similar because they became more negative (more positive in the case of *NEGINC*) and more statistically significant.

Although the instrument we use may be questionable (as all instruments are), at least we are able to affirm that, if endogeneity is present in our analysis, our results in tables 7.8, 7.9, and 7.10 are somewhat conservative in terms of the real impact that firm performance has on CEO and director turnover after endogeneity is explicitly taken into account. This larger effect after endogeneity is explicitly considered using instrumental variables is also present in Hermalin and Weisbach (1991) and Himmelberg, Hubbard, and Palia (1999).

Forced Turnover

As shown in table 7.5, our sample includes 131 CEO turnovers. However, the information in the database does not allow us to determine which of these CEO turnovers are forced and which are natural. We try to use the age of the CEO to control partially for this effect, but we find a negative and significant coefficient for the variable CEOAGE, probably capturing other effects, such as CEO entrenchment.

To find another variable that we may use as a proxy for CEO turnover, we have constructed a dummy variable that takes the value of 1 if the CEO is replaced by somebody outside the firm (not previously attending the board of directors) and 0 if the CEO is replaced by somebody inside the firm. We run a set of regressions using this variable, called *NEWCEO* (not shown here),[54] and, although the signs of the coefficients of *LROAA* and *LROEA* are still negative, they are not statistically significant. Our data set contains only 71 CEO turnovers in which the incoming CEO is from outside the firm.

Although there are few observations in which NEWCEO is equal to 1, our third performance variable, *LNEGINC*, is still statistically significant. Our coefficient for *LNEGINC* is 1.137925 (z = 2.490) for the random-effects model and 1.576682 (z = 3.001) for the fixed-effects model.

We construct another dummy variable, called *FORCED*, that takes the value of 1 if the CEO that was turned over has stayed on the board as principal director for at least one year and 0 otherwise. In only 65 cases is *FORCED* equal to 1. Even when the small number of observations is taken into account, all the performance variables keep the expected sign, and, in the case of *LROEA*, the coefficients are –0.305591 (z = –1.829) for the random-effects model and –0.5043 (z = –1.604) for the fixed-effects model.

Conclusions and Policy Recommendations

Results from a questionnaire survey we have conducted on corporate governance practices in República Bolivariana de Venezuela show that public companies exhibit relatively low overall corporate governance scores, especially in the categories of general principles and of officers and the board. The scores on shareholders and on disclosure and information are relatively better. Overall results from the questionnaire would give Venezuelan firms an index of 54.71 out of 100. To place these results in perspective, mean results for the 14 emerging markets analyzed in Klapper and Love (2002) have yielded a similar score of 54.11. Scores for the two Latin American countries considered in their paper are 57.26 (Brazil) and 61.63 (Chile). Empirical tests reported in the annex hereafter suggest that there exists a positive and significant pairwise correlation and Spearman rank correlation between each of the value measures computed (Tobin's q, the price-to-book ratio, and dividend payout) and the CGI. The correlation between each of the corporate governance subindexes and the CGI is positive, although it is not significant in all cases. Regression analysis is consistent with these results, which ought to be analyzed with care given the small size of the sample.

The univariate test and the Logit regression model provide strong evidence that Hypothesis 1 may not be rejected. Also, the univariate test and the Poisson and OLS regression models provide strong evidence that Hypothesis 2 may not be rejected, that is, performance seems to affect the departure of CEOs and directors in our sample of Venezuelan public firms. This finding is consistent with Gibson (2003) in that corporate governance mechanisms in República Bolivariana de Venezuela seem to ensure that a firm's poor financial performance increases the likelihood that the CEO and the directors will leave the firm, a necessary condition for any corporate governance system to work. The low *between-firm* variability and *within-firm* variability in our ownership concentration variables may explain their lack of statistical power in the regressions.

Our results have passed several robustness tests. We have used lagged performance variables and panel data fixed-effects models to reduce the potential endogeneity between CEO and director turnover and firm performance. Also, using an instrumental variable estimation, we have shown that, when endogeneity is taken explicitly into account, the negative relationship between turnover and performance becomes more negative and more statistically significant.

We have also shown that the relationship between CEO and director turnover and the *CEOAGE*, *CEOCHA*, and *MEDITU* control variables capture some preliminary evidence of CEO and director entrenchment; that is, the older the CEO and the more powerful and more longstanding the board tenure, the less likely it is that we will observe turnovers because of poor corporate performance.

Another interesting result is that, on average, when the CEO leaves the firm, the directors also leave. It therefore seems that the role of boards of directors in this sample of Venezuelan firms is not monitoring, but rather advising the CEO. This idea might be added to Yermack's (2004) conjectures that directors might be tempted to abandon the firm when the CEO leaves for at least two reasons: reputation and the workload involved in restructuring a firm. In the same vein, Fich and Shivdasani (2006) show that busy directors in the United States are more likely to depart boards following poor firm performance. Moreover, the legal framework in República Bolivariana de Venezuela makes directors responsible for the administration of the firm; consistent with this role, directors leave the firm when its financial performance deteriorates.

Our survey on corporate governance in República Bolivariana de Venezuela suggests that, despite recent improvements, a number of practices need to be revised. These include the following findings: (1) the majority of external auditors are not elected by the firm's audit committee, (2) external auditors are hired for consulting purposes, (3) only a few firms acknowledge having a corporate governance committee, (4) there is a lack of transparency in disclosing a company's ultimate ownership, (5) there is a relatively low level of protection for minority shareholders, and (6) there are unsatisfactory levels of disclosure of executive compensation.

Even tough investors are not well protected in República Bolivariana de Venezuela. The results presented here suggest that firms may reduce the cost of capital when they improve their corporate governance practices, which, in turn, may also enhance their market valuation and operating performance. As may be seen in tables 7D and 7E in the annex, a higher CGI in República Bolivariana de Venezuela leads to increases in both a firm's Tobin's q and its price-to-book ratio. More specifically, as table 7G in the annex shows, a firm may increase its Tobin's q and price-to-book ratio by improving its performance on the corporate governance category of officers and the board.

A policy we suggest is the elimination of the 1 percent sales tax on all stock transactions currently in place on the BVC. This tax was instituted in the early 1990s (and the capital gains tax eliminated), and it is applied regardless of whether the investor has made a profit or suffered a loss. This sales tax penalizes the short-term transactions that are essential to providing liquidity to the stock market. As a result of the introduction of this tax, traded volumes have decreased substantially, and the stock exchange has become less efficient.[55] To the extent that the existence of liquid and efficient stock markets is a necessary condition so that better corporate governance practices may be reflected in higher market valuations, the elimination of this sales tax may prove to be crucial, especially for small- and medium-size firms the shares of which would never trade in the form of ADRs in the United States.

Every effort to increase the supply of long-term funds to the market is critical for the survival of capital markets in República Bolivariana de Venezuela. Foreign investors have, for the most part, exited the BVC and are investing in the ADRs of the few Venezuelan companies that are trading in the U.S. markets since the strict foreign exchange controls were introduced in February 2003. The importance of local funds for the sustainability of Venezuelan capital markets is clear given that there is no sign these capital controls will be eliminated over the short or medium term. Increasing oil prices have helped the economy grow at rapid rates since 2004, although political uncertainty and the possibility of a reversal in oil prices have deterred private investments.

The CNV has been undertaking increasingly substantial efforts to bring small investors into the local stock market by organizing free courses on capital markets and holding an initial investor's fair in September 2006. A recent change in the law that regulates cajas de ahorro (a savings mechanism available to public and private employees) allows for the investment of a fraction of these savings in the stock market. On the other hand, as we mention at the beginning of this chapter, a pension law still needs to be discussed and approved by Congress.

Finally, as a way to gain investor confidence and promote better governance practices, state-owned banks such as Banco Industrial de Venezuela may follow a plan, similar to the initiative devised by the National Development Bank in Brazil, to reduce interest rates on loans for firms that commit to implementing better corporate governance practices.

Annex 7.1 Nonparametric Tests and Regression Analysis

In this annex, we present a brief analysis of three nonparametric tests (pairwise correlation, Spearman rank correlation, and a test of equality of means) on the relation between a set of three valuation measures (Tobin's q, the price-to-book ratio, and dividend payout) and the CGI for the sample of Venezuelan firms presented in table 7.2.[56] We resort to nonparametric tests because of the small size of our sample of firms and because our questionnaire survey was conducted for only one year (2004).[57] We also present results arising from our regression analysis.

La Porta et al. (1998, 2000b, 2002) contend and find evidence that better shareholder protection is related to a higher valuation of corporate assets. There is a relationship because outside investors are willing to pay more for corporate assets when shareholders are protected. Using data from the Investor Responsibility Research Center, Gompers, Ishii, and Metrick (2003) find that firms with fewer shareholder rights have lower stock returns and firm valuations. They take Tobin's q as their single valuation measure.[58] Fenn and Liang (2001) use dividend yields as their value measure.

Table 7A presents a pairwise correlation matrix for the CGI, its subindexes, and the three value measures. There exists a positive and significant correlation between each of the value measures and the CGI. The correlation between each of the corporate governance subindexes and the CGI is positive and significant at the 1 percent level in all cases. Among the corporate governance subindexes, only the correlation between officers and the board and each of the three value measures is positive and significant. The correlation between general principles and dividend payout is positive and significant. The correlation between disclosure and information and Tobin's q and between disclosure and information and dividend payout is positive and significant.

In table 7B we report the results of Spearman rank correlations between the CGI and its subindexes and the three value measures. The results for the CGI are similar to those presented in table 7A. They show a positive and significant rank correlation between the CGI and each of the three value measures. The rank correlation between each of the corporate governance subindexes and the value measures is positive, although it is significant in all cases, except in the case of disclosure and information.

Table 7A Pairwise Correlation Matrix for the CGI, Subindexes, and Value Measures

	Value measures			*Corporate governance measures*				
	Tobin´s q	*Price-to-book ratio*	*Dividend payout*	*CGI*	*General principles*	*Officers and the board*	*Shareholders*	*Disclosure and info*
Tobin´s q	1.0000							
Price-to-book ratio	0.7753***	1.0000						
	0.0001							
Dividend payout	0.4668**	0.2032	1.0000					
	0.0388	0.3901						
Corporate governance index	0.5388**	0.4287*	0.5167**	1.0000				
	0.0142	0.0593	0.0197					
General principles	0.3390	0.0498	0.5014**	0.5857***	1.0000			
	0.1437	0.8348	0.0243	0.0067				
Officers and the board	0.4466**	0.4462**	0.4011*	0.7908***	0.4923**	1.0000		
	0.0484	0.0486	0.0796	0.0000	0.0275			
Shareholders	0.3201	0.3585	0.1567	0.6141***	0.1663	0.2629	1.0000	
	0.1689	0.1206	0.5095	0.0040	0.4834	0.2627		

(continued)

Table 7A Pairwise Correlation Matrix for the CGI, Subindexes, and Value Measures *(continued)*

	Value measures			*Corporate governance measures*				
	Tobin´s q	*Price-to-book ratio*	*Dividend payout*	*CGI*	*General principles*	*Officers and the board*	*Shareholders*	*Disclosure and info*
Disclosure	0.4418*	0.2959	0.3805*	0.7632***	0.1965	0.4037*	0.3923*	1.0000
and info	0.0512	0.2053	0.0979	0.0001	0.4065	0.0776	0.0871	

Source: Compiled by the authors from the annual financial proxies and investor relations offices of the firms.
Note: Definitions of the variables are given in table 7.4.
* significant at 10 percent
** significant at 5 percent
*** significant at 1 percent

Table 7B Spearman Rank Correlations among the CGI, Subindexes, and Value Measures

Variable	*Tobin's q*	*Price-to-book ratio*	*Dividend payout*
Corporate governance index	0.4991**	0.5193**	0.6043***
	0.0251	0.0190	0.0048
General principles	0.3994*	0.1927	0.4420**
	0.0811	0.4157	0.0500
Officers and the board	0.3372	0.4012*	0.5981***
	0.1460	0.0795	0.0053
Shareholders	0.3764	0.3871*	0.2726
	0.1019	0.0917	0.2440
Disclosure and information	0.4995**	0.4315*	0.4323*
	0.0249	0.0575	0.0569

Source: Compiled by the authors from the annual financial proxies and investor relations offices of the firms.

Note: Definitions of the variables are given in table 7.4.

* significant at 10 percent

** significant at 5 percent

*** significant at 1 percent

Table 7C presents a two-sample t test of means with equal variances. The means of firms possessing a Tobin's q above the average are significantly different from the means of firms possessing a Tobin's q below the average. The same result is found when the test is run on the price-to-book ratio, but is not found when the test is run using our third value measure, dividend payout.

We then analyze firm value as a function of the CGI and its subindexes using regression analysis. Our analysis is similar to that presented in Leal and Carvalhal-da-Silva (2005) and in Lefort and Walker (2005). Unfortunately, as we mention elsewhere above, the results from regressions may not be taken as conclusive evidence because our sample size is very small. Of the 31 firms that answered the questionnaire, it is possible only to include 20 in the regressions. These were the companies for which meaningful market-related data existed during 2003 and 2004. The other 11 companies did not trade at all on the BVC or traded very infrequently during 2004. Considering these facts, it is difficult to argue that the local stock exchange is efficient. The following analysis linking good corporate governance practices to market valuation should therefore be viewed with care.

In figure 7A, we present scatter plots of our three value measures (Tobin's q, the price-to-book ratio, and dividend payout) and the CGI for

Table 7C Tests of Equality of Means: Two-Sample t Test with Equal Variances

	Mean	*95% confidence interval*	
(i) Tobin's q			
q above average	1.2219	0.9388	1.5051
q below average	0.7509	0.489	1.0128
combined	1.0099	0.8006	1.2193
difference	0.471	0.1049	0.8371
t = 2.7032			
P > |t| = 0.0146			
(ii) Price-to-book			
PTB above average	1.7482	0.9469	2.5495
PTB below average	0.8767	0.3836	1.3697
Combined	1.356	0.8607	1.8513
Difference	0.8715	–0.0601	1.8031
t = 1.9655			
P > |t| = 0.0650			
(iii) Dividend payout (DP)			
DP above average	0.8656	0.0394	1.6918
DP below average	0.3844	–1.4385	2.2174
Combined	0.7854	0.1099	1.4608
Difference	0.4811	–1.4132	2.3754
t = 0.5659			
P > |t| = 0.5840			

Source: Compiled by the authors from the annual financial proxies and investor relations offices of the firms.

Note: Definitions of the variables are given in table 7.4. According to the null hypothesis, the difference between the two means is equal to 0. The alternative hypothesis is that the means are different from 0.

* significant at 10 percent

** significant at 5 percent

*** significant at 1 percent

Figure 7A Scatter Plots: Value Measures and Subindexes of the CGI

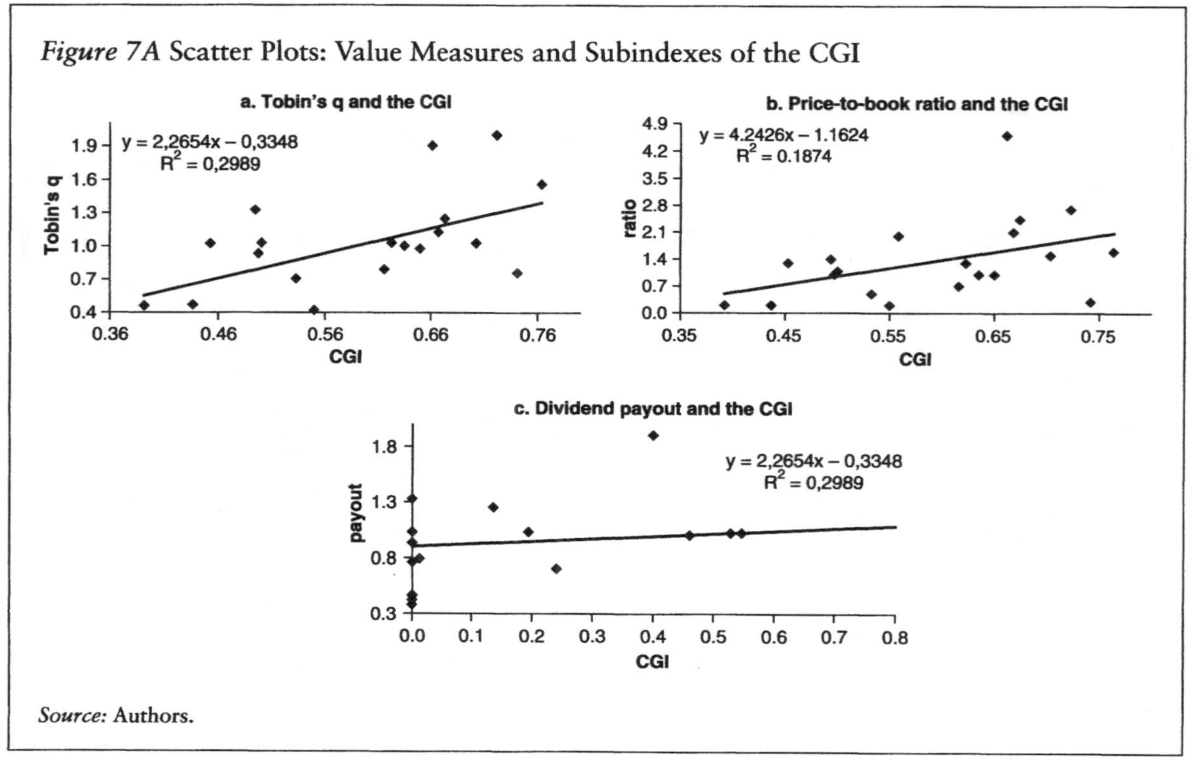

Source: Authors.

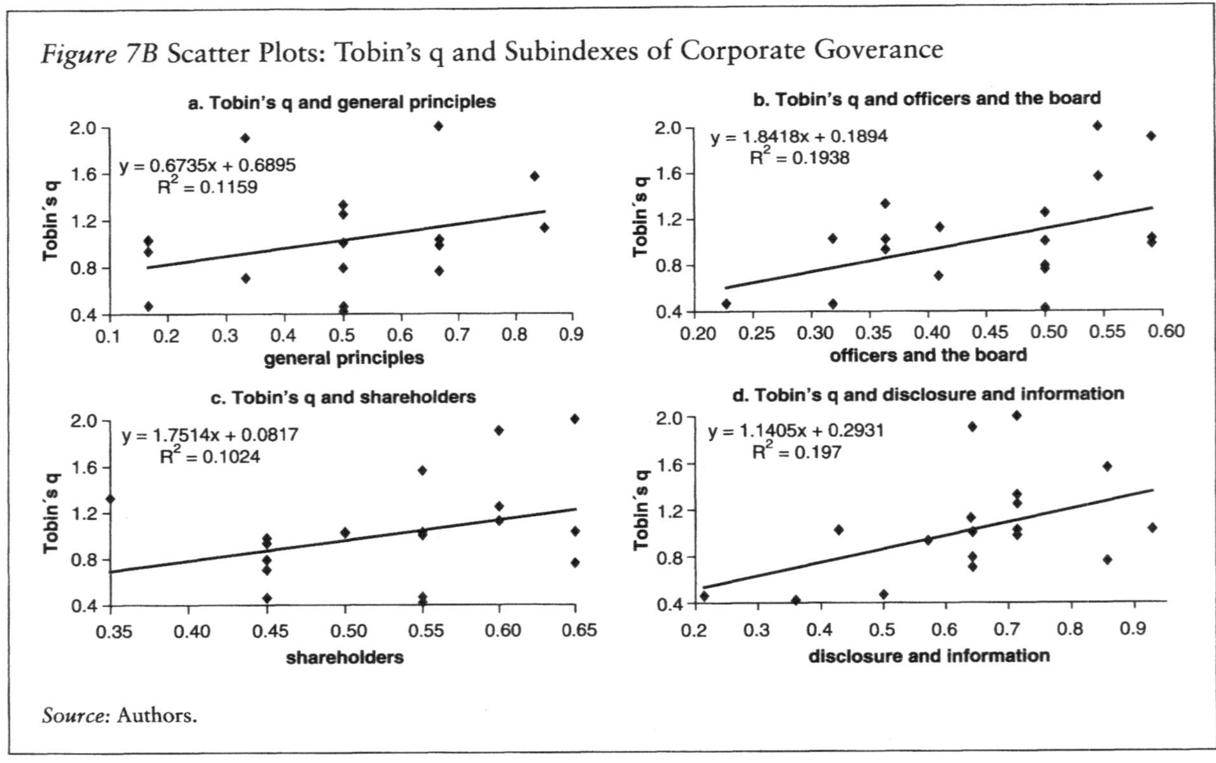

Figure 7B Scatter Plots: Tobin's q and Subindexes of Corporate Goverance

Source: Authors.

Figure 7C Scatter Plots: Price-to-Book Ratio and Corporate Governance

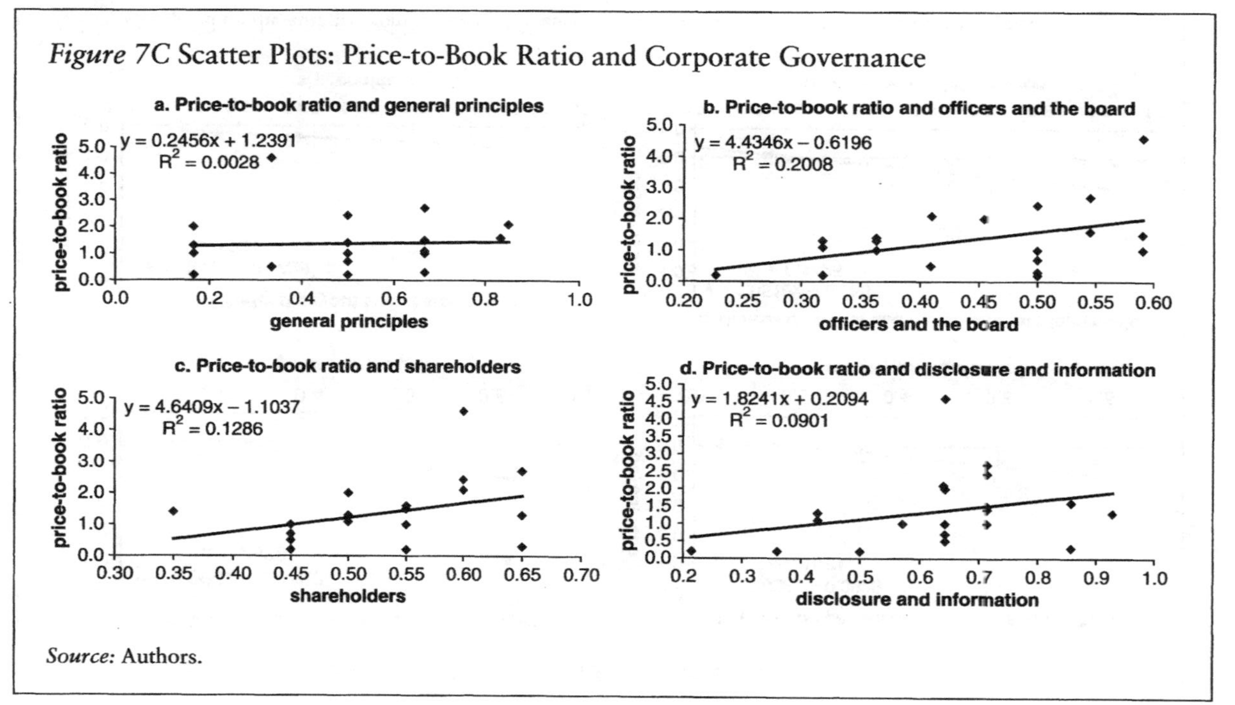

Source: Authors.

Figure 7D Scatter Plots: Dividend Payout and Corporate Goverance

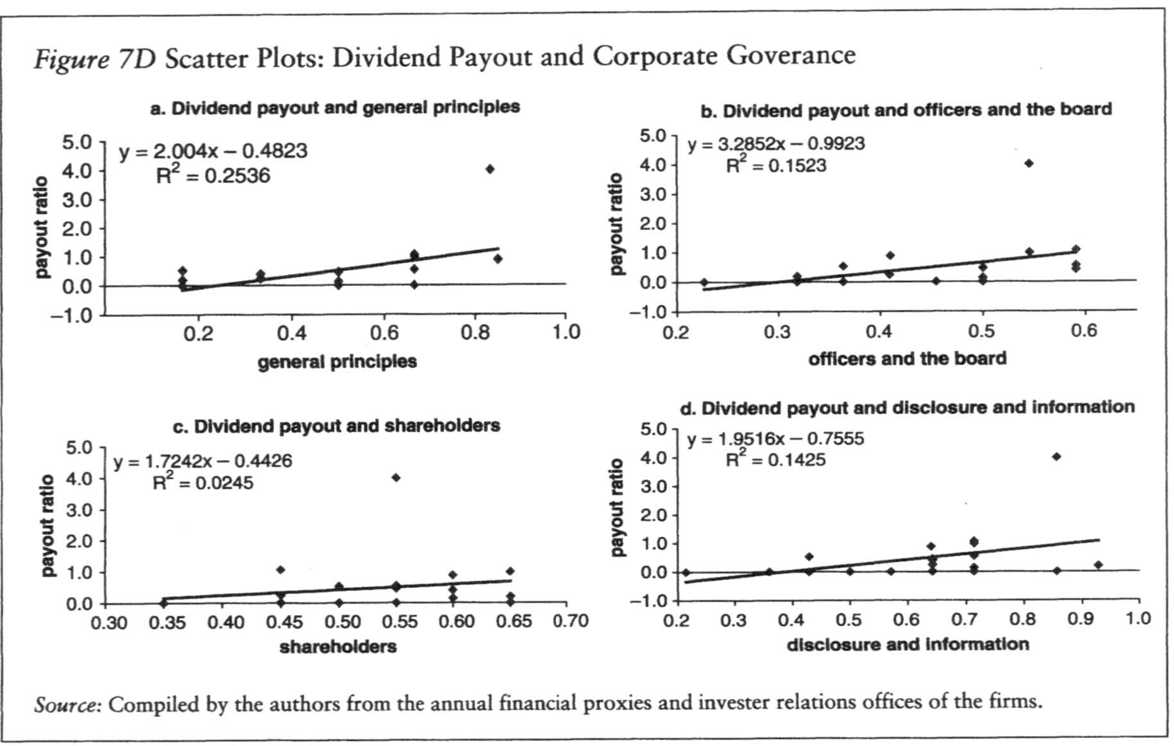

Source: Compiled by the authors from the annual financial proxies and invester relations offices of the firms.

these 20 listed firms. There is a positive relationship between each of the value measures and the CGI for the sample.

The scatter plots in figures 7B, 7C, and 7D present the relationship between each of the value measures (Tobin's q, the price-to-book ratio, and dividend payout) and each of the corporate governance subindexes (general principles, officers and the board, shareholders, and disclosure and information). In general, consistent with the nonparametric tests presented elsewhere above, the relationships between each of the corporate governance subindexes and each of the measures of value is positive and significant.

In the next tables, using regression analysis, we explore in more detail the relationships between the corporate governance subindexes and the measures of value. Table 7D presents regression results for Tobin's q on the CGI. Model 1 includes only the CGI as an explanatory variable. For a 1 unit increase in the CGI, Tobin's q increases by 2.24 percent. This result is both statistically and economically significant. The other models show other specifications in which different control variables (leverage, volatility, growth, ROA2, and size) are included. Unfortunately, given the small sample size, when a number of control variables are included in the same equation the degrees of freedom of the regression become too low. In general, the CGI remains positive and significant in these models. The only control variable that is significant is the ROA.

Table 7E shows regression results for the price-to-book ratio on the CGI. Model 1 presents only the CGI as an explanatory variable. For a 1 unit increase in the CGI, the price-to-book ratio increases by 4.21 percent. This result is both statistically and economically significant. The other models present other specifications in which different control variables (leverage, volatility, growth, ROA2, and size) are included. In general, the CGI remains positive and significant in these models. Once again, the only control variable that is statistically significant is the ROA.

Table 7F shows regression results for the dividend payout on the CGI. Once again, model 1 presents only the CGI as an explanatory variable. For a 1 unit increase in the CGI, dividend payout increases by 4.32 percent. This result is both statistically and economically significant. The other models present other specifications in which different combinations of control variables (leverage, volatility, growth, ROA2, and size) are included. In general, the CGI remains positive and significant in these models. No control variable is significant.

Table 7G presents regression results of value measures (Tobin's q, the price-to-book ratio, and dividend payout) on each of the four corporate governance subindexes. Interestingly, the only subindex that is significant in explaining each of the value measures is officers and the board. General principles and disclosure and information are also positive and statistically significant in explaining the payout ratio.

Table 7D OLS Regressions of Tobin's q on Corporate Governance Measures

	Dependent variable: Tobin's q						
Independent variables	*(1)*	*(2)*	*(3)*	*(4)*	*(5)*	*(6)*	*(7)*
Intercept	−0.3205	−0.3597	−0.2943	−0.3385	−0.2533	−0.0556	−0.4397
	t= −0.71	t= −0.79	t= −0.53	t= −0.73	t= −0.55	t= −0.07	t= −0.36
Corporate governance index	2.2429***	2.1370**	2.2297**	2.2549**	1.8651**	2.5010**	1.2637
	t=2.82	t=2.39	t= 2.60	t= 2.79	t= 2.42	t= 2.40	t= 1.23
Leverage		0.1837					0.4723
		t=0.46					t= 0.92
Volatility			−0.0012				0.0027
			t= −0.12				t= 0.21
Growth				0.0002			−0.0009
				t= 0.2			t= −0.91
ROA2					2.1336**		3.0586*
					t= 2.24		t= 2.00
SIZE						−0.0335	0.01786
						t= −0.41	t= 0.20
F-statistic	7.94***	4.52**	4.14**	4.08**	5.39**	3.96**	1.83
Significance F	0.0100	0.0266	0.0342	0.0357	0.0491	0.0388	0.1703
Adjusted-R^2	0.2900	0.3032	0.2906	0.2911	0.2709	0.2995	0.4461

Source: Compiled by the authors from the annual financial proxies and investor relations offices of the firms.
Note: Definitions of the variables are given in table 7.4. The Huber-White sandwich estimator has been used in all regressions.
* significant at 10 percent
** significant at 5 percent
*** significant at 1 percent

Table 7E OLS Regressions of the Price-to-Book Ratio on Corporate Governance Measures

	Dependent variable: price-to-book ratio						
Independent variables	*(1)*	*(2)*	*(3)*	*(4)*	*(5)*	*(6)*	*(7)*
Intercept	−1.1400	−1.3943	−1.0931	−1.1689	−1.0398	1.5610	1.1877
	t= −1.19	t= −1.60	t= −0.97	t= −1.21	t= −1.04	t= 1.35	t= 0.74
Corporate governance index	4.2100**	3.5341**	4.1888**	4.2312**	3.6353*	6.8480***	4.8099**
	t= 2.30	t= 2.19	t= 2.18	t= 2.28	t= 1.90	t= 3.37	t= 2.35
Leverage		1.1794					1.8585*
		t= 1.33					t= 1.88
Volatility			−0.0022				0.0114
			t= −0.10				t= 0.37
Growth				0.0003			−0.0041
				t= 0.15			t= −1.70
ROA2					3.2668**		3.6847*
					t= 2.25		t= 1.86
SIZE						−0.3418***	−0.3161*
						t= -3.10	t= −2.13
F-statistic	5.29**	3.91**	2.54	2.82*	5.31**	6.59***	1.78
Significance F	0.0337	0.0400	0.1087	0.0878	0.0161	0.0076	0.1798
Adjusted-R^2	0.1838	0.2791	0.1839	0.1840	0.2224	0.3550	0.3460

Source: Compiled by the authors from the annual financial proxies and investor relations offices of the firms.
Note: Definitions of the variables are given in table 7.4.
* significant at 10 percent
** significant at 5 percent
*** significant at 1 percent

Table 7F OLS Regressions of Dividend Payout on Corporate Governance Measures

	Dependent variable: dividend payout						
Independent variables	*(1)*	*(2)*	*(3)*	*(4)*	*(5)*	*(6)*	*(7)*
Intercept	−2.0900	−2.0314	−1.8944	−1.9552	−2.1552	−3.3833	−2.6549
	t = −1.58	t = −1.69	t = −1.16	t = −1.56	t = −1.55	t = 1.45	t = −1.12
Corporate	4.3200*	4.4808	4.2222	4.2299*	4.6835	3.0613*	3.7363
governance index	t = 1.74	t = 1.52	t = 1.57	t = 1.73	t = 1.67	t=1.93	t = 1.22
Leverage		−0.2778					−0.5388
		t = −0.33					t = −0.43
Volatility			−0.0088				−0.0147
			t = −0.52				t = −0.74
Growth				−0.0015			−0.0003
				t = −0.81			t = −0.13
ROA2					−2.0489		−1.4342
					t = −0.83		t = −0.47
SIZE						0.1634	0.1252
						t = 1.11	t = 0.88
F-statistic	3.04*	4.15**	3.62**	1.50	1.61	1.87	1.78
Significance F	0.0981	0.0342	0.0491	0.2517	0.2294	0.1846	0.1798
Adjusted-R^2	0.2670	0.2743	0.2709	0.2771	0.2879	0.3210	0.3460

Source: Compiled by the authors from the annual financial proxies and investor relations offices of the firms.

Note: Definitions of the variables are given in table 7.4. The Huber-White sandwich estimator has been used in all regressions.

* significant at 10 percent

** significant at 5 percent

*** significant at 1 percent

Table 7G OLS Regressions of Tobin's q, the Price-to-Book Ratio, and Dividend Payout

Independent variables	*Dependent variable: Tobin's q*				*Dependent variable: price-to-book ratio*				*Dependent variable: payout ratio*			
	(1)	*(2)*	*(3)*	*(4)*	*(5)*	*(6)*	*(7)*	*(8)*	*(9)*	*(10)*	*(11)*	*(12)*
Intercept	0.6895**	0.1894	0.0817	0.2931	1.2391**	-0.6196	-1.1037	0.2094	-0.4823	-0.9923	-0.4426	-0.7555
	t=2.99	t=0.46	t=0.12	t=.83	t=2.15	t=-0.65	t=-0.72	t=0.24	t=-1.14	t=-1.19	t=0.32	t=-1.03
General principles	0.6735				0.2456				2.0040**			
	t=1.54				t=0.22				t=2.47			
Officers and the board		1.8418**				4.4346**				3.2851*		
		t=2.08				t=2.13				t=1.80		
Shareholders			1.7514				4.6409				1.7242	
			t=1.43				t=1.63				0.67	
Disclosure and information				1.1405				1.8241				1.9516*
				t=2.10				t=1.34				t=1.73
F-statistic	2.36	4.33*	2.05	4.41**	0.05	4.52**	2.66	1.78	6.12**	3.24*	0.45	2.99
Significance F	0.1419	0.0521	0.1689	0.0499	0.8260	0.0475	0.1206	0.1986	0.0236	0.0889	0.5096	0.1008
Adjusted-R^2	0.0667	0.1490	0.0526	0.1523	-0.0526	0.1564	0.0801	0.0395	0.2121	0.1053	0.097	0.0949

Source: Compiled by the authors from the annual financial proxies and investor relations offices of the firms.
Note: Definitions of the variables are given in table 7.4.
* significant at 10 percent
** significant at 5 percent
*** significant at 1 percent

Taken together with the nonparametric tests, these results represent preliminary evidence of a positive relation between market value and governance in República Bolivariana de Venezuela. Our findings are similar to those of Leal and Carvalhal-da-Silva (2005) in the case of Brazil, and Lefort and Walker (2005) in the case of Chile.

Notes

1. See Shleifer and Vishny (1997) and Denis and McConnell (2003) for a complete literature review.

2. Using the Worldscope database, Gibson analyzed the largest public firms in Brazil, Chile, India, the Republic of Korea, Malaysia, Mexico, Taiwan (China), and Thailand.

3. Authors such as Lefort and Walker (2005) have argued that the observed high ownership concentration in Latin American economies makes the boards weaker than they are in developed economies, causing them to be a poor tool of governance.

4. See Brunello, Graziano, and Parigi (2000) and Volpin (2002) for a similar investigation in Italy and Renneboog (2000) for one in Belgium. See also Claessens and Djankov (1999) and Crespi and Gispert (1998) for somewhat similar studies on the Czech Republic and Spain, respectively.

5. See http://www.caracasstock.com.

6. For instance, Electricidad de Caracas, the second-largest firm in terms of market capitalization and traded volumes on the BVC, was the subject of a successful hostile takeover bid by the U.S. company AES Corporation in 2000. As a result, more than 80 percent of the stocks of Electricidad de Caracas no longer trade on the exchange.

7. See Garay (2001).

8. See Garay and Molina (2004).

9. See La Porta, López-de-Silanes, and Shleifer (1999).

10. Also, there are substantial institutional differences relative to other well-studied economies, such as Germany and Japan. In these countries, the corporate governance model is generally described as relationship oriented, whereby banks play a major role in monitoring management. See Shleifer and Vishny (1997).

11. See La Porta et al. (1997).

12. The Web site of the CNV is at http://www.cnv.gov.ve. The Venezuelan banking system is supervised by the Superintendency of Banks and Financial Institutions (Superintendencia de Bancos y de Otras Instituciones Financieras).

13. This index is constructed adding 1 if: (1) shareholders may mail in their votes, (2) shareholders are not required to deposit their shares prior to the general shareholders meetings, (3) cumulative voting is allowed, (4) an oppressed minorities mechanism is in place, (5) the minimum percentage of capital that entitles the shareholders to call an extraordinary shareholders meeting is less than 10 percent, and (6) shareholders have redemptive rights. The maximum value of this index is 6, and the minimum is 0.

14. This variable assesses the law-and-order tradition in the country and is constructed in the *International Country Risk Guide* (see PRS Group, various). The lowest possible score is 0 and the maximum is 10.

15. The other Latin America countries included in the sample (besides República Bolivariana de Venezuela) are Argentina, Brazil, Chile, Colombia, Ecuador, Mexico, Peru, and Uruguay.

16. Recently, the CNV issued a set of principles of corporate governance (principios de gobierno corporativo) that provides a stricter definition of the independent director. The principles also recommend that public companies should have an audit committee composed of independent directors. See the Web site, http://www.cnv.gov.ve.

17. We acknowledge that our results may be more optimistic about the current state of corporate governance practices in República Bolivariana de Venezuela than the general results presented in Klapper and Love (2002) for 14 emerging markets. This is because the results of those authors are based on the Credit Lyonnais Securities Asia (2001) study, wherein questionnaires were filled out by analysts. In our case, questionnaires were filled out by representatives of each of the companies.

18. Results from questions 20 and 49 are not reported.

19. The 12 other emerging markets studied in Klapper and Love (2002) are Hong Kong (China), India, Indonesia, Korea, Malaysia, Pakistan, the Philippines, Singapore, South Africa, Taiwan (China), Thailand, and Turkey.

20. Eighteen firms in our final sample were listed for less than 19 years on the BVC. Our panel is therefore unbalanced.

21. Note that we do not know whether the turnover was forced or natural. We do not think this lack of knowledge will bias systematically our results. In any case, if there is a systematic bias, it will make finding any connection between CEO turnover and a firm's performance more difficult. This issue is discussed in the section on Robustness Checks.

22. Notice that this result is basically the same as the one we have obtained on the questionnaire (see table 7.3).

23. See Shivdasani and Yermack (1999) for similar statistics corresponding to the U.S. market as of 1994.

24. See, for example, Shleifer and Vishny (1997); Hermalin and Weisbach (1998).

25. See, for instance, Demirgüç-Kunt and Levine (1995).

26. See International Finance Corporation (1999).

27. See Harvey (1995); Bruner et al. (2003).

28. See Weisbach (1988).

29. See Neter et al. (1996) for details.

30. See the subsection on the endogeneity problem for our analysis of the robustness of our results using an instrumental variables approach.

31. In each of the random-effects models, we calculate the Huber-White sandwich estimator of variance. This procedure validates standard errors even if the correlations within groups are not as hypothesized by the specified correlational structure.

32. See Kaplan and Minton (2006).

33. See Hermalin and Weisbach (1998).

34. See Wooldridge (2002).

35. Given the high ownership concentration in our sample of Venezuelan firms and the fact that the average firm in the subsample from 1996 to 2002 (where 55 percent of turnovers occurred) had been incorporated for a little more than 50 years, a possible explanation for the inverse relation between CEO turnover and a firm's performance might be a natural succession process, which is typical in family firms. However, when we check the new CEO's family name, it is not evident that CEO turnover is a response to a succession plan. Another possible explanation for the inverse relation between CEO turnover and a firm's performance is that the new generations (if, indeed, the observed CEO turnover is actually a family succession) choose to appoint professional managers to run the business. For instance, in the 1990s, the Venezuelan economy, like many other economies in Latin America, was liberalized, and many business sectors where open to foreign competition for the first time in decades. This novel environment demanded new, more professional

management skills. Notice that these two possible alternative explanations (succession and skills) are consistent with the negative relation between CEO turnover and firm performance.

36. For a thorough explanation of the specifications of this model, see Hausman, Hall, and Griliches (1984) and Neter et al. (1996).

37. For technical details, see Hausman, Hall, and Griliches (1984).

38. The estimation uses the Huber-White sandwich estimator of variance, as we do in the Logit regressions in table 7.8. This method produces valid standard errors even if the correlation within groups is not as hypothesized by the model correlation structure, an AR(1) process in this case.

39. On the first alternative, see Yermack (2004).

40. See Hausman, Hall, and Griliches (1984).

41. Recall that fixed-effects models lower the amount of variation in the data substantially because they ignore variations among firms and focus only on within-firm variations.

42. Also, we perform the same regression using the logarithmic transformation of *BODITU*, and the results remain unchanged in terms of the coefficient signs and their statistical significance.

43. The regressions are available upon request.

44. The results are available upon request.

45. All these regressions are available upon request.

46. See Jensen and Murphy (1990) and Morck, Shleifer, and Vishny (1988); for the emerging economies see Gomes (2000).

47. For the 51 firms in our sample, we have identified the shareholders with higher firm ownership (usually more than 10 percent of the firm book value); however, in 19 cases, the names of the ultimate owners have not been identified because of the existence of pyramidal structures, which are very common in República Bolivariana de Venezuela. In some cases, the ultimate owner has been identified for a period of time, but not for the entire 19 years of our sample.

48. See Hermalin and Weisbach (1991); Himmelberg, Hubbard, and Palia (1999).

49. We also use percent change in sales, lag value of unadjusted *ROA*, lag values of *INVTA*, and lag values of *PPTTOSALES* as instruments, with similar results.

50. See Opler and Titman (1994).

51. See Himmelberg, Hubbard, and Palia (1999).

52. Another concern is the application of the two-stage approach to estimate a nonlinear model using an endogenous variable. However, Angrist (2000) argues that this concern is more apparent than real because the coefficient estimation does not differ substantially when a nonlinear model is used.

53. The results are available upon request.

54. The results are available upon request.

55. See Garay (2001).

56. Note that we express caution about the potential problems arising from the use of market-related measures such as Tobin's q and price-to-book ratios in illiquid markets such as the BVC.

57. Of the 31 firms that answered the questionnaire it was possible only to include 20 firms in the tests presented in this annex. These were the only companies for which meaningful market-related data existed during 2003 and 2004. The other 11 companies did not trade at all on the BVC or traded very infrequently during 2004. A survivorship bias may be present in our results because the governance practices of the listed firms are probably better than those of delisted firms or of private firms. See Leal and Carvalhal-da-Silva (2005).

58. Demsetz and Lehn (1985), Morck, Shleifer, and Vishny (1988), and Bebchuk and Cohen (2004) also use Tobin's q as a valuation measure.

References

Angrist, J. D. 2000. "Estimation of Limited-Dependent Variable Models with Dummy Endogenous Regressors: Simple Strategies for Empirical Practice." NBER Technical Working Paper 248, National Bureau of Economic Research, Cambridge, MA.

Bebchuk, L. A., and A. Cohen. 2004. "The Costs of Entrenched Boards." NBER Working Paper 10587, National Bureau of Economic Research, Cambridge, MA.

Bhagat, S., and R. Jefferis. 2002. *The Econometrics of Corporate Governance Studies*. Cambridge, MA: MIT Press.

BVC (Bolsa de Valores de Caracas). 2003. *Anuario 2003*. Caracas: Bolsa de Valores de Caracas.

———. Various. *Anuario*. Caracas: Bolsa de Valores de Caracas.

Brunello, G., C. Graziano, and B. Parigi. 2000. "Ownership or Performance: What Determines Board of Director Turnover in Italy?" Discussion Paper 105, Institute for the Study of Labor, Bonn.

Claessens, S., and S. Djankov. 1999. "Enterprise Performance and Management Turnover in the Czech Republic." *European Economic Review* 43 (4–6): 1115–24.

Coles, J., and C. Hoi. 2003. "New Evidence on the Market for Directors: Board Membership and Pennsylvania Senate Bill 1310." *Journal of Finance* 58 (1): 197–230.

Conroy, R. M., W. Li, E. F. O'Halloran, M. Palacios Lleras, and R. F. Bruner. 2003. *Investing in Emerging Markets*. Charlottesville, VA: Research Foundation of the Association for Investment Management and Research.

Coughlan, A., and R. Schmidt. 1985. "Executive Compensation, Management Turnover, and Firm Performance: An Empirical Investigation." *Journal of Accounting and Economics* 7 (1–3): 43–66.

Credit Lyonnais Securities Asia. 2001. "Saints and Sinners: Who's Got Religion." CLSA Report, April, Credit Lyonnais Securities Asia, Hong Kong, China.

Crespi, R., and C. Gispert. 1998. "Board Remuneration, Performance Measures, and Corporate Governance in Large Spanish Companies." Unpublished working paper, Universidad Autónoma de Barcelona, Barcelona.

Dahlquist, M., L. Pinkowitz, R. M. Stulz, and R. Williamson. 2003. "Corporate Governance and the Home Bias." *Journal of Financial and Quantitative Analysis* 38 (1): 87–110.

Dahya, J., J. J. McConnell, and N. G. Travlos. 2002. "The Cadbury Committee, Corporate Performance, and Top Management Turnover." *Journal of Finance* 57 (1): 461–83.

Demirgüç-Kunt, A., and R. Levine. 1995. "Stock Market Development and Financial Intermediaries: Stylized Facts." *World Bank Economic Review* 10 (2): 291–321.

Demsetz, H., and K. Lehn. 1985. "The Structure of Corporate Ownership: Causes and Consequences." *Journal of Political Economy* 93 (6): 1155–77.

Denis, D. J., and D. K. Denis. 1995. "Performance Changes Following Top Management Dismissals." *Journal of Finance* 50 (4): 1029–57.

Denis, D. J., D. K. Denis, and A. Sarin. 1997. "Ownership Structure and Top Executive Turnover." *Journal of Financial Economics* 45 (2): 193–221.

Denis, D. K., and J. J. McConnell. 2003. "International Corporate Governance." *Journal of Financial and Quantitative Analysis* 38 (1): 1–36.

Domowitz, I., J. Glen, and A. Madhavan. 2001. "Liquidity, Volatility, and Equity Trading Costs across Countries and over Time." *International Finance* 4 (2): 221–55.

Farrell, K., and D. Whidbee. 2000. "The Consequences of Forced CEO Succession for Outside Directors." *Journal of Business* 73 (4): 597–627.

Fenn, G., and N. Liang. 2001. "Corporate Payout Policy and Managerial Stock Incentives." *Journal of Financial Economics* 60 (1): 45–72.

Fich, E., and A. Shivdasani. 2006. "Are Busy Boards Effective Monitors?" *Journal of Finance* 61 (2): 689–724.

Furtado, E., and M. Rozeff. 1987. "The Wealth Effects of Company Initiated Management Changes." *Journal of Financial Economics* 18 (1): 147–60.

Garay, U. 2001. "El Mercado Bursátil Venezolano: Evolución y Perspectivas." *Debates IESA* 6 (3): 48–50.

Garay, U., and C. Molina. 2004. "The Collapse in Venezuela's Financial Intermediation." Unpublished working paper, Instituto de Estudios Superiores de Administración, Caracas.

Gibson, M. 2003. "Is Corporate Governance Ineffective in Emerging Markets?" *Journal of Financial and Quantitative Analysis* 38 (1): 231–50.

Gilson, S. 1989. "Management Turnover and Financial Distress." *Journal of Financial Economics* 25 (2): 241–62.

———. 1990. "Bankruptcy, Boards, Banks, and Blockholders: Evidence on Changes in Corporate Control When Firms Default." *Journal of Financial Economics* 27 (2): 355–88.

Gomes, A. 2000. "Going Public without Governance." *Journal of Finance* 55 (2): 615–46.

Gompers, P. A., J. L. Ishii, and A. Metrick. 2003. "Corporate Governance and Equity Prices." *Quarterly Journal of Economics* 118 (1): 107–55.

Harford, J. 2003. "Takeover Bids and Target Directors' Incentives: The Impact of a Bid on Directors' Wealth and Board Seats." *Journal of Financial Economics* 69 (1): 51–83.

Harvey, C. R. 1995. "Predictable Risk and Returns in Emerging Markets." *Review of Financial Studies* 8 (2): 773–816.

Hausman, J., B. Hall, and Z. Griliches. 1984. "Econometric Models for Count Data with an Application to the Patents–R&D Relationships." *Econometrica* 52 (4): 909–38.

Hermalin, B. E., and M. S. Weisbach. 1991. "The Effects of Board Composition and Direct Incentives on Firm Performance." *Financial Management* 20 (4): 101–12.

———. 1998. "Endogenously Chosen Boards of Directors and the Monitoring of the CEO." *American Economic Review* 88 (1): 96–118.

Himmelberg, C. P., R. G. Hubbard, and D. Palia. 1999. "Understanding the Determinants of Managerial Ownership and the Link between Ownership and Performance." *Journal of Financial Economics* 53 (3): 353–84.

Huson, M., R. Parrino, and L. Starks. 2001. "Internal Monitoring Mechanisms and CEO Turnover: A Long-Term Perspective." *Journal of Finance* 56 (6): 2265–97.

International Finance Corporation. 1999. *Emerging Stock Markets Factbook 1999*. Washington, DC: International Finance Corporation, World Bank Group.

Jensen, M., and W. Murphy. 1990. "Performance Pay and Top Management Incentives." *Journal of Political Economy* 98 (2): 225–64.

Kang, S., and A. Shivdasani. 1995. "Firm Performance, Corporate Governance, and Top Executive Turnover in Japan." *Journal of Financial Economics* 38 (1): 29–58.

Kaplan, S. N. 1994a. "Top Executive Rewards and Firm Performance: A Comparison of Japan and the United States." *Journal of Political Economy* 102 (3): 510–46.

———. 1994b. "Top Executives, Turnover, and Firm Performance in Germany." *Journal of Law, Economics and Organizations* 10 (1): 142–59.

Kaplan, S. N., and B. A. Minton. 1994. "Appointments of Outsiders to Japanese Boards: Determinants and Implication for Managers." *Journal of Financial Economics* 36 (2): 225–58.

———. 2006. "How Has CEO Turnover Changed?: Increasingly Performance Sensitive Boards and Increasingly Uneasy CEOs." NBER Working Paper 12465, National Bureau of Economic Research, Cambridge, MA.

Kaplan, S. N., and D. Reishus. 1990. "Outside Directorships and Corporate Performance." *Journal of Financial Economics* 27 (2): 389–410.

Klapper, L., and I. Love. 2002. "Corporate Governance, Investor Protection, and Performance in Emerging Markets." Policy Research Paper 2818, World Bank, Washington, DC.

La Porta, R., F. López-de-Silanes, and A. Shleifer. 1999. "Corporate Ownership around the World." *Journal of Finance* 54 (2): 471–517.

La Porta, R., F. López-de-Silanes, A. Shleifer, and R. W. Vishny. 1997. "Legal Determinants of External Finance." *Journal of Finance* 52 (3): 1131–50.

———. 1998. "Law and Finance." *Journal of Political Economy* 106 (6): 1113–55.

———. 2000a. "Investor Protection and Corporate Governance." *Journal of Financial Economics* 58 (1–2): 3–27.

———. 2000b. "Agency Problems and Dividend Policies around the World." *Journal of Finance* 55 (1): 1–33.

———. 2002. "Investor Protection and Corporate Valuation." *Journal of Finance* 57 (3): 1147–70.

Leal, R. P. C., and A. L. Carvalhal-da-Silva. 2005. "Corporate Governance and Value in Brazil (and Chile)." Research Network Working Paper R-514, Research Department, Inter-American Development Bank, Washington, DC.

Lefort, F., and Walker, E. 2005. "The Effect of Corporate Governance Practices on Company Market Valuation and Payout Policy in Chile." Research Network Working Paper R-515, Research Department, Inter-American Development Bank, Washington, DC.

Martin, K. J., and J. J. McConnell. 1991. "Corporate Performance, Corporate Takeover, and Management Turnover." *Journal of Finance* 46 (2): 671–87.

Morck, R., A. Shleifer, and R. W. Vishny. 1988. "Management Ownership and Market Valuation: An Empirical Analysis." *Journal of Financial Economics* 20 (1): 293–315.

Murphy, K. J., and J. L. Zimmerman. 1993. "Financial Performance Surrounding CEO Turnover." *Journal of Accounting and Economics* 16 (1–3): 273–315.

Neter, J., M. H. Kutner, W. Wasserman, and C. J. Nachtsheim. 1996. *Applied Linear Statistical Models*. 4th ed. New York: McGraw-Hill.

Opler, T., and S. Titman. 1994. "Financial Distress and Corporate Performance." *Journal of Finance* 49 (3): 1015–40.

PRS Group. Various. *International Country Risk Guide*. East Syracuse, NY: Political Risk Services. http://www.prsgroup.com/icrg/icrg.html.

Renneboog, L. 2000. "Ownership, Managerial Control, and the Governance of Companies Listed on the Brussels Stock Exchange." *Journal of Banking and Finance* 24 (12): 1959–95.

Shivdasani, A., and D. Yermack. 1999. "CEO Involvement in the Selection of New Board Members: An Empirical Analysis." *Journal of Finance* 54 (5): 1829–53.

Shleifer, A., and R. W. Vishny. 1997. "A Survey of Corporate Governance." *Journal of Finance* 52 (2): 737–83.

Volpin, P. 2002. "Governance with Poor Investor Protection: Evidence from Top Executive Turnover." *Journal of Financial Economics* 64 (1): 61–90.

Warner, J. B., R. L. Watts, and K. H. Wruck. 1988. "Stock Prices and Top Management Changes." *Journal of Financial Economics* 20: 461–92.

Weisbach, M. S. 1988. "Outside Directors and CEO Turnover." *Journal of Financial Economics* 20: 431–60.

Wooldridge, J. 2002. *Econometric Analysis of Cross Section and Panel Data*. Cambridge, MA: MIT Press.

Yermack, D. 2004. "Remuneration, Retention, and Reputation Incentives for Outside Directors." *Journal of Finance* 59 (5): 2282–308.

Index

G

I

S

ECO-AUDIT

Environmental Benefits Statement

The World Bank is committed to preserving endangered forests and natural resources. The Office of the Publisher has chosen to print ***Investor Protection and Corporate Governance*** on recycled paper with 30 percent postconsumer fiber in accordance with the recommended standards for paper usage set by the Green Press Initiative, a nonprofit program supporting publishers in using fiber that is not sourced from endangered forests. For more information, visit www.greenpressinitiative.org.

Saved:
- 20 trees
- 14 million BTUs of total energy
- 1,782 lbs. of CO_2 equivalent greenhouse gases
- 7,395 gallons of wastewater
- 950 lbs. of solid waste

The authorized representative in the EU for product safety and compliance is:
Mare Nostrum Group
B.V Doelen 72
4831 GR Breda
The Netherlands

www.ingramcontent.com/pod-product-compliance
Lightning Source LLC
Chambersburg PA
CBHW021022210326
41598CB00016B/891

* 9 7 8 0 8 0 4 7 0 0 0 7 8 *